ISBN 978-1-5279-8531-5
PIBN 10999248

1 MONTH OF
FREE
READING

at

www.ForgottenBooks.com

By purchasing this book you are eligible for one month membership to ForgottenBooks.com, giving you unlimited access to our entire collection of over 1,000,000 titles via our web site and mobile apps.

To claim your free month visit:

www.forgottenbooks.com/free999248

English
Français
Deutsche
Italiano
Español
Português

www.forgottenbooks.com

Mythology Photography **Fiction**
Fishing Christianity **Art** Cooking
Essays Buddhism Freemasonry
Medicine **Biology** Music **Ancient
Egypt** Evolution Carpentry Physics
Dance Geology **Mathematics** Fitness
Shakespeare **Folklore** Yoga Marketing
Confidence Immortality Biographies
Poetry **Psychology** Witchcraft
Electronics Chemistry History **Law**
Accounting **Philosophy** Anthropology
Alchemy Drama Quantum Mechanics
Atheism Sexual Health **Ancient History**
Entrepreneurship Languages Sport
Paleontology Needlework Islam
Metaphysics Investment Archaeology
Parenting Statistics Criminology
Motivational

INDIANA ✓

70

SCHOOL JOURNAL,

ORGAN OF THE

STATE TEACHERS' ASSOCIATION,

AND CONTAINS DECISIONS OF THE

SUPERINTENDENT OF PUBLIC INSTRUCTION.

EDITOR AND PROPRIETOR:

WILLIAM A. BELL.

ASSOCIATE EDITOR:

GEO. P. BROWN.

VOLUME XXX.

INDIANAPOLIS:

No. 12, JOURNAL BUILDING.

1885.

STATE BOARD OF EDUCATION.

Isaac P. Gray, *Governor.*

John W. Holcombe, *Superintendent of Public Instruction.*

David S. Jordan, *President State University.*

W. W. Parsons, *President State Normal School.*

James H. Smart, *President Purdue University.*

Lewis H. Jones, *Superintendent Indianapolis Public Schools.*

John Cooper, *Superintendent Evansville Public Schools.*

John S. Irwin, *Superintendent Fort Wayne Public Schools.*

OFFICERS

OF THE

STATE TEACHERS' ASSOCIATION.

E. E. Smith, *President.*

Anna E. H. Lemon, *Recording Secretary.*

D. E. Hunter, *Per. Sec'y. and ex-officio Treasurer.*

W. H. Elson, *Chairman Executive Committee.*

INDEX.

INDEX.

INDIANA
SCHOOL JOURNAL.

| Vol. XXX. | JANUARY, 1885. | No. 1. |

THE KINDERGARTEN—ITS OBJECT, METHODS AND RELATION TO THE PUBLIC SCHOOL.

EMMA MONT. McRAE.

NOTHING else serves so well to distinguish between that dark-ness from which the race is emerging and the light that is dawning, as the increasing attention given to child-life— its needs, its rights, and its privileges. Nothing indicates more of hopefulness for the future than the recognition of the child's birth-right to be well born; that if through inheritance or other misfortune he be imbecile physically, mentally and morally, he is not to be sacrificed on the altar of human selfishness, but to be cared for in that higher humane spirit which recognizes in the humblest child the possibilities of a helpful man or woman. Victory to the strong has ceased to be the watch-word, and help to the weak has become the christianized sentiment of our civil-ization.

The child, whatever its natural capacity, needs nourishment adapted to its nature—it is weak, and therefore needs to be helped to grow strong. A Kindergarten is a garden for children. Before Friedrich Frœbel the idea of the development of the mind was entertained, but to him it was left to discover the best means for its growth. He, following in the footsteps of Pesta-lozzi, discovered the means for accomplishing what had been felt was the end to be attained in education, the harmonious de-velopment of the human being.

So much are people trammeled by their preconceived notions or the want of any definite ideas in regard to education, that it has been a difficult process to stem the tide of prejudice and ignorance. Many still look upon the Kindergarten as a place for play merely. The fact that play is natural to childhood serves only as an argument against it. What is natural certainly must be the very thing to be avoided. To mention that the child is happy in the Kindergarten as an evidence of its adaptability to its needs is received as a further argument against this paradise of little children. Although we may boast of our superior civilization there are still not a few who believe that a happy child in a happy school is abnormal. Frœbel realized the truth, that a child that is a natural child is a happy one, and that in its play it has the realization of the conflicts and victories of maturer life.

In this play, children call into being world after world and people them with creatures of their own fancy. "Deep meaning often lies in childish play." Through the medium of play, then, did it seem natural that the child should grow to be strong. Having this in mind Frœbel fashioned the Kindergarten gifts. What gifts! What a revelation to the hungering minds of the little ones. Oh, that these gifts might go into the hands of every little waif of humanity. But what of these gifts? What is their significance? Are they for amusement simply? Are the colored balls, the sphere, cylinder and cube, the various forms mere playthings, that may happen to awaken a thought in the little mind? Are they hap-hazzard forms that mean nothing? Rather they are the means of leading the child to appreciate color, size, shape and number. He will take into his consciousness these ideas because he sees with his own eyes, feels with his own hands. By the forms of cognition the child gains knowledge, by reproducing, recombining these ideas obtained from surrounding objects he may build rude forms which are living forms to the little builder, and by the forms of beauty or the symmetrical arrangement of parts the child has invention and taste developed. The time is not coming, it has already come when it will be demanded by the needs of modern life that a skilled hand accompany a trained mind. The demand for an industrial education is a just one and will make itself felt more and more until it can no longer be ignored by any who have the good of society at heart. Kindergarten training seems the best possible basis for an industrial education. The culture the child receives in the Kindergarten by feeling out with his hands step by step that knowledge which may make him either an artist or an artisan is the culture he most needs. It will not do to allow our young people to grow up without acquiring any skill of hand until they have a so-called intellectual education, hoping that after this they may enter the already over-crowded, struggling, dependent classes who seek to earn a living by their superior attainments. Helpless indeed will that young man, young woman be who, not only in the near future but in the present, finds himself, herself, only half prepared for life's duties and privileges, however brilliant has been the career at college. There are competing agencies with which there must be contact. If the machine has superseded the hand, a practical knowledge of science must make one able to master the machine. If the increase in population renders soil impoverished by unskillful farming, insufficient for proper sustenance, he must again call upon science to teach him that nature is not so prodigal of her gifts as to permit unrebuked such waste of her forces.

If the child is to be denied completeness in its education, if it be impossible for the college and Kindergarten both to be enjoyed, by all means let the first steps be taken on sure ground. Let rational methods start the child aright. Once let him have revealed to him all that can come through genuine Kindergarten training and even the narrow pedagogue having no higher conception of a teacher's work than that of a recitation hearer, may spend much fruitless effort in getting him back to be a pliant observer of second-hand ideas obtained by cramming.

Skill, industry and economy acquired by Kindergarten training are invaluable were there no other advantages. But when added to the skill obtained from drawing, sewing, modeling, the industrious habits fixed by pleasing and productive employment, and the economy which does not tolerate the waste of the smallest particle, there is that strongly fortified, independent, self reliant character which is the almost inevitable result of communion with the manifestations of divine truth in flower and fruit, seed-time and harvest, the birds and the birdlings, the child and its happy life.

The Kindergarten not only lays the foundation for industrial training, but it fits the child to be a social and moral being. It craves the society of those of its own age. Thus the Kindergarten affords him what the family does not. Here he finds companionship adapted to his needs. The just recognition of the rights of others which is fostered in the true Kindergarten, the forcible lessons drawn from nature herself tend to make of these little ones just, upright, reverent men and women. Precept upon precept, line upon line, is not sufficient to develop lovely character. What boy or girl has not been told that it is right to do right and wrong to do wrong? It is one thing to be polished on the surface, to have an admiration for righteousness, and quite another to be so well grounded as to have that inherent moral stamina which enables one to stand upon the firm foundation of self-confidence which arises from the steady growth of the moral nature. Pestalozzi taught that the faculties are developed by exercise. Frœbel added that the function of education is to develop the faculties by awaking voluntary activity. Action proceeding from inner impulse is the one thing needful. Frœbel says: "God's every thought is a work, a deed. Man must be a creator also. He who will early learn to recognize the Creator must early exercise his own power of action with the consciousness that he is bringing about what is good, for the doing good is the link between the creature and the Creator, and the conscious doing of it is the conscious connection, the true living union of the man with God, of the individual man as of the human race, and is therefore at once the starting point and the eternal aim of all education." The child in his relations needs something more than a mind stultified by unrelated facts of mathematics, geography and history. "In the creation, in nature and the order of the material world and in the progress of mankind, God has given us the true type of education," said Frœbel. Much harm, incalculable harm, is done true Kindergarten culture by the false pretenders who, by the use of the name, palm upon an unsuspecting public a spurious article and call it Kindergarten. It is unpardonable in any one to give children a few of the Kindergarten occupations and overlook altogether the deep meaning in all that is genuine in the teachings of Frœbel. It is far better that a child be left to its own sweet child-life, than that it be hampered by false teaching, especially under the name rendered so sacred by the fullness of its meaning.

The question arises: "Is it possible that in the few months, at most, that the child may enjoy this training, that he may be relieved from the mistakes of ignorance both in the home and in the school which he is to enter on leaving the Kindergarten"? It is fitting that the German fatherland should have given birth to the large-souled man who felt the need of proper training for the babies of the household, and hence worked hard and thought much that the mothers might become better fitted for their responsibilities. The earliest records of the sturdy Teutons show them to have felt that upon the mothers depended the success or failure of their undertakings. Popular education has done much to make the mothers of our time more worthy, more helpful, but it is true that even now, many homes are presided over by ignorant, frivolous or over-worked mothers whose lives are burdensome and whose children are coming up like weeds, without the care, the love which they need to make of them the sweet spirited parents of the next generation. It is not possible to undo the evil of these homes, but these are the children that need the influence of the true Kindergarten. For these children into whose lives comes so little of the true, pure side of life, there ought to be provided by the State this training which shall tend to make them happy, self-supporting members of society, rather than worthless consumers. Even those children of comfort and luxury who may have provided for them in the home the refining influences that cultivated taste may suggest miss the training which comes from the blending of the individual life in associated lives.

I believe the first step in the solution of the question, "How may public education keep pace with the demands of the times?" is to establish the Kindergarten as a part of the school system. The Kindergartens as a part of town and city school systems not only furnish to the children who need it most this desirable training, but they also provide the best possible facilities for the training of teachers for the primary schools. Graduates from the high school may enter the Kindergarten as volunteer assistants without pecuniary compensation and acquire a knowledge of the underlying principles of education. From an economic standpoint a school corporation can not afford to refuse this means of obtaining skill in the other departments of the school work. The principles of education are universal in their application. Frœbel's methods are the starting point in all genuine professional skill. When the threatening war-cloud lowers and the very life of the nation is in peril there comes a ringing appeal to arms that home and native land may be saved. Then from the farm, the work-shop, from the study, the counting-room, come thousands of brave men to do valiant service. Precious life-blood is poured out, and through this baptism of blood and fire wrongs are redressed and the dignity of the law maintained. Now since the State expects and enjoys such protection, is it not just that the State should provide the best possible instruction for all of her children. The provisions for the unfortunate classes already are liberal, and yet the imbecile, the deaf mute, the blind should have from the State the benefit of the Kindergarten. When every child, rich and poor, black and white, weak and strong shall be systematically educated, then will each be a law unto himself, and protection to the home and the government be assured.

The Kindergarten offers a solution to, "What shall be done with dull pupils?" It is often fortunate that they are too dull to absorb much of the bungling work called teaching. The wonder is that any children are bright enough to survive the experiments of untutored boys and girls.

But shall Kindergarten methods end with the Kindergarten ? By no means. It is a mistake to suppose that this transitional stage between the home and the school is to be wholly distinct from both. The Kindergarten should have something of the school and the school should have much of the Kindergarten. If the principles deduced by Frœbel be fundamental, be founded upon human needs and human organism, then they certainly can not be confined to a short period of a child's life. The difficulty in having the school carry on the thought of the Kindergarten arises from the misconception of the aims of the true Kindergarten. Its shadow only is carried into the school rather than its substance. Pupils never outgrow their need of individual self-activity, they never outgrow the need of that softening, beautifying spirit which was manifested by the great teacher himself. The mistake that primary teachers and teachers of higher grades make, is the taking for granted that clear conceptions are formed in the mind through the medium of the teacher's words. The teacher should not be satisfied with the shell, but should demand that the pupil arrive at the kernel, and not only that, but be able to express clearly the thought he grasps. The pupil knows the meaning of two and two when he handles two and two objects, he knows what a qt. means if he measures a qt.; he knows what a cord means if he pile up a cord of wood. He knows the fulness of the poet's inspiration if he be led to discover what the poet grasped in his wonderful conception. As he studies God's handiwork in the daisy he may say with the Poet Laureate :—

> " Flower in the crannied wall,
>   I pluck you out of the crannies,—
> Hold you here, root and all, in my hand,
>   Little flower—but if I could understand
> What you are, root and all, and all in all,
>   I should know what God and man is."

Speed the day when in every home there shall be more of the spirit of the Kindergarten, and in every Kindergarten there shall be more of the true home, and in every school the happy blending of the two. Then will come the union of Hercules and Minerva upon Mt. Olympus which shall typify the triumph of force and wisdom through the agency of unconquerable love.

Out of the struggles after the true, let us hope that we may come to the feet of childhood with an offering which shall vouchsafe so much of the world's best gifts as shall bring them into communion with the Creator's great storehouse of eternal truth.

ELEMENTS OF CHARACTER.

BY E. E. SMITH.

THE essence of a man is his character. Its measure is by content and extent—by that which the man is and by those whom the man affects. The stamp which a man has upon his inner life through nature, association and culture, is one phase of his being; the stamp which he tends to put upon the life with which he is associated and which comes under his influence, is another phase. These two do not always harmonize. The difference may lie in the nature of the man himself, and there may thus be diversity in unity. It may lie in his purposes, and hence give rise to that shadow often regarded as more precious than the substance—*reputation*.

Character would thus seem to have two phases, an active and a passive. The former may be the manifestation of the latter, or it may not. Before God and itself the soul stands naked; before the world it is clothed with a garment. The garment may be well-fitting and natural, and thus the true inner form be revealed; it may be ill-fitting or padded, and thus the inner form be concealed. In a thoroughly-formed character, one in which sincerity prevails—the two phases are complementary. And there is always strong hope for an honest man, it matters not whether he be honestly good or honestly evil. Upon a two-faced genius the devil has a triple mortgage. The chances are very large that the mortgage will be foreclosed and not lifted.

Character, then, is not a uniform but a variable quantity. It is a growth, a progression. The constancy or the inconstancy of this progression largely lies in two factors—natural disposition and education. The purpose of the latter may be simply to give direction and opportunity to the former, or to unmake and re-make it. It is insincere to deny that, morally as well as physically, the probability is that "when the fathers eat sour grapes, the children's teeth will be set on edge." Heredity, and the home influence of the first six years, do largely determine a child's character. When it enters the school-house door, its soul is usually in one of three conditions: The good angel prevails the bad angel prevails, or there is a state of "armed neutrality." The labors of the teacher are very largely devoted to the first and third of these conditions; his duty is mainly to the second. I hold it a more glorious thing to hunt up the one straying lamb, even though thereby one travels among the thorns of ingratitude, the sloughs of despondency, and the stones of injustice and misrepresentation, one and all, than to care for the nine who go not far away from the path leading to good pastures. It isn't such a hard task to train a good child; but it takes a master spirit to patiently, perseveringly and successfully train an evil one.

Character, as we have said, is a growth. In this growth there are three factors operative: disposition or tendency, habit, and reason. The two first mentioned may be described as indirect or automatic factors; the latter is the direct or systematic one. The essential element in the first of these factors is inclination; this carried into automatic action becomes *habit*, into systematic action becomes *reason*. For all ordinary occasions, and for the greater number of lives, the inclination toward the right and the habit of doing right, will be sufficient to keep the children on the safe side. But in the great emergencies of life, in the time of sore temptation and trial, when good seems to be evil and evil good, there is need of some stronger power,—of a moral, an intellectual and a spiritual stamina strong enough to hold the child's life firmly on the true course. Herein lies the necessity for great purposes, for lofty ideals, and for a well-regulated will.

The child's nature will unfold not alone because of the teacher, but also without a teacher, and even in spite of a teacher. It surely behooves the teacher, then, to see that its tendencies, its habits, its purposes and its aims are right. The method of doing this is to be determined by the object which the teacher has in view, and by the character so far formed of the child to be dealt with. This indicates two means of operation—the direct and the indirect. The former looks to implanting deep and solid principles of action and calls into full play the rational powers. The latter looks rather to the cultivation of the emotional and the philanthropic. In neither is it the purpose to extinguish the passions that spring strong in the young breast, but to regulate or to direct them in worthy channels.

The limits of this article will not permit a full development of the thought here. The following diagram may aid the reader and furnish food for reflection :

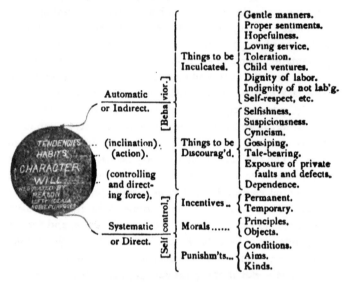

These two lines of influence affect the complete circuit of being, are mutually helpful, and, if rightfully employed will assist the child in securing the essential elements of a fully rounded out character.

THE GRUBE METHOD—II.

E. E. WHITE, LL. D.

It is conceded that the first lessons in number should combine equal as well as unequal groups of objects, or numbers, and that they should also separate groups of objects, or numbers, into equal as well as into unequal groups or parts. But the combining of equal groups of objects, or the adding of equal numbers, is not multiplication, and the separating of groups of objects into equal groups, or numbers into equal parts, is not numerical division.

The numbering of a group of objects determines how many ones in the group, and the adding of two or more groups determines the number of ones in their sum, but it does not follow that addition is a method of *counting by ones*. On the contrary, the pupil has not learned what may be called the alphabet of addition until he can give the sum of any two digital numbers *without counting*. Indeed the habit of counting by ones to ascertain the sum of two digital numbers is so pernicious that, in the first lessons in number, great care should be taken to avoid counting by ones in numbering, combining, and separating groups of objects, or numbers. If the primary lessons in number be properly graded, the pupils may be taught to number any group by adding one to the next smaller group, and then their perceptive power may be so trained that they can number groups at sight, not exceeding ten, combine the smaller groups that compose these groups, and separate them into parts *without counting by ones*. But whatever may be theoretically true on this point, the one practical result to be reached in the primary lessons in number is the power to give instantly the sum of any two digital numbers, *without counting by ones*.

It is true that the product of any two digital numbers is the number obtained by adding one of these numbers to itself continuously as many times as there are ones less one in the other number, but it does not follow that multiplication is a process of adding equal numbers. On the contrary, the pupil has not the alphabet of multiplication until he can give the product of any two digital numbers *without adding*. Indeed, it may be a question whether it is a good method of teaching the products of digital numbers to train pupils in adding one of the numbers to itself continuously. It is believed to be a better method to teach the pupil to find a product by adding what may be called the basal number to its next lower product. The product of 7 multiplied by 5 should be found, for example, by adding 7 to 28, the next lower product. This method is easily carried out in a properly graded series of lessons. It is similar to the process of teaching the word *traveler,* to a pupil who knows *travel*, by adding *er*. It would be not only unnecessary, but a waste of time, to consider the power of each letter in the word *traveler*, from left to right. This is not a parallel case, but it illustrates the principle involved.

The fact that the *processes* of addition and multiplication are not identical is obvious when illustrated by the written methods of adding and multiplying large numbers, as by adding twenty-four 225's and then multiplying 225 by 24. While the results reached are the same, the two processes are obviously not the same.

When multiplication proper is reached, the idea of *parts* should be successively dropped *as soon as the products of the digital number, two by two, are known*, and these pairs of numbers and their products should be associated in the mind *under the relation of factor*. The numbers 5 and 6, for example, should be associated with 30 as clearly and as *immediately* as they are with 11, and this factor relation should not be confused by the intrusion of the idea of parts. Indeed, the old method of committing to memory arbitrarily the products of the digital numbers would be better than the continued and persistent mixing of part and factor relations—provided always that the products of actual numbers, not figures, are thus memorized.

The factor view is not only of practical importance in the child's first lessons in number, but in teaching the multiplication of fractional numbers, and also in the multiplication of quantities in the higher mathematics. The product of a multiplied by b is ab, and the factor relation alone enters into the idea or concept of this product.

The fact that the process of separating a group of objects, or a number, into equal parts is not numerical division may be shown by separating 15 beans into 5 equal groups and then by dividing 15 beans by 5 beans. In the first process, there is neither a numerical divisor nor a numerical quotient; in the second process, 5 beans is the divisor, or measure, and 3 is the quotient. The first process separates 15 beans into equal parts, which is division only in a primary or mechanical sense; the second process, divides 15 beans by 5 beans, one of its *factors*, and finds 3, the other *factor*, and this is numerical division—the process which is fundamental in arithmetic and in the higher mathematics.

It is thus seen that division should be taught as the inverse of multiplication, and that both processes should be taught together. The fact that 3 times 4 or 4 times 3 is 12 involves the facts that 4 is in 12 three times and 3 in 12 four times, and when these *related* facts are taught together, the pupil sees the latter in the former, and he is thus relieved of the necessity of committing the division results, or quotients, to memory.

There is nothing gained by the attempt to teach division as a method of subtraction. It is true that the quotient shows how many times the divisor *may be* subtracted from the dividend, but this quotient is not found *by subtraction*. This may be clearly shown by dividing 625 by 25, and then by subtracting 25 from 625 as many times as possible. It is obvious that neither the processess nor the results are the same. The final result of the several subtractions is 0, and it is only *by counting*, or inspection, that the number of subtractions is determined. The quotient obtained by dividing 625 by 25 is 25. and, *as a consequence*, it is seen that 25 can be subtracted from 625 twenty-five times. This consequence is an interesting fact, but it does not show that division is a method of subtraction.

The fact that there are but two fundamental ideas or principles in arithmetic, synthesis or combination and analysis or separation, does not show that there are but two fundamental *processes*. Whatever may be true theoretically, there are in practice two synthetic processes—addition and multiplication; and two analytic processes—subtraction and division. Addition and subtraction synthesize and analyze numbers as composed *of parts*, and, being inverse processes, should be taught together. Multiplication and division synthesize and analyze numbers as composed *of factors*, and, being inverse processes, should be taught together.

It may be added that little children should not be confused by theories of numbers or processes. The essential thing for them is to master thoroughly the four fundamental processes with digital numbers, and this should be accomplished in the simplest, most natural, and, as a consequence, most effective manner possible.

ARE THE SCHOOLS RESPONSIBLE FOR THE HOODLUM ELEMENT?

BY D. E. HUNTER.

THE hoodlum is becoming a large element in society, and not only large, but dangerous. The origin of this dangerous element is looked for anxiously, and some think the responsibility for its existence, rests with the public schools. Fifty years ago it was not so large an element as to-day. Fifty years ago public schools were few. With the increase of public schools we find the increase of the hoodlum element in society. Shall we therefore conclude that the school brought the hoodlum? Fifty years ago railroads were few. Fifty years ago very few people ate tomatoes. Now railroads are numerous and tomatoes are in quite common use. Therefore railroads caused people to eat tomatoes. Fifty years ago there was no such thing as a magnetic telegraph, and there were no coal oil explosions. Now we have telegraph lines all over the country, and coal oil explosions are quite common.

Fifty years ago the schools of Indianapolis were not graded, and floods in the Ohio river were of rare occurrence. Now, the schools of Indianapolis are thoroughly graded and the Ohio river is playing the pranks of the Nile by overflowing its banks annually,

The only connection between the floods and city schools is, that, when the flood comes, announcement of the fact made at noon in these schools, fills a dozen to fifty barrels with potatoes, two hours later, and five hundred to one thousand loaves of bread are ready to go forward to the sufferers next morning. Coal oil explosions occur without the aid of telegraph lines, but the news of these explosions are carried by the telegraph all over civilization, and ought to, and doubtless do prevent their being more numerous.

People learned, without the aid of railroads, that the tomato was useful on the dining table, as well as ornamental on the parlor mantel. And so the hoodlum element has become numerous and troublesome, not because of the schools, but rather, in spite of the schools. The teachings of the schools are against hoodlumism. Morality was formerly taught at home; the opportunities for children to congregate in the streets, and amuse themselves as they pleased, without interference on the part of teachers and parents, were very few. If there are more hoodlums to-day than formerly it is because: *First,* There are more children. *Second,* They are under less restraint. *Third,* There are more opportunies and inducements to learn and practice wrong.

Hoodlums are usually, not always, found among those who are irregular in attendance at school, or do not attend at all. They are, almost always, found among those who have the free range of the streets of villages, towns and cities. What can the public school do in three to nine months for the boy that attends the street school twelve months in the year. Six to thirty hours per week in the public school, and eighty to one hundred in the street school. Would you banish the hoodlum from the next generation? Break up the street school, make home what it ought to be—attractive, pleasant, interesting. Do not have a carpet too fine for your boy's boot. Interest yourself in what interests your children, then you may lead them in the right way; but when you undertake to drive, you often find that they are as obstinate as yourself. Co-operate with the teachers and encourage the children to believe that their teachers and their parents are really their best friends.

HEALTH FALLACIES.

POPULAR MISCONCEPTIONS THAT OUGHT TO BE OVERTHROWN.

A writer in *Lippincott's Magazine* thinks that the health of the people would be brought up to a better condition if they were educated out of the following fallacies:

The idea that cold baths are healthy in winter and dangerous in mid-summer.

That rain water is more wholesome than "hard" water.

That bed rooms must be heated in cold weather.

That the misery of everlasting scrubbing and soap-suds vapors is compensated by the comfort of the lucid intervals.

That a sick room must be hermetically closed.

That it pays to save foul air for the sake of its warmth.

That "draughts" are morbific agencies.

That catarrhs are due to low temperature.

That even in midsummer children must be sent to bed at sunset, when the air begins to be pleasant.

That an after-dinner nap can do any harm.

That the sanitary conditions of the air can be improved by the fetor of carbolic acid.

That there is any benefit in swallowing jugfuls of nauseous sulphur water.

That rest after dinner can be shortened with impunity.

That out-door recreation is a waste of time.

That athletic sports brutalize the character.

That a normal human being requires any other stimulant than exercise and fresh air.

That any plan of study can justify the custom of stinting children in sleep.

USES OF "AS."

[T. Mais contributes to the educational column of the Rockville R... from the following examples of the uses of as, which may be helpful to some teachers.]

As:—

I. As a Noun.
1. 1—Subject of a transitive verb—as takes the lead.
2. 2—Subject of a copulative verb—as is is a hard word to understand.
3. 2—Object of a finite verb—John parsed as correctly.
4. 2—Object of an infinitive verb—please parse as.
5. 2—Object of a preposition—we talked about as in class.
6. 2—Predicate with a verb—this is not the as we were parsing over.
7. 2—In apposition—Mary wrote the word as in her day book.
8. 2—Nominative absolute—O, as, thy constructions are difficult!

II. As a Relative Pronoun.
1. 2—Object of a transitive verb—such as they are give I unto you.
2. 2—Predicate with verb—we will entertain as many as you desire.
3. 2—Subject of a transitive verb—we will send such as are ready.
4. 1—Subject of a copulative verb—I gave as much as come.

III. As an Adverb.
1. 2—Of degree limiting an adjective—I will start as soon as possible.
2. 2—Of degree limiting an adverb—I argued as I thought.
3. 2—Conjunctive of manner—he plows his corn as he can.
4. 2—Conjunctive of time—happy as I now am I may have sorrow.
5. 2—Conjunctive of degree—as you wish to study I will retire.

IV. As a Conjunction—as you wish to study I will retire.

V. As a Preposition—the Digger Indians use bugs as food.

DEPARTMENT OF PEDAGOGY.

This Department is conducted by GEO. P. BROWN, President State Normal School.

——:o:——

BOOKS AND READING.

BOOKS may be divided into two classes, containing respectively trash and literature. The trashy books are numberless and of every degree of worthlessness. Some are absolutely bad, others harmless, and still others have a positive value for persons in certain stages of development. What would have been trash to Dr. Franklin at the age of fifty, might have been of positive value to him when he first entered Philadelphia, ignorant of the habits and customs of polite society. Mrs. Southworth has been of real service to some young people who were struggling to pass from a rude order of society to a higher plane of social culture. Thus literary trash may become a valuable aid by serving as stepping stones to higher things. Of literature there are two kinds according to Dr. Quincy—the literature of power, and the literature of knowledge.

The literature of knowledge may be mastered for all the practical needs of life by a mastery of indexes after a sufficient foundation has been laid. To know where to find what one needs to know at any time is next to knowing the thing itself, and makes much less demand upon the memory. Since each one of us has but a limited amount of mental energy to expend it is important that it be used economically. If it is all spent in memorizing, none is left to be employed as power. There are individuals, and indeed a whole race of beings that are examples of this misdirection of energy. Who has not known the animated encyclopedia who knows everything and can use nothing? The Chinese are a race who for ages have cultivated only the memory, and who have made no progress for ages.

Knowledge is *not* power. It serves, however, an excellent purpose in giving a proper direction to power. Power without knowledge is a blind giant. Knowledge without power is helplessness made more helpless.

The literature of power must be mastered by grappling with

2

the thing itself. There is no short or easy road to the acquisi-
sition of it. It comes through the many times repeated experiences that are occasioned by the reading of this literature and
reflection upon it. Its growth is as imperceptible and unconscious as is the growth of physical strength. It is only by measuring ourselves at different periods that our growth becomes
apparent to ourselves. There will be no growth at all unless we
do in some measure come into the experiences of those whose
works we read. When we re-experience the thoughts and feelings of the greatest of the race we become participants in their
greatness. All powers grow through exercise; the lowest and
the highest. It is the function of this kind of literature to stimulate the activity of the highest powers of head and heart.

There are many good books, and a few great ones. That
book is the greatest, that reflects to every one who comes to it,
the best and greatest that is in himself. It portrays to each one
his own self-consciousness, be that large or small. It is often
said that one can see in a work of art only what he brings with
him. It is equally true that one will find in a great book only
what is in himself,—no more.

The genius is the man who can voice the profoundest self-
consciousness of his race. What he sees and portrays was by
them vaguely felt.

It is the test of genius that it can so portray this vague, unconscious consciousness of all, that each will recognize in it the best
expression of that within himself which he had no power to utter.
When this is done equally well for all minds, both the great and
the small, then do we behold the greatest triumph of genius.
When it is done for the cultured, but the expression is a sealed
book to the uncultured, then the portrayor falls so far short of
making the greatest of books.

Of books of this latter class it is truly said that "it requires
culture to appreciate culture."

The greatest of all the great books, judged by this test, is the
Bible. The Bible consists of a collection of books that for pro-
foundness of spiritual insight and simplicity of expression, it is
generally conceded, have never been excelled. The poorest and

the richest minds are alike unable to fathom its spiritual depths.

Our profoundest literary critics have selected four other books as second in rank.   These are:

The Illiad and Odyssey of Homer,
The Divina Comedia of Dante,
The Dramas of Shakespeare,
The Faust of Gœthe.

None of these bear the test of giving satisfaction to the uncultured.   It would seem that they were more wanting in this than some other books of acknowledged greatness.   Indeed, it now begins to appear as if no one of the critics in the past has discerned the true significance of these poems.   The learned in every age have seen enough in them, however, to proclaim them great, though they have not been eminently successful in explaining to the unlearned how they are great.

It would prolong this paper too much to finish what we started to say about the different classes of books, and to suggest an elementary course of reading to the readers of the Journal.   Further discussion will, therefore, be deferred until next month.

G. P. B.

EDUCATIONAL VALUE OF SCHOOL WORK-SHOPS.

The educational value of anything, is determined by the kind of mental activity that is stimulated by that thing.   What kinds of mental activity are stimulated in a school work-shop?

A comparison of these with those occasioned by the study of the branches in the ordinary school curriculum, will determine the relative value of the machine shop as an educational appliance.

In the school shop the boy constructs from a model.   He must first know his model.   This involves the activity of the powers of observation.   He must discriminate and compare.   In his discriminating he has analyzed the model into its parts, but in this analysis he has constantly seen these parts in their relation to the whole, or synthesized them.

In constructing a thing like the model, he also discriminates and compares part with part, and whole with whole.   Suppose he is to construct a square.

(1.) He must reduce his raw material to the proper dimensions; (2) he must cut the sides of equal length; (3) he must make his joints so that the sides shall form right angles when joined. Every movement of his tools involves also discrimination and comparison, and a slight degree of reasoning. I see no other mind activity involved in constructing this square, unless we shall say that the imagination has furnished an object which the mind substitutes for the model with which it compares the construction. In all constructing from a model, these are the only mental powers employed. They are the simplest forms of mind activity which the boy has been employing all his life. He is compelled now, if he is well taught, to make sharper discriminations and more delicate comparisons than he has been wont to make. If he is not well taught, he does not get even this discipline. What is meant by training the eye, is forming the habit of sharp discriminations and accurate comparisons. The training of the hand is to habituate the muscles to obey the commands of the mind.

Let the educational value of this exercise be compared with that of a free-hand drawing of a square from a model. To draw this square, he must (1) make as discriminating study of the model as before. The same analysis and synthesis is necessary. (2) He makes his own material for his construction, which consists of lines properly drawn to represent this solid upon a flat surface. This representation is a new problem which did not arise in the work shop. A new training of the eye is necessary, and a demand for the exercise of the judgment far greater than that required in the former construction. A similar discrimination and comparison of the model with the drawing, is required now as before; the same exercise of the imagination is involved. (3) There is also a similar training of the muscles to obey the will and of the eye to see.

Good teaching of the drawing of the square, gives all the forms of mental activity that were employed in the work shop, and those involved in perspective drawing in addition. More muscles are required in the work-shop than in the drawing room, and for this reason the work-shop may be more promotive of health.

It would seem from this comparison, that every form of mental action that was employed in constructing the square in the work-shop, is involved in constructing the square in the drawing room, and more. The only difference in those elements in which they are similar, is that the work-shop brings more muscles of the body into exercise. This, however, is of no special value, if this exercise is not needed to maintain the health, or if it can be obtained in some other way with the same economy of time.

What is gained in education, then, by the work-shop?

It is said that the boy gets used to the handling of mechanical tools. But of what importance is this to a boy who is not to be a mechanic? And to him that is to become one, the use of the tools is readily acquired by the lad who enters the shop with a mind well disciplined by the study of the ordinary school curriculum, and with an eye and a hand well trained by the practice of free hand drawing from the object.

It is claimed that the work-shop will encourage industry, whereas the school now educates the pupil out of his sphere, and thus encourages idleness.

The truth is, that but for the school no habits of industry whatever would be fostered in many children. In many families where the wolf does not stand at the door, and persistent effort by every member is not necessary to keep him out, the children are trained to no habits of industry. Many a pupil graduates from the high school without ever having known what persistent toil means. Nothing of the sort is demanded at home, and the home authorities unite with the child in preventing the enforcement of these demands in the school. The influences that such homes bring to bear upon school boards and teachers, make it next to impossible to enforce such industry in the school as shall fix habits of work that will go with the pupil after he leaves it. And yet, in spite of all these counter forces, the children educated in the schools are more industrious than those that have never been subject to its discipline, other things being equal.

But the home is more potent than the school, in teaching the child that it is not disgraceful to labor with one's hands. Every demand of the school is a demand for work, and recognizes the dignity of labor. If, after a child comes through the schools, he will not work at any honorable employment that his needs require or his position demands, he has either not done his work well in the schools, or else the family has filled his head with false pride that the school could not keep out.   G. P. B.

PRIMARY DEPARTMENT.

[This Department is conducted by Lewis H. Jones, Supt. Indianapolis Schools.]

——:o:——

PRIMARY LANGUAGE.

THE chief aim in giving lessons in language in the primary grades, is to develop the power to use language correctly and with facility. This power must then be formed into a habit by much practice upon the correct and elegant forms of expression.

But for the best results this power must have its beginning in intelligent comprehension of the simplest facts of language. The logical relation between the thought and its expression in words must not be violated. The charm of interest must enlist the emotional nature, and the drill of the teacher must transform the will of child into its automatic modes of operation in the production of the correct forms of expression. Often this order of procedure is violated by omitting everything except the drill; in which case the lesson becomes devoid of interest, and the entire subject of language becomes distasteful to the pupil.

Again, while the power to compose in writing correctly and readily, including the spelling of all words, is regarded as a test of culture, the ability to talk correctly and effectively is a much more practical power for the average citizen.

Add to this the fact that talking is the easier of the two processes, and the one in which the child has had most practice before school age, and it is easily seen that the larger part of the first in language and work in composition, even, should be oral description.

Simple themes—pictures of landscapes, with children at play— or interesting objects, as fruits or nuts—should be chosen. Each child should express his thought with some freedom; and above everything else, let him feel that whatever of correction is needed will be made in a kindly spirit. Excessive criticism, or any tendency on the part of the teacher at this early stage to ridicule the language of the child is fatal to that easy play of faculty so necessary to the composer.

In some one of the earlier lessons of the kind just indicated, the teacher should write the conversation of the pupils on the board, capitalizing and punctuating, without referring to either capital or mark of punctuation further than to use it correctly. In this way the correct form of the sentence becomes familiar, soon comes to seem appropriate, and at last it will be practiced by the pupil on due occasion. In later work, however, the pupils need to be taught the laws which govern capitalizing and punctuating.

If the teacher will take the care to write plainly on the board, pupils of the second year in school will be able to read what has thus been first said orally by the pupils themselves, and afterwards written on the board by the teacher. After several pupils have read, the teacher may begin to distinguish among the expressions by saying (as she points), "Read this sentence, Harry," or "Read the first sentence, Fanny," etc.

In this work there is no definition of a sentence attempted, for none could be understood by pupils of the age supposed. But the term is used appropriately by the teacher, and something of the meaning of the word is beginning to dawn upon the mind of the pupil. This much is in preparation for the understanding of such definition at a later period; and if the teacher will use the term as applied to sentences only, and never with reference to other groups of words, the pupils will by observation gather enough of the meaning through such use to enable him to understand the fine distinctions between the sentence on the one hand, and the phrase or clause on the other, whenever such distinction becomes the proper subject of his study.

NUMBER AND ARITHMETIC.

F. W. PARKER.

Work from 1 *to* 20 *inclusive. Ascertain with the greatest care just what the pupil knows of Number.* Begin with the number that is one larger than the one which the pupil really knows.

What is it to know a number? To know:

1. The number as a whole. Take 8.
2. The equal numbers in a number (division), IIII IIII—
   II II II II.
3. The equal numbers that make a number,
   (multiplication) IIII IIII
                    II II II II.
4. The equal parts of a number, IIII, IIII ½—II II II, II ¼.
5. Any *two* equal or unequal numbers that may be found in
   a number,
   (subtraction) IIII IIII—I IIIIIII
                 II IIIIII—III III IIIII.
6. Any two equal or unequal numbers that make a number,
   (addition) IIII IIII—I IIIIIII
              II IIIIII—III IIIII.

It will be seen that the representations of humbers in 2, 3 and
4 are identical to the eye. (1) The purpose of each operation
differs radically from the others. The purpose arises from a
special necessity fonnd for a particular kind of doing in essentially practical mátters. (2) We must find the quarts in pints
(the twos in), the yards in feet (threes in), hence the necessity
of finding the equal numbers in a number. (3) I have 6 quarts;
how many pints have I? 6 twos of pints, union of equal numbers. (4) If 8 apples are given to 4 boys, how many do I give
to each? Here 8 apples must be separated into 4 equal parts—
in order to find the value of one part. Comparison of 2 and 4.
In both cases I have the same number. In 2 I must know one
of the equal numbers, in order to find the number of equal numbers; in 4 I must know an entirely different thing, and that is
the number of equal parts, in order to find she value of one part.
Confusion of these operations that are essentially different is the
source of much trouble *in logical reasoning in arithmetic.*

*Do these five different operations cover all the essentials in the use
of a number?* This question may be answered by finding some
operation or fact not included in them. Addition is uniting two
or more numbers; how then, can, knowing any two numbers
that make a number cover the whole ground of the facts in addition? 2+4+3=9. When 6 is learned 2+4 is learned; when

9 is learned 6+3 is known, so that the union of more than three numbers is simply a repetition or review of *what has been learned before.*

In what order should these different operations be learned? The order should be derermined by the power of the child to discover the facts in the number taught. If he sees the equal numbers jn a number first, then it follows that he (one child) learns that first, or if he discovers first the equal numbers that make a number, a similar deduction should be made. A long series of investigations would bring an honest investigator to some safe conclusions. Certainly a child should learn what he discovers, and in the order of discovery.

Each child should be lead to discover for himself, with the slightest possible help, all the facts in a number. A discovered truth is often nearly learned in the discovery. Discovery employs the highest mental action, while unneeded help weakens, and in the end renders the helped helpless. Of one thing there is no doubt ; a child can discover every fact in a number for himself if the teacher lets him and leads him.

The means to be used in teaching number. The psychological definition of number is : Number is the limitation of things by ones. The mind in numbering limits things by ones (the smallest measure). We learn to do by doing the thing to be done. Limiting things by ones, is the thing to be done. We can not think of a number without thinking of a number of things. There is absolutely no other way to learn number than by numbering things, numbering not counting ; counting is ordinal—the fourth finger is four in counting. All the fingers are four in numbering. By the thorough and complete appiication of this definition to every step of numbers and arithmetical teaching, mental power is used in the most economical way, in gaining a knowledge of the limitation of things by ones.

It is best to have pupils handle the objects and make all the limitations for themselves. Pupils can not well discover the truth in objects held or manipulated by the teacher. Let them make and discover by making their own limitations and they will not be so limited in knowledge as they sometimes are. Put the work of limiting things by ones (numbering) in the hands of your pupils; let them weigh, measure, buy, sell, unite and separate. In this work, if properly condncted, childred will great pleasure.

When a pupil can limit things by ones unaided by the presence of objects, the use of objects thereafter for the definite limitation that is clear without their use, weakens mental action. Thes statement answers the question of when and how long, objects should be used in teaching numbers. They *must* be used for the purpose of gaining ideas of numbers and their relations; as well might we try to learn botany without plants, or zoology without animals; but when the ideas and their relations are in the mind, their use for the purpose of bringing into the consciousness *what is already in the mind,* cultivates a habit of mental laziness, of dependence rather than freedom. Objects must be used all through the study of arithmetic when new conditions are presented that can not be grasped by the pupils without objects. For example: money should be used in teaching interest, and blocks in cube root.—*Practical Teacher.*

THE SCHOOL ROOM.

[This Department is conducted by GEO. F. BASS, Supervising Prin. Indianapolis schools.]

——:x:——

"UNITS, TENS, HUNDREDS."

How many pupils have said the above without having the remotest idea of the meaning! The writer well remembers wondering what it all meant. He lived, however, and learned at a later day the meaning of the mystic words. His father, who "cradled" his wheat lived too. They both see the Twine-Binder doing the work of half dozen men. The Twine-Binder is in the school room, too. Great improvements have been made in teaching—as great as in farming. No new principle in mechanics was discovered to enable the inventor to make his great machine. No new principle has been discovered to enable the teacher of the "new education" to do better work. Both apply the old principle more intelligently. We are now ready to introduce a lesson that may be seen in many good schools of city and country.

The following is from observation : The class was composed of pupils who could represent numbers by one figure readily. The teacher placed a bunch of lamp-lighters on the ledge of the blackboard and asked a pupil to write over it a figure showing how many bunches she had placed there. The figure *one* was written. The teacher then placed, similarly, two, three, four and five bunches. The figures were placed above them as be-fore. These *bunches* were then passed to the pupils so that they might count the lighters in each bunch. As soon as the teacher saw a little fellow had completed the counting, she called on him for the result. The answer came clear and distinct, "Ten." Each little fellow was thus called upon and each gave the an-swer, ten. The agreement of answers seemed to please them for their eyes were sparkling and there was a happy expression on each little face. The teacher took advantage of this state of the class and said, "How many *tens* we have! Let us tie them up and put them back on the ledge of the blackboard and see how many we have." It was done, and one little girl was asked to count the *tens* and place a figure over the pile that she made to show how many *tens* she found. Many test questions fol-lowed, fixing in the minds of the pupils the fact that in each *ten* there are ten ones.

The teacher put the tens in the box and took *one lamp-lighter* and stood it on the ledge of the board and had a pupil place a figure over it showing how many. She then said: "We will now stand a bunch on a *ten* at the left of it." A figure was placed over it and the children were led to read it, "1 ten and 1 one." The lighters were then taken away and counted when it was found that there were eleven in all. The children were then told that they might call the expression *eleven*. They were told that the right hand figure always meant *ones* or *units*, that the next figure meant *tens*. Time was now *up* and class was dis-missed, and we retired. It then occurred to us that we had read in a former number of the Indiana School Journal an article on "Primary Number" that had given these ideas. We got the back number and re-read the article. We then saw that the same plan might be carried on into 12, 13, 14, 20, etc. That

"hundreds" could be presented by binding ten bunches together. We expect to visit this teacher again.

WRITING—POSITION, FREEDOM, EASE, RAPIDITY, AND HAND–WRITING.

[CONCLUDED.]

IN addition to good position, freedom, etc., as mentioned in
last month's article, there will be gained something not desirable—the writing will be scraggly—uneven in height, slant and
spacing, and both pupil and parent will think the writing not so
good as before; nor will it be as good in *form*, but quality of
line will be better.

It may be well to explain to the school (and parents, too, if
you can) that this will be the outcome of the work.

Before the school can become good business writers they must
pass through this stage—it can not be avoided—and if they are
not taken through during school life, they must go through
when they enter business with their chances for settling into a
good business hand much against them, as you can readily convince yourself by examining any business writing, or even your
own writing.

Here in Indianapolis a graduate of the High School obtained
a situation in a prominent business house, but could not hold it
because he could not write sufficiently well, but he had done
good school-boy writing.   Sad commentary.

If the pupil has now become master of his muscles he has
arrived at a point where a strict adherence to forms must be
rejected and the advice of a teacher endowed with good common sense is invaluable to him.

Let the teacher keep in mind now that excellent writing has
three leading features:

(1). It must be perfectly legible *at a glance.*

(2). It must bear marks of rapidity.

(3). A page should be beautiful.

In order to legibility no letter should be so made that if it
were standing alone it might be taken for any other letter or be
unintelligible; hight and spacing should be even and regular.

Give the pupil the greatest freedom for developing his own peculiarities so long as he does not mar either of the three leading features. No flourish. He will fill his paper full of the wildest kind if not prevented.

Finally, practice what you teach as far as your circumstances will permit.

RELATED IDEAS.

T. M—ă—n, (phonically). What did I spell, Johnnie?

J. Don't know.

T. Now listen carefully. Repeats with great emphasis. Now what is it?

J. Don't know.

T. Now think. What will you be when you are as big as your father?

J. (Sobbing). A dunce.

We laugh at such occurrences as this and dismiss them without ascertaining who made the first mistake, and probably the worst one. At first thought it may seem that the pupil is dull and that *he* made the mistake.

Let us look again. The teacher was trying to teach the word *man* by the phonic method. He had given the sounds correctly once, and the pupil having inherited some of his father's traits of intellect, was slow to comprehend. He then repeated the sounds, and yet the pupil could not tell what word was meant. The teacher then forsook his phonic method and attempted to have the pupil get the word from relations entirely outside the phonic method.

The pupil understood those relations better than the teacher did. Either his father was an acknowledged dunce, or else the boy had been told so frequently that he would be a dunce when he became a man, that he concluded it was better to say so at once.

Teachers often make mistakes as bad as this, and they are passed by unnoticed, because they do not happen to present the ludicrous as this one does.

Stick to your method.

TECHNICAL TERMS.

Shall we teach them to third and fourth grade pupils? **No.**
Why not? Are they not a convenience? Yes, but they **are**
usually learned to say by pupils of this age. They mean nothing. "Possessive plural" usually means very little to third and
fourth grade children.

It is nonsense to give a hard shell hickory nut to a small boy
and tell him to eat it. He can not crack the shell. Terms are
hard shells; they contain the meat but they must be cracked before the meat can be tasted. These young pupils can not crack
them. They do not know that they are worth cracking.

They may learn to "rattle these terms off" and make as much
noise as a small boy with a basket of hickory nuts at the top of
a pair of uncarpeted stairs.

Teach the pupil to form the possessive plural, but do not
bother him with the term nor a formal rule for forming it.

"COMMA, ONE."

"In the good old days of yore" we used to say the "stops"
as we read. "Ned, can you hop?" would have been read as
follows: "Ned (comma one) can you hop" (interrogation point
four).

Every thinking teacher now knows that the punctuation
marks do not indicate pauses. There are some teachers, however, who do not think, but teach as their teachers taught.

"MY RULE."

"This must be done just because it is my rule. I know it
will work injustice to several pupils, but it is my rule and I must
treat all alike."

But all are *not* alike and can not be. A teacher should be
greater than his rule.

EDITORIAL.

The JOURNAL enters upon its *thirtieth* volume with this issue. It . wishes a "Happy New Year" to each of its many friends, and will endeavor to continue to deserve their hearty support. The Journal's motto is, "Prove all things and hold fast that which is good"—it is therefore conservative and at the same time progressive. A *bona fide* subscription list of more than *5000* is a substantial endorsement of this course.

Special attention is called to the advertisements in this issue.

January 1, 1885, was fixed as the time when, with a few special exceptions, all deferred subscriptions to this Journal should be paid. Let those to whom this applies *remember*.

PRIZE ESSAY.—Do not fail to read the advertisement offering a prize to the person who will write the best essay on "The Value of Cyclopedias in the School-room, and the Best Manner of Using them." This has more than a common interest.

Persons sending money for this Journal can send amounts less than $1 in *two* and *one* cent postage stamps; no others can be used.

In asking to have the address of your Journal changed, please give the *old* address as well as the new, naming the county as well as the state.

An agent is wanted to raise a club for the Journal in every township in the State. Send for terms.

COTTON EXPOSITION.

The great Cotton Exposition at New Orleans had its formal open-ing Tuesday, December 16th. Gen. Carnahan, in the issue of the *Indianapolis Journal* under date of December 15th, gives his im-pressions of a visit to New Orleans. He says although the formal opening is December 16th, not one-fifth of the goods for the exposi-tion will be in their places at that date, and advises all who intend making a journey South to postpone it until the middle of January or first of February. This is rather discouraging to those who ex-pect to make a holiday trip to New Orleans, and it is to be hoped that the managers of the exposition will be more rapid in their move-ments than is predicted. To most people in the North a visit to New Orleans for the sake of the city itself will well repay the expense and time involved.

THE PRESIDENCY OF THE STATE UNIVERSITY.

The trustees of Indiana University have promoted Prof. David S. Jordan from the chair of natural science to the presidency of the university, to succeed Dr. Lemuel Moss. This is a marked compli-ment to Prof. Jordan, who is not yet 34 years of age. He is a New Yorker by birth, and is a graduate of Cornell University. He received his special stimulus in the natural science line from the noted Louis Agassiz, at Penikese Island.

Prof. Jordan's first teaching after his study with Agassiz was in the Indianapolis high school. In 1874 he was elected to the chair of natural science in Butler University. In 1878 he accepted the posi-tion in the State University which he has since filled. In addition to his regular work he has done work for the Smithsonian Institute, which has been highly appreciated. His special line in natural sci-ence is a fish-line. As an ichthyologist he has a reputation even in Europe. While ihcthyology is his specialty he stands high in several other of the natural science departments, and is by no means defi-cient in other departments of college work. His salary is $3000.

The trustees at the same meeting elected Horace A. Hoffman, a graduate of the University, and who is now taking a special course at Harvard, Professor of Greek, to assume his duties in the future.

RELIGION IN THE PUBLIC SCHOOLS.

Rev. A. Marine, of Indianapolis, one of the leading Methodist preachers in the State of Indiana, in a sermon preached on last Thanksgiving Day, made use of the following language, as reported in the *Indianapolis Journal:* " Religion is prescribed and forbidden to urge its transcendent claims outside its own sanctuaries and chosen altars of devotion by secular journalism and narrow partisan newspapers, while our entire public school system has become so remotely separated from all religious influence as to make itself felt and seen in the materialistic tendencies of our civilization. It is time that emphasis should be given to the fact that education without the religious element in it is a violation of every recognized principle of sound philosophy and every law of our being."

The above statement in regard to the public schools is frequently expressed by clergymen, and can be accounted for on one of two theories: (1) They are not familiar with what the schools are really doing; or (2) They use the word religion in the sense of sectarian dogma.

Having entered the public schools, as a pupil, about forty-five years ago, and having been connected with them in some capacity ever since, I feel competent to speak from personal knowledge, and the following statements are in accord with my experience, observation, and information:

Never before was the fact so generally recognized and so much insisted upon that the chief part of a child is its moral and religious nature; that intellectual training, unaccompanied by moral training, is a positive harm to a community, as it simply gives greater power for evil.

Never before was the standard of moral integrity so high for the teacher, and as a consequence, there were never before so many noble christian men and women engaged in teaching.

Never before was the necessity of moral training so frequently talked of and urged in teachers' meetings. Perhaps not a single one of the ninety-two county institutes held within the last six months in this State has missed having this thought urged upon it. With but few exceptions each day's session of these meetings is opened with religious exercises.

Throughout the country the rule is to open schools with religious exercises. The school in which the Bible is not read daily is the exception. There is not a normal school or college in the country in which the great masses of the teachers are educated and trained that does not open each day's work with the reading of scripture and prayer.

Furthermore, large numbers, I think it is safe to say a majority, of the teachers are church members, and a large majority of the remainder are regular attendants upon church services, and thus the great body of teachers are directly under the influence of the church. The parents who do most in determining the character of the schools attend church, as do also the children.

Now, if it is true, as Mr. Marine charges, that the schools are failing

3

in one of their most vital duties, he and his fellow-preachers ought
to be ashamed of themselves. If, with the teacher and patrons, and
children looking to them for spiritual guidance, the clergy allow the
schools to drift away from their highest form of work, it is a sad commentary upon their own influence, and they should be ashamed of
themselves. If the charge is true then the preachers of the land are
more culpable than any other class of community.

But the charge is not true. Mr. Marine is mistaken, unless he
uses the term "religion" as many ministers do use it, in a narrow
sectarian sense. When it is realized that religion is not a theory,
not a creed, not even "a plan of salvation," but a *life*—a life lived
recognizing its relations to its fellow-men, and to "Our Father who
art in heaven," then it will be found that our schools as a whole *are*
doing a great work, not only intellectually but morally and relig-
iously. They are the great character builders.

OUR LOSSES IN EDUCATION.

"The first of the losses of the present system of education is the
loss of spontaneity and originality in the teacher."—E. E. HALE, in
North American Review for November.

This moves me to say that it is true, and is necessarily true. It
marks a stage in our progress toward rational spontaneity and originality. In so far as it indicates progress from a lower to a higher
grade of teaching it should be classed as a gain rather than a loss.

I will try to explain: There seem to be three stages in the advance of every one in the mastery of any vocation; which stages are
more or less clearly defined in different individuals.

In the first stage of knowledge there is a spontaneity and originality begotten of ignorance. The tyro has gotten the skin of something,—call it the teaching vocation,—and has mistaken it for the
thing. He is not troubled with any doubts. He acts with freedom
within these limits and transcends these limits with equal freedom,
being unconscious of their existence. He is enthusiastic, spontaneous and original, and will naturally kindle the enthusiasm of his
pupils. They will be "waked up," and some of them will "blaze"
their own way through difficulties where the teacher is powerless to
help them. But there comes a time in that teacher's growth,—unless
he fossilizes into a pedagogue,—when he breaks through this skin
and discovers that there is something beneath which he has not yet
explored. Now comes the period of timidity and uncertainty. He
is not so sure of his ground. He looks around for some support.
In his bewildered condition he is inclined to lean upon the arm of
revered and trusted authority. He dons the working harness of
some one else, but it chafes him. His glance below the surface has

revealed that there is a law or method belonging to teaching which he feels that he must know. He tries to get it second-hand. It is not his own and it trammels him. He has lost enthusiasm, spontaneity and originality. He takes some method ready-made and proceeds to fit himself to it, paring here and padding there. If he stops here he will crystallize into a mere formalist. He becomes one of the washers in the Walpurgis night of Faust. His last state is worse than his first. He is an illustration of that line in Pope that,

"A little learning is a dangerous thing."

In his third stage he has passed out of his state of bondage to method into that freedom which the knowledge of the principles of all method confers. He has discovered what are the true purposes of education, and has gained a theoretical and experimental knowledge of how to direct the child in his acquisition of knowledge so as to realize most nearly these purposes. His knowledge of both mind and matter makes him free in the construction of his own methods. Now he becomes again "spontaneous and original," but his freedom is the freedom of knowledge, not of ignorance. His enthusiasm, too, is tempered by discretion. He knows what can and what can not be done, and loses no time in his essays after the impossible.

Neither he nor his school will be as demonstrative as it was in his first stage. There will be less "cavorting about" and more settled, strong pulling.

* * * * * * * *

Now I believe that every teacher must go through these three stages of growth. If he passes through them by the road of experience he is generally well along in that period called the prime of his mental and vital powers, before he has well entered the third stage. A thorough training under the direction of those who have themselves passed over the road, will enable a young teacher to attain this third stage of knowledge much sooner than he could arrive at it by experience alone; but he will never fully enter it except through experience, whatever may be his preparatory training.

* * * * * * * *

Now there will be stages in the development of the teaching vocation in the world that will correspond to these periods of their growth in the individual. There has been a time when the teachers of this country were free because they were ignorant of the existence of a science or even of an art (in any true sense) of education. All that they were supposed to know was the subjects which they were expected to teach.

For the past few years, teachers as a class have been in that transition stage from the first to the third. They have magnified method unduly. They have even exalted it over scholarship. The scholarship of our teachers throughout the country is shamefully poor. What hope is there of enthusiasm, spontaneity, or originality when the teacher himself is feeding upon the husks of the subject he is teaching. They have not stopped to learn what to teach, but have been vainly reaching after the how, and in this have pinned their faith to the sleeve of some revered authority, and so have become mere organ grinders. As Mr. Hale says they have lost the "spontaneity and originality" of former times. He seems to imply that this loss is due to the "present system."

But the present deplorable condition is a necessary phase in our growth. Let us pray, however, that our development be not arrested here. The public schools and our public school system can only be saved from destruction at the hands of an indignant people by the teachers' passing on into the stage of the freedom of knowledge. The system is all well enough. It is the inefficiency of the teacher, and failure to comprehend the reason of his existence as teacher that is the matter with the schools.   G. P. B.

THE GIRLS DIDN'T GO.

The Western Reserve College was established about sixty years ago, and of course admitted only young men. About twelve years ago women were admitted. Recently, by reason of a large gift the name of the college was changed to Adelbert, in honor of the donor's only son, and was removed from Hudson to Cleveland, Ohio.

From all the testimony that reaches us the young women maintained themselves creditably in scholarship and deportment, but for some unaccountable reason all the members of the faculty, except the president, petitioned the board of trustees to exclude the ladies on the ground "that women would break down in health; that they needed not the *same* education as men, but something to fit them for the duties of wife and mother; that a separate college must be built with 'diploma certificates' instead of degrees; that boys would be deterred from coming to a college which woman's attending always made second rate"!!

As may be imagined Cleveland was greatly agitated over this proposition. It was discussed through the newspapers, from the pulpits, in the shops, and at the firesides. The trustees appointed a committee to take the subject under consideration and make a report. This committee sought the views of leading educators who had tested co-education, and could therefore speak from experience. The following indicate the uniform testimony received:

James B. Angell, Pres. Michigan University, wrote: "Most of the evils feared by those who opposed the admission of women were not encountered. We made no solitary modification of our rules or re-

quirements. The women did not become hoydenish; they did not
fail in their studies; they did not break down in their health; they
have graduated in all departments; they have not been inferior in
scholarship. We count the experiment here a success."

G Anderson, Pres. Chicago University, replying to the objection
on the part of young men, wrote: "In one instance, during my
presidency of six years, one or two young men left one class because
they could not successfully compete with two young women in the
class, and I did not, under the circumstances, mourn their departure.
I have never had the slightest trouble from the association of the
sexes."

Chancellor Manatt, of Nebraska University, wrote: "This question sounds like a joke in this longitude. As well ask if a girl's being
born into a family turns the boys out of doors. It rather strengthens
the home attraction. So in the university."

A. D. White, Pres. Cornell University, wrote: "Having gone
through one more year, making twelve in all since women were admitted (to the "annex"), I do not hesitate to say that I believe their
presence here good for us in every respect. There has not been a
particle of scandal of any sort, and no trouble."

Prof. Moses Coit Tyler wrote: "My observation has been that,
under joint system, the tone of college life has grown more earnest,
more courteous and refined, less flippant and cynical. The women
are usually among the very best scholars, and lead instead of drag,
and their lapses from good health are rather, yes, decidedly, less numerous than those alleged by the young men."

President Warren, of Boston University, wrote: "My convictions
grow stronger and more decided every year. The only opponents
of co-education I have ever known are persons who know nothing
about it practically, and whose difficulties are all speculative and
imaginary."

Many other opinions to the same effect might be given, but the
above will suffice. The report of the committee contains the following:

"The harem is Mohammedan; the monastery and nunnery are
Romanistic. Separate education of the sexes was the natural outgrowth, or rather the belief on which both rest, that the sexes can
not associate together without danger and harm. Opposed to these
is co-education, the latest and best growth of Christianity."

The girls were victorious by a vote of 12 to 6.

ANSWER TO QUERIES.—The capital of Louisiana according to the
latest geographies is Baton Rouge. Louisiana is divided into par-
ishes instead of counties.

BLOW-HARD ADVERTISING.

The *National Normal Exponent* takes exceptions to what the Journal in its October issue had to say as to its method of advertising.

The answer of the *Exponent* is in keeping with the advertising, and is therefore characteristic, and would not have received further notice were it not for the fact that the Journal's article is construed to be an attack on "independent normalism." No criticism was made upon "normalism" of any kind. The Journal has as high regard for "independent normals" and "independent *Exponents*" as it has for state institutions, when they do as honest work. The Journal estimates a school or a paper solely by the work it does.

The term "University" is justified by Mr. Holbrook on the ground that his school contains a large number of departments, and because other institutions not so large are called "universities."

Because "some little institutions" have assumed a name which they have no right to, is hardly a sufficient reason why their example should be followed. And the *number* of branches taught and *number* of teachers employed will hardly make a "university" without regard to the extent of the course of study. An institution that admits students before they are ready to enter an ordinary high school, and then graduates them from some of its departments in a single year, and from many if not every one in two or three years, is hardly worthy the name University—remembering that "university" means *higher* and *beyond* the college. To drag down the name of the highest institution of learning and apply it to a school whose chief work is teaching the common branches, does not lift up the lower school, but it does cheapen and make meaningless the high title. The tendency now is to abuse the word "university" in the same way in which the word "professor" is abused. There are getting to be so many "professors" that one can achieve most notoriety by adhering to the plain title Mr.

Mr. Holbrook say, "This institution (The National Normal) is the founder of a *system* of education. Are you not aware of it?"

The Journal is compelled to confess ignorance as to any such *system* of education. It has seen extraordinary claims as to its ability to do as much for a student in *one* year as an "old fogy college" can do in *three*. It has also noticed a *system*-atic tendency to magnify whatever was done at the normal and to minify whatever was done in other schools. Aside from these characteristics the Journal has in its long years of observation discovered nothing of importance that was *original*.

Mr. Holbrook has no right to complain, as he does, at being criticised. Within the range of the Journal's extensive acquaintance it knows of no other person who has indulged so freely and so relentlessly in the criticism of other institutions as has he. The last issue of the *Exponent* furnishes ample proof of this.

The Journal will repeat what it said in its former article, viz.; that the National Normal has done and is doing much good work; but the good work is not original in the sense claimed, and the original work ("the only authoritative," etc.) is not good.

The pages of the Journal are at the service of Mr. Holbrook if he wishes to set forth a few of the characteristic features of his "new system of education."

QUESTIONS AND ANSWERS.

QUESTIONS BY THE STATE BOARD FOR NOVEMBER.

THEORY OF TEACHING.—1. Show that the teacher does not make the rules of the school, but that he must be obedient to them equally with the pupils.

2. What is the value as discipline of the maintenance of silence in the school room?

3. Describe the process of forming a habit.

4. Name the different ends for which the school exists.

5. What is meant by the organization of a school?

ORTHOGRAPHY.—1. How many elementary sounds in the English Language?

2. (a) Into what three general classes are these divided?
(b) Give an example of each.   a=6 b=4.

3. How many sounds has e and g? Illustrate each.   2 pts, 5 ea.

4. How many and what sounds compose the word receipt?
2 pts, 5 each.

5. Spell the plural of beau, die (a stamp) corps, valley, folio.

6. Spell ten words dictated by the Superintendent.   10 pts, 5 ea.

PENMANSHIP.—1. Describe your method of distributing and collecting copy-books.

2. In teaching penmanship what should receive attention first?

3. Describe the *Arm Rest.* The *Hand Rest.*

4. Give your method of criticising the work of your pupils.

5. Analyze a, b, c, A, C.

NOTE.—Your writing in answering these questions will be taken as a specimen of your penmanship, and will be marked 50 or below, according to merit.

PHYSIOLOGY.—1. What is anatomy?

2. Where and how does nutrition take place?   2 pts, 5 each.

3. By what organs are the different parts of the body connected?

4. Describe a muscle.

5. What are the nature and effect of true exercise?   2 pts, 5 ea.

6, What is the general action on the food in digestion?

7. Describe the lungs, with diagram.

8. (*a*) Is cold bread more healthful than hot bread?
(*b*) Why?   a=2; b=8

9. What nerves are included within the skull?

10. To what extent and for what purpose is breathing under control of the will?   2 pts, 5 ea.

GRAMMAR — 1. How many and what elements in every sentence? Why must every sentence have them?

2. What is the ground for dividing sentences into Declarative, Interrogative and Exclamatory?

3. How does the simple sentence differ from the compound or complex sentence?

4. Name and explain two of the leading relations that exist between the members of a compound sentence?

5. What is the difference between a subordinate clause and a substantive clause?

6. Should we say, "I feel bad," or "I feel badly"? Why?

7. Give all the participial forms of the following verbs: *lay, recite, write.*

8. Parse the nouns in the following: "John being industrious, he was soon appointed leader."

9. State and illustrate the offices of the compound personal pronoun?

10. Correct the following, giving reasons: *a.* "I can solve this problem easier than that." *b.* "I want to go very bad." *c.* "This lesson is awful hard."

READING.—1. What relation has reading to all other branches of study?

2. What are the chief ends to be attained in teaching reading in the common schools?

3. What preparation should children in the Second Reader be required to make for the reading lesson?

4. Name five American authors that you would recommend children to read.   5 pts, 2 each.

5. What is mechanical reading, and how is it to be avoided?   2 pts, 5 each.

6. Read a paragraph of prose and a stanza of poetry selected by the Superintendent.   25 each.

ARITHMETIC.—1. What is a common multiple? A least common multiple? Why invert the divisor in division of fractions? What is a square? A cube?   5, 2 each.

2. What is a ratio? Give the rule for stating a problem in simple proportion.   5, 5

3. A commission merchant sold 1300 barrels of flour, at $5.75 a barrel, receiving a commission of 3½%, and invested the net proceeds in coffee at 25 cts. a pound, first deducting 2% commission, how many pounds of coffee did he purchase? What was his entire commission?   5, 5

4. The duty on 1250 yards of silk, at 40% ad valorem, was $1,100, what was the invoice price per yard? For how much per yard must the importer sell the silk to clear 20%?

5. What is the amount of $192.60 for 1 yr. 5 mo. 19 da. at 9%?

6. What is the equated time for the payment of $340, due May 10th, 1870; $450, due June 10; $560, due July 15; and $650, due August 10?

7. From ¼ of a pound of Troy take ⅜ of an ounce. Proc. 5, ans. 5.

8. There is a circular field 40 rods in diameter, what is its circumference? How many acres does it contain?   5, 5

9. A man paid $8100 for two farms, and ⅜ of the cost of the larger farm was equal to ₇⅝ of the cost of the smaller, what was the cost of each?   5, 5

10. If 100 lbs. be carried 20 mi. for 20 cts., how far may 10100 lbs. be carried for $60.60?

GEOGRAPHY.—1. Name and locate the Tropics, and tell why they are so located.

2. Name and describe the different forms of government existing among civilized people.

3. Name the political divisions of North America in order, beginning with the most northern. Give capitals of each.

4. Name and locate five seaboard cities of the United States.

5. Give location of Quito, Vienna, Canton, Marseilles and Galveston.

6. Where is Cape May? Mobile Bay? Island of Corsica? San Joaquin River? Wasatch Mountains?

7. Where is Birmingham? Rouen? Prague? Munich? Naples?

8. What countries border on France? What is the government of France?

9. What countries are separated by the Adriatic Sea? What large city is located on this sea?

10. Name five rivers of Africa.

U S. HISTORY.—1. What evidence is there that this country was inhabited by an earlier and more civilized people than the Indians?
10

2. What relation does the rise of the Huguenots in France have to do with the settlement of the southern part of the U. S. Territory?
10

3. How did the war in Europe for the Spanish succession cause war in the American colonies?   10

4. What celebrated English statesmen, early in 1775, tried to obtain justice for the colonies? What was the reply of one of them to Lord North's proposition to all the colonies to tax themselves for the benefit of Great Britain?   5, 5

5. What American obtained aid of the French for the colonies in the Revolution? What variation from court etiquette, made in his favor, showed the high estimation in which he was held?   5, 5

6. Name three important events in Van Buren's administration. What gave rise to the expression "fifty-four, forty, or fight?" How was the matter settled?   5 pts.

7. What is the Ordinance of 1787? What relation has this instrument to the subjects of slavery and education in the States erected from the N. W. Territory?   5, 5

8. When was Fort Sumter captured? What was the numerical proportion of the men engaged on the two sides? What was the result of this capture?   4, 3, 3

9. In colonial times the slave interests were North, at the time of the Civil war they were South; what caused this change?   10

10. Describe the battle of Nashville, in which Thomas so literally destroyed Hood's army.   10

ANSWERS TO STATE BOARD QUESTIONS PRINTED IN DECEMBER.

READING.—1. The method of teaching children the meaning of words should begin with teaching the words themselves. The natural order is: the familiar object, the oral representative or name, the written representative, or word. Sufficient repetition to fix the association of these in the mind should be made—no more. Too much assistance will fail to place the proper responsibility upon the child for his part of the work. Motions may be taught the child by corresponding actions, or by referring to corresponding actions with which he is well acquainted. Others, later on, by analogy with those which he knows. Knowledge of relations as expressed by prepositions and conjunctions will naturally be learned by the association of objects and actions. All of these may be associated, interest kindled, and the impression deepened by incidents, pictures, drawings, etc. As the pupil advances in age he may by degrees be taught the proper use of the dictionary and the cyclopedia. Also the combinations of the given word in other connections than the one given in the reader, its ready use in composition, etc.

2. In reading. the pupil should take the book in the left hand, the thumb and little finger upon either page in front, the other three fingers being used as a support. The left upper arm should be nearly vertical beside the body, the lower arm extending forward

and toward the center of the front of the body, slightly upward but nearly at a right angle. The right arm should hang beside the body. One foot should be in advance of the other, and at an angle of 60° to the one upon which the support of the body mainly depends. The trunk should be erect and the head inclined slightly forward. Ease, grace, comfort, naturalness, accommodation to the eye, are the elements to be determined.

5. A good method of teaching a Fourth Reader class is the following: When the pupils have reached the recitation benches and been quietly seated, let each one, in perfect silence, read carefully the first verse for—say two minutes. Then let such a pupil as the teacher may designate close his book, rise and state the meaning of the verse in his own words. If the teacher is not satisfied, he may call upon another pupil to explain in like manner. When the teacher and the class are satisfied as to the statement, the pupil giving it correctly may then be called upon to read the verse. If he does not, in his reading, bring out the full meaning of the passage read, all will see it and note wherein his rendering is defective. One verse read properly and understandingly in this way is of more value to the class than ten verses read carelessly, or read without an analysis of both the thought and its method of expression on the part of the pupils.

PHYSIOLOGY.—1. Anatomy, physiology and hygiene are the divisions of physiology in the wide sense. Anatomy teaches the mechanical parts and relations of the body, or of its organs; physiology, in the strict sense, treats of the functions of the organs and systems of the body; hygiene states the conditions necessary to a normal or healthful state or action of the body, or of its parts.

3. Digestion is partly a chemical, partly a mechanical process. It consists, essentially, in reducing the food to such a condition that its nutritious elements may be readily absorbed and used by the various tissues of the body.

4. The principal ingredients of food are complex organic substances derived from plants and animals. A small amount of inorganic material is used also—chiefly for the supporting tissues.

5. A healthful diet is good in quality, moderate in quantity, varied in kind, and adapted to the particular life of the person using it.

6. Cooking meat gelatinizes its white fibrous tissue and makes it more easily chewed and more easily digested. Agreeable flavors are also developed and parasites, if any, destroyed. The principle advantage derivable from cooking vegetables is to change the raw starch into a more easily digestible state.

8. The body *may* be kept too clean. The use of too much and

too strong soap may remove the oil secreted by the sebaceous glands, a certain portion of which is necessary to a healthful condition of the skin.

9. Nerve matter is composed of fibres, cells, blood vessels, connective tissue, etc. The fibres are found in both branches and centers, but the cells are found in the centers only. Around a nerve is the outer sheaf, or perineurium; within this the funiculi, or cords, held apart by the connective tissue, and each within a sheath of its own, known as the neurilemma. Within this last sheath are the real nerve fibres, consisting of (*a*) the sheath of Schwann; (*b*) the fatty or medullary sheath, or coating; (*c*) the axis cylinder, or core, the essential part of the fiber, and continuous from the nerve center to the organ in which the nerve ends.

SCIENCE OF TEACHING.—1. The seats of a school-room should be placed so that pupils would not have to face the light. The light should come from the left and back, or from the left alone, and from the upper part of the windows.

2. Ventilation received from the top of the window is not likely to strike the children in such strong and direct currents as when admitted below.

3. Voluntary attention implies an exercise of will; involuntary attention implies only attractiveness of object or subject. Voluntary attention implies control of the will—the chief end of education.

4. The ideal school must develop *all* the powers of the child—moral, mental, and physical. The mental and moral can not be manifested except *through* the physical. Good thinking and good morals alike depend much upon good health.

5. The mind can do its best work only when free from annoyances, hence the great importance of a spirit of kindness and good nature in the school.

GEOGRAPHY.—1. The Polar Circles are 23½° from the Poles. They mark the extreme point beyond the poles that the rays of the sun reach when the sun shines vertically upon the Tropic of Cancer and Tropic of Capricorn, respectively.

2. Commerce is trade. Carried on between two different countries, as Great Britain and United States, it is styled foreign commerce. Carried on between two parts of the same country, as New York and San Francisco, it is termed domestic commerce. •

3. Madrid, Rome, Constantinople.

4. The European cities enjoy a much milder climate than New York. The warm currents of air from the Sahara and the modifying influences of the Mediterranean Sea cause this difference.

5. The Atlantic Slope is a narrow strip of land between the Alleghany Mountains and the Atlantic Ocean. It has many rivers, and

is very fertile. The Central Plain, lies between the Alleghany and Rocky Mountains. It slopes gently from each range of the mountain, and near the centre, forms the basin of the Mississippi River. The Great Western Plateau embraces all territory west of the central plain. This is rugged and contains many lofty mountains.

6. Hides, Peruvian bark, red pepper, spices, rose-wood and mahogany.

7. Rio Janeiro.

8. Sardinia, Corsica, Sicily, Candia, Cyprus.

9. Caspian Sea, White Sea, Baltic Sea, Black Sea, and Sea of Azof.

10. The British claim possession of India, which includes Hindostan, a part of Farther India, a part of the western coast of the Malay peninsula, and the islands of Ceylon and Singapore. The exports of British India are cotton, rice, opium, tobacco, sugar, jute, indigo, coffee, cocoa-nuts, cinnamon, spices, etc.

U. S. HISTORY.—1. Pennsylvania differed in that the land was all owned by one man—the proprietor—who planned the enterprise. He made it "a free colony for all mankind," permitting the people to govern themselves without any interference, and securing them against Indian hostility by making a compact of peace with the red men. It agreed with *some* other colonies in that it was a refuge for the persecuted in other lands.

2. They honestly believed that it was their duty to control religious beliefs, and to suppress any heresies that might arise. The unwise conduct of some among the Quakers and others in opposition to the government drew upon themselves the condemnation of the Puritans.

3 Jealousies between the French and English, and a disputed claim to the lands west of the Alleghanies, along the Ohio River.

4 The Mecklenburg Resolutions announced the principle which is embodied in the Declaration of Independence.

5. Because they were contending for a principle, not for a reduction of taxes.

6. New York. Rhode Island.

7. That an extended credit system and speculation are destructive to business, and that the public safety is to be secured through the legitimate avenues of trade.

8. (*a*) Dred Scott decision. (*b*) John Brown's raid into Virginia. (*c*) The secession of seven States, and the organization of the "Confederate States of America."

9. (*a*) The people in that part of Virginia being Unionists, the separate State of West Virginia was organized, 1863. (*b*) The Union forces.

10. (*a*) General Butler. (*b*) The claim that slaves were property. (*c*) The slaves flocked in large numbers to the Union lines, and the practical result was the weakening of the South.

GRAMMAR.—1. A predicate may be simple, complex, or compound. The part that makes the assertion, without modification, is generally called the simple predicate: as, "The rain *is falling.*" It is complex when modified by a phrase or a clause, or by both: as, "The boy recites well in all his studies because he is a diligent pupil." Compound—"He recites in the morning and studies in the afternoon." Most predicates may be modified by a word, phrase, or clause. Some intransitive verbs, like *become, seem, appear,* etc., require as complement a predicate *noun* or a predicate *adjective :* as, "The man became *president,*" "He appears *cheerful,*" etc.

2. You are not going? He will accept the offer? They usually express doubt or surprise.

3. A simple declarative sentence. *I* is the simple subject unmodified. *Shall certainly be at the train in time* is the entire predicate. *Shall be* is pred. verb, modified by *certainly,* an adverb of *affirmation,* and also by the prep. phrases *at the train* and *in time—* the first being an adverbial modifier of *place,* the second, of *time.*

4. *Both, and,* copulative; *either, or,* disjunctive; *therefore, hence,* illative; *for, because,* causal; *but, yet,* adversative.

5. *That Franklin was a great philosopher* is admitted by all (subject). All admit *that Franklin was a great philosopher* (object). He held the opinion *that Franklin was a great philosopher* (appositive). My opinion is *that Franklin was a great philosopher* (predicate).

8. Webster's and Worcester's Dictionaries. Each is the author of a dictionary. The sentence as it stands implies joint authorship. I went to Mr. Smith, my old teacher's home, or, I went to the home of Mr. Smith, my old teacher. This is somebody else's work. A complex term annexes the sign of possession to last word.

10. I speak to whoever speaks to me. The object of "to" is the clause. "I speak to whomever I know," is correct, *whomever* being the object of *know.* I give it to whoever comes. It is not necessary to supply the antecedents.

ARITHMETIC.—1. Interest is the premium paid for the use of money. Amount is the sum of principal and interest. Principal is the sum of money for which interest is paid. Usury is any rate of interest higher than the legal rate. Discount is the amount deducted from a debt for its payment before it is due.

2. Ratio is the relation between two numbers of the same kind expressed by their quotient. A couplet is the two terms of a ratio. A simple proportion is an equality of ratios. A compound proportion is an equality of two

ratios. A compound proportion is an equality of two ratios, one or both of which are compound. Four numbers are in proportion when the ratio of the first to the second is equal to the ratio of the third to the fourth.

3. $\frac{6}{11} - \frac{5}{11} = \frac{1}{11}$. $890 = \frac{1}{11}$ of his property.
   $890 \times 5 = \$4450$, daughter's share.
   $890 \times 6 = \$5340$, son's share.

4. $\frac{4+\frac{1}{2}}{7-\frac{1}{3}} = \frac{4\frac{1}{2}}{\ldots}$. $\frac{4\frac{1}{2}}{\ldots} = \frac{1}{2}\frac{4\frac{1}{2}}{\ldots}$. $\frac{4\frac{1}{2}}{\ldots} = \frac{7}{8}\frac{1}{2}\frac{1}{2}$. $\frac{1}{2}\frac{1}{2}\frac{1}{2} - \frac{1}{2}\frac{1}{2}\frac{1}{2} = \frac{1}{11}\frac{1}{2}\frac{1}{2}$ increase.

5. $12\frac{1}{2}\% = \frac{1}{8}$. $650 \times 8 = \$5200$, A's.
   $62\frac{1}{2}\% = \frac{5}{8}$. $5200 = \frac{5}{8}$ of B's. $\frac{1}{5}$ of $5200 = \$1040$, $\frac{1}{8}$ of B's income.
   $1040 \times 8 = \$8320$, B's income.

6. \$ .972 proceeds on \$1 for given time, plus 3 days. $1944 \div \$.972 = \$2000$. Answer.

7. $10000 - \$2300 = \$7700$. $4 + 3 = 7$. $7700 \div 7 = \$1100$. $1100 \times 4 = \$4400$, first man's share. $1100 \times 3 = \$3300$, second.

8. $\sqrt{(69)_2 + (92)_2} = 115$ rods. Ans.

9. $\sqrt[3]{69934528} = 412$. Ans.

10. $\frac{2}{3} = .66666666 +$.
    $\sqrt{.66666666} = .8164 +$. Ans.

MISCELLANY.

KNOX COUNTY is taking steps towards the educational display at New Orleans.

WABASH COUNTY enrolls 150 of its teachers as members of "Indiana Reading Circle." Good!

THE COLLEGE RECORD is the paper published by Union Christian College at Merom. It is a very creditable sheet.

STARKE COUNTY, under the superintendency of H. C. Rogers, held one of its best institutes this year. The teachers in this county are steadily improving.

GEO. W. YOUNG, Superintendent of Ripley county, has issued a circular to the teachers of his county urging them to join the Reading Circle, and to do it *at once*, that no time be lost.

GINN, HEATH & Co. have in preparation a text-book on Temperance by Axel Gustafson, the author of "Foundation of Death," a book that has of late attracted much wide-spread interest.

AN address on denominational education was delivered by J. J. Mills, President of Earlham, at the New York yearly meeting of Friends, held at Glens Falls, in June last. It has been printed in pamphlet form, and can be obtained by addressing President Mills. It will well repay the reading.

VAN ANTWERP, BRAGG & Co have bought out the school publications of Jones Bros. of Cincinnati. Their list of school books will now include Milne's series of Arithmetics, Ridpath's Histories, and Forbriger's Drawing Tablets.

JENNINGS COUNTY enrolled 110 out of its 128 teachers, the first half day. This record is hard to beat. Superintendent Conboy secured this prompt attendance, not by giving an additional per cent. on license for attending, but by *deducting* from the grade of examination for license two per cent. for each day missed from the institute.

VERMILLION COUNTY held a two days' Association at Dana, the Friday and Saturday following Thanksgiving. It was fairly well attended, and the exercises were very creditable. Superintendent Johnson was kept from attending by some unexpected court business, he being an attorney. The teachers of Vermillion average well.

THE LEONARD SCOTT PUBLISHING Co , of Philadelphia, offer 15 prizes, amounting in the aggregate to $500, for essays on Shakesperian subjects. Their object is to stimulate the study of the great English dramatist in the home circle, as well as in colleges and schools. Any one desiring particulars in regard to this can address as above.

THE Manual of St Joseph County Schools, Calvin Moon, Super-intendent, contains an account of the formation of a Teachers' Library Association. Such a movement can not be too highly commended. If a similar organization could be started in each county in the State the result would be a telling one upon the general intelligence of its population.

WALTER WALLACE, principal of Fourth Ward School, Columbus, has prepared a set of cards containing facts about authors, libraries, colleges, etc , to be used in games by young people. They can be played and used so as to be very entertaining as well as instructive They can be used with great advantage for a Friday afternoon's exercise. For further information address Walter Wallace, Columbus.

COINCIDENTS.—In the ninety two names of county superintendents of schools there are four instances of duplicates of surnames. We have C. W. Osborne of Union, and G. A. Osborne of Grant; H. C. Rogers of Stark, and A. E. Rogers of Hendricks ; B. F. Johnson of Benton, and A. J. Johnson of Vermillion ; S. W Axtell of Greene, and W. F. Axtell of Monroe. There is neither a Brown nor a Jones in the list, and there is but one Smith. • • •

MONTGOMERY COUNTY is steadily moving to the front The grading of the schools is becoming general. The average length of the school term for the county is seven months. The average advance on teachers wages is thirty-seven cents a day. Superintendent Cantley has clear ideas, and works to definite ends. Last year he revoked the licenses of two teachers, because they refused to conform to the regulations laid down by the county board. The attendance at the normal last summer reached 100.

HANCOCK COUNTY.—New Palestine dedicated a magnificent school building on November 22, 1884. Addresses were delivered by State Supt. Holcombe, Supt. Harlan of Marion county, Supt. Dobbins of Shelby county, Supt. Smith of Hancock county, and J. H. Binford of Greenfield. This building reflects credit on the trustees of New Palestine, Ernest H. Faut, C. H. Kirkhoff and Wm. A. Wood, and township treasurer Sylvester Waggoner. Wm. A. Wood has charge of the schools.

PARKE COUNTY.—The annual two-day meeting of the teachers of Parke county took place at Rockville November 28-29. The trustees in this county give one day's salary if the teachers attend both; so it *pays* to be present, and the meeting as usual was large. The teachers in this county take a lively interest in their work and make careful preparation for all exercises. Two days were spent profitably and pleasantly. Friday evening was devoted to an oratorical contest. Four teachers—two ladies and two gentlemen—engaged in it. The judges, James H. Smart, R. G. Boone, and Cyrus W. Hodgin, awarded both prizes to the ladies. County Superintendent W. H. Elson is doing a excellent work.

HENRY COUNTY.—The annual institute of Henry county, commencing August 11th, was in every way the most successful ever held in the county. The enrollment reached 160. The success of the institute of 1884 was due largely to the good management of Supt. W. R. Wilson, who is very popular with his teachers, and who spared no pains to secure good instructors. Among these W. H. Payne, of the Michigan University, deserved special mention for his efficiency as an institute worker. C. W. Hodgin and Miss Furby, of Richmond, and others rendered aid which was greatly appreciated. Taking into consideration the high grade of our teachers and the excellent condition of our schools, we think Henry county is entitled to a place in the front rank. MARK P. TURNER, Sec'y.

STATE NORMAL NOTES.—The Winter term opened December 1st, with an unusually large attendance. It has been found necessary to employ an additional teacher for the remainder of the school year. The school has been fortunate in securing the services of Mr. Elwood Kemp, formerly teacher of History in this school, but more recently a student at Harvard University. Mr. Kemp is a teacher of extraor-

4

dinary ability. The regular faculty now numbers fifteen, besides the critic teachers and the teacher of the Kindergarten.

Another class will enter immediately after the holidays. Those expecting to enter before the Spring term should come in at that time. ' The fifteenth annual report of this school is now ready for distribution. It is an unusually large volume, containing much matter that will be of interest to the friends of the institution.

LAKE COUNTY held its institute, December 15-19, at Crown Point. It was better attended than usual. The first morning 70 teachers were present and 82 enrolled before night. The second day the enrollment reached 100. The whole number of teachers in the county is 130. The principal workers were Capt. H. A. Ford of Detroit, Michigan, Miss Teressa J. Crocker, elocutionist, of Logansport, and G. L Voorhes, W. C. Belman and L. M. Bassett, home talent. The work generally gave good satisfaction. Prof. Ford has been repeatedly recalled to this county. He gave an evening lecture, and Miss Crocker gave two evening entertainments. In this county each teacher when examined pays fifty cents as an institute fund. To such the evening entertainments are all free. Frank Cooper, the County Superintendent, seems to have his work well in hand.

SUPERINTENDENTS' MEETING.

The Superintendents of Eastern Indiana and Western Ohio held a very interesting and profitable meeting at Winchester December 5 and 6. There was a good attendance, and the discussions, which took a wide range, were entirely informal, and entered into by all present. The meeting was organized by electing J. J. Mills chairman, and E. H. Butler, secretary.

The first session was held on Friday evening, and the topics, "How Can a Superintendent Best Expend His Time and Energies," and "School Appliances," were taken and thoroughly discussed. The former topic was opened by Superintendent Treudley of Union City, who said: "There is a tendency on the part of many superintendents to engage in the mechanical work of the school rather than that which will be suggestive to teachers. A superintendent should do a great deal of reading, not only of a professional nature, but it should extend far beyond it. He should be a hard student. He thought it profitable for a superintendent to teach a part of the time." President Mills thought that a Superintendent should not only read himself, but direct the reading of his teachers. He ought to know what his teachers do by visiting them, and his visits should be made in such a way as to make his teachers feel comfortable. He should have a clear conception of the work he is to do. The discussion of this subject was further participated in by R. I. Hamilton, Superintendent of Anderson Schools, Cyrus W. Hodgin of the Richmond Normal, Supt. W. W. Wirt of Portland, Prof. Hobbs, of Ridgeville, and E. H. Butler. The subject of "School Appliances" was opened by C. W. Hodgin, who said that a good teacher was about the best appliance of the school. "We need comfortable houses, plenty of light, good books, blackboards, etc." President Mills thought the best appliance was the proper use of ten skillful fingers. We do not use the crayon and board enough. Supt. Treudley explained the use of the sand-box in teaching geography and history. After further discussion Supt. Hamilton suggested that on to-morrow we discuss the question of preparing one class of pupils for the duties of life, and at the same time prepare another class for college. C. H. Wood, principal of the Winchester High School, made some remarks on the same subject.

The first subject taken up on Saturday morning was, "The Best Methods and Aids to Language Teaching and Primary Number." Supt. Hamilton opened the discussion by saying that language instruction is commenced in the first year in the Anderson Schools, and oral instruction is extended to the sixth year. The discussion was lively and interesting, and was participated in by all the superintendents present. Committing memory gems and reading standard literature were strongly recommended as aids in language culture. Supt. Luckey of Decatur, thought Peaslee's Graded Selections too difficult for pupils for whom they were intended.

"Supplementary Reading" was the next topic on the program. President Mills thought there was a tendency to diffuseness in supplementary reading. He thought the best results were obtained in the higher grades by an exhaustive study of a few selections. The subject was further discussed by Supts. Hamilton, Treudley, Hodgin and others.

"Recess or no Recess" was discussed in a vigorous manner. Superintendents Treudley and Luckey were the only advocates of indoor recess The former explained the methods adopted at Union City, which consisted of two five minutes rests each forenoon and afternoon; one in doors and one out of doors

"How to Conduct Teachers' Meetings" and the High School question were subjects of animated discussion.

A committee consisting of Superintendents Treudley, Hamilton and President Mills was appointed to report on a High School course of study at a future meeting.

So well pleased were the superintendents with the success of the meeting it was unanimously agreed to hold another sometime during this school year, and Superintendents Hamilton, Cromer and E. H. Butler were appointed to arrange a program. Union City was selected as the place.   E. H. BUTLER, Secretary.

INDIANA TEACHERS' READING CIRCLE.

OUTLINE OF

Work in Brooks' Mental Science, for Jan., 1885. Subject: Memory, Pages 127-168.

I. DEFINITIONS OF TERMS.

1. Tenacious Memory, (131) 2. Experience of Sense, (135). 3. Refreshing the Memory, (138) 4. Relation of Ideas, (142). 5. Learning by rote, (161). 6. Conservative (as applied to mind). 7. Resuscitative. 8. Redintegration.

"The relations which bind perceptions together are likenesses, unlikenesses, and dependence."—*Johonnot.*

"Committing to memory the verbal construction of others can aid a pupil very little in acquiring the power to construct for himself."—*Johonnot.*

"Every feeling, every thought, every purpose, abides with the mind forever." (This in connection with item 6 above.)—*Day.*

II. DISTINCTIONS OF TERMS.

1. Association and Suggestion.

"The power to control the succession of ideas, very much depends upon the habits formed in establishing these associations."

2. Recognition and comparison. 3. Remembrance and recollection. 4 Memorizing and recalling. 5. Strength of memory and strength of mind.

III. ITEMS OF SPECIAL PROFESSIONAL IMPORT.

1. Difference between retention and recollection. 2. The fact of latent modifications of consciousness. (See page 131.)

1. "Mind is the whole of which consciousness is a part."

2. "Our knowledge is mainly potential not actual."

3. "Consciousness sees but 'one idea at a time, and is conscious of that idea only for the present moment."

4. "After education has presented ideas to consciousness those ideas fall back into consciousness."

5. "The educated man is more conscious, extensively and intensively, than the ignorant peasant; but the process of development does not increase what man is actually conscious of, so much as he *can* be conscious of."

6. "That the mind acquires most of its knowledge unconsciously may be seen by a little reflection on the ways in which our experience has been acquired."

7. "Repetition and interest are the two means of mentally receiving ideas."

(NOTE.—These seven quotations are made from the article: "The Unconscious in Education," by John Edward Maude, to which reference was made in November Out, lines It is thought the extracts may be especially valuable in this connection.)

3. Means of increasing readiness of memory.

"As is the earnestness of attention, so is the duration of remembrance, or the distinctness and readiness of recollection."

"One's memory will serve him in proportion as he really trusts it."—*Alden.*

"The art of memory is the art of paying attention."—*Jos. Payne.*

"The pupil should learn something thoroughly; and refer everything to that."—*Jacotot.*

"In order to train the memory, the child must be held responsible for its use."—*Hewett*

4. Distinctions between products of memory and those of imagination. Page 137.

5. The Law of Association.

6. Relation of memory culture to modern education.

"The retentive faculty is the faculty that most of all concerns us in education."—*Bain.*

"The memory of youth differs in kind as well as degree from that of maturer years. The youth remembers facts; the man relations and laws. Youth collects materials; old age uses them. In childhood susceptibility is more active; in youth, retentiveness; in manhood, readiness."—*Wayland.*

"It must be borne in mind, that, with the young, memory is strong and logical perception is weak. All teaching should start from this undoubted fact. It sounds fascinating to talk about understanding everything, learning all thoroughly, and all these broad phrases which plump down on a difficulty and hide it. Put in practice they are about on a par with exhorting a boy to mind he does not go into the water till he can swim."—*Thring.*

IV. SUMMARIES.

1. The elements of memory. 2. The laws of retention. 3. The laws of recollection. 4. The methods of culture.

V. NOTES.

1. "One of the questions deserving careful consideration in education is, 'what ought to be forgotten.'"—*Donaldson.*

2. "At the first it is no great matter how much you learn, but how well you learn it."—*Erasmus.*

3. "Experience teaches that a child will retain in its memory only what is incorporated into its life."—*Dr. Schwab.*

4. The memory should be made a store-house of such facts as are good material for the other powers of the mind to work with."—*Quick.*

5. Along with this lesson should be re-read preceding pages 76, 114-123.

METHODS OF INSTRUCTION.

Talks on Teaching—pages 95–119.

I. *Number Defined.*—(Number may be defined as "the how many" of any thing or things. This is number considered correctly. Of number considered abstractly the author does not treat, and very properly, for it belongs to the department of pure mathematics.)

Especial attention is called to the emphasis that the author places upon the importance of learning numbers by the use of objects.

What can be done with numbers? (Just what can be done with the things. Separate things can be combined into one group. So separate numbers can be combined into one by the process of addition or multiplication) What is the difference between these two processes? What is the difference between subtraction and division? What other operation is possible with numbers? What is the purpose of teaching arithmetic in schools? (Information and discipline.) In what does the educational value of the study of arithmetic consist? Process of teaching arithmetic.

1. First discover what the child already knows. Be careful not to mistake knowledge of words for that of things. What tests would you apply to find out whether the word *four* expresses the idea of *number* four to the child?

2. Make the child ready and accurate in the fundamental operation so far as it attempts to learn them. When is knowledge automatic?

2. What time should be taken to learn numbers to ten? Why?

4. When should the child begin to learn written number? Why?

5. When should the use of objects be discontinued? Why? How long should he be in learning numbers to one hundred?

6. How should fractions be taught to a child? Illustrate by the use of an object, as an apple, the meaning of ½ of ⅓ of ¼.

7. What is the educational value of the formal analysis so common in teaching mental arithmetic? What is the caution to be observed if it is used?

THE SANITARY CONVENTION AT LAFAYETTE.

A Sanitary Convention under auspices of the state and local boards of health was held at Lafayette November 18th in the chapel of Purdue University. The attendance was small, but the papers and the interest were unusually good.

Pres. Smart, in a very happy vein, gave the welcoming address, in which he indicated the great importance of the subject under consideration and the disposition people have rather to pay doctor's bills than to keep from being sick.

The first paper upon the program, by Dr. E. S. Elder, Sec'y State Board, Indianapolis, outlined in a brief but very interesting way the work of the State Board for the year and the problems under consideration by it.

Prof. H. A. Huston, of Purdue University, developed "The Value of the State Weather Service to Public Health," showing many facts new even to reflecting persons, and accompanying his paper by illustrative diagrams. Prof. R. B. Warder, of Purdue, explained the operation of "Wolfert's Apparatus for the Examination of Air," in a very practical and instructive manner. Two of the most excellent addresses were by Hon. Will Cumback, of Greensburg, on "Politics and Sanitation," and by Hon. T. H. Willard, Bedford, on "Sanitation, an Index to Civilization."

Other papers were read on "Conflict of Vital Forces—How Modified by Sanitary Law;" "Habits in their Relation to Sanitation;" "Some Legal Points in the Practical Application of Drainage Laws;" "Some of the Defects in our Present School System;" "Contagious Diseases not Considered Dangerous;" "Some Facts about Milk Sickness, with Measures of Prevention;" "Impure Water as a Source of Disease;" "Clothing and Climate;" "The Drainage of Farm and Waste Lands as a Sanitary Measure;" "Heredity in its Relation to Insanity and Diseases of the Nervous System."

Many of these papers would be of value to teachers and parents. The subject is one needing profound consideration.

GEMS OF THOUGHT.

He that is good in making excuses is seldom good at anything else.—*Franklin.*

Many a little makes a mickle; beware of little expenses; a small leak will sink a great ship.

> Learn to make the most of life,
>   Lose no happy day;
> Time will never bring thee back,
>   Chances swept away.   —*Anon.*

Wherever the speech is corrupted the mind is also.—*Seneca.*

Habit, if not resisted, soon becomes necessity.—*St. Augustine.*

> He liveth long who liveth well;
>   All else is being thrown away;
> He liveth longest who can tell
>   Of true things only, done each day.   —*Bonar.*

> Knowledge is proud that he has learned so much;
> Wisdom is humble that he knows no more.   —*Cowper.*

Our greatest glory consists not in never falling, but in rising every time we fall.—*Goldsmith.*

Such is an *ignis fatuus.* You may follow it to ruin, but never to . success. Things don't turn up in this world till somebody turns them up.—*Garfield.*

'Tis the mind that makes the body rich.—*Shakespeare.*

The most difficult thing is to know thyself.—*Thales.*

He lives long that lives well, and time misspent is not lived—but lost.—*Fuller.*   •

> He that has light in his own clear breast,
> May sit in the centre and enjoy bright day;
> But he that hides a dark soul and foul thoughts
> Benighted walks under the mid-day sun;
> Himself is his own dungeon.   —*Milton.*

> Count that day lost whose low descending sun
> Views from thy hand no worthy action done.
>   —*Staniford.*

> Distrust that man who tells you to distrust;
> He takes the measure of his own small soul
> And thinks the world no larger.   —*Ella Wheeler.*

Our acts make or mar us. We are the children of our own deeds.
                                      —*Victor Hugo.*

> All, who joy would win,
> Must share it: Happiness was born a twin.   —*Byron.*

> Man's inhumanity to man
> Makes countless thousands mourn.   —*Burns.*

PERSONAL.

L. M. Bassett has charge of the Hobart schools.

M. W. Harrison remains in charge of the Anderson schools.

W. C. Belman is serving very acceptably his second year at Hammond.

A. L. Stevenson is serving his second year at the head of the Lowell schools.

B. B. Harrison is superintendent at Waterloo, and is winning a great victory.

John W. Perrin, formerly of Newport, is now in charge of the schools at Catlin, Illinois.

G. L. Voorhees, a graduate of the University of Wisconsin, is superintendent of the Crown Point schools.

Anson Buckley is now at work in the State Superintendent's office, giving his time chiefly to educational exhibit matters.

T. J. Sanders is still doing good work at Butler. He has two popular lectures on The Great North American Glaciers that are well worth hearing.

J. F. W. Gatch, formerly principal of Ladoga Normal, will have charge of Hope Normal School, *vice* John Mickleborough, who has returned to Cincinnati.

Jas. R. Hart, former superintendent of Switzerland county, is now at the head of the Thorntown schools, which are full and doing well.

Chas. O. Thompson, Pres of Rose Polytechnic Institute, delivered an address before the Michigan State Teachers' Association, Dec. 29th, on "Technology in the Public Schools."

Jessie Stretch, formerly of Camden, Ind., writes that she is *herding* at Winfield, Kansas. Has 220 children, first primary, with an average attendance of 145. Fannie Stretch, formerly a teacher at Battle Ground, this State, is also engaged in the city schools at Winfield, Kansas.

Hubert M. Skinner, head clerk in the Department of Public Instruction, owing to over-work, has been "under the weather" for the past month. Mr. Skinner is an indefatigable worker, and in addition to the work of the office which he done well, he has done a vast deal of outside literary work.

BOOK TABLE.

The Fountain is the name of a monthly magazine for boys and girls, published at York, Penn., by W. H. Shelly. It is one of the *very best* that comes to our table.

Littell's Living Age, which has been published for forty years, is a weekly magazine which gives a re print of the best matter in the standard magazines of England and the Continent. It is not too broad to say that nearly the whole world of authors appear in The Living Age. Price $8.00 per annum; with the School Journal, $9.25.

D. Lothrop & Co., of Boston, are doing an excellent work for the children. *Wide-Awake* is one of the very best magazines for boys and girls that is published. The quality of the reading matter is of the highest standard, the illustrations are of the finest, and the paper smooth as could be desired. *Our Little Men and Women*, for a young class of readers, is charming and cheap. It would make most valuable supplementary reading matter for a primary school. Price $1.00 a year.

The Atlantic Monthly for 1885 will contain a series of papers by Oliver Wendell Holmes, entitled "The New Portfolio"; also the following serial stories: "A Country Gentleman", by Mrs. Oliphant; "The Princess Casamassima", by Henry James; "A Marsh Island", by Sarah Orne Jewett; "The Prophet of the Great Smoky Mountains", by Chas. Egbert Craddock. This magazine is not illustrated, but is filled with the best thoughts of the ablest writers of the age. Price $4.00. Houghton, Mifflin & Co., Boston, are the publishers

With the December number *Harper's Monthly Magazine* will complete its thirty-fifth year. Leading features in the volume for 1885 are: New serial novels by Constance Fenimore Woolson and W. D. Howells; descriptive illustrated papers by Millet, Gifford, Abbey, Gibson and others. The December number in illustration, general style and make-up, is simply beautiful. While the Monthly Magazine stands in the front rank, *Harper's Weekly Bazar* and *Young People* are each leading periodicals in their respective departments. Price of Magazine, Weekly, Bazar, each $4.00 per year. Young People, $2.00.

The Great Temperance Controversy; A Plea for the Fallen. By
R. L. Fletcher.

This book is a series of lectures, eleven in number, covering the
ground in its various phases. It is radical, and takes a strong stand
in favor of *prohibition.* Whatever may be one's views as to the
means to be employed in the suppression of intemperance, there can
be no difference of opinion as to the vital importance of the question,
and full and free discussion can but result in good. Persons wishing to post themselves as to the facts and phases of the temperance
problem will find this book helpful. It is published by the author
at Indianapolis.

Analytical Elocution. By James E. Murdock, Cincinnati: Van
Antwerp, Bragg & Co.

This is not what most "Elocutions" are, viz., a book of selections
preceded by a few pages of suggestions, principles, and rules. The
book contains over 500 pages, but the "selections" occupy only
about 66 pages; the remaining pages being devoted to a thorough
scientific discussion of this subject in all its phases. No man in the
United States stands higher as an elocutionist than does Mr. Murdock. The book is the result of his study and practice for more
than fifty years. Price, $1.

Professor Hadley's Greek Grammar has been revised and in part
re-written by Frederic De Forest Allen, of Harvard University. A
casual glance at the book makes one think that it is the old book of
his college days, in a new dress. More careful examination, however, reveals many important changes through the entire book, only
a few of which can be noted:

1. Marking the doubtful vowels when long. 2. Calling the "connecting vowel" a part of the tense stem. 3. Making First Aorist
stem "lusa." 4. Reducing the nine classes of verbs to seven. 5.
Classified verb-list revised, forms of Attic prose and poetry distinguished by two kinds of type. 6 Syntax of the modes, having
adopted many of the excellent features of Prof. Goodwin's Greek
Grammar, especially the distinction of general and particular suppo-
sitions, and the arrangement of final clauses.

No teacher of Greek can afford to be without the revised edition of
Hadley's Greek Grammar. D. Appleton & Co., publishers.

On and after the first of January, 1885, *The Christian Union* will
be enlarged by the addition of eight pages. It will then become a
thirty-two page paper, and will contain more reading matter than
any other religious weekly newspaper in the world. Many popular
features will be introduced, which will make its columns for home
reading unusually varied, graphic and interesting. Its editorial and
literary departments will be enlarged, and will represent the best
work of the best men on all topics—religious, political, social and
literary It will give its readers during the coming year several serial stories of a high order, together with productions of many of the
most distinguished writers in this country and abroad.

This is without question the best non sectarian religious paper
published. It is *not* denominational, *not* composed of church news,
not a theological paper, *not* made up of stale sermons and weekly
scraps, *not* a story paper; but *it is* a christian newspaper, progressive, comprehensive, helpful, fearless, clean, fresh, interesting, and

religious in the highest and best sense. The editors are Lyman Abbott and Hamilton W. Mabie. Price $3. Address, The Christian Union, 20 La Fayette Place, New York City.

BUSINESS NOTICES.

Do YOU expect to buy a Piano or Organ? If so, do not buy till you have called upon Theo. Pafflin & Co., 82 and 84 north Pennsylvania street, Indianapolis. Low prices, easy terms and fair dealing, is the motto of this house. See advertisement on the 4th cover page.

TEACHERS desiring to attend a *Normal School*, or those wishing a situation or an increase of salary, should send for a sample copy of *"The Educational World."* Address,
1-12t. W. SAYLER, *Editor, Logansport, Ind.*

EXCURSION TO NEW ORLEANS.—New Orleans Excursion Tickets are now on sale at the Ticket Offices of the Jeffersonville, Madison & Indianapolis Railroad Co. For rates and time of trains, call upon or write to nearest Agent, Jeffersonville, Madison & Indianapolis Railroad Company, or to H. R. Dering, Assistant General Passenger Agent, Indianapolis, Ind.   1-3t

THE best route between Indianapolis and Fort Wayne, is by the C, C., C. & I. to Muncie, and then by the Ft. Wayne, Cincinnati & Louisville. This is the shortest and best. For information in regard to these roads, inquire of W. J. Nichols, Indianapolis, General Passenger Agent of the first named road, and of R. E. Kinnaird, Fort Wayne, General Passenger Agent of the other road.

1884.   CHRISTMAS—NEW YEAR.   1885.

EXCURSION RATES FOR THE HOLIDAYS.

Chicago, St. Louis and Pittsburgh R. R., J., M. & I. R. R. and the I. & V. R. R.—In accordance with their usual custom, the above named lines announce the sale of cheap excursion tickets to and from all stations during the Christmas Holidays. Tickets will be sold on December 24th, 25th and 31st, 1884, and January 1st, 1885, and will be good for return passage until January 2d, 1885, inclusive. The rates will be low, affording everybody an opportunity to spend Christmas and New Year among relatives or friends at a distance, or to visit the large cities and other points of interest located on the lines controlled by these Companies. Upon application, Agents of any of the above Companies will cheerfully furnish time of trains, rates of fare and further information.   1-1t

CONSUMPTION CURED.

An old physician, retired from practice, having had placed in his hands by an East India missionary the formula of a simple vegetable remedy for the speedy and permanent cure of Consumption, Bronchitis, Catarrh, Asthma, and all Throat and Lung Affections, also a positive and radical cure for Nervous Debility and all Nervous Complaints, after having tested its wonderful curative powers in thousands of cases, has felt it his duty to make it known to his suffering fellows. Actuated by this motive and a desire to relieve human suffering, I will send free of charge, to all who desire it, this recipe, in German, French or English, with full directions for preparing and using. Sent by mail by addressing with stamp, naming this paper, W. A. NOYES, 149 Power's Block, Rochester, N. Y. 10-9

OUR NEW SCHOOL AIDS are the best and cheapest system for conducting schools in good quiet order. Each set contains 150 pretty chrome credit cards. 50 large beautiful chromo merit cards, and 12 large elegant artistic chromo excelsior cards, price per set $1; half set 50c. 500 new designs brilliant artistic chromo school reward, excelsior, merit, credit, diploma, birthday, easter, friendship, remembrance, address, visiting, christmas, new year, scripture and gift cards at at $5, 10, 15, 20 and 25c. per doz. Large set samples 20c. If you do not care to order samples send any amount you wish; stating number and kinds of cards wanted and we will surely please you. Price list, order blanks, return envelopes free All postpaid by mail. Stamps taken Please send a trial order. Fine Art Publishing Co., Warren, Pa.   10-1y

TO THE TEACHERS OF INDIANA.
GRAND PRIZE ESSAY,
ON THE TOPIC:
THE VALUE OF CYCLOPAEDIAS IN THE SCHOOL-ROOM, AND THE BEST MANNER OF USING THEM.

As a premium for the best essay on the above topic, the undersigned offers one full set of Johnson's Universal Cyclopaedia, in 8 volumes, Half Turkey Morocco Binding, price, at reduced rates, $42 00. This is not only a most desirable addition to the Library of any teacher, but it is also a work of the highest order. In evidence of this I append a few short testimonials:

Hon. A. R. Spofford, Librarian of Congress, says:

"Johnson's Cyclopaedia answers more questions satisfactorily that any other work of reference in the Library of Congress."

Prof. Geo. P. Brown, President Indiana State Normal School, says:

"We have several sets of other Cyclopaedias and six sets of Johnson's. We make more use of Johnson's than of any other, and probably more than of all others."

James Colgrove, of Chicago, a gentleman thoroughly posted in books, says:

"Johnson's will give more accurate information of such a character as is wanted by the great majority of those who have occasion to use Encyclopaedias than any other."

Rev. E. A. Bradley, Rector of Christ Church, Indianapolis, says:

"It is the fullest and most compact thesaurus, for its size and price, in print."

Rev. H. A. Edson, Pastor Memorial Church, Indianapolis, says:

"It puts a whole library in small compass for very little money—which has ordinarily been accessible only to the rich."

Prof. H. S. Tarbell says:

"I know of no Cyclopaedia better adapted to the busy man who wishes also to be an intelligent one."

Prof. L. H. Jones, Supt. of Public Schools, Indianapolis, says:

"I believe Johnson's Cyclopaedia to be the best and most convenient work for constant use of any now before the public."

Prof. Richard Boone, A. M., Supt. of Frankfort Schools, says;

"In the Frankfort Schools there are nine sets of Cyclopaedias, and I have no hesitation in recommending Johnson's as being for all purposes, regardless of price and size, the best and most frequently consulted of all."

Dr. A. W. Brayton says:

"I would not exchange my Johnson's Universal Cyclopaedia for any single general work of reference which it has been my fortune to consult. It is in compact form, 8 volumes, large page, clear type, and contains more matter, more topics, better treated, than the 16 volumes of the American, and is better in every respect, and costs three-eights as much."

CONDITIONS.

1. The competition is open to any person actively engaged in educational work in the State of Indiana.

2. The essays, consisting of not more than 1500 words, will be prepared, signed by a fictitious name enclosed in sealed envelope marked " Prize Essay," and placed in my hands on or before March 1st, 1885 These envelopes will be opened only by awarding committee.

3 At or about the same time, each writer will place in my hands another sealed envelope containing his real and fictitious names. These envelopes will not be opened until after the award has been made.

4. The successful or Prize Essay, is to be my property. All others will be returned to writer if desired

5 I have invited Hon Jno W. Holcombe, Supt of Public Instruction, Prof. Geo. P. Brown, President of Indiana State Normal School, and Prof L. H. Jones, Supt. of Public Schools, Indianapolis, to act as Judges.

HIRAM HADLEY, Indianapolis, Ind.,
116 North Pennsylvania Street.

I͵NDIANA

SCHOOL JOURNAL.

| Vol. XXX. | FEBRUARY, 1885. | No. 2. |

ENGLISH LANGUAGE AND LITERATURE IN THE HIGH SCHOOL.

W. W. PARSONS. STATE NORMAL SCHOOL.

IN the discussion of this subject it is assumed that the average student enters the high school early in his fifteenth year, and completes his course therein in his nineteenth year. What is his intellectual status at the close of his study in the grades, first, as to character and extent of knowledge possessed; and second, in respect to the stage and degree of his mental development and activity? These are important considerations in determining the nature and order of the subjects in English to be taught in the high school.

Entering the lowest grade of the public school at six, the pupil has had eight years' systematic instruction in the fundamental branches. But it is to be remembered that a considerable portion of this period is devoted to the simplest elements of knowledge, to the mastery of the mere tools of learning. The number of the child's acquisitions, during the first few years of his school life, other than these simple instruments of learning, is very limited. It should also be borne in mind that knowledge possessed at the age of fourteen or fifteen has been acquired and is retained under the lower and more obvious connections. It is information chiefly, not knowledge. Those higher bonds of association—means and end, causation, design and the like—under which facts and information are converted into organized knowledge, the pupil of this age knows but little about. Instruction below the high school must ever be on the elements of the common branches, the facts of these bound together under thought connections which the immature mind can ccmprehend. Five studies in English receive attention more or less fully during the first eight years of public school instruction, namely; spelling and pronunciation—word work; grammar, which limits its attention to the sentence; reading, which seeks to give the pupil the twofold power of comprehending and also of adequately expressing the meaning of printed discourse; and composition, whose aim is to confer skill in building the simple forms of discourse which the business and social worlds require. As regards English, then, it may be assumed that the pupil, on leaving the grades, has a working knowledge of these elements. He spells and pronounces fairly his own vocabulary; he avoids at least the serious violations of the rules of grammar in his own sentence building; he can with ease comprehend the thought of ordinary printed discourse, and render it intelligently; and he has a reasonable command over the common elementary forms of communication. Less than this the grade work must not be content with; more can not be reasonably required.

In what phase of mind unfolding do we find the pupil at this period? The first years of the high school may properly be called a transition period; indeed, we might characterize the entire four years occupied by the high school course as a transition from the activity of sense, fancy, memory and the lower forms of imagination, to judgment, abstraction, reasoning, and the reflective processes generally. It is at this time that the pupil passes from the knowledge of the individual to the knowledge of the general; from fact to principle; from spontaneous association of objects to their rational connections. In other words, he begins the organization of his knowledge, and this is thinking.

These premised, it will be the principal aim of this paper to show what subjects in the field of English language and literature the high school course should embrace, with the reasons therefor, what their logical sequence and what salient phases of subject-matter each presents for study. From the stand-point of the present discussion, this necessitates a brief analysis of four distinct, but related studies, namely; English grammar, rhetoric, English literature, and advanced or reflective compusition. Such a course provides for a thorough study of the two higher language forms—the sentence and the discourse—in all their important phases, while it is to be supposed that pupils are held for the correct spelling and pronunciation of words in all subjects.

The high school should give one daily lesson during the entire first year to a thorough, comprehensive study of the English sentence. The reasons are obvious. The close, scientific study of the sentence, which alone can give real freedom in and power over this element of expression, is impossible below the high school. If for the fruitless endeavor to teach formal, technical grammar in the sixth and seventh years, we were to substitute regularly graded exercises in all the simple forms of discourse, thus teaching children to write their own live thought as freely as they speak it, and defer the study of grammar as a science until the high school is reached, we should only do that which the simplest understanding of the pupil's capacity, and the difficulty of the subject alike requires.

Logically considered, the sentence is the first really significant language form. Words, as words, that is, as denoting isolated, unrelated ideas, are without meaning. Words are significant only when connected in the sentence, as ideas have meaning only when related in thoughts. The sentence is the unit of language, as the judgment—its corresponding thought form—is the first product of mind. Every act of mind is an act of judgment. The sentence derives its whole meaning as a language form from the fact of expressing this primary result of mind. And this fundamental fact is the basis of scientific grammar. The study of grammatical analysis, of rules, inflections, classifications and kindred subjects is largely a waste of energy, except as these are seen in vital connection with the thought modifications which determine them, which they originate to express. To study these sentence forms in immediate connection with their living meaning, to make real to the student this association at every point, is the province of scientific or reflective grammar. This is not a process of perception or imagination, but an act of severe reflection, requiring a high degree of abstraction and self-consciousness—processes to which the average pupil in the grades is almost a stranger. Therefore, I repeat, the reflective study of the sentence must be deferred till the high school is reached.

The sentence has been called the unit of expression. All the higher forms of language and literature instruction presuppose this knowledge of and command over the sentence. There can be little satisfactory work in building the higher forms of discourse, without this foundation. The student whose sentence structure is chiefly spontaneous, not grounded on principles, through reflection, will be hampered at every step in the attempt to organize systematic discourse. The knowledge of this form grammatically considered, is also the foundation for the study of the sentence in the rhetorical view. Grammar stops with simple accuracy; rhetoric, so far as it relates to the sentence, assumes accuracy, and adds whatever will render the sentence effective. Instruction in literature, equally with advanced composition and rhetoric, assumes and requires this knowledge of the sentence. An extended experience in teaching this subject warrants the statement, that the greatest difficulty encountered in teaching the English classics is this imperfect knowledge of the classical English sentence. This knowledge can not be acquired by children. The difficulty in comprehending Bacon, Shakespeare, or Milton, is not their peculiar use of words, the figurative language employed, nor the historic and other allusions. In addition to the abstruseness of the thought itself, for which language is in no way accountable, is the long, complicated sentence structure, so strange to the beginner because so unlike the sentence of common life. Let any one examine the average sentence of either of the three writers named, and test for himself the correctness of this view. The grammar work of the grades must deal with what the pupil can understand, with the forms which appeal to his own conscious experience. It is held, therefore, thet it should be the ruling aim of the first year's instruction in English in the high school to ground the pupil thoroughly in the knowledge of the primary language form—the sentence.

What should be the type of the instruction in English during the second year? We are to remember now that the pupil, before entering the high school, had thorough drill in the conventional forms of communication, and also in writing from his own thought the elementary forms of definition, illustration, example, comparison, narration and description. The first year in the high school has been given to a thorough study of the sentence from the scientific point of view.

It is at this stage of his progress in English that rhetoric may be of the greatest service to the student. Its function is twofold; first, to supplement all the language work that has preceded it; and second, to broaden the function for the work in English yet to be done. In the first view rhetoric is to add a knowledge of the esthetic qualities of language; in general, whatever makes it effective, in addition to being accurate. It will view language in each of its types—the word, the sentence, the discourse ; but chiefly with reference to their literary qualities. So far as it leads to a re-study of words, it will be to supplement the mere accuracy of sound and form as taught by pronunciation and spelling, with a knowledge of the truly literary and esthetic qualities of words; clearness, melody, harmony, suggestiveness and the like. Likewise, in its view of the sentence, accuracy of construction as taught by grammar is assumed. But to this rhetoric adds that body of principles relating to the arrangement of sentence elements which arise in the effort to make the most effective presentation of the thought. In other words, the sentence is both a grammatical whole and a rhetorical unit. The student is lead to make a study of all the qualities of style based upon both the understanding and the feelings, including the leading types of figurative expression. But while designed to aid the pupil to make his own discourse effective, this knowledge serves equally the end of preparing for the study and interpretation of literature. Next to the understanding of the sentence grammatically, as a condition to the study of literature, comes this knowledge of the matter presented by rhetoric. Every page of literature employs the rhetorical qualities of language, and these, along with the principles of the sentence, are to be the student's main instruments in penetrating to its thought. While these three language forms are undergoing this critical study through the second year, the rhetorical principles learned are to be applied in all the constructive language work of the year, regular exercises in which should not be omitted after the first year.   This work will at every advance deepen his understanding of the instruction given below the high school, and ground him in the logical and rhetorical use of language.

We are now at the end of the second year in the high school. A glance back over the instruction thus far given by the school will show that the student has been drilled in every phase of language.   The word in respect to pronunciation, spelling, and meaning; the sentence practically before it was possible for its principles to be comprehended, and afterwards in its theoretic or scientific view; discourse, first, analytically as in reading, and second, in its constructive phase, as in composition.   And to all this has been added a re-study of the three—the word, the sentence, and the discourse—with 'a view to comprehending their rhetorical principles.   The pupil should now be, in a fair degree, the master of the tools of language.   Not that he is the experienced architect, or skilled artisan; these are the results of a life's endeavor.   But having mastered the principles of both, he has fulfilled the first conditions necessary to becoming either.

The student is now prepared for the most advanced work in English; and to the two fundamental phases of this—analysis and synthesis—it is held the last two years of the course should be given.   The analytic view will consist in the interpretation of the permanent literature of the language; the constructive will instruct and discipline the student in building the reflective forms of discourse—the varieties of exposition and argument. It is not meant that these should be entirely separate in time, as they are mutually helpful when carried on together.   They are here separated for convenience of treatment.

What and *how* in English literature for the high school, are important questions.   It is a most inadequate conception of the possibilities of this subject that makes it principally a study of the biography of literary characters, though this, held in due subordination, has a place in the work. It is not the individual's actual life in the world, however interesting the events of this in themselves may be, that the great writer weaves into his literary product; at least, these can have place in it only so far as they can be made images or symbols of universal content. His truly individual life is matter of little concern. Nor is that a correct theory which adds to the biographical view a list of the author's works, accompanied by the running comments and explanations of the editor, however intelligent these may be. To study a literary product is to come into direct contact with the living thought of the writer himself, not some one else. He who would slake his thirst with the purest draught must drink close up to the fountain head. A great system of literature, like that born of the English mind, is the noblest product of a people's spiritual life. It is the highest embodiment of their highest aspirations. The actual life of a people finds expression in history, science, and such forms; their ideal life, that is, their truly rational life, is borne to the ages on the wings of imagination. This is to be studied in their art, and mainly literature, the highest and most plastic form of art. Here we find their theory of human life; their glimpse of eternity; their profoundest insights into what is rationally and, therefore, universally true and beautiful. Their mountain-height visions into the world's ethical order are here enshrined in permanent living art forms. The transcendant excellence of that great body of literature produced by the English-speaking race is its recognition and emphasis of the world's moral and ethical order. It seizes man in the world of thought and action and portrays the immutable and eternal consequences of human deeds. It gives what humanity feels to be a solution of its problems. In its highest phases, it seizes the ever-recurring problems of human life and destiny and projects them into sensuous forms for the contemplation of the race.

If this is literature, does it need argument to establish for it a place in the education conferred by the high school? If it is the function of education to lift the individual to the rank of his that is, to endow him with the culture of his whole race, one fail to see the important means to this end supplied by literature of the English language? Moreover, this is the universally accessible form of the world's fine art. The sculpture, painting, and architecture of world interest and value are not accessible to the student. Except in favored instances, he is barred from participation, in the highest sense, in the great musical creations of his race. But the best thought of humanity is placed on his table for a trifle. Shall not the school unseal this volume and let its contents enter into his thought and life? It is the view of this paper that a daily lesson during not less than the third year of the high school should be given to a systematic study, in the order of their development, of the classical and permanent literary products of the English mind. Complete wholes or products of those great spiritual guides of the race should be made the subjects of direct instruction; those whose writings have made the greatest impress on the thought and life of the world; those whose solutions of life questions remain the fixed and established anchorage of the race. A term in this way with Chaucer, Spenser and Bacon; a second with Shakespeare and Milton; and a third with Coleridge, Wordsworth, Tennyson, and a triplet of American writers, will do two things: first, it will arouse a permanent interest in, determine a method for, and establish a habit in, the study of the classical literary creations of the English race; second, it will form the best possible introduction to the study of universal literature, into which the seers of the age have put their highest and clearest visions.

A brief statement may now be made of that phase of instruction in English which has been termed reflective composition. It is assigned to the last year in the course because it most fully presupposes all the forms of English thus far studied, as well also for the reason that it involves the highest degree of reflection and the largest fund of information. It supposes the word, the sentence, and a knowledge of rhetorical principles. It will engage and test the full measure of the student's power acquired in every field of study in his course. It will require not only the knowledge of every phase of English studied; but history, science, mathematics, observation and reflection will all serve him. It is proposed that a year's instruction shall be given upon those advanced forms of discourse in which are presented most subjects designed for instruction and to influence men's views, convictions and actions. They deal with what is abstract to a degree, general or comprehensive in thought.

It is readily seen that all knowledge exists either as ideas or judgments, or both. What is individual and concrete in these two realms belongs to the lower division of composition; it appeals to sense and imagination. But what is general and comprehensive in idea and thought, is subject-matter for advanced composition. The varieties of discourse dealing with the general may be grouped under two heads, exposition and argument. It will be seen that a single word or term, such as education, law, state, government, mental growth, may hold an amount of thought which it requires an essay or a volume to expand and exhibit. And so of the comprehensive judgment. It is the end of one division of instruction in composition to give the power to unfold by the proper means such ideas and judgments, that through their elements, they may be grasped and retained by those addressed. Composition is directly based upon the science of mind, since it is mind addressing mind. Consulting the means by which the general and complex is apprehended, it will, in this department, instruct the student in the systematic use of definition, analysis, contrast, example, illustration, and all the devices employed to present and amplify what is abstract and difficult.

In the field of argumentative discourse, the instruction may take two forms: first, the study of models that are within the student's grasp; and second, exercises in writing the simple forms of argument, carefully guarding the selection of subjects that lie within the student's experience and thought. The power to weigh conflicting facts, testimony, principles and reasons, and so to marshal these in orderly arrangement as to produce logical conviction, can not, it is true, be expected at the age of eighteen or nineteen years. But the definition of reason and argument, the principles relating to the arrangement of arguments in both direct proof and refutation, and exercises in simple argumentation, are all within the power of the senior in the high school. In the practical view, such instruction may be made direct preparation for that independence of judgment and conviction on the part of its member, of which the world which the student is to enter, stands in so great need.

The theory of instruction in English in the high school, as here outlined, proposes a continuous line of study from the beginning to the end of the course. The main positions advanced may be thus summarized: The first year is to be given to the scientific study of the sentence, for the reasons, first, that such instruction is impossible in the grades; second, it alone can give the fullest command of the sentence; and third, it is necessary to all the higher instruction in English. The second year is to be devoted to a continuation of the practice in writing the simple forms of discourse studied in the grades, and to the rhetorical view of the word, sentence, and discourse; thus giving immediate opportunity for the application, in the pupil's own product, of the rhetorical principles of language. The third year is to be given to representative permanent literary products in language, with three ends in view: first, to excite an interest in, and give some knowledge of, classical English literature; second, to teach a method of studying this; and third, to introduce the student to universal literature. To the fourth year is assigned the theoretic and practical work in the reflective discourse forms—exposition and argument.

Skill in any and all departments of this instruction is to be acquired by faithful and persistent practice in doing, under competent guidance. Accompanying every theoretical phase, it is the belief that there should be regular and methodical exercises in construction. This is the absolute condition to excellence in writing, as it is the safest and surest test of language power.

PEDAGOGICAL RHETORIC.

BY A. TOMPKINS, SUPT. FRANKLIN SCHOOLS.

The school exists,—1. As a formal organization evolved from an idea. 2. As an organization struggling to realize the idea that gave it birth.

Thus the school has two lines of progress,—1. The progress in developing its organs, its form and conditions of work. 2. Its progress in realizing the idea for which it was organized.

So much have our energies been exhausted in the first phase of progress, that we have given little attention to the nature, steps, and principles in the process of the work for which our machinery was devised. Our geographies and stump-orators glibly praise our ample school fund and our elaborate school system, but say nothing of skillful manipulation of ideas in forming the mental life of the pupil. The great body of teachers are most interested in the mechanics of the profession—plans of examination and promotion, forms of drill and schemes of marking, gradation and graduation, statistics, etc.

All this is necessary and in the natural order of progress. But in this rapid evolution of form, in our effort to adjust a part to every needed function as it arises, in our admiration of the beautiful system, we have forgotten that the organization has a work to do, and have thus lost the end in the means. Form and parade are sought as things in themselves. Even in the recitation, the culminating point of school work, the question is, "What is the formula for teaching this or that?" The demand for this has been so great that abnormal schools have sprung up all over the State, whose professed business is to give us formulas for doing things.

So much have we emphasized the system and the formula of its work that we have unconsciously exalted the forms of knowledge above the reality. Quantity of result is sought rather than character of mental effect. All the formulas, rules, dates, and isolated facts in the subjects that may be hit with the indispensable ten questions must be pounded in by the effective drill of the machinery, with shameful indifference to the mental needs of the pupil.

This, with the practical tendency of the age, has made the teaching of subjects for their own sake the characteristic phase of school work; and hence, means and methods of drill in securing measurable products are at the expense of a conscious plan of evolving the potential individual by means of the subjects taught. How to use our machinery to bring the objective face to face with the subjective for the development of the latter has not been attempted with any systematic effort. We may have discussed the problem in general terms; we may have grown elegant over the new education as a beautiful theory, but we work on as we have always worked; either because satisfied with mechanical manipulation and square-inch products, or from want of a clear comprehension of the nature of the educational process and an abiding faith in its non-percentable results.

It will be a hopeful day for the schools of Indiana when educational thought turns from the discussion of general questions, side issues, and non-essentials, to discussions of the essential nature of the educational process, and the scientific application of means in carrying out the process.

This is the next step in our progress; and it is the purpose of this paper, by a comparison with an outline of rhetoric, to give the general features of this needed phase of progress and some definite suggestions as to the means used in the educational process.

Rhetoric is the science and the art of discourse, the purpose of which is to affect the mind, by means of ideas, conveyed through symbols. This gives three chapters in the science and art of rhetoric. The first, to deal with the purpose of discourse— the effect it is to have on the mind. The second, to deal with the ideas by which the mind is affected. The third, to deal with the means of bringing the ideas in contact with the mind, that they may affect it. The definition and outline of pedagogics is identical with the above.

Pedagogics is the science and the art of affecting the mind, by means of ideas, conveyed through symbols. This gives three chapters in the science and art of pedagogics. The first, to deal with the purpose of teaching—the effect to be produced on the mind. The second, to deal with the ideas by which the effects on the mind are to be produced. The third, to deal with the means of bringing the ideas in contact with the mind that they may affect it.

The writer about to make a piece of discourse asks: 1. What

effect do I want to produce? Do I want to instruct the intellect, cultivate the emotional nature, or determine the will in a new course of conduct? 2. What ideas have I by which I may produce this desired effect? 3. How can I best carry these ideas to the mind that they may have the desired effect? i. e., how may I write effectively?

The teacher—the artistic teacher—asks the same questions. The laws and principles that pertain to the purpose, to the thought and to the style of the writer, pertain also to the purpose, to the thought and to the style of the teacher; only the latter point differing, and differing only as the conditions differ; for we control the receiving mind when we teach it, but do not when we discourse to it.

Hence, the first element of professional knowledge on the part of the teacher is a clear comprehension of the nature of the effect to be produced on the soul of the pupil—an aim, an effect, an ideal to be born out of the struggling life of the pupil. Not an immediate effect, but remote, determined by the range of the pupil's unfolding life—effects whose value can only be judged by the aim of life itself; since the aim of life and the aim of school are one. Till such an aim become the organizing idea in the work of the teacher, he will follow a trade and not a profession; he will be an artisan and not an artist.

It is not necessary here to describe this aim. It has been told over and over again from the writers of Greece down—in uncertain tones at first, but clear and positive for the two past centuries. We understand its general meaning, but we have not made it a part of our professional life, as is shown by the absence of any systematic plan consciously followed to reach the aim in which we profess to believe. We accept the doctrine of the purpose of education as logically correct, but refuse, either from want of professional faith, or because the material pressure of the age forces us to the so-called practical ends of knowledge, to accept its guiding light, by which only we can work out a scientific educational process. The great body of teachers are not discussing a definite, organic plan of work to develop the powers of the soul—how by means of the subjects of study to train the intellect in power, habits, and forms of thought; how by means of the beautiful to refine and strengthen the emotions, and chasten the imagination; how, by means of the aspiring self in the pupil, to determine the will to seize and hold, as an eternal guide of conduct through all varying fortunes, the ideal of life—the possible self. In this the essential line of progress we have done nothing. We teach on unconscious that a subject has a mission to fill in the mental economy of the pupil, and that the ideas in the subjects must be organized and presented with a definite end in view. In the last State Association it was said that as long as text-books in a certain subject were made as they are, the teaching of that subject must be as it is. This is the type of many statements which imply that the *means* determine the *end*. Ask the teacher what she accomplishes in English language in the first year high school, and she will tell you that she uses Powel's How to Write. What do you accomplish in Physical Geography? We use Guyot. Now if these answers had been different the ends would have been different. We have here no thought of subordination of means to end which characterizes professional work.

We need to shift our point of view from the *subjects* taught to the *individual* for whom they are taught. The subjects must be reduced to a means, and the ideal in the pupil exalted to an organizing purpose in all educational efforts. And here progress necessarily stands in her own light. For indeed it is difficult, in a system whose highest point of development is rigid, uniform examination of teachers, and of pupils for graduation from the district schools—in a system which makes answers to questions its final test of efficiency, and thus puts a premium on immediate, ponderable results, not to aim our work at the subject, rather than at some unseen and remote effect on the mental habit of the pupil, and which must be accepted by our faith in the laws of spiritual growth.

Suppose us to have changed our point of view and to be determined in making the most of the pupil by *means* of the subjects in making the purpose of life and the purpose of school work the same, and by means of the subjects to help realize life's purpose, and we are at once under the necessity of stating how by means of the subjects this may be done.   This is the second chapter in the science and art of pedagogics, and corresponds to the second chapter of rhetoric, which discusses how to affect the mind by means of ideas.   This is the unwritten chapter. The course of study is fixed both by law and logic; the field of study is given to us along with the mind, but we have worked out no rational plan of conducting the educational process.

An outline of this second chapter is suggested by a further comparison with rhetoric.

[TO BE CONTINUED.]

THE SCHOOL ROOM.

[This Department is conducted by GEO. F. BASS, Supervising Prin. Indianapolis schools.]

——:o:——

"CRITICISMS."

THE Fourth Reader class was reading, and Mary had just finished reading the first paragraph, when critisms were called for.   The word "criticisms" caused much vigorous swinging of hands by many members of the class.   We began to feel sorry for Mary.

The teacher, by a nod of her head, gave permission to a certain pupil to make his criticisms known.   He was followed by another and another until all the hands had been mowed down. The criticisms were about as follows :—

Said *uv* for *of;* left out *the;* kept voice up at the end of the third line; *hǎlf* for *hälf;* omitted *t* in *must;* mumbled; read too fast; stood on one foot; held book too low; etc.

Each "criticism" was followed by a "yes" from the teacher, with that peculiar inflection that asks for more.   The pupil was asked to read again and correct these mistakes—somewhere from ten to fifteen of them.   The patient and long suffering Mary tried again, and again brought the house down on her.

The teacher did not believe in reading for her pupils, so she asked the best reader in the class to show Mary how to read it.

Mary tried again, but received another shower of "criticisms."
What was the trouble? Mary had too many things to think
about at one time. If she had been asked to read one sentence
and correct *one* mistake she could probably have succeeded.
Then, if the teacher and class had made her feel that she had
been successful, she would have read again and again until *all*
her mistakes had been corrected. "One thing at a time" is a
good motto in teaching. Give the pupil credit for every success,
or partial success. Read sentence by sentence, keeping one
point prominent until *all* mistakes are corrected. Lastly, read
the whole paragraph as a kind of review.

It should be remembered that the above criticisms are all on
the mechanical side of reading. There is another and much
neglected side—the thought side.

THE WRONG QUESTION.

A PUPIL in an arithmetic class was asked, "What month is
November?" He said, "Ninth month." The teacher then
undertook to lead the pupil to correct his mistake by questioning him. This, by the way, is one of the best plans to correct
mistakes. Care must be taken to ask the *right* questions. The
following is what occurred in this case :—

Tr. Now, George, what is the last month of the year?"
Geo. December.
Tr. Well, what number is it?
Geo. The twelfth month.
Tr. Well, now, what *is* the ninth month?
Geo. November.
Tr. (To another pupil.) What month *is* November?
Pu. The eleventh month.
Tr. Certainly.

The teacher asked the right question when he asked what the
last month of the year is and its number; but when he followed
with "What *is* the ninth month?" he asked the *wrong* question,
because he called the pupil's attention to the very thing he did
not want. The pupil had no use for the "ninth month." Hav-

ing called to the pupil's mind the fact that December is the 12th month, he should have asked what month precedes ·December, and then "What month is November?"

Questioning is a great art that should be studied carefully by every teacher. Form the habit of studying your own questions. When you think your pupils are slow to take a subject that you have presented on the "development plan," analyze your questions and see whether they did not mislead the pupil.

PRIMARY DEPARTMENT.

[This Department is conducted by LEWIS H. JONES, Supt. Indianapolis Schools]

——:o:——

PRIMARY LANGUAGE.

A FTER the exercises indicated in the preceding article of this series, there should follow a conversation between pupils and teacher upon some theme. A picture, with a large number of objects represented in it, forms a suitable subject. Let pupils make statements and ask questions about the objects represented in the picture. The teacher should write both the statements and the questions on the board as they are given, being careful to punctuate and capitalize each correctly.

From the exercise of the preceding day children would refer to the different expressions on the board as sentences. Ask a pupil to take a pointer and touch a sentence that asks about something. To another say, "Read the question which that sentence asks." To another, "Find a sentence that does not ask anything, but simply tells something. Read what that sentence tells." Pursue this line of work for a little while, having pupils thus distinguish the sentence that "asks something" from the one that merely "tells something." Presently say, "You may find an asking sentence, Mary." "Read the question which that asking sentence asks, Fannie." "You may find a telling sentence, Henry." "Read what this telling sentence tells, Robbie." Thus each child has divided the collection of sen-

2

tences into two kinds, and has seen what each kind may appropriately be called from its use.

Review the sentences with reference to capitalization and punctuation. "Read a telling sentence, Annie." Refer to the capital at beginning and to the period at the close. "Who can find another sentence in this group, beginning with a capital and ending with a period?" Mary can do so. "Think whether it is an asking sentence or a telling sentence." They soon decide that it is a telling sentence. Have children find all the telling sentences in the group, and observe that each begins with a capital and closes with a period. Generalize the idea by saying that what they have found is true of all telling sentences when properly written.

Begin now to review the asking sentences. Each is seen to begin with a capital and close, not with a period, but with a question mark.

The other two forms of sentence—the commanding sentence and the exclaiming sentence—are by their nature a little more difficult of comprehension. They may therefore be delayed a little; though when they are taught, the method of presentation here outlined for *telling* and *asking* sentences will be found equally adapted to their introduction.

In addition to the statement that "a commanding sentence begins with a capital and ends with a period," we must also teach that "the name of the person or thing commanded must be separated from the other part of the sentence by a comma."

In order to complete the study of the kinds of sentence, take the readers which the children may chance to be using—Second Readers or Third Readers, as the case may be—and practice searching for a special kind, as the *telling* sentence, or the *exclaiming* sentence; letting each child read the sentence found, and letting all decide upon the correctness of the work.   ·

Give on a subsequent day a reproduction lesson, by referring to a particular picture in some book used by all the children, as their reader, and require the pupil to "write two *telling* sentences about this picture," or "write three *asking* sentences about things that you see in this picture," etc., etc. It is an interesting exercise for pupils to read, in the next recitation in language, from their slates or paper, the various sentences thus obtained. Each pupil should be held responsible for telling what kind of sentence he thinks each is, and for describing the mode of capitalizing and punctuating each. If rightly managed the conversation induced is worth as much in language culture as is the written exercise. Indeed, cultivated conversation on proper themes of study is largely the occupation of the true school.

The exercises indicated in this brief paper may be condensed into a few lessons, and the essential facts of the subject be thus learned; or they may be profitably expanded into many weeks of practice in speaking and in writing the simple English sentence. The leading factors in determining which course shall be pursued, are, age of pupils, skill of teacher, time that can be spared from other work, etc., etc.

In either case there is little technicality, but much practice in speaking and writing; a notable example of "learning to do by doing" in an intelligent and orderly way.

DEPARTMENT OF PEDAGOGY.

This Department is conducted by GEO. P. BROWN, President State Normal School.

——:o:——

"LEARNING TO DO BY DOING."

COL. F. W. PARKER may be styled the modern apostle of the educational doctrine enunciated by the phrase above quoted. Indeed, so prominent and influential has he been in the advocacy of certain educational ideas that his own name has been more than once attached to his doctrine. Parkerism is a term of somewhat frequent occurrence in educational writings. What we shall say will refer to the doctrine and not to the author. Personally he is worthy of the highest respect and admiration of all who esteem a generous, large-hearted, enthusiastic lover of the children, who desires to make their school-life pleasant and profitable. ·

The *dictum*, "Learn to do by doing," has been made to

do such a varied service in the vague and undiscriminating writings of many of this day that we were gratified to have the phrase defined by one whom the advocates of one of the "new educations" of our time will accept as authority. Mr. Parker said, substantially, in a recent address before the teachers of Indiana, that all activity, whether mental or physical, is *doing* in the meaning of the maxim. That to perceive, to remember, to imagine, to judge, to reason, and the like, are *to do*. That the objective manifestation of our mental activity is but one kind of doing. That there is a subjective, internal, spiritual activity that is as truly *doing* as is any objective manifestation of it.

This seems but another way of expressing the time-worn truth that the law of the growth of any power, mental or physical, is by the exercise of that power. To acquire the power of observing, one must practice observation. If one would cultivate his imagination he must exercise it. To acquire power in judging and reasoning one must judge and reason. To deny all this would be to imitate the fond but timid mother who advised her son to learn to swim, but urged him never to go into the water. To "learn to do by doing" seems to mean, after all, that the different faculties of the mind are to be strengthened, and facility in their use is to be acquired by the exercise of these faculties. Also, if I would acquire manual skill of any kind it must be through practice of those muscles of the body that combine to produce the desired result. This, then, is the corner stone of that structure called the "New Education."

' How many of us have been New Educationists all our lives without knowing it! Now that we have had the fundamental doctrine of the New Education defined by so high an authority, and have found it to be identical with the fundamental doctrine of every teacher and psychologist for the last hundred years, viz., that "the law of all growth of power is through the exercise of that power," let us beat our swords into plow-shares and our spears into pruning hooks and bend all our energies toward the proper application of this law of nature to the education of the child.

The only difference that can arise among teachers is respecting the extent and mode of application of this law. It is a great satisfaction to learn, as we have learned from such excellent authority, that there is no difference in doctrine among intelligent teachers. A difference in either extent or mode of application may be sufficiently great, however, to justify discussion.

In the application of this law, for instance, Mr. Parker inveighs against the study of Grammar, saying with Richard Grant White, that since the English is virtually a grammarless tongue, the methods of study of Latin and Greek are inapplicable to English. If by Grammar is meant inflection only, then this statement is substantially true. But the grammar of any language includes much more than inflection. The grammar of the Latin or Greek language, even, is largely devoted to the presentation of the science of sentence construction. English grammar is almost wholly devoted to this. If the province of grammar is to teach the laws and principles of sentence construction, it is nonsense to call the English a grammarless tongue. Mr. Parker says that time spent in the study of English grammar is vainly spent; is worse than wasted. That the way to learn the English language is to use it correctly. And here he seems to lapse from his original definition and adopts the popular meaning of "learning to do by doing." A conscious knowledge of the principles and laws of sentence construction he does not think to be needful. He would seem to rest satisfied with an empirical knowledge gained by practice in the use of language under criticism. He would rely upon the education of the ear and the eye. All the learner would be able to give as a reason for the incorrectness of a sentence would be, "it does not sound right," or "it does not look right." He has "learned to do by doing" in the sense in which that phrase has been understood by all except the apostles of the "New Education."

Those who advocate the retention of grammar in our school curriculum hold that it is important that the learner, when he has reached a certain stage of knowledge by this process of "learning to do by doing," shall advance to a higher stage of knowledge in which other and higher faculties of mind are brought into exercise. He shall be taught to turn his thought back upon what he has thus learned, and be led to discover and formulate the laws of language which he has been unconsciously obeying under the lead of his teachers. In doing this he acquires powers of generalizing and classifying that his former methods of study did not exercise, and he learns to do this by doing it. He is now able to criticise his own language and that of others from another and higher basis than sound or sight. Until he can construct a sentence in conscious obedience to the known laws of his language, he has no adequate knowledge of his language.

Our criticism on Col. Parker as to this point is not that he would have his pupils learn to do by doing, but it is that he would not have them learn enough things by doing them. He would seem to limit the study of language to the cultivation of the ear and the eye, giving only a perceptive stage of knowledge of it. We would extend it to the cultivation of the powers of generalization, classification and judgment. Making the pupils' knowledge of his language rational as well as empirical.

That this rational study is begun too soon in many schools and great injury done thereby, is generally conceded by intelligent teachers. But Mr. Parker not only condemns the commencement of grammar at too early a period, but even its study altogether.   G. P. B.

MINUTES OF THE INDIANA STATE TEACHERS' ASSOCIATION.

· Held in Plymouth Church, Indianapolis, Dec. 29–31, 1884.

MONDAY EVENING, December 29.

The thirty-first annual meeting of the Indiana State Teachers' Association was called to order by Prof. E. E. Smith, Chairman of the Executive Committee.

The retiring President, Dr. J. S. Irwin, of Fort Wayne, having been delayed on a late train, telegraphed that he could not be present.

H. B. Hill, Supt. of Dearborn county, President-elect, delivered his inaugural address, his subject being,

"A RETROSPECTIVE AND A PROSPECTIVE VIEW OF INDIANA'S SCHOOL SYSTEM."

He said the city schools have added the appliances so necessary to a perfect instruction. In this they have done well. In the country the schools are yet held in insufficient buildings, and the terms are short. Thus it appears that the school system of the State is unequal. The country schools are not receiving the proper attention of the people. If a better class of teachers is needed, or if, in short, they are not doing the work for which they are designed, how can the result desired be obtained? One remedy is a uniformity in the length of the school terms and amount of salaries in town and city. Until a uniform term is had it will be impossible to successfully grade them. The short term schools are taught by the inferior teachers, and thus the pupils of such schools are the losers in a twofold manner. If I were asked what is to day the most pressing need of the country schools, I would promptly reply, a more cultured class of teachers. The direction of a whole generation is in the hands of the school teachers of the present day. I put the teachers higher than the preacher, lawyer, and doctor. I put God first, then mother, then teacher, then minister.

The successful teacher should know the law of mind growth and the science of education. His chief delight is in doing the greatest good to those whom he is training up Nine tenths of mankind owe their weal or woe to their early education. The parents and school officers of Indiana must demand that the teachers shall be competent, and the doors of the schools must be closed against the incompetent.

The compensation of a teacher must be equal to the demands made of him. The present compensation is not respectable. The average school pays the average teacher the enormous sum of $240 annually. He must be an honest man, keep within the bounds of his salary, and have a nice little sum in bank at the end of the year. So says a college professor. I am in favor of a compulsory educational law. The question that every one has a right to do as he pleases, so long as he interferes with the rights of no one, admits of argument. The dissemination of education is essential to the safety of the government; therefore, no one has a right to grow in ignorance. The person who grows up in ignorance is discriminated against. We are told that upon the hands of many children depends the livelihood of their families, and that they can not be spared to go to school. These children are not able during school age to labor. Some States have adopted laws forbidding the employment of children under certain age. This is to prevent them from becoming a care to the State. If some stock raisers should treat their stock as they do their children, they would be arrested for cruelty to animals. We ask for a law to protect such children; both in their rights and physical training.

J. M. Olcott moved that a committee be appointed to formulate and present the system advocated in the paper, and distribute the same before the people throughout the State.

D. E. Hunter moved to amend by appointing a committee of five to work and consult with the State Superintendent in presenting the plan to the Legislature now about to assemble. He said:

That every advance in school work made in this State during the last thirty years had its origin in this association. We must have the lower grades come up to the higher. There can be no good grade work while there is such a difference in length of school term in the different parts of the State, or even in the different parts of the same county.

W. A Bell indorsed the idea of increasing the school term, and formulating the arguments of the President's paper, but he saw difficulties in the way of a proper presentation of the argument to the Legislature. If a school tax, local or general, is asked for, it will be said, and properly, that we have all that we need. We have all the laws we need in favor of the schools, but what we want is the education of the public sentiment up to the point of the proper utilization of the laws we already have.

The Chair appointed the following committee:

Supt. John W. Holcombe, John M. Olcott, D. E. Hunter, F. D. Churchill, Geo. F. Bass, and J H. Martin.

E. E. Smith moved that a committee of three, on resolutions, be appointed. The following committee was appointed:

W. W. Parsons, J. C. Eagle, and W. H. Caulkins.

D. E. Hunter nominated Mrs. Annie E. H. Lemon, of Spencer, for Assistant Secretary. Mr. Hunter named as Assistant Enrolling Secretaries, E. R. Smith, of La Fayette, and Walter Wallace, of Columbus.

R. A. Ogg moved that a committee of intelligence, to inform teachers and school men of vacancies, be appointed. R. A. Ogg and W. A. Bell were appointed. Association adjourned.

TUESDAY, 9:00 A. M.

The Association was called to order, and prayer was offered by Supt. J. C. Eagle, of Edinburg.

The first paper of the morning was presented by Mrs. E. A. Blaker, Prin. Indianapolis Kindergarten. Subject,

"THE FRŒBELIAN IDEA."

She said: Some one has said "Whenever we have learned to take an interest in a man's opinions or his public actions and influence we naturally desire to know more of his life, to see what cirucmstances went to form his character, what peculiar impulse or purpose shaped his destiny." The history of Frœbel is so closely connected with his opinions and work that one of his disciples felt that he could not analyze his theory without analyzing his life

Although he did not have the influence of his mother on account of her death, yet he believed himself to have inherited from her his own imaginative and esthetic spirit.

Frœbel's class was the model of the school. He had an opportunity to let teachers and parents see the advantages of his method of instruction. His idea was a high one, and he felt his need of going more deeply into methods of instruction and education.

What is education ? What do the means of elementary instruction set forth by Pestalozzi signify ? What is principally the object of instruction? In answer to the last he says, "Man lives in a world of objects which act upon him, on which he wishes to work ; thus he must know them according to their nature, their character, and their relation to each other and himself." The objects have form, then come size Everything is unity ; everything rests in, proceeds from, strives for, leads and returns to unity ?

To him the universe was God's expressed thought, the study of its laws, the study of God's plan of development. Frœbel was not a mere theorist His soul was in his work He recognized the truth, "That to live one's self is the true and proper education. It was his duty to aid humanity in the fulfillment of its destiny ; as humanity is made up of individuals, he applied himself to a search for a plan of individual development. He was convinced that Nature's law for growth was motion, and he began with play, or the spontaneous activity of the child.

His method of education exerts an influence over the whole being of the child, lays a foundation for future life work, develops body and soul harmoniously, gives clearness and precision in the use of the hand and of language, and inculcates a love of God and man."

Discussion of the paper was opened by D. M. Nelson, Supt. of Jasper county, who presented the following ideas:

All who have the care of the young should be deeply interested in this subject. It had been ably said in the paper that Rousseau gave the standing point to the modern education. The mind had been regarded as a tablet upon which the educator might write anything he chose. Rousseau showed us that education is a growth like that of the plant, and that the child is developed according to organic law ; not only its body but its mind is an organism Pestalozzi emphasizes this, and the importance of home education, and the careful study of the individuality of the child All instruction in the school should be verified in the experience of the child. A large part of the education of mankind comes through their daily employm nts.

This idea gives rise to two modern institutions; agricultural colleges, institutions of technology, and the kindergarten system.

Frœbel believed that the analogies he saw in nature held true of the mind ; he believed in the harmony between mind and matter, and the principles of the development of the physical and mental world. He watched the growth of the child and saw that its great characteristic was its restlessness, physical restlessness showing itself in the movements of the body, and mental restlessness showing itself in the curiosity to examine everything within its reach. Its desire to imitate men and women is shown in its plays, and to imitate forms of life and beauty is shown in its attempts at drawing. Frœbel noticed in the child's plays that its social organism goes out toward its fellow-beings, and said, "This is the great activity that leads it onward into the possession of all its powers."

The children's garden, or kindergarten, is a place where the children are cultivated as the gardener cultivates his plants, and takes most care of the little ones that are most likely to be injured. The main idea is the education of the child through its spontaneous activities. The child should never know that he is being instructed, but amused and played with all the time.

W. A. Bell said: Almost all parents live *for* their children, but there are not very many who know how to live *with* their children. There is a marked distinction between these two. Apply this to teacher of little children; the teacher should live *with* the children in mental work. She should not stand above and talk down to them, or at them, but put herself into sympathy with them. She should think with the child, and in that way stimulate its activity and allow it to develop itself; let it do its own work, guided by the teacher. This principle applies to all the lower grades.

Geo. P. Brown said he thought the Frœbelian thought was that man was to be educated for *freedom*. In this he differed from the educators of his time. He held that this great world is identical with the little world within the child. The process of education has been the identification of these two worlds, and his freedom is to come from the realization of that identity. Frœbel recognized man as a social being, and established a school to develop social equality. The child is the property of the state and the state should educate it. The child must be brought out of the family into communion with his fellows. This is the fundamental idea of Frœbel.

"THE MORAL EDUCATION OF THE YOUNG,"

an address by Rev. O. C. McCulloch, of Indianapolis, will appear in a future number of the Journal.

The third paper,

"PROFIT AND LOSS OF THE GRADED SCHOOL SYSTEM,"

was read by D. D. Luke, Supt. of the Ligonier schools. In his paper Mr. Luke presented the following ideas:

The pupils in our city and town schools are classified in different rooms with respect to their ability and proficiency, and are placed under different teachers as they advance from grade to grade. The same system of grading prevails to a marked degree in the district schools.

The efficiency of any system in subserving the interest involved in their object must be judged by the results produced; since the graded system, in so far as it meets to a good advantage the requirements of sound culture, indispensable to a liberty loving and industrial citizenship is profit, its shortcomings are loss. The marked principle of civilization is division of labor, and the graded school system, being the prime factor in economic culture, conforms with the general principle in making its grades and assigning work to teachers. This principle is of great advantage in that it gives increased skill, the teacher better knowledge of her work, saves time in changing from one subject to another, affords better means for the teacher to invent, as a means to an end, and increases the adaptation of physical and mental abilities The principle of division of labor is a disadvantage in that it tends to enervate the operator because it does not give full activity to the development of body and other functions Also by the division of labor the teacher and pupil incur a loss in individuality, and the more marked the grades become the more nearly will the system approximate machine work. These tendencies may be compensated by the teacher's devoting a certain portion of her time to studies outside of her profession, thereby broadening her knowledge and keeping pace with the world of thought. The influence is of advantage with respect to discipline of the school, by affording better opportunities for the management of large masses; also, it affords to the people better means of intellectual discipline. The value to the pupil in this respect arises from the skilled labor of the teacher in her special line of work.

With respect to the pupil's physical and intellectual training there occurs a loss in the general health of the pupil, and through the mistaken idea that sound training is measured by the number of studies the pupil goes through in his school course The chances of a pupil's getting through with the average course of high school with sound and mental sensibilities are about as one to three; the pupil will either fail or come out with a smattering of what he had gone over. The tendency to reading trashy literature is chargeable to the methods of study practiced in graded schools; pupils hurried through the course have no time to practice thought; and for this reason, dislike to read subjects requiring thought.

Minds not given to thought can not be expected to read anything requiring thought, and certainly for one to read a good book simply for the reading, is a waste of time. If our young people are to be led to read standard works, a desire for knowledge and a thirst for information must first be created. The way to cultivate a taste for good literature is not to force good books into the hands of the young for the sake of literature, for rest assured no good will come from such a course; but to train pupils to think and investigate new trains of thought for themselves. The tampering with literature or history as it is done in the average school, makes these studies distasteful, so much so that when the pupil leaves school he views them as a thing to be loathed. With the experiences of the past to guide us, there is no reason why the graded school system can not be made the most efficient instrument of sound culture and progressive civilization ever devised by man.

The afternoon session was introduced by a recitation, given by Master Bertie Feibleman, well rendered and much enjoyed.

"EDUCATION—A WAY, A METHOD, OR A SCIENCE,"

a paper read by G. F. Kenaston, Supt. of Attica schools, contained the ideas presented in these words:

Education is the development of the faculties of the intellect, sensibility and will, and the training of them into harmonious action in accordance with the laws and principles of their nature and growth. Education is, or should be, the science and art of the culture and instruction of the human being, not simply an empiric method or way. A method is a special mode of practicing and unfolding an art, and must necessarily vary according to the age of the pupil, the knowledge of the teacher, subject-matter, the conception of the mind of the materials upon which we work or the object aimed at. An art is a practical display of science. It aims to accomplish a definite work by rational methods. The art of educating or teaching is the means and methods used by the teacher to influence, instruct, and train his pupils. Science seeks to find and classify the unchangeable laws and principles underlying the art, and give a rational basis for the methods for applying it.

Education as an empiric way or method is practicing the most difficult of all arts without any knowledge of its principles. The function of the science of education in relation to the art, the practice, and the methods of teaching, is to give us a deeper insight into the nature and conditions of successful teaching, to show the various ways each and all of the faculties develop, and the influences and methods best adapted to call them into full and harmonious exercise, to give the laws and conditions of their growth, which the teacher should supplement with the methods and means of experience.

Just as the physician sees the elements needed for bone and muscle, so the teacher who knows the revelations of psychology and educational history, will be able to detect and carry out scientific methods of training the faculties at their proper time and with their proper food. For are we not artists; the mind the clay upon which we work? Like the carpenter and the goldsmith we should know the attributes and capacities, resources and faculties of our material, how far it will yield to the treatment, and how far and when resist. Mental science has as close relation to our work as mathematics has to the astronomer or surveyor. It is the spirit, enthusiastic interest. luminous personal influence that gives life. Nothing can take the place of the great hearted, rich souled, cultured man or woman.

After a short recess, Mrs. R. A. Moffitt, of Rushville high school, recited "A Shadow," to the delight of all the audience.

Col. F. W. Parker, of Normalville, Ill., delivered the annual address, having for its subject, "Learn to Do by Doing." (A full report of this will be given in next number of the Journal.)

The following committee was appointed to nominate officers:

1st District—Wm. McK. Blake, Evansville; 2d District—W B. Creager, Sullivan; 3d District—R. A. Ogg, New Albany; 4th Dist.— J. A. Carnagey, Madison; 5th District—A. E. Rogers, Clayton; 6th District—J. M. Bloss, Muncie; 7th District—C. S, Olcott, Indianapolis; 8th District—W. H. Elson, Rockville; 9th District—J T. Merrill, La Fayette; 10th District—P. H. Kirsch, Rensselaer; 11th District; H. S. McRae, Marion; 12th District—John S. Irwin, Fort Wayne; 13th District—Elias Boltz, Mishawaka.

In the evening session Wallace Bruce, of Poughkeepsie, New York, lectured on

"WOMANHOOD IN SHAKESPEARE."

He said that in presenting the subject he was conscious of present-in the two best known words of the English language—Shakespeare and woman. In an age like ours, which derives its inspiration from the future and which delights in the practical, it seems strange to go back so far to find out what was thought of woman. He spoke of Shakespeare as having four heroines to one hero, and he regards that as the true ratio. It is said of his plays that if they were all put upon the stage at once it would require over seven hundred perform-ers, aside from attendants, etc., and yet no two of his characters are alike. I saw recently a picture of Shakespeare and his friends, all his characters passing in revie v before him. Standing out from the gloom and sadness of his male, we see the relief afforded by his female characters, with a few exceptions models of their sex.

The speaker divided his subject into three divisions : the romantic, the domestic, and the heroic. Under the first head comes Miranda, the character given in the Tempest. In the world of romance no character seems so fair and beautiful—a vision even purer and sweeter than the fourth book of Milton's Paradise Lost. Romances have well been termed the salt in the ocean of life which keeps its waters pure and wholesome The picture of Ferdinand and Miranda is worth a thousand homilies on culture. Like a clever artist Shakespeare de-velops character with a few well chosen touches.

From the life of Ophelia we learn that no life is a failure, which has been truly and honorably spent. Love is the great educator of life. These characters represent the love of early womanhood.

Shakespeare's domestic ideal is the realization of the romance and love dreams, of which our novelists and writers only write. They stop at [the conclusion of the romantic, as if that were the end of happiness and love and peace. But Shakespeare goes on. His Catharine is one of the ideals of domestic life. Indeed, Hawthorne says she is the womanliest woman of all Shakespeare's characters. To know the right, and to do it, is the crowning glory of manhood and womanhood. Contrast this character with that of Cleopatra, with all her vices and cruelties. Cordelia, in her fidelity to her father, is another character It is true she suffered disgrace and was banished, but she comes at last to be her father's comforter at his bedside. Of all his characters, Cordelia speaks the least, but says the most.

In this life we are controlled by circumstances which we either make or accept; just how made the centuries have been trying to solve. Portia and Jessica are next in the list of heroines. Portia, in the court at Venice, presents a perfect picture of the heroic woman in her exposition of the law governing the case, and her admixture of the sentiment of mercy in the strict administration of the law be-tween Antonio and the Jew, Shylock. This trial scene is to be placed next to the trial of Paul before King Agrippa. Madam De Stael said "Courage and weakness are the true bonds of the sexes," and there is a world of meaning in it. Equality does not mean identity. The mass of women do not look to masculine fields for a place to labor, nor should they, for there is room for them in their own field.

WEDNESDAY MORNING, Dec. 31.

The President in the chair, R. A. Ogg, of New Albany, conducted the devotional exercises. A paper,

"PERSONALITY IN TEACHING,"

was read by Miss Ella E. Munson, late principal of the Mitchell public schools. These are some of the good ideas her paper contained:

In the atom is the soul of the universe; in the drop of blood fresh from the human body is the wellspring of life; in the seed is the life, the heart of the forest; in the dew drop the possibility of an ocean; but in man is the soul, the spring, the heart, the possibility of a nation. In a Socrates we see the soul of an ancient philosophy, of an Athens; in a Luther, the fermenting spirit of a fifteenth century, the spring of modern thought; in a Napoleon, we see all the possibilities of a French people; in the mental accumulations of centuries in an Emerson, we see the alert, moving, speculative American. Men, individuals, make circumstances Individuality, strong marked characters, and their influence mark the advancing steps of civilization, and retracing its progress we only retrace their lives and character. If, as has been said, individual development is the model of social progress, surely the fashioning of that model for good or for evil, the laying of the foundation of the society of the future, both in the moral and intellectual world, lies pre-eminently with the teacher. Does the profession, as it exists to-day, possess all the essentials for accomplishing such a high and holy purpose? Though we have had Huxleys, Bains, and Herbert Spencers to discourse to us on the true philosophy of education, yet the application of these principles by modern educators seems almost as an entire perversion of the very life and purpose for which they labored

The question of education resolves into the query, not what shall I do best to satisfy the needs of the child, that spirit of the future; but the old Grecian principle, how can the child best meet the requirements of my methods? Is this the true plan? The hope that you may put zinc and copper into the crucible and bring out the shining gold is no more impossible than this all-pervading principle, that method can make the teacher. Nowhere else do we find such demands as are made on the teacher.

The principle that may be applied successfully to our pupil, or to one school, may be of no avail with another; for the avenue that would lead to the good and redeeming of one, would in many cases produce dangerous results in another. As no one can exert an influence beyond what he promises himself, or produce a desire in others beyond that for which he is striving, there must emanate from the teacher this alert, penetrating, originating spirit; his precepts and examples must accord with the influence. How few recognize this responsibility, or realize that the word of to-day becomes the thought of to-morrow!

Prof. Carhart, of DePauw University, discussed this subject in a short paper which the Journal will hereafter publish.

"THE ELEMENT OF TRUST IN GOVERNMENT,"

a paper read by Mrs. Harriet E. Leonard, principal of Jefferson School, Fort Wayne, said:

The element of trust in government takes note of the primal occasion for and use of authority, considers the different forms of government and their applications, as shown in the history of nations, finds the essential qualities of successful administration to be wisdom, justice and goodness, suggests that t. e persons lacking these in character, at least. should not be found directing or restricting the activities of others; that the highest success in government is found in the confidence inspired and reposed by the individual practice of that which is most estimable in mankind—believes that the careful study of the laws of the mind and of the child-nature will enable the teacher to stimulate that which is noblest and best in her pupils—that Indiana, having a small percent of foreign parentage, has less occasion to beat the bodies, and more opportunity to draw out the minds of her growing citizens than many of her sister States, and by a wise supervision and careful administration has proven much that is possible and worthy of imitation of the power of trust in government.

In the discussion of the subject, Mr. R. A. Ogg, of New Albany, said:

You have had presented to you the origin and histroy of government, and the application of the general idea to the school room. I will add that it seems to me we should take into consideration the elements of trust on the part of the governing toward the governed. The object and aim of government is to secure good conduct and to develop right character. The great question that most concerns us, is how far may we trust our pupils and, by means of that trust, secure good conduct in the school room and the development of right character. We want good conduct because without it we can not do good work; we must have it for our own sakes, but more for the sake of those we teach. It is our duty to determine how far we may trust our pupils with safety It is important that the teacher should show to the pupils confide ce in their honesty, earnestness, and their desire to do right When we feel that we can trust our pupils, we have done much for them. Yet while we find a sense of honor possessed by some in such a degree that we feel that they will take no advantage of opportunities for wrong doing, we have others whom we can not trust at all. It is well to repose all the confidence in the pupils that we dare; it will elevate their ideals for themselves and fit them better for the duties of citizenship.

The trust that the governed have in the one who is governing is at the basis of all good government. He who would govern well must have the confidence of the governed. If they have not confidence in his honesty, his government is an injury to them. They should be made to feel that the teacher is their friend. The great power Dr. Arnold possessed was the power to make his pupils feel that he was their friend; and when he punished, it was for their good.

The third paper of the morning,

"THE CITIZENSHIP OF THE TEACHER,"

was presented by Edward Taylor, of Vincennes. In the presentation of his subject, Mr. Taylor said:

The teacher sustains a dual relation to the government: first, that relation which arises from his office as an agent of the State in training citizens; second, that which arises from his own citizenship. The maintenance of schools at public expense is an act of self-preservation, which is an instinct of society, as of individuals. Our "conscript fathers" knew, as well as we, that ignorant suffrage is a continual menace to the Republic. In some of our States the illiterate voters are in the majority In Indiana they hold the balance of power These may, by combination, become a Samson to destroy our temple. Foreign immigration is reducing our per cent. of illiteracy The training of the will, sometimes as untrained as the zebra, to the authority o the school, will prepare the pupil for obedience to the law. Man is not a good citizen by nature, but only by discipline. Public intelligence and virtue are our best security against the dangers which beset republics.

The teacher should be one who forms, not one who follows, public opinion. He should be a positive, and not a passive receiver of other men's opinions He need not keep his eye on the weathercock, nor walk the middle line of neutrality. Let him be bold enough to avow and defend truth as he understands it. Let him nail his theses to the door, and modestly advocate them.

Politics is said to be a "muddy pool," but no teacher should be too immaculate to step into it. He need not be a rancorous partisan. He should scorn the party whip, and seek his affiliation where his principles are best reflected If called to places of trust under the State, the teacher should not hesitate to accept. The unknown is widening faster than the known. The age is asking more questions than it answers. Let the teacher do his part to help the world on to a right solution. Let him be hopeful of the coming day, when under an ideal government, nobler than Plato's republic, greater than More's Utopia, our country shall be a fraternity in which "the inquiry of one shall be the concern of all."

"THE TEACHERS' READING CIRCLE."

President J. J. Mills, of Earlham College, chairman of the Executive Board of the State Teachers' Reading Circle, made following report:

To the Indiana State Teachers' Reading Circle:

In accordance with the resolutions adopted by the Association one year ago, we have framed a plan of Organization and Course of Study for "The Indiana Teachers' Reading Circle." The purposes and plans of the Reading Circle were presented to the county superintendents at their annual convention in June last. A deep interest in the enterprise was manifested by them, and the Board of Directors would express their obligation for the valuable suggestions brought out in the discussion of the subject by the superintendents. As a further evidence of their co-operation in the work, we are glad to mention the fact that 90 out of 92 county superintendents of the State have consented to act as managers of the Circle in their respective counties.

The plan of Organization and Course of Study were laid before the teachers of the State through the educational journals and by circulars sent out by the Educational Department of the State at as early a date as practicable under the circumstances, but after the meeting of the Teachers' Institutes in a number of the counties of the State, so that the organization of the Circle in those counties could not be made under the most favorable circumstances this year.

Difficulty has also been experienced in securing a sufficient supply of text-books in some lines of reading, which has proved a source of hindrance in our work. County managers have been unable to complete their list of members, and, consequently, the returns from many counties have not yet been received

But notwithstanding these unfavorable conditions, the board is able to report an encouraging interest in the enterprise throughout the State. A careful estimate based upon reports received to date, show a present membership in the Circle of 3000 in round numbers. Until further returns shall have been received, it will be impracticable to give a report of the financial condition of the Circle.

H. M. SKINNER, *Secretary.*   J. J. MILLS, *President.*

J. M. Olcott moved that it be made the duty of the Reading Circle Board to report to this convention annually.

AFTERNOON SESSION.—The President introduced Miss Margaret Lawrence, of Frankfort, who read a paper on

"THE EXAMINATION QUESTION."

She said that the examinations in our public schools are, under the present limitations in school work, trustworthy measures of either a pupil's acquired knowledge or mental growth, is doubtless a mistake. The mistakes are in our school system; arrangement of our courses of study; the periodicity of examinations, where such practices exist; imperfect teaching and faulty questions, one, or all, are active agents in lessening the value commonly attached to them as measures of either knowledge or power of pupils. Examinations do not always express the class work of the pupils; they do not indicate the growth in mind-power of the pupil—the latter being shown rather by the earnest, continued effort; the increasing ability to study with well defined purpose and method, careful, original thought, and the aroused spirit of investigation—all of which appear in daily work rather than through the examination average.

Promotions by examinations alone do an injury to those pupils whose circumstances will not permit them to take the entire course, as they thus often leave the school with much less information and power than they might have if individual necessities were more often considered.

If a certain percent be obtained, the work is pronounced good; but many a pupil has carried an excellent record of percents into the world, and found himself unable to solve the simplest problems. Before the special work, he as a member of society has been called to do, he has stood ignorant and helpless.

4

Examinations certainly hold a more important place in the school economy than their real value justifies; and, without question, the work of pupils would be no less thoroughly and carefully done if they were less frequent in their occurrence, if greater importance were attached to daily, persistent effort, and if real growth in self-directing and self-controlling power were made the stronger aim of all endeavor.

While discussing the subject "Examination Question," F. D. Churchill, Supt. Aurora schools, said:

I do not agree with the paper when it says that examinations hold a more important place in the school economy than the existing circumstances justify. They are not held perhaps oftener than once a month; in some schools I am glad to say that periodical examinations are not held at all, but when the subject is completed. When you consider the object of the examination, I do not believe you will be inclined to say that it is too often. The object of the examination is not to give the teacher an opportunity to find out what the pupils know, nor is it for the benefit of the teacher; but it is for the benefit of the pupils.

The examination is of value to the pupil in that it teaches him to express in writing what he has learned, and there is no more practical exercise. It the second place it teaches him to concentrate his thoughts. Until he has acquired the power to fasten his mind on a subject and hold it there he is not educated. What teacher has not thought, as he looked upon his school on examination day, "If I could but get as earnest work every day, how much greater would be the results!" The examination day is the day of all days when you get concentrated effort from your pupils.

It is of great value to the pupil in that it requires him to make an effort to retain facts in his mind: without it he would perhaps prepare his lesson merely for the recitations, and afterwards they would pass out of mind. Knowing that examination is coming, the pupil will make an effort to retain the facts, and there is a probability he will always retain them. An exercise of such value can not hold too great a place in the school-room.

The last exercise was an address by Dr. E. E. White, of Cincinnati, upon the

"PHILOSOPHY OF TEACHING."

The speaker began with the statement that education as an art is based on the nature of the being educated, and hence the devising of an effective method of school education involves a knowledge of the educable nature of children and youth. The best method of reaching this knowledge was shown by a clear and masterly analysis of psyichical processes and phenomena, as revealed in consciousness.

The order of activity and maturity of the intellectual faculties was then shown to be, first, the presentative or perceptive, next representative, and lastly the thought powers. This order was shown to be a psychical necessity. The activity of the higher powers is conditioned upon the activity of the lower. This is also true of the three thought powers. Reasoning is conditioned upon formal judging and both on conceptive generalization.

How early the several faculties awaken into activity, and their relative strength and activity at different ages can only be determined by a careful study of children in the light of psychology Dr. White presented the results of his investigations by a chart which showed graphically the growth of the mental powers of the average child.

The facts thus reached were next considered in the light of what was called the leading axiom of pedagogy, to-wit: "Instruction, both in matter and method, must be adapted to the capability of the pupil."

Six important principles of teaching were stated and applied, as follows:

1. There is a natural order in which the faculties should be exercised and the corresponding kinds of knowledge taught.

2. There is a variation in the relative attention to be given the different faculties and the corresponding kinds of knowledge in the successive grades of school.

3. The primary concepts and ideas in every branch of knowledge must be taught objectively in all grades.

4 Oral teaching and text-book study are complementary means of school education, the former being largely preparatory to the latter.

5. In the teaching of any art clear and correct ideas must precede and guide practice. The common maxim, "We learn to do by doing," is only a half truth

6. A true course of study for elementary schools cuts off a section of presentative, representative, and thought knowledge each year.

W. A. Bell moved that the Association return a vote of thanks to Dr. White for his able and instructive lecture. Carried with emphasis.

E. H. Butler presented the following report:

To the Members of the Indiana State Teachers' Association:

We, your committee, appointed to recommend two persons to fill vacancies in the Board of the Indiana State Teachers' Reading Circle, beg leave to recommend Mrs. R. A. Moffitt, of Rushville, and Will J. Houck, Supt. of Jay county.

Respectfully submitted, FLO. CARPENTER,
O. P. McAULEY,
E H. BUTLER.

Hiram Hadley moved to amend the report by substituting the names of Geo. P. Brown and Mrs. Emma Mont. McRae, to be their own successors. The report was so amended and adopted.

J. M. Olcott made the following report:

Your committee, appointed to draft an address to the General Assembly, which should embody the recommendations of the President's inaugural address, and such other recommendations as may seem desirable, and confer with the State Superintendent as to the best mode of laying such an address before the General Assembly, would respectfully report they have performed the duties assigned them.

Your committee submit for your approval the following address to the General Assembly:

To the Honorable, the General Assembly of the State of Indiana:

The State Teachers' Association, in convention assembled, in the City of Indianapolis, December 31, 1884, in the earnest desire for the increased efficiency of the common schools, and for securing to all the people better and more extended privileges, most respectfully recommend to your honorable body the enactment of legislation to secure the following ends:

1. Uniform terms for all schools of the same class, which shall not in any case be less than eight school months.

2. The provision of a sufficient fund for the maintenance of the county institute.

3. Reform of the township institute system.

4. The guaranty of school privileges to all the children of Indiana, by the enactment of a mild and well-guarded compulsory education law, applicable to children between the ages of eight and fourteen years.

5. The introduction among the requirements for a teacher's license and the subjects of instruction in district schools, of the elements of industrial drawing, to be taught as a part of the subject of penmanship

We believe that by this measure the efficiency of teachers to teach every branch of study would be greatly increased by the acquisition of skill in graphic illustration, and that the penmanship of pupils would be improved at the same time that they were gaining a skill which would be of great practical value to them

Respectfully submitted,   J. M. OLCOTT,
J. P. MATHER,
GEO. F. BASS,
D. E. HUNTER,
F. D. CHURCHILL,
Committee.

The State Superintendent agreed to publish the above in his report to the Legislature.

E. E. Smith made the following report:

Your committee, to whom was referred the report of the State Superintendent of Public Instruction upon the matter of ornamentation and improvement of school houses and lots, would respectfully report:

1. That we view with pleasure the excellent progress made in this work by the joint committee of this Association and of the State Horticultural Society; and we can but feel that these disinterested but earnest efforts to improve the æsthetic and hygienic features of our schools and their surroundings, must ultimately result in great good.

2. That we suggest the appointment of the following committee to continue this work on the part of this Association: Hon. J. W. Holcombe, Cyrus W. Hodgin, W. H. Ernst, R. A. Smith.

3. That we appreciate the hearty co-operation with us of the committee of the State Horticultural Society, and we instruct the com-

mittee from this body to express to them, in some appropriate way, our determ·nation to continue the work so auspiciously begun.

Very respectfully, E. E. SMITH,
W. H. ELSON,
J. H. MARTIN,
Committee.

TREASURER'S ANNUAL REPORT.

D. E. Hunter, Treasurer I. S. T. Association, *Dr.*

Dec. 28—Cash on hand..................................	$100 58
31 Cash from members............................	141 75
Cash from Grand Hotel	50 00
	$292 33

Contra.

Dec. 29—Postage and exchange	$1 20
Envelopes	3 75
Membership Cards..............................	1 50
Expressage....................................	1 80
Drayage......................................	35
Stationery....................................	4 10
Expenses of Executive Committee...............	24 00
Expenses of Col. Parker........................	24 00
Expenses of E. E. White......................	3 50
Expenses of Wallace Bruce....................	60 00
Rent of Church.............	50 00
Recording Secretaries..........................	11 00
Permanent Secretary...........................	12 00
R. R. Secretary and Postage....................	17 00
Recording Statistics...........................	12 00
Amount....................................	$226 20
Dec. 30—Paid W. A. Bell, for expenses of Dr. Thompson's address, ordered by Association Dec. '83·····	25 00
Total amount.............................	$251 20
Jan. 7, 1885—Cash on hand...........................	41 13
	$292 33

NOTE.—Since the above report was made out, the committee on Prof. Thompson's address has returned $6 25 of the $25 received. The expense, therefore, of printing and distributing the address was $18 75.

Respectfully submitted, D. E. HUNTER,
Per. Sec. and Treas. I. S. T. A.

The report of the Committee on resolutions was not received, the chairman, W. W. Parsons, having ^gone home without submitting it.

The Association adjourned after the election of the following officers, which were nominated by the committee appointed on Tuesday:

President—E. E. Smith, Purdue University.

Vice Presidents—Mrs. Sheridan Cox, Kokomo; Edward Taylor, Vincennes; M. J Mallery, Danville; W. M. Blake, Evansville; Dr. C. R. Dryer. Fort Wayne; J. P. Mather, Warsaw; J. A. Carnagey, Madison; W. M. Rank, Lafayette.

Secretary—Mrs Anna E. H. Lemon, Spencer.

Executive Committee—W. H. Elson, Parke Co., ch'n; R. A. Ogg. New Albany; L. H. Jones, Indianapolis; D. M. Nelson, Rensselaer; and W. F. L. Sanders, Cambridge City.

SAMUEL LILLY, *Secretary.*   H. B. HILL, *President.*

LIST OF MEMBERS ENROLLED.

ALLEN CONNTY.—John S. Irwin, Harriet E. Leonard, Charles R. Dryer, Fort Wayne; W. S. Walker, Monroeville.

ADAMS Co.—G. W. A. Luckey, Bertha M. Luckey, Decatur.

BARTHOLOMEW—Hugh S Quick, Walter Wallace, Columbus.

BOONE—S. N. Cragun, O. C. Charlton, H. M. La Follette, Lebanon.

CARROLL—B. W. Evermann, Mrs. B W. Evermann, O. C. Sterling, Camden; S B. McCracken, M. B. McReynolds, Emma Shealy, Katherine McReynolds, Kate A Crawford, Winnie C. Scott, Carrie Cory, Ella Arbuckle, Delphi.

CASS—J. K. Walts, Francis M. Spraker, E. A. Hunt, J. C. Black. Logansport.

CLARKE—Miss Frances C. Simpson, Jeffersonville.

CLAY—Belle E. Jones, Eaglesfield.

CLINTON—Emma Killgore, Colfax; Mary E. Mustard, Amanda Elliott, Lizzie Jacques, Margaret Lawrence, C. E. Newlin, Frankfort; Alice Miller, Kilmore.

DEARBORN—Louise Severin, F. D. Churchill, H. B. Hill, Anna Suter, Aurora.

DECATUR—W. P. Shannon, Greensburg.

DELAWARE—Alta Stiffler, Florence Carpenter, Kate S. Garst, M. A McClure, J. M. Bloss, W. R. Snyder, A. W. Clancy, Muncie; L. G. Saffer, Selma.

DAVIESS—W. F. Hoffmann, S. B. Boyd, D. E. Hunter, Wash-. ington.

FAYETTE—J. S. Gamble, Connersville.

FLOYD—Chas. F. Coffin, D K. Armstrong, Robert A. Ogg, Lizzie Pearson, Fannie Fawcett, New Albany.

FOUNTAIN—G. F. Kenaston, Attica; V. E. Livengood, Jas. Burgliam, Ida E. Livingood, Covington.

FULTON—Mary C. Brown, Minnie A. Brown, Rochester.

GIBSON—J. E. Calhoun, Owensville.

GRANT—Ryland Ratliff, H. S. McRae, E. M. McRae, Marion.

HANCOCK—Flora Love, R. A. Smith, E. W. Felt, Frank O. Fort, J. V. Martin, Greenfield.

HENRY—C. W. Harvey, New Castle; W. D. Kerlin, Springport.

HENDRICKS—Milton J. Mallery, Danville; Maggie J. Carter, T. J. Charlton, R. Kate Beeson, Elva T. Carter, Geo. W. White, Plainfield; A. E. Rogers, Clayton.

HOWARD—Sara Ellis, Mrs. Sheridan Cox, S. A. G. Woody, Sheridan Cox, J. C. Leach, C. M. Piercy, Kokomo; Jos .W. Parker, New London.

HUNTINGTON—L. Hanman, Harriet A. Leets, Huntington.

JASPER—D. M. Nelson, Remington ; A. E. Coen, Alice Irwin, P. H. Kirsch, Jas. A. Burnham, Rensselaer.

JEFFERSON—J. H. Martin, J. A. Carnagey, Geo. C. Hubbard, O. E. Arbuckle, Madison.

JENNINGS—Amos Sanders, North Vernon ; S. W. Conboy, W. S. Almond, Vernon.

JOHNSON—J. C. Eagle, Edinburg ; Kittie E. Palmer, A. Tompkins, Jennie S. Tompkins, Franklin.

JAY—Will J. Houck, Portland.

KNOX—Edward Taylor, Vincennes.

KOSCIUSKO—E. M. Chaplin, John P. Mather, Viola Strain, Margaret Wilson, Warsaw.

LAWRENCE—F. P. Smith, Bedford ; Lula Munson, Ida Y. Burton, Lizzie W. Parke, Laura F. McCoy, C. W. McClure, W. E. Lugenbéel, Mitchell.

MADISON—Dale J. Crittenberger, Anderson ; W. L. Williamson, Pendleton.

MARION—Frances E. Husted, Cumberland; A. C. Shortridge, Alice McCord, J. C. Buchanan, Hattie Maning, A. R. Rankin, Delia Curtis, Isaac Roose, H B. Jacobs, Alice B. Thomas, L. P. Harlan, M. E. Nicholson, Amelia W. Platter, Agnes Jordan, Jesse H. Brown, W. H. Bass, Geo. F. Bass, W. A. Bell, W. W. Grant, T. J. McAvoy, L. H. Jones, T. G. Alford, John W. Holcombe, Mrs L. G. Hufford, Geo. W. Hufford, Nellie H Loomis, Mrs. Mary P Currie, Hubert M. Skinner, Lucy V. Gosney, Indianapolis : B. M. Blount, M. A. Husted, Irvington ; W B Flick, Lawrence.

MONROE—James K. Beck, Bloomington.

MONTGOMERY—T. H Dunn, Mary D. Howard, Flora C. Mitchell, Crawfordsville ; W. W. Ewing, Ladoga ; O· B. Hultz, New Market ; Andrew G. Yount, Yountsville.

MORGAN—J. R. Starkey, Martinsville ; Ella R. Tilford, Monrovia.

NOBLE—D. D. Luke, Ligonier.

OWEN—Samuel Lilly, Gosport ; O. P. McAuley, Anna E. H. Lemon, S. E. Harwood, Mrs. S. E. Harwood, Mrs. R. J. Aley, R. J. Aley, Jo Ahern, Spencer.

PARKE—C. O. Matin, Annapolis ; B. C. Hobbs, Bloomingdale ; Mary A. Cox, Tillie Cox, Colomia ; W H. Elson, Mrs. W. H Elson, Lin H. Hadley, Rockville ; Martha A. Lindley, Martha C. Lindley, Sylvania.

PIKE—A. C. Crouch, Petersburg.

PORTER—Clara Stevens, Valparaiso.

PUTNAM—John M. Olcott, Joseph Carhart, L. E. Smedley, Greencastle.

RANDOLPH—S Albert Arbogast, J. W. Denny, Parker ; E. M. C. Hobbs, Ridgeville ; C. H. Wood, E. H. Butler, H. W. Bowers, Annie Tabbott, Winchester.

RUSH—Margaret M. Hill, Lena Martin, Bailey Martin, Carthage ; Mrs. R. A. Moffitt, John L. Shauck, James Baldwin, May Hackleman, Rushville.

SCOTT—T. J. Shea, Lexington.

SHELBY—G H. Campbell, Morristown ; A. E. Mowier, Shelbyville.

ST. JOSEPH—Elias Boltz, Mishawaka.

SULLIVAN—W. B. Creager, Sullivan.

SWITZERLAND—M. C. Walden, Vevay.

TIPPECANOE—J. C. Eckhart, Colburn; Alexander T. Reid, Dayton; M. C. Stevens, L. S. Thompson, Ed. R. Smith, E. E. Smith, W. H. Caulkins, Oscar J. Craig, J. T. Merrill, J. H. Smart, Jennie Smiley, La Fayette; Annie Lindsay, W. J. Bowen, Stockwell; W. W. Mershorn, Transitville.

TIPTON—A. D Moffet, Tipton.

VANDERBURG—W. McK Blake, Edward A. Clarke, Evansville.

VERMILLION—A· A. Parker, Mate L. Holmes, Newport.

VIGO—G. W. Thompson. W. H. Wiley, Ruth Morris, G. P. Brown, A. R Charman, J. T. Scovill, O. P. Jenkins, W. W. Parsons, Howard Sandison, N. Newby, Alpheus McTaggart, M. Seiler, Mrs. Lizzie Byers, A. E. Humke, Terre Haute.

WABASH—H. W. Charles, Wabash.

WASHINGTON—J. A. Wood, Salem.

WAYNE—Eli Jay, J. J Mills, Emma A. Shover, Annie M. Brown, J. N. Study, T. A. Mott, Penina Hill, D. W. Dennis, Mattie C. Dennis, Richmond; Susie Harding, W. F. L. Sanders, Jennie E. Horning, Cambridge City

WHITE—Lizzie Holmes, Brookston.

Illinois—Mrs. L. F. Brockway, Isabel Downey, Gertrude Clark, Chicago; E D. Bosworth, Farmer's City; Jessie La Grange, J. W. Merrill, Paris.

Ohio—E. E. White, John P. Patterson, Cincinnati; Geo. H. Caraway, Fort Recovery.

Michigan—Ella E. Munson, Muskegon.

Total enrollment, 263; attendance about 450.

D. E. HUNTER, *Per. Secretary.*

PROCEEDINGS OF THE HIGH SCHOOL SECTION OF THE STATE TEACHERS' ASSOCIATION.

PLYMOUTH CHURCH, INDIANAPOLIS, }
Monday Afternoon, Dec. 29, 1884 }

The first session was called to order at 2 o'clock P. M., by Pres. C. P. Doney, of Logansport.

The first paper read was by Principal H. G. Woody, of Kokomo, his subject being

THE HIGH SCHOOL—ITS PLACE IN EDUCATIONAL ECONOMY.

Notwithstanding the fact that there are those who would talk the High School out of existence, and who argue that it has no place either in educational or political economy, still I think my task comparatively easy, for the High School not only has a place, but it has found its place. My business, therefore, is not so much to work out a course for the High School as to discover what its course already is, and to determine its influence upon the educational universe.

However much thought and money the state may expend upon its schools, its policy is worthless, unless it contributes to the strength and perpetuity of the state and the happiness of its citizens. On this truth is founded our school system. But it is no less a truth than this: The American home is the bulwark of American liberty.

Then our first proposition reduces to this: The educational policy of the state is as nothing, unless it shall contribute to the domestic felicity of its citizenship. Here the High School has a place. Without removing the pupil from the sacred influences of his home, it affords him the advantage of more than a common school education. We may not measure the helpfulness of the home to the boy or the girl of fourteen years to eighteen years of age; but we recognize the fact of its existence as we do that of mind and life. Happy is he, who, born with a good home, enjoyed its blessings well up to the close of his school days.

Business life demands keenness of perception, reach of memory, breadth of mind. Everything else being equal, the boy trained to see from the beginning to the end of a complex mathematical deduction, trained to note the relations of the various equations, taught to eliminate the non-essential and retain the essential,—I say such a boy will see farther into a business transaction than the boy without such power. With the former, business is a problem; with the latter it is a venture. In a nation like this what can be more practical than enlightened citizens—men who can fathom their country's needs, and who can not for one moment be misled by the deceits and tricks of the demagogue. In the late canvass of this state, the central committees of the two great parties had on their books the name of over 20,000 voters classed as "cattle."

The highest culture is the most truly practical. The most perfect development gives the best citizenship, and the highest order of citizenship is the maximum of the practical. This the high school does not give; but while affording to thousands a primary knowledge of the sciences, mathematics, and the languages, she has been a feeder to higher institutions of learning. An eminent college President said: "We have no very exact data upon which to base our statement, but the opinion here is that the general organization of high schools has increased the standard of work and also the attendance at college."

Better still, the high school holds a healthful influence over the Grammar Schools It is unto them a compulsory education statute without the compulsion. It is the goal to which every pupil looks. It is the something better and higher, only a little beyond. So it becomes an inspiration. Let the high school, under an inefficient principal, become weak, disorganized and disorderly, and the grammar schools, too, though under the best instructors, decline On the other hand, a full, active, energetic high school is a sure index to full schools the city over.

The high school takes precedence to the state's higher institutions of learning. I am not of the number of those who think the university a burden too onerous for the state to bear, or that it does not more than repay the people all it costs; but I hold that the high school is nearer the public heart and life. It is not only of the state but of the neighborhood and the home. The university is off yonder, the pride of a distant city; the high school is at the very doors of the people, the boast of each town and city. The university does a great deal for the hundreds, the high school accomplishes much for the thousands. The university becomes the Alma Mater of only such as are able to defray the expense of a collegiate education, of which tuition is the smallest item; the high school numbers among its graduates a large plurality of poor boys and poor girls, and gives them an education so practical as to open to them the doors of the

business world, or becomes to them the stepping-stone to higher intellectual attainments. The high school of the people and for the
people is deservedly popular. All the township graded schools of
the state striving, in the course of study and in discipline, to imitate
or surpass the high school, stand as so many proofs of the fact that
the high school has a place in the hearts of the people.

In opening the discussion of Mr. Woody's paper, J. C. Black said
the high school has a tendency to make popular the common school,
the lower grades. The rich and influential citizens patronize the
high school in preference to the private schools and academies; and
thus the high school popularizes the common school.

The high school practically prepares pupils for the business of life.
It does the work of elevating public sentiment   It is preparing the
men and women who are soon to take the places of our present political leaders, and elevate the standard of statesmanship. The high
school fits the teachers for their work. Formerly the country schools
furnished teachers; now the high school does it. The high school
is an incentive to the pupils in the lower grades; it gives them an
aim. It leads them on to effort until it sends many to college; and
thus many become educational leaders, who might have led very
different lives but for the influence of the high school. It is the poor
man's college. The child does not learn to reason intelligently in
the lower grades; in the high school he learns this. Thus the high
school systematizes what has been learned before.

S. E. Harwood, of Spencer. emphasized the thought that the high
school is the poor man's college. He said that only about 25 per
cent of the high school graduates enter college, perhaps not that
many. Hence it is the high school that fits most of the men and
women for their life-work.

E. H. Butler, of Winchester, spoke of the danger we are in, in the
high school, of giving the pupils the impression that the high school
course will fit them for life. He urged that we ought to encourage
the pupils to go to college; that many pupils are financially able to
go to college if they had proper encouragement. He suggested that
a committee be appointed to recommend a high school course for
the entire state.

G. F. Kenaston, of Attica, spoke of a custom in Massachusetts,—
the state pays $100 to each pupil for each year he completes in the
high school. The children are educated for the state, not for the
parents; hence the state encourages them, and they are educated
for citizenship and taught to think of the questions they must answer
when they take their places as citizens.

METHODS OF TEACHING THE ENGLISH LANGUAGE AND LITERATURE IN THE
HIGH SCHOOLS OF INDIANA.

W. W. Parsons followed, speaking on the above subject. This
paper is published in full in another place in this Journal.

E. E. Smith, of Purdue University, opened the discussion of Prof.
Parsons' paper. His remarks will be printed in a future number of
the Journal.

Dr. Charles R. Dryer, of Fort Wayne, next read a paper on

THE SCIENTIFIC METHOD AND ITS EDUCATIONAL VALUE.

Whatever may be the judgment which future generations will pass upon this nineteenth century, and whatever estimate they may form of the character and value of its contributions to civilization; one thing is certain, the achievements of pure and applied science will constitute one of the most important factors to be considered by the future historian and philosopher To say that we live in an age and country of remarkable scientific and industrial activity is to repeat one of the tritest observations of the day. The telephone, the telegraph, and the locomotive carry to the remotest neighborhood and to the humblest child the demonstration of realities of which the Oriental never dreamed, and speculative philosophy never caught sight, realities which would have petrified the sages of Greece and Rome with astonishment.

If I were learned enough and witty enough I would like to lead you in imagination through the incidents of a day with Socrates in New York; to invite you to accompany him through Broadway, Fifth Avenue and Wall Street, to look with him from the Brooklyn bridge upon the shipping in the East River, to visit with him warehouses and elevators, docks and markets, the Postoffice, the Custom House and the Stock Exchange, the Tribune and the Equitable buildings, Central Park and the Grand Central Depot, the Western Union Telegraph and the Bell Telephone offices. I would like to report the questions he would ask, and especially the answers of New Yorkers to those old stock questions of his, "What is piety?" and "What is virtue?" I would like to depict, if they could be painted, the emotions all these things would arouse in his sagacious mind, to move you to laughter at the absurd contrasts and the ridiculous relations between the mind of the man and his surroundings; aye, and to move you to tears for very pity of his bewilderment and chagrin. When he is thoroughly convinced that against iron and steam and electricity even Socratic irony is powerless; when in the face of the stupendous revelation of modern life, the product and creation of that physical science which he despised, he stands at last dumb, I would take him home to Xantippe, *full* for once in his life, filled with the conviction that old things have passed away and all things are made new.

That there ought to be a literary or clerical class of limited extent who should keep alive the Socratic learning and culture, I do not dispute; there should be no law to prevent any one from acquiring that culture, if he wants it; but for the masses, here and to-day, the *prima facie* evidence in favor of education in harmony with the spirit of the age is sufficient to throw the burden of proof upon the advocates of the classics; and very strong and cogent reasons must be shown to justify the retention of Latin and Greek in the public schools. The people have use for scientific knowledge, that is for information concerning the results of scientific discovery, "mere information," as some like to call it. Yet no one has been able to show why a knowledge of rocks and soil, of rivers and lakes, of wind and rain, of grass and trees, of beasts and men, a knowledge of our whole physical environment is not as valuable as a knowledge of history, of literature, or of art. It is the duty of the public schools to impart scientific knowledge; and there can be but one correct method of imparting it, the scientific method

Prof. Clifford has given us the whole subject in a nut-shell. "Science," he says, "is the getting of knowledge from experience, on the assumption of uniformity in nature, and the use of such knowl-·edge to guide the actions of men."

If there is any subject which ought to be taught and can be taught ·strictly according to the scientific method, it is chemistry Yet if even the very best school text-books are used, how is it taught? Is the pupil called upon or permitted to make the smallest induction for ·himself? Is he not told, not only what he is to see in an experiment, but also what conclusion he is to draw from it? An incorrect con-·clusion independently reached may be worth more to the pupil than a correct one learned from the book.

Our text-books are too good; they tell too much; and whatever the intention or the ability of the teacher, as long as such books are in the hands of the pupils, he can not teach according to the scien-tific method. The pupils are in the habit of learning from books; they can not learn in any other way unless they are helped to; they will not learn in any other way unless they are compelled to.

Science should be taught because to the youth of this day and gen-·eration scientific knowledge is useful. Science should be taught be-cause the scientific method furnishes such mental exercise in seeing and thinking as no other kind of study can furnish. But beyond and above these, the practical argument and the mental discipline argu-ment, lies another consideration which transcends all others, viz: science should be taught because scientific knowledge acquired by the scientific method tends to produce a higher type of culture than the world has yet seen.

The subject being opened for general discussion, Geo. P. Brown admitted the importance of the subject and of all that had been stated in the paper, but thought that the importance of this subject had been over-estimated in the paper. He claimed that the paper over-stated the case in claiming that we could better afford to lose all the prin-·ciples given us by the early philosophers, than to lose what we have gained since Bacon. He said we should not under-rate the method of Plato, while we extol the scientific method. Both methods are important. He insisted that reasoning from the general to the par-·ticular is just as scientific as reasoning from the particular to the general.

Under the head of miscellaneous business several committees were appointed. It was unanimously agreed that some steps should be taken to make a uniform course of study for the various high schools of the state; and it was decided to appoint a committee to consider this subject, and make a full report at the next annual meeting. It was agreed that the committee should consist of seven, and that in it there should be representatives of the State University, State Normal School, Purdue University, and the Indianapolis High School.

On motion of Elias Boltz, of Mishawaka, the President appointed the following: R. G. Boone, of Frankfort, chairman; Mrs. Emma Mont. McRae, of Marion; W. W. Parsons, of the State Normal; E. E. Smith, of Purdue University; J. K. Beck, of the State Univer-·sity; L. H. Jones, of Indianapolis; W. M. Blake, of Evansville.

Prof. D. W. Dennis, of Earlham College, read the first paper, discussing

METHODS OF TEACHING SCIENCE IN THE HIGH SCHOOLS.

Wordsworth puts both sides of a common question: in his "Exposition and Reply" he says:

> "Come forth into the light of things,
>   Let Nature be your teacher.
> One impulse from a vernal world
>   May teach you more of man,
> Of moral evil and of good
>   Than all the sages can.

Truth ought to be labeled *verus proteiformus;* it looks so many ways; it so defies aphorism, postulate, proverb and formula. "Learn to do by doing" is fine; but suppose the lesson is how the pyramids were built, or how the Atlantic cable was laid, or better still, how the world was made. "Induction and Bacon, not deduction and Aristotle, is the road to natural science." Yes, but what if the lesson is the law of gravitation. Induction and experiment on this one point employed Sir Isaac Newton for 17 years. Has the boy as much time for a single item? The time-honored illustration of what induction is—Sir Humphrey Davy's generalization which led to the discovery of the metals of the alkalies employed the best scientist of his day for many times as long a time as our best schools can give to chemistry. The great Agassiz was wont to say with characteristic modesty: "I have done one thing, viz; I have shown that the embryology and growth of the fish reveals the same changes from spawn to adult fish as are recorded in the rocks from the introduction of the type until now." Shall we now employ a competent student for a good portion of his life in reaching the same conclusion inductively? or shall we give him the result in 30 minutes, and give him the method by which it was reached in such time and by such illustrations as we can, and then direct his powers to some new problem of like importance?

"Observation! teach observation; teach the child to observe; the eagle's eye is necessary for the boy." Yes, and sufficient as well, if it is the object to make an eagle of the boy. But how shall we get this observing, discriminating habit? Not by training the eye, the ear and the hand, certainly, but by training the man. That the hand becomes another hand, when guided by an intelligent mind, has been borrowed from a Massachusetts school-master and placed upon the statute books of England. Science we believe should be so taught in the high school as to stimulate and strengthen every mental faculty. Observation should be trained to quickness in noting every detail.

Skill in experiment should always be acquired by the student of science; but on this point mistake is easy, for experiment is fascinating, study often irksome, and experiment without study makes the operator, not the scientist. One experiment, with careful reflection on its meaning, is worth a hundred without. Ask the clever analyst why his muriatic acid and his silver nitrate will give a precipitate, and it will generally appear that his initial step has been taken a hundred times without a thought that looked beyond interpretation.

Science teaching should also seek to train the student in the independent use of books, as the only available source, in any particular case, of a large amount of useful information. The study of the known in science should mainly be pursued by acquisition from books and subsequent verification, for the very reason that original investigation of the known in any one science, even if pursued under skillful direction, would not be possible in the longest lifetime, to say nothing of a four years' course in school, divided up among the various branches.

Finally, science teaching, last of all things, should not be discouraged with any problem however great. In nature nothing is small, for truly may nature claim,

"Time is my fair seed-field;
Of time I'm hero."

J. P. Naylor, of the Indianapolis high school, opened the discussion, which he made very interesting by the use of apparatus.

HOW TO MAKE THE LIBRARY DO MOST SERVICE TO THE SCHOOL

was the next subject for consideration, upon which James Baldwin, of Rushville, read an invaluable paper. It will appear in full in the Journal.

In discussing the question, Supt. T. H. Dunn, of Crawfordsville, said: To get the best results from the library, the teachers must know what is to be found in it. Pupils need guidance, and the guidance is to be expected at the hands of their teachers; but the blind are not fit leaders for the blind. With State Board of Education, leading out with systematic work, and with our own committee and its work, the Indiana State Teachers' Reading Circle, there is much broadening work being done by teachers in their effort to keep abreast with the wide awake thought and action here at home, and those who do keep abreast, will soon be conscious of a familiarity with books, and even of a mastery over books, which will fit them for this leadership.

By the downright study of some books, by a much lighter reading of some others, by conversations about others, or reading reviews of them, and even by turning intelligently through others, the teacher of geography and spelling may become the pupil's teacher and guide in the library. He will often have the opportunity of saying, "You will find a charming story on this subject in the library, in such and such a book. I would like to have you tell me something about it to-morrow."

In order to get good results from the library, it must needs be a good one—not made up wholly of what we technically call good books, for that would not be a good library for the school. I quote an appeal: "Remember, if the child is ever to love reading, we must have room left him to exercise a little choice. And do not forget that, beyond the region of mere information, there is the whole domain of wonderland, of fancy, of romance, of poetry, of dreams and fairy tales. Do not let us think scorn of that pleasant land, or suppose that all the fruit in the garden of the Lord grows on the tree of knowledge. Wonder, animosity, the sense of the infinite, the love of what is vast and remote, of the strange and the picturesque, all these things are not knowledge in the school sense of the word; but they are capable in due time of being transformed into knowledge—nay, into something better than knowledge—into wisdom and insight and power."

This is out of the question. In the library work, which has been the greater factor in the education of so many—in this work, if the teacher be able for it, is the opportunity to build with reference to the pupil's individual bias.

OFFICERS FOR THE ENSUING YEAR.

President—Mrs. R. A. Moffitt, of Rushville.
Vice President—Elias Boltz, of Mishawaka.
Secretary—R. J Aley, of Spencer.
Ex. Com.—Supt. T. H Dunn, of Crawfordsville; A. D. Moffett, of Tipton; G. W. Hufford, of Indianapolis.

C. H. Wood, *Secretary.*   C. P. Doney, *President.*

INDIANA COLLEGE ASSOCIATION.

The Colloge Association met this year in the parlors of the Bates House. The meeting was well attended, and the exercises were of more than usual interest.

Prof. J. C. Ridpath was the President-elect, and took for the subject of his address "The True Evolution." It was a masterful effort, and was a defense of the development theory set forth by Charles Darwin. At the same meeting David S. Jordan, President of the State University, read an address on Charles Darwin, which Prof. P. S. Baker, of DePauw, heartily endorsed. So Darwin and his development theory had a good time in the Association.

Prof. R. B. Warder, of Purdue, read a paper on "The True Place of Industrial Education." He would teach a few manual industries in the common schools and cultivate accurate perception of common things, but would not give technical instruction in colleges.

Prof. Alma Holman, of DePauw, gave reasons why natives are better than foreigners as instructors of "Modern Languages."

Prof. J. L. Campbell, of Wabash, read a very instructive address on the "Present Conditions of the Physical Development of Indiana." Dr. A. W. Brayton, of Indianapolis High School, followed with an equally interesting paper on the same subject.

Prof. J. L. Campbell was elected President for the coming year; Prof. R. B. Warder, Secretary; and Prof. D. W. Dennis, of Earlham College, Treasurer.

JOINT TEACHERS' MEETING.—The teachers of Randolph county and of Dark county, Ohio, held a joint meeting in Winchester, Ind., January 24th. About 70 of the Ohio teachers came over, the Randolph teachers turned out well, and the meeting was a profitable one. The church in which the meeting was held would not comfortably seat the audience in the afternoon. Our crowded pages this month prevents a more extended notice.

EDITORIAL.

Persons sending money for this Journal can send amounts less than $1 in *two* and *one* cent postage stamps; no others can be used.

In asking to have the address of your Journal changed, please give the *old* address as well as the new, naming the county as well as the·state.

An agent is wanted to raise a club for the Journal in every township in the State. Send for terms.

PURDUE UNIVERSITY.—The writer spent a day at Purdue University, and was pleased with what he saw. It is a pleasure to note that President Smart has been able to take up the excellent work done by Dr. White, and carry it forward without a perceptible jar to the institution. There has been a steady growth in the University since Dr. White first took charge of it, and it is highly creditable to President Smart that, under the circumstances, he has been able to keep the institution steadily on the up grade.

Almost every Chair is filled by a specialist, and the work done is certainly most practical. It must be seen, to be appreciated. The school deserves the hearty support of every one interested in industrial education.

THE STATE TEACHERS' ASSOCIATION.

Most of the space of the Journal is devoted this month to a report of the proceedings of the State Teachers' Association. The report is very complete and full. The reports of the addresses will be found unusually full and correct. The meeting was not as large as that of last year, but the exercises were above the average in point of merit. E. E. Smith, chairman of the executive committee, deserves credit for his efficient management. H. B. Hill made an excellent presiding officer, and deserves commendation. The Journal is compelled to make its annual criticism: The program was too full, and so required too much rushing, and left too little time for miscellaneous discussion of papers. Two papers for each half-day, with discussions, and recesses for forming acquaintances, are ample.

The High School Section was very largely attended this year, and was both interesting and profitable, but interfered materially with the main association by holding meetings at the same hours. This conflict should be avoided in the future if possible.

OUTLINES FOR THE READING CIRCLE have been omitted this month. The committes are informed that but few circles are up with the outlines in their reading, and it was thought best to allow them to catch up. Circles that are up will of course go right on with their reading. Attention is called to the report on the Reading Circle printed in the minutes of the State Association. Favorable reports are received almost daily.

THE NEW ORLEANS EXPOSITION is now fully in shape and is richly worth visiting. Those who went to New Orleans during the holidays, while there were hundreds of car-loads of material not yet in position, reported themselves well paid They said that there was already a great deal more in position than they could look at in a week, and then they got to see "the sunny south." Since the railroad fare is reduced to less than a cent a mile hundreds of people will be able to do what they have long desired to do, but felt that they were not able to afford it, viz; visit the fair south.

TEACHERS' STATE CERTIFICATES.

At a meeting of the State Board of Education, October 17, 1884, on the recommendation of the Superintendent of Public Instruction, the Board made the following order concerning the examination for State Certificates:

It is Ordered, That the examination for Teachers' State Certificates be divided into three parts, and that the questions, prepared by the State Board of Education, be submitted to applicants in the several counties by the county superintendents, on the last Saturdays of February, March, and April of each year.

ON THE LAST SATURDAY OF FEBRUARY—*Forenoon:* Arithmetic, Grammar, Geography. *Afternoon:* Geography, Physics, United States History.

ON THE LAST SATURDAY OF MARCH—*Forenoon:* Algebra, Reading, Science of Teaching. \ *Afternoon:* Physical Geography, Zoology, U. S. Constitution, Moral Science.

ON THE LAST SATURDAY OF APRIL—*Forenoon:* Geometry, Literature, Orthography. *Afternoon:* Rhetoric, Botany, General History, Penmanship.

That applicants for State Certificates must have taught school not less than forty-eight months, of which not less than sixteen shall have been in Indiana. They shall present to the county superintendent, before entering upon the examination, satisfactory evidence of good moral character and professional ability, and pay five dollars each, the fee prescribed by law, which can in no case be refunded.

4

That the county superintendents shall, immediately after the close of each examination, send the manuscripts, testimonials, and fees of applicants, to the Superintendent of Public Instruction. The manuscripts shall be examined and graded by the members of the State Board, and certificates shall be granted to those applicants who make a general average of *seventy-five per cent.*, and do not fall below *sixty per cent.* in any subject.

The above circular explains itself. There should be hundreds of teachers and superintendents in the State who will gladly avail themselves of this opportunity, on general principles. *Besides*, the present Legislature is likely to enact a law requiring county superintendents to hold a State License. Such a bill has been introduced.

Persons expecting to be examined should notify their county superintendent at once.

QUESTIONS AND ANSWERS.

QUESTIONS BY THE STATE BOARD FOR DECEMBER.

THEORY OF TEACHING.—1. Describe the nature of the products of each of the three classes of intellectual faculties.

2. Distinguish between a perception, a conception and a judgment.

3. What is the value of phonic spelling in primary schools?

4. Why is it better to use pleasurable than painful motives to influence pupils?

5. Why is the offering of prizes a bad means to employ in a school?

ORTHOGRAPHY.—1. What syllable in the word Evansville is the penult?

2. When is the letter *y* a vowel? Give two examples.

3. How many and what sounds has the letter *i*? Give words illustrating its different sounds. 2 pts, 5, 5

4. What is the use of silent letters?

5. Write one important rule to serve as a guide to the spelling of a class of words.

6. Spell ten words dictated by the superintendent. 10 pts, 5 ea.

READING —1. In teaching reading why should attention be given to the authorship of selections?

2. Give two reasons in favor of ccasional concert reading.

3. What is the use of punctuation?

4. Mention two uses of the dictionary in connection with the reading lesson. 2 pts, 5 each

5. Name the methods that are most common in teaching primary reading. State which you prefer, and give reason for your preference.

6. Read a paragraph of prose and a stanza of poetry selected by the superintendent.   25 each

PENMANSHIP.—1. Name five important things which should receive attention in teaching penmanship.

2. Describe the manner of holding the pen.

3. Name the kinds of movement usually employed in writing.

4. What is meant by form?

5. Write the principles from which the small letters are formed.

NOTE.—Your writing in answering these questions will be taken as a specimen of your penmanship, and will be marked 50 or below, according to merit.

GEOGRAPHY.—1. How many and what races of men are there?

2. Name the chief inland waters of the United States.

3. Name five ports on the Great Lakes in the order of their importance.

4. Name five of the important manufacturing towns of the United States, and the manufactures for which each is chiefly noted.

5. What are the three chief agricultural productions of the West Indies?

6. Bound Spain.

7. Name the forms of government of the six largest countries of Europe.

8. Name five great rivers of Asia.

9. Name the five largest European capitals.

10. Name five rivers of Indiana, and tell to what system each belongs.

PHYSIOLOGY.—1. Name two characteristics of healthful clothing.
                                                2 pts, 5 each

2. Describe the sympathetic system.

3. How do nerves of sensation differ from nerves of motion?

4. Describe the structure of a long bone, with diagram.

5. *a* State the difference between voluntary and involuntary muscles. *b* Give examples.   a-6, b-4

6. Why is a *variety* of food necessary?

7. *a* What is respiration? *b* What is its immediate object?
                                                a-4, b-6

8. Describe the blood.

9. How are the nerves protected?

10. Why should the teeth be kept perfectly clean?

ARITHMETIC.—1. Define bank discount. Bonds.   5, 5

2. What is arithmetic? Cancellation?   5, 5

3. Define a common multiple. A complex fraction.   5, 5

4. A, at the age of 40, effects an insurance on his life for 4 years, for the sum of $8,000, at the rate of $1.80 on $100 per annum; what was the annual premium?   proc. 5, ans. 5

5 Required the cost of a draft of $8,500 for 60 days, at 6 per cent, exchange being 1⅓ per cent. premium?

6. The capacity of a cistern is 2,400 gallons, and is filled with water by a pipe which pours into it 9 gal. 3 qt. a minute. By a leakage, 1 gal. 3 qt. 1 pt. is lost every minute during the time of filling. In what time will the cistern be filled? State by proportion.
                              Statement 5, ans. 5.

7. What is the width of a park in which stands a flag-staff 240 feet high, from the top of which to one side of the park is 300 feet, and to the other side 400 feet?

8. What is the cube root of 1860867?

9. What is the interest of $496 for 2 years, 3 months and 18 days at 6 per cent?

GRAMMAR.—1. State the office performed by each infinitive in the following:

    a Man never is, but always to be, blest.
    b. Freedom has a thousand charms to show.
    c. He appears to be thoughtful.

2. Where should the relative pronoun *who* be used in preference to *that?*

3. Correct the errors in the following, giving reasons:
    a. Whom do you suppose it is?
    b. It was supposed to be he.
    c. It was Paul, him who wrote the epistle.

4. State the leading differences between the participle and the infinitive.

5. State the use of each participle in the following:
    a. Ayr, gurgling, kissed its pebbled shore.
    b. John, being tired, did not go.
    c. The messenger came running.

6. Correct the errors in the following, giving reasons:
    a. I laid the book on the table.
    b. If my friend was only here he would help me.
    c. I had never known how short life really was.

7. Define comparison as applied to the adjective. What classes of adjectives admit of comparison?

8. Give the principal parts of each of the following verbs: Come, do, fall, go, lie (to recline).

9. Parse the verbs in the following: "It is acting the evil that is destroying him."

10. Change the verbs in the following to the corresponding active or passive voice without changing the meaning of the sentence: "They apprehended that he might have been carried off by the Gypsies."

U. S. HISTORY.—1. What people claim to have been the original discoverers of America? Historically who were the real discoverers of North America?   5, 5

2. Who discovered Florida? Why did he give it that name? What was his ultimate fate?   3, 3, 4

3. In the charters to the first English colonies what were the two chief objects recited as the principal purposes of the settlement? 5, 5

4. What acts of Parliament and the British Government led to the Declaration of Independence?   10

5. What was a remarkable feature in the defeats of Washington during the Revolution?   10

6. Was the sympathy of the French with the colonies manifested chiefly by the government or by private individuals?   10

7. Describe briefly Burr's conspiracy.

8. When and why was the Republican party formed?

9. What were the peculiar features of Lee's surrender?

10. Why was the colonial charter of Georgia surrendered to the crown?

ANSWERS TO STATE BOARD QUESTIONS PRINTED IN JANUARY.

PHYSIOLOGY.—2. Nutrition takes place wherever there is a tissue to be nourished. The materials are prepared through the processes of the digestive canal and its accessories and then carried to the tissues by the blood-current. The nutritive elements pass out through the capillary walls, bathe the tissues, and so much as is needed is absorbed, the remainder ·passing into the lymphatic vessels and returning to the heart.

5 A muscle is an irritable, elastic tissue, whose chief property is said to be contractility. It is subject to excitement by nervous or electric stimulus, by a blow, etc., and unless used will deteriorate both in quality and power. Exercise is a necessary condition of muscular development. Through proper exercise, in pure air, amid pleasant surroundings, with proper food, the muscles are toned up, become of a deep red color, firmer, larger and stronger.

6. The general action on the food in digestion is the changing of so much of it as requires changing from its present indigestible condition to a state of solution suitable for dialysis. This process is partly mechanical, partly chemical,—the latter being effected through the acid and alkali juices of the alimentary canal.

7. No nerves, properly speaking, "are included within the skull." The twelve pairs of cranial nerves, however, branch off from the nerve centers within the skull and pass (1) to the nose; (2) to the eyes; (3) to the muscles of the eyeball and of the upper lid; (4) to

a muscle of the eyeball; (5) to the teeth, the lower part of the nose, the muscles over the forehead and eye-lids, the pharynx, the palate, the lower part of the face, the tongue, the salivary glands, and the lower lip; (6) to muscles of the eyeballs; (7) to muscles of the scalp and the side of the face; (8) to the ears; (9) to the posterior portion of the tongue, to the mucous membrane of the pharynx and æsophagus, and to the middle ear; (10) to the lungs, heart, stomach, æsophagus, pharynx, and windpipe; (11) to muscles about the shoulders; (12) to the muscles of the tongue and of the hyoid bone.

10.   Breathing is but slightly under the control of the will, in order that so important a function may not have any "patent-medicine" experiments practiced upon it. We may increase or decrease the rapidity of respiration,—the former, if continued, usually producing dizziness, and the latter, an involuntary effort on the part of the respiratory muscles to resume their accustomed rate. Proper and timely breathing exercises are useful in bringing all the respiratory muscles into play, and in developing the size of the pleural cavity.

READING.—1.   Reading is the key to all other branches of study. It enables one to comprehend the thought contained in them, and, if necessary, to give it oral expression. It is thus seen to be a language study, and should be properly associated and connected with the other language studies in the curriculum of the school.

2.   The chief ends to be attained in teaching reading in the common schools are, briefly enumerated: (1) Sight-knowledge of the forms of words; (2) knowledge of the meanings of words as associated with other words in expressing thought; (3) ability to quickly comprehend the meaning of the thoughts thus expressed; (4) ability to express these thoughts in other words than those of the author; (5) ability to give correct oral expression to the thoughts found in the written or printed page; (6) by supplemental reading to lead the pupil gradually to have a fondness for reading of a useful and instructive kind. By judicious selections and the relation of interesting particulars, the skillful teacher can beget in his pupils a desire for a healthful and beneficial literature.

· 3.   In preparing for a future lesson in the Second Reader, the teacher should first pronounce each of the words in the list preceding the lesson, requiring the pupils to pronounce and then spell them after. If there be any word of unusual meaning, or of a meaning difficult to be understood, such word should be explained by the teacher *before* the lesson is studied by the pupil. The pupils should then be required, (1) to so study the words in the list that they can promptly pronounce them at sight; (2) to read the lesson assigned so carefully that they can give the meaning of each word in the list *as used in the lesson;* (3) to be prepared to give orally, with closed book, the substance of the selection assigned; (4) to be able to spell the words in the list.

4. Five American authors, whose works children can safely read, are Louisa M. Alcott, "Grace Greenwood," T. B. Aldrich, T. W. Higginson, Mary Mapes Dodge.

5. Mechanical reading arises from too much imitation of the teacher, lack of comprehension of the thought to be expressed, lack of acquaintance with the forms, the sounds and the meanings of the words, and from lack of interest in the lesson. The errors mentioned suggest their own remedy.

U. S. HISTORY.—1. The existence of extensive mounds and earthworks in the basins of the Mississippi and the Great Lakes. The remains prove that these mound-builders understood arts with which the Indians were unacquainted.

2. The Huguenots fleeing from persecutions in France, settled in large numbers in South Carolina and further south.

3. When Louis XVI of France placed his grandson upon the throne of Spain, the English declared war against France to preserve the "balance of power." The French and English colonies in America were necessarily involved in the quarrel.

4. (*a*) Pitt, Barre, Fox, Burke. (*b*) That "it was like trying to put out a conflagration with a bucket of water."

5. (*a*) Benjamin Franklin. (*b*) He was excused from wearing the court costume, and allowed to wear his plain dress.

6. (*a*) A great financial panic. (*b*) The Canadian rebellion. (*c*) The settlement of the northeast boundary between the United States and British Possessions. The dispute in regard to the boundary between British America and Oregon led to the use of the expression, "Fifty-four, forty or fight," which was the boundary line demanded by one party. A compromise was effected, by which the boundary was fixed at 49°.

7. The "Ordinance of 1787" was a bill passed by the last Continental Congress providing for the government of the Northwest Territory. It was a compact which could never be repealed; and provided that there should be neither slavery nor involuntary servitude within its borders; and that "schools and means of education shall forever be encouraged."

8. (*a*) April 14, 1861. (*b*) Seven thousand Confederates to seventy Federals. (*c*) Civil war.

9. Slavery never flourished in the North, because the climate was unfavorable and public sentiment opposed to it. On the cotton plantations of the South slave labor was very profitable, hence it took deep root in that part of the Union.

10. When Gen. Thomas, who had been shut up within the forti-

fications of Nashville, was fully prepared, he sallied out and in two days of severe fighting drove the Confederate forces from their entrenchments. Hood's army, in a demoralized condition, was driven beyond the Tennessee.

ARITHMETIC.—3. 28287 lbs. of coffee; $403.06=entire commission.

4. $2.20=invoice price per yd.; $3.69 selling price.

5. $218.07.

6. July 5th.

7. 9 oz. 14 dwt.

8. 125.664 rds.=circumference; 7.854 acres.

9. $3240; $4860.

10. 60 miles.

GRAMMAR.—1. The subject, predicate, and copula. We can not express a complete thought without them.

2. A thought may be expressed in the form of a declaration, a question, or an exclamation. The *imperative sentence* is used to express our feelings in the form of command or exhortation.

3. The simple sentence has but one subject and one predicate. Simple: "One *touch* of nature *makes* the whole world kin." Complex; "*Fools rush* in where *angels fear* to tread." Compound: "A *fool speaks* all his mind, but a wise *man reserves* something for hereafter."

4. The members may have a *copulative* conjunction as connective: as, "The lightnings flashed *and* the thunders roared." They may be connected by an *adversative* conjunction: as, "The spirit is willing, but the flesh is weak." The connective may be illative also.

5. Every substantive clause is dependent in its nature, but not every dependent clause is used substantively. Substantive clause: "*What you say* is not true." Adjective clause: "The pupil *who studies hard* may become a scholar." Adverbial clause: "The thief ran *when he saw the officer.*"

6. I feel bad. *Feel* is a verb of incomplete predication and requires the adjective form here because it describes the condition of the subject.

7. Active: Laying, having laid. Passive: Being laid, laid, having been laid. Active: Reciting, having recited. Passive: Being recited, recited, having been recited. Active: Writing, having written. Passive: Being written, written, having been written.

8. *John* is a noun, proper, masculine, third, singular, nominative case, used absolutely before the participle *being*. *Leader* is a noun, common, masculine, third, singular, nom. case by predication after *was appointed*, a verb in the passive voice.

9. It may be used to *emphasize* the subject, as, "The man *him-*

self did the work." It may be used to represent *reflex action*, as, "The boy hurt *himself.*"

10. (*a*) I can solve the problem more easily than that. The manner of solving is described, and hence the adverb is required. (*b*) I desire (want) to go very much. Improper use of the word *bad*. (*c*) This lesson is very hard.

MISCELLANY.

THE SOUTHERN IND. NORMAL COLLEGE at Mitchell, W. E. Lugenbeel, President, is reported in a healthy condition.

SULLIVAN COUNTY reports over 150 members of the Reading Circle. This is the largest number yet reported from any one county.

CARROLL COUNTY is well organized in its school work. Most of the teachers are in the Reading Circle and doing efficient work. Superintendant Evermann is leading the van.

HARTFORD CITY.—The high school has recently received, through the kindness of Harry C. Russey, several hundred valuable mineralogical specimens. Mr. Reed is still superintendent of schools.

TERRE HAUTE.—The high school here numbers 337, and is of a high grade. W. W. Byers is principal. The city schools are moving on smoothly and doing good work under the supervision of W. H. Wiley.

The Home and School Journal is the name of a little semi-monthly paper just started at Pierceton, Kosciusko county, published by I. H. Beyerle, with Supt. D. Anglin as editor, and F. McAlpine as associate editor—Price $1. The number before us contains some good articles.

NEW PALESTINE contains one of the finest township school buildings in the state. W. A. Wood is principal of the school. A joint township teachers' meeting held there January 10th, was largely attended, pleasant and profitable. County Supt. R. A. Smith has the faculty of organizing helpful meetings.

WHITLEY COUNTY held its institute during Christmas week,—the attendance was fair and the interest good. The work for the first three days was done exclusively by W. F. L. Sanders, of Cambridge City, and W. A. Bell. Mr. Sanders remained all the week and did excellent work. The work done by the home teachers the last two days is highly commended. The fact that the superintendent could pay Prof. Swing $60 and expenses for a lecture and then clear money on him speaks well for the teachers, and for the citizens of Columbia City. Supt. Adair is highly respected by teachers and citizens.

SHELBYVILLE.—A recent monthly report of the schools published in the local papers, gives the following figures, which indicate well for Supt. W. H. Fertich and his teachers: Enrollment 898; daily attendance 803 (the largest ever reached); percent of attendance 95; neither tardy nor absent, 500 (the largest number ever reached).

WHITE COUNTY.—The institute in this county was held during New Year's week and was fairly well attended. The work was principally done by home talent, and was well done. George P. Brown of the State Normal, and W. A. Bell were present one day each, and did acceptable work. Wm. Guthrie, the superintendent, is active and persevering, and seems to be doing good service.

The Bryant & Stratton Business College of Indianapolis has added to its departments a Normal Training School, under the personal direction and instruction of Prof. Eli F. Brown, as announced elsewhere in this number of the Journal. Students attending the Normal School will be admitted to the Institute of Penmanship, under the direction of Prof. E. J. Heeb, and to any of the special studies of the Business College.

INTERNATIONAL CONGRESS OF EDUCATORS.—It is proposed to hold at New Orleans, in connection with the National Superintendents' Convention, an "International Congress," beginning February 23d and continuing to the 28th. The indications are that the meeting will be large and include many of the leading educators of the country, and a few foreign representatives. An extensive program has been arranged and the meeting will be an important one.

D. E. HUNTER, Supt. of the Washington schools, has in preparation a set of "Primary Reading Charts." The charts will be so arranged as to harmonize with any ordinary primary Reader. Mr. Hunter has had long years of experience as superintendent of schools and in doing primary work in teachers' institutes, and has also had the experience of preparing another set of Reading Charts; we may therefore expect the forthcoming charts to be based on practical experience and be fully abreast of the times. Mr. Hunter is not likely to let any good point escape him.

ST. JOSEPH COUNTY.—The institute held during the Christmas week was one of the best ever held in the county, and perhaps one of the best ever held in the state. In this county each teacher examined pays an institute fee of 50 cents, and this fund, with the $50 from the county, enables the superintendent to employ the best talent. W. W. Parsons, of the State Normal School, and Cyrus W. Hodgin, of the Richmond Normal, did all the work, and it is not necessary to say it was well done. County Supt. Calvin Moon is a splendid leader, and he has an excellent county board at his back.

PLYMOUTH.—The tenth anniversary of the opening of the school building was celebrated by a series of exercises extending through several days and evenings. The day exercises were not ordinary recitations, but exhibited some of the results of work done; and the evening exercises consisted of songs, recitations, plays, etc., and were in the nature of entertainments. The object seems to have been to "keep the schools before the people," something too often neglected. R. A. Chase has been superintendent all these years, and has reason to be proud of his work. Perhaps no other building in the state, in use so long, is freer from marks or defacements of any kind.

HENDRICKS COUNTY.—The first annual meeting of the Hendricks County Teachers' Association that convened at Danville on the 19th and 20th of Dec., was attended by about 90 teachers. Although the weather was extremely cold teachers from all parts of the county were present on the first morning. The program, though a long one, was followed with but two or three exceptions. The papers and discussions would have done credit to a State Association. Quite a number of pupils and trustees of the county were in attendance.

The Oratorical Contest which took place on the evening of the 19th was an affair of which Hendricks county justly feels proud. The contestants were C. E. Morgan, principal at Brownsburg; Wilbert Ward, principal at Clayton ; J. W. Riddle, principal at Pittsboro ; Miss Mollie Mitchel of the Clayton schools, and Miss Carrie S. Green of the Pittsboro schools. The prizes were awarded to Mr. Morgan and Miss Mitchel. The judges were Governor Porter, Sen. Campbell, Hon. John V. Hadley, Miss Mary Krout, Miss Cora Campbell, and Rev. U. C. Curry.

Every one present at the meeting of the Association pronounced it a decided success. Supt. A. E. Rogers is doing excellent work in the schools.

PERSONAL.

E. A. Allen is in charge at Rising Sun.

J. Humphrey is principal at Churubusco.

W. A. Munger is chief school director at Larwill.

M. L. Galbreth is principal of the Collamer schools.

J. A. Hancock is principal of the Farmland schools.

F. D. Churchill is superintendent of the Aurora schools.

Cassius M. Walden is the new Supt. of Switzerland county.

F. D. Haimbaugh is serving his 4th year as Prin. at Brookston.

S. A. Chambers, formerly of this state, still holds the reins at Henderson, Ky.

Jésse Lewis, a graduate of the State Normal, is principal of the Xenia schools.

E. M. C. Hobbs, a graduate of the State Normal, has charge of the schools at Ridgeville.

J H. Neff is serving his third year as principal at Bunker Hill, and is deservedly popular.

Walter S. Smith, formerly Supt. of Marion county, is principal of the Owenton, Ky., high school.

J. M. Stallsworth, formerly of Clark county, this state, is now principal of a normal school at Glascow, Ky.

H. B. Boyd, Supt. of Daviess county, has prepared a "Teacher's Report" that seems concise and complete.

John Mickleborough has resigned the principalship of the Hope Normal School and returned to Cincinnati.

N. W. Bryant has been for six years principal of the Acton schools, and he will open his fourth normal term in April.

C. M. Merica, Supt. of DeKalb county, has been "enjoying" poor health this winter, and yet has kept his work going.

R. E. Pretlow is principal of the Bloomingdale Academy. Susan R. Harrison and Edwin Morrison are associate teachers.

W. F L. Sanders, author of "Sentence Analysis," is serving acceptably his second year as Supt. of the Cambridge City schools.

Charles S. Taylor, who has been connected with the Goshen high school for the past six years, has resigned, to take charge of the schools at Plainfield, Ill.

W. J. Speer, formerly editor of the *Northern Ind. School Journal*, is now principal of the South Whitley schools. This is a graded township school, and numbers 220 pupils.

T. J. Sanders, Supt. of the Butler schools, has contributed the geological chapter to the History of DeKalb County, now in preparation. Mr. Sanders has been making natural science a specialty for some years.

Lewis H. Jones, who was last summer promoted to the superintendency of the Indianapolis schools, is managing the work in such a way as to render general satisfaction to school board, teachers and patrons.

H. S. Tarbell, formerly Supt. of the Indianapolis schools, now Supt. of the schools of Providence, R. I., recently read an evening address before the fortieth annual meeting of the Rhode Island Institute of Instruction.

Prof. Geo. W. Hoss, formerly one of Indiana's leading educators, and many years editor of this Journal, has found his double work too heavy, and has sold *The Educationist* (Kansas), and is devoting his entire time to his duties as Professor in Baldwin University.

Dr. E E. White has been doing some very acceptable institute work in Pennsylvania and other states. His lectures on psychology attract special attention. We learn that Mr. White is now at home (Walnut Hills, near Cincinnati), for a six-month work in his library, presumably to complete his educational books, which the educational public will be glad to see.

Hiram Hadley, of Indianapolis, in offering a premium for the best essay on "How best to use Encyclopedias in Schools," is doing a good educational work and deserves support. See his advertisement in January Journal.

Wm Irelan began teaching at Burnettsville twenty-nine years ago, and is still in charge. In the mean time he has lost nine years by attending college, serving in the army, and teaching a short time at one other place. He wears well.

Walter Sayler, of Logansport, editor of *The Educational World*, principal of "The American Normal College," and head of a "Teachers' Agency," has secured the control of *The American*, published at Valparaiso. This looks like business

Smith Hunt, formerly of Columbia City, and who has for several years been teaching in Iowa, has recently been elected President of the Iowa Agricultural College. Judging from newspaper reports no educational man in Iowa stands higher than does Mr. Hunt. He is well remembered in this state as an affable, attractive gentleman, and a good teacher, and his Hoosier friends are a little surprised that he should have dropped the vulgar cognomen Smith and taken in its place Leigh. "What's in a name?"

BOOK TABLE.

Educational Weekly is the name of a new paper started January 1st in Toronto. It is a 20-page 3-column paper, stitched and trimmed. It looks well and reads well. Price $2.

Babyhood is the name of a new magazine just started in New York. It is not for babies, as the name would indicate, but for parents, especially mothers. The suggestions in regard to the rearing of children are certainly valuable. Caring for babies should be made a study and reduced to a scientific basis. Address 18 Spruce St.

The Chemical Review is the name of a magazine recently issued at Franklin, Ind., devoted to applied chemistry. It is published every six weeks, by the James Chaffee Chemical Laboratory, Franklin College. It contains much that is of interest not only to the chemist, but to every one who wishes useful information in regard to chemical facts in every-day life.

Our crowded pages this month prevents the insertion of several notices of books now before us. Among these books are the following: "Oral Lessons in Number" (for teachers), by E. E. White, Van Antwerp, Bragg & Co.; "Temperance Physiology," by Mary H. Hunt, A. S. Barnes & Co.; "Lippincott's Science Series," Physiology; "How we Live, or the human body and how to take care of it," by Johonnot and Bouton, D. Appleton & Co.; "Eclectic School Geometry," "Classics for Children," "Kingsley's Greek Heroes," and Primer and First Reader, Ginn, Heath & Co.

Elements of Zoology. By C. F Holder, Fellow of the New York Academy of Science, and J. B Holder, M. D., Curator of Zoology, American Museum of Natural History, Central Park. New York: D. Appleton & Co.

This text-book is designed for use in higher schools and academies.

Its peculiarities are that it employs simple rather than technical terms; it encourages students to become investigators and collectors, and suggests best methods for collecting and preserving specimens; it treats at length of the economic value of animals. The book is handsomely illustrated and seems well suited to the purpose of the authors.

BUSINESS NOTICES.

TEACHERS DESIRING POSITIONS, and Educational Institutions in want of TEACHERS, please address

☞   TEACHERS' AGENCY,

☞   152 Griffith St.,

☞   FORT WAYNE, IND.

Its peculiarities are that it employs simple rather than technical terms; it encourages students to become investigators and collectors, and suggests best methods for collecting and preserving specimens; it treats at length of the economic value of animals. The book is handsomely illustrated and seems well suited to the purpose of the authors.

BUSINESS NOTICES.

TEACHERS DESIRING POSITIONS, and Educational Institutions in want of TEACHERS, please address

☞   TEACHERS' AGENCY,
    ☞   152 Griffith St.,
      ☞   FORT WAYNE, IND.

PRIZES FOR ARITHMETIC.

$600.00.

The publishers of THE SCHOOL SUPPLEMENT purpose issuing a new book on the subject of ARITHMETIC to offer as a premium with their paper. Rather than pay an individual author a sum of money to prepare such a book as they require, the publishers have divided the sum—*Six Hundred Dollars*—which they propose to offer into *One Hundred and Twenty Prizes*, arranged in *eight groups* of $75 each. To correspond with these eight groups of prizes, they have divided the whole subject of Arithmetic into the following *eight departments:*

(1) Addition, Subtraction, Multiplication, Division. (2) Factors, Multiples, Fractions, Decimals (3) Denominate Numbers (4) Practical Measurements. (5) Percentage, Trade Discount, Profit and Loss, Commission and Brokerage. (6) Interest, Partial Payments, True and Bank Discount, Stocks. (7) Insurance, Taxes, Exchange, Proportion, Partnership. (8) Miscellaneous Practical Exercises and Problems.

Each group of prizes the publishers have subdivided as follows: Five first prizes of $10 each; five second prizes of $3 each; and five third prizes of $2 each. *All teachers and students may compete* for these prizes upon the following conditions:

Each must send to the publishers, as early as possible, a *set of ten examples in Arithmetic* based upon the work included in some *one* of the eight departments already named. The *correct answers* (not solutions) to the ten examples must also be given. The examples need not necessarily cover the whole work of the department. Each competitor may enter for prizes in as many departments as he chooses, but no *one* competitor will be awarded prizes in more than five departments.

The Prizes will be Awarded for the fifteen best sets in each department. The arbitrators will take into consideration the originality and practical character of the examples, and their general adaptation to public, grammar, and high school work.

The *Three Hundred* sets of examples which the arbitrators consider the best will be published in book form. Each set will be printed complete, and the name of the compiler will be inserted with it. Together with the *three thousand Examples* secured in this way, the book will contain an entirely new and novel treatment of the whole subject of Arithmetic. The printing and binding will be the best that modern workmanship can turn out.

Every person who sends a set or sets of examples must send therewith ONE DOLLAR as his or her subscription to THE SCHOOL SUPPLEMENT for one year. A copy of the ARITHMETIC will be mailed FREE to every subscriber on the second day of February, 1885 The latest date for receiving sets of examples in departments 1, 2, 3 and 4, will be January 5th, 1885, and in departments 5, 6, 7 and 8, the latest date will be January 10th, 1885. The one One Hundred and Twenty Prizes will be mailed by P. O Order or Bank Draft to the winner on the second day of February, 1885 The complete results of the competition will be published in the *Supplement.* Any further explanation or information necessary will be sent cheerfully upon application.

The School Supplement is, without any exception, the best school paper published. Though its publication was commenced less than a year ago, its fame has already spread from California to Newfoundland, and from British Columbia to Florida Its subscribers represent every State and Province The *Supplement* is an Educational Journal on an entirely new plan. It is profusely illustrated, and contains lessons in all the school subjects The current numbers contain biographies of noted authors and statesmen, with large, beautifully engraved portraits; short stories for school-room; interesting sketches; maps and illustrations; readings and recitations; lessons in practical arithmetic and grammar; hundreds of sentences for correction; illustrated lessons in astronomy, standard time, correspondence, mensuration and railroad geography; anecdotes of authors; practical exercises for primary pupils; prize competitions for pupils' work, and numerous miscellaneous articles. Sample copies will be mailed to those who have not seen the paper, for *Eight Cents* in stamps.

SPECIAL OFFER.

The publishers will continue to mail a new book FREE to all their subscribers on the first day of February of each year. A few hundred copies of their 1884 book still remain on hand It is an *Examination Manual*, and it contains over 2,000 questions and exercises in all the common and high school branches. This is a very valuable book, many thousand copies having been disposed of during the year. It contains 175 pages, beautifully printed and bound A copy will be mailed FREE to every new subscriber until the stock is exhausted. Those, then, who subscribe at once, whether competing for the Arithmetic Prizes or not, will receive one book by return mail, one book on the second day of February, 1885, and *The School Supplement* for one year—all for *One Dollar*. Please enclose eight cents with your one dollar, to pay the postage of the *Examination Manual*. Mail all letters to either one of the following addresses:

EATON, GIBSON & CO., EDUCATIONAL PUBLISHERS BUFFALO, N. Y.

OR EATON, GIBSON & CO., EDUCATIONAL PUBLISHERS, TORONTO, CAN.

The SUPPLEMENT and premium books are mailed from both places. All letters are answered promptly.
2-

INDIANA
SCHOOL JOURNAL.

Vol. XXX.　　　　MARCH, 1885.　　　　No. 3.

CHILD NATURE.

EMMA C. STOUT.

[Read at Teachers' Holiday Institute, held at Jonesboro, Grant Co., Dec. 27, 1884.]

"Childhood is the bough where slumbered
Birds and blossoms many numbered."

THE teacher's hand may make the glorious harmony of future years, his sunshine of sympathy may aid in the perfection of rich fruitage, or his cold neglect may chill and dwarf the buds of promising thought. This subject is one of rapidly growing importance to our profession. Perhaps many would be better qualified for their work if they would spend more time upon the study of child nature and less upon mathematics or some other abstract science. Woman's pen is introducing a new era in the little world of juvenile literature, and by a hasty review we can see that the purest and noblest men, whose names appear upon the roll of authors, have been devoted students and lovers of children. Our ideal poets revel in the theme. Whittier's "Barefoot Boy" and "School Days," Longfellow's "Children's Hour" and "Maidenhood," and Tennyson's "Children's Hospital" are poems which once read glide into our imagination, a pure stream of delight that ripples on forever. The deep thoughts of Emerson never reach our inmost nature more touchingly than in the sublimely beautiful passages of "Threnody," and even the dignified music of Bryant pauses in lofty flight to sing of the "Little People of the Snow."

· Children are near to Nature's heart, and the mother or teacher who would make the highest success of physical, mental and spiritual development must reach them through their natural dispositions and tendencies; otherwise originality is crushed and individuality becomes mere affectation. The general characteristics of childhood upon which we can build permanent qualities for a worthy manhood or womanhood are ambition, perseverance, activity, vivid imagination, apt imitation, conscientiousness, love, and reverence. There are, of course, some "side issues" to this general outline; the perseverance may in some cases amount to wilfulness or obstinacy, the activity may degenerate into mischievousness. But the good in child nature preponderates over the evil, and therefore the good may be more fully and rapidly developed if a master hand strike the keys. But the work of the teacher is often marred because he has too many keys to strike at once, and in wisely planning for the majority some are left to grind out discord. Yet from this great diversity some teachers are so discerning that they bring out a harmonious unity. From the native quality, ambition, a wise teacher will inspire an honest pride in perfect lessons and a healthy emulation in striving to excel in points of order as well as in mental pursuits, for children glory in doing something that is hard to do. Through activity the busy fingers and brain can be turned into channels of industry. By giving them plenty to do, and the secret is,—a pleasant way in which to accomplish their tasks—mischief may be driven into the back ground. Children live in an atmosphere of poetry and imagination, and if in the preparation of their lessons they are allowed to weave in some of their native fancies they will be busier, happier, and accomplish more than with merely the text-book placed before them.

Upon this principle rests the great popularity of the Kindergarten system, which may be partially introduced into every country school-room with beneficial results. For instance, in the Second and Third Reader grades, the reading lessons are usually short, and the illustrations give the pupil something to think about beside what they see in the text. After questioning them so as to arouse a train of thought, the teacher might say: "Now we will suppose that this picture is not a picture, but that you are walking along and meet this little boy and girl in a field; after you have properly prepared the lesson in the book I shall write a story of the picture on the board—that is, I shall write a part of one and you may complete it." The teacher writes as follows, when the proper time comes for such work:

"One — day I met a — bcy and girl in a — field. The grass was —, some — flowers grew by the — brook. The girl's eyes were — . She wore a — dress, a — apron and a — bonnet. The boy carried a — cage in which was a — bird."

The variety of these stories will be surprising, for no two will be exactly alike unless there be a conference. The exercise may be made valuable as a drill in spelling, punctuation, writing, composition, and language.

In arithmetic the same play on the imagination can be indulged without the least harm to numerical calculations. The teacher writes on the board the bare sums, $6 + 2$; $22 + 33$, etc., the lesson to be brought to recitation on slates, and adds: "Now, I tell you a story every morning, and I want you after you finish each sum on your slate to tell me a story about something like this,—"As I came to school this morning I saw 6 men riding along the road in a big green wagon, and 2 men gathering corn in a field; therefore, I saw the sum of 6 men and 2 men, which are 8 men." Or, "I had 6 white marbles, and John gave me 2 blue ones," etc. These exercises should be repeated from memory so as to make a useful drill in analysis and language.

In geography the same pleasing story telling may be followed by taking imaginary journeys by rail or by ship. Some may object to this plan, but the children will not if it be agreeably presented, and through it all they are developing original thought and expression which after all is the best part of an education. It is daily assisting them in becoming practical grammarians, good conversationalists, and logical thinkers. Children who prepare their lessons in this way will never make a bugbear of essay and letter writing, for their style of expression will be developed in equal proportion to other mental powers. Teachers understand child nature sufficiently well to know the value of object lessons. They learn a great deal more through their eyes than their ears.

But it takes a deeper study to make a success of their moral than of their mental development. Here is proven the old adage that "The road by precept is long, while that by example is short and sure." In every community there is a stream of coarse slang, rude jokes and unpleasant gossip, and some of the children drink constantly from these impure waters. The teacher may strive to launch his pupils upon the counter current, and yet an hour on the play ground may often undo what the precepts of mother and teacher have been months in building. In the moral training the teacher may again do effective work by story telling—stories that embody a truth worth impressing. Give them sketches of biography, and then tell them to go home and search their books or question their elders for the name of the hero. For points of order give them stories of Careful and Careless, or Willful and Obedient personified. The advice is far more impressive than if given in the usual manner.

Teachers are largely responsible for the views of life adopted by their pupils. A little girl in defining duty said: "It most always means something you had rather not do."

Do we give our pupils such an impression? One who is in sympathy with childhood can easily teach children to look upon duties not as disagreeable tasks, but as bright jewels in the crown of a useful, happy life.

It is said that a child learns more in the first five years of its life than in any such period afterward, and this fact makes the position of primary teacher very important. The early sunbeams cast the longest shadows, the bird songs are sweetest, the flowers are brightest. Then let teachers magnify their office; their training, words and influence are the early impressions in the morning of life of our coming men and women. The humble teacher is as it were a missionary to an enchanted land, preparing its inhabitants for toilsome journeys and noontide heat, but losing them from sight when they enter the busy ways of life.

"LEARNING TO DO BY DOING."

COL. F. W. PARKER.

[Address delivered before the State Teachers' Association, Dec. 30, 1884.]

THE following is an abstract of his address, minus the force of his gestures and facial expressions, which added much:

I am happy to greet my brethren and sisters of the great State of Indiana. It has been my fortune to be a Buckeye temporarily, and for a short time to be a Sucker, but never until to-day to be a Hoosier. It may be that many of the faults in the Quincy system are due to that fact.

You will find my text on the program. You have probably found it elsewhere. It has been found throughout the past. It is found in the Bible. "He that doeth my will shall know of the doctrine." The subject I present is one that will bear study, and as you have often talked about it and discussed it, you will excuse me if I enter upon it in a pretty dry way.

The things that must be done should be learned by doing them. The first question I ask is, "What is doing?" A man can think and express thought. What else can he do? This beautiful church is a manifestation of thought on the part of the architect. A man can manifest thought by drawing, by oral and written language, and by music. And all these manifestations of thought re doing.

But this is a question of education. To me the things done are of great value to mankind. This church is of importance to the multitude that meet here. The oration is of importance to those who listen, and also to those who may read it, and its educational value is of immediate importance to the one who utters it. I utter my thought, and in that action my mind receives strength. The manifestation of thought has its effect upon the mind and the emotions.

Creating the thing to be expressed is doing. I trust you are doing something now. If you are thinking, are you not doing something? The artist, creating a beautiful work of art, is doing something; his mind is moving in the creation of that which shall live for ages. The philosopher analyzes, and though he may sit silent for hours he is doing. What is *not* doing then? The memory takes care of itself. As one is thinking, these thoughts pass into memory to reappear again. Doing is the manifestation of thought, but there must be something done before the doing. When I am forming an ideal, when I am creating what I should be, am I doing? This learning to do by doing covers all the ground; things that have to be done, must be done by doing them; this is the straight and narrow way that leads to education. Of course it is a psychological question, and should be studied as such. Dogmatic statements have little effect unless supported by careful reasoning.

If this sentence covers the whole ground, what is its application? It is like the eleventh commandment, everybody believes it and some practice it. I have only to go to my own history as a school teacher to discover its application. I try to learn to do things by doing something else. It has been the fault of many teachers to try to learn a thing by going around the main question.

Take Reading, which is one of the great subjects of our work in school. It brings inherited power face to face with inherited knowledge; it is the means of opening the door to the past. What is reading? I know what I thought it was, and as I thought, so I pursued it. I believed that teaching reading was teaching pronunciation, and I taught pronunciation.

Another says reading is emphasis. Did you never think that the child can emphasize better than any teacher can teach him? Why it is impossible for a child to have a thought and not emphasize it properly; but it is possible for a teacher, or a minister, or a reader, who has an orotund voice.

The child has learned to talk by a method in vogue since the days of Adam, and he has learned to talk beautifully; the merry voice of childhood is an example for our great elocutionists. Booth has said, "When I wish new lessons in elocution I go to the child." Listen to the child as he admiringly exclaims, "O see those beautiful flowers!" Then think of his going into the school-room, and under the most careful training, changing that beautiful voice until we hear him say, "O—see—those—beauti-ful—flowers!" We, are artists, you know, and that is the product of our teaching.

What is the mistake? I think it is that we do not learn to do by doing. Reading is getting thought; it is thinking by means of printed words. Talking is a means of teaching reading, but when it is used as the end the work all goes wrong.

What is spelling? The way I taught it, it was the laborious description of printed words by naming one letter after another. When is there any need for oral spelling? You know we spell only when we write. Suppose you have pronouncing lessons. Pronunciation is the correlative of spelling; spelling is forming the word with the pen or pencil; pronunciation is making the form of a word with the vocal organs. We pronounce when we have thoughts to utter; that is the economical way of training the child to pronunciation. The thought demands expression, and the child practices uttering thoughts because he has them. But the teacher has divorced spelling from the utterance of thought, and made it a cold, hard thing; and, therefore, the teaching of it is an extravagant use of time. When a child learns to talk with a pencil, every sentence he writes can be written under the influence of thought, and he can be trained to utter thoughts correctly, so that no time may be taken outside of this for spelling. The spelling-book should be hung up as a relic of the past, and I suppose it is banished from three-fourths of the counties in Indiana.

Take Language as an example of learning to do by doing. Lindley Murray was a good man, for whom we should all have respect. He tried to help the children. There was not much for them to do. The Latin and Greek had grammars. Ergo, said Lindley Murray, there must be a grammar of the English. The way to learn English was to learn it as the Latin had been taught, and so he made a grammar. He did not know that William the Conqueror had cut off the inflexions of the English and made it a comparatively grammarless language. He made his book, then the children were doomed. He never understood it himself, and I do not suppose he understands it now If he does, he can not b so happy as we hope he is.

"I love, thou lovest, he loves." That song was sung again and again. Now, my friends, those words, when you mean them, are beautiful; but what is the use of compelling our children to say them. Parsing! I parsed Paradise Lost, and it has been "lost" to me ever since, and I can not see any beauty in Milton. I put myself at those old desks again, and think of those rules in grammar and those long lists of prepositions, and I can not see into the grand beauty of Milton.

Now if grammar will help us to grasp thought deeper and broader, let us have grammar. But if children do not gain thought better by it, then grammar teaching is wrong. Parsing was a very simple matter, but somebody invented something more than parsing. Sentences were divided up and each part given a name. O those names! I thought I was wicked when I refused to learn them, but that was the first indication of goodness in me.

Teaching develops thought, thought demands expression. Every thought we utter reflects back upon itself; the expression of thought is the means of developing thought.

Take up Arithmetic. In this, if you do not understand anything, call it abstract. Charity covereth a multitude of sins, but it does not cover abstractness. Children can not reason. They have to learn a great mess of words, and after a while the reasoning comes to them. Think of multiplying or dividing a fraction by a fraction! What a beautiful thing it is to find the greatest common divisor! I am always finding the least common multiple. If there ever was a humbug, it is spending one fourth of the time in learning figures. The natural sciences, God's thoughts in nature wait—for what? For a great mess of figures to be learned, that fill the soul with nothing but rubbish? That is what you are doing to-day. I believe if you would teach zoology, botany, and mineralogy, the children would learn more of arithmetic than by your teaching arithmetic itself.

The great error is we do not discriminate between the means and the end. The child knows a great deal when he enters the school-room, and we try in an artificial way to teach him to do what he can already do and do well. What things must be

done? Those things that make the man; that make the best of the child. It is the teacher's sublime mission to work out the design of God in humanity; we call that design character. In this blessed country every child is privileged to be a king. The time has come when every child is to be trained into true sovereignty. Those things that make character are to be taught in the school.

What a tangle we are getting into! Fifty studies in twelve years! A great many of these having no other purpose than to train children to do what somebody may do in future life. The subjects should be governed by the power gained in the character-building of the children. The amount taught should be that which will give the highest power; and that which develops character the best way should be taught in the schools. What we have to do is to discover what is best. Character is made up of habits. Habit is a tendency to do that which we have done. The whole character is formed by doing, and character is all that we are. There is no neutral ground. You are developing morality or immorality in the child. I believe the greatest sin is selfishness, and the greatest virtue is that laid down in the eleventh commandment, love for others. Every school should be a miniature republic, each for all and all for each. We are all builders of this great republic, and we are training the children to steal systematically. Everything is done to get percent. By this we are training children into immorality. The percent system is a curse to this country. Just as though there was not pleasure in study! I would banish every marking system from the land.

You train the children into the will power. Suppose I suppress your wills for about eight years. I can have you sit up straight without your knowing why you do it. I can punish you, or worse still, I can give you a reward. I have entered a school where the school did not look at me. To me the sight was painful. If I feel gloomy and want anything to cure me, I go into the lowest primary, where a gleam of sunshine goes through me and I feel better all day. But in this school they did not look at me. They were asked question after question;

"I love, thou lovest, he loves." That song was sung again and again. Now, my friends, those words, when you mean them, are beautiful; but what is the use of compelling our children to say them. Parsing! I parsed Paradise Lost, and it has been "lost" to me ever since, and I can not see any beauty in Milton. I put myself at those old desks again, and think of those rules in grammar and those long lists of prepositions, and I can not see into the grand beauty of Milton.

Now if grammar will help us to grasp thought deeper and broader, let us have grammar. But if children do not gain thought better by it, then grammar teaching is wrong. Parsing was a very simple matter, but somebody invented something more than parsing. Sentences were divided up and each part given a name. O those names! I thought I was wicked when I refused to learn them, but that was the first indication of goodness in me.

Teaching develops thought, thought demands expression. Every thought we utter reflects back upon itself; the expression of thought is the means of developing thought.

Take up Arithmetic. In this, if you do not understand anything, call it abstract. Charity covereth a multitude of sins, but it does not cover abstractness. Children can not reason. They have to learn a great mess of words, and after a while the reasoning comes to them. Think of multiplying or dividing a fraction by a fraction! What a beautiful thing it is to find the greatest common divisor! I am always finding the least common multiple. If there ever was a humbug, it is spending one fourth of the time in learning figures. The natural sciences, God's thoughts in nature wait—for what? For a great mess of figures to be learned, that fill the soul with nothing but rubbish? That is what you are doing to-day. I believe if you would teach zoology, botany, and mineralogy, the children would learn more of arithmetic than by your teaching arithmetic itself.

The great error is we do not discriminate between the means and the end. The child knows a great deal when he enters the school-room, and we try in an artificial way to teach him to do what he can already do and do well. What things must be

done? Those things that make the man; that make the best of the child. It is the teacher's sublime mission to work out the design of God in humanity; we call that design character. In this blessed country every child is privileged to be a king. The time has come when every child is to be trained into true sovereignty. Those things that make character are to be taught in the school.

What a tangle we are getting into! Fifty studies in twelve years! A great many of these having no other purpose than to train children to do what somebody may do in future life. The subjects should be governed by the power gained in the character-building of the children. The amount taught should be that which will give the highest power; and that which develops character the best way should be taught in the schools. What we have to do is to discover what is best. Character is made up of habits. Habit is a tendency to do that which we have done. The whole character is formed by doing, and character is all that we are. There is no neutral ground. You are developing morality or immorality in the child. I believe the greatest sin is selfishness, and the greatest virtue is that laid down in the eleventh commandment, love for others. Every school should be a miniature republic, each for all and all for each. We are all builders of this great republic, and we are training the children to steal systematically. Everything is done to get percent. By this we are training children into immorality. The percent system is a curse to this country. Just as though there was not pleasure in study! I would banish every marking system from the land.

You train the children into the will power. Suppose I suppress your wills for about eight years. I can have you sit up straight without your knowing why you do it. I can punish you, or worse still, I can give you a reward. I have entered a school where the school did not look at me. To me the sight was painful. If I feel gloomy and want anything to cure me, I go into the lowest primary, where a gleam of sunshine goes through me and I feel better all day. But in this school they did not look at me. They were asked question after question;

"I love, thou lovest, he loves." That song was sung again and again. Now, my friends, those words, when you mean them, are beautiful; but what is the use of compelling our children to say them. Parsing! I parsed Paradise Lost, and it has been "lost" to me ever since, and I can not see any beauty in Milton. I put myself at those old desks again, and think of those rules in grammar and those long lists of prepositions, and I can not see into the grand beauty of Milton.

Now if grammar will help us to grasp thought deeper and broader, let us have grammar. But if children do not gain thought better by it, then grammar teaching is wrong. Parsing was a very simple matter, but somebody invented something more than parsing. Sentences were divided up and each part given a name. O those names! I thought I was wicked when I refused to learn them, but that was the first indication of goodness in me.

Teaching develops thought, thought demands expression. Every thought we utter reflects back upon itself; the expression of thought is the means of developing thought.

Take up Arithmetic. In this, if you do not understand anything, call it abstract. Charity covereth a multitude of sins, but it does not cover abstractness. Children can not reason. They have to learn a great mess of words, and after a while the reasoning comes to them. Think of multiplying or dividing a fraction by a fraction! What a beautiful thing it is to find the greatest common divisor! I am always finding the least common multiple. If there ever was a humbug, it is spending one fourth of the time in learning figures. The natural sciences, God's thoughts in nature wait—for what? For a great mess of figures to be learned, that fill the soul with nothing but rubbish? That is what you are doing to-day. I believe if you would teach zoology, botany, and mineralogy, the children would learn more of arithmetic than by your teaching arithmetic itself.

The great error is we do not discriminate between the means and the end. The child knows a great deal when he enters the school-room, and we try in an artificial way to teach him to do what he can already do and do well. What things must be

done? Those things that make the man; that make the best of
the child. It is the teacher's sublime mission to work out the
design of God in humanity; we call that design character. In
this blessed country every child is privileged to be a king. The
time has come when every child is to be trained into true sovereignty. Those things that make character are to be taught in
the school.

What a tangle we are getting into! Fifty studies in twelve
years! A great many of these having no other purpose than to
train children to do what somebody may do in future life. The
subjects should be governed by the power gained in the character-building of the children. The amount taught should be that
which will give the highest power; and that which develops
character the best way should be taught in the schools. What
we have to do is to discover what is best. Character is made
up of habits. Habit is a tendency to do that which we have
done. The whole character is formed by doing, and character
is all that we are. There is no neutral ground. You are developing morality or immorality in the child. I believe the greatest
sin is selfishness, and the greatest virtue is that laid down in the
eleventh commandment, love for others. Every school should
be a miniature republic, each for all and all for each. We are
all builders of this great republic, and we are training the children to steal systematically. Everything is done to get percent.
By this we are training children into immorality. The percent
system is a curse to this country. Just as though there was not
pleasure in study! I would banish every marking system from
the land.

You train the children into the will power. Suppose I suppress your wills for about eight years. I can have you sit up
straight without your knowing why you do it. I can punish
you, or worse still, I can give you a reward. I have entered a
school where the school did not look at me. To me the sight
was painful. If I feel gloomy and want anything to cure me,
I go into the lowest primary, where a gleam of sunshine goes
through me and I feel better all day. But in this school they
did not look at me. They were asked question after question;

"I love, thou lovest, he loves." That song was sung again
and again. Now, my friends, those words, when you mean
them, are beautiful; but what is the use of compelling our children to say them. Parsing! I parsed Paradise Lost, and it has
been "lost" to me ever since, and I can not see any beauty in
Milton. I put myself at those old desks again, and think of
those rules in grammar and those long lists of prepositions, and
I can not see into the grand beauty of Milton.

Now if grammar will help us to grasp thought deeper and
broader, let us have grammar. But if children do not gain
thought better by it, then grammar teaching is wrong. Parsing
was a very simple matter, but somebody invented something
more than parsing. Sentences were divided up and each part
given a name. O those names! I thought I was wicked when
I refused to learn them, but that was the first indication of goodness in me.

Teaching develops thought, thought demands expression.
Every thought we utter reflects back upon itself; the expression
of thought is the means of developing thought.

Take up Arithmetic. In this, if you do not understand anything, call it abstract. Charity covereth a multitude of sins, but
it does not cover abstractness. Children can not reason. They
have to learn a great mess of words, and after a while the reasoning comes to them. Think of multiplying or dividing a fraction
by a fraction! What a beautiful thing it is to find the greatest
common divisor! I am always finding the least common multiple. If there ever was a humbug, it is spending one fourth of
the time in learning figures. The natural sciences, God's thoughts
in nature wait—for what? For a great mess of figures to be
learned, that fill the soul with nothing but rubbish? That is
what you are doing to-day. I believe if you would teach zoology, botany, and mineralogy, the children would learn more of
arithmetic than by your teaching arithmetic itself.

The great error is we do not discriminate between the means
and the end. The child knows a great deal when he enters the
school-room, and we try in an artificial way to teach him to do
what he can already do and do well. What things must be

done? Those things that make the man; that make the best of the child. It is the teacher's sublime mission to work out the design of God in humanity; we call that design character. In this blessed country every child is privileged to be a king. The time has come when every child is to be trained into true sovereignty. Those things that make character are to be taught in the school.

What a tangle we are getting into! Fifty studies in twelve years! A great many of these having no other purpose than to train children to do what somebody may do in future life. The subjects should be governed by the power gained in the character-building of the children. The amount taught should be that which will give the highest power; and that which develops character the best way should be taught in the schools. What we have to do is to discover what is best. Character is made up of habits. Habit is a tendency to do that which we have done. The whole character is formed by doing, and character is all that we are. There is no neutral ground. You are developing morality or immorality in the child. I believe the greatest sin is selfishness, and the greatest virtue is that laid down in the eleventh commandment, love for others. Every school should be a miniature republic, each for all and all for each. We are all builders of this great republic, and we are training the children to steal systematically. Everything is done to get percent. By this we are training children into immorality. The percent system is a curse to this country. Just as though there was not pleasure in study! I would banish every marking system from the land.

You train the children into the will power. Suppose I suppress your wills for about eight years. I can have you sit up straight without your knowing why you do it. I can punish you, or worse still, I can give you a reward. I have entered a school where the school did not look at me. To me the sight was painful. If I feel gloomy and want anything to cure me, I go into the lowest primary, where a gleam of sunshine goes through me and I feel better all day. But in this school they did not look at me. They were asked question after question;

"I love, thou lovest, he loves." That song was sung again and again. Now, my friends, those words, when you mean them, are beautiful; but what is the use of compelling our children to say them. Parsing! I parsed Paradise Lost, and it has been "lost" to me ever since, and I can not see any beauty in Milton. I put myself at those old desks again, and think of those rules in grammar and those long lists of prepositions, and I can not see into the grand beauty of Milton.

Now if grammar will help us to grasp thought deeper and broader, let us have grammar. But if children do not gain thought better by it, then grammar teaching is wrong. Parsing was a very simple matter, but somebody invented something more than parsing. Sentences were divided up and each part given a name. O those names! I thought I was wicked when I refused to learn them, but that was the first indication of goodness in me.

Teaching develops thought, thought demands expression. Every thought we utter reflects back upon itself; the expression of thought is the means of developing thought.

Take up Arithmetic. In this, if you do not understand anything, call it abstract. Charity covereth a multitude of sins, but it does not cover abstractness. Children can not reason. They have to learn a great mess of words, and after a while the reasoning comes to them. Think of multiplying or dividing a fraction by a fraction! What a beautiful thing it is to find the greatest common divisor! I am always finding the least common multiple. If there ever was a humbug, it is spending one fourth of the time in learning figures. The natural sciences, God's thoughts in nature wait—for what? For a great mess of figures to be learned, that fill the soul with nothing but rubbish? That is what you are doing to-day. I believe if you would teach zoology, botany, and mineralogy, the children would learn more of arithmetic than by your teaching arithmetic itself.

The great error is we do not discriminate between the means and the end. The child knows a great deal when he enters the school-room, and we try in an artificial way to teach him to do what he can already do and do well. What things must be

done? Those things that make the man; that make the best of
the child. It is the teacher's sublime mission to work out the
design of God in humanity; we call that design character. In
this blessed country every child is privileged to be a king. The
time has come when every child is to be trained into true sovereignty. Those things that make character are to be taught in
the school.

What a tangle we are getting into! Fifty studies in twelve
years! A great many of these having no other purpose than to
train children to do what somebody may do in future life. The
subjects should be governed by the power gained in the character-building of the children. The amount taught should be that
which will give the highest power; and that which develops
character the best way should be taught in the schools. What
we have to do is to discover what is best. Character is made
up of habits. Habit is a tendency to do that which we have
done. The whole character is formed by doing, and character
is all that we are. There is no neutral ground. You are developing morality or immorality in the child. I believe the greatest
sin is selfishness, and the greatest virtue is that laid down in the
eleventh commandment, love for others. Every school should
be a miniature republic, each for all and all for each. We are
all builders of this great republic, and we are training the children to steal systematically. Everything is done to get percent.
By this we are training children into immorality. The percent
system is a curse to this country. Just as though there was not
pleasure in study! I would banish every marking system from
the land.

You train the children into the will power. Suppose I suppress your wills for about eight years. I can have you sit up
straight without your knowing why you do it. I can punish
you, or worse still, I can give you a reward. I have entered a
school where the school did not look at me. To me the sight
was painful. If I feel gloomy and want anything to cure me,
I go into the lowest primary, where a gleam of sunshine goes
through me and I feel better all day. But in this school they
did not look at me. They were asked question after question;

"I love, thou lovest, he loves." That song was sung again and again. Now, my friends, those words, when you mean them, are beautiful; but what is the use of compelling our children to say them. Parsing! I parsed Paradise Lost, and it has been "lost" to me ever since, and I can not see any beauty in Milton. I put myself at those old desks again, and think of those rules in grammar and those long lists of prepositions, and I can not see into the grand beauty of Milton.

Now if grammar will help us to grasp thought deeper and broader, let us have grammar. But if children do not gain thought better by it, then grammar teaching is wrong. Parsing was a very simple matter, but somebody invented something more than parsing. Sentences were divided up and each part given a name. O those names! I thought I was wicked when I refused to learn them, but that was the first indication of goodness in me.

Teaching develops thought, thought demands expression. Every thought we utter reflects back upon itself; the expression of thought is the means of developing thought.

Take up Arithmetic. In this, if you do not understand anything, call it abstract. Charity covereth a multitude of sins, but it does not cover abstractness. Children can not reason. They have to learn a great mess of words, and after a while the reasoning comes to them. Think of multiplying or dividing a fraction by a fraction! What a beautiful thing it is to find the greatest common divisor! I am always finding the least common multiple. If there ever was a humbug, it is spending one fourth of the time in learning figures. The natural sciences, God's thoughts in nature wait—for what? For a great mess of figures to be learned, that fill the soul with nothing but rubbish? That is what you are doing to-day. I believe if you would teach zoology, botany, and mineralogy, the children would learn more of arithmetic than by your teaching arithmetic itself.

The great error is we do not discriminate between the means and the end. The child knows a great deal when he enters the school-room, and we try in an artificial way to teach him to do what he can already do and do well. What things must be

done? Those things that make the man; that make the best of the child. It is the teacher's sublime mission to work out the design of God in humanity; we call that design character. In this blessed country every child is privileged to be a king. The time has come when every child is to be trained into true sovereignty. Those things that make character are to be taught in the school.

What a tangle we are getting into! Fifty studies in twelve years! A great many of these having no other purpose than to train children to do what somebody may do in future life. The subjects should be governed by the power gained in the character-building of the children. The amount taught should be that which will give the highest power; and that which develops character the best way should be taught in the schools. What we have to do is to discover what is best. Character is made up of habits. Habit is a tendency to do that which we have done. The whole character is formed by doing, and character is all that we are. There is no neutral ground. You are developing morality or immorality in the child. I believe the greatest sin is selfishness, and the greatest virtue is that laid down in the eleventh commandment, love for others. Every school should be a miniature republic, each for all and all for each. We are all builders of this great republic, and we are training the children to steal systematically. Everything is done to get percent. By this we are training children into immorality. The percent system is a curse to this country. Just as though there was not pleasure in study! I would banish every marking system from the land.

You train the children into the will power. Suppose I suppress your wills for about eight years. I can have you sit up straight without your knowing why you do it. I can punish you, or worse still, I can give you a reward. I have entered a school where the school did not look at me. To me the sight was painful. If I feel gloomy and want anything to cure me, I go into the lowest primary, where a gleam of sunshine goes through me and I feel better all day. But in this school they did not look at me. They were asked question after question;

and if the teacher had played upon a key-board with wires attached to the children they could not have responded quicker. We are to train independent citizens; to train men to use their wills. By suppressing their wills? We wonder at elections that men can be bought and sold, and yet we are training them to this thing in the school room. All training that does not follow nature is depriving the child of his mental and moral power.

The trouble is we know too much about teaching already; we are not serious enough, not prayerful enough. We learn the truth by searching for it; we will find it if we search earnestly and prayerfully for it. We do not live up to our opportunities. The meeting of the college faculties here to-day is the grandest thing I have seen. When the colleges reach out to help us, if we join together, and study the subject, first asking, What is this we teach? if we follow that question, and follow this great rule, "Learn to do by doing," I believe the teachers, by earnest, thoughtful, persistent study, giving attention to this greatest of all works, the building of this great republic, are to be a power in the land; to stand as leaders of the people, guides of the children, and a power in all the work of the country. .

Let us put aside everything like dogmatism and conceit, and become as little children in the study of this great subject.

METHODS OF TEACHING THE ENGLISH LANGUAGE AND LITERATURE IN THE HIGH SCHOOLS OF INDIANA.

E. E. SMITH, PURDUE UNIVERSITY.

Prof. E. E. Smith, in opening the discussion of Prof. Parsons' paper, read at the State Association and printed in last month's Journal, said:

I am sure I but express the sentiment of this body when I bear testimony to the excellence of the paper just read. There remains for me but to emphasize some of the points presented, and, possibly, to suggest something in the way of a method of execution of the ideal course just outlined.

It is a hopeful sign that such thoughtful attention has, for the past few years, been given to the *what* and *how* of instruction in English. Both the principles and the methods of this work, in all the grades, have undergone careful examination and practical revision. And for a wise reason. Full command of the mother tongue underlies and conditions accurate work in every line of study. Whether the pupil study or recite the facts of geography, the inductions of arithmetic, or the analysis of science, he must use his power over speech to give these expression. Ideas formulated in clear-cut terms, not those enveloped in mists and separated by chasms, accomplish effective results.

It is well, then, that we recognize this dependence upon language of all work done by the pupil, and so make a common-sense gradation of the work in English. The method of this gradation must depend upon three things: the changing condition of the pupil's mind, his needs at particular periods of his work, and the relations of the study to what precedes and follows. The question arises, then, are these conditions such as to make the ideal course of study outlined practically operative now? In the main, I should say *Yes;* in some particulars, *No.*

It is not believed that the best results can be accomplished now by giving the whole of the first year in the high school to "the scientific study of the sentence." The pupil's previous preparation will not justify work wholly analytic at this period. Synthetic work, or the study of the art of the sentence, should be made a part of this work, and, according to my view, is of fully as much value to the pupil as analysis, parsing, etc. I should further suggest a modification of this work for the first year, for the present and until the work in language in the grades will enable the teacher to dispense with this addition, by devoting the first term to the *study of words.* By this I mean, not the study of words from the æsthetic standpoint wholly, (as in Rhetoric), but words in their origin, derivation, shades of meaning, comparative value in speech, etc. This I should supplement by teaching the pupils *how to get acquainted with the content of the words.* I am sure that the experience of every teacher present will justify the statement that the pupils come to us from the grades sadly deficient in their knowledge of and control over words,—especially in other relations than those with which routine has associated them. Here, then, seems to be an important condition of the best higher work, which condition is not met by the present instruction in the grades.

But I would not be understood, Mr. Chairman, to in any way depreciate the importance of the scientific study of the English sentence. It certainly must gratify all true lovers of our mother tongue to see a deliberate stand taken in favor of a systematic, intelligent study of its forms and its powers of expression. We shall in this way come at last to realize that the English language is in a transitional state, and that its rules of grammar are not fixed, but changeable. That it is a living speech, not a dead one; that it is governed by use, not by form; that it is based upon the laws of thought and the growth of mind in each age, and is not simply a machine operated by cranks. Heretofore, the best authority in grammar has usually been the man who could in the shortest time show the absolute and fixed-from-all-eternity form and construction which a certain expression has, and what an ignoramus the other fellow was who couldn't perceive this.

No, the pupil's mind is now sufficiently matured for an intelligent study of grammar, so that it will be to him something more than mere task-work in committing definitions, generalizations, etc., and in making pens for words from which the class or the teacher was sure to release half or more of them.

Following this work in Grammar should properly come the work in Rhetoric, enabling the pupil to extend his efforts in the direction of discourse, to add polish to his own composition and to recognize the lights and shades manifested in the artistic constructions of standard writers. He is thus, as Prof. Parsons has said, rightly prepared to take up work in Literature.

To the splendid view opened up to us in the paper of what is contained in a people's literature and what may be gained by its study, I would simply add the following things in the way of the *what* and the *how*.

I. Of the WHAT: 1. A brief biography of those authors whose words are to be studied, looking not so much to the chronology of their lives as to those idiosyncracies in themselves and those peculiarities in their surroundings which will serve to explain the character and the purpose of the productions considered by the class. 2. Arranging recapitulations or diagrams of the growth and development of literature in different periods. 3. The philosophy of this growth—things determining both the form and the substance of the literature of a particular period, with indications of its effect upon social, religious, or political life. 4. Standard works of various periods, in which may be found the growth of mind, the change in language, the social, domestic, civil and industrial pursuits of a nation, together with the motives and aspirations underlying these, and the varying forms in which the author's thoughts are expressed. 5. Knowledge of books and of how to use them.

II. Of the How: 1. By suitable recapitulations or other diagrams. The work of the first printing press may be illustrated. 2. By queries philosophically arranged, *i. e.*, leading to a special line of thought in investigation on the part of the pupil. The best results can not be accomplished by isolated queries, but by queries so grouped (with suitable references for the pupils) that the student may find a purpose in his work and an object gained by its completion. 3. By actual study of the times, customs, purposes, words, figurative references, plots, characters, etc., portrayed by authors. 4. By suitable essays, discussions, etc., all having a certain tendency, and in which the aim of the teacher is operative but not recognized by the pupil. Thus the work seems to be original and the conclusions reached the result of his own reflection, to the student. I remember—(here the speaker was cut off by the rap of the chairman's gavel).

PEDAGOGICAL RHETORIC.

BY A. TOMPKINS, SUPT. FRANKLIN SCHOOLS.

The effective writer or teacher must know the classes of ideas, and the thought relations involved in knowing each.

All the ideas by which another mind is affected in teaching or writing are either individual or general ideas. If individual ideas they are wholes as existing in space at a given moment—space wholes, or wholes as changing in successive portions of time—time wholes. These two kinds of individuals give rise to two processes of discourse, description and narration. Likewise the general notion, or class gives rise to two processes of discourse—exposition, setting forth the nature of a class; and argumentation, proving the truth of a general proposition. These four processes of writing correspond to the four processes of teaching. Each process is determined by the kind of thinking required to know the ideas; hence, there are certain habits of thought cultivated in thinking each class of ideas. Whether the ideas be presented for their own sake or for the sake of habits of thought, the teacher must know the kind of thinking required to know each class of ideas and what habits of thought are formed in each case.

Each space object—the word, the picture, the plant, the animal, the common object, the town, the state, the world, the human body, etc., to be known must be thought under the relation of whole and part; and the object as a whole, and also each part, must be thought in the relations of use, position, form, size, and attributes. Systematic drill in thinking thus fixes habits of method, completeness, and thoroughness. Each thought relation in the hands of a skillful teacher has a definite educational value.

Thinking the use of the apple, the pencil, the eye, the earth, and the relation of their position, form, size, attributes, and parts to their use fixes an essential habit and fundamental form of thought; and thus is something more than a means of gaining a knowledge of these objects. The pupil who can not hold in mind the use of the earth and by this interpret its mathematical relations, and organic parts, may be posted in geography, but is not educated in it, and has missed the best means of cultivating the powers of comprehensive judgment.

The habit of locating definitely an object of thought, whether it be in the field of space or in the field of thought, is as essential to the pupil's mental make-up as it is to the knowledge of the object.

The habit of passing the mind around the form of the object, of intellectually grasping it, of seeing the other and the opposite side of things, is of as much importance as drawing and geometry, which are based on form. Here the pupil gets his first lessons in thinking clearly—in seeing an object as separated and bounded from other objects. Clear thinking goes for much in life. It is characteristic of the strong, accurate mind, and should be cultivated with the utmost care by requiring the pupil to bound every idea with which he deals, whether it be a material object or an emotion of the soul.

The means of discipline is further increased by the relation of whole and part. With this the pupil gets his first training in thinking an object distinctly—in seeing its parts in their mutual relation and in their relation to the whole. This habit ranks with clear thinking, and both are fundamental in the well-trained mind. Is it not essential to the educational process that the teacher consciously train to this habit by the means already thrust upon her? Is she to see nothing in an object lesson on the chair, in which the pupil traces its boundaries, and thinks in order its parts in their spatial and use relation to each other and the whole, but the knowledge which the pupil gets of the chair? Is the pupil to think the parts of an apple in their adaptation of attribute and position to the end of the whole to gain a knowledge of the apple, which he knew before? Object lessons are not given for information, but to make the child's thought definite, to train it how to think, to bring it from vague dream-land and give its thought the form it must take in gaining a knowledge of the world.

A large body of school work consists of individuals changing in time; as, the plant in its development, physiological processes, the story in the reader, movements in history, etc. The form of thinking and the method of treating one of these individuals serves for all.

The prominent feature of the time whole is a change to accomplish a purpose. Change implies time + cause + result. The change consists in a succession of steps, giving the relation of whole and part. The habit of thought cultivated in bounding an event in space and time, and distinguishing its parts, is the same as for the space whole. The peculiar activity here required, and which gives it a special educational value, is the comprehension of a series of changes organically related to a fixed purpose. Indeed, it is by this form of thought that we reach the conception of final cause and watch its struggles upward to realize itself in the true, the beautiful, and the good.

Quite another kind of thinking is required in treating the class, or general nature. The class must be thought as to the content of attributes and extent of individuals, giving rise respectively to the processes of definition and division. In the first, the pupil is required to search for common, essential attributes; and thus cultivate the habit of distinguishing between essentials and non-essentials—a most important habit in any walk of life. In this we pass beyond outer resemblance and come to the essence of things. Yet with this powerful means at hand, and the need of such habits more than knowledge, we yet, either give the definition on faith, or are satisfied with the most inaccurate boundaries of the class defined. This is because we value more a lump of knowledge than mental precision.

In the further study of the class, the pupil is required to search for likeness and difference in the members to find a basis for dividing the extent of the class. With this basis in mind the pupil works out the divisions of the class, comparing and contrasting, and thus carefully discriminating each division from the other on the basis assumed. The habit of accurate discrimination that may be cultivated by this means ought to go for much along with the knowledge gained; yet we ignore it in practice. In dividing the class words into parts of speech, as usually taught, does the pupil work out his basis and determine what classes there must be, and what is the common and differencing attributes in the classes; or does he receive the classes without thinking them? Does he know when the class is exhausted on the basis used; or would he not receive another page of divisions if given to him? And this slipshod work is found wherever the teacher deals with the class—found in spite of our highly functionized school system.

Besides the process of exposition, setting forth the nature of the class, we have the process of argumentation, proving the general proposition. In this the mind is trained to detect the steps that lie between a premise and a conclusion. Training in this has been more satisfactory than with either of the other classes of ideas; yet, we find a strong tendency to reach a conclusion by committing the steps in the argument. This will probably be true as long as conclusions are valued more than the training which may be secured by reasoning out the conclusion, and as long as text-books—especially in algebra and geometry—contain the printed argument for the pupil.

This partial suggestion on the four classes of ideas may indicate what is meant by a plan of carrying out the educational process. This rational process requires a knowledge of these four classes of ideas, and the kind of thinking required to know each; not only that the ideas be fully conveyed, but that certain types of mental habit be formed in connection with each kind of thinking. In presenting any idea the teacher must be immediately conscious of the activity required and know the intellectual value of the habit to be formed. This is a conscious application of ideas to evolve and form the mind; it is the wielding of ideas with a definite purpose.

(To be continued.)

THE SIGNS $+$, $-$, $\times$, $\div$.

N. NEWBY.

1. In finding the sum of several numbers whose symbols are connected by $+$ and $-$ it is immaterial in what order the combinations be made. The numbers may be combined in succession from first to last, from last to first, or the positives may be grouped into one sum, the negatives into another, and these two sums combined for the ultimate result.

2. It is generally agreed that the sign $\times$ or $\div$ takes precedence over $+$ or $-$; thus $3 + 4 \times 2 = 11$. Also $8 - 6 + 2 = 5$, etc.

3. It is not generally agreed, however, in what order the

2

processes indicated by $\times$ and $\div$ shall be performed when $+$ or $-$ does not intervene. Writers on the subject are not agreed upon the result indicated by $12 \div 2 \times 3$. Some announce the result to be 18, while others assert that it is 2.

4. In Algebra two letters (symbols of quantity) written with no sign between them, as ab, are viewed as representing a *product* of which each of the letters is a *factor; i. e.*, the sign $\times$ is understood between them. $a \times b$ and ab are virtually considered as identical expressions. $a \times b \div c$ is, therefore, identical in signification with $ab \div c$; and hence $8 \times 6 \div 3 = 48 \div 3 = 16$. For the same reason $a \div b \times c$ is identical in signification with $a \div bc$; and hence $16 \div 2 \times 4 = 16 \div 8 = 2$. Reasoning from the *general* (algebraic) interpretation to the *particular* (arithmetical), the sign $\times$ is found to take precedence over $\div$.

STATE NORMAL SCHOOL.

Written for the Indiana School Journal.

SCHOOL-TEACHERS.

ROSALIE D. HAMBLEN.

"O, the school-teacher's work, it is easy enough
    For people too lazy to work,
Who have plenty of money and nothing to do
    But hard, honest labor to shirk."
Yet, the parent is willing to go to the field
    And yield up his darling and joy,
To the teacher who as he says "Don't do no good,
    And don't know as much as my boy".

If he's pleasant and gentle and good to the boys,
    "No lickin', no larnin'," they say.
If he brings in the rod and gets threatning and cross
    They take the dear children away.
If in school there's the tales of the good little ones
    "He's pinching," "She's pulling my hair,"
Or, "The boy that you told to stand up on the floor,
    Sat down on his seat over there,"

"He is partial and cross and he can't do the sums!"
    Still, the teacher works faithfully on,
Preparing and filling the mind with rich store
    To be used when life's work is begun.
Patience, teacher, your work's not on deck nor in field,
    Yet an army of minds you command.
The machine that makes judges and fills senate halls
    Is turned by the pedagogue's hand.

CLAYTON, IND.

THE SCHOOL ROOM.

[This Department is conducted by Gzo. F. Bass, Supervising Prin. Indianapolis schools.]

————:o:————

COMPOSITION.

TO be able to write a composition two things are necessary, (1) something to say—facts; (2) ability to say it in written language—compose. In former days some teachers ignored both these requisites. Pupils were simply told that they *must have a composition by next Friday.*

These facts may be obtained through spoken or written language, from pictures, or from the objects themselves. The ability to compose comes by practice—not blind practice. We do *not* learn to do right by practicing the wrong. This practice must be guided by the teacher.

To decide which method to use in obtaining the facts for a composition the following should be considered: age and mental condition of pupils; what the available objects are;—for example, it would be the height of nonsense to send third year pupils to a cyclopedia for facts. If the school is six miles from any library it is hardly practicable for them to visit the library to consult books to obtain facts.

Objects are always to be found and they are cheap. Trees, animals, and inanimate objects are plenty, but it is not always easy to get the object we wish into the school-room. Pictures are good and can be obtained easily. Every teacher can get them without cost. The readers and geographies are full of them. Write descriptions of them. Begin with the lower grades and with simple pictures. In Appleton's Third Reader, p. 64, is a suitable one for third year pupils. The following plan was used in a third grade by a teacher:

The pupils were asked to look at the picture and decide what the picture represents. This is a valuable exercise in itself. Many grown people fail to see what a picture means. These pupils were inclined to say, "It represents a little girl." "It represents five boys and a girl." "It represents winter," etc. By a series of questions the teacher led them to see that the maker of the picture intended to tell us that this little girl is taking a sleigh-ride. The next point they decided was what the chief object of the picture is. (1) The little girl is the chief object. This was written on the board by the teacher. Each of the following statements was obtained from the pupils and written on the board by the teacher: (2) She is sitting in a sled. (3) It is a small sled. (4) It is a hand-sled. Pupils were then asked to put the four statements—facts—into one sentence without using the word and. Quite a variety of sentences were written. The chief object of this picture is a little girl riding in a small hand-sled.

(To be continued.)

"I DON'T THINK SO."

"JAMES, who has been there, knows what they should do." The pupil is asked to tell the kinds of pronouns and give the case of each.

Pupil. *Who* is a personal pronoun.

Tr. "I don't think so."

Pu. Who is a relative pronoun.

Now, if the teacher had said "I don't think so," the pupil would have said "Interrogative." But he didn't say so. He said, "Yes, why do you call it a relative pronoun?" If the pupil had dared to answer honestly he would have said, "Because you would not let me call it a personal pronoun." He did *not* answer this way. He said, "It is a relative pronoun because it relates to some preceding word, and connects clauses." The words that follow *because* form the last part of the definition in the book used. Now this seems all right, but a few questions might have developed the fact that all this pupil had been 'doing' was learning things to say. Ask such as follows:

Does it relate to a word, or words? Tell what word or words it relates to. What clauses does it connect? Why is it not a personal pronoun?

"Who is in the nominative case." Why? "Because it is the subject of a sentence." "What sentence?" Pupil gives the whole sentence, thereby showing that he does not understand case. The teacher says, "I don't think so." The pupil attempts to make some change, but blunders more and more. Teacher asks "What is the subject of *knows?*" Pupil is led to think, "What is it that knows?" The answer readily comes, "James."

"What verb is who the subject of?" "Has been." "What sentence is it subject of?" "Who has been there." It is evident that the pupil guessed that who is used in the nominative case, and then undertook to guess a reason for its use. "I don't think so" will not correct his error. Correct questioning *will* lead him into proper habits of thinking.

"SHALL WE ADD OR SUBTRACT?"

"Two persons start from the same place and travel in different directions; one travels at the rate of 20 miles an hour, and the other at the rate of 35 miles an hour. How far apart will they be in 9 hours?"

The above example sometimes brings the question at the head of this article. The *easiest* thing for the teacher to do is to tell the pupil *what* to do. "Add 20 miles and 35 miles and multiply the sum by 9."

But this does not strengthen the pupil's power to interpret the conditions of the problem presented to him. He should be *led* to see what he must do. He then learns to interpret by interpreting, not by "doing something else."

Ask questions that he can answer by an intelligent reading of the example. How far did the first person mentioned travel in one day? How far did the second travel? How far were they apart at the close of the first day? How do you find how far apart they are? How many times this distance will they be apart at the end of 9 days? How do you find 9 times any number? Do not insist upon a set form of analysis. If more of this kind of work were done and less of the so-called "analyzing" of the division of one fraction by another, we would have better thinkers in the upper grades.

A whole recitation may sometimes be profitably spent on one problem. There seems to be a feeling among some teachers that *ten* examples must be explained at each recitation. Make haste slowly. Teach for the sake of the pupil, not for the sake of the problems.

PRIMARY DEPARTMENT.

[This Department is conducted by Lewis H. Jones, Supt. Indianapolis Schools]

——:x:——

PRIMARY LANGUAGE.

WHEN pupils are able to distinguish "telling sentences," "asking sentences," "exclaiming sentences," and "commanding sentences," one from another, as indicated in the preceding article of this series, they are ready for intelligent practice in the use of each in familiar discourse, written and oral. Pupils in the latter half of the second year in school, or the first half of the third year, can easily write the answers to simple questions written on the board by the teacher, or can easily fulfill some simple written direction in the construction of short sentences classified as above. After all, it is constant *practice* in the *use* of language, under judicious criticism, that gives accuracy and facility in speech; and these two qualities of style are fundamental to the superstructure of elegant utterance which the student rears only in the later years of his school life.

While engaged in securing this practice, oral and written, with the language forms already learned, the wide-awake teacher will usually involve some one new point; thus engaging the interest by the new element, and securing practice in the old with the new. Thus pupils of the age referred to in this article need to know how to spell and capitalize the days of the week and the months of the year. At the time devoted to the language lesson on some particular day, then, she may teach the spelling of the name of each day of the week. At the time devoted by the same class to the study of language, she may direct the attention of pupils to that part of the blackboard on which she has written plainly such requirements as these :

1. Make a telling sentence about the third day of the week.
2. Ask something about the seventh day of the week.
3. What day of the week is to-day?

In a similar way the names of the months, as soon as their spelling and meaning have been taught, may be involved in the practice upon classes of sentences.   If the above work seems a little difficult for written work at first, the teacher has only to give an oral exercise or two on the giving of sentences and the answering of such questions; then the writing may follow as review of what was said orally in the recitation.

The possibilities of this work broaden rapidly when once it is rightly begun.   The difference in spelling and use of a word in the different grammatical numbers and cases will give innumerable opportunities for varying the exercise.   At first the work is a spelling lesson.   "Spell the word cat so as to make it mean more than one."   "What is the form of the word bird that means but one and shows ownership?"   Child spells.   "That means more than one, and shows ownership?"   The proper placing of the apostrophe is of course a part of the spelling; but as the use of the apostrophe is closely united to the meaning of the word in a definite use, the work is not completed until pupils have learned to place each word in all its forms into appropriate sentences.

A pupil that has correctly filled the blank in, "The (horses') manes are long," will fail when asked to fill the blank in, "All (horses) have manes," unless his attention has been called to the fact that "have" in the last sentence shows the ownership, and hence the apostrophe is not needed.

It is evident that what is most needed here is much practice in the use of these words, properly spelled, in appropriate sentences.

BEGINNING LONG DIVISION.

MOLLIE SMITH.

So MANY teachers have trouble with beginners in division that I will give my method of teaching it, in hopes that it will prove a benefit to some one else.

First give your pupils small numbers, as $\frac{8}{2}$; $\frac{12}{3}$; showing them that by this we mean eight can be divided into two equal parts, each of which will contain four, or that four can be taken away from eight twice. Be sure to teach the names of the terms dividend, divisor, and quotient, and why so called.

After they can divide numbers that are contained an even number of times, take some with a remainder, as, 19|4; 24|4; show them as before that 19 can be divided into three equal parts, each of which will contain six, with one odd one, which we will call a remainder.

The next step is to give them examples of three or more figures, as, 216|2; 480|4. A careful teacher can easily have a class understand the *why* of these various steps by a few judicious questions.

If the class have properly mastered the different steps given, they will have no trouble with larger divisors, and you may give them such examples as, 240[16; 469[21; 786[30; and a few in which the quotient will contain a cipher, as, 1863[9. You can now gradually enlarge both dividend and divisor, and you will be surprised at the advancement your pupils will make.

I am sure this method of taking one step at a time (and that thoroughly) is so much easier, more thorough, and consequently more pleasant than to assign the examples in the text-books and tell the pupils to "follow the rules," that I cordially commend it.

DEPARTMENT OF PEDAGOGY.

This Department is conducted by GEO. P. BROWN, President State Normal School.

——:o:——

BOOKS AND READING.

IN a previous article a distinction was made between what has been called the "literature of power" and the "literature of knowledge." We will now consider briefly the different sources from which our literature has sprung.

There are as many departments of literature as there are of human activity:

1. Man is an intelligent being. As such he has accumulated in books a vast store of knowledge. Some of these contain mere statements of fact. They give "information" which may

serve as data for conclusions, but are not so employed. Others are books of science. They arrange the discovered facts under some law and explain them by referring them to the principle from which they originated. Others still, are books of philosophy. They deal with the principles of the different sciences and explain them by referring them to one first and absolute principle that is the source of all that is. These all belong to "the literature of knowledge," but the second and third classes of books belong also to the literature of power. It is through scientific and philosophic study that the intellectual powers are developed, and man is able to rise to a mastery of his environment.

2. Man is also an emotional being. Because of this element in his nature he has produced many books on religion, ethics, and fine art; besides innumerable productions in sculpture, painting, and architecture. Literature as a fine art is what is meant by the term "literature" when contrasted with the terms "science" and "history." Science expresses what man has *known*. Fine art is this *knowledge* "touched with the emotion" of the beautiful, and expressed in a beautiful form. Because of the influence of emotion upon the will, literature as a fine art was called by De Quincy "the literature of power."

3. Man is a being that wills. That department of literature that best displays the activity of this element of his nature is history. History recounts the deeds of men. Science and literature recount the thoughts and emotions of man; history makes known to us his deeds. Thus we have the inner and the outer man portrayed.

He who would lay claim to any degree of literary culture and have that claim allowed, must have some acquaintance with the literature of these three departments.

It is the purpose of this paper to name a few books in the departments of Literature and History that will serve to introduce the reader, who needs introduction, to these two realms. The general method observed is to begin with what is near and proceed to what is more remote.

Of American Literature the representative prose authors are

Hawthorne and Emerson, while Longfellow, Bryant and Lowell may be considered representative poets.

English prose Literature may be divided into Essays and Novels. The essays of Macauley, Carlyle, Matthew Arnold, and Addison are especially valuable, while the novels of Walter Scott, George Elliott, Thackeray and Dickens represent four great types of fiction. The English poets suggested are Tennyson, Wordsworth and Shakespeare. The student should read with these the twenty little volumes entitled English Men of Letters, and Shakespeare should be read with the aid of the commentaries of Mr. Denton J. Snyder, who has greater insight into true literary criticism than any man in America, in the opinion of many competent judges.

History may be divided into history proper and biography. In history proper it is suggested that in addition to some good school text-book on the History of the United States, the United States of Freeman's Historical Course be read together with the series of volumes known as the American Statesmen series. Another series known as the Epoch series should also be at hand to be read with the other histories of the times of which they treat. Green's Short History of England may be followed by Justin McCarty's History of Our Own Times. Carlyle's French Revolution, Liddell's History of Rome, and Smith's or Curtius's History of Greece, followed by Hegel's Philosophy of History will make a good preparation for the great books in history beginning with Herodotus.

Every teacher should read, also, a history of Educational Theories. Probably Browning's, published by Harper Bros., and Quick's Educational Reformers, are the best of the small books.

Biographies of persons prominent and influential in giving direction to affairs of State or in Art or in Education should be read with the history of the time of each. Among the many excellent books are Irving's Life of Washington, Carlyle's Life of Cromwell, Irving's Life of Columbus, Plutarchs' Lives, Grimm's Life of Goethe, Grimm's Life of Michael Angelo, Dean Stanley's Life of Dr. Thomas Arnold, and the Life of Horace Mann.

The greatest of all books is the Bible, which should be studied not alone for the inspiration and guidance it gives in matters of religion, but for its history and literature. One of the best companion books to study along with it is Clark's History of Ten Great Religions.

This course is elementary and partial, but if carefully and diligently pursued it will do much toward arousing to activity the literary and historical spirit, and giving one the power to determine his own further course.   G. P. B.

IS THE GRUBE METHOD OF NUMBER UNPHILO-SOPHICAL?

By which is meant, is the Grube Method one that is unfitted to the minds of children that are beginning to learn to combine numbers? This is an important question in this State, for this method is in use substantially in a large number of primary schools. It is claimed that it is unphilosophical for the reason that it proposes to teach together two different relations of numbers; to-wit, the *part* relation and the *factor* relation.

It is claimed, moreover, that these relations are fundamentally different, giving rise to fundamentally different processes. That addition deals with the part relation of numbers, while multiplication deals with the factor relation, which is so different from the part relation that they have nothing in common. If this is true, then that feature of the Grube Method which teaches the four processes together should be discontinued for the reason that the child can best learn one thing at a time. This does not forbid the teaching of addition and subtraction together, for subtraction is involved in addition. If I know that 3 and 5 are 8, I must know that 3 from 8 leaves 5.

But we are taught by authority the most excellent in the opinion of all of us, that the process, 3 and 3 are 6, is fundamentally different from the process 2 times 3 are 6. That the latter process is not involved in the former; which means that I may know that 3 and 3 make 6 without knowing that 2 times 3 are 6, because the one is a process resulting from considering the part

relation of numbers, while the other results from the consideration of the factor relation of number, which is a relation not involved in the part relation, but is fundamentally different. I
think we will all agree that if this is true we should at once abandon the teaching of the four arithmetical processes together in
the beginning of number study. Hence the practical importance of a proper solution of this question.

Before much progress can be made toward a satisfactory answer it will be necessary to define clearly what is meant by the
factor relation.

When I am asked to add 5 to 7 I understand that both 5 and
7 must unite to make the sum. I may be so unpracticed in the
use of numbers that I have to add 5 to 7 by adding one at a time,
or counting. This is the mere alphabet of addition. Practice
in combining numbers enables me to see 12 immediately as the
sum of these two numbers. I may learn by frequent repetition that 7 and 5 are 12, and I remember it so perfectly that
when the sum of 7 and 5 is asked for, the number 12 presents
itself at once. I am not conscious of counting, and if I do actually count, the process is instantaneous, without effort, and
performed unconsciously.

When I am asked to multiply 7 by 5, what should I understand by it? Am I to think that 7 and 5 both enter into and
"compose" the product? I think not. The number 5 does
not enter into the product in any way. It stands to the mind
simply as the indicator or sign of the number of 7's that are to
be taken. It seems as if 5 times 7 in its most natural and most
evident signification means that 7 is taken 5 times. The product is "composed" of a number of 7's only. The number
5 merely indicates how many of these 7's shall compose it. The
factor relation of numbers would seem to be that they are so related to each other that one of them, called the multiplier, stands
as the indicator of the number of times the other, called the multiplicand, is to be taken. The amount resulting from thus repeating the multiplicand is the product.

Now I may be so unpracticed in this combination of numbers
that I have to think the process thus: 7–14–21–28–35. This

is counting by 7's, or the continuous addition of the same number. When I have memorized the fact that 7 taken 5 times is 35, then, when 7 and 5 are united in the mind under this factor relation,—or the idea of multiplication,—the number 35 immediately presents itself.

The alphabet of multiplication is the adding of equal numbers. But multiplication proper is the use of the sums of groups of equal numbers that have been stored up in the memory.

It may be said that when I multiply 225 by 24 the process is fundamentally different from what it is when I add twenty-four 225's together. But the difference is more apparent than real. If I had learned the multiplication table to 24 times 225 I think there could be no question but that the multiplying of 225 by 24 would be merely the calling up in the memory of the sum of 225 taken 24 times. But not knowing the multiplication table so far I break up my multiplier and multiplicand into parts so small that I can make use of the table of sums of equal numbers that I have learned.

I divide the 225 into 200, 20, and 5, and the 24 into 20 and 4; or in actual practice I consider simply the numbers 2 and 2 and 5 in the multiplicand, and the numbers 2 and 4 in the multiplier, and rely upon a mechanical placing of the different products and their subsequent addition to secure the proper result.

From this analysis it would seem that the processes of multiplication and addition are not fundamentally different but are fundamentally the same, and that they can be taught together without violating any fundamental law of teaching.   G. P. B.

THE NEW IN THE OLD.

* * * * The model teacher of all time, was the humble Nazarene carpenter. He taught as one who saw, and therefore with authority. Socrates, Plato and Aristotle were his great predecessors. Many who have followed him have discovered his "secret and his method," and have become great in consequence. Nothing essentially new has been discovered in recent times. Educational reformers, ancient and modern, agree substantially as to the purpose and method of education.

A more analytic knowledge of the mind to be trained, and of the matter to be used in the training, has led to a more analytic knowledge of the method to be pursued. The teacher of the present ought to be able to see more *distinctly* than did the teacher of the past, both the *what* and the *how* of his teaching; but his function is the same as that announced by Socrates,—"to assist at the birth of souls",—and in essentially the same way.

The race has not been suffering all these years from want of educational seers. It has had them in every age. The want has been in its ability to see what its seers unfolded. Some one has said that "it takes a long time to get a great idea into the heads of the race." There are so many little Socrateses and Comeniuses now at work driving into the heads of the people the great idea of these great teachers, that there is greater hope than ever before that it may come to prevail. Each one has his little hammer fashioned after his own peculiar notion, that he wields in his own way, which he may have christened "New Education," perhaps, but they are all driving away at the same idea. It will come to prevail more and more, provided the workmen do not get to quarrelling over the fashion of their hammers, and the peculiar sweep of their blows.

The great idea is that education is the process of the birth of a soul. When a soul has been well born in the Socratic sense, all will have been done for it that education can do. It is well born when it has been raised from the dominance of sense into that of reason.

This process has its side of *knowledge* and its side of *doing*. The child must be taught both to know and to do. And since conduct is three-fourths of life, the great importance of learning to do is evident. There is a much-quoted saying of the old masters current in these times, that "one is to learn to do by doing." This would scarcely be recognized by Comenius in the use to which it is put by some of us moderns. He evidently wished to emphasize the fact that the true process of knowledge is a double-sided one. The error that he combated, was that *knowledge* is education. Doing is the other side of the process, and each side is necessary to the existence of the other.   G. P. B.

The "open winter" has "compassed us on every side."

EDITORIAL.

W. A. BELL, Editor-in-Chief and Proprietor.

GEO. P. BROWN, Pres State Normal School, Associate Editor and Editor of the Department of Pedagogy.

LEWIS H. JONES, Superintendent of Indianapolis Schools, and Editor of the Primary Department.

GEO. F. BASS, Supervising Principal Indianapolis Schools, and Critic in Training School, Editor of The School Room Department.

A. W. BRAYTON, Prof. of Natural Science in the Indianapolis Schools, is Editor of the Popular Science Department.

Prof E. E. WHITE, Ohio; Prof. E. E. SMITH, Purdue University; HUBERT M. SKINNER, Chief Clerk Dept. of Public Instruction; JAS. BALDWIN, Supt. Schools Rushville; HOWARD SANDISON, W. W. PARSONS, and MICHAEL SEILER, of State Normal School; EMMA MONT. MCRAE, Principal Marion High School; H. S. TARBELL, late Supt. of the Indianapolis Schools, are frequent contributors.

Many other able writers contribute occasional articles to the JOURNAL. Should all those be enrolled as "Contributing Editors" who contribute one article or more a year the list could be indefinitely extended.

This large list of special editors and able contributors insures for the readers of the JOURNAL the best, the freshest, the most practical thoughts and methods in all departments of school work.

The Miscellaneous and Personal Departments of the Journal will not be neglected, but it places special emphasis on its large amount of unequaled practical and helpful educational articles.

Persons sending money for this Journal can send amounts less than $1 in *two* and *one* cent postage stamps; no others can be used.

In asking to have the address of your Journal changed, please give the *old* address as well as the new, naming the county as well as the state.

An agent is wanted to raise a club for the Journal in every township in the State. Send for terms.

In connection with the report of the address of Col Parker on "Learning to do by doing," printed on another page, it will be worth while to turn to the February Journal and read what Mr. Brown says on the same subject.

A REMINDER.—A few of the readers of the Journal have not yet had their names transferred to the "paid" list. Will not this general "reminder" be sufficient?

THE NEW ORLEANS EXPOSITION is in full blast. Persons who have seen both claim that this far exceeds in extent and intereest that of the Centennial Exposition at Philadelphia. Rates by river and by rail are low, and thousands are taking this opportunity to visit the South and the Crescent City. March 16th is fixed upon as Indiana's Day at the exposition.

THE SCHOOL TROUBLE AT SHELBYVILLE.

Owing to certain statements that have been extensively circulated through the papers, affecting the conduct of W. H Fertich as superintendent of the Shelbyville schools, the Journal feels that justice to Mr. Fertich calls for the following presentation of the case:

Mr. Mitchner, a prominent citizen of the place, has sued Mr. Fertich for $2000 damages, and, in his complaint, alleges that on a cold morning, when the mercury in the thermometer showed 18 degrees below zero, his daughter reached the school house a few minutes late and was refused admission, and being compelled to return home for an excuse froze her feet and otherwise suffered greatly. The complaint affirms that the rule is oppressive and the treatment inexcusable, etc., and hence the damages asked.

The newspapers taking for granted that the bill of complaint in court was entirely true, not only published the allegations but gave vent to commentaries that were not at all complimentary to either the good sense or humanity of the superintendent, and in addition took occasion to rail at the "system" in the public schools.

As the trial has not yet taken place the defense has not been published, but the Journal is assured from a reliable source that Mr. Fertich will prove that he was not in the building at the time referred to, but at another school building, looking after the comfort of the children ; that the door of the school-room was locked during opening exercises, but that the hall was provided with a good heater and at that time was at a temperature of from 60 to 65 degrees; that the superintendent's office was open and warm, and accessible to tardy pupils; that the girl in returning home did so without the knowledge or consent of either her teacher or the superintendent, and in so doing violated a positive rule of the school ; that the rule concerning tardiness was in force many years before Mr. Fertich was made superintendent, and that it is not arbitrarily enforced

This statement is made without Mr. Fertich's knowledge or suggestion, but as a matter of justice, as his side of the case should certainly go with the other.

All school regulations are made for ordinary conditions, and a teacher who has enough common sense to teach a decent school will have sense enough to disregard a rule when an extraordinary condition of things demands it.

If Mr. Fertich has been guilty of deliberately sending a child home for an excuse under the circumstances narrated, he should be made to pay the fine, and be not only dismissed from his place, but ruled out of the profession ; but if entirely innocent of all such charges, as the Journal is compelled to believe until he is *proved* guilty, then he is entitled to the sympathy of his fellow-teachers, and they should take pains to vindicate his good name.

THE TEACHERS' READING CIRCLE.

The Educational Weekly, in its issue of February 14th, contains
an article on the Reading Circle, filled with false accusations and
base insinuations, and does gross injustice to the board of directors.
That no injustice may be done by misinterpretation, the language of
The Weekly is given verbatim. After preliminary remarks in regard
to the Circle it says:

"Several features have unfortunately crept into the organization
which were not contemplated by those who first suggested the propriety of such an organization. It was not at first contemplated that
the directors should be paid for their services, and we are still of the
opinion that they should not be, for there are plenty of competent
teachers in the state who would be very willing to make out the Outlines gratuitously. It was not at first contemplated that there should
be an annual squabble for position on the board of directors, as was
witnessed at the State Association last winter. It was expected that
after *kind solicitation,* enough *pro bono publico* spirit among the
teachers of the state could be found to fill up the board, and by
"taking turns" it would not prove burdensome to any. It was not
intended that the Teachers' Reading Circle should carry "loaves
and fishes" to be sought as a prize, nor yet that its honors should be
trampled upon.

That members of the board should have their legitimate expenses
paid, while devoting their time exclusively to the work of the Circle,
is not objectionable, provided there be means secured in a proper
way to defray their expenses. But in a voluntary association, made
expressly for the *mutual* benefit of the members thereof, we do not
see clearly by what authority, other than by common consent, a fixed
tax is levied upon the membership by the board, nor yet by what law
of apportionment any money thus collected is distributed among the
members of the board," etc.

How it is possible in the same space to do greater injustice to a
body of honorable, high minded, self sacrificing people, is hard to
imagine. The board is composed of J. J. Mills, President of Earlham College; R. G. Boone, Supt. Frankfort schools; Emma Mont.
McRae, Prin. Marion high school; Mattie Curl Dennis, teacher in
Earlham College; H. B. Hill, Supt. Dearborn county; John C. Macpherson, Supt. Wayne county; Hubert M. Skinner, chief clerk of the
State Superintendent; and Geo. P. Brown, President State Normal
School.

Other persons as capable and as honorable doubtless could have
been selected, but it is hardly possible that a more reliable, more
trustworthy board could have been named. Individually and col-
lectively they stand even above suspicion, and yet this article *insin-*

3

nates that they are without authority imposing a tax that it may be "distributed among the members of the board," and that Mr. Brown and Mrs. McRae "squabbled" to retain their places on the board for the sake of the "loaves and fishes."

Now the facts are these:

(1) The State Association *empowered* this board to organize a Reading Circle, which was done, fixing a fee of 25 cents for *necessary* expenses. The power to organize and conduct the Circle carries with it the power to pay necessary expenses.

(2) The organization has taken a vast deal of work—the keeping of the records; the receiving of moneys and keeping an account thereof; the overseeing of orders; the answering of innumerable letters of inquiry, etc., etc. The most of this work has necessarily fallen upon Mr. Skinner, the secretary, and for it the directors have voted him the enormous sum of $25, not half what it is worth.

Aside from this not one cent has been paid to any member of the board for services. In the organization it was absolutely necessary to meet and determine the details of the plan, select books, etc. In such cases actual expenses and nothing more were paid. The *insinuation* that members are paid for making out the "outlines" of study is utterly groundless, as not one cent has ever been paid for such work and no one doing the work has ever thought of charging for it.

If *The Weekly* did not know the above facts before publishing its libelous article, it was inexcusably ignorant, for they were near at hand and could have been had for the asking. No correction it can now make will undo the wrong it has inflicted upon the board, and the check it has given the circle. There was no shadow of excuse for the article.

SUPERINTENDENCY OF SCHOOLS.—It is now generally conceded, not only by teachers but by all, that wise supervision is absolutely essential to the highest efficiency of schools, both county and city. It has been many years since even old fogies have objected to supervision in cities; so it is almost startling to read in *The Educational World*, edited by Walter Sayler, Prin. of the Normal School at Logansport, that a superintendent is a "figure-head." It predicts that in the future schools "will not be under the tyrannical supervision of that 'figure-head' known as 'The Superintendent.' If the school board of a town or city would look after the interests of the school, instead of paying a large salary to a pompous, narrow-minded superintendent, we believe that much better results would be obtained."

This is pernicious doctrine, and certainly can not find support in Indiana in this advanced stage of its educational progress.

GEOGRAPHICAL.—At this writing, February 23d, Lake Michigan is frozen from shore to shore opposite Milwaukee, a condition never before known.

THE REPORT of the State Superintendent contains the complete Outlines of Reading Circle work for all the months preceding this issue. Teachers who are late joining the Circle, and those who have mislaid their Outlines or who failed to obtain them, will be thus enabled to make up the work and go on without interruption. Mr. Skinner's Outlines on History are supplied for the missing months in the report, and will also be found in this issue of the Journal.

COMPLIMENTARY.—The Journal does not often intrude upon its readers what its friends say of it, and begs pardon for presenting the following, which is a sample of many others:

MR. W. A. BELL—*Dear Sir:* I want to take a few moments of your time—just enough in which to express my appreciation of the Indiana School Journal. The last number seems to be about the best. The articles are well calculated to raise the standard of teaching. We need such articles to keep before us the fact that teaching may be and must be a profession. The Journal is doing much not only to impress that fact, but to lead the teachers to make greater efforts to advance toward the ideal set forth.   * * *

The above is especially appreciated as it comes from one of the best city superintendents in the state, who is a comparative stranger to the editor.

QUESTIONS AND ANSWERS.

QUESTIONS BY THE STATE BOARD FOR JANUARY.

THEORY OF TEACHING.—1. Show that discrimination is the mental activity first employed in learning.

2. What are the products in knowledge resulting from discrimination?

3. State three of the principal laws of memory that the teacher needs to regard.

4. What is method? What is a natural method?

5. What is the value of a knowledge of diacritical marks in learning to read?

ORTHOGRAPHY.—1. What is the distinction between a vocal and a sub-vocal? Name 5 of each.   2 pts, 5 each

2. Write the possessive plural of man, sky, rogue, valley, and ally.

3. Spell another word that is the same in pronunciation as each of the follow ng: faint, write, claws, hoard, row, ring, straight, isle, rain, and slay.

4. What is the difference between a diphthong and a digraph? Illustrate each by two words. 2 pts, 6, 4

5. Define orthœpy and orthography. 2 pts, 5 each

6. Spell ten words dictated by the superintendent 10 pts, 5 each

PHYSIOLOGY.—1. (a) Should we eat when tired? (b) Give reasons. a=3, b=7

2. What is Human Physiology?

3 Describe a cell.

4. What organs are protected by the skull?

5. Name two great purposes of the bones. 2 pts, 5 each

6. Describe the brain, with diagram.

7. What is the relation of the nerves to the will?

8. What is the function of the skin?

9. (a) What is the best mode of cooking meat? (b) Why?
a=4, b=6

10. Why should underclothing be kept clean and frequently changed?

GEOGRAPHY.—1. Define climate and give four of the chief causes of variations of temperature.

2. Contrast the Gulf States with those of the Great Lakes as to agricultural products, and account for any differences that may be found.

3. What is a zone? Name the zones.

4. Name ten of the leading agricultural products of the United States.

.5. Name the provinces that compose the Dominion of Canada. Name the capital of the Dominion.

6. Name the two principal seaports of the west coast of South America.

7. Name the five largest rivers in Europe.

8. Name the Greater Antilles, and tell to what nation each belongs.

9. What are three agricultural products of China?

10. Name the most important British possessions in Africa.

GRAMMAR.—1. State what the underscored words in the following sentences modify: (a) He is speaking *positively*.
(b) He, *positively*, is speaking.

2. Write a sentence that shall contain all the different kinds of modifiers which the subject of a sentence may have. Designate.

3. Class the following sentences both as to form and meaning:
(*a*) With heaven who can contend?
(*b*) Thou shalt not kill
(*c*) You are not gone yet.

4. What is the order of the elements in the declarative sentence? What in the interrogative?

5. Write a simple sentence containing nouns used in four different constructions.

6. Into what three general classes can the different parts of speech be grouped? What are the sub-classes under each general class?

7. Explain and illustrate the difference between an abridged compound sentence and a simple sentence having a compound element.

8. Punctuate the following, giving reasons:

(*a*) The benevolent man is esteemed the penurious despised.

(*b*) There is good for the good there is virtue for the faithful there is victory for the valiant.

9. What classes of words join adjective clauses to the words they modify? Illustrate.

10. State the office performed by each subordinate clause in the following:

(*a*) It is certain that he went.

(*b*) The report, it is said, is false.

(*c*) We are told that an open sea surrounds the pole.

ARITHMETIC. — 1. What is domestic exchange? Foreign exchange? 5, 5

2. The principal, time, and interest being given, how find the rate per cent?

3. If from a flock of 1200 sheep $\frac{1}{4}$ were sold at one time, and $\frac{1}{5}$ of the remainder at another, what per cent. of the flock was sold?

proc 4. ans. 6

4. How many bushels of wheat will fill a bin 8 ft. long, 5 ft. wide, and 4 ft. deep? proc. 4. ans. 6

5. A and B can do a piece of work in 12 days, B and C in 9 days, A and C in 6 days; how long will it take each alone to do it? 4. 3. 3

6. How many gallons of water will a cistern contain which is 7 feet long, 6 feet wide, and 11 feet deep? proc. 6. ans. 4

7. If a man walk 2044 rods in $\frac{7}{15}$ of an hour, at that rate how far will he walk in $1\frac{1}{2}$ hours?

8. The length of a wall, by a measuring line, was 543 ft. 8 in., but the line was found to be 25 ft. 5.25 in long, instead of 25 ft., its supposed length; what was the true length of the wall? Solve by proportion. Statement 5, ans 5

9 A room is 20 ft. long, 16 ft. wide, and 12 ft. high; what is the distance from one of the lower corners to the opposite upper corner?

10 The side of a cubical vessel is 1 foot; find the side of another cubical vessel that shall contain 3 times as much.

PENMANSHIP.—1.   How many kinds of lines are used in writing?
Define each.

2.   What is meant by a head line?   By a base line?   By a top
line?

3.   What is meant by main slant?   Connecting slant?

4.   Name the principles from which the capital letters are formed.

5.   Analyze h, u, m, A, U.

NOTE.—Your writing in answering these questions will be taken as a specimen of your
penmanship, and will be marked 90 or below, according to merit.

READING.—1.   To what extent and for what purpose would you
use the word method?

2.   Give two essential characteristics of good oral reading.
2 pts, 5 each

3.   Name and define two kinds of emphasis.   2 pts, 5 each

4.   What is silent reading, and how may the ability of pupils to
read silently be cultivated?   4, 6

5.   Write a sentence which asks a question and requires the falling
inflection.

6.   Read a paragraph of prose and a stanza of poetry selected by
the superintendent.   2 pts, 25 each

U. S. HISTORY.—1.   What four European nations principally settled North America?   Which of them most largely settled the present territory of the United States?   5, 5

2.   Name two events, important for this country, that took place
in 1732.   5, 5

3.   What were the general views entertained by the English Parliament as to the relations borne by the colonies to the mother
country?   10

4.   What was the "American Association?"   What was its connection with the Declaration of Independence?   5, 5

5.   What naval officer proved of great service to Washington?
In what American novel are his exploits celebrated?   5, 5

6.   What was Dean Tucker's remedy for the rebellion of the colonies?   What would have been the probable result of its adoption? 5, 5

7.   How was the war of 1812 terminated?   What was the pecu-
arity of the document?   What was the advantage to the U. S.? 3, 3, 4

8.   What three clauses of the Constitution destroy all ground for
the rebellion of the Southern States?   10

9.   Why did Sherman say that he would furnish Hood with rations
to march on Nashville?   10

10.   What was the peculiar position of Tennessee in the reconstruction of the South?   What act led to the impeachment of President Johnson?   5, 5

ANSWERS TO STATE BOARD QUESTIONS PRINTED IN FEBRUARY.

READING.—1. It is well to give some attention to the authorship of selections in teaching reading—more or less as the circumstances may suggest—because pupils receive hints as to who are standard writers and what are standard writings. Often a pupil will be pleased with a selection, look up the book from which it is taken, and thus begin a series of incidental reading that may be of much advantage.

2. Occasional concert reading may be pleasant as a variety, may encourage timid pupils, may aid some in getting certain expressions which they would not otherwise get, or may be useful as a general oral drill.

3. The purpose of punctuation is simply to show the grammatical relations and logical dependence of the various parts of discourse. It is chiefly valuable in silent reading.

4. The dictionary may be used in ascertaining the correct pronunciation of words, as also of letters. With pupils in the Second or Third Reader classes, there is danger in the use of the dictionary unless under the immediate supervision and direction of the teacher. The meanings of words become confounded. With older pupils, the various meanings and synonyms may be compared and discriminations made, etc.

5. The methods most common in teaching primary reading are the phonic, the alphabetic, the word, and the combined. The latter is preferred, as thereby the weakness of one may be supplemented by the strength of some other. One thus has the advantage of all.

PHYSIOLOGY.·· 1. Healthful clothing should fit the body comfortably, but not so closely at any point as to interfere with the normal action of any organ. It should also protect best those parts of the body which are most liable to be affected by changes of the atmosphere.

2. The sympathetic nervous system consists, primarily, of a double chain of ganglia and connecting nerves extending on both sides of the spinal column from the base of the brain to the coccyx. There are twenty-four pairs of ganglia, the two chains uniting in the forty-ninth ganglia at the coccyx. Secondly, the nerves branching off from these ganglia communicate with the cranial and the spinal nerves, and also pass to various organs of the body.

3. Nerves of sensation differ from nerves of motion in that the former transmit impressions from the nerve termini to the nerve centers, and the latter transmit volitions or reflections from the centers to the termini.

5. Voluntary muscles are those which act when directly stimulated by the will; involuntary muscles act automatically. Exam-

ples: of the former, the biceps, the triceps, the gastrocuenims. etc.; of the latter, the heart and the diaphragm; of the two combined, the muscles of the eye-lids.

6. Variety of food is pleasant because there is a variety, and also because no one article of food contains materials for all the tissues of a mature body.

9. The nerves are protected: (1) by their location; (2) by the sheaths in which they are enclosed.

10. The teeth ought to be kept clean at all times, as the accumulations of food between them cause fermentation and decay; because it tends to cause one to have a less offensive breath, and because it saves bills and pains at the dentist's.

U. S. HISTORY.—1. (*a*) The Norsemen (*b*) The English under the command of John Cabot.

2. (*a*) Ponce de Leon. (*b*) Partly in honor of the day of discovery, Pascua Florida, and partly to describe the wealth of vegetation. (*c*) Mortally wounded by an Indian arrow, he died in Cuba, 1521.

3. To establish plantations in America, and to form colonies without the hope of christianizing the natives.

4. The English government attempted by law to control and restrict the trade and manufactures of the colonies. The Writs of Assistance, the Stamp Act, the Boston Port Bill and other tyrannical measures aroused the colonists to indignant remonstrance. To the protest of the Continental Congress against the quartering of soldiers among the colonists the King returned a contemptuous denial, and despairing of receiving any just recognition of rights from the English government, the Declaration of Independence was passed.

5. Instead of succumbing to defeat, Washington, by his energy and strategic skill, won brilliant victories, that inspired the soldiers with new courage, and revived the hopes of the country.

6. At first, by individuals; after Burgoyne surrendered, the French government became an open ally of America.

7. Burr formed a treasonable scheme, whose object was to raise a military force, invade Mexico, and separate the Southwestern States from the Union. He was suspected, arrested and tried, but was acquitted "for want of sufficient proof."

8. (*a*) "The Republican party was born in Michigan, on the 6th day of July, 1854."—*Zach. Chandler*. (*b*) To prevent the extension of slavery, and to "battle for the first principles of the Republic."

9. The peculiar feature of Lee's surrender was the liberality of the *terms*. Officers and men, having given their word of honor to fight no more against the United States, were permitted to return to their homes.

10. The liberties of the Georgia colonists were greatly restricted

by the trustees under the charter. At last, wearied by the complaints of the colonists, the trustees surrendered their charter to the crown.

GRAMMAR.—1. The first completes the meaning of the predicate. The second is used as an adjective and modifies the noun *charms.*

2. *Who* is generally preferred to *that* in explanatory clauses.

. 3. (*a*) Who do you suppose it is? (You do suppose it is *who.*) *Who* is nominative after *is.* (*b*) "It was supposed to be *he,*" is correct. (*c*) It was Paul, *he* who wrote the epistle; "he" must be in the same case as "Paul."

5. (*a*) "Gurgling" is used adjectively and modifies the noun "Ayr." (*b*) This sentence may mean: John, *who was tired,* did not go; or, John did not go, *because he was tired.* According to the first sentence, *being* has an adjective force, modifying John. In the second sentence it expresses cause, and modifies *did go.* (*c*) The messenger came running, *running* has the force of an adverb of manner, modifying *came.*

6. (*a*) The sentence is correct. (*b*) This is a supposition contrary to the fact, and the subjunctive is required in the conditional clause. The sentence should read, "If my friend *were* here," etc. (*c*) I had never known how short life really *is.* Universal truths require the present tense.

8. Come, came, coming come; Do, did, doing, done; Fall, fell, falling, fallen; Lie, lay, lying, lain.

9. *Is* is an irregular, intransitive (neuter) verb, indicative, present, third, singular, agreeing in person and number with its subject *it,* or "acting the evil," for which *it* stands. *Is destroying* is a regular, transitive verb, active, indicative, present, third, singular, agreeing with its subject *that.* It is the progressive form.

10. It was apprehended by them that the Gypsies might have carried him off.

GEOGRAPHY.—1. The races of men are Caucasian, Ethiopian, Mongolian, Malay, American (Indian), Australian. The first three are sometimes called the primary, and the last three the secondary races. Some authors make fewer and some more races.

2. Lakes Superior, Michigan, Huron, Erie, Ontario are the chief inland waters.

3. The five ports on the great lakes in the order of their importance are Chicago, Cleveland, Buffalo, Detroit, Milwaukee.

4. Five manufacturing cities—Pittsburgh, iron, glass and nails; Lowell, cotton goods; Lynn, boots and shoes; Manchester, locomotives, hardware, calico; Worcester, cotton and woollen goods, pistols, locks, wire, musical instruments, etc.

5. Sugar, tobacco, coffee.

7. Russia, abolute monarchy; Great Britain, Prussia, Austria and Spain are limited monarchies; France, republic.

9. London, Paris, Vienna, Berlin, St. Petersburg.

10. Wabash, White, White Water, Kankakee, belong to the Mississippi system; St. Joseph belonging to the Great Lake system.

THEORY OF TEACHING.—1. The powers of the mind embrace *intellect*, which produces ideas, thoughts, reflection; *sensibility*, which gives rise to f elings, emotions, sensations, desires, etc.; and *will*, which accounts for all volition, voluntary action, choosing, determination, etc., etc.

2. *Perception* is that power of the mind by which we gain a knowledge of the outward world through the senses; *conception*, or generalization, is the power of forming general ideas. It is derived from *con*, to gather, and *capio*, to take, hence taking or binding together; *judgment* is the power of perceiving agreements or differences of objects of thought. It compares one object with another and the mental product is called a judgment. The expression of a judgment in words is called a proposition.

3. Phonic spelling in primary schools will aid in developing the vocal organs, in distinct articulation and enunciation. It is often carried too far.

4. Painful motives distract the mind and disqualify for study, while pleasant motives stimulate and enable the mind to do its best work.

5. Prizes are harmful because they usually stimulate only the few who do not need to be stimulated, while they discourage the many who become indifferent. Besides prizes are unworthy motives to place before children, and they frequently lead to rivalry and dishonesty.

ARITHMETIC.—1. Bank discount is a deduction made by banks for paying a note before it becomes due It is the interest upon the face of the note for three days more than the time specified. Bonds are written instruments given to secure the payment of a sum of money at a specified time.

2. Arithmetic is the science of numbers, and the art of numerical computation. Cancellation is the omission of one or more factors of a number.

3. A common multiple of two or more numbers is a number which each of them will exactly divide. A complex fraction is one having a fraction in one or both of its terms.

4. $.8000 = $80 hundred. $1.80 × 80 = $144, the annual premium.

5. $1\frac{7}{8}$% of $1 = $.01$\frac{7}{8}$. $1 + $.01$\frac{7}{8}$ = 1.01\frac{7}{8}$. 63 days + 6 = $.0105 b. d. on $1. 1.01\frac{7}{8}$ − $.0105 = 1.0082\frac{1}{2}$. $1.00825 × 8500 = $8570.125, Answer.

6. (9 gal. 3 qt.)—(1 gal. 3 qt. 1 pt.(=)7 gal. 3 qt. 1 pt.) or 63 pts. 2400 gal.=19200 pts. 63 pts. : 19200 pts. : : 1 min. : $\frac{19200 \times 1}{63}$ = 304$\frac{48}{63}$ min. or 5 hr. 4$\frac{48}{63}$ min.

7. $\sqrt{(300)^2 - (240)^2}$ = 180 ft. $\sqrt{(400)^2 - (240)^2}$ = 320 ft. 180 ft. + 320 ft.=500 ft., Ans.

8. $\sqrt[3]{1860867}$ = 123.

9. Int. on $1 for 2 yr.=$.12; for 3 mo. $.015; for 18 days $.003 $.12+ $.015+$.003=$.138, but on $1 for given time, $.138×496=$68.448, Ans.

MISCELLANY.

ANSWER TO QUERY.—The capital of Dakota is Yankton.

PURDUE UNIVERSITY has 180 students this term. It has matriculated 220 students this year.

Messrs. E. L. Kellogg & Co., educational publishers, announce their removal to 25 Clinton Place, N. Y.

THE School of Pharmacy at Purdue University has closed for this year. The session expired February 9th.

THE schools in Rensselaer are reported to be in their most prosperous condition. P. H. Kirsch is superintendent.

MONTICELLO.—The manual shows the schools of this place in good condition. Wm. M. Sinclair is Supt. and Geo. W. Isham is principal of the high·school.

THE Richmond Normal School has gained fifty per cent. this year over the attendance of last year. Those in attendance speak very highly of its work.

Henry Hoffman, of Blunt, Dakota, has started a weekly school journal. It runs 16 pages not quite so large as the pages of this paper. Its success is certainly doubtful in that "far off country."

The Ripley county manual of public schools is a compact, carefully arranged pamphlet of 48 pages, and contains full information on school matters. In it Supt. Geo. W. Young makes some pertinent suggestions.

LADOGA.—The Central Normal located here is doing well. The enrollment this term is over 150, while the prospects for next term are excellent. A. F. Knotts, a graduate of the Valparaiso Normal, is principal.

HAMILTON COUNTY.—The teachers of Hamilton county held a joint meeting at Noblesville February 14th. Judging from the program the meeting must have been profitable. Supt. A. H. Morris makes a success of whatever he undertakes.

St. Joseph County has now 104 members of the Reading Circle; 83 percent of the district teachers are in it, while only 20 percent of the city teachers belong. This is an excellent showing, especially for the teachers who are directly under the charge of Supt. Moon.

Brownstown.—The high school will graduate a class of eight this year. The schools are prospering. A good supply of chemical and philosophical apparatus has been secured by the efforts of the principal and teachers. The efficient principal, C. L. Hottel, will re-open the Brownstown Normal May 4th.

Pulaski County.—The manual for the schools of this county, published by Supt. W. E. Netherton, is the largest, fullest, most comprehensive, yet received. It contains everything about the county system and about the state system of education, and a *few* pages of advertising. Supt. Netherton never does things by halves.

Ligonier.—Supt. D D. Luke has had charge of the Ligonier schools for many years, and is doing excellent work. He is a person who thinks for himself and works for the best results. His last report is very full and is put up in excellent style. A new feature is that for each child a report is published of days present, times tardy, time lost by tardiness, deportment, and average percent of scholarship

Indianapolis.—In the schools here classes are promoted regularly twice each year. This of course brings a new class to the high school in the middle of the year. Until within two years the midyear class has been small, and its graduation was delayed to the close of the year with the main class. For the past two years these classes have been graduated at the middle of the year on the completion of the course of study. The last class numbered twelve. W. W Grant is succeeding well as principal of the high school.

The Fountain County Teachers' Association convened in Covington, February 6th and 7th, and was certainly the most successful ever held in the county. The instruction the first day was given by home talent · On the evening of the 6th Co Supt. Elson, of Parke, addressed the teachers and citizens on the subject, "Uses and Abuses of the School Funds." This was well received W. A Bell, J M. Olcott, and W. T. Fry were present the second day and gave some very valuable suggestions on school government. Judge Davidson and Mr. H H. Docterman, two prominent lawyers of Covington, instructed the Association in a manner that was heartily endorsed. There was a full attendance. It was decided to make this a permanent organization to be held annually.

V. E Livengood, Sec'y.   J. G. Glasscock, Pres't.

MEETING OF CITY SUPERINTENDENTS.—A meeting of city and town superintendents will be held in Union City March 13 and 14 The first meeting will be held on Friday evening at 7 o'clock, and the meetings will be continued over Saturday. The discussions will be entirely *informal.* The following are some of the subjects proposed : 1. What can we do in the direction of Industrial Education ? 2. The place of Drawing in the School Curriculum. 3 What constitutes an Ideal School ? 4. Relation of Superintendent to School Board. 5. What Training is necessary to Successful Teaching ? 6. Can our Course of Study be so arranged as to promote pupils faster ? 7. The Library in Schools. 8. Should the course of instruction in our schools be modified ? and others.

J. J. Mills, R. I. Hamilton, and F. Treudly will report a "High School Course of Study." This meeting is not confined to superintendents of Eastern Indiana and Western Ohio, but all superintendents and others that feel disposed to come are cordially invited.

ST. JOSEPH COUNTY.—The Board of Education at a special meeting in January, resolved in favor of—(1) A uniform term of school of not less than eight months ; (2) A uniform course of study and grading country schools; (3) A compulsory school law; (4) Paying teachers for attending township institutes; (5) No change in the present law governing the license of teachers or the election of county superintendents.

In this county by vote of the county institute and by the board of education it has been the custom for two years past for each teacher on being examined to pay to the superintendent for institute purposes 50 cents each. The board resolved not to employ teachers refusing to pay this tax.

The teacher's institute recommended that in order to stimulate and secure higher culture among the teachers that the trustees should pay higher wages to such as passed an examination upon civil government, physiology, geography, science of teaching, general history, mental science, and algebra. Superintendent Calvin Moon is a moving power.

JAY COUNTY.—Will J. Houck, Supt. of Jay county, is scarcely surpassed by any superintendent in the state in his zeal and efficiency in pushing forward the cause of education in his county. In order to secure what he wanted he arranged and published a Register especially adapted to securing proper grading, enrolling, reporting, stimulating pupils, encouraging attendance, etc. He has provided for uniform examinations twice each year for promotion. Every pupil is examined whether ready for promotion or not. Promotions are made on an average of 85 percent, not falling below 65 percent on any one branch.

The schools are divided into eight grades. At the close of each year the questions prepared by the state committee for graduation from the common schools are submitted to those finishing the seventh year's work, and those who pass are given their diploma, and are promoted to the eighth grade, which is called the "post graduate year's work." Persons completing satisfactorily the post graduate course are given "trial certificates to teach.

A school exhibit, made up in part of papers prepared at these uniform examinations, is made an important part of each county fair. Teachers are required to report the names of pupils enumerated but not enrolled in schools, together with reasons for non-attendance; and also the names of parents of such children. This helps the attendance. •

A large number of the teachers in the county are in the Reading Circle, and all in all Jay county seems to be in a healthy condition and on the up-grade educationally.

THORNTOWN.—A joint township association was held at Thorntown February 13th and 14th, which was largely attended and was a marked success. R. G. Boone, of Frankfort, gave an excellent address Friday evening, and A. G. Alford, Indianapolis, made an address Saturday P. M., which pleased all who heard it. Co. Supt. LaFollette read a valuable paper on "Literature in Common Schools." Supt. Hart, of the Thorntown schols, was active in making everybody "at home." He is doing good work in his schools.

SOUTHERN INDIANA TEACHERS' ASSOCIATION.

EIGHTH ANNUAL MEETING,

To be held at College Hall, Mitchell, Ind., April 2 and 3, 1885.

PROGRAM.

THURSDAY MORNING, 10 o'clock.—Opening Exercises. Address of Welcome—Rev. R. J. Parrs, Mitchell, Ind. Address of Retiring President—A. M. Sweeney, Supt. Dubois Co. Inaugural Address—D. S. Kelley, Supt. of schools at Jeffersonville. Miscellaneous Business. Appointment of Committees.

AFTERNOON, 2:00 – Paper—The Progress of Educational Thought, E. A. Ryan, President of the Vincennes University. Discussion opened by D. E. Hunter, Supt. schools Washington, Ind. Paper—The Limit in the Practical in Teaching, C. F. Coffin, Supt. schools New Albany. Discussion opened by J. R. Hamilton, Supt. Jackson county schools. Paper—Our County Schools, S. E. Boyd, Supt. ...... county. Discussion opened by N. F. Smith, Prin. schools Troy, Ind. Paper—Esthetics in Common School Education, Mrs.

Alice Bridgman, Asst H. S., Salem, Ind. Discussion opened by O. T. Dunagan, Prin. schools, Shoals, Ind. Miscellaneous Business—Appointment of Committee on Officers.

EVENING, 7:30. — Address — Primary Instruction, John Cooper, Supt. schools, Evansville, Ind. Address—Common School Room Diseases, Dr. H. Stillson, Prof. Science, Southern Indiana Normal College. Paper—Natural Science in Elementary Schools, Prof. O. P. Jenkins, Natural Science, State Normal, Terre Haute.

FRIDAY MORNING, 9 o'clock.—Opening Exercises. Paper—Will-Power, Prof. J. K. Beck, Prin. Preparatory Dept., State University. Discussion opened by Hon. J. M. Bloss, Supt. schools, Muncie, Ind. Paper—Our High Schools, Frank M. Stalker, Prin. schools, Orleans, Ind. Discussion opened by Walter Wallace, Prin. Fourth Ward School, Columbus, Ind. (*Recess.*) Address—Independent Normalism as a New Education, Prof. R. Heber Holbrook, Vice-President National Normal University, Lebanon, Ohio. Talks on Primary Teaching—Miss Ellen J. Strader, Bloomington schools; Miss Mary Glover, Bedford schools; Miss Alice Whitaker, Spencer schools.

AFTERNOON, 1:00 —Paper—Education and the Spirit of the Age, A. H. Kennedy, Supt. schools, Rockport, Ind. General Discussion. Paper—Negative Factors in Educational Problems, A. J. Snoke, Supt. schools, Princeton. Paper—Part of the Teacher in the Development of Civilization, G. L. McIntosh, Lawrenceburg, Ind. General Discussion—Reports of Committees.

Executive Committee. — W. E Lugenbeel, chairman, Mitchell; R. A. Ogg, New Albany; W. W. Fuller, Booneville; C. W. McClure, Mitchell; D. H. Ellison, Mitchell; A. Tompkins, Franklin.

Music Committee.—Miss Dora Stroud, Mitchell; C. F. Coffin, New Albany; Miss Jessie Robertson, Mitchell; Miss Jennie Day, New Albany; Miss Eva L. Lydall, New Albany; D. S. Kelley, Jeffersonville. The exercises will be interspersed with first-class vocal and instrumental music.

FRIDAY EVENING—Social Entertainment.

ANNOUNCEMENTS.

Railroad Rates.—Reduced rates have been secured on the O. & M. R. R., the L. N. A. & C. R. R., and connecting lines. Write at once to C. W. McClure, railroad secretary, Mitchell, Ind., for orders on the agents of the various roads for excursion tickets. *State particularly the roads over which you desire to travel.* Tickets good going March 31, April 1 and 2; returning, until April 5th.

Hotels and Boarding.—Mitchell is abundantly supplied with good hotels and private boarding houses. Hotels, $1 to $1 50 per day; private boarding houses, $1 per day; private families, $1 per day.

Committee of Reception.—Persons, on arriving, will be met at the trains by members of the Reception Committee. Every train—day or night—will be met.

Arrivals of Trains.—Trains on the O. & M. R. R. arrive from the East at 11:40 a. m., 11:40 p. m., and 1:09 a. m ; from the West at 5:50 a. m., 2 39 p. m , 3:30 p. m., and 2:39 a. m. L. N. A. & C R. R., trains arrive from the South at 10:26 a. m. and 10:26 p. m.; from the North at 5·46 p. m. and 5:00 a m.

Length of Papers—No paper or address is to exceed 30 minutes. The person who opens the discussion will be allowed 10 minutes; all others will be limited to 5 minutes. The object is to secure variety of work.

School Work.—All members of the Association who arrive on Wednesday morning or evening will have an opportunity to witness the working of the various departments of the Mitchell public schools on Wednesday, and of inspecting the work done in all the departments of the Southern Indiana Normal College on Wednesday and on Thursday morning. The latter institution will have all its regular classes in session before the hours of opening the meetings of the Association every day, but the exercises of the convention will be attended by the students and teachers in a body.

Notices in the Papers—It is earnestly requested by the committee that all persons who receive these programs will place notices of the meeting of the Association in their county papers.

All teachers who desire the progress of the "New Profession" are cordially invited to attend.   W. E. LUGENBEEL,

Chn. Ex. Com., Mitchell, Ind.

INDIANA TEACHERS' READING CIRCLE.

OUTLINE OF

Work in Brooks' Mental Science, for February, 1885—Pages 169–199. Subject: "The Imagination."

I. TERMS TO BE EXPLAINED.

1. Ideal, idealize. 2. "Train of thought," page 174. 3. Spontaneity. 4. "A plastic power," page 186. 5. "Great guess," p. 189. 6. "Inductive thought," p. 189 7. "Elastic thread of gravity," page 179.

II. TERMS TO BE DISTINGUISHED.

1 Idea and ideal. 2 Memory and imagination. 3 "New Combinations" and "new creations" 4 Imagination proper, and fancy.

NOTE.—To say that a careful and familiar knowledge of the terms (words and phrases) used, is of the first importance is to say what every one believes to be true, but what few persons resolutely put into common practice. These first two items should, then, be constantly used.

III. BIOGRAPHIES.

Concerning the persons referred to in these two chapters, it is enough to say, that from Demosthenes in his political oratory, to Cuvier with his fossils and bones, every character is representative, in the culture and exercise, of a far-reaching and efficient imagination.

IV. PROFESSIONAL ITEMS.

(a) *Relation of Imagination to Memory.*

1. "For the materials necessary to its processes, imagination depends, immediately, upon memory; remotely, upon perception."
—*Munsell.*

2. "What is ordinarily called learning, whether by oral communication or by books, is not simply an exercise of memory; it involves an exercise of imagination as well."—*Sully.*

(b) *The Principle of Suggestion in Imagining.*

1. "Had Columbus been without imagination, he would not have discovered America."—*Winslow.*

2. "The teaching of the science of Geography depends almost entirely upon the power to use the imagination."—*Parker.*

(c) *The Power of Idealizing Sense-Perceptions.*

1 "The child turns his perceptions into conceptions and plays with them :—this is imagination."—*Rosenkrans.*

2. "The imagination of mechanical inventors has been chiefly exerted in devising schemes for getting hold of, guiding, governing, or modifying the forces of nature."—*Jardine.*

3 "Next to the direct action of the senses, imagination is the most important, in its length, breadth and depth of all the mental powers."—*Parker.*

(d) *Relation of Imagination to Thinking.*

1 "Imagination is as necessary to philosophy as to poetry."—*Bascom.*

2. "Nearly all the great discoveries of science have been the result of an effort of imagination."—*Jardine.*

3. "Imagination is indispensable to the processes of true science."—*Munsell.*

(e) *Relation of Imagination to Character.*

1. "The sound and proper exercise of the imagination may be an aid to the cultivation of all that is virtuous and estimable in human character."—*Abercrombie.*

(f) *Influence of an Acquaintance with Art—Pictures, Literature.*

V. QUOTATIONS.

There are given in this lesson eight familiar quotations from three equally well-known authors. With one exception, possibly, the

4

books are such as may be found in every neighborhood, and the gems are well worth tracing up. Besides, their connection with the imagination is both close and important.

VI. SUMMARIES.

1. The forms of Imagination.
2. The products of Imagination.
3. The laws of Imagination.
4. The limits of Imagination.
5. The sphere of Imagination.
6. Methods of cultivating the Imagination.

(*a*) "The gratifying of children with the literature of imagination is a matter for parents as much as to give them country walks or holiday treats."—*Bain.*

(*b*) "A strong native bent to imaginative activity, requires to be guided rather than resisted or frustrated."—*Sully.*

Note.—Special reference should be made, also, to an address delivered before the Indiana Teachers' Association at Indianapolis, by Supt. H. S. Tarbell, and published in the Indiana School Journal, June, 1883. This article is an appropriate supplement to the February Mental Science. R. G. B.

OUTLINES OF HISTORY FOR DECEMBER.
Barnes' General History—Pages 73-108.

First Week.—The splendid maritime achievements of the Phœnicians—the path finders of the ancient world—are subjects of peculiar interest to the student. The voyages of these primitive navigators should be carefully traced upon a map or globe.

1. The influence of their commerce upon the world, in distributing the arts, sciences and customs of many nations, with their material products, abroad over the earth.

2. The influence of this commerce upon public spirit at home.

3. Carthage, her rise and fall. Date of the former. (Virgil's account of Queen Dido, in the Æneid, is a gross but pardonable anachronism.)

4. From what regions did the Phœnicians acquire, and to what regions did they carry art and culture? From whom was the first alphabet derived?

5. Native arts—astronomy, mining, pottery, dyeing.

6. Religion—Baal, or Bel Moloch. Astarte, or Ashtoreth. The influence of the Phœnician Queen upon the kingdom of Israel. (I Kings, XVI)

Second Week.—The Jews. 1. Origin of the Jews; The Sojourn in Egypt; The Return to Palestine. 2. The Exodus; The date compared with that of the discovery of America. 3. The Conquest of Canaan, as related in the book of Joshua. 4. The Jews under the Judges—(See the book of Judges.) 5. King Saul. 6. King David;

The new Capital; The Psalms. 7. King Solomon; The great Temple; The Proverbs, Canticles, and The Preacher. 8. The Division; Israel and her Captivity; Judah and her Captivity. 9. The Restoration of Judah. 10. Civilization; The Jewish Commonwealth; Character of the Mosaic laws; Mitigations of Oriental Cruelty.

NOTE.—Jerusalem consisted of three parts: 1. The old town of Salem (Gen. xiv. 18). 2. The hill to the South, wrested from the Jebusites by David, (II Samuel V), called by him Mt. Zion, and built up with splendor for the new capital. 3. Mt. Moriah, the hill to the eastward, added by Solomon as the site of his temple, (I Kings, VI). The old capital was Hebron, where Abraham was buried.

Third Week.—The third of the five great Empires—the Persian. 1. The romantic story of Cyrus. 2. The fulfillment of prophesy in his career. 3. Cambyses and Egypt. 4. Darius I, and the Satraps; Susa, the Sushan of Scripture—(Esther I, 2.) 5. Oriental Despotism; Oriental Etiquette. 9 Persian Literature; The Zend-Avesta. 7. Why the Greeks considered the Persians "barbarians," in spite of their luxuries; What elements of true civilization were wanting. 8. Peculiarities of Persian Art. 9. Persian Religions; The Magi. 10. Oriental status of Women. 11. The Persian army. (Perhaps the most interesting portion of the history remains to be told, in connection with that of Greece. These accounts of Persian warfare will be of interest hereafter.)

Fourth Week.—The Hindoos. 1. Their relations to us, as Aryans of a common parentage; Physical differences resulting from the long separation; Other differences; The time of the migration; Re-union of the sundered branches in British India. 2. The system of caste; Have we lost it or have they acquired it, since the separation? 3. The Sanskrit; The literature, extent and quality; The Rig Veda. 4. The ancient religion of Brahminism. 5. Buddha, or Gantama, the great reformer; Driven from India, his religion takes root in other lands, and China is degraded into a disgusting superstition; The character of Gantama.

SUNDAY READINGS (SUGGESTIVE).

First Sunday.—I Kings, XVIII; Ezek. XXVIII, XXVI.

Second Sunday.—Selections from Exodus, Joshua, Judges, Samuel and Kings.

Third Sunday.—Isaiah XLV, 1-4, (a prophesy written more than a century before Cyrus was born.)

Fourth Sunday.—Arnold's "Light of Asia." (This is published in cheap form, and is worth perusal.)

OUTLINES OF HISTORY FOR JANUARY.

Pages 109-135.

First Week.—The Chinese. 1. Antiquity of the nation; Ching Wang and the Great Wall; Ultimate triumph of the Tartars. 2. Isolation, and its results; Visit of Marco Polo. 3. Chinese literature.

4. The religions; Boodhism; Taoism; Confuscius (Kong Fu Tse) a philosopher rather than a false prophet; His Silver-Rule compared with the Golden Rule of the Savior. '

Second Week.—The Greeks. 1. The earliest seat of Western civilization; Difference between the Western and the Eastern civilizations 2. Geographical features of Greece, and their influence on the Greeks. 3 The Greeks a people, rather than a nation; Their origin; Bonds of union. 4. Legends; The Argonauts, and the War of Troy. 5. The return of the Heraclidae, compared with the return of the Israelites to Canaan. 6. Greek colonies. 7. Divisions of Greece.

Third Week.—Athens and Sparta. 1. The kingdom of Sparta; Lycurgus and his laws; Results of his system. 2. The Republic of Athens; Draco and his laws; Solon and his laws. 3. The tyrants, or kings; The triumph of Democracy. 4. The first Persian inroad. 5. The second expedition; The defense of Greece; The battle of Marathon, which "saved the civilization of the world." (Everything pertaining to this most important engagement should receive careful study.) 6. The effect of this battle on Greece; on Athens; on Sparta; on Miltiades. 7. Themistocles and Aristides; The system of ostracism; Its injustice

Fourth Week.—The third Persian expedition. 1. Sparta's first part of the war; Leonidas and Thermopylae. 2. The Athenian victory at Salamis; The fleet; The "wooden wall" of the Athenians; The flight of Xerxes. 3. Final conflicts. 4. Results of the war. 5. Magnitude of the undertaking.

OUTLINES OF HISTORY FOR FEBRUARY.
General History · Pages 135-153.

First Week—1. The career of Cimon. 2. Pericles, and the triumph of Democracy. Modes of educating the populace. 3. Athenian civilization and culture. 4. How an inland city was made a seaport. 5. Exhibitions of Athenian sport.

Second Week.—1. The *real cause* of the great war between the Greek States. The *occasion* of the war. 2. How the States were arranged in the two great parties to the conflict. 3. The conduct of the war. The terrible siege of Athens. 4. The perfidy of Pausanius. The heroic defense of Platea, and the destruction of the city. 5. The scheme of Alcibiades. His traitorous conduct, after his deposition. The fate of the expedition. His recall by the fickle Athenians, and his second deposition. 6. The fall of Athens. 7. Her continued supremacy in literature and art. The thirty tyrants, and the re-establishment of Democracy.

Third Week.—1. The third Persian war. How Greece became involved. 2. How victory was turned into defeat. 3. The retreat

under Xenophon. Its remarkable character. 4. A fifth war with
Persia. Greeks again the aggressors. 5. Persian gold triumphs
Decline of Sparta. 6. The Washington of Greece—Epaminondas.
Leuctra and Mantinea. The fall of Thebes. The Theban Phalanx.

Fourth Week.—1. In what respect was Macedon to be considered
a Greek State? 2. Philip's ambition to be recognized as a Greek.
His success. He craftily insinuates himself into Greek affairs. 3. The
opposition of Demosthenes. 4. The Macedonian Phalanx. 5. Anecdotes illustrating the character of Philip. His death. 6. Alexander, The destruction of Thebes. 7. The conquest of Persia. The
conquest of Egypt, and the new city on the Mediterranean. The advance into India. 8. Alexander's death. 9. His plans. His influence on the history of the world. 10. In what respects was Alexander's empire a *Greek* empire? 11. Did Alexander really conquer
the world, as legend states?

NOTE.—It is not generally spoken of as the Greek Empire, since that term is used to
designate the eastern division of the Roman Empire of centuries later.   H. M. S.

————o————

METHODS OF INSTRUCTION.

Talks on Teaching—pp. 101-120.

When shall the writing of numbers be commenced? Not until
the number *ten* has been thoroughly learned, says the author. What
must the child know to have a thorough knowledge of ten? How
long will it take a child entering school at the age of six to acquire
this knowledge? Why should not children be taught to count to 50
or to 100 the first year? The author recommends the teaching of
the four fundamental operations simultaneously   What are the reasons for this? What are the arguments against it? (The Circle
should study the papers that have appeared in the last three or four
numbers of the School Journal on the "*Grube Method,*" written by
Dr. White and the editor the Ped. Dept. of the Journal) These
questions are of fundamental importance and should be carefully
studied. What reason is suggested why the written form of numbers
should not be taught as early as the written form of words? Especial attention is called to the suggestions of the text as to the method
by which the child shall learn to associate the *idea* of number with
the figures, and thus avoid the common error of teaching the child
figures instead of numbers: How much and what should be taught
the second year? How much the third year? What are the abuses
of formal analysis? When should the use of objects cease? Note
especially the teachings of the text in regard to leading the pupils to
discover all new processes for themselves. Reflect upon the definition of education as " *The generation of power.*"   G. P. B.

GEMS OF THOUGHT.

Growth is better than permanence, but permanent growth is better than all.—*Garfield.*

The shaping of our life is our own work. It is a thing of beauty, it is a thing of shame, as we ourselves make it.—*Ware.*

Young men talk of trusting to the spur of the occasion. That trust is vain. Occasion can not make spurs. If you expect to wear spurs you must win them. If you wish to use them you must buckle them to your own heels before you go into the fight.—*Garfield.*

GOOD RULES.

The following rules are commonplace enough, but we can assure our readers that if they will observe every one of them, they will be anything but commonplace men and women:

Don't stop to tell stories in business hours.
If you have a place of business, be found there when wanted.
No man can get rich sitting around stores and saloons.
Have order, system, regularity, and also promptness.
Do not meddle with business you know nothing of.
Pay as you go.
Learn to think and act for yourself.
A man of honor respects his word as he does his bond.
Help others, but never give what you can not afford to, simply because it is fashionable to give.

OLD SAYINGS.

As poor as a church mouse, as thin as a rail;
As fat as a porpoise, as rough as a gale;
As brave as a lion, as spry as a cat;
As bright as a sixpence, as weak as a rat.

As proud as a peacock, as sly as a fox;
As mad as a March hare, as stout as an ox;
As fair as a lily, as empty as air;
As rich as Crœsus, as cross as a bear.

As pure as an angel, as neat as a pin;
As smart as a steel-trap, as ugly as sin;
As dead as a door-nail, as white as a sheet;
As flat as a pan cake, as red as a beet.

As round as an apple, as black as your hat;
As brown as a berry, as blind as a bat;
As mean as a miser, as full as a tick;
As plump as a partridge, as sharp as a stick.

As clean as a penny, as dark as a pall;
As hard as a mill-stone, as bitter as gall;
As fine as a fiddle, as clear as a bell;
As dry as a herring, as deep as a well.

As light as a feather, as firm as a rock;
As stiff as a poker, as calm as a clock;
As green as a gosling, as brisk as bee;
And now let me stop, lest you weary of me. [*Selected.*

PERSONAL.

E. O. Ellis is principal of the Fairmount schools.

T. A. Clifton is in charge of the Williamsport schools.

R. H. Harney is serving his second year as Supt. at Lebanon.

E. C. White is giving good satisfaction as principal of the Albion schools.

Geo. W. White is teaching a good school in the Friends' Academy at Plainfield.

A. Knight, a graduate of Earlham College, is principal of the school at Sugar Plain, near Thorntown.

J. F. Scull still has charge of the Rochester schools, and his recent report shows everything on the *up-grade.*

J. G. Scott is principal of the New Providence Normal School, which will open its third term March 30th, and become a permanent institution.

W. H. Wells, for many years Supt. of the Chicago schools, and recognized as one of the leading educators of this country, died at his home in Chicage January 21st.

A. G. Alford, who is well known in Southern Indiana, is giving entire satisfaction to school board and patrons, as principal of the Indianapolis South Side High School.

James B. Irwin, who had represented the house of Van Antwerp, Bragg & Co. for more than twenty years, and perhaps the best known man in Ohio, died recently at his home in Dayton.

Samuel E. Harwood, Supt. of Spencer schools, wishes to do institute work during the coming summer. Will teach any of the branches required, but prefers language and literature.

E. E. Smith, Professor of English and History, who is serving his eighth year in Purdue University, has recently been elected a member of the Modern Language Association of America.

J. F. Snow, Supt. of Adams county, has been sick for about two months, and is just getting out. Notwithstanding this drawback the school work moves on, and about 40 percent of his teachers have entered the Reading Circle.

Miss Mary E. Nicholson, for many years teacher of history and literature in the Indianapolis high school, now principal of the Indianapolis training school, has recently been elected a member of the American Historical Society.

S. S. Parr, formerly connected with the State Normal School, and now editor of *School Education*, published at St. Paul, Minn., has been elected Professor of Didactics in De Pauw University. Several years since, when W. A. Jones, then president of the normal school, was relieved of class work, he selected Mr. Parr to carry on his work in didactics, which he did with marked success. For several years past Mr. Parr has achieved success as an institute worker, city superintendent, and editor of the Minn. State Journal of Education. Of the several new enterprises recently undertaken at De Pauw this is the most important, and Mr. Parr will make a notable addition of ber already strong faculty. The Journal heartily welcomes him back to the educational field of Indiana.

W. H. Venable, author of U. S. History, two different volumes of poems, and of innumerable educational articles, and at present principal of Chickering Academy, Cincinnati, O., is willing to do some institute work in Indiana the coming season.

FORT WAYNE COLLEGE.—This college was re-organided about a year ago and started off on new footing with new life. The work it does is of a high order and will bear investigation. W. F. Yocum, the president, is one of the best scholars and one of the best men in the state.

BOOK TABLE.

The Journal of American Orthœpy is published by C. W. Larison, Ringos, N. J. Any one interested in fonics will find this little book helpful.

The Current, published in Chicago, although only about one year old, has taken rank with the best literary papers in the United States. It is simply *first-class*.

Boys and Girls' Atlas of the World, by James Monteith.. New York and Chicago : A. Barnes & Co.

This atlas, in addition to a good variety of maps, including one of New York City and vicinity, contains all the important facts about area, population, cities, rivers, mountains, productions, etc. It is "handy" and will certainly be in demand. Price 50 cents.

Application of Psychology to the Art of Teaching. By W. N. Hailman. Boston: Willard & Small.

The above is a little book of only 40 pages, being a prize essay. The American Institute of Instruction offered a prize for the best essay on the subject named. Thirty were received and the award was given to Prof. Hailman, superintendent of schools at LaPorte, Ind. The award was an honor to the writer, and is sufficient commendation to the essay. Just now, when the relation of psychology to teaching is claiming so much attention, this little book will have special interest It is too much condensed to be of much value to the novice in the line of thought, but it is full of suggestion to those who have some knowledge of mental science.

ton's Chart-Primer—Exercises in Reading at Sight, and e and Color Lessons for Beginners. By Rebecca D. Rickoff. k: D. Appleton & Co. C. E. Lane, Chicago, Western Agt.

Without any question this is the most beautiful primer yet printed. Many of the charming pictures are colored—all are suggestive—and the child must talk about them whether he will or not. The best thought of the best primary teachers is here embodied, and the work of taking the first lesson in reading is changed from a task to a pastime. Every primary teacher should see the book.

Stories for Young Children. By E. A. Turner. Boston: Ginn & Heath. Harold Smith, Chicago, Western Agent.

This is a little book of 85 pages, bound in paper, which can be purchased for 15 cents It is designed for supplementary reading in schools. The stories are short, simply told, and adapted to Second and Third Reader pupils We can hardly imagine anything better adapted to the use for which it was intended than this book. Ginn & Heath are furnishing many *standard* works for older children to be used as extra reading in schools.

The St Nicholas continues to stand at the head of magazines for boys and girls. Good reading for the youth is being appreciated more and more as time goes on, and in the near future a good juvenile paper or magazine will be regarded as a *necessity* in every family where there are children. Good reading increases information, cultivates taste, fixes good habits, and is the best possible preventive to idleness, bad company, and vice. Teachers should do what they can to encourage their pupils to take and read good papers. The St. Nicholas, published in New York by the Century Company, ranks with the best.

The Century began in November last to publish articles on the different battles of the late rebellion by prominent persons engaged in these battles, on both sides. These articles have given to the magazine a great boom. The February issue, containing General Grant's article on the Battle of Pittsburg Landing was originally 180,000; other editions were demanded and to date over 200,000 copies have been sent out. The March issue is 190,000. While these war articles are an attractive feature, the other departments of the *Century* are kept up to the highest standard. Address Century Co., New York City. Price $4; club price, with the Journal, $4 85.

Oral Lessons in Number. By E. E. White, LL. D. Cincinnati: Van Antwerp, Bragg & Co.

This little book supplies a long-felt want; viz, a carefully planned and skillfully arranged course of lessons beginning with the "first steps" and continuing through the first three years' work in number. Dr. White has taken great pains to develop the subject step by step in a clear and natural manner, and at the same time has suggested processes of teaching and states concisely the principles involved.

Primary number can be best taught orally, and yet but few teachers can arrange a systematic course of instruction. This book is just what the teacher needs, and the gain to pupils can not be estimated. Whether Dr. White's criticism on the Grube Method is fully endorsed or not, it must do good, as it will cause thought, and will serve to break up a tendency towards mechanical routine methods. The book must find a large field of usefulness.

The January-February number of EDUCATION fully sustains the high character of this able educational magazine. Supt. Long, of

St. Louis, leads in the discussion of "Intellectual Training in Normal
Schools," and Prest. Hunter, of the New York City Normal School,
has an article on the "Necessity and Growth of Normal Schools."
Prof. Anderson, of Aberdeen, Scotland, writes of "The Æsthetic
Element in Education," and the second article of M. Greard, of
France, on "The Spirit of Discipline in Education." Mrs. Hopkins
treats of "The Memory Faculty," in her course in Psychology.
Prest. Bicknell's Annual Address before the National Educational
Association at Madison, appears in full in this number   Other arti
cles are "The Lost Atlantis," by Mrs. Knight; "Quintilian's Educational Theory," and Foreign Notes. This number is embellished
by a steel engraving of Louis Prang, the celebrated art publisher of
Boston. This magazine embodies the best literature of the teaching
profession   Price $4 00; single copies, 75 cents. Address New Eng-
land Publishing Company, Boston.

BUSINESS NOTICES.

WHERE TO ATTEND SCHOOL.

1. Where you can get good instruction in whatever you may wish to study.

2. Where you can get good accommodations and good society.

3. Where rates are cheapest.

4. Where things are just as represented or all money refunded and travel-
ing expenses paid.

Send for special rates, and try the Central Indiana Normal School, at Ladoga, Ind. It is the cheapest school in the state.

FORT WAYNE COLLEGE ranks with the best in the state. See advertisement on cover page of this Journal. Send for catalogue. Address the president, W. F. Yocum, Fort Wayne.

INSTITUTE WORK.—Prof. W. H. Venable may be engaged to teach and
lecture at Institutes in June, July or August. His favorite subjects are History, Literature, Rhetoric, and Pedagogics. Address him at Station C, Cincinnati.   3-4t

PENNSYLVANIA EDUCATIONAL BUREAU. — *Business transacted in every
State and Territory—Old and Reliable.*—Hundreds of teachers have been
supplied in the past. The manager is Superintendent of the Public Schools
of Allentown, and has a professional experience of twenty-five years. Many
teachers wanted. Register *now*. For application form and list of testimonials,
address L. B. LANDIS, Manager, 631 Hamilton St., Allentown, Pa.   3-4t

TERMINAL RAILROAD FACILITIES IN WASHINGTON CITY.—The Station of
the Pennsylvania Railroad is the only first-class Station in the city; it is located on Pennsylvania Avenue, in the center of the town, in close proximity
to all the leading hotels, and within two minutes walk of the Capitol building.
The Station used by the other line reaching Washington from the West, is a
second-class building, located in a hollow, on a back street, and unless stran-
gers arriving by that line take carriages, they will encounter more or less difficulty in reaching their places of abode.

TEACHERS desiring to attend a *Normal School*, or those wishing a situation or an increase of salary, should send for a sample copy of "*The Educational World.*" Address, W. SAYLER, *Editor, Logansport, Ind.* 1-12t.

The fourth year of the Acton Normal School, conducted by N. W. Bryant, assisted by Miss Cora M. Smith, of Butler University, and a full corps of competent teachers, will open Wednesday, April 8, 1885. For catalogue and information, address the principal, N. W. Bryant. 2-2t

TO THE NEW ORLEANS EXPOSITION.—The favorite route to New Orleans is via the Indianapolis & St. Louis R'y, "Bee Line Route," via Mattoon, Ill. Only one change of cars. From Mattoon the route is via the Illinois Central R'y, through Cairo, Jackson, Tenn., and Jackson, Miss. Tickets on sale at Bee Line office, No. 2 Bates House. W. J. Nichols, Pass. Agt. 2-3t

EXCURSION TO NEW ORLEANS.—New Orleans Excursion Tickets are now on sale at the Ticket Offices of the Jeffersonville, Madison & Indianapolis Railroad Co. For rates and time of trains, call upon or write to nearest Agent, Jeffersonville, Madison & Indianapolis Railroad Company, or to H. R. Dering, Assistant General Passenger Agent, Indianapolis, Ind. 1-3t

THE best route between Indianapolis and Fort Wayne, is by the C., C., C. & I. to Muncie, and then by the Ft. Wayne, Cincinnati & Louisville. This is the shortest and best. For information in regard to these roads, inquire of W. J. Nichols, Indianapolis, General Passenger Agent of the first named road, and of R. E. Kinnaird, Fort Wayne, General Passenger Agent of the other road.

THE INDIANA, BLOOMINGTON & WESTERN RAILWAY,
INDIANAPOLIS, Feb. 17, 1885.

TO WHOM IT MAY CONCERN: I wish to caution the public against one Howard Saxby, who, I understand, is representing himself as Manager Advertising Department I. B. & W. R'y. Any letters he may show purporting to give him authority to represent this company in any capacity, are false. He has no authority to advertise this road in any manner whatever.

Yours truly, H. M. BRONSON, Gen'l Ticket Agent.

AMERICAN ANTIQUARIAN AND ORIENTAL JOURNAL.—This is a bi-monthly illustrated magazine, published in Chicago, Ill., and edited by Rev. S. D. Peet, assisted by gentlemen residing in New York, Philadelphia, Washington, and various other places. The Contributors to the Journal are all gentlemen who are well known for their scholarship. The most of them are citizens of the United States, but some are residents in England, France, Greece, China, India, Africa, and remote countries. The Magazine has a Department of Correspondence, which may be regarded as a most interesting feature. This is sustained by gentlemen who are engaged in original research in various parts of the globe, and who furnish the results of their investigations for publication to us directly. Subscription price, $4.00 per year. To Teachers for a trial year, $2.00. 2-3t

EXCURSION TO WASHINGTON.—On the fourth of March, every fourth year, multitudes of people assemble at the National Capital to take part in and to witness the ceremonial which invests with imperial authority the uncrowned monarch of the Great Republic. The preparations for the inauguration of the next President are being made upon a scale which promises a display of unprecedented grandeur and magnificence. Washington, in the winter season, is one of the gayest capitals in Christendom, and the festivities incident to the inauguration of the chief magistrate will render it doubly attractive. The vicinity of Washington abounds in places of historic interest. Mount Vernon, the resting place of the first President, is reached by a short steamboat ride upon the bosom of the majestic Potomac, the National Cemetery at Arlington, where thousands of heroes sleep, and the National Soldiers' Home are also within easy access.

There can be no question as to the pleasure to be derived from a visit to Washington, and the only question is, how to get there at a reasonable cost. To meet this query the "Pennsylvania Lines" will sell excursion tickets at extremely low rates. They have placed in service elegant Eastlake Day Coaches and Pullman's Palace Sleeping Cars, which will form solid through trains from Cincinnati, St. Louis, Chicago, Toledo and Cleveland to Washington City. The Pennsylvania Lines are superior to any on the continent in construction, equipment and efficient service. "Security, Certainty and Celerity" is their motto. Their lines traverse a section unsurpassed in rich and varied scenery.

OUR SUPERINTENDENTS OF PUBLIC INSTRUCTION.
By HUBERT M. SKINNER.

Revised and corrected from the sketches published in this Journal, printed fine paper, with newly engraved portrait of each Superintendent. Sent by mail on receipt of fifty cents. Only a limited number printed. Order at once, of Hubert M. Skinner, Indianapolis, Ind.

INDIANA
SCHOOL JOURNAL.

Vol. XXX.   APRIL, 1885.   No. 4.

LINCOLN LEAFLETS.

HUBERT M. SKINNER.

TWO tall and beautiful monuments rising from the soil of Illinois, one by the Sangamon river and one by the great Lake, are of special interest to students of American history. They mark the last resting places of the two great statesmen on whom was centered the attention of America—and indeed of the civilized world—in the years immediately preceding the great war. Douglas triumphed over Lincoln in 1858, and Lincoln triumphed over Douglas in 1860. They were personal friends.[1] The issues on which they were arrayed belong wholly to the past, and no longer divide us. In recalling the stirring events of their campaigns no bitter feelings rise, and no appeal is made to partisan bias. The issues were squarely presented and earnestly debated, and were decided, as American issues must be, by the people. It is of President Lincoln that I wish to speak in these pages. Since all concede his greatness and his goodness, and since his name is far removed from the divisions and questions of to-day, may not teachers and pupils unite, as the twentieth year circles over his tomb,[2] in exercises which shall be a token of affectionate remembrance, and in repeating the sentiments with which he touched the chords of humanity and spoke to all the future?

The most remarkable popular debate in American annals, and in some respects the most remarkable in all history, was that of the senatorial compaign in Illinois in 1858. The excited interest with which it was attended, its protraction through many weeks and through widely different localities and communities,[1] the rush of many thousands to hear, the endless reproduction in the newspapers of every State, the comments of the millions who practically constituted the audience, the sharply drawn issues, the perfect candor of the debaters (who answered each the most searching questions of his opponent), the momentous character of the conclusions drawn—all these strange accompaniments rendered the senatorial canvass in reality a canvass before the nation and before the world, a canvass which can be likened to no other, and one which pre-determined at once the choice of the two champions as standard-bearers in the presidential canvass of two years later.

———

Singularly contrasted were the speakers in the Great Debate. Proud in the consciousness of his powers, matchless in eloquence, small in figure but splendid in the magnetism of his presence, graceful in gesture, cold, self-possessed and lofty in scorn or glowing in the passion of appeal, was Judge Douglas, the Senator of a dozen years, the hitherto unchallenged master in the field of controversy. Opposed to him was the Rail Splitter. Six feet two in his stockings, lank and ungainly, unprepossessing of visage save in the kindliness of his smile, without art or polish, but with earnestness and solemnity born of the great crisis, with honesty of purpose that none in all the throng could question, and with homely phrases that reached the heart, was Abraham Lincoln, who had dared to challenge the Little Giant to a joint discussion. Answering to the polished oratory of the Senator were the solemn earnestness and the quaint and irresistible humor of this man of the people.

———

Very remarkable was the political situation in 1858. The Democratic party was rent in twain. At the head of one division was the Administration. The leader of the other was Judge Douglas. Opposed was the young and rapidly growing Republican party; the old Whig party had gone out of existence. It was thus a three sided issue, for the Republicans met their divided opponents with a solid front. The positions of the three opposing parties may be stated briefly thus:

"It is both the right and the duty of Congress to *protect* the institution of slavery in all the Tearitorḷes."— *The Administration party.*

"It is both the right and the duty of Congress to *prohibit* the institution of slavery in all the Territories."— *The Republican party.*

"It is neither the right nor the duty of Congress to protect or to prohibit the institution of slavery in the Territories. The matter must be decided by the people of each Territory for themselves."— *The Douglas party.*

In their sentiments the Republicans were no less divided than the Democrats, though they were united in action. "Of strange, discordant and often hostile elements," said Mr. Lincoln, "we gathered from the four winds." Sentiments held by members of that party in northern Illinois were vehemently repudiated by members in the central and southern parts. To unite in action people of opposing views was the task set before both debaters. Never was presented to public men a greater temptation to equivocate and to play a double part; and yet never was debate conducted with greater candor on both sides. Perhaps never before was the American public so thoroughly instructed upon the real character of the issues to be decided.

———

The presidential campaign of 1860 was but a continuation of the same debate by the same debaters[4] To complicate matters still further, a fourth party arose, which was non-committal as to policy, proclaiming as its platform only "The Union, the Constitution, and the enforcement of the laws." A popular majority was impossible, under the circumstances. Mr. Lincoln received a *plurality* of the *popular* votes,[5] and a *majority* of the *electoral* votes,[6] and was legally elected.

———

The burden of responsibility borne by President Lincoln, the prolonged and terrible war in which he was engaged, the freeing of the slaves, the death of the President in the hour of final victory—all these are matters known to all and personally remembered by many of the readers of the Journal. They need not be related here. From the remarkable utterances of Lincoln I have selected the following extracts, which I believe will be of interest to all readers of the Journal, and which may be of value to teachers and pupils in some such way as I have suggested. They reveal more perfectly than description can portray the character of that remarkable man who stood at the helm of our Ship of State through the storm and peril of a gigantic war— of that man of whom his conquered foes have unfeignedly said, "He was our best friend."

" 'A house divided against itself can not stand.' I believe this government can not endure permanently half slave and half free. I do not expect the Union to be dissolved—I do not expect the house to fall—but I do expect it will cease to be divided."—*Key-note to the Illinois campaign of '58, Springfield, June 17.*

"My friend has said to me that I am a poor hand to quote Scripture. I will try it again, however. It is said in one of the admonitions of our Lord, 'As your Father in Heaven is perfect, be ye also perfect.' The Savior, I suppose, did not expect that any human creature could be perfect as the Father in Heaven. But he said, 'As your Father in Heaven is perfect, be ye also perfect.' He set that up as a standard; and he who did most toward reaching that standard, attained the highest degree of moral perfection. So I say in relation to the principle that all men are created equal; let it be as nearly reached as we can. If we can not give freedom to every creature, let us do nothing that will impose slavery upon any other creature."—*Chicago speech of July 10, 1858.*

"Now it happens that we meet together once every year, sometimes about the fourth of July, for some reason or other. These 4th of July gatherings, I suppose, have their uses. If you will indulge me, I will state what I suppose to be some of them.   *   *   *   *

We hold this annual celebration to remind ourselves of all the good done in this process of time, of how it was done, and who did it, and how we are historically connected with it; and we go from these meetings in better humor with ourselves—we feel more attached, the one to the other, and more firmly bound to the country we inhabit. In every way we are better men in the age and race and country in which we live, for these celebrations.: But after we have done all this, we have not yet reached the whole. There is something else connected with it. We have besides these men—descended by blood from our ancestors—among us, perhaps half our people, who are not descendents at all of these men; they are men who have come from Europe themselves, or whose ancestors have come hither and settled here, finding themselves our equals in all things. If they look back through this history to trace their connection with those days by blood, they find they have none; they can not carry themselves back into that glorious epoch and make them selves feel that they are part of us. But when they look through that old Declaration of Independence, they find that those old men say that 'We hold these truths to be self-evident, that all men are created equal'; and then they feel that that moral sentiment taught in that day evidences their relation to those men; that it is the father of all moral principle in them, and that they have a right to claim it as though they were blood of the blood and flesh of the flesh of the men who wrote that Declaration,—and so they are. That is the electric cord in that Declaration that links the hearts of patriotic and liberty-loving men together, that will link these patriotic hearts as long as the love of freedom exists in the minds of men throughout the world."—*Chicago speech, July* 10, 1858.

"I hold that there is no reason in the world why the negro is not entitled to all the natural rights enumerated in the Declaration of Independence—the right to life, liberty, and the pursuit of happiness. I hold that he is as much entitled to these as the white man. I agree with Judge Douglas, he is not my equal in many respects—certainly not in color, perhaps not in moral or intellectual endowment. But in the right to eat without the leave of anybody else, the bread which his own hand earns, he is my equal and the equal of Judge Douglas, and the equal of every living man."—*The Great Debate; Ottawa.*

"I think the authors of that notable instrument (the Declaration of Independence) intended to include *all* men, but they did not mean to declare all men equal *in all respects.* They did not mean to say all men were equal in color, size, intellect, moral development or social capacity. They defined with tolerable distinctness *in what* they did consider all men are created equal— equal in certain inalienable rights, among which are life, liberty, and the pursuit of happiness. This they said, and this they meant. They did not mean to assert the obvious untruth that all were then actually *enjoying* that equality, or that *they* were about to *confer* it immediately upon them. In fact, they had no power to confer such a boon. They meant simply to *declare the right*, so that the enforcement of it might follow as fast as circumstances should permit. They meant to set up a standard maxim for free society, which should be familiar to all; constantly referred to, constantly labored for, and even, though never perfectly attained, constantly approximated, and thereby constantly spreading and deepening its influence and augmenting the happiness and value of life to all people, of all colors, everywhere."—*The Great Debate; Alton.*

"A duty devolves upon me which is perhaps greater than that which has devolved upon any other man since the days of Washington. He never could have succeeded except for the aid of Divine Providence, upon which he at all times relied. I feel that I can not succeed without the same Divine aid which sustained him; and on the same Almighty Being I place my reliance for support. And I hope that you, my friends, will all pray that I may receive that Divine assistance, without which I can not succeed, but with which success is certain."—*Farewell speech at Springfield, Feb.* 11, 1861.

"I am but an accidental instrument, temporary and to serve for a limited time; and I appeal to you to constantly bear in mind that with you, and not with politicians, nor with presidents, nor with office seekers, but with *you* is the question, "Shall the Union and shall the liberties of this country be preserved to the latest generations."—*Bates House speech at Indianapolis, Feb.* 11, 1861.

"I have often inquired of myself what great principle or idea it was that kept this Confederacy so long together. It was not the mere matter of the separation of the Colonies from the mother-land, but that sentiment in the Declaration of Independence which gave liberty not alone to the people of this country, but, I hope, to the world for all future time. It was that which gave promise that in due time the weight would be lifted from the shoulders of all men. This is the sentiment embodied in the Declaration of Independence. Now, my friends, can the country be saved upon that basis? If it can, I will consider myself the happiest man in the world if I can help to save it. If it can not be saved upon that principle, it will be truly awful. But if this country can not be saved without giving up that principle, I was about to say that I would rather be assassinated on this spot than surrender it."—*Independence Hall speech, Philadelphia, Feb.* 21, 1861.

"Why should there not be a patient confidence in the ultimate justice of the people? Is there any better or equal hope in the world? In our present differences is either party without faith of being in the right? If the Almighty Ruler of Nations, with His eternal truth and justice, be on your side of the North or on yours of the South, that truth and that justice will surely prevail, by the judgment of this great tribunal of the American people."
—*First Inaugural, March* 4, 1861.

"In your hands, my dissatisfied fellow-countrymen, and not in mine, is the momentous issue of civil war. The government will not assail you. You can have no conflict without being yourselves the aggressors. You have no oath registered in Heaven to destroy the government, while I have the most solemn one to 'preserve, protect.and defend' it. I am loth to close. We are not enemies, but friends. We must not be enemies. Though passion may have strained, it must not break our bonds of affection. The mystic chording of memory stretches from every battle-field and patriot grave to every living heart and hearthstone all over this broad land, will yet swell the chorus of the Union, when again touched, as surely they will be, by the angels of our better nature."—*First Inaugural.*

"Now, therefore, I, Abraham Lincoln, President of the United States, by virtue of the power vested in me as Commander-in-Chief of the Army and Navy of the United States in time of actual armed rebellion against the authority and government of the United States, and as a fit and necessary war measure for suppressing said rebellion, do, on this 1st day of January in the year of our Lord one thousand eight hundred and sixty-three, and in accordance with my purpose to do so proclaimed for the full period of one hundred days, from the first day above mentioned, order and designate as the States and parts of States wherein the people thereof are respectively this day in rebellion against the United States, the following, etc.

And by virtue of the power and for the purpose aforesaid, I do order and declare that all persons held as slaves within said designated States and parts of States are, and henceforward shall be, free; and that the Executive Government of the United States, including the military and naval authorities thereof, will recognize and maintain the freedom of said persons.   *   *   *

And upon this act, sincerely believed to be an act of justice, warranted by the Constitution upon military necessity, I invoke the considerate judgment of mankind and the favor of Almighty God."—*Proclamation of Emancipation, Jan.* 1, 1863.

"The world will little note nor long remember what we say here, but it can never forget what they did here. It is for *us*, the *living*, rather, to be dedicated here to the unfinished work they have thus far so nobly carried on. It is rather for *us* to be here dedicated to the great task remaining before us, that from these honored dead we take increased devotion to the cause for which they gave the last full measure of devotion; that we here highly resolve that these dead shall not have died in vain; that the nation shall, under God, have a new birth of freedom; and that the government of the people, by the people, and for the people, shall not perish from the earth."—*Gettysburg Cemetery Dedication, Nov.,* 1864.

"With malice toward none, with charity for all, with firmness to do the right as God gives us to see the right, let us strive to finish the great work we are in, to bind up the nation's wounds, to care for him who shall have borne the battle and for his widow and his orphans; to do all which may achieve and cherish a just

and a lasting peace among ourselves and with all nations."—
Second Inaugural, March 4, 1865.

1. Both friendship and patriotism dictated the last words of Douglas to
his sons: "Stand by the Constitution! *Stand by the President!*" At the
river of death the Little Giant sent forth to the millions a bugle-call for the
Union. He passed away in June, 1861.

2. Mr. Lincoln expired on the morning of April 15, 1865. His remains
were entombed on the 4th of May, and were translated to the new sepulcher
on the 15th of October.

3. The following were the appointments of the Great Debate: Ottawa,
August 21; Freeport, August 27; Jonesboro', Sept. 15; Charleston, Sept. 18;
Galesburgh, October 7; Quincy, October 13; Alton, October 15. Preceding
and interspersed with these appointments were fifty other addresses by Mr.
Lincoln, in as many cities and towns, and perhaps the same number by Mr.
Douglas. These virtually formed a part of the Great Debate.

4. The Little Giant was nominated at Baltimore in April; the Rail Splitter
at the "Wigwam" in Chicago, in May. Both had continued the debate
through 1859 in various States.

5. The vote stood as follows:

        The Republican party—Lincoln............ 1,886,452.
        The Douglas party—Douglas............... 1,375,157.
        The Administration party—Breckenridge, 847,953.
        The Union party—Bell.... .... 590,631.

Thus there were nearly a million more votes cast against Mr. Lincoln than
for him.

6. The electoral vote stood as follows:

        The Republican party—Lincoln............ .... 180.
        The Administration party—Breckenridge......... 72.
        The Union party—Bell....... ... . 39.
        The Douglas party—Douglas .... 12. ·

The votes cast for Douglas reveal an absurd difference between the electoral
and the popular verdicts.

PEDAGOGICAL RHETORIC.

BY A. TOMPKINS, SUPT. FRANKLIN SCHOOLS.

ON this basis, we must reconstruct our knowledge of the subjects. We must be able to determine what the organization of
the matter and the treatment of the ideas must be, and not be piece-
meal receivers of fragmentary facts served up in some convenient
form, on the page. The teacher, as well as the writer, must be
able to construct upon the inherent laws of the ideas. The sub-

ject must be worked into an educational means, by analyzing it into the classes of ideas, and thus determining the thought relations involved, and what power, habit, and tone of thought can be cultivated. Only this is professional knowledge of the subject; and only he who has a definite plan for making a subject an educating power is a professional teacher.

So far in the progress of our schools, teachers have not been held responsible for the kind of thinking their pupils do. We have not brought criticism down to the mind developing process in the recitation. If the school building and furniture is of the latest and best, if the general machinery of the school is up to a high state of organization; if in the recitation the class is prim and formal and give out the assigned work (no matter what) without failure, all is well. No matter what opportunities are lost to fix the essential habits of character, no matter what outrages are committed on the growing mind of the child, if the machine runs smoothly and grinds out *some* product. We must make the criticism on the process itself, not on the process of carrying on school work, but on the mental process of dealing with ideas, not the outside but the inside process.

When we require pupils to think these four classes of ideas as each class requires, their study and recitation will assume a different character. The pupil trained thus, in studying the human heart will know where to begin, how to proceed, and when he is done. He thinks the thing. The imagination creates it and he surveys it face to face. He methodically proceeds from a determination of its use to its position and relation of its position to its use; to its form and relation of its form to its use; to its size and relation of its size to its use; to its attributes and how these condition its use; to its parts with their relation to each other and to the whole This pupil will study the heart and not the book, but will use the book in learning about the heart. He will search other sources than the text. When he comes to the class he is ready to talk. He has no trouble to remember his lesson, and does not ask if it is the first paragraph on the next page. And the teacher can use, without disconcerting the pupil, the topical, question, or any other method which he may have adopted as *his method!* The pupil can talk continuously and methodically, and can write a complete description if required. As a pupil is ordinarily trained to study he will gather such fragmentary facts as he can force in the memory from fragmentary paragraphs. If the text should treat the matter fully and methodically he has no organizing habit to embody the parts, and when reciting must recall the points as given to him, and not as he sees them in their relation to the object itself. This pupil can not talk continuously unless he recites the text, which he will have to do or be propped up by isolated questions. His vacant stare will betray the nervous strain to remember things read and not seen with the mental eye.

Besides the habits named that might be formed in connection with each class of ideas, many others would be listed and provided for by the professional teacher : as, the habit of accuracy and truthfulness, especially in mathematics; liberality and toleration in history, patience and industry in all, etc.

If it seem that all this is too much on the side of mental discipline and not enough on the side of knowledge, it need only be said that the methods of gaining discipline and knowledge are at heart one. A perfect method of either requires a perfect perfect method of both. If a subject is taught so as to secure the most perfect discipline nothing more could be done to secure the knowledge. Besides, this doctrine is now much needed to check this high pressure system of teaching facts. We can not avoid this doctrine if we accept the development doctrine of education.

But it is not only that the writer and teacher present ideas to another mind to affect it with knowledge and discipline, they present these ideas to affect the emotional, the æsthetic nature. This is the purely literary phase of the work of both, and consists of the poetic conception of ideas and the tuning of life to a higher tone. As Hawthorne lifted the Old Town Pump into the literary atmosphere till it gushed sweet rills for thirsty souls in other lands, so the teacher is to lead the pupil to poetic conceptions of the meanest objects—to idealize them into something pure, noble, and beautiful. The pupil should not leave the object a cold, dry thing, the product of the categories of thought, but should lift it to the level of the emotional nature—should endow it with life by the poetic imagination. This will induce a glowing habit of soul which warms into poetic light common-place things, and will do much to relieve the dull tedium of every day life. There are certain ideas which reach directly the emotional nature and purify it, as those formally treated in drawing, music, and literature; but those intellectual ideas counted valuable for their own sake, if not elevated into the higher light, are apt to chain life to a world of material fact and make it monotonous and flat, without light, shade, or color. This elevation of ideas in teaching corresponds to figures of speech in writing, and as the latter elevates the tone of discourse, so the former elevates the tone of teaching.

But the work of the teacher and writer would be fatally incomplete if they presented *ideas* to train and instruct the intellect, and to purify and intensify the emotional nature, if they should not present them so as to determine the will in a course of conduct—the oratory of teaching. The pressing need of the schools is for something more definite to be done by way of giving pupils a correct notion of life—a regulative purpose to govern conduct. It is to little purpose to give a pupil power if he does not know how to limit and direct it. He should be led to create the true ideal of life and stimulated to send the current of his being out after it.

Thus the writer and the teacher present ideas to the mind for three purposes—to affect the intellect, the sensibility, and the will; and by four processes—description, narration, exposition, and argumentation. This completes the outline of the second chapter of pedagogics, which treats of affecting the mind by means of ideas.

When the writer or the teacher has fixed his purpose and has mastered the ideas by which he is to accomplish his purpose, the question of style presents itself: "How can he best convey the ideas from his mind to the one to be affected? The ideas must pass through some medium and suffer loss by friction. The medium must be interpreted, and so part of the energy of the interpreting mind is taken from the thought conveyed to the medium. A perfect medium would be perfectly transparent, so that the thought would be as perfect in the receiving mind as in the giving mind. The naked thought would pass entire from one mind to the other. In perfectly clear language we seem to lay directly hold of the content and are not conscious of a conveying instrument. This law of style which requires a transparent medium lies at the bottom of all the rules on this subject, and with a probable exception, at the bottom of all the rules of presenting a subject to a class. The teacher fixes her purpose and arranges the ideas, and then appears before the class with this problem: "How can I cause their minds to lay hold of the ideas without waste of time and energy on something not necessary in gaining the ideas?

The third chapter of pedagogical science and art deals with this problem. It corresponds to the chapter of style in rhetoric. A brief illustration is all that is intended here.

If the teacher uses unnecessary words or speaks in loud harsh tones the pupil's attention is diverted to these. If questions are not clear or are ambiguous energy is wasted in finding out what is wanted. If a lesson is indefinitely assigned, or work given for which pupils are not prepared, much worry and needless work are occasioned. There is loss of effort by trying to convey by words what would be more directly conveyed by an illustration or an example. But the one great violation of this principle in teaching is that style of teaching which requires the pupil to study the medium instead of the ideas conveyed. This is done in committing definitions not understood, and in reciting pages of matter, notes and all, as given in the text. It is a common thing for a class to spend half their time and strength in fixing the points in the order and form of the book for purposes of recitation. The teacher should use every art known to the writer to engage the sympathy, awaken interest, and arouse the activity of the learner, and to remove every necessity for unnecessary thinking.

Sometimes the writer chooses to make the medium not only clear but beautiful, as in the poetic form. Likewise the work of the teacher should be beautiful in form, which, with the figurative conception of ideas, constitutes æsthetic or poetic teaching.

THE ADVANTAGES OF OUR SYSTEM OF EXAMINATIONS.

BY MARY HADLEY.

[Read before the Parke County Teachers' Association.]

OUR SYSTEM OF EXAMINATIONS is understood to mean the system adopted for our State, and thus for our county, as the State provides for uniformity of system by counties.

It is an outgrowth of a condition of the State (pre-existing) which demands intelligent citizenship. And as far as this outgrowth is normal, is our system one of advantage and competent to meet the demand.

The term *system* implies a combination of parts into a whole. Also a connected view of the truths pertaining to some department of knowledge or to some scheme for obtaining certain ends.

We are instructed to discuss the topic on program from the stand-point of one department of the subject *only*—namely, that of a system of examinations for *teachers*. This divides the length of the discussion by about two. The word "advantages" suggests that we are to speak of the merits rather than the demerits of the system. This again limits the discussion and disarms it to some extent of the weapon of comparison and contrast.

Our topic thus abreviated opens a field for discussion which is yet broad enough for the limited time and ability of a teacher of public schools who is patron to and servant of the system. All systems of examinations for teachers propose to guarantee to the *taught*, the competency of the *teacher*. Hence the *propriety* of a system.

Our system, by a plan of gradation by percents, attempts to approximately measure the capacity of the teacher for the work to be done. In whatever this test fails, the deficiency is supplemented if not entirely complemented by the estimate which is placed upon professional ability, moral worth, adaptability, and actual success in the work of the school-room.

The plan involves a two-fold test: 1st, a test of the teacher's knowledge of text-books; 2d, a test of his professional skill. The first test has been copiously and in some cases unscrupulously criticised, both as to method and subject-matter. If those employed to administer the system are in any way deficient in ability or fidelity to their trust, such deficiency is chargeable to them and not to the system. The circumstance of trafficking in state board questions, which occurred during the official term of ex-Supt. Bloss, together with its exposure and punishment, gives evidence that there is "a power behind the throne" to vindicate the integrity of the test.

This brings us to consider the *efficiency* of the test. If the questions employed are of doubtful, general or particular interest, or should they be strikingly in harmony with the course of instruction given at some isolated institution of learning with which some member of the board is conversant (a charge often made), or should they fail to test, in some degree, the applicant's professional skill, they are to the extent of these deficiencies circumscribed and shorn of their purpose. But if our state board has recognized the fact that every teacher who throngs the public school mart is *not* the *ideal* teacher, and has so framed its questions as to make it possible (by some energetic clambering up), for the demand for teachers to be supplied, its action must savor of expediency though its questions may not be those it would dictate as the ideal ones.

Having said this much for expediency, we wish to discuss the second test (that of professional skill), from a proposition which we think so expedient that in the near future its verification is destined to relieve our system of its greatest embarrassment— viz., every teacher should have *professional* skill before ENTERING upon the duties of his profession.

Hence necessarily a professional training. This is required of *other* practitioners, and if the teacher would dignify his calling with the title of "profession" he can not expect less of himself. A physician does not presume upon the faith of any community without producing a diploma of professional skill. He can not insist that he be allowed to practice for a few years even, at only the possible sacrifice of health and life, in order that he may attain to that professional skill which can and should be secured without this. Then inasmuch as mal-practice upon the mind—the immortal part of our being—is more disastrous than such practice upon our physical being *can* be, the teacher should not so presume.

Aside from a knowledge of text-books, every effort of the teacher in the direction of professional skill, moral excellency and general knowledge, secures for itself its own legitimate reward. But that system which offers the best *inducement* for such attainment, may justly claim most in the scale of advantage. For illustration interview the average patron of the average public school community or district in regard to the success of the school work of the place, and he will say of a certain teacher, "He is a fine scholar, but he failed in discipline." Or of a certain other teacher, "He wasn't much of a scholar, but *some how or* RUTHER he had a WAY about him which made his pupils all like him." This "WAY" he had about him evidently meant his school management—an important part of which is discipline. His ability to direct and control others is an outgrowth of a habit of self-control. This means *moral excellency*, which some how or other (though the fact may not always be discerned), weighs largely in the scale of estimation placed upon us by those to whom we would make our labor acceptable.

On this point issue may be taken. And it may be insisted that ability to govern is not inherent in moral force of character; but that those morally depraved often govern best. On this point we would take issue, by agreeing that there are exceptions to the first proposition—that of the power to control being inherent in moral character. But the proposition that depravity can not control admits of NO exception. Depravity may *command*, and through advantage of position or desparado courage *enforce*—but *govern never!* A *despot* may rule—only a KING can govern. Emerson says, "The reason why men do not obey us is because they see the *mud* at the bottom of our eyes."

Professional skill, moral force, and general intelligence have long been recognized by the law which dictates Our System of Examinations for Teachers. But not so fully as by the recent amendments (to the system), which places these attainments at a premium.

THE GRUBE. METHOD AGAIN.

BY E. E. WHITE.

THE first reading of the editorial (associate's) in the March number of the Journal gave me the impression that it was intended to answer the objections to the Grube method urged in my two former contributions, but a more careful reading suggests that the editorial may be designed to be a somewhat independent contribution to the general discussion, my articles being used as a sort of scaffolding for this purpose. This view seems reasonable since the main objection to the Grube method stated and considered, is *not mine*. We quote :

"It is claimed, moreover, that these relations [*part* relation and *factor* relation] are fundamentally different processes. That addition deals with the part relation of numbers, while multiplication deals with the factor relation, which is so different from the part relation that they have nothing in common."

And again :

" But we are taught by authority the most excellent in the opinion of all of us, that the process, 3 and 3 are 6, is fundamentally different from the process, 2 times 3 are 6."

The editorial then proceeds to show that these two relations are *fundamentally* the same and concludes that, for this reason, "they can be taught together without violating any fundamental law of teaching."

If I correctly understand the meaning of "fundamental", I do not hold or teach the views above cited. On the contrary, I hold that multiplication has its *genesis*, or *fundamentum* if preferred, in addition, and have taught that both addition and multiplication embody a common principle—there being "but two *fundamental* principles in arithmetic, synthesis and analysis"

2

—and, besides, my method of teaching the products of the digital numbers is based on and embodies the fact that multiplication has its *genesis* or basis in addition.*

My positions are that the *part* relation and the *factor* relation in mathematics are not *identical*, and that the processes of addition and multiplication (also of subtraction and division) are not *identical;* and I further hold, with Prof. Edward Olney, that the connection between these two relations and the corresponding processes is not so immediate and practical as to necessitate or justify the teaching of addition, subtraction, multiplication, and division together *from the first.*

But whatever may have been the purpose of the writer, the editorial is the clearest and strongest statement of the supposed philosophic basis of the Grube method that I have seen, though it strangely leaves the union of subtraction and division without defense. Permit me, however, to add that, in my judgment, the argument fails to show that the method is philosophical, and to ask whether the conclusion reached is not clearly a *non sequitur.*

We would submit that it does not follow that two processes may or should be taught together because the one has its genesis in the other, or because they have a common basis. The three thought processes called conception, formal judging, and reasoning all have their basis in the act of *comparison*, and, in this sense, they are "fundamentally" the same; but it does not follow that the three faculties called conception, judgment, and reason should, *from the first*, be exercised together and the corresponding kinds of knowledge taught together.

If there be a principle of teaching that is "fundamental" it is the fact that there is a natural order in which the different faculties of the mind should be exercised and the corresponding kinds of knowledge taught; and it follows that, if there be a natural or logical sequence in the processes and principles of mathematics, this sequence should be observed in teaching them. The two inverse processes of multiplication and division naturally and logically follow the inverse processes of addition and subtraction,

---

* See "Oral Lessons in Number," pp. 120–145.

and hence we hold that the ignoring of this sequence is a violation of a fundamental principle of teaching.

The only sure philosophic basis for the Grube method is the *identity* of the processes of addition and multiplication and of subtraction and division. (Is there any significance in the fact that the editorial makes no reference to subtraction and division?) It must be shown that there are but two numerical processes, addition and subtraction, and that every so-called product is and must be found by *adding*, and that every so-called quotient is and must be found by *subtracting*.

This brings us to the decisive inquiry, Are the processes of addition and multiplication in mathematics *identical?*

It does not follow that they are identical because the one has its genesis in the other. True marriage, for example, has its genesis or basis in mutual love, but marriage and mutual love are not identical relations.

It does not follow that the processes of addition and multiplication are identical because the number denoting the product of any two integers may be obtained by adding one of these numbers continuously to itself, nor because the expression 5 times 7, for example, may be equivalent to 7 taken 5 times. There are many persons who in childhood arbitrarily memorized the forty-five digital products and have multiplied numbers all their life *without consciously adding*. I now multiply 320 by 4 without consciously adding 320 to itself and without consciously adding the 2 tens to itself or the 3 hundreds to itself. Nor will it do to assert that whatever I may be conscious of, I do actually find the product by adding. This involves the psychical absurdity that the mental process of which I am conscious has no existence, while a process of which I am not conscious actually exists! When a theory runs beyond or deeper than consciousness I can not follow it, and there is the suspicion that it is an unsubstantial basis for a method of teaching.

The evident truth is that howsoever the products of the digital numbers are first learned, the *process* of multiplying numbers is differentiated from the *process* of adding, and the two processes are not identical but are distinct—I do not say "fundamentally different." As evidence of their distinct character, I cite the fact that the processes and results of addition and multiplication are uniformly expressed by different words and these are not inter-changeable. No mathematical terms are more distinct than the terms *add* and *multiply, sum* and *product; subtract* and *divide, dif-ference* and *quotient.* Moreover, the *part* signs, + and —, and the *factor* signs, × and ÷, run through mathematics from ele-mentary arithmetic to the calculus, and they never indicate the same process. $a \times b$ never means $a + b$, and $a \div b$ never means $a - b$.

· This difference is also shown by the fact that while the num-ber denoting the product of two *integral* numbers may be found by adding one of the numbers continuously to itself, it is not true that the product of *any* two mathematical quantities may thus be found. This may be shown by an attempt to find *by addition* the products of $\frac{1}{4} \times \frac{1}{3}$, or $\frac{1}{a} \times \frac{1}{a}$, or $\frac{x}{s} \times \frac{1}{y}$. The entire sign and terminological language of mathematics is based on the fact that there are four distinct *processes.*

But my objections to the Grube method as used in American schools are *practical*, as well as philosophical. Five years ago I found that this method was used, with more or less fullness, in many of the graded schools of Indiana, and I have since taken some pains to ascertain the practical success of the method. I have the testimony of more than a score of the superintendents and principals of city and town schools in the State that the re-sults of the method are not satisfactory—to express the testimony mildly. Since reading the editorial in the March Journal, I have fortunately had the opportunity of witnessing a first-year exercise in number by the Grube method. The class was composed of very bright first year pupils and the teacher was very skillful and "at home" in the use of the method. The lesson was devoted to the number 8. So long as the lesson was confined to the combining of the parts of 8 and the separating of 8 into its parts, the drill was admirable, the pupils showing a clear perception of processes and results; but as soon as the teacher passed over to the *factor* relation and introduced the word "times", the num-bers used were in several instances misplaced and the mental confusion of the pupils was otherwise evident, and, when a little fellow passed to the black-board and wrote $1 \times 5 + 3 = 8$, the entire expression of the pupils showed that they were using signs without clearly perceiving what was signified. When the teacher skillfully passed from the taking away of the parts of 8 to the division of 8 by one of its parts, the mental uncertainty of the little ones was still more marked, and the climax was reached when a six-year old wrote on the black-board, $8 + 5 = 1$ (3). The exercise, so admirable in most respects, reminded me of the earnest and skillful drills in the oral analysis of problems to which the young pupils in the Cleveland schools were subjected thirty-three years ago, when "Mental Arithmetic" was a school hobby. The Cleveland pupils gave with amazing glibness the most logical analyses of problems; the teachers understood the language used and saw the logic (at least some of them), and *they supposed that this was true of their little pupils.* Who now believes that these children were the remarkable logicians they seemed to be?

Permit me to add that I have never witnessed a Grube drill in number with *first-year* pupils, when this mental uncertainty and confusion and consequent mechanism were not apparent, and I have certainly seen the work of as skillful primary teachers as the average teacher employed in our schools.

It is both a philosophical and a practical mistake to introduce the factor term "times" or to use the factor signs, $\times$ and $\div$, in first-year instruction in number. I also doubt the wisdom of using even the part signs, $+$ and $-$, in first year lessons, and it is clearly an error to use the formal *equation*. This technical mathematical language is an actual hindrance to the normal progress of little children.

There is a natural and logical sequence of numerical processes, the inverse processes of addition and subtraction *preceding* those of multiplication and division, and this sequence should be carefully observed in the first lessons in number.

It is believed, Mr. Editor, that it is time to call a halt in the unquestioning use of the Grube method.

The north pole seems to be on a southern cruise, as it were.

THE SCHOOL ROOM.

[This Department is conducted by GEO. F. BASS, Supervising Prin. Indianapolis schools.]

——:o:——

THEY DIDN'T READ IT.

"IF a carpenter earn $84 in one month and spend $56, how much will he save in five months?"

The above was given to an average third-year class in good condition. The pupils were not frightened by an examination. It was given during the usual study hour as regular daily work.

The class made an average of zero. Several got the correct answer, but by an entirely senseless method. They found the sum of $84 and $56 and labeled it "Answer." The problem is peculiar in that this process gives the same answer as the proper process gives. The majority of the class did it this way. The rest, excepting one boy, subtracted $56 from $84 and called the remainder the answer. The "one boy" solved by the proper plan, but made a mistake in computation.

There is nothing unique in this occurrence. Such things have disgusted and discouraged many a teacher, even in the higher grades. Why do such things occur and recur?

Pupils and other people are apt to do what they have been doing recently. The last thing these little people had been doing was adding. They had been reviewing addition and subtraction in solving concrete examples. They had solved more in addition than subtraction. So we found that the majority of the class added. They saw two numbers with the dollar sign prefixed. The 5 months did not attract them; they had not been dealing in months as much as they had in dollars. The problems they had solved during their school life always required the dollar sign to be used, but frequently other concrete numbers had not entered into the solution. Hence without thought, but just through force of habit they added or subtracted.

While the work was being done it was noticed that many began to solve the problem before they read it—in fact it was found afterwards by questioning the pupils, that many of them never did read it.

The Remedy.—Have the pupils form the *habit* of reading very carefully each problem before they begin to solve it. *How* shall this habit be formed? Suggestion: Ask them to read the problem silently, after which put the same kind of questions that are used in a reading recitation to ascertain whether the pupils have comprehended the thought.

What is asked for in this problem? How much does he earn in one month? How much does he spend in one month? How much *must* he save in one month? How many months does he save this amount? How much, then, *must* he save in *five* months?

This kind of work takes time and patience. Thought grows slowly. Habit is formed by often repeating a thing. Habit of thinking is not an exception. A teacher who follows the plan suggested may not get "over" much in one recitation, but the habit of reading and understanding the conditions of the problem before beginning to solve it will be formed, which is worth more than ten guesses, even though they be "percented" by the teacher each day and returned to the pupil on the following day for another guess, if he were *unlucky* in his first guess.

COMPOSITION.

REFERRING to the article on this subject in the March number of the Journal, it will be seen that the following were given by the pupils and placed on the black-board by the teacher; and that the pupils were asked to put them into one sentence without using the word *and*:

(1) The chief object in this picture is a little girl. (2) She is riding on a sled. (3) It is a small sled. (4) It is a hand-sled. When these were combined by the pupils they were asked to read from their slates. It was found that the sentences were *not all exactly alike.* There was quite a variety. A few follow: "The chief object of this picture is a little girl riding in a small hand-sled." "The chief object of this picture is a little girl who is riding in a small hand-sled." "A little girl riding in a small hand-sled is the chief object of the picture."

How is she dressed? To this question many answers differing in form were written on the slates. "In a large warm shawl, and she is bundled up so that we can see only her face."

When they were asked to put this additional fact into their sentence they were enthusiastic in their efforts to accomplish it. There was not a face in the room that said "I am writing a dry, dreary, disgusting composition"—*not one*. All seemed happy, and very soon bright eyes said, "We are ready." Again a variety of sentences was read. Thus, patiently, from day to day, were they led on and the composition grew gradually, but surely, and when it was done it was the pupil's composition and no partnership affair—half teacher and half school—the individuality of the pupil entirely swallowed up.

By skillful questioning, the following statements were gotten from the pupils from day to day, and placed on the board to be combined as has been suggested above. Sometimes the teacher would give the pupils a connecting word that might be used; as, which, that, who, and, when, etc. The teacher also indicated which ones should be put into one statement, and which of these statements should be placed in one paragraph:

The sled is at the top of the hill. It is a large hill. Four boys are pulling the sled. They are jolly looking boys. They pull by a long rope. Both ends of the rope are fastened to the sled. One boy is waving his cap. He is in front. One has fallen down. He has dropped his book. He is in the rear. They all have fur caps. They have good warm clothes. They have high boots. There is a boy at the left. His head and ears are tied up with a long scarf. He is watching the fun. He has two books under his arm. This is a picture of a country scene. I think so because I see a rail fence in the back part. The picture makes one think of the fun we have going to school when the snow is on the ground.

After these had been combined in sentences written on the slate, and after they had been read and criticised, the pupils were required to write the composition on paper. A meager outline which suggested the facts and the order of presenting them was furnished.

PRIMARY DEPARTMENT.

[This Department is conducted by Lewis H. Jones, Supt. Indianapolis Schools.]

——:o:——

PRIMARY LANGUAGE.

WHEN pupils have mastered the four classes of sentences by the method indicated in the preceding paper of this series, they may be said to have in their possession the tools for the remaining work in Language. Each new fact is to be learned in its proper connection for its appropriate place in some one of the four kinds of sentence.

For this reason the conversation of teacher and pupils during the lesson in language, should be composed of wholes,—units of language—sentences.

It is frequently best in the recitation in Arithmetic, or even in Geography, in which the thought is dominant, and the language from subordinates, to accept fragmentary expressions; but in the language lesson, in which the purpose is to harmonize the thought and the language form, and to explain the latter by means of the former, it is best that all the forms used be complete.

In all highly inflected languages, construction is dependent on the change of meaning produced by the change of form in the individual words which compose the sentence; in English there is the added fact of a change of meaning of a word by change of its position in the sentence.

In both of these cases the fact is, when first learned, equally arbitrary; but after one has heard the correct construction oft repeated in respect to thoughts that are of deep interest, there is developed a *standard of taste*, which rejects all that does not harmonize with what has thus become habitual. The development of this standard of taste is, after all, the most important end of primary instruction in language.

These preliminary remarks indicate plainly a method for the teaching to children the few inflections that are needed to prevent the common and gross mistakes which are heard among the uncultivated :

1. The simple fact—the various forms of a word and the meaning of each.

2. The use of each form in sentence about some familiar theme, so as to express precisely the relation of ideas which the theme demands.

3. Much practice in oral and written composition demanding the use of the various forms in their appropriate meanings—first, in elliptical sentences, and second, in original sentences on definite new themes.

These three steps will be developed in another article.

LATE AGAIN.

[READ THIS TO THE PUPILS.]

"Half a minute more, ma'am, and you'd have missed the train!"

Yes; and very probably she would have deserved to have missed it. It does sometimes happen that one can not help it, but in nine cases out of ten the cause of being too late is just a habit of trifling and putting off every thing to the last. Very likely this lady had plenty of time, but she trifled with her packing, and trifled with her dressing, and trifled in getting to the station; and now with her trifling she teases the porter, who manages to get her pushed into the train just as it begins to move, at the risk of being knocked down and crushed under the wheels.

Which of you is it who is always making that noise by coming in late in the morning to school? Never do it again. Be punctual—that is, be in time in all your engagements. You have no right to keep people—and especially older people—waiting for you. To be careless in keeping an appointment shows a real want of conscientiousness; and yet some of those who are the very worst in this respect will never admit they are in the wrong. Their watch misled them, or "they did not think it was so far on," or some excuse or other is always ready.

Boys, if you go on thus, you will never get on in business. The great General Washington of America once had a secretary who was often late at his desk, and was always laying the blame on his watch. "You must get another watch," said the General at last, "or I must get another secretary."—*Ex.*

DEPARTMENT OF PEDAGOGY.

This Department is conducted by Geo. P. Brown, President State Normal School.

————:o:————

SIR WM. HAMILTON defines a science to be a complement of cognitions that are logically arranged and are true. This makes a science to consist of a group of ideas properly arranged; or it is classified knowledge. This definition must be liberally construed or it will lead to error. It may be asked whether the science of Botany, for instance, has not existed ever since vegetable life began. One interpretation of this general definition of science would forbid me to call Botany a science until the facts and laws of the process of plant life had been discovered by some human being and set out in logical order. Only what has been found out and properly organized is science. It is the product of the human mind, and has no real existence outside of it. Destroy all human beings and all science would vanish. This would give science a transitory, or at least a contingent existence.

But if we consider the processes in the vegetable world as an expression of the conscious thought of an intelligent being, then the complement of ideas embodied therein has an existence independent of the human mind. The science of Botany then is seen to be an objective reality which I may or may not discover, but which exists whether I discover it or not.

Considered from this point of view Botany is not constructed by the learner, but is discovered. It exists wherever vegetable life exists. When I discover it I "think God's thoughts after him.' From this view Botany is not a human, but a divine creation. Man may come into possession of more or less of this knowledge by a study of the objects that embody it. But whether he knows much or little or nothing of it, the thing exists all the same.

There are some sciences of human origin, such as language for example, which are a spontaneous, unconscious creation of man, before he comes into a conscious scientific knowledge of them.

Is there a science of teaching? Education is the process by

which the individual changes from the natural state of a mere animal, to that spiritual state of knowledge and self-control in which he comprehends the world and becomes obedient to ethical laws. This process is the activity of an energy or principle called growth, that produces certain definite results. This principle is stimulated to activity primarily by attacks made upon the senses by their environment. A perfect environment would result in a perfect process.

To know this process would be to know the science of education. To know and supply the environment necessary to stimulate this process would be to know and practice the Art of education.

The school is an institution that has for its purpose the supplying of this environment to the child during that period known as school life, for a portion of each year. The science of school teaching is the principles, laws, and facts that determine the process of his education, during this period.

The art of school teaching is the actual supplying of this environment by the teacher, in obedience to the dictates of the science.

Teaching has been defined by Mr. Dickinson to be the act of "presenting objects of thought (either subjective or objective), to the learner's mind as occasions of knowledge or mental development."

This is but another way of saying in the terms used in this discussion, that teaching is the supplying of the environment necessary to stimulate that mental activity that will result in knowledge and mental development. All the teacher can do is to supply the conditions for this activity. When the favoring conditions have been supplied, and all of the distracting influences removed, all has been done that can be done. The education of the child can result only from his own effort. The law of education is the law of self-activity. Every child must educate himself.

There is a science of education since there is a process of mental growth that is obedient to natural law. There is a science of teaching for the same reason. The teacher who has discovered this science may make conscious application of it to the training of the pupil by presenting such objects of knowledge to his mind as will stimulate the activities required for his proper education in each stage of the development of his powers.

It is our intention to present in subsequent numbers of the Journal an outline of the science of teaching as seen from our own point of view. Comparatively few facts and fewer laws have yet been discovered. But enough is known to make it evident that the science exists. Much yet remains to be discovered before this science can be properly set out in systematic form. G. P. B.

INTEREST.

INTEREST is derived from *iuter*, meaning *between*, and *est*, from *esse*, meaning *to be*. Literally, therefore, interest means *it is between*. This indicates that there are two things, between which is a third thing. On one hand is the untrained mind with its natural disinclination to continuous effort in a given direction, and on the other hand, a certain subject or lesson requiring close effort to master it. To master the point of knowledge requires attention. But attention by its literal meaning signifies effort. It means *a stretching to*—the very thing that the untrained mind is averse to. Whatever stands between this tendency of the mind to avoid continuous effort, and the knowledge, the mastery of which requires effort, and thereby attaches the mind to its work, is interest. Attention is the concentration of the mental faculties upon a given subject. It is therefore, an act of will, and is based upon motive. The motive is interest of some kind. Every lesson requires effort. It is essential therefore, especially in primary work, that the lesson be interesting.

Interest is the basis of attention. 'Attention in the child is feeble, and capable of but limited continuance. It grows stronger by exercise, and interest is the great promoter of its exercise, and thereby of permanency in the knowledge gained, or the power of memory.'

Interest may be introduced into a lesson, and the attention

gained, by appealing, among others, to either of four laws or motives :— The law of activity;

The law of curiosity;

The law of sympathy;

The law of power.

The pupil is by nature inclined to mental and to manual activity (though not continuous as necessary for mastery).

He should, therefore, not be a passive listener, but should be led to exercise his mind upon the material presented.

His manual activity should also be employed, whenever the progress of the work permits.

Curiosity exists by nature, and may be very strongly excited; it is gratified by the imparting of information on topics, and in a manner suited to the pupil's capacity.

The teacher who speaks to the intelligence of his pupils, and interests their feelings, imparts to the subject interest, and thereby gains and holds their attention. It has been said that nothing which excites the wonder or kindles the delight of pupils, is soon lost by them.

Under the law of sympathy, interest and attention will exist in the pupil in proportion to the kind and degree of personal ascendency which the teacher has obtained. If this be well established, the pupil will make great efforts to enter into the work of the teacher, both from his instinct of imitation, and the happiness which he derives from sympathy. In such a case, what the one is interested in, will be just what the other is; so completely does the pupil enter into the mind of the teacher, that he eagerly tries to anticipate the line of action which he feels the teacher intends to follow. Hence the importance of genuine interest in work, as manifested by the teacher; it fixes the attention almost without the consciousness of either that there is effort being exerted. If the pupils see that the teacher's interest is awakened, and his curiosity excited by the idea of making some new observation, or ascertaining some new fact, they will soon try to anticipate the discoveries.

If they observe him to be interested in the study of flowers, in determining the elements of climate, or in tracing the relations existing between natural features and the habits of man, they will be delighted with the same. "Example, emulation, curiosity, the most natural stimulants at an age when pleasure is so vividly enjoyed, and the idea of utility is so indistinct, will all act in unison."

The law of power is employed to awaken the interest and attention whenever there is a recognition of information or of mental or manual power on the part of the pupil.

Later in the work the idea of utility may be employed in connection with this law; as when the relation of the subject-matter to mental or manual power is shown.   HOWARD SANDISON.

ARITHMETIC—DEDUCTIVE.

"ARITHMETIC is by pre-eminence deductive or demonstrative, and exhibits in nearly a perfect form all the machinery belonging to this mode of obtaining truth.   Laying down a very few first principles, either self-evident or requiring but little effort to prove them, it evolves a vast number of deductive truths and applications."—*Bain.*

Most of the child's first conclusions reached in the study of numbers are inductions.   A certain truth is observed of a particular fact or process.   The same truth is observed of another, and so of a large number of facts.   The child comes at length to expect the observed truth as an accompaniment of every similar fact to which his attention is called.   He observes that if he multiply the dividend the quotient is correspondingly multiplied. He observes the same truth in a large number of cases, hence he concludes that multiplying the dividend (in *ail* cases) multiplies the quotient.   He has not tried all cases that might arise, and hence he can not give any better reason for his conclusion than that such is true of the cases already tried—that as yet he has found no exception.   But if he be pressed he admits that he is not sure but that exceptions might occur.

After a few months, perhaps years, the pupil finds himself in a mental condition that enables him to grasp the principle in its *general* aspect.   He knows its truth independently of any and all verifications of it by trial.   The very nature of the relations sustained among the terms of division asserts its truth.   He s:es in it its own verification—he sees it as *self-evident.*

When the pupil has, by the insight of the reason, thus grasped a general truth he is master of all the particular truths that fall within the scope of the general.   He is no longer compelled to grope from particular to particular, alternately hoping and doubting the correctness of his conclusion.   To give this mastery over particulars is one of the purposes of a course in mathematical study.

As already stated, in the earlier study of numbers, conclusions more or less general are reached by means of particulars—external objects being freely resorted to as illustrations.   Indeed at first the child does not clearly distinguish between an outward object and his *idea* of the object.   Too many pupils never rise out of this objective and inductive way of proceeding.   They thus fail to derive the chief power which a course in mathematics is designed to give if properly pursued.   1. To reach and formulate general truths in the light of properties and relations inhering in and among the facts contemplated.   2. To recognize a *particular* as belonging to a *general* already cognized.

When the pupil is strong enough to grasp axiomatic truths, his course in Arithmetic should gradually change from the inductive to the deductive.   In beginning the study of a new topic, or branch of the subject, the essential terms are accurately defined and illustrated, that the pupil may know the exact limits of the field he is to explore.

The relations existing among the facts defined are next carefully traced.   By virtue of these relations certain truths are seen to exist of necessity;—i. e., these truths, or principles can not be otherwise with the relations as they are, and the relations can not be otherwise with the definitions as they are.   The principles determine the order in which the involved processes are to be performed.   If the pupil have *mastered* the definitions and principles, he can not fail in the processes except in the matter of accuracy in computation.   N. Newby.

Protection of the law is most claimed by those who violate it.

EDITORIAL.

W. A. BELL, Editor-in-Chief and Proprietor.

GEO. P. BROWN, Pres. State Normal School, Associate Editor and Editor of the Department of Pedagogy.

LEWIS H. JONES, Superintedent of Indianapolis Schools, and Editor of the Primary Department.

GEO. F. BASS, Supervising Principal Indianapolis Schools, and Critic in Training School, Editor of The School Room Department.

A. W. BRAYTON, Prof. of Natural Science in the Indianapolis Schools, is Editor of the Popular Science Department.

Prof E. E.WHITE, Ohio; Prof. E. E. SMITH, Purdue University; HUBERT M. SKINNER, Chief Clerk Dept. of Public Instruction; JAS. BALDWIN, Supt. Schools Rushville; HOWARD SANDISON, W. W. PARSONS, and MICHAEL SEILER, of State Normal School; EMMA MONT. MCRAE, Principal Marion High School; H. S. TARBELL, late Supt. of the Indianapolis Schools, are frequent contributors.

Many other able writers contribute occasional articles to the JOURNAL. Should althose be enrolled as "Contributing Editors" who contribute one article or more a year the list could be indefinitely extended.

This large list of special editors and able contributors insures for the readers of the JOURNAL the best, the freshest, the most practical thoughts and methods in all departments of school work.

The Miscellaneous and Personal Departments of the Journal will not be neglected, but it places special emphasis on its large amount of unequaled practical and helpful educational articles.

Persons sending money for this Journal can send amounts less than $1 in *two* and *one* cent postage stamps; no others can be used.

In asking to have the address of your Journal changed, please give the *old* address as well as the new, naming the county as well as the state.

An agent is wanted to raise a club for the Journal in every township in the State. Send for terms.

ERRATA.—In the third paragraph on page 191 the eighth sentence should read, "The mystic *chords* of memory, *stretching* from every battle-field," etc.

THE Report of the State Superintendent has been unavoidably delayed on account of the printer, but is now out. A number will be sent to each county superintendent for distribution in his county.

THE FIRST ASSOCIATION.—Through the kindness of Dr. E. E. White, we have, in pamphlet form, the minutes of the *first* State Teachers' Association, held Dec. 25, 1854—hence one year older than this Journal. It contains many interesting items which will be given at a future time. It may be stated here that Horace Mann, one of the world's greatest educators, was present and made an address.

3

The reports from Washington state that the Commissioner of Education, Hon. John Eaton, has been asked to resign. If the "civil service" rules are to apply any place, certainly they should include this purely educational office. But if a change is to be made and a democrat is to have the place, the Journal knows of no better qualified man than James H. Smart of Indiana. He possesses high qualifications for that office—it is exactly in his line.

NATIONAL EDUCATIONAL ASSOCIATION.—A letter from the president, F. Louis Soldan, of St. Louis, gives the information that the National Association will hold its next meeting at Saratoga, July 14-18. All the inducements of reduced fares on railroads and at hotels etc have been guaranteed. The popularity of Saratoga as a "watering place" is world-wide, and the points of attraction within easy reach are numerous.

The first choice of places for holding the Association was Washington City, but no local inducements at that season of the year could be secured. Pres. Soldan will leave nothing undone to make this meeting equal to the best.

DEATH OF CHAS. O. THOMPSON.—The President of the Rose Polytechnic Institute at Terre Haute, Charles O. Thompson, died at his home March 17th, of rheumatism of the heart. He was a native of Vermont, and about 42 years old. He assumed the presidency of the Institute at its opening, March 7, 1883. He had for several years prior to this been at the head of a technic school at Worcester, Mass., and had met with great success. Perhaps he had no superior in the United States in his field of education. He was a man of great mental vigor, and whatever he did or said indicated a reserved latent power. In his untimely death not only does Rose Polytechnic Institute, and the State of Indiana, but the cause of education in the entire country suffer a great loss.

TO SCHOOL TRUSTEES, SUPERINTENDENTS AND TEACHERS:—After conferring with Mr. J. G. Kingsbury, of the State Horticultural Society's committee on the celebration of Arbor Day by the schools, I have decided that it is not necessary to again call together the joint committee on that subject, as the plan laid out last year can very well be followed again this season. I therefore appoint Friday, April 10th, as ARBOR DAY for the public schools, and recommend that wherever possible trustees, superintendents, and teachers make suitable preparations and do what can be done toward beautifying their school grounds, with the accompaniment of appropriate literary exercises. This Department can not furnish programs this year.

Very truly yours,   JOHN W. HOLCOMBE,
March 10, 1885.   *Sup't Public Instruction.*

The above speaks for itself. The importance of planting trees on and around school premises is so manifest as to need no urging. Let every teacher take the lead and enlist trustees, parents, and older pupils, and see to it that something is done. Plant forest trees—these are cheapest and best. Go to work.

TRAINING FOR NURSES.—The Flower Mission Training School for Nurses has made arrangements with the authorities of the Indianapolis City Hospital for giving two years' training to women desirous of becoming professional nurses. Those wishing to obtain this course of instruction must apply to the Superintendent of the Training School, upon whose approval they will be received into the school for one month on probation.

The most acceptable age for candidates is from twenty-one to thirty-five years. Applicants are received at any time during the year, and candidates from country and towns desired. Those who prove satisfactory will be accepted as pupil nurses, after signing an agreement to remain two years. A sufficient sum is allowed for the dress, textbooks, and other personal expenses, and is in nowise intended as wages, it being considered that the education given is a full equivalent for their services. The pupils are boarded and lodged free in the Nurses' Home. In sickness nurses are cared for gratuitously.

Such a calling insures an honorable position and good wages. Further information will be given on application in person or by letter, to Miss Hunt, Supt. Training School, City Hospital, Indianapolis, Ind.

MEMORIAL DAY FOR LINCOLN.

On April 15th will occur the 20th anniversary of the death of Abraham Lincoln. It is customary to celebrate the birth-days of authors, and much good is thus accomplished. In this way the writings and inspiration of the best men and women are infused into the lives of those participating.

Lincoln was not an author, and yet his noble life and his living words are the inheritance of the ages. Mr. Hubert M. Skinner has prepared an article, which appears elsewhere in this Journal, composed of a few of the utterances of Mr. Lincoln, and has suggested that it might be made the basis of a memorial service in our schools on April 15th. The article indicates extensive reading and excellent taste and does Mr. Skinner much credit.

Will teachers take this suggestion which the Journal *heartily* endorses, and make the 15th inst. an occasion to teach some interesting history, and what is more, give some valuable lessons on "humble living and high thinking," on the higher law of justice and eternal right as opposed to expediency, and on patriotism.

A THREATENED CALAMITY.

Judge J. T. Allison, of Switzerland county, has declared the local tuition school tax unconstitutional. The present law is the same in spirit and substance as the one declared unconstitutional by Judge Perkins in 1857. The present law has never been tested before the Supreme Court, and there is a difference of opinion among lawyers as to the result when it is submitted to that body. To cut off the local tuition tax is to cut down the term of every school in the state except in one or two cities. In many of the country schools the term would be reduced to two and three months.

It is to be earnestly hoped that the Supreme Court will reverse the decision of Judge Allison, and thus avoid a great calamity.

UNCONSCIOUS TEACHING.

"It has long been my opinion that we are all educated, whether children, men, or women, far more by personal influence than by books and the apparatus of the school-room. The privilege of sitting down before a great, clear-headed, large-hearted man, and breathing the atmosphere of his life, and being drawn up to him and lifted up by him, and learning his methods of thinking and living, is, in itself an enormous educating power."—*Garfield.*

Mr. Garfield never said a truer thing. The unconscious tuition is what does most in the formation of character. The man, the woman, is always more than the teacher. The person who is simply a teacher may drill well, may manage the machinery of the school well, may fill the mind of the pupil with facts, but lacks power to inspire to higher living. Only a person who possesses character can develop character in others. Education, reading outside the narrow professional limits, culture—these alone can give a person the grasp of thought and substratum of character essential to the best teaching.

THE WEEKLY *VS.* THE READING CIRCLE BOARD.

The *Educational Weekly* in its issue of February 14th contained a criticism on the work of the Directors of the Reading Circle. This article the Journal in its March issue criticised and charged that it did gross injustice to the directors.

A second article in the *Weekly* March 14th makes a second article in the Journal necessary. The *Weekly's* first article said: "Several features have unfortunately crept into the organization [board of directors] which were not at first contemplated. * * * It was not at first contemplated that the directors should be paid for their services, and we are still of the opinion that they should not be, for there

are plenty of competent teachers in the state who would be willing to make out the outlines gratuitously. It was not at first contemplated that there should be an annual squabble for position on the board of directors, as was witnessed at the State Association last winter. _*
* * It was not intended that the Teachers' Reading Circle should carry 'loaves and fishes' to be sought for as a prize. * * * We do not see clearly by what authority, other than by common consent, a fixed tax is levied upon the members by the board, nor yet by what law of apportionment any money thus collected *is distributed among the members of the board.*"

The Journal in its article, in order to vindicate the board from the charges made in regard to the misappropriation of money, stated the facts, which are these:

1. The power given the board to organize the Circle carried with it the power to provide a plan for paying necessary expenses.

2. That not one cent has been paid to any member of the board for services, except a small fee to the Secretary, who had to do a great deal of work.

The Journal stated in as strong language as it could command that this article was outrageously unjust to the board. The *Weekly* in its second article, instead of acknowledging its mistake in a frank and manly way, undertakes to crawl out of its difficulty through an "auger hole," and displays an animus which but few will commend. This is the way it does it It says: "Instead of saying members of the board *are* paid, we say we do not see how they *can be*. We do not think they are paid for their services."

The *Weekly* must give its readers credit with very little power to understand language if it expects them to take such a forced interpretation of what it stated.

It starts out with saying that "certain features have crept into the organization that were not intended," and the first one named is that "it was not intended that the directors should be paid for their services," etc., and then goes on to speak of "loaves and fishes," and of collecting money and distributing it among the members of the board."

If this does not charge the board with taking pay for services, what does it mean? Has it any meaning? Is it possible to put any other construction upon it? If the *Weekly* "does not think that they are paid for their services," then it has written itself down a defamer of the board, or convicted itself of putting forth an editorial article that is simply *drivel* and nonsense.

The *Weekly* goes on to say: "In regard to insinuations against the board, no one knows better than the Journal that the Weekly intended no charge or insinuation whatever against the board as a whole, and for the Journal to try to so torture our language as to make it reflect upon other members of the board than those intended is, to say the least of it, unfair. In order to avoid personalities our article was so written that it could be easily read between the lines by the parties concerned, and thus no unnecessary publicity given to it."

Here is the "milk in the cocoanut." The *Weekly* wishes to make a covert thrust at some member of the board against whom it has a private grudge, and so makes its charges against the whole board expecting the "parties concerned" to "read between the lines."

Will the *Weekly* explain how it expected the teachers throughout the state to know that when it said "board" it did not mean board, but meant a single individual of that board. If it has not lost its wits entirely, it must know that, with the exception of a very few persons who happened to know the feeling of the *Weekly* toward a certain member of the board, its readers would understand that the whole board was charged. Does it not see how it is utterly impossible that they should understand otherw.se? And yet to make this attack on *one*, it slandered *seven* whom it concedes innocent, and did not correct the wrong until the Journal's article compelled it to do so.

If the *Weekly* will point out a word or sentence in its first article that would enable the masses of its readers to "read between the lines," and even *guess* that it meant one and not all, it will relieve itself of a very embarrassing predicament.

The last article of the *Weekly* goes on to say: "The Journal says we insinuated that 'Mr. Brown and Mrs. McRae squabbled to retain their places on the board for the sake of the loaves and fishes.' The Journal knows the *Weekly* insinuated no such thing. * * Every one who attended this meeting of the Association knows very well that Mrs. McRae had nothing to do with the squabble for position on the board, and no one ever thought of preferring such a charge against her; but every one knows just as well that Mr. Brown and his friends precipitated the squabble for the reason that Mr. Brown's name was left off."

Here it is again. Every teacher in the state who read the proceedings of the Association knows that the time of Mr. Brown and Mrs. McRae had expired on the board and that they were re-elected. How could teachers know from the language of the *Weekly* that it did not include both in its charge of "squabbling" for "loaves and fishes"? Mrs. McRae is favorably known to thousands of teachers who did not attend the Association, and how were they to know that Mr. Brown, and not she, was meant? Besides, the so-called "squabble" took place late in the afternon of the last day of the Association, after a large majority of those who had been in attendance had left for home. How could those who were not present at that closing hour know that both were not included?

Whatever the *Wekly* may have *intended*, the fact remains that it
did charge the *board* with levying a tax without authority and distributing the money "*among the members* of the board," and that it
did include Mrs. McRae in its charge of "squabbling" for "loaves
and fishes." The language of the *Weekly* will admit of no other interpretation.

If the *Weekly* wished to criticise Mr. Brown, why did it not do so
in a straight forward way, and not "wash its dirty linen" before the
public at the expense of its friends?

The Journal will not discuss the "squabble" further than to say
that there are those who think it *originated* with a select few who
seem to be very anxious to "take turns" lest the work should be
"burdensome to any." That there was opposition to the re-appointment of Mr. Brown and Mrs. McRae on the part of a few individuals
on personal grounds can not be truthfully denied; that there were
those who opposed their re-appointment because of honest difference
of opinion is equally certain.

The friends of Mr. Brown and Mrs. McRae (for the friends of both
were equally active,) ignored entirely all personal considerations and
advocated their re-appointment on two grounds: 1. That they had
been faithful and efficient members, and having served less than one
year, while the regular term is four, they should be allowed to carry
into execution the work they had so carefully planned   That while
there was room for honest difference of opinion as to the work mapped
out it was too early to pass judgment upon it, but few "Circles" having done as much as half of one year's work.

2. In appointing the board originally, the effort was made to represent as far as possible all the varied school interests, and at the
same time time to represent the different sections of the state, not
going too far from the centre. (This last to avoid long journeys and
expense and secure attendance upon meetings.)

By the removal of Mr. Mills from Indianapolis and Mrs. Dennis
from Bloomingdale, Parke county, both to Earlham College, *four*
out of the eight members were in the extreme eastern line of counties. The report of the committee at the Association proposed to
take away the only representative left to the western part of the state
and give it to an eastern border county, thus giving the extreme east
five out of the eight. On these grounds and these alone the Association voted "by a large majority" to retain the present incumbents.
The persons nominated by the committee were both highly respected
persons and well qualified for the place, and not one word of criticism, so far as the Journal heard, was uttered against either, and no
disrespect was intended in the vote. Nobody voted *against* them,
but *under the circumstances*, a large majority felt compelled to vote
for Mr. Brown and Mrs. McRae.

In the light of the *Weekly's* unjustifiable attack upon Mr. Brown it is only just to him to say that notwithstanding the fact that he has attended more meetings of the board and committees than have any other member, he has not only *not* received pay for his services, but has not received one dime for his expenses even, nor does he expect to accept a cent.

QUESTIONS AND ANSWERS.

QUESTIONS BY THE STATE BOARD FOR FEBRUARY.

SCIENCE OF TEACHING.—1. Why is it difficult for a child to change from purely oral instruction to text-book study?

2. Why will a child comprehend much better what is told to him or read to him than he will what he reads himself?

3. Show that the great reliance in elementary moral instruction must be in inculcating habits of obedience and cultivating the social and sympathetic emotions.

4. Why in the first lessons in teaching children to read is it best to teach words as wholes?

5. Show that the transition period from oral instruction to the study of the book is one of the most difficult and important periods of school education.

READING.—1. Name five American prose writers and one of the works of each.

2. Why is it after so much time is spent in teaching reading that we have so few good readers?

3. Name three points you consider essential in the preparation of a lesson in the Third Reader by the pupil.

4. Ought advanced classes to stand or sit during the reading exercises? Why?

5. Name three purposes for which a dictionary should be used in the preparation of a lesson in the Fifth Reader.

6. Read a selection chosen by the superintendent.

GEOGRAPHY.—1. Name and locate five of the gulfs and border seas of Asia.

2. What is the North Pole of the earth? In what direction from it, and in what zones, are the following places: Upernavik, St. Petersburg, San Francisco, London, and Buenos Ayres.

3. Bound New York. Name and locate the five largest cities of New York.

4. Why is the climate in Western Europe milder than it is in the same latitude in North America? Give reasons.

5. Locate accurately the following: Pensacola, Milwaukee, Belfast, Berlin, Canton.

6. Locate the following islands, stating the direction of each from the nearest country and to what government each belongs: Porto Rico, Malta, Iceland, Candia, and the Bahamas.

7. What and where is each of the following: Java, Odessa, St. Roque, Cairo, Honduras

8. What countries in Europe have a republican form of government?

9. Name the highest mountain in S. America. What mountains between France and Italy?

10. Bound Asia. What is the most densely populated country in Asia? Its capital, its form of government, its chief exports?

PENMANSHIP.—1. Show by a diagram the relative length of g, p, t, s, l.

2. What is meant by *form?* In what manner does a careful study of *form* aid in making a good penman?

3. How many kinds are used in writing? Define each kind.

4. Analyze a, h, u, N, F.

5. What is meant by principles?

NOTE.—Your writing in answering these questions will be taken as a specimen of your penmanship, and will be marked 50 or below, according to merit.

PHYSIOLOGY.—1. Describe the alimentary canal.

Explain respiration.

Describe the optic nerve.

4. How is near-sightedness produced?

5. What is the fontanelle?

6. Make a diagram showing the bones of the arm.

7. Distinguish between sensory and motor nerves.

8. Describe the labyrinth of the ear.

9. Describe the structure of the heart.

10. Describe the structure of a gland. Name five of the largest glands in the human body.

HISTORY.—1· Of what country was Columbus a native? Under whose auspices did he discover America?   5, 5

2. What attempt was made by the Huguenots to establish a colony in this country? What was the result?   5, 5

3. How did European wars cause the inter-colonial wars?   10

4. What two *surrenders* had the greatest influence upon American success in the Revolution?   5, 5

5. What authority had Jefferson for the *Louisiana purchase?* From whom was it bought?   5, 5

6 What was the principal cause of the Mexican war? What purchase was necessary to settle it entirely?   5, 5

7. When was Indiana admitted as a State? What other States were erected from the Northwest Territory? 5 pts

8. What connection had the clause in the Constitution concerning the slave trade with the civil war? 10

9. What cause led to the Bull Run defeat? What effect did this defeat have on the North? 5, 5

10. What led to the impeachment of President Johnson? What was the result of the trial? 5, 5

GRAMMAR.—1. When should a child begin the study of technical grammar? Why?

2. Write a compound and a complex sentence. In what do they agree? How do they differ?

3. State the grounds for classifying sentences as Declarative, Interrogative, Imperative, and Exclamatory.

4. How does a preposition differ from a conjunction?

5. Name all of the parts of speech in the following sentence:
"And is a conjunction when it is used to connect sentences."

6. Analyze the following sentence:
"To be or not to be; that is the question."

7. Parse the *italicised* words in the following sentence:
"I told *him to go*, but *his going was prevented*."

8. How do relative pronouns differ from personal pronouns?

9. Correct the following and give reasons:
"Your dress sets well."
"It seems to be him."
"I believe it to be he."
"Webster and Worcester's Dictionary."
"I knew of him being a musician."

10. Give the corresponding passive forms of the following verbs:
Set, raise, has laid. Shall have written, is reciting.

ARITHMETIC.—1. How far does a man walk while planting a field of corn 285 feet square, the rows being 3 feet apart and 3 feet from the fences?

2. A man bought 25 sheep for $56; if he had bought 3 more for the same sum, how much less per head would he have paid?

3. Find the least number which, divided by 2, 3, 4, 5 and 6, leaves a remainder 1 each time.

4. Define cube root and illustrate by finding the cube root of 2315.68.

5. Define the terms Insurance, Policy, Premium, Interest, and Amount.

6. The interest of $560 for 2 years, 8 mos., 15 days, was $106.40; what was the rate per cent.?

7. If 7 men can mow 35 acres in 4 days, how many acres can 10 men mow in 3⅓ days? By analysis.

8. Chicago is 843 miles west of Boston. When it is 9 o'clock A. M. at Chicago, what time is it at Boston, allowing 51 miles for a degree of longitude?

9. A ladder 39 feet long stands resting its whole length against a perpendicular wall; how far must it be drawn out at the bottom that the top may be lowered 3 feet?

10. What will it cost to cover a floor 40 feet by 32 feet, with matting 4 feet wide, at $1.20 per yard?

ORTHOGRAPHY.—1. Into what general classes are the elementary sounds of the English language divided? Give examples.

2. What are substitutes? Give five examples.

3. What are cognate sounds? Give four examples.

4. Accent the following words: Mischievous, contrary, disputant, discipline, and microscopy.

5. Indicate the accent and the phonic spelling of the following words: Vicar, provost, shire, heroine, and melee.

6. Spell ten words pronounced by the superintendent.

ANSWERS TO STATE BOARD QUESTIONS PRINTED IN MARCH.

ARITHMETIC.— 1. Domestic exchange is that which is made between different places of the same country. Foreign exchange is that which is made between different countries.

2. Divide the principal by the product of the interest and time in years.

3. $1-\frac{1}{2}=\frac{1}{2}$; $\frac{1}{2}-(\frac{1}{2}$ of $\frac{1}{2})=\frac{1}{4}$; $\frac{1}{2}=50\%$.

4. $\frac{1\times\frac{1}{2}\times4\times1728}{2150.4}=128\frac{4}{7}$ bushels.

5. A and B can do $\frac{1}{12}$ in one day.

B and C can do $\frac{1}{9}$ in one day.

A and C can do $\frac{1}{8}$ in one day.

$\frac{1}{12}+\frac{1}{9}+\frac{1}{8}=\frac{11}{24}$, twice the work.

$\frac{1}{2}$ of $\frac{11}{24}=\frac{11}{48}$, once the work.

$\frac{11}{48}-\frac{1}{12}=\frac{7}{48}$, C's work in one day.

$\frac{11}{48}-\frac{1}{9}=\frac{1}{24}$, A's work in one day.

$\frac{11}{48}-\frac{1}{8}=\frac{5}{48}$, B's work in one day.

$1\div\frac{7}{48}=10\frac{2}{7}$. C can do it in 10⅔ days.

$1\div\frac{1}{24}=14\frac{4}{7}$. A can do it in 14⅔ days.

$1\div\frac{1}{72}=72$. B can do it in 72 days.

$\frac{1\times8\times11\times1728}{11\frac{1}{2}}=3456$ gallons.

7. 2044 mi.÷7=292 mi. in $\frac{1}{15}$ hr. $1\frac{4}{15}=\frac{29}{15}$. 292 mi.$\times$29=8468 miles.

8. 25 ft. : 25 ft 5.25 in. : : 543 ft. 8 in. : ——. Reducing and solving we have 553 ft. 2.17 inches.

9. $\sqrt{20^2+16^2+12^2}=28.28+$ft.

10. $\sqrt[3]{1728\times3}=17.3+$inches.

U. S. History. — 1.　Spanish, English, French, and Dutch. French, Spanish, and English.

2.　Georgia was settled under Oglethorpe, completing the number of the Colonies which rebelled against Great Britain, and George Washington was born, under whose military lead the revolution was successfully prosecuted.

3.　That they were simply outposts, occupied for the benefit of the mother country, whose inhabitants had political rights when in Great Britain, but were virtually expatriated when in the Colonies; that all emoluments and incomes created in them belonged of right to the home government, as proprietors, and were to be collected in any manner, and from any source that would produce the greatest amount for that government; that any hardships resulting from this course to the colonists were more than counterbalanced by the benefits to the government; in fact, that the home government was everything, and the colonies nothing.

4.　It was a body of Articles, the object of which was to put a stop to all importation from, and exportation to Great Britain or any of its dependencies until the oppressive acts of Parliament were repealed. It even forbade the importation of, or purchase of imported slaves after a certain date. This was signed by the entire Continental Congress, and by large numbers of others. It preceded the Declaration of Independence, in which the principles of the association were embodied; and the Spirit, that led to the association, led also to the Declaration.

5.　John Paul Jones. J. Fennimore Cooper's Pilot.

6.　That Parliament should declare the colonies separated from the mother country, until they humbled themselves to ask for forgiveness and restoration. The independence resulting from the Revolution would have come without the war.

7.　By the Treaty of Ghent. The real cause of the war was not mentioned in the treaty, notwithstanding which the very silence was a waiver of right by Great Britain to do that for which she fought, impress seamen on our vessels.

8.　The three clauses of Section 10, of Article I.

9.　Because so long as Hood, with his strong army, reinforced by Forrest's cavalry, remained in the South, Sherman could not successfully make his raid into Georgia, or prosecute his intended march to the sea.

10.　Tennessee, having promptly ratified the Fourteenth Amendment, was at once restored to her place in the Union, while the remaining Confederate States were subjected to provisional governments. His attempt to remove Edwin M. Stanton from his position as Secretary of War, in violation of the Tenure-of-Office Bill.

PHYSIOLOGY — 1. We should eat when we are hungry, but it is well not to eat so much if we are wearied as well as ahungered. The muscles of the body, internal and external, are somewhat relaxed and indisposed to work, the flow of the blood is sluggish, and the nervous stimulus is likely to be wanting, when we are tired. The exhaustion of the system itself suggests moderation if not abstinence.

2. Human Physiology treats of the functions of the tissues and organs of the human body.

3. A cell, so found in the human body before change by differentiation, (*e. g.*, a white blood-corpuscle), is a small, soft, delicate granular mass of irregular shape but usually somewhat circular and about $\frac{1}{1000}$ of an inch in diameter. Its essential parts are the *nucleolus*, the *nucleus*, and the granular *cell-body*.

4. The skull protects the brain (including the cerebrum, cerebellum, pons and other ganglia), the cranial nerves and the medulla oblongata..

5. Two great purposes of the bones are, (1) to assist in locomotion; (2) to protect more delicate parts of the body.

7. The nerves bear a double relation to the will: they convey to the brain those sensations which may arouse the feelings and thus through desire or antipathy call the will into action; or they may convey the volition to whatever muscle the will desires to call into play.

8. The skin has several functions: (1) With its fatty lining, it is a warm covering for the body; (2) It affords protection to the delicate nerve-fibrils, and thus enables us to touch and not be pained; (3) It is an excretory organ; (4) It regulates the temperature of the body; (5) It may discharge part of the functions of the lungs when those bodies are not in good working order.

9. The best method of cooking meat depends upon the purpose you have in view. Broiling, boiling, baking, are good in the order named. The poorest way to cook meat is to fry it. Whatever method preserves the juices without hardening the tissues so the gastric juice will not act upon them, is a good method.

10. Under-clothing should be kept clean for the sake of self-respect. Besides, gases and waste from the body are constantly becoming entangled in its meshes. Unless frequently changed, there is danger that these be reabsorbed and thus injure the very means nature has provided in part for the purification of the system.

READING.—1. The Word Method, as its name indicates, begins with and has for its purpose the immediate association of the thing with its oral and written representative. The written equivalents of the oral terms are to be acquired by the pupils, not synthetically, not piece by piece or sound by sound, as in the Alphabetic and Phonic Methods, but as wholes with which they are in part already acquainted. This process may be continued until the pupils themselves begin to realize that the words are made of parts or sounds, or until they begin to read short sentences with ease. Then the analytic and the synthetic processes may profitably be combined.

2. Two essential characteristics of good oral reading are distinctness of enunciation and accuracy of expression.

3. Silent reading is, essentially, the acquisition of the thought expressed upon the written or printed page. The power to do this may be cultivated by requiring pupils to state orally the substance of their reading lessons; to study carefully for a minute or two some quotation unexpectedly written upon the board by the teacher just before the recitation, and then to state its meaning; to make analyses of certain portions of the lesson;—in short, any exercise which will develop the perceptive and the realizing powers of the mind, will sharpen the intellects and quicken the sensibilities, must tend to cultivate silent reading. Of course it is understood that the reading matter is within the comprehension of the average pupil.

GEOGRAPHY.—1. The climate of a country is the general condition of its atmosphere in regard to heat and moisture. Climate depends upon (1) distance from the equator; (2) elevation above the sea level; (3) prevailing winds and ocean currents; (4) distance from the sea.

2. In the Gulf States is the great cotton belt, with sugar and rice in the moist coast regions, and oranges in Florida. In the region of the Great Lakes the leading agricultural products are corn, wheat, oats, potatoes, and hay. The difference in the products of the two sections is due chiefly to the great difference in climate.

3. A zone is a broad belt or division on the earth's surface parallel to the equator. The zones are Torrid, North and South Temperate, North and South Frigid.

4. Wheat, corn, cotton, rice, sugar, oats, barley, rye, potatoes, tobacco.

5. Nova Scotia, Prince Edward Island, New Brunswick, Quebec, Ontario, Manitoba, British Columbia, form the Dominion of Canada. Its capital is Ottawa.

6. Valparaiso and Callao are the two chief seaports on the west coast of South America.

7. Volga, Danube, Dnieper, Don, Rhine.

8. The Greater Antilles are Cuba, Hayti, Jamaica, Porto Rico. Cuba and Porto Rico belong to Spain; Jamaica belongs to England; Hayti is independent.

9. Tea, rice, and cotton.

10. Cape Colony, Natal, and the Province of Transvaal are the most important British possessions in Africa.

GRAMMAR.—1. (a) *Positively* is an adverb of manner, and modifies *is speaking.* (b) A *model* adverb, and qualifies the entire sentence.

2. The subject may be modified by a word, phrase, or clause, as, "The earnest desire of my friend, that I might have a pleasant journey, was fully realized."

3. (a) It is an interrogative sentence expressed in the rhetorical form for emphasis. The sentence means no one can contend with Heaven. (b) "Thou shalt not kill" is declarative in form but expresses a command. (c) "You are not gone yet?" is an interrogative sentence in the form of a declaration.

4. (a) The subject, copula, and predicate. (b) The verb or auxiliary part comes before the subject.

5. "A nation's character is the sum of its splendid deeds."

6. (a) Principal elements; as, noun, pronoun, verb. (b) Subordinate elements; as, adjectives and adverbs. (c) Connectives, as, conjunctions and prepositions.

7. (a) "Reading maketh a full man : conference, a ready man ; writing, an exact man," is an example of an abridged compound sentence. (b) "Webster was *a statesman and an orator*, is an example of a simple sentence containing a compound element.

9. (a) Relative pronouns and subordinate conjunctions. (b) The man *who is industrious* will prosper. (c) The belief *that the soul is immortal*, has been entertained by all nations.

10. (a) "That he went" is the subject of the sentence. "It" is the anticipative subject. (b) "It is said," is parenthasized, and, by some authors, is called an independent or foreign element. (c) The subordinate clause is the object of "are told."

THEORY OF TEACHING.—1. The first power of the mind developed, aside from mere consciousness, is *discrimination.* The child first sees differences. It knows the difference between a familiar face or voice and a strange one. It distinguishes between its mother and other members of the household. It knows each member of the family. *Discrimination* is the principal element in all primary learning.

2. The products resulting from discrimination are : The clearly defined mental pictures of external objects ; also the conclusions reached by comparison.

3. The three principal laws of memory are : 1. The mind remembers in proportion to its *activity*—the degree of *attention.* 2. *Repetition.* 3. *Association* and logical relation.

4. A *method* is a plan or rule of action. A *natural method* is one founded on logical principles.

5. In learning to read "diacritical marks" are of little value.

Theoretically they enable the child to determine the correct pronun-ciation of words without the aid of the teacher ; *practically* the child learns the proper pronunciation from the teacher. The child makes but little practical use of diacritical marks until old enough to use a dictionary.

MISCELLANY.

MILTON.—The schools here, which have for four years been under the supervision of R. W. Wood, are reported in excellent order.

RICHMOND NORMAL —Very encouraging reports come from this school, both as to attendance and character of work done. Cyrus W. Hodgin is at the head.

A great lake, "probably as large as Lake Superior," is believed by some to exist in the great unexplored region east of Hudson Bay. A Canadian expedition, eqnipped for an 18 months stay, started in June last to look for it.

THE PRIZE ESSAY ON CYCLOPÆDIAS.—Hiram Hadley desires to inform those interested, that he has received fourteen essays. These are now in the hands of the examining committee.

CLINTON. — J. H. Tomlin, Prin., Mary E. De La Bar, and Alice Rupp, all graduates of the State Normal, have been re-elected for next year. This means good work done in a satisfactory manner.

NEWTON COUNTY.—Supt. Hershman is making arrangements for a grand educational exhibit and contest in his county. The prizes offered for best work amount to over $60. The plan taken will cer-tainly arouse great interest.

PARKE COUNTY.—A copy of questions for graduation indicate great care and much skill. Only well-taught and well-posted students can pass the ordeal, and a certificate in Parke county stands for some-thing. Supt. Elson is doing a good work, and he has a good corps of teachers to help him.

There is to be a Summer School, comprising Normal Training, Mathematics, Science, Art, Music, Elocution, and Bible study, at Monteagle, on the top of Cumberland Mountain, in Tennessee, be-ginning June 30th. Prof. L. S. Thompson, of Purdue University, is to have charge of the Art Department.

MONROE COUNTY.—The law suit over the office of examiner in this county is at an end, and Wm. T. Axtell is now the recognized and undisputed Supt. Owing to the unsettled state of affairs the work for the schools has not been so effective as it otherwise would have been, but the prospects are encouraging for the future.

CONNERSVILLE.—The schools are still prospering under the direction of J. L. Rippetoe, who has been Supt. for *seventeen years*. The schools celebrated Washington's and Longfellow's birth-days.

FAYETTE COUNTY.—The teachers of this county held an association at Connersville, March 21st, which was well attended considering the lateness of the season, and it was a good meeting. Supt. Gamble has had charge for ten years, and the schools of the county are well organized and in a prosperous condition. Fayette stands well.

CORRECTION.—Last month's Journal stated that Yankton was the capital of Dakota. It did it on the authority of three of the latest geographies, and on the strength of the fact that the Supt. of Public Instruction dates his official letters at Yankton. Later information says that Bismark was made the capital in 1883, but that there is a strife now going on to change it to Pierre.

FRANKLIN COUNTY.—The schools in this county, under Supt. M. A. Mess, are doing better and better work each year. No township in the county runs its schools less than six months, while there are two of the largest townships that run nine months. The total number of teachers required in the county is 117, and the club for the Journal sent by Supt. Mess is 107—pretty good. Of course the schools will improve.

THE STATE NORMAL SCHOOL has opened its spring term with a large attendance, and the work is moving on in its wonted vigorous style. As a strictly normal school it has few equals in point of thoroughness and scientific teaching.

Prof. McTaggart is trying the experiment of putting beginners in Latin at once at work on Cæsar and teaching them *grammar* as it is demanded. He is so far well satisfied with the-results.

INDIANAPOLIS.—The new High School building in Indianapolis was dedicated March 6th with appropriate ceremonies. Addresses were made by Mayor McMasters, ex-Gov. Porter, State Supt. J. W. Holcombe, Geo. P. Brown, W. A. Bell and others. The building is the finest in the state and complete in every regard, and yet neither gaudy nor expensive.

W. W. Grant is the efficient principal of the high school, and he directs the work of 14 associate teachers.

BARTHOLOMEW COUNTY.—The 4th Wednesday in May next has been set apart as commencement day for the public district schools of Bartholomew county; and the large hall in the Central School Building in Columbus is fixed upon as the place for holding such commencement exercises. The applicants for diplomas from each of the school corporations of the county whose *general average* shall

4

be highest in each corporation, shall be entitled to represent it by reciting an original essay, or other production, on said commencement day. W. T. Hacker is Supt.

L. P. Harlan, who has served as Supt. of Marion county for four consecutive terms, is not a candidate for re-election, and will retire at the close of his present term in June. Doubtless a great many other superintendents would be willing to step aside if they could step into an easier position worth $1800 a year.

NATIONAL EDUCATIONAL ASSO'N PROCEEDINGS.—The committee in charge of the publication of the proceedings of the meeting of 1884 have informed me that the volume is now ready for delivery to members. This will be an unusually large and valuable volume, and, as the cost of sending it *by mail* to all the members will be about $500, and as many members may have changed their residences since the time of the meeting, it is deemed advisable to request those who desire to have this volume sent to them by MAIL, *to forward to the undersigned;* without delay, their *present address* in full, also 15 cents toward payment of postage on the volume. If your address has been changed from the place given, please state—*First*, what address you gave; *Second*, what your present address is. The volume will be promptly mailed to all who respond to the above requests. N. A. CALKINS, *Treasurer*,
124 East 80th Street, New York City.

TIPPECANOE CO. NOTES.—The Normal Review Term for teachers and for those desiring to prepare for the Freshman Class, opens at Purdue the 2d of April. The prospects are good for a large attendance. The regular instruction is supplemented by lectures from Pres Smart and Profs Craig, Smith, Thompson, Barnes and others.

Graduating exercises for those completing the common school course have been held recently at Romney and at Dayton. At the conclusion of the regular program a short address was delivered at the former place by Prof. L. S. Thompson, and at the latter place by Prof. E E. Smith.

The Schools at Chauncey, under the charge of Ed. R. Smith, principal, and three assistants, have the largest attendance for years. It is reported that the work is enthusiastically and satisfactorily done.

Misses Anna Hall and Kate Andrew, two of the best teachers in the Centennial School at Lafayette, are also two of the most active members of the local teachers' Reading Circle. Co. Supt. Caulkins is a member of the same circle.

INDIANA TEACHERS' READING CIRCLE.

OUTLINE OF

Work in Brooks' Mental Science, for April, 1885—Subject: The Understanding. Pages 201–236.

I. TERMS TO BE STUDIED.

1. Comparison, pages 202–3, 213, 229. 2. Prescind, page 208. 3. Symbolical Concepts, p. 219. 4. Differentia, p. 222. 5. Derived Judgments, pp. 234–5. 6. "Ghosts of departed qualities," p. 205. 7. Animality, pp. 219, 222, 230. 8. Rationality. 9. Privativa, pp. 220–1. 10. Proximate Species, p. 222. 11. Nominalism.

II. TERMS TO BE DISTINGUISHED.

1. Thought knowledge and Sense knowledge, pp. 98, 117. 2. Attention and Abstraction. Re-read pp. 67–8, 75–9, 121–3. 3. Extent and Content. 4. Clear and Distinct—referring to concepts. 5 Proposition and Sentence. 6 Thinking and Judging. 7. A Judgment and The Judgment. 8. Abstract Ideas and general ideas, p. 209.

III. ITEMS OF SPECIAL PROFESSIONAL IMPORT.

1. The relation of Abstraction to Perception.

"With no other powers than those of perception, consciousness and original suggestiveness, our ideas would be all of individuals. Abstraction is that faculty of the mind by which from individual, concrete, conceptions, we form general and abstract ideas."— *Wayland.*

2. The relation of Abstraction to Memory.

a. "To know a thing implies the remembrance of it. Only when the memory is well stored with distinct images, and series of such images, can the higher operations of the understanding be carried out."—*Sully.*

b. "The understanding has as its chief auxiliary the faculty of reproduction."—*Kant.*

3. The Formation of Concepts.

a. "Until we have been struck with the resemblance of things that also differ we do not make a beginning in abstraction."—*Bain.*

b. "Abstraction implies a high exercise of the power of voluntary attention, acting in opposition to what is impressive or interesting."—*Sully.*

c. "It must not be supposed that the child fashions an entire concept at one time or in systematic way. The process of Abstraction is a slowly progressive one."—*Sully.*

d. "Conceptions are but the reflex of what has been observed in the sense. These conceptions have no more, and no less reality than belongs to the original sense of observation."—*Seelye.*

4. Symbolical Conceptions. See p. 219.

5. The Formation of Judgments.

   a. "Reasoning is a process; judgment, a decision. Reasoning prepares the way for a result; judgment is the result. To understanding we apply the epithets, *strong, vigorous, comprehensive, profound;* to judgment, those of *correct, cool, unprejudiced, impartial, solid.* The sound judgment is one of the highest attributes of humanity."—*Wins'ow.*

6. The value of General Ideas. See p. 223.

   a. "The power of generalizing is the chief distinction between an educated mind and the rude, uncultivated one."—*Ogden.*

R. G. B.

——o——

METHODS OF INSTRUCTION.
Talks on Teaching—pp. 120-137.

GEOGRAPHY.

Define Geography. "Structural Geography." Show the relation of geography to other natural sciences. In what sense is geography a science? It has sometimes been called a hybrid science: Why? After abstracting from Geography what belongs to Physics, to Chemistry, to Botany, to Zoology, to Geology, to Mathematics, to Anthropology, to Meteorology, and to any and all other sciences, what would be exclusively geography?

One purpose of the study of geography is to fix in the mind clear, comprehensive pictures of the form of the surface of the earth as a whole, and of the forms of its different parts. How can this best be done? Show that this subject affords excellent opportunities for cultivating the imagination. Indeed, it is only by the constant use of the imagination that geography can be taught at all. State the evil of relying upon maps. When should maps be introduced? When should elementary geography begin? What preparation should be made for it? Of what should the first year's work in elementary geography consist? Note the suggestive questions on page 130.

Having completed the preliminary study of geographical forms, what parts of the earth's surface should the child first construct in his imagination? Method of doing this? Why should not the child begin with a study of school grounds, and then make a study of the township, then of the county, then of the state, etc.?

Explain what is meant by the maxim "From whole to part." What is the place of mathematical geography in the geographical course? Why is moulding preferable to drawing the forms of the different continents, etc.?

The author's suggestions about teaching geography are of great value and deserve to be thoroughly studied by every teacher. Nothing better has ever been said.

G. P. B.

GENERAL HISTORY.

Barnes' General History—Pages 153-177.

First Week.—It was the mission of Alexander to diffuse the Greek language and civilization over the earth. Calling himself a Greek, he gathered about him Greek generals, philosophers, artisans and authors. His empire was of short duration. From its ruins four Greek kingdoms immediately sprang into existence. Of these the most interesting in its history is Egypt—not the Egypt of Abraham and the Pharaohs and Joseph, but the Egypt of the Ptolemys and Cleopatra and Mark Antony and Julius Cæsar.

1. Ptolemy I and his wise policy. The new elements of the population. The predominant speech. 2. The new city. The Pharos. The Mausoleum. The original Suez Canal. 3. The Alexandrine Library. The great work of the seventy Jewish doctors. (This book alone cost the king $2,500,000). The vast number of the volumes. 4. The great school. Its museum. Its gardens. The numbers in attendance. In what respect was it the greatest school in the history of the world? The famous names connected with it. Its influence on the world's measurement of time. Its influence on science. Its later influence on religion. 5. The end of the Ptolemy line, after nearly three centuries of rule. The romantic story of Cleopatra. Egypt swallowed up in the Roman Empire. 6. The Greek kingdom of Thrace and Asia Minor. Its short duration and its annexation to the kingdom of the East. 7. The Greek kingdom of the East. New cities founded. The Syrian Antioch. Pergamos, and the English word derived from its name. Their absorption by the Roman dominion. The one kingdom which was *not* conquered by the Romans. Pontus and its surrender to the Romans. 8. The kingdom of Macedon and Greece. The incursion of the Barbarians, and their expulsion to Galatia. The Achaean and Aetolian Leagues. "All roads lead to Rome." The history of this kingdom ends as end those of the others. 9. Greece as a Roman province As it is to-day, so was it in the time of Horace and Cicero—a land of departed greatness, of sentiment, of song and story.

Sunday Readings.—The prophesy concerning Alexander (the "King of Grecia") and the four Greek kingdoms—Daniel VIII, XI, 3.

Second Week.—If it be an instructive study to analyze the civilization of any nation or race, especially is this the case with Grecian civilization. Though Gibbon may have overestimated the influence of that civilization upon the development of our own, it is yet difficult to comprehend the extent of our indebtedness to early Greece.

1. The fabled celestial descent of the Athenians. Their social orders. The dignity of Athenian manhood. 2. The employments deemed honorable. Those deemed degrading. The examples of

Solon, Aristotle and Plato. 3. The three classes of the population of Sparta. 4. Difference between the literature of the Greeks and those of other ancient peoples. The Greek literature not a *dead* literature even at this day. 5. The dawn of epic poetry. The rhapsodists, their lyre and odes. The joining of many odes to form an extended poem. 6. Homer. Traditions concerning him. Doubts concerning his existence The theory of the doubters. The work of Dr. Schliemann. (Mrs. Schliemann recently arrayed herself for a portrait in the veritable jewels of Helen of Troy, as Dr. Schliemann believes them to be.) Antiquity of the poem. How was it preserved until the invention of writing? 7. The story of the Iliad. Characteristics of the poem. Alexander's fondness of the poem (page 151), The Odyssey. 8. The poems of Hesiod. The martial songs of Tyrtaeus, and the fulfilment of the oracle's prophesy. Archilochus. 9. The Tenth Muse (The story of Sappho's suicide by leaping from the Lady's Cape—the Leucadian Promontory—is not now believed). Alcaeus, her lover, rendered familiar in our day by the translation of his best poem by Sir William Jones. 10. Anacreon. His odes (translated into elegant English verse by Tom Moore.) Simonides and the Epigram. 11. Pindar and his odes. Respect paid him on the destruction of Thebes.

Third Week.—1. The origin of the drama. It must be remembered that the modern drama had an entirely separate origin, and is not modeled after the classic drama at all, as modern epics are modeled after classic epics. Bacchanalian revels. The poet's crown. 2. The character of the classic drama. Prologue, epilogue and chorus. 3. The Tragic Trio of the Golden Age. 4 Eschylus. Prometheus Bound. The story of Prometheus (Read Willis's Parrhasius.) 5. The Attic Bee. The character of his works. King Oedipus. (The reader is recommended to study carefully the story of Oedipus and to read a translation of the drama. It is often called the greatest of classic tragedies. I incline to the opinion expressed at Oxford, that Philoctetes, the "Classic Crusoe," is "the masterpiece of the Athenian stage." It will well repay the reader to peruse the Philoctetes. If these tragedies are not accessible, he will find in Milton's Samson Agonistes a faithful representation of Greek tragedy.) The Science Philosopher. His characters. His advanced thought. 7. Comedy. Aristophanes and his historic personages. Menander and his representative but fictitious characters.

Fourth Week.—1. The Father of History. His life; His travels; His subjects. 2. Thucydides. His great work; His style contrasted with that of Herodotus. 3. Xenophon. The Anabasis. The earliest conversational memoirs. 4. Demosthenes. His Oration upon the Crown. 5. The Seven Sages. 6. The Academy. Plato's philosophy. 7. The Lyceum, Aristotle and the Peripatetic school.

Aristotle's philosophy. 8. The Epicureans (Acts XVII 18). 9. The Stoics and the Painted Porch. Zeno and his philosophy. Diogenes and the Cynics.

PERSONAL.

W. H. Fertich has been re-elected Supt. of the Shelbyville schools for next school year at an advanced salary.

J. V. Coombs, well known in this state, is now president of the Kansas College, located at Burlington, Kan. He is also editor of the *Kansas School Journal*.

J. A. Kibbie, Supt. of the schools at Kendallville, according to reports in the papers, has been compelled to flee the state, for a crime toward young ladies in his school, not proper to mention in these pages.

Cyrus Smith has just entered the employ of the book house of A. S. Barnes & Co. His field is to be Indiana and Michigan, with headquarters at Indianapolis. Mr. Smith has a host of warm friends in both these states who will be glad to see him "on the road" again.

Maurice Thompson, the Poet and Archer, of Crawfordsville, has been appointed by the Governor State Geologist, instead of John Collett, who has served in that capacity for many years past with great acceptance. Gov. Williams disregarded politics and appointed Prof. Collett on account of his high qualifications. Had qualification alone been considered the change would not have been made.

Anna P. Brown, sister of Geo. P. Brown, died of congestion of the lungs, in Zionsville, Feb. 24th. Miss Brown has been one of the faithful workers, and for more than twenty years has devoted her life to the welfare of others. When the State Association appointed editors for the *School Journal* Miss Brown was for several years editor of the Primary Department. At the time of her death she was teaching a kindergarten in Zionsville. "She hath done what she could."

BOOK TABLE.

A Method of English Composition. By T. Whiting Bancroft, Prof. of Rhetoric and English Literature in Brown University. Boston: Ginn, Heath & Co.

This work is designed not to supplant other text-books on Rhetoric, but to be used in connection with them. Though adapted to advanced classes, its plan and method are clear and simple. In the hands of a skillful teacher, it will be found to be a valuable aid in securing practical results.

The Eclectic Complete Book-Keeping. By Ira Mayhew, LL. D. Cincinnati: Van Antwerp, Bragg & Co.

The importance of book-keeping as a practical study is generally recognized. This book is somewhat elementary, but contains all that enters into ordinary business transactions, and whatever there is beyond must be learned by experience in actual business.

Methods of Teaching History. Boston: Ginn, Heath & Co. This is intended to be the first of a series of books forming a Pedagogical Library. It contains discussions of methods in teaching History from the pens of experienced historical teachers, and will be found most helpful and suggestive to those less experienced who desire to methodize their teaching of this subject. The second part of the book contains classified lists of works of reference, including not only histories so-called, but works of fiction or poetry, which may be regarded as side-lights in the study.

The Dorcas Magazine, a periodical devoted to the interests of WOMEN and the HOME, has completed its first year's work. Its pages are filled with plain directions for making an infinite variety of useful and decorative articles, and its aim is evidently not only to help women to employ their time in a useful and pleasing manner, but also to be of service to those whom necessity compels to labor.

There are thousands of women throughout the land supporting themselves by the aid of the Crochet-hook and Knitting-needle, to whom the *Dorcas* is invaluable. The Patterns given are selected with care and taste, and the working directions, which, by the way, are printed without abbreviations, are tested by an expert, to prevent mistakes. Knitting, Netting, Crochet-work, all kinds of Embroidery, and Artistic Needle-work are treated in its columns. $1 oo per year. Sample copies 10 cents. Address, DORCAS, 872 Broadway, New York City.

B. W. Evermann, Supt. of Carroll county, and well known in Indiana, has issued, through Jansen, McClurg & Co., of Chicago, an *Animal Analysis*, especially designed to accompany Jordan's Manual of Vertebrate Animals. There are five different forms, one for Mammals, Birds, Reptiles and Fishes respectively, and a fifth form that may be used as occasion demands. There are spaces for recording 120 species of the eight or nine hundred back-boned animals of the northeastern United States. It stands to Analytical Zoölogy as Apgar's Plant Record does to Systematic Botany. It is neat and cheap, and can be used advantageously as a record and description book with any Zoölogy, and especially by field naturalists and amateurs who wish to keep some account of the species they become acquainted with either in school or field. Mr. Evermann is one of several who have been special students under Dr. Jordan at the State University in Natural History, and thus have been enabled to commence independent and original work.

BUSINESS NOTICES.

THE "Monon" route to Chicago from Indianapolis is several miles the shortest, and is now running two trains daily. See advertisement.

TEACHERS desiring to attend a *Normal School*, or those wishing a situation or an increase of salary, should send for a sample copy of "*The Educational World.*" Address, W. SAYLER, *Editor, Logansport, Ind.*   1-12t.

Capt. H. A. Ford and Mrs. Kate B. Ford, former editors of the *Northern Indiana Teacher*, both well and favorably known in this state, will make engagements to do institute work this summer. Their address is Detroit, Mich.

IF you wish to go to Cincinnati by the road that will take you through the most delightful country, take the C. H. & D. This road runs through Rushville, Connersville, Liberty, Oxford, O., Glendale, O., and Green Lawn Cemetery, near Cincinnati.

WANTED—A few good canvassers for Johnson's Universal Cyclopoedia. The best and the cheapest. None but men of intelligence and good character need apply.   HIRAM HADLEY, Gen'l. Manager,
4-1t   116 North Pennsylvania street, Indianapolis.

INSTITUTE WORK.—Prof. W. H. Venable may be engaged to teach and lecture at Institutes in June, July or August. His favorite subjects are History, Literature, Rhetoric, and Pedagogics. Address him at Station C, Cincinnati.   3-4t

TO THE NEW ORLEANS EXPOSITION.—The favorite route to New Orleans is via the Indianapolis & St. Louis R'y, "Bee Line Route," via Mattoon, Ill. Only one change of cars. From Mattoon the route is via the Illinois Central R'y, through Cairo, Jackson, Tenn., and Jackson, Miss. Tickets on sale at Bee Line office, No. 2 Bates House. W. J Nichols, Pass. Agt.   2-3t

EXCURSION TO NEW ORLEANS.—New Orleans Excursion Tickets are now on sale at the Ticket Offices of the Jeffersonville, Madison & Indianapolis Railroad Co. For rates and time of trains, call upon or write to nearest Agent, Jeffersonville, Madison & Indianapolis Railroad Company, or to H. R. Dering, Assistant General Passenger Agent, Indianapolis, Ind.   1-3t

PENNSYLVANIA EDUCATIONAL BUREAU. — *Business transacted in every State and Territory—Old and Reliable.*—Hundreds of teachers have been supplied in the past. The manager is Superintendent of the Public Schools of Allentown, and has a professional experience of twenty-five years. Many teachers wanted. Register *now*. For application form and list of testimonials, address L. B. LANDIS, Manager, 631 Hamilton St., Allentown, Pa.   3-4t

WANTED—A lady of sense, energy and respectability in every county and township, to distribute circulars and canvass for an article of great convenience and value to her sex. Important and indispensable to lady teachers and clerks. $3 to $5 per per day can be easily earned by any lady by giving it a portion of her time. It costs nothing to make a trial. You can earn as much during vacation as you have the past winter. Send stamp for full particulars.
                    HOME MANF'G Co., 15 Vance Block, Indianapolis.

INDIANA
SCHOOL JOURNAL.

Vol. XXX.   MAY, 1885.   No. 5.

THE LIBRARY IN THE SCHOOL.

JAMES BALDWIN, RUSHVILLE, IND.

[Read before the High School Section of the State Teachers' Association.]

How shall the library be made to do most service to the school? To my mind, the weightiest question before the teachers of the country to day, is a question of books—not of text-books, but of books that are really books. What books to read, and how to read them—this is the problem which confronts us with regard to ourselves. By what means can reading matter of a healthful, wholesome nature be placed in the reach of all our pupils, and how shall we lead them into habits of methodical and gainful reading? These are the questions which have a bearing upon the duties which we owe to those entrusted to our care and instruction.

A love for reading is not necessarily a virtue; the time spent in the study of printed pages is not always time spent profitably; the perusal of many books may lead rather to mind-shrinkage than to mind-growth; a taste for literature, so-called, is too often a vitiated or misguided taste, working disorder and disease in its possessor; a library may be a deadly curse, instead of a benefactor and a blessing, to those for whose pleasure or profit it has been established. Since these things are so, what question can deserve a more careful attention than this: *How shall the library be made to do most service to the school?*

First, and above all other requisites—indeed, before it is worth our while to discuss the question of means and methods—the teacher who is to have anything to do with this matter, must be thoroughly qualified for his work. He must be acquainted with books—a knower and a lover of books; otherwise, all will fail. It is not enough that he should possess a merely passable knowl-edge of general history, or of literature, or of mental science, or of pedagogics; he must know the books which contain the best thoughts of the greatest thinkers on these subjects. Besides hav-ing in his mind a store of historical knowledge—a knowledge of dates and events, of causes and results—he must know what are the most trustworthy authorities, ancient and modern, and where to find this or that statement or opinion, and how much is its probable value. He must be able to indicate to his pupils a course of reading on any given subject, and to cite them to those passages or chapters which have a present bearing on their studies. He must acquaint himself with the character and literary worth of the works of Rawlinson, and Smith, and Ebers; of Grote, and Curtus, and Cox, and Felton; of Mommsen, and Merivale, and Arnold, and Gibbon; of Milman, and Stanley, and Hallam, and Guizot; of Hume, and Knight, and Freeman, and Green, and Froude, and Macaulay, and Lecky; of Bancroft, and Hildreth, and Parkman, and Gay, and McMaster. He must know, too, the books which his younger pupils will like best to read in this line of historical study—the books of Miss Yonge, and of John and Jacob Abbott, and of Lanier, and of Coffin, and many oth-ers. All these he should know so well that he shall make no mis-take in recommending the best reading matter to his pupils.

Again, to have some acquaintance with the history of English literature— to know, for instance, that Chaucer wrote the Can-terbury Tales, that Shakspeare is without a rival in the domain of poetic thought; that Milton, when old and blind, composed the grandest epic in our language; and that Longfellow, if not the greatest, is certainly the best loved of American poets,—to know these things and a thousand facts like them, is but a small part of the knowledge which every teacher ought to possess. He should be acquainted at first hand, not through the medium merely of manuals and reviews, with all the master-pieces of English literature,—the works of Lord Bacon; the dramas of

Shakspeare, and Marlowe, and Ben Johnson; the "Faerie Queene;" Milton's "Comus" and "Paradise Lost;" the "Spectator" of Addison; Dean Swift's great satires; Goldsmith, and Boswell, and Burke, and Burns; The Waverley Novels; Lamb's "Essays of Elia;" the "Idylls of the King;" and very many other works which can not here be named. These, I say, the teacher who aspires to the directorship of a library or of the use of any part of it, should know sufficiently well to be able to give his pupils intelligent guidance in the manner of using and reading them. Then he will not be found stumbling by the way,—advising children to read Herbert Spencer's "Fairy Queen," or directing them to study Bacon's Poems—unless, indeed, he believes that Shakspeare's plays were written by the Lord Chancellor; nor yet will he be found tripping into the statement that one of the greatest living authors is Mr. Eclectic, nor falling into the error of admitting Peck's "Bad Boy" into the library, under the impression that it is a very amusing and harmless book.

"If the blind lead the blind, both will fall into the ditch." You may set it down therefore in letters which can not be erased, that without this *knowledge of books on the part of the teacher*, the best chosen library will fail, wholly or in great part, to accomplish the ends for which it was founded; and the boasted "cultivation of a taste for reading," of which we talk so much, will become either a matter of merest chance, or a miserable cheat and farce.

The second thing necessary to promote the usefulness of the library is, that those who take part in its management shall have right and clear ideas concerning its scope and the objects to be reached through its means.

I take it that the chief end to be aimed at and hoped for, in the foundation of every library, is to provide the means by which an appetite for the best and most profitable reading may be planted and encouraged. The teacher who shall so shape and guide the tastes and judgment of his pupils that, when they leave school, they may safely choose their own reading, will not have fallen far short of having done his whole duty,—he will have educated them to educate themselves. And yet, how seldom is this done or even thought of? "The statistics of our public libraries," says Mr. Hudson, "show that some cause is working mightily to prepare the young for delight only in what is both morally and intellectually mean and foul." While the school and the school library fail "to set up the needed safe guards of taste and habit against such a result," can we say that they are doing all that is expected or demanded of them?

Besides this training of the taste and guiding of the judgment, there are other important objects to be reached through the help of the library. A good collection of books, wisely used, will prove to be the teacher's lieutenant and best helper. In the library the pupil finds out thousands of facts not set down in the text-books; he gains the habit and the power of looking carefully into things, and finding out the truth about them for himself; his eyes are opened, and the horizon of his thoughts lifts and widens; and the blue skies and far-away hills of a new world are, by-and-by, laid open to his sight. Then, again, the scholar who has learned to use books rightly, learns that aside from their utilities which are "endless and priceless," they offer him amusement, "more innocent, more sweet, more gracious, more elevating, and more fortifying," than any that is offered to him elsewhere. The genuine pleasure derived from an acquaintance with the best books can not be over-estimated; and the making of this pleasure possible is one of the true objects of the school library. The pupil who acquires a fondness for good books and right reading, needs no discipline; this very fondness will act both as a spur and rein, to urge forward and to restrain. The library which fails to accomplish all the results just named, will fall far short of doing the most service to the school.

Let us suppose, now, that being a knower and a lover of books, as you ought to be, and having fully satisfied yourself as to the objects which you desire to attain, you are ready to begin the establishment of a library in your school. The first question is one of means and funds. How shall the books be procured? To make your library do the greatest service, it must be, in the strictest sense, a *schooi* library. Your philanthropy, no doubt, is as broad as your ambitions are lofty; but if you try to cater to the multitudinous appetites of the public, and at the same time to serve the best interests of your pupils, you will fail twice. Let the town provide its public library, if it will, your field of labor is in the school. The influence of your efforts will, by-and-by, reach the public; and it will be of greater worth than it could possibly have been, had your means and strength been expended in providing that kind of literature craved for and demanded by the multitude.

But books are costly, and school boards are sometimes economical: how shall the funds with which to purchase even a small library be secured? If your school board will levy a tax for that purpose, as the law allows and provides, you need have no anxiety on that point. (Refer to the School Law of Indiana, sections 4524 and 4525.)

Yet even should the necessary funds be placed thus easily within your reach, I am inclined to think that your library will do most service to the school if it is bought and paid for, in part, by your own efforts and those of your pupils, without relying wholly upon the aid of others. To willing workers, many ways and means will suggest themselves. One way is by the formation, among citizens and pupils, of a library association. Members of this association understand that the library is, and shall always be, first and chiefly for the benefit of the school. A life membership may be had, we will say, for twelve dollars, and three years may be allowed for the payment. Merchants, lawyers, clergymen, laborers, school children—all can become members if they wish; and but few are so poor that they can not afford one cent a day for the infinite riches to be derived from the use of a serviceable, well chosen library. Even in a small town, fifty life members ought to be enrolled, thus insuring you a fund of six hundred dollars payable within the first three years. But it will not do to stop here; other means of adding to the library revenue must be adopted. Allow me to suggest a public entertainment now and then, adapted to the tastes and habits of the community and to your own resources. These entertainments— be they festivals, or dramatic representations, or oratorical contests, or school "exhibitions"—of course entail much labor; yet

if properly managed, they will detract nothing from the efficiency
of the ordinary work of the school, but will serve rather to awaken
and keep alive a deeper interest in all that pertains to the intellectual progress of your pupils.

Another method of adding something to the revenue, and at
the same time to the serviceableness of your library, is to make
your pupils feel from the beginning that the library is—in part,
at least—their own. The most common possession to be appreciated at its full value, must cost us something. Hence, it will
be found profitable to encourage your pupils, some to become
life members of the association, others to purchase cards of temporary membership at the nominal cost, say, of not more than
one cent per week; while those who are unwilling or unable to
pay anything should receive cards free of charge, but be expected
to help along on all needful occasions with their labor. Each
school-room, or each class, might be encouraged to form an association of its own, with its own special rules and its own officers, but auxiliary to the main association. Thus, while no
hardship is imposed upon any one, pennies which would otherwise be spent thoughtlessly and foolishly, are cheerfully given
for the buying of new books; and, at the same time, pupils are
led to the acquisition of ideas of liberality and a worthy feeling
of public enterprise.

Still other means of adding to the library fund might be named,
but I forbear. No one should regard it as a great misfortune if
but little aid is granted in the shape of public moneys. If you
deserve a school library you will find some means of getting it.
And if that library is to do most service to the school, it must
cost both you and your pupils some sacrifices in the way of labor
and self-denial.

Having now procured the means with which to make the first
purchases, the next question is, what shall we buy? The selection will depend to a large extent, of course, upon the character
of the community in which your school is located, and the age
and capacity of your pupils. The first thought, often, is to buy
a large number of books of reference. Such works are of immense value to any school, almost indispensable, in fact; but

they are usually made to answer only one of the purposes for which the library is intended, namely, that of giving information. Through them alone, you will hardly succeed in directing the pupil's judgment in the choice of books, very far in the right course; you may add something, but not enough, to their ability for independent research; while in the perusal of the matter-of-fact statements of a cyclopedia, not many of them will be able to find "sweet, gracious, or elevating amusement." A due proportion, therefore, of reference books should be chosen, but not too large a proportion. Let us content ourselves, if our means are limited, with one good, first-class cyclopedia—not too costly, but always first-class—and a few other reference books of the most indispensable kind; and let us spend the bulk of our funds for books of a miscellaneous character and, if possible, a more general usefulness. For the younger pupils, we shall select the purest, noblest books for children, shunning, not only all kinds of trash, but all kinds of "goody-goody" books, those which are filled with sentimental gush, or are over-burdened with what is popularly termed "useful knowledge," presented in a formal, distasteful manner. Here we shall have the best versions of the old fairy tales: Grimm's and Andersen's and Laboulaye's; "Alice in Wonderland," and the "Water Babies," and Hawthorne's "Wonder Book," and "Robinson Crusoe," and the best edition of the "Arabian Nights;" and books about animals, and stories from history, and the good old-fashioned "Rollo Books" and "Franconia Stories," and very many more.

For pupils of the sixth grade, we shall seek books which will supplement their work in geography—books of travel, and wholesome stories of adventure; the "Bodley Books," and "Hans Brinker," and the "Zig-zag Journeys," and the adventures of the "Three Vassar Girls," and some books on natural history, and a few of the best and sweetest poems in the language. For those of the seventh grade, we shall choose Colonel Knox's "Boy Travellers," and some other books of the same kind; and Abbott's series of "American Histories" and "Pioneers and Patriots;" and Hale's "Stories of Adventure," and of "War," and of "Discovery," and of the "Sea;" and Towle's "Heroes of History;" and Coffin's series of historical books; and Eggleston's "Famous Indians;" and many more of like character. For the eighth grade, we shall buy standard works on American history, both for reading and for reference, such as the works of Bancroft and Hildreth and Lossing and Parkman and Prescott and Ridpath and Gay; and we shall have Abbott's biographical histories and some choice books of travel; and Irving and Longfellow, and Bryant, and Whittier; and Lanier's Boys' Books; and Wood's Natural History; and Miss Buckley's admirable volumes on Natural Science; and the larger part of Scribner's Library of Wonders. For the ninth grade and the high school, we shall select, first, a choice list of books on English history, so as to provide for a systematic course of reading in that branch of study; we shall choose, also, the best books on Greek and Roman history, and on the history of the Middle Ages; and to those we shall add the best popular works on science, and as large a collection as possible of the standard English classics, and the most trustworthy works on literary criticism.

Having now completed our selection of books, we look about us and inquire: Of whom shall we buy? When it becomes known that we are on the point of purchasing books, we shall not lack advisers. We shall doubtless be waited upon by accommodating gentlemen, some of whom know more about our wishes and needs than we ourselves can ever know, and are only too anxious to sacrifice themselves for our benefit. One has a wonderful book called "The Silver Goblet," which contains in condensed form the wisdom of the world; thousands of people buy it, but not one person has been known to read it. Another has a cyclopedia which, he declares, is simply all the libraries of the world concentrated into fifteen or twenty volumes; if it is what we want—a first-class cyclopedia at moderate cost— we shall buy it. A third has a hundred-volume library of the publisher's own selection, which he offers to us for a hundred dollars—a fine bargain, if the list includes the books we need most. Shall we buy our books of agents? If we depend entirely upon doing this, we shall often pay dearly for our books, because many of them will prove worthless to us in the end. If we make our own selection, we can scarcely fail to get what we want; and if we buy direct from trustworthy wholesale dealers, we can often secure such discounts as will make our books cheaper than they can possibly be bought through the aid of a third party. Good cyclopedias can not, of course, be obtained in any other way than from the publishers' authorized agents; and the same is true with reference to several other standard and altogether indispensable works. Book agents have done, and are still doing, a great educational work by putting good books into families and communities where otherwise no reading-matter, especially of the better kind, would ever be admitted or called for. The point I wish to emphasize is this: For our school library, we shall buy of agents only when we know that, by doing so, we shall get just the book we need at the best possible rates.

The value of a library depends, not so much upon the number of its volumes, as upon their character. Hence, donations of books, unless such books are known to be valuable, are not generally to be depended upon for the increasing of a library. Books so secured are often worthless volumes which the donor is glad to get rid of, and whose presence on your shelves is an ever visible reminder of their inferiority. Patent Office Reports and other public documents add but little to the value of a school library, and might as well be kept out of sight. If you want to cultivate a relish for what is pure and wholesome, keep clear, not only of trash, but of useless lumber.

Having procured our books, we must next consider the means for their preservation from injury or loss. Our book-cases, although cheap, should be neat and attractive in appearance, with glass doors, and with the shelves neither too near the floor, nor so high that the topmost row of books can not be reached with ease. Each book should have its own place, or compartment, being separated from those next to it by partitions, or slides, which can be adjusted to the size or thickness of the volume. Each compartment is numbered, beginning at the left hand end of each shelf; and the name of the book is pasted beneath. Each book also is numbered, and its number designates the compartment in which it belongs. Thus, the book numbered 12: 3, belongs in case 1, on the second shelf, and in the third space from the left; the book numbered 35: 35, belongs in case 3, on the 5th shelf, and in the 35th space. You will observe that in this plan of numbering the first figure denotes the case, the 2d the shelf, and the figure or figures to the right of the colon, the number of the space or compartment. We shall arrange our books, so far as possible, with reference to the character of their subjects and the grade of pupils for whom they are designed. We shall put covers on none of them, save the cyclopedias and dictionaries, and perhaps a few others which are most liable to receive rough handling; for I have noticed that, as a general rule, books will last longer and be better cared for if the binding be left in full sight; we look upon their handsome exteriors and learn to admire and love them as the faces of our friends. We shall next catalogue our books, noting the price and the place of each, and then we shall be ready to begin the use of them.

The problem of problems now presents itself in a most emphatic manner: *How to make the library do most service to the school.* Shall we invite our pupils to come and choose what they like best? Nine times in ten they will make mistakes, and the tenth time they will choose unwisely. Children are not expected to know books so well that they can safely choose their own reading. If you would make the library do the most service to your school, you must be, not only a director and an adviser, but you must be the autocrat of that library. It is for you to select the books which each pupil is to read, having due consideration, of course, for the peculiarities of his tastes, and needs; and it is for you to see that the books which you give him are read in such manner as shall be of the greatest possible benefit both to him and to his class. By no other means will you be able to guide and properly regulate his reading, or cultivate his judgment with reference to the true worth of books. Assign to the pupils of each class those books which have the most direct bearing upon their studies. To the class in United States History we would give books relating to the early discoveries, the history and the geography of America, and the resources and government of our country; to the class in English History, the best standard works on England and its people; to the students of Latin and Greek, books on ancient history, and classical mythology and literature; to pupils studying geography, books of travel and adventure, and works on natural history; to students of civil government, works on political economy; to students of literature, the master-pieces of poetry and fiction and eloquence, not only of England and America, but of the world.

To name the books most valuable for these classes, or to indicate courses of reading to be pursued, would exceed the limits and the design of this paper. I have elsewhere* given such lists, and have suggested courses of study which may be adapted to readers of every degree, whether private students or pupils at school. Having selected and assigned the books that are to be read, it remains to adopt some means of measuring the work accomplished, and of testing its worth. One or two examples of plans actually and successfully tried, will illustrate some of the methods by which the reading of library books may be made both pleasurable and highly profitable.

Suppose we have before us a class in English history. To the first pupil, we have given the first volume of Green's History of the English People; to the second, Yonge's Young Folks' History of England; to the third, Thierry's Norman Conquest; to the fourth, Hughes's Life of Alfred the Great; to the fifth, the History of William the Conqueror; to the sixth, Tennyson's Harold; to the seventh, Bulwer's Harold; to the eighth, Abbot's Richard the First; to the ninth, Howard Pyle's Robin Hood; to the tenth, Ivanhoe. They use the text-book simply as an outline and for reference; and they have access, also for reference, to Hume and Knight and Freeman and Lingard in English history, and to Hallam and Guizot and Gibbon and other authorities for matters pertaining to the middle ages. Each pupil is required, once a week, to stand before his class and talk about what he has read. If there are ten pupils, two will talk each day. A good plan at the beginning of this work, is to require those who are to talk, to write on the black-board each

---

*The Book Lover, a Guide to the Best Reading. Published by Jansen, McClurg & Co., Chicago, 1885.

morning before school, a set of questions relating to that which they have read,—these questions to serve the purpose of prompters or pointers, and to be answered, in the course of his talk, by the one who has written them. Here is a list of questions prepared by pupil No. 1, after the class has been reading several weeks:

"GREEN'S HISTORY OF THE ENGLISH PEOPLE," pp. 78–82.

1. What was King Ælfred's greatest service to the English people?

2. What books did he cause to be written, and why?

3. What was the state of learning in England at the beginning of his reign?

4. Tell about the schools which he founded, and the teachers which he placed over them?

5. What did he, himself, think of the work which he had accomplished?·

6. Give an account of the voyages of Ohthere and Wulfstan?

7. What was the Anglo-Saxon Chronicle?

8. To what may be traced the beginning of the English navy?

9. Who were the Danes, and what was their character?

10. Give an account of Ælfred's death.

And here are the questions prepared at the same time by pupil No. 10:

"IVANHOE." CHAPTER XXXVII.

The Trial of Rebecca.

1. Describe the place in which the trial of Rebecca was held.

2. Describe the dress and manner of the Grand Master and of other Knights Templars present.

3. Of what was Rebecca accused?

4. What were some of the rules by which the Templars were governed?

5. Who were some of the witnesses, and what was their testimony?

6. In what sort of estimation did the court hold Higg the son of Snell, and why?

7.   Why did Bois-Guilbert say nothing?

8.   What were thought to be some of the sure evidences of
witchcraft in those days?

9.   What chance of life was still left to Rebecca, and how
was she reminded of it?

10.   What was meant by the trial by combat, and how were
such trials usually conducted?

These questions are answered connectedly in the course of
the pupil's talk; and although they are not formally referred to,
they serve to the hearers the purpose of helps in pointing out
and fixing in the memory the main things talked about.   To-
morrow, those who have listened to day will be questioned on
the leading features in the life of Alfred the Great, on the history of the Knights Templars, on some of the superstitions peculiar to the middle ages, and on the methods of trial by combat.
Having been led up to these subjects in a manner which has
awakened their livliest interest, they are inspired with a desire
to know more about them, and many of the pupils repair voluntarily to the reading-room in order to consult the reference books
there; and each one unearths some new item of information or
interest which, to morrow, will be made the common property
of the class.   Before a week has passed and the time has come
for Nos. 1 and 10 to continue their talks, every pupil has fixed
thoroughly in his mind all the valuable points connected with
these lessons, and will be able, if called upon, to talk about them
intelligently.

"Slow work," did you say?   True, each pupil will read
through only two or three books in a year, this way; but he
makes them his own; and he also gets the pith and the kernel
of all that the other members of his class read.   He learns, too,
to read with a purpose in view; and he acquires the power and
the habit of digesting what he reads.   He avoids the pit-falls of
desultory reading.   He becomes able to stand on his feet in the
presence of listeners, and to talk correctly and logically on subjects of interest to him.   He learns to investigate the truth of
that which he reads, and to look on both sides of things; and
when desired to do so, he can write in a logical manner, neatly
and accurately, the substance of any information he has obtained

lists of questions and answers, given at state and county examinations of teachers. The fact that many teachers buy *question books*, and subscribe to journals because they contain lists of questions and answers, is a reason why publishers supply the demand; but is the demand creditable to anybody?

The cramming system is condemned with much show of earnest protest, in every normal school, teachers' institute, text-book on education, and pedagogical paper; but the crammers continue to cram, multiplying machines and appliances to expedite every crammatory art. The state and county examiners cram so as to cram their certificate-seeking victims, who, in their turn cram to cram their devoted pupils, who also cram, cram, cram. Yet, from the college president down to the tiniest lisper in the kindergarten we will agree in saying and almost swearing that the "cramming system is a great and growing evil." Which is sincere, the popular protestation, or the popular practice?

The Harvard and the Yale "Examination Questions" are issued in large editions, and students in preparatory schools are advised to "coach up" by means of them. Almost every college, academy, and high school, prints in its annual catalogue or report the questions that have been used in written examinations. What is the benefit expected from all this?

The writer of this one day not long ago entered a room in a high school in a western city, on the eve of examination, and felt a little ashamed of himself to discover that the teacher in the room was pronouncing to her class a long list of questions on history from printed slips that had been saved up from similar occasions in years past. Thus accident revealed to embarrassed eyes and ears the cramming machine in oily operation.

Perhaps the reader will ask, "Well, what of it? what harm in it?" That is the very question to be asked, pondered, discussed, and decided. What *is* the harm in cramming? Are the question books a blessing or a curse? Do they aid teachers and pupils in education, or do they really retard scholarship and growth of character?

Or is the question merely one of use and abuse? Is the abuse e than compensated for by the legitimate use? or does the abuse outweigh the use, and therefore put the said questionable question-books and lists in the catagory of cigarettes and whisky?'

My dear Mr. Bell, I desire only to state the questionable question, not to make an argument. But, for one, I have no hesitation in saying that my experience and judgment lead me to the opinion that the cramming method is almost wholly evil, and that such publications as I have referred to tend to aggravate the evil. However, if I am at fault, I am open to persuasion, and would be glad to be "confuted in error."

CINCINNATI, OHIO, March 8, 1885.

HOW MUCH CONSCIOUS TEACHING?

BY S. S. PARR.

NEARLY or quite all teachers consciously use the faculty of memory in their pupils. Certain ideas, or ideas and statements, or statements alone are required to be fixed in memory. Very often this goes no further than memorizing text. If such practices employ memory consciously can not observation, imagination and judgment be as consciously employed in common school work as is this faculty? To answer this question intelligently, one needs to examine the meaning of the conscious use of any faculty. It means nothing more than use under the will of teacher or pupil, or both, or, stated differently, to call a faculty into action when wanted and let it lie dormant when not wanted.

No special obstacles seem in the way of using observation, imagination and judgment as consciously as memory. The Grube method, which uses objects in building up the conceptions of numbered objects and numbers, employs observation consciously. Putty maps, map drawing and illustrative objects are attempts at the same in geography. These devices also employ memory and imagination; judgment, too, in its smaller sense. Experiments in physics, as usually conducted, have conscious observation as their object. Imaginary journeys, descriptions, scenes, events and persons, of course, attempt the employment of the faculty of imagination under direction of the teacher's will. Judgment

2

is more difficult to direct than any other faculty of the intellect, since the higher we ascend in the scale of powers, the less they are under outward direction. But every subject, if it be well taught, affords scope for the judgment in its higher and lower phases. Arithmetic is especially valuable as affording drill in that phase of reasoning which deals with the relation of whole and part as applied to space, to numbered objects, and to degrees of intensity. Geography and history are the universal field for the judgment, as they are for man and his actions. All the thought-relations—substance and attribute, whole and part, cause, comparison and purpose—find abundant place. The same is true of reading, word-study, and the elements of the natural sciences.

Teaching will be efficient just as it consciously or unconsciously calls all the faculties into play in due proportion, neither over-working nor neglecting any. The great weakness of unconscious teaching lies in its failure to call all the faculties into action. The weakness of conscious teaching is a lack of freedom,—a certain stiffness and formality that often results from methods and devices that are imperfectly mastered. If freedom of recitation and thought can be secured, unquestionably better results come from conscious than from unconscious teaching. The difference is that between thoughtful selection and blind chance. We are constantly cited to mechanics of various kinds, who are said to do their work well without knowing how they do it. Their unconsciousness of action is greatly overstated. It is true likewise that a good teacher (i. e., one who follows good methods in the main, with poor devices and means) with a poor method, is better than a poor teacher (i. e., one who has no invention and no adaptability) with a good method. The words "good" and "poor" describe the process of calling the right faculties into action at the right time, or the reverse. The tendency of present teaching is certainly toward a conscious use of faculties.

The new chemical laboratory and the new museum of the State University at Bloomington are rapidly approaching completion. Both are very handsome and very well-arranged buildings.

ONLY A PROVERB.

THOMAS BAGOT.

NEARLY every one has heard and perhaps quoted the proverb, "All that glistens is not gold," the authorship of which is usually accorded to Shakespeare. The facts in the case are, however, so far as I can discover, (1) that Shakespeare did not write the proverb at all in the exact form given, and (2) that it dates far earlier than Shakespeare's time even in the form he used.

In Merchant of Venice, Act II, Sec. 7, Shakespeare makes the Prince of Morocco say, "*All that glisters is not gold,*" but this, while equivalent to, is not the same as the form under consideration. George Herbert, who was a middle aged man at the time of Shakespeare's death, renders it in the same words in his Jacula Prudentum, and Edmund Spenser, a cotemporary of Shakespeare for thirty-four years, says in Faerie Queen, Bk. II, Canto 8, Stanza 14, "*Gold all is not that doth golden seeme.*" John Middleton, too, who survived Shakespeare only eleven years, and from whose "Witch" Shakespeare is supposed to have taken much of the material for "Macbeth," in "A Fair Quarrel," Act V, Scene 1, has, "*All is not gold that glisteneth.*"

It makes little difference which of the persons named above first gave utterance to the proverb in the form that best suited him, since, as we shall see, it did not originate with any of them.

John Heywood, who died the year after Shakespeare was born, when Spenser was only eight years of age, and sixteen years before Herbert came into the world, says in his proverbs, "*All that glisters is not gold,*" which is just exactly what Shakespeare and Herbert said in after years, and equivalent to what Middleton and Spenser said. But the proverb was not original with Heywood. John Lydgate, who died in 1460, forty years before Heywood's birth, wrote in "On the Mutability of Human Affairs," "*All is not golde that outward shewith bright,*" and in Chaucer's "Chanones Yemannes Tale" we have, "*But all thing, which that shineth as the gold, ne is no gold.*" Chaucer died in the year 1400, twenty-seven years after Lydgate's birth, and may have received the proverb from some of his predecessors, but I have never noticed it in any earlier writers.

Among later writers it is rendered in various other forms. For instance, Dryden in Part II of "The Hind and the Panther," has it, "*All, as they say, that glitters is not gold,*" and Thomas Gray in Ode II, Stanza 7, puts it, "*Nor all that glistens gold.*" Even Charles Lamb does not deviate far from the beaten path when he says, "*All is not soot that looks like soot.*"

The present form of the proverb, "All that glistens is not gold," is only a modified and modernized form of those given. It seems to have come from the crucible in which the others have been smelted, and to have been adopted by general consent.

CRITICISM ON STATE BOARD QUESTIONS.

THE Indiana system of examining and licensing teachers is very generally held to be superior to the systems of other states. Yet in its results it is not exempt from criticism. During the past month the critics have been unusually numerous and active. A long and not commendable article in the *Logansport Journal* has been widely copied in the state, and has called general attention to the work of the State Board in the preparation of the question lists. It is perhaps a popular belief among the teachers that the strictures of the critics are not wholly unjustifiable. Certainly the Board will not claim to be infallible, and a prevailing opinion, even though ill founded, is entitled to some attention. Hence we feel perfectly free to call the attention of the Board to what seem defects.

To those who urge that a uniform examination for all of the state is undesirable, in view of the diversity of the text-books used, we would say that the Board is right in assuming that something more than a mere text-book knowledge is necessary to the teacher—that in whatever locality he may teach, and whatever books he may use, he requires a general knowledge that will enable him to discuss *topics* rather than books, and to teach subjects rather than pages. Is there not danger, we may be asked, that the Board will go too far beyond the text-books, and ask questions which belong to the repertoire of a specialist, rather than to that of the general student? Very likely. But the fault is rather with the *working* of the system than with the system itself. It is very difficult to devise a perfect mode of questioning. Questions should not be such as can be fully answered by a simple "yes" or "no," since they set too high a premium on guess-work. They should be somewhat general. To call for a specific date, unless it be one of great importance, is not a good plan. If dates must be called for, let the question leave something to the choice of the examinee. If he do not remember the particular one-out-of-ten in the mind of the questioner, he may know the other nine, and they may be just as important And in history there are many things which are not of sufficient importance to be deemed a test of scholarship. For instance, it seems hardly wise to ask what General Santa Anna remarked to General Crittenden, or what General Marion said at dinner, or who kissed Doctor Franklin in Paris, or what John Van Buren said to Queen Victoria, or what Dean Tucker thought about the Revolution, or what novel recounts the exploits of a naval officer that was of great service to General Washington. A well posted county superintendent, with the help of four histories, including Ridpath's large one, and an encyclopedia, is unable to find answers to all the history questions. True, all these matters are subjects of interesting anecdote, and are perhaps worth remembering. But they are not worthy of serious study, or necessary to a teacher's preparation for his work. Possibly Dean Tucker's views are an exception to this statement; but whether they are or not, Dean Tucker is effectually shut out from the knowledge of most teachers by the omission of all reference to him in most library editions of American history.

The questions in arithmetic should be simple tests of the knowledge of arithmetical principles, rather than tests of endurance, in view of the fact that the physical test is at best severe. The questions on "theory" contain questions that can only be answered by a student of mental philosophy. This is hardly fair to the masses of teachers who have never studied this subject.

These ideas are the ideas of the Board, and are followed in the main, and our question lists have a high reputation in other states. That an occasional question should fail to be up to the standard is by no means surprising, in view of the large number of different ones to be supplied and the limited time that the members have to devote to the work. Furthermore, it is absurd to hold the President and Secretary accountable for the work of the entire Board simply because they sign the lists. * * *

The Journal admits the above semi-criticism in order to thus call the attention of the Board to certain strictures that are being made upon parts of its work, and in order to give it the opportunity of explaining certain things that will throw light upon some matters not well understood.

The Journal will say this much for the Board: that while individual questions may be open to criticism, as a whole they are good. Also, the Board has for years purposely made a few questions each time a little in advance of or outside of the smaller text-books, in order to encourage study and advancement on the part of teachers.

Let it be remembered that it is *not* an easy matter to prepare several lists of questions at a time on a subject, and have each list comprehensive, and each question a model, and yet not repeat questions; and further, that it *is* an easy thing to criticise questions that somebody else makes.

THE SCHOOL ROOM.

[This Department is conducted by Geo. F. Bass, Supervising Prin. Indianapolis schools.]

GUESSING.

THERE is probably no worse habit in the schools than that of guessing. Teachers and pupils frequently indulge in it. The teachers in explaining things to the children often guess that this or that plan will reach the pupils and make the matter plain. Quite frequently in the examination for a certificate, the teacher guesses the answer. But the greatest harm is done by teaching in such a way that pupils are afforded an opportunity to guess.

"Which is the capital of Ohio, Cincinnati or Columbus?" is a kind of question that makes guesses. The pupil has only *one* chance to miss. He takes his chance. Who wouldn't, as a last resort, especially when he knows he will be counted a "failure" if he misses *one* question, and will be detained a half hour to "make up" his lesson?

"Did you give an orange to James?" "No, Sir; John gave it." In the above sentences, which words should receive emphasis? The *question*, in this case, is all right, provided the school has not formed this bad habit of guessing. If they have, several hands will be up before you have fairly finished your question. Call on some pupil quickly and he will give you a very prompt answer. He may say, "*You*." if he does, don't say "Yes," but ask another question to test him as to whether he guesses. Why? Now if he says that he thinks James has an orange and thinks that some one *gave* it to him, but does not know *who*, you may be certain that he did *not* guess. Now, suppose some one reads the answer emphasizing *gave*. You ask, "Is that right?" Nine in every ten will say, "No, Sir." Why will they? Because you have invited them to guess. You say, "Well, what is wrong?" "He should not emphasize gave; he should emphasize *John*." "Yes," you say. You are in a hurry; you have only ten more minutes for this recitation and you must hear fifteen more pupils read, because if you do not some pupil may say, at home, that you did not call on him in reading to-day.

Since the time is short, use it to the best advantage. Do not say "Yes" unless you are certain the pupil knows why the word *John* should be emphasized. Ask for the meaning given when that word is made emphatic. Call on pupils to use their judgment and decide which is right and which is wrong. If read the way the pupil read it, call attention to the reading of the question;—"Did *you* give James an orange?" What does the questioner wish to know? "He wishes to know *who* gave the orange."

Answer the question by reading the words of the book.

THE EXAMINATION.

THERE *is* some good to be gained by a written examination; not much can be gained from the percents. They are only pointers—indicators, as the hands of a clock. I look at the clock when the position of the sun shows that it is mid-day, and the hands by pointing to certain *figures* show 9 *o'clock.* I know something is wrong, but I do not know what. I listen, the clock ticks. I say, "No, it has not stopped." I must look further to find out what is wrong.

I look down a row of percents—say, *percents,*—and find a 36. Something wrong, I do not know what. I call for the paper the pupil presented. There is nearly no writing. I must read it carefully. I do not know just what is the trouble, but I know more than I knew. I may need to have a talk with the teacher and talk over the course. I may need to see the teacher at the recitation. I may need to do the teaching myself. After a time, I may or may not know just what is wrong, but I know more than I did. I see that the *percent* started me on my tour of investigation. As the teacher myself I must go over the very same work. I must have a private talk with the pupil and test the work itself. Self-criticism is very valuable.

The examination has a tendency to remind us that we need to re-examine our own work. We may think we have presented the subject in a philosophical manner—even according to the method, and yet the examination may remind us that we are not reaching the pupil. We may think the subject has been taught thoroughly, and that the pupil has had to *do* the work, we may flatter ourselves that he has learned "to do by doing"; the method when the child knows *what* to do and does it; the examination may disclose the fact that he has not done them enough. I examine my method of presentation and find it about right, but find that the pupil is still a failure. I conclude that he needs more practice—more *doing.*

LANGUAGE LESSON.

Fill the blanks with the proper form of *Louis, Mr. Ross, fly,* work and sparrow.

—— mother has no one else to send.
—— horse was frightened by the music.
All —— wings are transparent.
At the close of ten —— work vacation begins.
The boys had found some —— nests near the ball ground.

2. Fill the blanks with the proper form of *water*, *waves*, and *princess*.

The boat was drawn to the —— edge.
You noisy —— roll higher up the strand.
"We do not dare," the —— reply.
What was the —— reply?
She was dressed like an Indian —— .
The —— dress was of deer-skin.

3. Which of the sentences above is a command? Which is a question? Which contains a quotation?

4. Fill the blanks with some form of *do*, *go*, *come*, and *choose*.

He —— his work and —— to school early.
If he had —— to play, he could not have —— so soon.
Has the teacher ——?
Have you —— a good subject for your composition?

The above exercise was given as a written examination to test the pupils in their knowledge of language as far as they had been taught. On reading their papers it was found that many had failed to use their common sense, and some did not know the proper forms of the words. Such sentences as follows were found on several papers: "Mr. horse was frightened by the music." "The Indian dress was of deer-skin." Remember the word "Indian" is not one of those from which they were to choose. "All sparrows' wings are transparent." By questioning afterward it was found that only one pupil in the class knew what *transparent* means. Common sense would have said, "Don't use a word that means nothing to you."

But some one says, "You can not expect children of this grade to have as much judgment as you suggest." Proper teaching will give them this power to judge. This examination surprised the teacher, and the papers were handed to the children and a lesson, substantially as follows, was given:

Tr. In the first sentence, whose mother is meant?

Pu. Louis's mother, (orally).

Tr. Why not Mr. Ross's mother?

Pu. Because Mr. Ross is a man, and his mother would not send him on an errand.

Tr. Spell the form of Louis that you used.

Pu. Louis's.

Tr. What does it mean?

Pu. It means one and shows ownership.

Tr.　Who most likely owned the horse, the boy or the man?

Pu.　The man.

Tr.　Mary, what will you put in the next sentence?

Mary.　Mr. Ross's.

Tr.　Spell it, Mary.　Mr period, capital R–o–double s, apostrophe–s.

Tr.　Why not put Mr. alone?

Pu.　Because it don't make no sense.

Tr.　Because it *doesn't* make *any* sense.　What does transparent mean?

Pupils looked blank.　Finally one little fellow in the back part of the room put up his hand rather hesitatingly, and the teacher said, "Well, Tommie?"

Tommie.　What you can see through.

Tr.　Tommie is right.　Anything that we can see through is transparent.　Name something that is transparent.

Pupils (looking at the windows).　Tr. Class.　Pu. Glass.

Tr.　How many of you have looked at a sparrow's wing? at a fly's wing? (nearly all had).　Which one can you see through? Class.

Pupils.　The fly's wings.

Tr.　Which of the words must we take to fill the blank? class.

Class.　Fly.

Tr.　What must the form that we use mean?　Susie.

Susie.　It must mean more than one.

Tr.　How do you know?

Susie.　Because the word *all* means more than one fly.

Tr.　What else must it mean?

Pu.　It must mean ownership.

Tr.　Write on the board the form that means more than one.

Pu.　Flies.

Tr.　What must we do to make it show ownership?

Pu.　We must add an apostrophe.

Tr.　Yes.　Add it.

This is slow work but it is good work.　The pupil has been led to think about the things that he *must* think about to properly fill the blanks given.　This kind of work will teach him to use his common sense.

The third sentence is faulty because it contains a word that was not in their vocabulary. They should not have undertaken to fill the blank at all. It was a mere *guess* on their part.

There is material enough in this set of questions for another lesson of this sort, but not half enough in the whole set for one *guess* lesson.

PRIMARY DEPARTMENT.

[This Department is conducted by Lewis H. Jones, Supt. Indianapolis Schools]

——:o:——

PRIMARY LANGUAGE.

WHEN taught by the appropriate methods, the different forms of nouns and pronouns, the verbs and adjectives, may be learned practically by pupils so immature that it would be useless to attempt to teach to them the declensions, comparisons and conjugations as arranged in most grammars. The child often learns the meaning of a word by the position in which he finds it in a sentence. This is especially true of the different forms of the same word after the root meaning has been learned by experience, since the variation is made for the better expression of some special relation of ideas; which relation of ideas makes up the real meaning of the new form of the word chosen for its expression. Thus every child early learns the meaning of the word *ring* as applied to a bell. If now the different forms of this word, as ring, rings, rang, (has, have or had) rung, be used correctly in conversation by the teacher, with respect to the bell, pupils will easily and readily learn the peculiar *relative time* implied in each form. But since the power to use language after the meaning of the words has been learned is dependent on the perfect association of word and meaning in memory, there must be much drill of some kind in order to secure such memory; so that when afterward a child has just such relationship of ideas to express, the proper form of the appropriate word will suggest itself through the force of the law of association. This is of course but another way of forming intelligently a *habit* of *correct usage.*

Three different steps in the practice necessary to insure habitual correct use suggest themselves. They vary in degree of difficulty, and therefore suggest the order of their employment.

1. (*a*) Oral use of the different forms of the word "ring" by the teacher in full sentences, illustrating by actions with the bell the precise relative time of each act, as indicated by the different forms of the word used. (*b*) Oral recitation (or reading) by the pupil of prepared sentences, written on the blackboard by the teacher in which the precise relative time of imagined (or remembered), actions with the bell are correctly indicated by the different forms of the word "ring."

2. The filling of blanks by pupils in sentences in which the precise relative time of imagined (or remembered) actions with a bell are made evident by the context. Pupils supply the appropriate form of the word to *accord* in meaning with the relative time indicated by the context. In this work the pupil should have before him on the black-board, a list of the "forms of 'ring,'" from which to choose.

Some such arrangement as this would serve:

FORMS OF THE WORD RING.

rings
ring
rang
rung { have
has
had

Some little explanation should be made in reference to the different words "have," "has" and "had;" that when one of them is used the others are omitted; or better, use "have," "has," or "had" whenever you use "rung."

This division (2) also admits of subdivisions *a* and *b;* i. e., oral, and written.

3. Write original sentences about the ringing of the bell. Each sentence should be brought to the criticism of teacher or class, or of both; for pupils learn much from the work of the other members of their own classes.

. There is of course in all this work no need to say anything about modes or tenses, person or number of the verb; not even necessity for any speaking of "ring" as a verb at all; only call it the word "ring" and speak of its "forms." The personal pronouns offer fine opportunity for similar treatment. Thus the work might appear in this way:

FORMS OF *I.*

I	me	my
mine	we	us
our	ours	

Then come the elliptical sentences in which the mystical relations of "person" and "number" are made plain by the context:

1. —— have done —— work.
2. He spoke to —— .
3. This is —— book.
4. That book is yours; but this one is —— .
5. —— are going to the city.

With the "forms of I" and the elliptical sentences before pupils, an oral lesson should precede the written, so as to give opportunity for criticism of poor selections. A little help given at the right time will develop the power to choose rightly, and will elevate the standard of taste in the use of language. This culture of taste is, as I have before indicated, the chief end of a course in language training.

THE A B C OF NUMBER.

"WE will do some buying and selling to-day. Look over the goods, and tell me what there is to sell."

Boxes of matches (empty boxes); thimbles (clay); marbles (clay); spools of thread (empty spools); lozenges (paste-board disks); sticks of candy (colored sticks); pencils, papers of pins, papers of needles, pin-balls, apples, pears, plums, grapes, peaches, oranges (clay); hat-pins (splints); pens, toy watches, toy tools (paper); postage stamps, pictures, cards, sand-paper, blotting-paper, narrow ribbon, narrow lace, newspapers, envelopes, star books, pencil tablets.

"George may be salesman, and set his own prices, but he is not to charge more than fifteen cents for any article."

Teacher. Nellie may run to the store, and buy a thimble for herself, and a paper of No. 10 needles for me. (She is given a ten-cent piece.)

Nellie, at the store. I wish for a thimble for myself, and a paper of No. 10 needles.

Salesmen. Thimble two cents, needles five cents, and three cents, are ten cents.

T. Frank may buy a small bottle of ink and a half-dozen pens. (Frank is given a five-cent piece and two three-cent pieces.)

Frank. I wish for a bottle of ink and a half-dozen pens.

S. Bottle of ink five cents, pens five cents, and one cent, are eleven cents.

T. Harry may buy two sheets of coarse sand-paper, and this morning's paper. (Harry is given a five-cent piece and two two-cent pieces.)

S. Two sheets of sand-paper four cents, and the newspaper three cents, and two cents, are nine cents.

T. Annie may buy three two-cent postage stamps, and two sheets of white tissue paper. (Annie is given four three-cent pieces.)

S. Three two-cent stamps six cents, two sheets of tissue-paper four cents, and two cents, are twelve cents.

T. Willie may buy a half-dozen apples and three peaches. (Willie is given two threes and a five.)

S. Six apples three cents, three peaches six cents, and two cents, are eleven cents.

T. Nettie may buy what she wishes to buy, and tell me about it afterwards. (Nettie is given some money.)

T. Henry may buy anything he wants, and tell me about it afterwards. Joe may buy two sticks of candy and a watch. Tell me about the purchase when you return.

Each child tells me about his purchase after he returns. This exercise will require some tact on the teacher's part at first, that it may run smoothly; but after a few exercises the children will price the goods fairly, and count out change in a business-like way. The exercise tests the children's power to apply their knowledge of number, acquaints them with prices of small articles, and gives practice in handling money.

The prices of the different articles may be written upon the board before the class exercises, thus:

Oranges 05	Paper of pins 06
Apples 02	Thimbles 02
Grapes 03	Ribbon per yard . . .05
Pin-balls 05	Paper and needles . . .10
Lead pencils . . .05	Hat-pins 02

These are not arithmetic diversions, but legitimate means of training to a knowledge of numbers.

I attach great importance to applied number. Nice little problems about articles the children themselves buy, about things they see and do, about facts in nature, as the number of toes a cat has, the number of wings a butterfly has, the number of legs a fly has; about numbers applied arbitrarily, as the days in a week, the things in a dozen, the things in a score, the sheets of paper in a quire, the months in a year, the gills in a pint, pints in a quart, quarts in a gallon, in a peck, in a bushel.

I have selected a few which I have heard:

If I tell John to lower half the windows in this room, how many will he lower?

If you have three holidays in the winter term, and two in the summer term, how many holidays do you have in both terms?

Mary writes three words, rubs out two words, and then writes three more words; how many words will she have to show me?

If Annie, Jennie, and Ned keep their hands under the table, how many hands are hidden away?

If Harry, Jennie, Robert, and Frank stand squarely upon two feet, how many feet will rest nicely upon the floor?

If there are four persons in your family, but one goes away to visit, and two of your friends come to visit you, then one of these goes away, how many persons will there be in your family?

If you have four errands to do, and forget half of them, how many do you remember?

If you drop six kernels of corn into each hill, and a worm eats one, a crow eats two, and one dies, how many are left to grow?

One mile is half the distance I walk every pleasant day. How far do I usually walk?

If you owe me six cents, and pay me in two-cent pieces, how many two-cent pieces do you give me?

If George writes the word "cup" six times, erases the word twice, and writes it over again, how many times does he write the word? .

My watch loses six seconds a day, and my brother's watch gains two seconds a day. If the watches are together one morning, how much will they differ in time the next morning?

If a boy earns two cents a day, Tuesdays and Fridays, and one cent for each of the other days, how many cents will he earn during the week?

What three unequal pieces of money make six cents?

A coffee-cup holds two gills; how many cupfuls make a pint?

If your hat, coat, and book are lying on the chair, and your rubbers, mittens, and boots are scattered about on the floor, how many things must you pick up?

Exercises like these make children think before they act, cultivate reason, impress facts, awaken interest, and put knowledge in a form to use. Their office is not solely to test for facts. They furnish the best opportunity for understanding language, and for showing power to reason. I never aim to make the conditions puzzling, but give fair and open questions. I always require the problem to be illustrated when there is any hesitation in understanding it. I believe in a great amount of illustrative work to show me what the children are thinking about, and to help the child to think more clearly.

In all work with numbers, proceed by steps, following the law of dependence and of simplicity. It is not always best to finish one subject before taking up another. It is certainly very much simpler to take the first step in addition, in subtraction, and in multiplication, before taking the second step in addition; very much simpler to take some steps in fractions and in mensuration and in denominate numbers before taking all the steps under the four fundamental rules.

Many books give quite clearly the different points under a

single subject in their order, but I know of none which gives subjects in the order in which you will want to present them, if you make a logical analysis of the subject of number, for teaching. So you have chiefly to depend upon your own study.

There is no text-book calculated to be of much help to the child during the first four years. He needs none in recitation, and the work which he does by himself is represented by figures; so a book which contains a great deal of number work expressed in figures, and in the last part some examples, with blanks for figures, which figures he is to supply, and then solve the problems, is the only one that he can use. Such a book would greatly aid the teacher in the matter of time.

Notation and numeration are taught step by step, as occasion requires, and the principles acquired gradually, without effort on the part of the child.

No subject offers so many opportunities for mental activity to children just beginning school life, as simple number. In no subject is it possible to lead them to do, to talk, and to think, as in number. Every lesson makes a special demand upon their powers of close attention and of quick response. There is no subject that they enjoy more, none they take more pride in studying.

Do not forget that tact enters into all work, and that no one of the suggestions made will be of value without it. Tact is born of sympathy, and sympathy is the kingdom of heaven in all teaching. Seek it first, and all other things shall be added unto you There is no child but is responsive to our personal interest in him, and there are few children who will be interested in their work without it.—*Miss E. M. Reed, in New York School Journal.*

The telegram sent west some days since stating that Secretary Lamar had asked for Commissioner Eaton's resignation, and to which the Journal referred last month is, we learn from trustworthy authority, incorrect. Our informant says that, "He has not even hinted that such resignation is desired, and it is believed that he appreciates fully Gen. Eaton's work—especially in the South." We are glad to make the correction.

3

DEPARTMENT OF PEDAGOGY.

This Department is conducted by Geo. P. Brown, President State Normal School.

------:o:------

THE USE AND ABUSE OF OUTLINES.

Much reliance is placed upon "teaching by outline" by teachers. Such gross abuses of this method have been sanctioned by some who advertise themselves as educational reformers, and who wield considerable influence among the young and less thoughtful class of teachers, that a word of caution is needed.

We shall attempt to state fairly the uses and abuses of this plan of teaching as they appear to us.

The purpose of an outline is to employ the memory of the eye to assist in retaining in the mind the order of the ideas that compose a science. This is done by arranging upon black-board or paper words and phrases that express these ideas more or less perfectly, in a certain arbitrary order. He who understands the order of arrangement and knows the ideas will be able to see in this outline what ideas are co-ordinate and what are subordinate, and how each idea stands related to the others. But to make this arrangement of words and phrases signify anything, the ideas that they represent must be first known and their relations discovered. When they have been thus carefully studied then the mechanical outline may bring the memory of the eyes to the aid of the other retentive faculties involved and assist them in holding these ideas in their proper relations.

It is also true that the black-board may often be profitably employed to aid in teaching for the first time the relations in these ideas, for the reason that it is always well to bring the senses to the aid of the imagination, the reason and judgment whenever it can be done.

Outlining is especially valuable in reviewing a topic or science, for the purpose of fixing in mind the prominent ideas, after a careful study of the topic has been made.

It is a great abuse of outlines when they are made the principal object of study. In such cases the mechanical outline of a subject is substituted for the subject itself; the study of words and their arbitrary arrangement with a very vague idea of what the words mean is put in the place of the study of ideas and their logical connection; the sense of sight is employed to the neglect, if not utter exclusion, of the imagination, the judgment and the reason. What is learned and remembered is the verbal outline.

To one ignorant of the subject, and even to one familiar with it, such a student seems to know a great deal so long as he is allowed to do all the talking. But how soon is the illusion dispelled when some questions testing the knowledge of what the outline expresses are asked. His seeming erudition is found to consist of words of learned length and thundering sound.

And the worst and most criminal feature of this fraud is that the innocent, confiding, gullible student really thinks he has something valuable when he has nothing.

This cruel deception often finds a more lasting lodgment in the mind from the stimulants that are skillfully applied to his self-pride and egotism. Poor fellow! He really thinks he has learned more in three months by the outline method than he could have learned without it in a year. It is not until he gets out into the world and comes into competition with those who have some knowledge and some intellectual training that he finally and painfully discovers that he knows nothing. He finds that his magnificent possessions are but apples of Sodom.

It is in part by this abuse of the method of outline study that some color of truth is given to the boasts of some schools whose advertisements we have read that by their new methods they can teach a student more in two years than they can learn in other schools in six. The students, as we have said, come through having the appearance of knowing something because they can rattle through a mass of skeletons of sciences that are indeed veritable dry bones.

The device of outlines is not a new discovery. It has been used by generations of teachers. But it seems to have been left for our time to exalt this means into an end and to go about, as Carlyle says, rattling this dry skin. And it is as true educationally as it is commercially, that the number is legion of those who are ever trying to get something for nothing. There are a few who succeed in doing this in the commercial world, but education can not be so obtained.

G. P. B.

HOW TO PRONOUNCE ARKANSAS.

ED. JOURNAL: The question is frequently asked, "If *Arkansas* spells "Arkansaw," why does not *Kansas* spell "Kansaw"? Allow me to ask: If *dough* spells "do", why does not *rough* spell "ro"? The pronunciation of geographical names is explained by their history. The name *Arkansas* was given to a settlement made by the French two hundred years ago—in 1685. It was pronounced "Arkansaw" then, and has been ever since, the pronunciation being handed down in an uninterrupted succession of generations of inhabitants. With Kansas the case was entirely different. It was not settled until within comparatively recent years, and was settled wholly by English speaking people, who pronounced the name according to ordinary English analogy. There was no other pronunciation handed down from a remote past. Nine thousand nine hundred and ninety-nine people out of ten thousand in Arkansas pronounce the name "Arkansaw," and the ten-thousandth will if he lives there long enough.

SK.

EDITORIAL.

The editor having spent the last month in New Orleans, asks that any mistakes in proof-reading, or shortness in miscellaneous news, or lateness in the appearance of the Journal may be charged to the usual source of all such mistakes and deficiencies—the ever conven- ient clerk.

THE NEW ORLEANS EXPOSITION.

This exposition is a great one. In some regards it is not equal to the Centennial Exposition, but in others it far exceeds it. Indiana's state exhibit is only creditable, except in its educational department, where it ranks with the best. The excellence of the educational ex- hibit is attested by impartial, competent judges. The writer speaks what he has learned *on the ground*. State Supt. Holcombe has done himself and the state credit.

The Exposition will well repay a visit to New Orleans, and this is the best season to see the "Sunny South." A person who is inter- ested in leaving his Arctic climate, and for a few days bathing in balmy air of spring, again to return to his wintry abode, should come here in February or March, but he who wishes to see *The South* in its wealth of verdure and flowers should come now. To see the South, May is a hundred fold better month than February.

New Orleans itself is well worth a visit. We speak from experi- ence and say—*It will pay to visit the World's Exposition at New Orleans.*

ELECTION OF COUNTY SUPERINTENDENTS.

By the law there must be an election of county superintendents the first of June. The Journal wishes to reiterate what it has often said before, viz: that great care should be taken in this the most important officer in the county. No other officer has such vital rela- tions with so many people. No other officer has it in his power to exercise so much influence for good. His work is for all classes, rich, poor, black, white, without regard to politics, religion, or rela- tionship.

In the selection of these superintendents trustees are called upon to discharge the most responsible and most important of their official duties. In this selection trustees should rise above politics, above sectarianism, above relationship, above personal friendship, and have in mind only the highest interest of the children of the county.

A man who is not capable of rising above all these side issues and voting for a superintendent solely upon his *merit* is not the man for trustee.

In making this choice of superintendent, other things being equal, the present incumbent should have the preference. Experience is valuable in any line of work. In this office it takes about all the first year to inaugurate and put into successful operation any systematic plan of work, and a term of two years only prepares a person for his best work. A man who has had two years experience is worth much more in the office than a new person of equal ability.

This is not a plea for the retention in office of incompetent or unfaithful superintendents, neither is it a plea for even a good man if a much better one can be had, but is a plea for the exercise of the best judgment, to the end that the "great right arm of our school system" may be strengthened and not weakened in the election to take place in June.

LADY COUNTY SUPERINTENDENTS—WHY NOT?

Why not elect, in some of the counties, ladies to the office of county superintendent? In Illinois some of the most efficient superintendents are ladies, and the Journal can see no reason why the same thing might not be true in Indiana. True, a former Attorney General gave an opinion to the effect that the superintendent is a *county officer*, and that a county officer must be a *citizen*, and that a woman is not a citizen, in the office holding sense. But it is also true that the man who framed the law which gives women the right to serve on school boards, is a good lawyer and *intended* the law to include all school offices. It is also true that not only he, but many able lawyers hold the opinion that the county superintendency is not in any true or legal sense a *county office*, and that women are eligible.

The Journal would be exceedingly glad to see a good woman elected in some of the counties, and then if any one chooses to contest the election the courts could decide the matter.

REPORT OF THE SUPT. OF PUBLIC INSTRUCTION
For the Years ending August 31, 1883–4.

Supt. Holcombe's first Biennial Report is before us, and deserves special mention. It contains information on many subjects connected with education, and will compare favorably with reports heretofore issued from this office.

Part First discusses, (1) the Indiana System, setting forth its main features and their dependence and relations, and gives also a brief history of the growth of the system; (2) various amendments needed in some of the details of the system—this especially, for the legislature did nothing in this line; (3) State Teacher's Certificates, modified plan of examination, conditions, sample questions, etc.; (4) Teachers' Institutes, county and township, with uniform outlines for each; (5) Uniform Course of Study for the county schools and questions for graduation from the same; (6) High School Commissions; (7) Celebration of Arbor Day; (8) Inter-State Educational Convention; (9) Teachers' Reading Circle; (10) State Exhibit at Madison; (11) Higher and Special Instruction; (12) Analysis of Statistics, etc.

Part Second contains, (1) Biographies of State Superintendents, by H. M. Skinner, chief clerk of Supt.; (2) Proceedings of County Sup'ts Association; (3) Essays of County Sup'ts on various topics; (4) Statistical Tables; (5) General Index.

The following are a few facts gleaned: Total enumeration of children, 722,851, an increase in one year of 3,816; No. enrolled, 501,142, of whom 8,903 were colored. The percent of children enrolled for the entire state is 64; the highest percent by any county is 88, and that is reached only by Kosciusko and La Grange; the lowest percent is 23, by Brown county. The counties making the largest enumeration are Marion, 45,283; Allen, 25,078; Vanderburg, 20,831: those making the smallest enrollment are Ohio, 1,772; Stark, 2,161; Union, 2,504. Number of teachers employed, 13,302, of whom 6,481 are females.

SCHOOL LEGISLATION.

Few laws were enacted by the late General Assembly that affect the school system of our state, nor are those of special importance which were passed. The following presents in brief summary the changes made and the appropriations voted.

SURPLUS DOG TAX.—Section 8 of the act approved April 13, 1881, is considerably altered by an amendment presented in the Senate and numbered 108. Hereafter, township trustees will retain all surplus arising from the dog tax, after paying for the sheep killed, unless such surplus exceeds fifty dollars, on the first Monday in March; and in case the sum does exceed fifty dollars at that time, the amount is to be turned into the county treasury, to constitute a "dog fund" from which other trustees may draw, if they have not been able to pay for all the sheep killed in their townships. On the second Monday in March all that remains of the "dog fund" is to be given to the schools in like manner as the interest on the Congressional School Fund. This last would appear to be a somewhat indefinite statement.

PRIVATE LIBRARIES.—Where there is a library established by private donation, worth one thousand dollars or more, and secured to the use of all the people of the township, the township trustee may levy and collect annually a tax of not more than one cent on the hundred dollars, and pay the same to the trustees of the said library, for its care and enlargement.

LIBRARY BUILDINGS.—With the consent of the county commissioners, the township trustee may erect or extend a building for such library, and collect therefor a tax of not more than five cents on the hundred dollars for not more than three years. These two provisions are to be found in the act numbered 100, which originated in the House. It contains an emergency clause.

PAYMENT FOR LIBRARY BUILDINGS ALREADY ERECTED.—City school trustees who have erected library buildings or purchased real estate for such purposes, according to Sections 4524-5-6 Revised Statutes of 1881, and who are not able to pay the same from the revenues therein prescribed, may pay for the same from any of the special school revenue. This act (324, Senate) contains an emergency clause.

A METROPOLITAN LAW.—In cities of over seventy thousand population, the offices of city treasurer and city assessor are abolished. The county treasurer is to conduct the city's finances, and is to give a separate bond to the school commissioners for the safe keeping of moneys belonging to the "school city," and is otherwise instructed somewhat minutely as to his new functions. This act is numbered 182 (Senate).

COUNTY TREASURERS' SETTLEMENTS.—The act numbered 322 (Senate) cuts away a great deal of red tape, and the wonder is that it was not passed thirty years ago. At the semi-annual settlement the State Auditor is to give the county treasurer a warrant on the state treasury for the state school revenue collected in his county; and when the State Supt. of Public Instruction makes his semi-annual apportionment, the State Auditor shall draw a warrant on the State Treasurer for any deficiency. County treasurers will pay or receive any surplus, accordingly as they receive by the apportionment less or more than their counties contribute. Thus the great bulk of the revenue will not be carried to the capital and back twice a year. This act contains an emergency clause.

RELIEF OF TRUSTEES.—Several acts were passed for the relief of trustees who, through the bank failures of last year, lost the school money entrusted to their care, and were liable for the deficits thus created.

THE STATE UNIVERSITY.—Indiana University receives in the general appropriations the total sum of thirty-six thousand dollars, as follows:

Annual expenses................................. $23,000 00
Building repairs, library, museum, apparatus, etc.... 13,000 00
                                                     ──────────
   Total..................................... $36,000 00

STATE INDUSTRIAL SCHOOL.—Purdue University receives the same total sum as Indiana, as follows :

Annual expenses................................. $24,000 00
Buildings and machinery......................... 12,000 00
                                                 ──────────
   Total..................................... $36,000 00

STATE NORMAL SCHOOL.—The State Normal School receives an aggregate of ten thousand five hundred dollars (in addition to the twenty thousand dollars apportioned annually by the State Supt. of Public Instruction), as follows :

Annual expenses................................. $10,000 00
Library... 500 00
                                                 ──────────
   Total..................................... $10,500 00

Among the bills which were generally desired, by the people, but which failed to pass, were those relating to the instruction of youths in the physiological effects of stimulants and narcotics, and to the township institutes. As regards the former, there is not so much need for positive *law* on the subject, as for an interest on the part of the teacher. In our state we have a way of anticipating the law in many things relating to the school system. In fact, our system is a growth, largely outside of the letter of the law.

The State Supt. of Public Instruction provided last year for the instruction of all the teachers in the state in the effects of stimulants and narcotics, when he issued his Outline of Institute Work, and it is supposed that all conscientious teachers will make a practical use of the work of the institutes.

─────

There was a meeting of superintendents and graded school teachers at Elkhart on April 18th. The following subjects were on the program for discussion: 1. Graduation and its data; 2. The Over-work of Pupils; 3. What changes are needed in our course of study? 4. Can the course of study be so arranged as to promote pupils faster? 5. How can we interest pupils in the reading of good literature? 6. Essential qualifications of the teacher.

Supt. Elias Boltz seems to be a moving educational spirit in that section of the state.

─────────

Under the new arrangements for State Licenses about sixty persons have applied. This is a great increase over the number applying in any former year, and the plan is certainly a good one.

QUESTIONS AND ANSWERS.

D.

QUESTIONS BY THE STATE BOARD FOR MARCH.

SCIENCE OF TEACHING —1.   What is memory? State the difference between a perfect and an imperfect memory of any thing.

2.   At what age will children memorize with greatest ease?

3.   What is the evil of trying to make pupils learn what requires the activity of the reasoning powers before these have become active?

4.   What is concrete knowledge? What is abstract knowledge?

5.   Which of the above kinds of knowledge are most interesting to a child? Why?

READING.—1.   In what grade should pupils be supplied with dictionaries, and for what purpose should they be used?

2.   What is an aspirated tone? Give an example that should be read in that tone.

3.   Of what use are punctuation marks? Illustrate.

4.   How will you prevent your pupils from reading poetry in a sing-song tone?

5.   Name the inflections used in reading, and give the use of each.

6.   Read a paragraph of prose and a stanza of poetry selected by the superintendent.

PHYSIOLOGY.—1.   Can a nerve, once cut, be healed again? Illustrate.

2.   Describe the villi of the intestines.

3.   Explain to what degree animal heat is constant.

4.   Describe the action of the crystalline lens of the eye.

5.   Why do we not see objects inverted?

6.   Describe the epiglottis.

7.   Describe the movements of the heart.

8.   Describe the function of the liver.

9.   Describe the valves of the blood vessels.

10.   What effects are produced by want of natural sleep?

HISTORY.—1.   What led Columbus to the discovery of America? 10

2.   What people claims to have discovered this country before Columbus?   10

3.   What connection had the settlement of New York by the Dutch with the "Anti-Rent" troubles in Tyler's administration?   10

4.   Name four indirect, and the direct cause of the Revolutionary War.   5 pts

5.   Describe briefly the connection of Franklin with the Revolutionary War.   10

6.   What difficulty connected with the territory which now forms Indiana had Washington's administration?   10

7. What two commanders were noted for successful operations in the war of 1812, and also in the Mexican War?   10

8. What connection had the Mexican War with the Civil War? 10

9. What celebrated march during the Civil War had much to do with closing it? What was the immediate effect of this march? 5, 5

10. Have the results of the Civil War been an injury or a benefit to the seceding States? Why?   3, 7

ORTHOGRAPHY.—1. Write and punctuate the abbreviations of the following words: Received, volumes, pages, manuscripts, Doctor of Medicine.

2. Write five sentences, and in each use one of the following words correctly: Cholor, vane, dulest, venial, serge.

3. Indicate the proper pronunciation of these words: Won, jugular, seine, tiny, satire.

4. Give a table of the consonants that have more than one sound.

5. In how many ways may the sound of *e* in *her* be represented? Give them.

6. Spell ten words selected by the superintendent.

PENMANSHIP.—1. What is meant by the analysis of letters?

2. Which capitals should be commenced three spaces above the base line?

3. What is meant by spacing? What space should be allowed letters in a word?

4. Where should the shade occur in *t* and *d*?

5. Analyze *i, b, j, n, y*.

NOTE.—Your writing in answering these questions will be taken as a specimen of your penmanship, and will be marked 50 or below, according to merit.

GEOGRAPHY.—1. Name all the countries of North America in order of position, commencing with the most northerly. In order of size, beginning with the largest.

2. Name the capital of each of the ten leading countries of Europe.

3. Name the three greatest wheat producing countries of the world. The greatest rice market of the United States   The greatest rice producing country of the world.

4. Bound Brazil; give some idea of its size compared with three other countries, and a statement of five of its most important exports.

5. Describe the location of Rome, Canton, Quebec, St. Petersburg, and New Orleans.

6. Contrast the Northern and the Southern States of the Union as to agricultural products, and account for the differences you notice.

7. Name the five leading agricultural countries of Europe. The five leading mining countries.

8. Name in order the waters passed through by a vessel that goes directly from New Orleans to Liverpool. With what would it likely be loaded?

9. Name all the cities of the United States that exceed 500,000 in population.

10. Locate the following five cities: San Francisco, Tokio, Quito, Paris, and New York.

GRAMMAR.—1. Name the different elements of a sentence, and state what kinds of modifiers each may have.

2. State in full the difference in the use of the adverbs in the following sentence: "He is probably honest, but he is exceedingly unpopular."

3. How is the passive form of the verb made from the active?

4. Correct the errors in the following, giving reasons:
    a. I feel badly.
    b. The child behaves bad.
    c. I had rather go as stay.

5. Write the correct plural of each of the following: Piano, valley, dwarf, mouse-trap, General Smith.

6. Give the present and past participle forms of each of the following verbs: Write, lay, set, receive.

7. How does the infinitive differ from the finite verb? How resemble it?

8. Analyze: "It is believed that the moon is not inhabited."

9. How does the compound sentence differ from the simple sentence with a compound subject or predicate? Illustrate each by an example.

10. Write a sentence that is interrogative in form but declarative in meaning.

ARITHMETIC.—1. A boat in crossing a river 500 yds. wide, drifted with the current 360 yds.; how far did it go? In extracting the sq. root, why double the root already found for a trial divisor?

2. A's gain is $1,800, B's $2,250, C's $3,200; A's capital was in 6 months, B's 9 months, and C's 14 months; how much of the capital, $27,450, did each own?

3. Find the face of a 90 day note, which, discounted at 7% per annum, yields $1,235 40. Analyze.

4. Find the discount of $6,344.25, due in 23 days; rate of interest 5%. What is the difference between a debt not due and its present worth?

5. Find the amount of $1,883 for 1 year, 4 mos., 21 days, at 9%. What is the difference between simple and compound interest?

6. A garrison has food to last 9 months, giving each man 1 lb. 2 oz. a day; what should be a man's daily allowance, to make the food last 1 year 8 months?

7. Divide 36.72672 by .5025. Give the rule for pointing off the quotient in the division of decimals.

8. What order or orders will a figure in the tenths' place, multiplied by a figure in the hundredths' place, have? What is the effect of annexing or omitting ciphers at the right of a decimal?

9. Reduce $\frac{4\frac{1}{16} \text{ of } 2\frac{2}{3}}{5\frac{1}{4} - 4\frac{1}{2}}$ and $\frac{1}{7} \times (100 - 1\frac{1}{2} + \frac{3}{18})$ to their simplest forms.

10. A bought $\frac{1}{4}$ of a farm of 219$\frac{1}{2}$ acres, and sold $\frac{3}{4}$ of his part to C; what part of the whole, and how many acres did he sell?

ANSWERS TO STATE BOARD QUESTIONS PRINTED IN APRIL.

ARITHMETIC.—1. $(285-6)+3=93$ spaces. 94 rows required. 279 ft. $\times 94=26226$ ft.; 26226 ft.+273 ft., distance across the field from first row to last,=26499 ft., or 5 mi. 6 rd., Ans.

2. $56+25=\$2.24$, cost per head of first lot. $\$56+(25+3)=\$2$, cost per head of second lot. $\$2.24-\$2.=24$ cents, Ans.

3. L. C. M. of 2, 3, 4, 5, 6 is 60; 60+1=61, Ans.

4. One of the three equal factors. 13.2+taken three times will produce the given number.

5. An indemnity against loss. A written contract between the company and the insured. Amount paid for the insurance. Money paid for the use of money. Sum of principal and interest.

6. 2 yr. 8 mo. 15 da.=$\frac{48}{18}$ yr. $\frac{1}{8180} \times \frac{108.40}{81} \times \frac{1}{13.5}=.07+$ Ans., 7%.

7. 7 men will mow $\frac{1}{4}$ of 35 A. in 1 day,=$\frac{35}{4}$ A. 1 man will mow in 1 day $\frac{1}{7}$ of $\frac{35}{4}$ A.=1$\frac{1}{4}$ A. 10 men will mow in 1 day $10 \times 1\frac{1}{4}$ A., $\frac{25}{2}$ A. In 3$\frac{1}{2}$ days they will mow $3\frac{1}{2} \times \frac{25}{2}$ A.=41$\frac{3}{4}$ A.

8. 343+51=16$\frac{1}{17}$ degrees. $\frac{1}{15}$ of 16$\frac{1}{17}$=1$\frac{11}{17}$ hrs.=1 hr. 6 min. 7$\frac{1}{17}$ sec.

9. $\sqrt{39^2 - 36^2}=15$ ft., Ans.

10. $\frac{12 \times 11 \times 11.10}{4 \times 3}=\$128$. Ans.

HISTORY.—1. Of Genoa, in Italy. Ferdinand and Isabella, King and Queen of Arragon and Castile, in Spain

2. Admiral Gaspard de Cologny, sent out a colony of Huguenots under Jean Ribault, which landed on the coast of Florida, sailed up the river St. John, and founded Port Royal. The whole colony perished when Ribault was in France on a visit. A second attempt to found a colony was frustrated by their own dissensions and quarrels.

3. The various nations tn Europe which had colonies in this country, transferred the seat of war to it as far as they could to save expenses at home, while the national animosities which continued here, aided in bringing on and keeping up a condition of warfare.

4. The surrender of Burgoyne, and that of Cornwallis.

5. Really none. He was authorized to purchase a small portion of the Southern part to open up the Mississippi River to our commerce, but his commissioners found a willingness on the part of the

French to sell the whole for a remarkably small sum, and assuming powers which they had not made the purchase, in which they were sustained by Jefferson, and afterwards by Congress. Napoleon I.

6. The annexation of Texas, whose independence had not been recognized by Mexico. The Gadsden purchase of property beyond the Gila River.

7. In 1816. Ohio, Illinois, Michigan, Wisconsin, and a small point of land in Minnesota.

8. The slave trade was one of the commercial interests of New England, to which the South was opposed. As a compromise the trade was legalized for a term of 20 years. As the North furnished no field for enlarged slave labor, and the invention of the cotton gin made that labor eventually of great value in the South, it came about that when the slave trade ceased by the constitutional limitation it had become important to the South. Ceasing to be valuable to the North, the doctrine of abolition soon became strong, resisting which the South gradually drifted into the Civil War.

9. The general demand at the north that our army be moved on to Richmond, while from want of time and a clear apprehension of the real difficulties in the undertaking, our army was largely unprepared. On the contrary the South were well prepared, and had a more certain knowledge of the conditions existing. Furthermore their success in reaching Washington, would in all probability have put them in possession of means and appliances, whose use might have rendered the successful operations of the North an impossibility. The defeat roused the North to a clear sense of the magnitude of the struggle, and aroused an indomitable spirit of patriotism which having right and justice for its objects, could not fail of eventual success.

10. His attempt to remove Edwin M. Stanton from the War Department in violation of the tenure-of-office bill. It failed for want of a constitutional majority on the vote against him, resulting in a "Scotch verdict" of not proven.

PHYSIOLOGY.—1. The alimentary canal is the digestive tube opening anteriorly through the mouth, posteriorily through the anus. It is lined with mucous membranes, and has three enlargements— the pharynx, the stomach, and the large intestine. In its passage through this canal, the food is acted upon by five different juices— the saliva, the gastric juice, the intestinal, and pancreatic juices, and the bile.

2. Respiration is the act by which the body takes in oxygen and gives off carbonic acid and other impurities. It is performed chiefly through the lungs, but partly by the skin.

3. The optic nerve is a branch of the second pair of cranial nerves. These spring from the optic thalami and the corpora quadrigemina, unite in the optic commissure underneath the cerebrum,

and then, after a partial interchange of fibres, pass on to the eyeballs.

4. Near-sightedness is due to an elongation of the eye-ball from front to back, so that parallel rays of light, entering the cornea, are focused in front of the retina. Concave spectacles remedy the defect.

5. The fontanelle is the space within the roof of the skull where the three lines of sutures tend to meet in the cranium of the new-born child, but which is temporarily covered with a thin layer of cartilage. The beating of the heart can be readily perceived at this point.

7. Sensory nerves carry impressions toward the cranial or spinal centers; motor nerves carry volitions or reflex actions outward from these centers.

8. The labyrinth is the internal ear. It consists of chambers and tubes hollowed out in the temporal bone. Externally, it communicates through the oval and round windams with the middle ear; internally, it communicates by means of the auditory nerve with the brain. Its divisions are the vestibule, the cochlea, and the semi-circular canals.

9. The heart is a hollow muscle. It has four cavities : two above, with thin walls—the auricles; two below, with thick walls—the ventricles. The right side receives from the body partly prepared blood, impure blood and lymph, which it pumps to the lungs; the left side receives pure blood from the lungs, which it pumps to the various tissues of the body. The heart lies in a loose sac lined with serous membrane. It is lined with fibrous membrane. Its walls are composed mainly of striped muscular tissue.

10. Glands are organs of the body whose form is various but whose essential parts are a layer of cells, a basement membrane beneath and a capillary network of blood-vessels. The function of a gland is essentially secretive. Some of the larger glands of the body are the liver, the pancreas, the spleen, the kidneys, the salivary glands, etc.

READING —1. Five American prose writers, with one work of each: Washinffton Irving, "The Sketch-Book"; Oliver Wendell Holmes, "The Guardian Angel"; Ralph Waldo Emerson, "Representative Men"; Henry David Thoreau, "The Excursions;" James Fennimore Cooper, "The Last of the Mohicans."

3. Three things important in the preparation of a lesson by a Third Reader pupil are: Such a knowledge of the thoughts of the lesson that he can give their substance in his own language; such a knowledge of the words of the lesson that he recognizes them at sight; such a knowledge of the words of the lesson that he can compose other sentences with these words properly placed in them.

4. It is better for advanced classes to stand whilst reading: (*a*) They acquire the habit of taking and maintaining a good posture; (*b*) Their position thus enables them to have a better use of the respiratory and vocal muscles; (*c*) They may learn to be graceful, composed and at ease when afterward presenting themselves before an audience.

5. In the preparation of a Fifth Reader lesson, the dictionary may be used, (*a*) for pronunciation, (*b*) for accurate definition, (*c*) for synonymous words, (*d*) for mythological references, (*e*) for the explanation of foreign phrases, etc., etc.

GEOGRAPHY.—1. Okhotsk Sea—separates the peninsula of Kamtchatka from Siberia: Sea of Japan—separates the Japan islands from the mainland: Yellow Sea—separates Corea from the continent: Bay of Bengal, east of India: Persian Gulf, between Arabia and Persia.

2. The North Pole is the northern extremity of the earth's axis. All other places on the earth's surface are south of the North Pole. Upernavik, in north frigid zone; St. Petersburg, in north temperate zone; San Francisco and London, in north temperate zone; Buenos Ayres, in south temperate zone.

3. New York State is bounded on the north by Lake Ontario, St. Lawrence River and Province of Quebec; on the east by Lake Champlain, Vermont, Massachusetts, and Connecticut; on the south by the Atlantic Ocean, New Jersey and Pennsylvania; on the west by Pennsylvania, Lake Erie, and Niagara River. The five largest cities of New York are New York City, at the head of New York Bay; Brooklyn, on the west end of Long Island; Buffalo, at the east end of Lake Erie; Albany, in the eastern part of the state on the Hudson River; Rochester, in the western part of the state, on the Genesee River.

4. The greater mildness of the climate if Western Europe is due to the warm current of the Gulf Stream which washes the coast. The eastern coasts of North America are also chilled by the cold waters of the Arctic current.

5. Pensacola is in the northwestern part of Florida, on Pensacola Bay: Milwaukee, in the eastern part of Wisconsin, on Lake Michigan: Belfast, in the northeastern part of Ireland, on Belfast Lake: Berlin, near the central part of Germany, on the River Spree: Canton, in the southern part of China, on the coast.

6. Porto Rico is east of the island of Hayti; belongs to Spain: Malta, south of Sicily, in Mediterranean Sea; belongs to Great Britain: Iceland, is east of Greenland; belongs to Denmark: Candia, southeast of Greece, belongs to Turkey: The Bahamas are east of southern Florida, and belong to Great Britain.

7. Java is an island of the East Indies, southeast of Sumatra:

Odessa, a city of Russia, on the Black Sea: St. Roque, a cape, the most eastern point of South America: Cairo, capital of Egypt, near the Delta of the Nile: Honduras, a political division of Central America.

8. France and Switzerland.

9. (*a*) Mt. Aconcagua, in Chili. (*b*) The Alps.

10. Asia is bounded on the north by the Arctic Ocean; east by the Pacific Ocean; south by the Indian Ocean; west by the Red Sea, Mediterranean, Marmora, Black, and Caspian Seas; by the Caucasus Mountains, the Ural River and Ural Mountains. China is most densely populated. Its capital is Pekin; government, a despotism; chief exports, tea and silk.

GRAMMAR.—2. *a.* "Get wisdom; and, with all thy getting, get understanding." *b.* "'Will you walk into my parlor?' said the spider to the fly." *c.* They agree in having more than one proposition. *d.* The propositions differ in rank. A compound sentence consists of two or more *independent* propositions, while a complex sentence consists of one independent and one or more *dependent* propositions.

3. Most of our thoughts are expressed in the form of an assertion. The interrogative and imperative forms afford brevity, variety, and emphasis; as, "I ask you whether you will go," is assertive. Interrogative, "Will you go?" Assertive (form of command), "I ask you to go." Imperative, "Go." We use the exclamatory form to express strong feeling or emotion.

4. Prepositions connect related words; or, a word with a clause when the clause is the object of a preposition. Conjunctions connect words, phrases, and clauses. Prepositions govern the objective cas; conjunctions do not affect the case of words.

5. "And (noun) is (copula) a (indef. article) conjunction (noun) when (conj. adverb) it (per. pronoun) is used (verb) to connect (infinitive) sentences (noun).

6. Simple sentence containing an independent element. *That* is the subject, *is* the copula, and *question* the predicate. *To be or not to be* is used absolutely.

7. *Him* is a pronoun, personal, masculine, third, singular, indirect object of *told; to go* is an infinitive, present, used as the direct object of *told; his* is a personal pronoun, possessive case, and limits *going; going* is a participial noun, nominative, and the subject of *was prevented; was prevented* is a verb, regular, transitive, passive voice, indicative, past, third, singular, and agrees with its subject *going.*

8. By their form, personal pronouns (generally distinguish) grammatical persons and can not be used as connectives. Relative pronouns may refer to persons or things without change of form and are used as connectives in subordinate clauses.

9. Ycur dress sits (or fits) well. The intransitive verb *set* is incorrectly used for *sit*. It seems be be *he: he* must agree, in case, with *it*. I believe it to be *him: him* and *it* must be in same case. "Webster's and Worcester's Dictionaries," since each is the author of a Dictionary. The phrase, as it stands, implies joint authorship. I knew of *his* being a musician. Possession is implied.

· 10. Be set, be raised, has been laid, shall have been written, is being recited.

SCIENCE OF TEACHING.—1. Because he is obliged to get the knowledge through a new channel. All the knowledge he has gained from words heretofore has come through the sense of hearing.

2. The *telling* of it gives an earnestness and attractiveness that the printed language can not convey.

3. A child is more likely to do what he has done. A story only shows what some one else has done. This will never form a habit of doing. It may awaken a desire to do, but the main dependence for the forming of a moral character must be in doing for the reason just mentioned.

4. Because it is exactly analagous to the way he has learned the spoken word. It is first known as a whole.

5. No. 1 tells why it is difficult. It is important because if he is not properly taught to interpret printed language he will have no power to gain knowledge from books. This will shut off the greatest avenue to the knowledge of the world.

MISCELLANY.

The total enrollment at Purdue University is 260 for the year.

There were 40 graduates from the Tippecanoe county common schools this spring.

The capital of West Virginia has just been changed from Wheeling to Charlestown.

Forty new students entered the Preparatory Class in Purdue University the Spring Term.

Mr. Hailman is at the head of the La Porte schools. We continually hear good reports of his work.

The Purdue commencement this year will be on Thursday, June 11th. There are eleven seniors. Lectures will be given on Monday, Tuesday and Wednesday evenings, June 8th, 9th, and 10th, before the Undergraduates, the Art Club, and the Scientific Society.

4

Edinburg schools are in a flourishing condition. The high school will graduate ten pupils this year. J. C. Eagle is the efficient superintendent.

THE NATIONAL EDUCATIONAL ASSOCIATION will be held this year at Saratoga, N. Y., and Pres Soldan is hard at work to make it a success in all regards.

The Rensselaer schools close the first week in June. They have never had so prosperous a year. Supt. P. H. Kirsch is an earnest, painstaking, capable worker.

The third annual announcement of the of the Pleasant Lake graded schools indicates enterprise and good work. H. H. Keep is principal and D. S. Gilbert trustee.

J G. Scott will open a Review Term of the Borden Institute, at New Providence, Ind., July 7th. He will be assisted by I. R. Weather, Sup't of the Cannelton schools.

St. Joseph county will have about twenty graduates from her country schools this year. We received a very handsome "commencement card" from Stover's school of Clay township. Mr. Moon has done good work for the schools of St. Joseph. Keep him at it.

Supt G. H. Kenaston, of Attica, seems to have stirred up quite a literary and educational spirit. Not only has he aided in securing a school library, but he is now actively employed in securing a general circulating library. He has been taking notes at the Purdue, the Wabash, and the De Pauw libraries.

W. N. Hailman, Supt. La Porte schools, and his wife, Mrs. Endora Hailman, both well known throughout the United States as leading kindergartners, will open a Summer School for the training of kindergarten and primary teachers, at Saratoga, N. Y., July 20th, immedeately following the meeting of the National Educational Association.

MARION NORMAL COLLEGE is the name of a new normal opened at Marion, with Joseph Tingley as president. Prof. Tingley was for many years connected with Asbury University, and his prominence as a scientist is generally conceded. In later years he has conducted a scientific department in connection with the Central Normal at Danville.

We hear good reports from Goshen. They have twenty-three teachers, all of whom belong to the Reading Circle. This work, it is thought, is having a good effect on the schools. There are more than 1200 pupils enrolled, and the average attendance on number belonging is over 95 per cent. W. H. Sims is the moving power. He is re-elected for another year. Served him right.

The school at Liberty Mills closed on April 3d, by an entertainment given by the high school. The reports from the school are very flattering. W. A. Fisk is the efficient leader.

Jesse H. Brown, Supervisor of Drawing in Indianapolis schools, can be engaged for general Institute work in July and August. Mr. Brown also makes a specialty of normal instruction in Drawing in institutes.

THE PROCEEDINGS OF THE SOUTHERN TEACHERS' ASSOCIATION were unaccountably mislaid and not discovered till the space was all filled, and this explanation is crowded in at the last hour The proceedings will appear next month, and thus the permanent record will be kept.

We have received some Reading Tablets prepared by the lowest primary grades of the Laporte schools. The stories are taken from their regular language work and are very good indeed. We add one of the letters which would throw credit on some older heads. From this letter we can form a pretty clear general idea of what these chil dren are doing.

LA PORTE, INDIANA, Feb'y 26, 1885.

My Dear Cousin:—I go to school every day and we learn to read and write. We march, and I am the leader. We work in clay, and cut and paste. I am in the Second Reader. We have tablets and lay pretty designs on the tables. My teacher had us speak pieces last Friday.   Your loving cousin,   DAISY HUNTOON.

REPORT OF THE SUPERINTENDENTS' MEETING
Held at Union City, March 13th, 14th, 1885.

Pursuant to an arrangement made by the Sup'ts of graded schools at a meeting held at Winchester in October, 1884, a second meeting was held at Union City March 13 and 14, 1885 At this meeting the following Sup'ts were present: Messrs. Bloss, McRae, Study, Butler, Reed, Hobbs, Wirt, and Treudley of Ind., and Messrs. F. G. Cromer, P. E. Cromer, Zemer, Woodbury, and Fall from Ohio. Besides these Mr. Woods, Prin. of Winchester high school; Mr. Frank, teacher of science in the Greenville high school; and Mr. Hiram Hadley, of Indianapolis, were present.

The following subjects were canvassed: 1. What Constitutes an Ideal School? 2. How can we best use the School Library? 3. What Training is necessary to successful Teaching? 4. Which is better, Township or County Supervision?

Besides these views were interchanged upon various subjects, among which may be mentioned Examinations, Punctuality, etc.

The discussion of the second topic was not heard by the secretary. As for the first topic it was said that in such a school the teaching of elementary science would be made very prominent, and would be made to underlie the teaching of language; that the superintendent would have no teaching to do, finding adequate use for all his powers in the instruction of his teachers, and the testing of the progress of the pupils; that the great work set before the school would be the development of the power to think; that it would create the ability to know how to acquire and use knowledge and see the relations of principles; that pupils here would be filled with the desire to learn. Further discussion took the very natural turn of inquiry into the causes thwarting the progress of schools, among which were cited roller-skating, protracted meetings, etc.

Respecting the third topic it was agreed that whatever might be the training, essential to it was the faculty for teaching which is inborn and not created. With this, training enhances the value of the teacher. Without it all training is rendered more or less inefficient. The interesting question was raised as to the value of normal schools in the training of teachers. On this point it was said that one great danger lay in the fact that too many normal students were not sufficiently informed, and that in consequence the teaching of these was apt to become lifeless and formal, unless saved by a strong substratum of common sense. The question was propounded whether for the true teaching of elementary science previous laboratory training was not essential. To this question the secretary understood that the superintendents would return an affirmative answer, although the conclusions were not well defined.

Further report of what was said and done is not necessary, save the action of the superintendents on the high school course of study. In adopting the following course as on the whole the best, in their judgment, the superintendents assumed that it had been preceded by an eight years course of study; that pupils could read and write well; that they could give expression to what they know in reasonably clear, accurate language; that they were posted in geography and were familiar and ready with the main principles of business transactions.

HIGH SCHOOL COURSE OF STUDY.

Mathematics, Science, Language, History.

First Year—Arithmetic, Physiology, Crammar, U. S. History.
Second Year—Algebra, Phys. Geography, Rhetoric, Gen. History.
Third Year—Alge. $\frac{1}{2}$, Geom. $\frac{1}{2}$; Physics, Eng. Lit., Gen. History.
Fourth Year—Geom. $\frac{1}{2}$, Arith. $\frac{1}{2}$; Chemistry, Eng. Lit. $\frac{1}{2}$, Gram. $\frac{1}{2}$; Constitution $\frac{1}{2}$, U. S. History $\frac{1}{2}$.

On the above course the following points were made:

1. A large majority would put U. S. History in the eighth year,

in which case they would substitute for U. S. History the study of English Classics.

2. The study of Rhetoric should look largely toward Grammar.

3. Chemistry was to be taught only on the condition that laboratory practice was possible. Otherwise the superintendents agreed that the study of Botany would afford the next best scientific study to be taught, especially during the fall and spring. During winter some other science, as Geology, might be pursued. But it was agreed that so far as these sciences, as Zoology, Geology, Astronomy, etc., were concerned, the personal taste of the teacher ought to be the determing element, from the fact that he could far better teach a subject he enjoyed.

4. In case pupils desired to go to college it was agreed to give the last three years of the language course to Latin. In addition it was agreed by the majority that in the study of Algebra the work in an ordinary book like Wentworth's or Loomis's ought to proceed as far as logarithms; that plane geometry and trigonometry were better than plane geometry alone, or plane and solid alone; that in case pupils should study Latin it were best to have the grammar and reader in the first year, Cæsar in the second, and Virgil in the third.

In the various discussions Holtze's Elements of Physics and Miss Youman's Botanical Course were very highly recommended for training in elementary science. Houston's Physical Geography, Wentworth's Geometry, and also Welch's Essentials of Geometry were recommended for high school study. Guyot's was deemed the best of all Physical Geographies, though a little too heavy for high school use. The reviews of the common branches ought to be carried on with strict reference to the principles involved.

The above seems to me to be a fair report of the proceedings of the meeting, which the secretary was instructed to draw up for publication On motion it was agreed to hold another meeting next year not later than October.

The universal expression on the part of the superintendents was that the meeting had been a great success. It is proper to say that in the conference on the high school course of study Mr. McRae was absent, and that the report as a whole was adopted with only one dissenting voice, that dissent being based upon the belief that two years to general history was too much Further, it was understood that the effort to draw up a high school course of study was in no sense designed to anticipate the work of the committee appointed at the Indianapolis meeting, but as an aid to the formation of such a course of study as might lead to uniform adoption throughout the state by reason of its adaptation to high school conditions.

F. TREUDLEY, *Secretary.*   J. N. STUDY, *Chairman.*

INDIANA TEACHERS' READING CIRCLE.

OUTLINE OF

Work in Brooks' Mental Science, for May, 1885 — Subject: The Nature of Reasoning. Pages 237-273.

I. Terms to be Studied.

1. Syllogism. Page 242.

"The syllogism is based on classification."—*Schuyler.*

"The truth is not, perhaps, as generally comprehended as it should be, that all valid reasoning is syllogism; that is, it is reducible, in its ultimate analysis, to the form of a syllogistic. This is apparent from the very definitions of reasoning, which, however variously they may be stated, all agree in recognizing it as a process of *mediate* knowledge, i. e., a process by which we know one thing in and through another; but this is just the essential element in syllogistic reasoning."—*Munsell.*

2. Premise. Major Term. Minor Term.

3. Enthymeme.

"Every enthymeme may be expanded into a syllogism."
—*Porter.*

"Practically, in reasoning, men do not use formal syllogisms, but enthymemes; suppressing such premise as is familiar to both both speaker and hearer."—*Munsell.*

4. Verification.

"Scientific knowledge differs from the so-called knowledge of common life, chiefly in being verified knowledge"—*Ward.*

"No belief is to be trusted which can not be verified. The verified alone is known."—*Ibid.*

"Inductive reasoning is little else than the cumulative verification of the given proposition."—*Ibid.*

II. Terms to be Distinguished.

1. Judgment and reasoning.
2. Analysis and reasoning.
3. Reasoning in a circle—and begging the question.
4. Hypothesis and theory.

"Investigations guided by intelligent hypotheses have led to nearly all the great achievements of scientific progress."— *Atwater.*

5. Analogy and induction.

"That likeness of phenomena in certain respects leads us to infer likeness in others is a fundamental fact in the reasonings of life."—*Hopkins.*

"Identity, sameness, resemblance, analogy, are various degrees of likeness."—*Bascom.*

"Nearly all the reasonings pertaining to practical life are reasonings from analogy."—*Alden.*

Said an attorney: "A perfect perception of analogies would make a perfect lawyer."

6. Analogy and metaphor.
7. Analogy and example.
8. Observation and experiment.

"The instruments of analysis are observation and experiment; those of synthesis are definition and classification."—*Stewart.*

"Observation is passive experience."—*Herschell.*

"Every experiment is a question addressed to nature. Every experiment, worthy of the name, is a prophesy."—*Schelling.*

"To observe and follow law is the peculiar characteristic of reason."—*Tittman.*

"The observation is preparatory to the induction, but no part of it."—*Hopkins.*

"Experiment is only another name for observation employed with a definite design."—*Porter.*

"The remedy for false inductions is to be found in careful and repeated observations."—*Winslow.*

9. Induction and deduction.

"Inductive method=analytical method=method of discovery. Deductive method = synthetic method = method of instruction."—*Jevons, Ward.*

"Deduction is a process of identification."—*Bain.*

"The underlying axiom of induction is 'the uniformity of causation.'"—*Hopkins.*

"To success in induction, the power of sure and ready deduction is also essential. The law of gravitation was no sooner suggested to the imagination of Newton, in the question, 'Why not?' and sanctioned by the approving answer, 'It is very probably true,' than the additional thought, 'if so, what follows?' put him upon the act of deduct on."—*Porter*

"Inductive reasoning deals only with probabilities."—*Bascom.*

"By far the larger part of the reasoning of natural science and of every day life, is of the inductive character; creeping from resemblance to resemblance, and unable to affirm of its best conclusions that they are demonstrative."—*Bascom.*

III. Items of Special Professional Import.

1. Mathematical reasoning.
2. Analogy in language.
3. Deductive reasoning.
4. Inductive reasoning. See Johonnot, page 162.
5. Testimony. Authority.

IV. Summaries.

1. Laws of the Syllogism.
2. Basis of Deduction.
3. Basis of Induction.
4. The Criteria of Induction.
5. The dangers of reasoning by analogy.
6. Conditions of belief.

——o——

OUTLINES OF GENERAL HISTORY FOR MAY.

Barnes' General History – Pages 178-☞

Greek education and art are subjects no less interesting in our own time than Greek literature. The advocates of the New Education appeal to the master teachers of the Greeks in respect of method and theory. A knowledge of the orders of classic architecture is necessary to an appreciation of many of our noblest structures. The music and the paintings of the Greeks have passed away, beyond restoration; their sculpture remains, incomparable in beauty and power of influence. Greek mythology is a necessary concomitant of Greek poetry and art. On no account, it is to be hoped, will the reader fail to master the work allotted to this month. It is a key to a vast treasury of entertainment and profit. He will use through life the education gained.

First Week.—1. Greek libraries From what words are *paper* and *style* derived? 2. The school age. Hours of work. Studies pursued by the Athenian youth. Compare with the proverbial "Three R's" of early western schools. Corporal punishment. Attention paid to morals and manners. 3 The character of Spartan education. The Spartan ideal, contrasted with that of the Athenians. 4 The three styles of Greek architecture—the simple and massive Doric, the graceful Ionic, and the elaborate Corinthian. The Doric has no pedestal. Note how the styles are sometimes blended. 5. Imaginative character of the Greek religion. Gods and demi-gods. The gods real Greek characters. The home of the gods. Greek and Roman names for the same deities. 6. The supreme god, the god of the sea, and the god of the lower world. How are they designated in poetry, painting and sculpture? 7. The god of war; The god of manly beauty, of poetry and song; The god of eloquence, the messenger of heaven; The god of wine. The symbols of each. The Apollo Belvidere is the ideal of manly beauty. The wings of the messenger god were not attached to the shoulder blades, like those of the angels as depicted by Christian artists, but were attached to his feet and to his cap. The petasus (see Dictionary) The caduceus, and its meaning (see Dictionary). 8. The blacksmith god; volcanoes supposed to be his forges; his fall from heaven, and his consequent lameness.

Second Week.—1. The queen of heaven, both sister and wife of Zeus, or Jupiter. Her symbols. Her disposition. 2. The goddess of wisdom. Her singular origin. Her symbol. 3. The goddess of love and beauty, and her origin. Her symbol. The quarrel about the golden apple. 4. The goddess of hunting. How represented. Her great temple at Ephesus. (Read the interesting account given in Acts, Chapter IX. 5. The goddesses of agriculture and of the domestic hearth. The cup-bearer of the celestial banquets. 6. The Three Graces. The Three Fates. The Three Hesperides. The "golden apples" in the Garden of the Hespérides were probably the oranges of Africa. The Three Harpies. The Three Gorgons. The Three Furies. 7. The Nine Muses and their origin. Pegasus. (See Dictionary). The theory that they dictated the songs of poets. The commencing lines of every epic poem illustrate this theory. Note the first verses of Pope's Iliad, Dryden's Aeneid, and Milton's invocation in the Paradise Lost. 8. Divination.

Third Week.—1. The Greek oracles. Dodona. Delphi. The most celebrated oracles in Greece. How the response was obtained. 2. The Olympian Games. The olive wreath The Pythian Games. The laurel wreath. The Nemean Isthmian Games, and the wreaths of parsley and pine. 3. The Panathenaia. 4. The Feast of Dionysos. 5. Character of ths plays in the Dyonisiac theatre at Athens; masks and costumes; (Greek plays at Harvard, and the costumes used—see Century Magazine); chorus; length of plays. 6. Greek marriages and marriage ceremonies. 7. Funeral ceremonies and customs. 8. Greek armor, arms and chariots; war ships and engines.

Fourth Week.—The scenes in the real life of the Greeks are especially instructive and entertaining, and should receive full and careful attention.

TO MANAGERS AND MEMBERS OF READING CIRCLE.

GENERAL STATEMENT.

If there has been any question as to the permanence and success of the Teachers' Reading Circle, it is effectually answered by the experience of the year now drawing to a close. Latest reports from 51 County Managers give assurance that of ths large membership enrolled a majority amounting almost to unanimity are convinced of the value of the work. Both the course and the management for the first year were of necessity largely experimental; neither has been exempt from criticism; on the contrary, many valuable suggestions have been received, and these have been offered not in the tone of complaint, but in the way of friendly suggestion to the Board.

ADVANTAGES

Should it be asked what are the advantages offered to the readers of the course, it may be replied they are three-fold:

(1) The work of the course has been carefully arranged. The need of both general and professional culture has been constantly kept in view. To have carefully followed the course is of no slight value. The personal benefit will be incalculable: 3,000 teachers of the state, reading and thinking along uniform lines of the best progress in thought, must dignify their work. The first advantage then is a professional and moral one.

(2) The honors to be conferred upon members who complete the course are not empty, meaningless, or to be cheaply esteemed. Certificates are to be issued only upon satisfactory completion of the work. No complimentary certificates will be given. Examinations, while free from catch questions and obstructions, will be made fair and sufficient tests of the work done.

(3) Finally, there is a practical advantage that will commend itself to every teacher, and which will be of itself worth all the needed study and expense.

The Course of Reading proposed is in the line of the preparation required by the State Board for securing teachers' license. For the current year the questions prepared on Science of Teaching have been based upon the Reading Circle outlines. On the strength of numerous suggestions, appeal will be made at once to the State Board to substitute the results of this examination for the usual monthly examination in Science of Teaching. The severe physical strain and mental weariness incident to the customary long examination of applicants in a single day will be relieved by this division of work and efficiency will be given to the study of professional literature.

INSTRUCTIONS TO COUNTY MANAGERS.

(1.) Examinations over first year's work will be conducted by County Managers, in their respective counties, the third Saturday in June (June 20), 1885.

(2) All are entitled to their examinations who have, (*a*) completed the work assigned, and (*b*) paid to the County Manager the examination fees (noted elsewhere in this circular.) Members who have not finished the entire course, may take examination over the one or two completed branches and be credited for what is done.

(3) Examinations will be conducted on the plan of the regular monthly examinations for teachers' license, questions being printed on slips and forwarded to Managers in sealed packets.

(4) Manuscripts of applicants, together with the examiner's fees, will be forwarded to the Secretary of the Board of Directors (H. M. Skinner), immediately following the examination.

(5) Papers will be graded by the Board of Directors, and statements of standing forwarded to the several members.

(6) County Managers will collect of each applicant a fee of

twenty-five (25) cents, which shall constitute a fund from which the per diem of County Managers shall be paid.

(7.) The importance of securing a large representation at this first examination must be obvious to all. County Managers will do themselves credit and Reading Circle interest great good by acquainting teachers with the time and conditions of the examination, and the need to complete the year's work at once. Record will be preserved at the Secretary's office, of all membership credits, and unfinished work may be brought up afterward; but it is advisable that each year's work be finished at the time prescribed.

(8.) As nearly as convenient County Managers will please inform the Secretary by postal card, as to number of question lists desired.

(9.) The business of the current year must be closed by the first day of July, 1885; full and complete returns of all fees and membership lists should be in by that date.

STATISTICAL REPORTS.

The forthcoming address of Mrs. E. Mont. McRae will display in particular the financial and other statistics of the Circle. County Managers are requested to secure its republication in local papers, following its appearance in educational journals.

SECOND YEAR'S WORK.

Provision is making for the continuation of the Circle work during the following school year pursuant to the original plan for a graded course. A circular will be issued at an early day setting forth in full the course to be followed, together with instructions to County Managers concerning the admission of new members, etc.

For the Board: RICHARD G. BOONE,
HUBERT M. SKINNER,
Committee.

————o————

TO THE TEACHERS OF INDIANA:

The remarkable success of the Chautauqua course of home reading and study, has encouraged effort in the direction of special courses of reading adapted to the peculiar needs of the teacher. While this home study never can be to the individual what personal contact with the live teacher is, still much useful knowledge and inspiration as well, may come through carefully selected reading.

There is an ever increasing demand for teachers who have a knowledge above and beyond the mere subject-matter of the so-called common branches. It is fully realized by intelligent people everywhere, that it is not possible for the teacher to have sufficient grasp of any subject which he knows only as an isolated set of facts or fancies. Subjects in their relations must be mastered by the teacher of the future. It need not be replied that some teachers have neither money nor leisure to pursue a course of reading which shall the better fit them for their work. It must be, as it has ever been, that present sacrifice must be made for future good. There ought to be years of preparation in the hope of doing better work and of receiving better compensation. All over the world, notably in our own country, there is an intellectual awakening. People are thinking, investigating, getting abreast of the age. Teachers must not be behind. The times demand broader culture, more exact training, and a higher manliness. To heed this increasing demand is not only a duty but a necessity.

The Indiana Teachers' Reading Circle was organized with the purpose of helping the teachers of the state to attain a greater degree of professional sk ll, and in addition, a broader knowledge in general lines of thought,—history, science, and literature.

That the purpose of the Reading Circle is being realized, is evident from the very favorable reports received from a large number of the counties in the state. These are all the more encouraging in view of the fact, that unavoidable delays were caused in the opening of the year's work. Many county superintendents have reported a very hopeful outlook for the coming year, who have as yet done but little.

Over eleven hundred members of the Circle have been officially reported. More than eighteen hundred books on mental science alone, having been sold, it is known that many more than those officially reported are pursuing the course prescribed, in whole or in part.

In view of the fact that a teacher's course of reading which might meet the needs of existing conditions was largely an experiment, members of the Board of Directors have invited suggestions and are ever ready to heed most cheerfully advice from any and all sources. That this Circle has been and may be to a far greater extent a wonderful power for good is not to be doubted. In order that it be the means of the greatest possible good, every teacher should feel in honor bound to give it such support as is commensurate with its helpful aim.

If the first year's reading has even not yet been commenced, the time to begin is at once. Do not delay. Let as much be done as can be in order that your next year's school may be better. By membership in the organization a great advantage is derived in the purchase of books at a much reduced rate, so that the expense becomes but $3.35 for the entire year's reading.

The Secretary's report of membership (by counties) and of receipts and expenditures, as rendered at the last meeting, was as follows:

Bartholomew	26	Madison	12
Boone	4	Newton	48
Cass	26	Orange	8

Carroll	81	Posey	3
Clark	61	Randolph	17
Daviess	17	Ripley	23
Delaware	35	St. Joseph	103
Dubois	47	Sullivan	127
Elkhart	59	Tippecanoe	23
Floyd	32	Union	12
Franklin	14	Vanderburgh	13
Gibson	4	Warrick	74
Grant	11	Wabash	152
Howard	16	White	30
Jackson	16		
Jennings	9	Total	1123
Jay	4	Fees received	$280 75
La Grange	11	Expended	80 08
Lake	3		
Marion	2	On hand	$200 67

It was only by careful management of the Bureau that the expenses for printing, postage, clerical work and individual expenses of the Board for a year and more were kept down to so small an amount.

Although the Reading Circle is a voluntary organization, under the control of the State Association, still its work is in harmony with that of the "State Board of Education." Very soon the attention given to this course of reading will show itself in the greater fitness of those taking it, for higher recognition in the form of better certificates.

Very respectfully,   EMMA MONT. McRAE,

For Board of Directors.

GEMS OF THOUGHT.

The devil never tempted a man whom he found judiciously employed.—*Spurgeon.*

Vice is attended with temporary felicity, piety with eternal joy.—*Bayard.*

We should ask not who is the most learned, but who is the best learned.—*Montague.*

> Trifles light as air,
> Are to the jealous, confirmations strong
> As proofs of holy writ.   —*Shakespeare.*

Honor and shame from no conditions rise,
Act well your part, there all the glory lies.   —*Pope.*

The star spangled banner in triumph shall wave
O'er the land of the free and the home of the brave.—*Key.*

Not myself, but the truth that in life I have spoken,
Not myself, but the seeds that in life I have sown,
Shall pass on to ages,—all about me forgotten,
Save the truth I have spoken, the things I have done.
—*H. Bonar.*

Take the open air,
The more you take the better ;
Follow nature's laws
To the very letter.   —*Anon.*

Avoid in youth luxurious diet,
Restrain the passions' lawless riot,
Devoted to domestic quiet,
  Be wisely gay ;
So shall ye, spite of age's fiat,
  Resist decay.   —*Horace Smith.*

When misrepresented, use no crooked means to clear yourself.
Clouds do not last long.—*Spurgeon.*

There is a broad distinction between character and reputation, for
one may be destroyed by slander, while the other can never be
harmed, save by its possessor.—*Holland.*

Let'pleasure be ever so innocent, the excess is always criminal.—
St. Evremond.

If you do what you should not, you must bear what you would
not.—*Franklin.*

To err is human ; to forgive divine.—*Pope.*

Truth crushed to earth, shall rise again ;
The eternal years of God are hers :
But error, wounded, writhes in pain,
And dies amid his worshipers.   —*Bryant.*

Seek the right, though the wrong be tempting,
Speak the truth at any cost.   —*Anon.*

There's room enough on every hand
For men of muscle, brain and nerve.—*Wallace Bruce.*

To live and die and never try
To do some good, some comfort give ;
If selfish life is all of life,
'Twere better for us not to live. —*J. Wallace Young.*

Habits are soon assumed, but when we strive
To strip them off,—'tis being flayed alive.   —*Cowper.*

PERSONAL.

N. J. Stith, of La Grange, Ark., seems to be doing a good educational work in his neighborhood.

Lewis H Jones has been unanimously re elected Sup't of the Indianapolis schools for the coming year His work has been successful and satisfactory to the board, the teachers, and the public.

George F. Bass, one of the most efficient supervising principals in the Indianapolis schools, will engage to do institute work the coming summer. He has had much successful experience in this kind of work. He will also engage to give evening lectures at Institutes and and Summer "Normals."

D. F. Lemmon, who for many years had been Supt. of Harrison county, having been promoted to a lucrative county office, C. W. Thomas was appointed his successor. Mr. Thomas did not get an even start with the year's work, but he has been energetic and done good service.

W H Wiley, Supt. of the Terre Haute schools, recently read a paper before a literary club on England, in which he showed careful study of both the past and current history of the country. Mr. Wiley is certainly an admirer of the English character. A lengthy report of the paper was printed in the *Terre Haute Gazette.*

John A. Steele, vice-president of Central Normal College, at Danville, died May 5th. Since the death of Pres. Adams, Prof. Steele has had control of the business management of the college, and his business ability not less than his teaching power gave him high standing with all who knew him. He leaves a large field of usefulness in the prime of life, and hosts of former students and friends will learn of his death with deep regret.

BOOK TABLE.

Home and School is the name of a neat 4 column 8-page paper published at Owensboro, Ky. The name indicates the character of the paper. W. A. Hester is editor and W. E. Parish business manager; both formerly Indiana teachers. The Journal wishes them success.

Chinese Gordon: The Uncrowned King, is the title of a handsome ribbon-tied book, by Laura C. Holloway, which Funk & Wagnalls have just issued. It is the compilation from Gordon's private letters of his sentiments regarding life, duty, religion and responsibilities, and can but prove a timely addition to Forbes' "Life." A portrait of Gordon, in mourning border, adorns the cover.

Teacher's Notes on Mathematical Geography is the title of a 28-page pamphlet recently printed by Michael Seiler, of the State Normal School. It indicates a line of study that is logical and complete, and makes the study of Physical Geography simple and natural. These "Notes" are suggestive and will not only save Mr. Seiler and his students much writing, but will be helpful to any teacher who desires a comprehensive, connected view of this subject.

Mind in Nature is the name of a new, neatly printed, monthly magazine. It purposes to give information, in ordinary language, that the wayfaring may understand, in regard to all psychical questions. It will give a full *resumé* of all the investigations and reports of both the English and American Societies of Psychical Research. The first two numbers have reached us. We read them both with great interest. Judging from these numbers, it is deserving of liberal support. One dollar secures it a year. It is published at Chicago by the Cosmic Publishing Company, 171 West Washington St.

Mental Science and Culture, by Edward Brooks. Lancaster, Pa.: Normal Publishing Co.

A knowledge of the human mind lies at the foundation of all thoughtful, effective work on the part of the teacher, and this fact is daily becoming more and more prominent. In a few years all examinations for license to teach will include questions on *mental science*. The above book is one of the best on the subject, as it applies the science to practical educational problems. It is the one adopted by the Indiana Reading Circle.

BUSINESS NOTICES.

WANTED—By an experienced teacher, position to teach Latin, German, or higher English branches. High school or academy preferred. Can give good references. Address, FRANCES E. HUSTED, Cumberland, Ind.

TEACHERS desiring to attend a *Normal School*, or those wishing a situation or an increase of salary, should send for a sample copy of *"The Educational World."* Address, W. SAYLER, *Editor, Logansport, Ind.* 1-12t.

INSTITUTE WORK.—Prof. W. H. Venable may be engaged to teach and lecture at Institutes in June, July or August. His favorite subjects are History, Literature, Rhetoric, and Pedagogics. Address him at Station C, Cincinnati. 3-4t

EXCURSION TO NEW ORLEANS.—New Orleans Excursion Tickets are now on sale at the Ticket Offices of the Jeffersonville, Madison & Indianapolis Railroad Co. For rates and time of trains, call upon or write to nearest Agent, Jeffersonville, Madison & Indianapolis Railroad Company, or to H. R. Dering, Assistant General Passenger Agent, Indianapolis, Ind. 1-3t

PENNSYLVANIA EDUCATIONAL BUREAU. — *Business transacted in every State and Territory—Old and Reliable.*—Hundreds of teachers have been supplied in the past. The manager is Superintendent of the Public Schools of Allentown, and has a professional experience of twenty-five years. Many teachers wanted. Register *now.* For application form and list of testimonials, address L. B. LANDIS, Manager, 631 Hamilton St., Allentown, Pa.   3-4t

WANTED—A lady of sense, energy and respectability in every county and township, to distribute circulars and canvass for an article of great convenience and value to her sex. Important and indispensable to lady teachers and clerks. $3 to $5 per per day can be easily earned by any lady by giving it a portion of her time. It costs nothing to make a trial. You can earn as much during vacation as you have the past winter. Send stamp for full particulars.

HOME MANF'G Co., 15 Vance Block, Indianapolis.

RAILROADS.—The L., N. A. & C. has begun the work of rejuvenating its equipments and roadbed. The Indianapolis & Chicago Division will receive due attention. J. H. Pierson, chief engineer, was in the city to-day, having passed over the Indianapolis Division to inspect the new wire fence and other improvements just completed. Ballasting will begin soon. The company is building an entire new passenger train for this division, consisting of elegant coaches and parlor cars, and Colonel Emmett says that no outfit that enters the Union Depot will outshine the " Monon's " new equipment.

At the Spring change the time will be materially shortened, which will reduce the time to about six hours between Indianapolis and Chicago. Through trains will also be run between Indianapolis and Grand Rapids, Mich., without change. If you have not been over the Monon Route, you have so far missed a fast and pleasant ride.—*Evening News.*

5

INDIANA
SCHOOL JOURNAL.

| Vol. XXX. | JUNE, 1885. | No. 6. |

THE HIGH SCHOOL QUESTION.

JOHN W. HOLCOMBE, SUPT. OF PUBLIC INSTRUCTION,
At the Dedication of Indianapolis High School Building.

THE high school argument has been made, the fight has been fought in this State, and the high school is accepted as an essential part of our common school system. Yet, as we have been advised that we ought often to re-examine the grounds of our beliefs however well settled, such an occasion as this ought not to pass without some inquiry into the principles upon which our public education in its different parts and institutions is based. The question is a large one, and but a small part of it can be gone over in the time allowed this evening.

The familiar proposition that the State has a right to educate because intelligence is essential to good citizenship—from which it follows that it has a right to educate only so far as may be necessary to make good citizens—certainly needs re-examination. That the justification of the State's expenditures for education, is the necessity of securing intelligence among the people, so that they will in turn preserve and maintain the State, is an inversion of ideas and an argument at variance with the genius of our institutions.

For what is the State? The French king, inheritor and perfector of an autocratic despotism, said, "The State, that is I!" The Spartans conceived the State as the corporate unity of all, absorbing into itself all powers, all rights; before which the individual stood stripped of every essential attribute of personal liberty. The French king might have said consistently, "If I give my people a certain kind of training it will be to the advantage of the State, that is to *my* advantage. I will give it them. May I not do that I will with mine own?" The Spartan government in effect said this. It assumed control of every citizen in his childhood and relaxed not its hold till old age, training his heart to devotion to Sparta, his intellect in cunning for its service; his body in the hardships, discipline and tactics of war, for its aggrandizement and defense, regulating his domestic relations, practically destroying his private life,—and all for the State, nothing for the man.

But with us, what is the State? Is it the Governor—recently named Porter, to-day named Gray? Or is it the entire body of men who administer the public business—state, county, city, town, and township officers, including school trustees and superintendents? But perhaps it were safer not to attempt a precise definition of our notion of the State. It is at any rate very different from the Spartan's, still more different from the French king's. It is the *res publica*, the *commonwealth*, the interests that are public and common to all the people. What these interests are, after the few general classes always entrusted to the governing agency, may give rise to differences of opinion. Various socialistic and communistic theories are based upon the belief that the control of government should be extended over a greater or less number of interests beyond those usually committed to it. But, in this country at least, the maintenance of schools is undertaken by society in its corporate capacity; the property of all contributes to the common education. In this we are communists; but we are a practical people, and do not take fright at names. A communistic practice that proves to be of general advantage we adopt. But, if the distinction be appreciable, the people establish and support schools not in their political capacity as a State, but in their corporate social capacity.

The support of education at the public expense is justified on the grounds of ability, economy and the general good, without special reference to civic duties. From the general diffusion of knowledge results, of course, a higher citizenship, better government, a more perfect State; but to say that the State educates the people to make them good citizens is to substitute effect for cause.

May we not say instead, "The people, wishing to give their children and to secure to the community the benefits of education, find that they can do this cheapest and best and with greatest advantage to society by means of free common schools." There is the all-sufficient justification of the system. No need to elaborate strained theories as to the right and power of the sovereign State. It is a purely economic and social question, not hard to understand.

It will not be doubted that the average tax payer secures the education of his children in the public schools cheaper than he could in private schools. The amount he pays in school taxes is less than he would otherwise pay in tuition for equal advantages. This is true of the large majority, the people of small and moderate means. The system is justified to them on the score of economy.

The case is somewhat different with the wealthy. The greater their wealth, the larger their tax. Many contribute far beyond the mere cost of educating their own children. Some also have no children, and yet must contribute in proportion to their property. Do these receive any return commensurate with their outlay? They do, beyond a doubt. They are benefited in their property. What would be the shrinkage in values in this city if the public schools were forever swept away! The panic of '73 would not compare with it. If property-holders reflect well on this point they will never complain of the school taxes.

But many contribute nothing—the poor who pay no taxes. To them the free schools are a precious boon, affording to their children the means of escape from poverty and crime.

Ignorance and poverty are inseparable. Careful calculations based on the statistics of several States show that a common school education adds fifty percent to the productive power of the laborer, an academic education one hundred percent, a collegiate education from two to three hundred percent. Also, that of the illiterate about one in ten is a pauper, while of the educated the paupers are but one in three hundred. Whence it may be inferred that ignorance is the very probable road to poverty, while education is the almost certain way to competence.

The statistics of crime are not less instructive. An examination of the returns of twenty States show that one-sixth of the crime is committed by persons wholly illiterate, one-third by persons wholly and substantially so, and that in proportion to numbers there are ten times as many criminals among the illiterate as among the educated.

Property-holders can therefore well afford to maintain schools in which the non-taxpayers enjoy equal privileges; for if the outlay for this purpose were cut down to any great extent, it is not rash to say that for every dollar so saved two would be paid for the support of paupers and the punishment of criminals. Thus the free school is again justified to the tax-payer on the score of economy alone.

But there are other considerations. Cyrus the Younger said that the greatest ornament to a prince was to be surrounded by prosperous and happy friends, So we may say that the greatest ornament to a citizen is to live in the midst of prosperous and intelligent fellow-citizens. The greatest addition to his dignity, his personal and social privileges, his opportunity for an elevated enjoyment of life, is secured by residence in a cultivated community. Such a community can be created only by the general diffusion of knowledge; for the average can not be higher if a large number be left in ignorance.

But while admitting the need and utility of free schools affording instruction in the elementary branches of learning, many doubt the advantage to society at large, and hence the right of society to maintain the high school. It can be supported, they say, only in cities and towns, and in these it is reached by but a small proportion of the pupils; so the people ought not to be taxed to sustain an institution so limited and so partial in its benefits.

The charge that the entire State is taxed to support high schools in cities and towns may be answered by a general denial.

In nearly every instance the high school is entirely supported by the community which enjoys its benefits. This city for instance, with a lower rate of taxation than is permitted to townships and towns, not only maintains her entire graded system for nearly ten months in the year, but out of her abundance contributes many thousand dollars for the payment of teachers throughout the State. The aggregation of wealth here produces a large revenue, the aggregation of population makes it possible to furnish instruction at a less rate per pupil than in the country. The same is true of all centres of population in proportion to their wealth and numbers.

But confining the question within the city limits, can we justify the maintenance of the high school, which is patronized by so few? I think we can.

The term high school is perhaps misleading, as suggesting a school different in kind and separate in some way from the grades below, which are often spoken of as the common schools. Such is not the case. The high school is as much *common* in every proper sense as the lowest primary grade. In the words of the constitution, it is equally open to all and tuition in it is without charge. It is merely the continuation, without break or interruption, of the graded course of study as far as the number of pupils desiring advanced instruction will justify its being carried. Upon what other principle can the course of study be abridged? There are but half as many pupils in the fifth year as in the first primary. If those grades only are to be kept up which accommodate the greatest number an average might be struck and all above the fifth year abolished.

By the immemorial custom and law of the English-speaking race the age of majority is fixed at twenty-one years. All our institutions, statutes and social arrangements tally with that theory. So it is held that a person is entitled to school privileges till he is twenty-one years of age. As Socrates would have asked, Is he entitled to receive instruction suited to his advancement or not suited to it? The answer is obvious, as to most of Socrates' questions. As the conditions of life adjust themselves the larger number of pupils in the schools will be young, under fourteen;

but many will remain after that age, some will be willing to remain as long as they can receive instruction suited to their needs. Such instruction should be furnished whenever a sufficient number desires it. It should not be a question of the grade but of the number of pupils. If this be sufficiently large to justify the employment of teachers and assignment of rooms for their benefit, they ought to be accommodated. It is not appreciably more expensive to provide for fifty pupils instruction in advanced studies than to teach the same number the elementary branches.

This principle applies to all times and places. The country district is not prevented from maintaining higher grades by lack of money, but by lack of numbers. When the numbers are collected the money is forthcoming. As a neighborhood becomes thickly settled the district school expands into a graded school, growing as the population grows, and as the village becomes a town and the town a city the school develops into a graded system, the higher departments, in such a city as this, surpassing in variety and extent many colleges of fifty years ago.

Even on the citizen-making theory the high school can not be dispensed with. Reading, writing, and arithmetic may qualify a man to cast an intelligent vote, if he uses these acquirements to advantage; but the collective citizenship of the State must furnish much more than voters. The citizen is now a voter, now a legislator, now a judge, and now a governor. If the State undertakes to make good citizens she must give the men who will fill all the positions incident to citizenship the means of qualifying themselves for their duties.

But whatever theory we may prefer, the return to the public and to every individual upon an investment in a high school is rich and abundant. It is a center of elevating influences, drawing up all the lower schools, awakening the ambition of the young, and making for the ambitious a way to the "career open to talent." More than any other agency it raises the average intelligence, and the general tone of thought and manners, sending into the homes of the people disciplined minds, enlarged views, refined tastes, and somewhat of that admirable but indefinable condition of mind and heart called culture—qualities belonging to the realm of infinite values, not to be measured in gold;—making "the poor man's hour of leisure richer than the baron's of old time." The high school is essential to the dignity of the city and the well-being of the citizens.

ÆSTHETICS IN COMMON SCHOOL EDUCATION.

·MRS. ALICE BRIDGEMAN, SALEM, IND.

FIFTY years ago the influence of our common schools upon the formation of the child's habits and character was comparatively small. When children attended school three months of the year and the remaining nine worked by the side of father or mother, the impressions made at school were often modified and obliterated by the home training. Then the teacher's business was the intellectual training of his pupils. Little else was required or even expected; indeed, the shortness of the school year forbade the attempt to do more than teach the rudiments of the required branches of study. Manners and morals were taught at home, if at all, and whatever of culture, refinement and beauty entered child-life originated in the home. Parents held themselves responsible for the conduct and well-being of their children, and taught them honesty, truthfulness and politeness by precept as well as by example.

In this age of busy boarding-house life for parents, and I may add street life for children, there is small chance for many a boy and girl to learn systematically anything not taught in the school, unless indeed it be something he ought not to know.

Many parents from necessity, some from indifference, shift the responsibility of their children's training upon the teacher, and when the result proves unsatisfactory cry out against the teacher, the school and the system.

While we object to this injustice, we can but admit that more is demanded of us than of our predecessors. The increased length of the school year, the multiplied school books, the numberless school appliances, all increase not only our opportunities for better work, but our obligations. Since then with us rests the burden of this matter, it is of the greatest importance that we appreciate the magnitude of our work—the education of the children. Definitions of education are numerous, but for present purposes it is sufficient to say that it consists of the harmonious development of all the powers. Any thing less than this falls short of true education. Every mind with which we have to deal is in its nature three-fold, æsthetic, moral, and intellectual. Any system of education which neglects any one of these is defective.

In years past we devoted ourselves almost exclusively to intellectual training. In institutes, conventions and associations we discussed how to teach Arithmetic, Geography, History, and Grammar. Methods, good, bad and indifferent were presented ad libitum, ad infinitum, often ad nauseam. Our work, in school and out, was directed into this channel, and indeed with no small gain to teachers and schools.

In the natural course of events we next turned our minds to the idea of moral culture as a part of our duty, and whereas this all-important matter had been left to the individual consciences of teachers, lessons in right acting now became a part of every well arranged course of study.

And now, the importance of this phase of education being well established, is it not time for the advocacy of the cultivation of the æsthetic nature? Our definition certainly includes this if such a nature exists.

We are all aware that we possess the idea of the beautiful. The smallest child instinctively recognizes some objects as beautiful, others as not. The idea of beauty is a necessity, and is common to all mankind. This is of itself a sufficient reason for its cultivation and development. Haven says, "The beautiful differs from the good in that the good always proposes some end to be accomplished—some obligation to be performed—while beauty proposes no end, acknowledges no obligation. It differs from the true in that the true is not expressed under sensible forms, is abstract, and addresses itself to reason, not to the senses." In other words, the true, the beautiful and the good are coördinate and can not be separated. Indeed they are three expressions of the mind of God.

Remembering this we shall not underestimate the beautiful nor the faculty by which we cognize it. It is natural that we ask ourselves, however, what benefits will follow the training of this? The first of these, in order of time at least, is the pleasure which arises from the contemplation of beauty. Perception of beauty is at once followed by the enjoyment of it, the intensity of the enjoyment depending upon the natural or acquired susceptibility to beauty. This susceptibility is a natural gift, varying in intensity in different individuals, and like all other native endowments is capable of improvement, or it may become so blunted by misuse as not to respond to the occasion. If this be true it becomes our duty to offer the opportunity for its exercise and encourage its manifestation.

Beauty indeed lingers everywhere. We need not seek it in art, we need not search for it in foreign lands—all about us lies the great illustrated book of nature—on every side hang God's pictures. The blue sky, the red and golden sunset, the towering oak, the daisy at our feet, we too often overlook in our search for the beautiful. The trained taste finds pleasure in the commonest, meanest object. Wordsworth says:

> The meanest flower that grows
> Oft gives me thoughts too deep for tears.

Poets have not hesitated to introduce into their writings the common things of life. Bryant's "Lines to a Water-Fowl," Whittier's "Snow Bound," Longfellow's "Village Blacksmith," are illustrations of how many beautiful thoughts may be awakened by objects in themselves insignificant and commonplace.

The ability to see beauty in common, every-day things is a power of no small value, being the source of a pleasure which often serves to lighten the heavy burdens of life. The pleasures of beauty are not only open to all, but are pure, harmless, and capable of increase. The exercise of the æsthetic faculty only serves to increase and develop it, the indulgence of the taste for beauty renders it more susceptible.

The pleasures of sin and sense fall upon the taste. The indiscretions and vicious indulgences of the youth soon become distasteful and hateful to the mature man. Seldom does an old man pursue the phantom follies of a wicked youth, and when he does how repulsive the sight. On the other hand, how pleasant the thought that a cultivated taste is a source of happiness which only grows deeper as the years roll by.

The constant gratification of this taste not only conduces to its development but the passive appreciation of beauty leads to the production of beauty. The artist is inspired by art; the study of music is a necessary step in the education of a composer; the mind of the embryo poet is unconsciously moulded by the rythm of the songs that he sings, the poems which he reads. As teachers we have abundant opportunities to know that like begets like. It is quite safe to suppose that some, at least, of the material of our future artists, sculptors, musicians and architects is to-day in our hands; how are we shaping it? The influence of school life to-day will tell upon the music, painting and oratory of the next decade.

The relation of the cognition of beauty and intelligence will repay a moment's attention. It is of course true that the skillful education of any power of the mind must produce a similar growth or effect upon others. Especially is this the case with two faculties so nearly akin as the æsthetic sense and the cognitive. The exact, clear perception of the beautiful is only possible through the exercise of cognition; on the other hand a nice perception of the forms of objects is necessary to a knowledge of them. The highest beauty can not be comprehended without a high degree of intelligence, since its vividness depends upon the correct interpretation of its idea. Beauty and intelligence are inseparably connected and influence each other. The relation between beauty and goodness is, as we have already suggested, even more intimate. The study of art keeps one familiar with the highest beauty which is moral in its nature, being the expression of high ideals—the contemplation of natural objects naturally. "A cultivated æsthetic sense rejects not only the ugly but impure and evil," leads to the contemplation of the attributes of God.

Since then we have seen that the development of our æsthetic nature tends to make us wiser, happier and better, does it not become our duty to give this work our attention? Can we ask more as a passport to favor?

The branches of study which are calculated to awaken and develop this faculty are painting, sculpture, music and discourse. As to painting we have little to say, as the impracticability of teaching painting as a part of our common school work is apparent. Form may be equally well taught by drawing, while the idea of color may be developed incidentally. Drawing has well been called the art of learning to see. To the teaching of this branch the utilitarian may object; to him the most potent argument we may advance is the report of an eastern school, in which it is stated that a number of children from the public school, in addition to the regular school work, in two years, by spending four hours each week became so proficient in drawing, modeling and wood-carving as to sell their work for good prices. A manufacturer even offered to employ forty of the class, and the worth of their services was estimated at nine dollars per week, each.

Where is the boy or girl who has not at some time drawn pictures in school and suffered reproof. Why not direct this natural desire, and instead of the hideous carricatures of other pupils and perhaps yourself, help to copy, then to create forms of beauty. A class of fifth year pupils, after a year's work under a careful teacher, were able to reproduce from memory easy patterns of oil-cloth, carpet, wall paper (containing no curved lines), analyze the figures, and to invent designs of considerable beauty. Was the time wasted? Surely the habit of close observation and neatness will manifest itself in the other work of the children and prove of sufficient value to repay the expenditure of time and patience, aside from the less visible but no less important result of increasing the love of the beautiful and laying the foundation of geometrical knowledge.

Music is one branch of study much neglected in the majority of schools. While it is the province of this paper to speak of these subjects as means for the development of the æsthetic sense, I may add that aside from this music is a powerful aid to right feeling and consequently to good order. Plato says in speaking of the education of the Greek youth, ''The teachers look carefully to virtuous habits: and rhythms and harmonies are made familiar to the souls of the young that they may become gentle and better men in word and action." Even when music can not be taught systematically, as it should be, it is possible, especially with small children, to teach them to produce pleasant musical tones and to avoid certain habits which so inflict the nerves of sensitive people.

Against the pursuit of these studies is urged the objection that many children have no talent for drawing or music. Granted; but a great many children have no talent for arithmetic and grammar, and yet you do not omit these from their work.

When we speak of literature as a means of æsthetic culture we mean not the English literature of most high school courses, which too often consist of tables of births, deaths, and works of men whose writings the class will never see, but the study of the lives, characters and books of a few of the men who have given us noble thoughts, chaste language and beautiful imagery. This may begin very early in the life of the child, much earlier than we sometimes think. We too often underestimate children's powers of interpretation and delay this culture until the enemy, in the shape of flashy, sensational literature, has taken possession. The influence of a child's reading can hardly be overestimated. We read of a boy who has robbed his father, bought a revolver and started west, and we think, if indeed the paper does not state, he has been reading sensational stories—and we are generally right. We have so much faith in the power of evil—have we none in good? The proverb "Evil communications" has no antithesis, but should have—Good company mends bad manners. Where may better company be found than in good books? Good company, which can not itself be contaminated, can not fall into disrepute.

In no other department of æsthetics is it so necessary that the individual taste should be correct. A correct eye for color is an advantage, a correct musical ear is a desirable accomplishment, but neither is of any moral value. A man who knows not red from blue may be a good citizen and a noble man; a woman may wear purple strings upon her green bonnet, and otherwise be an ornament to society; but a man or a woman with a taste for the weak or vicious in literature can not but be influenced mentally and morally by his inclinations. Correct taste in this matter as in all others is the result of training, not a native endowment. The child, the savage prefers bright red, blue, green, or yellow; the cultured taste is disgusted with excess of color. This difference is owing to culture. A child reared among the Esquimaux comes to regard the blubber of the whale as a delicious morsel. The same child in different surroundings might even relish human flesh. To children of our own country these things are loathsome. Sounds, which to a Chinaman are sweet music, are torture to the ear of an American or European.

In all these cases the effects of education are very apparent. In literature its influence is not less. A child constantly surrounded with trashy or evil books, although not encouraged to read them, unconsciously forms a taste for it without knowing that anything better exists. Who is to blame? Certainly not the child, and yet he is the loser. Why not replace all this objectionable matter by standard works of fiction, history, science and poetry, and thus lead the child to form imperceptibly a habit which can only be acquired later in life by great effort. Many young men and women read certain books because they are recommended to them by persons in whose judgment they have confidence—read from a sense of duty—because they are said to be improving, but find no pleasure in them; when, if a taste for these had been cultivated, what is now a dreary, irksome task would be a source of delight. A taste for good books is worth more to a boy or a girl from our high schools than a college course without it. When I say this I repeat the thought if not the words of more than one eminent educator.

Aside from these studies in which attention is especially given to the æsthetic nature, in many other ways may aid be incidentally given. *In Botany and Geology nothing is lost by calling attention to the beautiful colors and forms of the objects of which they teach. The interest is only increased. In Reading attention may be called to the scenes described, the figures used. Indeed the opportunities lie all about us if we but seize them.

The surroundings of children should be such as to awaken, or at least appeal to their admiration. No child can help being influenced by the objects with which he is daily brought in contact. How many school boards and trustees take into consideration the beauty of the location chosen for the new school house? It is a shame that in this country of cheap land and well to-do people, the most barren, ugly, comfortless spot in the district is ever chosen because of its cheapness. Ugly bare walls, dirty walks, untidy floors complete the picture of which the architect makes the outline and the teacher fills in the color.

In a certain wealthy county the new court house, a model of of architecture, is furnished with neat carpet and matting and heavy handsome chairs, and yet in the largest town of that county teachers do not dare carpet even the rostrums of their rooms unless at their own expense. Men whose minds are mature, whose tastes are developed, surrounded by objects of beauty; children, with minds open to impressions, in dreary, bare rooms with, it may be, an untidy teacher! Flowers, pictures and statuary are a part of the furniture of the ideal school room.

There remains yet one point to be noticed, which is of itself of sufficient importance to become the subject of another paper; I mean the observance of certain days as anniversaries or festival occasions. The beautiful custom of celebrating the birthdays of Authors is becoming quite general and is doing much to awaken interest in the lives and works of our own countrymen, at least, beside bringing teacher, pupil and parent into closer relation upon the ground of a common sympathy. Of general interest and of even more practical value, perhaps, is the observance of Arbor Day, although not general as yet. This institution, *of itself*, embodies a beautiful sentiment as well as wisdom and forethought; but the introduction of the custom of tree planting among the school children was the happiest thought of all. Children are in this way brought face to face with nature, and taught to admire and love her works. This love will grow as the tree grows; and though dear to heart of the planter, these living monuments will be even more so to his descendants.

The ash trees planted by the hand of Washington are objects of deep interest to every visitor at Mt. Vernon. How dear to every loyal heart the old liberty elm of Boston Common! Oliver Wendell Holmes in writing of this subject says, "I have written many verses, but the best poems I have produced are the trees I planted on the hillsides overlooking the meadows. Nature finds rhymes for them in the recurring measures of the seasons. Winter strips them of their ornament and gives them, as it were, a prose translation, and summer re-clothes them in all the splendid phrases of their leafy language. It is enough to know that when we plant a tree we are doing what we can to make our planet a happier dwelling place, for those who come after us, if not for ourselves."

Finally, let us put beauty and happines into the lives of our pupils, knowing that in so doing we are fitting them for happier and better manhood and womanhood.

A PROPOSED CHANGE IN THE METHOD OF CONDUCTING A STATE TEACHERS' ASSOCIATION.

BY F. TREUDLEY.

Two years ago, at the meeting of the State Teachers' Association, Prof. E. E. Smith, of Purdue University, moved the appointment of a committee to which should be referred a plan of his looking to the increase of the efficiency of the Association in its work. This committee consisted of himself as chairman, and Messrs. Sandison, Ogg, and myself. If there was a fifth member his name has passed from my memory.

The plan of Prof. Smith met the approval of the committee and was reported substantially to the Association as worthy of adoption. But the lateness of the hour, the anxiety of the members to get through with the business, the backwardness of the committee in defending their action under these circumstances, together with the remark that the plan had been tried and failed, conspired to defeat the recommendation and it was dropped. But it seemed to me wise then, and capable of greatly increasing the value of those educational meetings, and subsequent reflection confirms my belief. The suggestion made was very simple, and its substance I shall embody in conclusions of my own, with reasons for them.

In my judgment the benefits which, as teachers we ought to obtain from these meetings, may be summed up in a general way under these three heads:

1. The relaxation afforded by change of scenes and associates, and the pleasure and inspiration gained by personal contact with old and new friends.

2. The broadening of our conceptions of our work and the enlargement of our knowledge of what is going on in the educational world and the ideas that are being wrought out.

3. Special help and suggestion in the line of our individual work.

I hold that while the first two points are admirably realized by our meetings, the last is not. And besides the many remarks I have heard made in the same line of criticism by teachers, as proof that the statement is true, I may cite the fact that the high school teachers felt it necessary to organize a special section for discussion of questions arising in their own field, and that the superintendents of city schools have made several attempts at the same thing in the last few years—while the continuance of the College Association appears to me additional proof that although in our great educational meeting we have many things in common which we may serve, still there are fields of inquiry and work lying outside the sphere of its present operations for aid which we must seek in narrower circles. The counsel and experience of those who have made specialties of them as at present conducted I testify that the net results capable of application to immediate use by the average teacher is very small and disproportionate to the effort made to gain it. And I ask also if we could so arrange it as to bring the combined experience of *teachers* in the various departments of instruction to bear upon specific educational work, would not a great gain be made not only for those who participate but for those who listen, and for the work in general.

I know of no way of accomplishing this better than to break up the Association into sections, which shall hold sessions during a half of each day. I would have sections for consideration of questions pertaining to the work of: 1. Primary Teachers; 2. Grammar Grade Teachers; 3. High School Teachers; 4. City Superintendents; 5. County Superintendents. I would make no changes in the general manner of conducting the Association save that it should resolve itself into sections to meet in the afternoons and take the whole of this time. This would leave the evenings and forenoons to be filled as they now are.

To carry this out successfully I think that it would be necessary to obtain rooms for the sections as convenient to each other as possible; that it should be understood that the meetings in sections should be informal, of a conversational character; that the best talent obtainable in the state for carrying on or leading these discussions should be called to the work; that the questions should be special not general; that each section should have its own officers and be under its own management as to the subjects and general character of the discussions.

I can not but think that if I were a primary teacher I would deem it a great privilege to spend three afternoons in company with the best primary teachers in the state, and learn how they teach their pupils to read, write, draw, spell; how they keep little hands and heads busy; how they mould human nature and the implements they have to do it with. And as a superintendent of schools I feel that if I could say to the instructors in our primary grades that teachers of established reputation from the best schools in the state would conduct afternoon sessions for them especially, showing how and why they do as they do—the actual methods employed in their schools for mental development, and that in the conduct of these meetings abundant opportunity would be given for the thousand and one questions that teachers want to know *particularly* about, I would have a weightier argument for their attendance than any I now possess. And what is true of this department is true of any other.

This plan is adopted by the National Teachers' Association, and while it is true it consists of a far larger number of persons

2

competent to lead in discussion, still I think it would be far from creditable to assume that our Association could not muster enough teachers able to do the work proposed.

It was objected that the plan had been tried and failed. I am informed by competent authority that the great reason for the failure lay in the fact that the general meeting was maintained at the same time, and for various obvious reasons diminished the interest in the work of the sections. It appears to me that it would be no slight gain to have a body of teachers at command to which those who determine what and how much shall be done in graded schools might go for counsel. I can not but think that the value of supervision of public schools would be enhanced did those engaged in it find ample opportunity for ascertaining the real opinions of those actually engaged in teaching. I submit that if you could gather the best primary teachers in Indiana and obtain from them a judgment as to when the pen should be first used and how—what ought to constitute the work in reading in each of the primary years—what amount of work in number may be attempted—and many other questions of similar import, that the report would be helpful and stimulating.

The best and most profitable educational meetings ever attended by me, so far as I personally am concerned, have been the superintendents' meetings held at various times. Here we gathered together, discussed questions informally, but endeavored to gather up the results, and whenever possible took votes on the best methods of procedure. If we had difficulties we stated them frankly and asked counsel. If any plans had been tried of special value we had the opportunity of explaining them. If any books bearing on special departments of work had been proved of value we noted them down.

With this plan we may well hold a meeting of three full days. If it should be said that it would impair the enthusiasm of the meetings by reason of the separations into small bodies, I answer that in these bodies teachers will get closer together and compensate for it. If it be said that comparatively few will thus meet, I answer that I do not believe it, and that if it be so we must still remember the value of the "remnant," and on no account let it die out for want of food.

But I have this remark to make, that in the general meetings the great majority of papers are listened to attentively by not more than a half or third of the teachers in attendance. Our Indiana teachers are undoubtedly an earnest body of men and women. They incur the expense of a trip to Indianapolis willingly and ought to receive every possible advantage.

Wisely managed I can see in the proposed change only a great additional inducement to teachers to come up to the capital for rest, recreation and instruction.

UNION CITY, IND.

DEPARTMENT OF PEDAGOGY.

This Department is conducted by GEO. P. BROWN, President State Normal School.

——:o:——

SCIENCE OF SCHOOL TEACHING—II.

THE true classification of the laws and facts of the growth of mind constitute the science of education. The principle of the science is the activity or energy manifesting itself in this growth. This principle follows certain laws in its activity. These laws can be discovered; (1) by observation of the facts of mind growth, and (2) by inferring from these facts what the laws are. If the observations are too few or are inaccurate the inference will not be a true expression of the law. One law of the development of this energy which we call mind, is that the first kind of action it performs is to discriminate between things. A thing to be known at all must be known as different, (1) from the self that knows it, and (2) from other things that are known. Until it is known as different it can not be known at all. Discrimination is the primary intellectual activity that must serve as the condition for every other and different act of intellect. Even if the objects known are simply acts and states of the soul they must be seen by the soul to be other than itself to be known at all, and each must be seen to be different from the others to be known with any distinctness.

It is through this power of discrimination that the mind comes by its knowledge of particular things. The entire objective world to the infant child is at first one thing. It discriminates this from itself, but knows it only as one object. By motion of the things themselves and of its own organs it is stimulated to discriminate one object from another and divides its one thing into many.

By continued repetition of this process in regard to the same thing, that becomes familiar; which is to say that the mind retains more and more of that knowledge which it acquires by these repeated acts of discrimination. When these acts of discrimination have been repeated for a sufficient number of times with the object present, a mental product will be formed and will remain as a permanent possession of the mind, which can be recalled when the object itself is not present.

The power to retain matures rapidly in children. This power is necessary to any complete discrimination, for unless the mind retained what it discriminated it would make only the same partial discrimination each time the object was presented, and no advancement in knowledge would be possible.

These two faculties, Discrimination and Memory, are accompanied by another that may be called Identification. This also makes a certain degree of development early in the infancy of the child. It is the power to see what is the same in different objects. It is the obverse of Discrimination. The latter discovers what each object has that others have not, while Identification discovers what is common to a number of objects.

It is by this power that the mind can group objects into classes. Unless the common attribute in things could be known there would be no such thing as separating objects into classes.

These terms, Discrimination, Memory, and Identification, name the three primary processes of the intellect. The mind must possess these powers in order that it shall be able to make any advancement in knowledge beyond that which is most rudimentary. It is in its superior power of Identification that the human intellect excells the intellect of the highest order of brutes. These can discriminate and remember, but they have only a slight power of discerning the likenesses in things. It is because of this power to see sameness in diversity that man is compelled to invent a language. He seeks some symbol by which to express this same-ness in things. Arbitrary signs that have no significance of their own are much better adapted to his use than are objects or signs that have an individual meaning. The hyeroglyphics of Egypt are much inferior to the words of the Greeks as modes of expres-sing what is common in things. Every word in our language is a word for the reason that it is the mark or sign of that which is common to a whole class of particular objects, either material or immaterial. Unless the mind had the power to discern what is common to many things there would be no language. When the child begins to use words with any intelligence it has begun to seize upon that which is the same in objects and give expression to it.

There is one other faculty of the intellect employed in learning that needs to be briefly considered. It may be called the power to create or construct new things. This is a power essentially dif-ferent from any of those mentioned. It is named by some the creative imagination. Mr. Bain and some others call it construc-tiveness. This is a power of later development than the other three. It is only after the mind has become stored with partic-ulars and some advancement has been made in the classification of things that the imagination begins to construct these things into new wholes.

There are two phases of the development of this power that need to be separately considered.

IS THE GRUBE METHOD OF TEACHING NUMBER PHILOSOPHICAL?—II.

I RECUR to this question again for the purpose of clearing away some cob-webs that seem to have gathered around my former article.

That addition and multiplication are fundamentally the same thing seems to be admitted by us all. The same is true of sub-traction and division.

That the *processes* of addition and multiplication are not iden-tical, i. e., *the same*, every one will admit. There could be no question as to the propriety of teaching them together if the processes were *identical*, for then they would not be two processes, but one.

The question recurs, "Are these processes so different that they should not be taught together?" Or, to state it differently, is the principle of teaching which requires that the thing to be taught shall be kept free from entangling relations, violated by teaching the four arithmetical processes together?

A rational method of seeking an answer to the question is to first make a careful analysis of the processes in question, and determine precisely what mental acts are involved in them.

This was attempted in a former article published in the School Journal of March, to which reference is made. The conclusion there reached may be summarized as follows: Addition, when the pupil has progressed beyond counting by ones, is merely recalling the sums of numbers that have been memorized. For example, the addition of 5 and 7 is remembering that 5 and 7 are 12. Unless this is remembered the sum must be obtained, as it was originally obtained, by counting. Now in addition the numbers whose sums are thus remembered are either equal or unequal. It is addition whether I say 7 and 7 are 14, or 8 and 6 are 14. The point insisted on is that if it is an act of addition and not an act of counting by ones merely,—which was called the alphabet of addition,—then the sum of these numbers must be remembered, and recalled when the numbers themselves are thought.

Addition as it is practiced is, therefore, the recalling of the sums of numbers that have been previously learned. Now the sums of groups of *unequal* numbers can be memorized, or we can memorize the sums of groups of *equal* numbers. When we exercise our memory of the sums of the groups of unequal numbers, or, rather, of groups of numbers without regard to whether they are equal or unequal, we are performing the process of addition.

The process of multiplication differs from that of addition in that we conceive the groups to be added to be equal, and we remember the sum of these groups of equal numbers. To illustrate: It is addition when I think that 8 and 7 and 6 are 21. So too it is addition when I think 7 and 7 and 7 are 21. But when the mind changes its attitude toward these latter numbers and thinks of them as three equal groups with 7 in each group, and thinks the aggregate of these equal groups to be 21, it has performed the mental process called multiplication. Multiplication is therefore thinking the sum of any number of groups of equal numbers that has been memorized. As counting by ones is the alphabet of addition, so counting by 2's or 3's or 4's, etc., is the alphabet of multiplication. The pupil has passed beyond the alphabet to the complete process when he uses his memory in recalling the sums of the different groups of equal numbers that he has memorized.

Such it seems to me are the mental acts involved in addition and multiplication. The processes of subtraction and division could be illustrated in a similar way. The only difference is that the process is analytic instead of synthetic.

In subtraction it is required that I separate part of a group of numbers from the group and determine how many remain. That is, I am to separate one group of numbers into two groups, without any regard to whether these groups are equal or unequal.

Division is the separating of a number into *equal* groups, and determining the number of groups, or it is determining the size of each of a given number of equal groups. In the one case the divisor represents the size of each group, and in the other case it represents the number of groups. This alternative that division involves makes the analysis of the process more complicated than is that of multiplication, but in each case division is but the subtraction of a constant quantity, and is as intimately related to subtraction as multiplication is to addition.

Now whether addition and multiplication can be taught together profitably must depend upon the ability of the learner to attend to two ideas at the same time. These are, (1) the idea of the *sum* of groups of numbers, and (2) the idea of the *equality* of the groups composing the sum. If he can not see that 2 times 3 is the same as 3 and 3, then these processes should not be taught together.

This is a question of practical experience which I do not know enough about to determine. It is very probable that in the very first steps of number study the idea of *sum* is all the little mind can hold at a time, without giving any attention to the equality or inequality of the numbers to be added. But it seems equally true that the child will very soon acquire the power to carry this second idea along with the other. When he is found to be able to do this he may be profitably taught addition and multiplication together.

What is true of these processes is equally true of subtraction and division, the two analytic operations.

I know that a little child five years of age, in my own household, seems to see that 2 times 4 figures are 8 figures just as clearly as she sees that 4 figures and 4 figures are eight; and it seems to me that she knows the latter all the better from knowing the former.' But it is not material to the question of the use of the Grube Method that the four processes be taught *from the first*. A child may be put to learning number in school too young, or before the age which that method contemplates. I think that a careful examination of children will show that when they can add small groups of numbers it is not long before they can multiply intelligently.

THE SCHOOL ROOM.

[This Department is conducted by Geo. F. Bass, Supervising Prin. Indianapolis schools.]

———:o:———

HELPING PUPILS.

MANY teachers unconsciously help pupils in the recitation. This is probably more frequently true in grammar than in any other study. Suppose the lesson is on *complements*. The pupil reads a sentence; as, "Gold is maleable," and not knowing what maleable means and not thinking it necessary to know, guesses that it is an object complement when the teacher shows signs of distress by some facial expression. The pupil notices this, and before the teacher has time to say a word, changes to *attribute complement* and follows this with the regulation reason for attribute complement which is, "It completes the predicate and belongs to the subject." This *may* all be done without the pupil's knowing either subject or predicate, or what is meant by "completes the predicate" or "belongs to the subject." The teacher showed surprise when the pupil said "object complement." The pupil then had only one more guess to make, and as he had learned the regulation reason that goes with the *other* complement his way was clear. Had the teacher showed no sign of displeasure the pupil would have sailed through just as smoothly. He would have said, "Maleable is an object complement because it completes the predicate and names the receiver of an act." Had the teacher said "Yes," and called for the next, he would never have once thought of changing.

REMEDY.

First, see that the pupils know what the words of the sentence mean. Do not allow them to attempt an analysis until this is done. Second, have them discover how each word is used in the given sentence: e. g. The word *gold* is used to name the object about which an assertion is made. The word *is* makes the assertion. The word *maleable* denotes a quality of gold— or of the object named by the *word* gold. It takes no rules of grammar to enable a pupil to do this. He is now ready for his grammatical knowledge—definitions; as, "The subject names that of which an assertion is made." Referring to the sentence with this definition in mind he will readily select the subject. Use the definition of predicate in the same way. Take the definition of complement—object and attribute. "The object complement completes the predicate and names that which receives the act." Refer to the sentence, "Have we any word that completes the predicate?" "Yes, maleable." "Does it name that which receives the act?" "No, it does not name at all." "Can it, then, be object complement?" "No." Take the definition of attribute complement and try it. "An attribute complement completes the predicate, and belongs to the subject." The pupil may not know what this definition means. Ask what the phrase "belongs to the subject" means. If he does not know, tell him that it means that the word denotes some attribute of the object named—or denoted by the subject of the sentence. He will then be able to put the word *maleable* into its proper class of complements. Let us remember, all the while, that this is done *not* for the sake of the' grammar, but for the sake of the pupil. His powers of discrimination are to be developed. This can be done only by taking time to question in such a way as to lead him to use his definitions and principles in a common sense way. Lead him to decide for himself. To give him a wink or nod and thereby cause him to make a mere guess is not "teaching the young idea how to shoot" and hit the mark.

RAPIDITY AND ACCURACY.

IT is insisted that a pupil should know instantly, on presentation, every possible combination of numbers from one to nine in addition; also, that he should be able to give instantly every combination of the multiplication table. This he must be able to do, if he is to be a practical accountant.

It is not enough for him to be able to give the correct result of a column of figures. He must do so with rapidity. We often find pupils counting fingers, or nodding the head for each *one* added: for example, 5+4=what? The pupil will say, "Five, six, seven, eight, nine," tapping his finger on the desk for each word after five. This is adding by ones, and is only the *first* step in addition. He should be taught to recognize 5+4 as 9 just as quickly as he would recognize m–a–n as man. When he has thus learned every possible combination in addition, he will be able to read the results in a column of figures as rapidly and accurately as he will a line of words.

To acquire this ability much repetition is needed. Drill, drill, drill. Preceding this drill there must be some patient slow work. It should be slow enough to allow the pupil to comprehend it. The tendency of teachers seems to be to give a question to a pupil in the explosive form of voice with the idea that it will startle him and make him quick,—often the words quick, quick, quick, follow to help—or force him along.

Lead him quietly and slowly to see that the combination 2 and 3 always produces 5. Do this by having him add the following: 2+3; 12+3; 22+3; 32+3; etc. Each result (which should be written on the slate or black-board,) ending in 5 will help to fix in his mind the law that 3 added to any number ending in two will give a number ending in 5. Drill on this combination until the pupil can recognize and state the result instantly. In this drill, when a pupil fails, refer immediately to the law mentioned above, by saying, "3 added to a number ending in 2 gives a number ending in what?" This leads the pupil to think of just the right thing, and prevents his falling into the habit of counting fingers, etc.

When drilling on the multiplication table, see to it that the combinations given to the pupils do not follow in any regular order. Saying it backwards and forwards is not enough to make the pupil give results of miscellaneous combinations instantly. If 11 × 11 are asked for, the chances are that a pupil who has learned the table in a certain order, will have to begin at one end or the other and work up to 11 × 11. Try yourself on your Latin endings.

Such exercises as the following are good tests. Have the pupils make numbers from 1—10 on slates, and require them to write answers only. (1) 5+9, (2) 7×9, (3) 9×4, (4) 8×3, (5) 6×7, (6) 7+9, (7) 18+7, (8) 95+8, (9) 78+4, (10) 5×7.

DON'T HURRY.

"HASTE makes waste." Do not hurry the children in the recitation. Take time to speak distinctly, but do not make your speech painfully distinct. Do not say "sev'n two" for seven and two. The way to do a great deal in a little time is to give your questions or directions distinctly and quietly, and to be *ready* with another as soon as the one given is answered. Much time is lost by just a little hesitation of the teacher after each answer.

We 'give ourselves away' in eager effort to 'draw others out.'

PRIMARY DEPARTMENT.

[This Department is conducted by LEWIS H. JONES, Supt. Indianapolis Schools.]

——:o:——

WHAT JOHNNIE'S TEACHER DID.

BY ELIZABETH PORTER GOULD.

"REMEMBER, Johnnie, it is just as necessary for you to clean your teeth when you go to bed as it is to say your prayers. So don't forget to do either, will you? Your prayers will be all the sweeter, coming from a clean mouth."

So said Mrs. Tay to her boy as she kissed him good-night, and then turned to Johnnie's school-teacher, who was spending the evening with her, and said: "I suppose that does sound very strange to you, but I am learning more and more the need of taking care of the body as well as the mind. If my aunt, who brought me up, had impressed upon me the necessity of taking care of my teeth when I was very young, I shouldn't have suffered from neuralgia as I have, or have been so ashamed to open my mouth. She insisted well upon my saying my prayers—and rightly, too—but never mentioned my teeth, or my stomach, as to that. Oh, I did grow up so ignorant about anything pertaining to my body!"

Now, to tell the truth, Johnnie's school-teacher was a little schocked when Mrs. Tay spoke to him as she did, but, in the few words which she said to herself, she saw a truth which, as she walked home by herself an hour later, grew more and more reasonable. And when, the next day, she looked around among her boys, ranging from nine to twelve years old, in a large public school, and saw in so many mouths the need of a tooth-brush, she realized, as never before, the necessity of making the matter as important as Johnnie's mother did. "Would that other mothers would do as much," she said to herself. "But if parents are so remiss in this matter, why is it not my duty, as a teacher, to do what I can to teach the sure laws of cause and effect? If a prayer is sweeter coming from a clean mouth, why is not a school lesson? And surely good teeth will be of as great value to these boys as much of the mere book-learning which they now receive, and to some, perhaps, more. I will do what I can, and I'll begin to-day, too. They will thank me for it, sometime, I know."

Thus Johnnie's teacher planned to herself, and made good her decision by requesting, just before school closed, that the boys be perfectly still, as she had something important to say. She then asked how many of them owned a tooth-brush. They evidently were very much surprised at the question, but not more so than she was when she saw how few owned such a thing, or had ever used one at all. She then said a few impressive words upon the urgent necessity of forming this habit of cleanliness in youth, and illustrated the subject by telling of the nature of teeth, and of two boys, one of whom was wise in season, and the other who suffered much from his negligence. As she was a woman who never hesitated to do any little charitable act within her means, right among the needy in her school, she promised to give to any boy who would use it a tooth-brush, provided his parents were not able or willing to do as much for him.

Her talk made a good impression upon the boys, so much so that after they were dismissed she heard some of them making great promises among themselves. If she had looked into the ante-room she would have seen several of them awaiting their turn to look at their teeth in the glass, while one boy had just left it with the remark, "I declare, I can never get them clean."

The teacher was wise enough to follow up the subject, as a part of her duty, by setting apart a little time at the close of each week's session in which to talk familiarly with the boys about the matter. After awhile, when she saw some good fruits of her labor, she embraced the opportunity to add some words relative to that other necessity of never allowing the use of any bad words —for what could be worse than bad words out of a clean mouth?

It so happened that the very next morning after this talk she had occasion to illustrate the subject in a way which was particularly striking. It seems that as she was going into the school-room she heard a boy swearing to another in such words as made her blood boil. She immediately took him and led him into a corner of the school-room, to remain there until the school had been duly opened. Then, before a lesson was recited, she took him out before all the scholars, and, then and there, washed out his mouth with a sponge wet in pure castile soap-suds which she had prepared; after which she talked earnestly and tenderly to the boys of the enormity of the crime of speaking in such a way the name of the Great Being who, if he should do what they called upon him to do, would bring down the most dreadful agony that could be imagined. She further said that there was a civil law against habitual swearing, by which even boys could be arrested; and then she warned them that in no easier way could habitual swearing be made than by boys getting into this dreadful habit during their school-days. She made the lesson truly effective, and it is safe to say that no boy in that school could easily forget that punishment in its bearings upon a clean mouth.

When every teacher fully accepts the meaning of education in the broad sense that Johnnie's teacher did, there will be a more general desire to supplement the regular school recitations with that personal interest which will lovingly work for scholars in any direction to prepare them for the best practical living in a practical world.—*Journal of Education*

A SWARM OF BEES.

B hopeful, B cheerful, B happy, B kind,
B busy of body, B modest of mind,
B earnest, B truthful, B firm and B fair.
Of all Miss B Haviour, B sure and B ware.
B think ere you stumble of what may B fall;
B true to yourself, and B faithful to all.
B brave to B ware of the sins that B set;
B sure that no sin will another B get.
B watchful, B ready, B open, B frank,
B manly to all men whate'er B their rank;
B just, and B generous, B honest, B wise,
B mindful of time, and B certain it flies.
B prudent, B liberal, of order B fond,
B uy less than you need B fore B uying B yond.
B careful, But yet yet B the first to B stow,
B temperate, B steadfast, to anger B slow.
B thoughtful, B thankful, whatever may B tide,
B justful, B joyful, B cleanly B side.
B pleasant, B patient, B fervent to all,
B best if you can, But B humble withal.
B prompt and B dutiful, and still B polite,
B reverent, B quiet, B sure and B right;
B calm, B retiring, B ne'er led astray,
B grateful, B cautious, of those who B tray.
B tender, B loving, B good, and B nign—
B loved shalt thou B, and all else shall B thine.

Indianapolis Times.

EDITORIAL.

W. A. BELL, Editor-in-Chief and Proprietor.

GEO. P. BROWN, Pres. State Normal School, Associate Editor and Editor of the Department of Pedagogy.

LEWIS H. JONES, Superintedent of Indianapolis Schools, and Editor of the Primary Department.

GEO. F. BASS, Supervising Principal Indianapolis Schools, and Critic in Training School, Editor of The School Room Department.

A. W. BRAYTON, Prof. of Natural Science in the Indianapolis Schools, is Editor of the Popular Science Department.

Prof E. E. WHITE, Ohio; Prof. E. E. SMITH, Purdue University; HUBERT M. SKINNER, Chief Clerk Dept. of Public Instruction; JAS. BALDWIN, Supt. Schools Rushville; HOWARD SANDISON, W. W. PARSONS, and MICHAEL SEILER, of State Normal School; EMMA MONT. MCRAE, Principal Marion High School; H. S. TARBELL, late Supt. of the Indianapolis Schools, are frequent contributors.

Many other able writers contribute occasional articles to the JOURNAL. Should althose be enrolled as "Contributing Editors" who contribute one article or more a year the list could be indefinitely extended.

This large list of special editors and able contributors insures fer the readers of the JOURNAL the best, the freshest, the most practical thoughts and methods in all departments of school work.

The Miscellaneous and Personal Departments of the Journal will not be neglected, but it places special emphasis on its large amount of unequaled practical and helpful educanonal articles.

Persons sending money for this Journal can send amounts less than $1 in *two* and *one* cent postage stamps; no others can be used.

In asking to have the address of your Journal changed, please give the *old* address as well as the new, naming the county as well as the state.

An agent is wanted to raise a club for the Journal in every township in the State. Send for terms.

ISLAND PARK ASSEMBLY, 1885.

The Island Park meetings for the coming summer promise to be of unusual interest. The schools embracing Music, Art, Elocution, German, French, Italian, Spanish, New Testament Greek, and Hebrew, and probably a School of Domestic Economy, will open Tuesday, July 7th. The seventh annual session of the Assembly will be open on Tuesday, July 14th, and close on Thursday, July 28th. The The Sunday School Normal Department will be under the personal direction of the Superintendent of Instruction, the Rev. A. H. Gillet. The Children's Class will be taught by Rev. N. B. C. Love. Among the lecturers to be present are Bishop R. S. Foster, Rev. T. DeWitt Talmage, Geo. W. Cable, Rev. John Alabaster, Prof. C. E. Bolton, Rev. Geo. Loring, Rev. J. B. Thomas, Miss Lydia M. Von Finklestien, Prof. Wm. I. Marshall, Wallace Bruce, Bishop Thomas Bowman. Prof. C. C. Case will have charge of the Department of Music, and among the special attractions are the Haydn Quartette, the Meigs

Sisters Vocal Quartette, and Prof. Chas. E. Underhill, Reader. A very large Oriental Museum, under the direction of Peter M. Von Finklestien, of Jerusalem. Brilliant Oriental Entertainments by Miss Von Finklestien and her Brother in the rich and elegant costumes of the East. Fine Stereopticon Entertainments, and Grand Vocal and Instrumental Concerts. For copies of The Assembly Record, containing detailed announcements, address, "The Assembly Record," Sturgis, Mich.

A CARD.

In an editorial in the April number of the Journal it was stated that I had not received anything from the treasury of the Reading Circle for my expenses, and that I did not intend to make any charge for the same. My expenses have been very light up to this time, because of certain privileges of travel granted to me, and it was my first intention to make no charge for them. But further reflection made it apparent that this course would be unjust to the other members who had not these privileges, and that my actual expenses should be paid, however small. I certainly have no desire to gain any cheap notoriety for charity toward the Reading Circle..

GEO. P. BROWN.

"RECESS OR NO RECESS IN SCHOOLS."

A committee of the National Council of Education made to that body at its meeting held in Madison, Wis , July 10, 1884, a report upon "Recess or no Recess in Schools." After discussion, the subject was referred back to the committee for further investigation, to be followed by another report in July, 1885. The subject is of vital importance, touching as it does the welfare of pupils in the schools of the country; hence the investigation assumes the widest scope. The committee seeks facts of experience, as well as theories based upon experience; any fact that bears directly or indirectly upon the subject will be very acceptable.

The scope of the investigation is indicated by the following questions, to which answers are solicited from superintendents of schools, principals, teachers, school officers, physicians, professional men of all classes, and parents. The first nine questions are directed especially to superintendents and and teachers; the rest of the questions are also directed to any persons who can give any information upon the points raised. The name and address of persons, particularly physicians, who have given attention to this subject, will be valuable aid; copies of reports or papers that discuss this subject are solicited. Send all communications to the sub-committee named below.

QUESTIONS.

I. Is the no-recess plan in operation in the schools under your supervision or instruction?

II. If it is, has any proposition been made toward the establishment of the plan, and what arguments prevailed against the proposition to introduce it?

III. Have you returned to the recess plan after a fair trial of the no-recess plan, and if so, what causes led to the change?

IV. What condition existed in and about your schools that prompted the officials to abolish the recess and adopt the no-recess plan, and with whom did the proposition originate to establish in your schools the no-recess plan—with the superintendent and teachers, with the board of education, or with the patrons?

V. How many hours of continuous confinement within the school-room are required daily, A. M. and P. M, of pupils in the several grades under your no-recess plan?

VI. What are the precise duties and privileges of pupils that have been substituted for those of the recess in the several grades of your school?

VII. Are physical exercises as a practical means of retaining and securing health in the school-room, an equivalent under your no-recess plans for the exercise afforded to pupils by an out-door recess?

VIII. What effect has the no-recess plan upon the management and government of your schools, especially in the matter of the pupil's habits in conduct?

IX. Is the no-recess plan extending among the schools in your vicinity?

X. How is the health of pupils affected in the following particulars by the no-recess plan, so far as your observation and experience extend?

NOTE.—State explicitly the nature and character of the examinations instituted to arrive at the facts and opinions which you recount in your answers to the questions asked under (a) to (e) below. Special inquiry is made about those children that have inherited or have developed weaknesses in the points enumerated.

(a) Does or does not the no-recess plan affect the duties and privileges of pupils in such a way as to develop or aggravate in any of them nervous irritation?—revealed by a tendency to or an absence from cerebral pains, inability to think or to act or to remember, weariness, coldness of extremities, want of blood in the brain, irritation of the sympathetic system of nerves—owing to continuous sedentary confinement in the school-room with its heated and perhaps vitiated air?

(b) Does or does not the no-recess plan affect the pelvic organs?—

3

revealed by a tendency to develop or aggravate irritation and disease of the kidneys, bladder, rectum, or by blood poisoning from retention of urine—owing to the failure of pupils tc comply regularly with the physical necessities under which they rest, to a lack of those physical exercises which tend to keep in a healthy condition the organs enumerated, and to the continuous confinement upon the seats in the school-room?

(*c*) Does or does not the no recess plan affect the eye-sight?—revealed by developing or aggravating enfeebled powers of those organs, owing to deficiency of out-door exposure?

(*d*) Does or does not the no-recess plan affect the nasal passages and lungs?—revealed by developing or aggravating catarrh or irritation of the lungs, owing to too continuous exposure to the dust, heat and air of the school-room?

(*e*) How do the physical exercises substituted by the no-recess plan for those of the recess affect, relatively, the rapidity of the pulse of pupils when it is compared to the rapidity developed in the exercises of the out-door recess?

Very respectfully submitted, J. H. HOOSE,
Sub-committee on Hygiene in Education.

STATE NORMAL SCHOOL,
Cortland, Cortland Co., N. Y., Jan. 7, 1885.

NATIONAL EDUCATIONAL ASSOCIATION.

The Association will meet at Saratoga, N. Y., July 14-18, 1885. The program has been issued, and offers strong inducements for a large attendance. Many of the leading educational problems will be treated by some of the ablest men of the country. Any one interested in this great cause can find abundance to interest and instruct. Meeting and hearing the prominent educators of the country will of itself repay the trip.

Hotel rates range from $1.00 to $2.50 per day. For information and to secure places in advance, address Geo. T. Church, Supt. of schools, Saratoga Springs, N. Y., stating just what is desired.

Railroad Rates.—All the principal railroads from the West will sell round trip tickets at *a fare and a third*   Tickets good going from July 1st to 13th, and good returning till August 31st. Numerous cheap excursions have been planned to various points of interest from Saratoga.

Indiana will be creditably represented on the program in the Association, and should send a large delegation. State Supt. Holcombe will have a paper be'ore the Supt's Department; Lewis H. Jones, Supt. of Indianapolis schools, will discuss a paper by W. T. Harris;

Geo. P. Brown, Pres. of the State Normal, will have an inaugural as President of the Normal Department, and he is also Secretary of the National Council; W. N. Hailman, Supt. of the La Porte schools, is President of the Kindergarten Section, and is its leader; W. F. M. Goss, of Purdue University, will have a paper in the Industrial Department. Besides these Supt.·Holcombe is Vice-President, H. B. Hill is Councilor, and W. A. Bell is State Manager.

The President of the general Association is F. Louis Soldan, of St. Louis, Mo., and he is leaving nothing undone to insure to the meeting the grandest success.

NORTHERN INDIANA TEACHERS' ASSOCIATION.

The meeting of the Northern Indiana Teachers' Association will take place at Island Park, Rome City, July 21st, and continue four days. Prof. Swartz, chairman of the executive committee Teachers' Association, reports that a very interesting and successful session is anticipated. An excellent program has been prepared, bringing out some of the foremost educational talent in the state. Papers will be read by the·fellowing persons: Supt. L. H. Jones, of Indianapolis; Miss Morden, of Logansport; Co. Supt. H. M. Lafollett, of Boone county; Supt W. H. Banta, of Velparaiso; Prof. W. W. Parsons, of the State Normal at Terre Haute; Miss Ada Baylor, of Wabash; and Supt. W. H. Sims, of Goshen. These papers will be discussed by prominent educators of the northern part of the state. The Island Park Association will be in session at the same time, thus affording the teachers an excellent opportunity to hear the excellent lectures that constitute a feature of the assembly. A more eligible place than Rome City could not be selected for the meeting, and no doubt the attendance will be large.

STATE CERTIFICATES.

The teachers recently examined, to whom the State Board of Education have issued State licenses, are R. J. Aley, Spencer; Hamlet Allen, Washington; P. A. Allen, Bluffton; John W. Barnes, Kokomo; R. G. Boone, Frankfort; O. C. Charlton, Lebanon; Mary E. Dick, Fort Wayne; A. H. Douglass, Walton; B. W. Everman, Camden; W. W. Fuller, Boonville; J. M. Gross, New Carlisle; G. L. Harding, Leesburg; B. B. Harrison, Waterloo; M. W. Harrison, Auburn; S. E. Harwood, Spencer; James H. Hays, Connersville; W. T. Hoffman, Washington; N. C. Johnson, Oakland; A. H. Kennedy, Rockport; C. W. McClure, Mitchell; H. H. Miller, Bremen; James H. Neff, Bunker Hill; J. W. Nourse, Rockport; Chs. N. Peak, Aurora; G. A.

Powles, Mishawaka; M. F. Rickoff, Nineveh; W. B. Sinclair, San Pierre; Amos Sanders, North Vernon; T. J. Sanders, Butler; J D. White, Greensburg; Phariba W. White, New Castle; Londonia Williams, Richmond; J. A. Wood, Salem; B. F. Wissler, Cambridge City. There are two others to whom licenses will probably be issued when the board obtains some information regarding their standing as experienced and capable teachers.

COMPLIMENTARY TO INDIANA.—Hon. Le Roy D. Brown, Supt. of Public Instruction in Ohio, has written State Supt. Holcombe a very complimentary letter regarding the Indiana educational exhibit at New Orleans. In it he says: "Your educational exhibit is a fine one in many respects. I doubt if Indiana ever before equaled it. Your work on country schools is exceptionally good, and shows what efficient supervision can do for the schools of rural districts. Ohio and other states without supervision need it badly, and some states with supervision need improvement in that line of work."

HIGH SCHOOL COMMENCEMENTS.—The Journal started out to make a notice of the high school commencements, but has been overwhelmed and is compelled to give it up. Never before were so many commencement programs received, never before was the average number of graduates so large, never before were the programs issued in such elegant style, and never before was there so much general interest taken in this higher education. If space would allow the Journal would be glad to make an extended notice of each commencement.

A GOOD IDEA.—W. H. Payne, of Michigan University, suggests the plan of holding a Conference of Reading Circle Managers from the various States at the National Association, and nominates J. J. Burns of Ohio, and Geo. P. Brown of Indiana to take the lead and provide for the meeting.

WRITING.—While the blackboard and writing-charts are indispensable in teaching penmanship, the young beginner needs his model no larger nor smaller than the letters he is expected to produce, and the copy should be placed immediately under his eye and as near his pencil as possible. To meet these conditions of successful teaching, the County Board of Education has adopted Hurst's Compend of Penmanship.

It begins with the teaching of drawing and writing simultaneously upon the basis of a uniform and proportionate division of space, an inch being the unit of measurement, beginning with the simplest form, and proceeding by easy and attractive stages to the completion of all the work required in our First Grade. The Compend, faithfully followed, presents the needed systematic design.—*From Supt. Macpherson's Explanation of Course of Instruction for First Grade for Wayne county.*

QUESTIONS AND ANSWERS.

QUESTIONS BY THE STATE BOARD FOR APRIL.

SCIENCE OF TEACHING.—1. What is imagination, as distinguished from memory?

2. Illustrate how the imagination may be employed in teaching Geography.

3. What is the method by which any faculty of the mind is cultivated?

4. Show that to educate a child is to establish certain habits of mind-action.

5. Show that there are two ways of fixing such habits, (1) by fixing the attention through awakening an interest, and (2) by repetition.

6. Show that if reliance is placed upon repetition alone, much time and energy is wasted.

READING.—1. What is the difference between accent and emphasis?

2. Define the two kinds of emphasis.

3. What is the distinction between pitch and force? Between force and rate?

4. What is a monotone? Give an example in which you would use it.

5. What is the principal object to be gained in teaching reading?

6. Why should a child be able to call every word in the reading lesson, at sight?

7. Read a selection chosen by the superintendent.

PHYSIOLOGY.—1. Distinguish between distilled and fermented liquors and their effects.

2. Describe the digestive fluids.

3. Describe the clotting of blood.

4. Describe the diaphragm.

5. Describe paralysis.

6. In what respects does the structure of the infant differ from that of the adult?

7. Describe the production of high and low notes by the voice.

8. Distinguish between arteries and veins.

9. From what causes is the air of the average school-room unwholesome?

10. Describe the cilia in the air passages.

HISTORY.—1. Why did Columbus first apply to the King of Portugal for aid in making his discoveries?

10

2. What colony adopted the first written Constitution? What was the character of the charter which consolidated the Connecticut colonies? 4, 6

3. What was the "Boston Tea Party?" 10

4. Wherein did Washington's defeats differ from the defeats of most generals? 10

5. Who was the inventor of the steamboat? On what waters was it tested? 5, 5

6. What was the cause of the war of 1812? How was this cause treated in the treaty which concluded war? 5, 5

7. What relation had the annexation of Texas to the Civil War? 10

8. What claim of the South as to their slaves justified the Emancipation Proclamation, apart from all idea of humanity? 10

9. What naval battle in the Civil War effected a complete change in naval warfare? 10

10. What was the "Trent affair?" What was its result? 5, 5

ORTHOGRAPHY.—1. What is the distinction between a vocal and a sub-vocal? Give five vocals and five sub-vocals. 2 pts, 5 each

2. Mark the sound of *ch* in the following words : charcoal, chasm, chautauqua, chimerical, and niche.

3. Indicate the pronunciation of the following words by the use of diacritical marks and accents : immobile, arbitrament, plethoric, illustrate, and peremptory.

4. What is the use of silent letters?

5. Give the ways in which the sound of *a* in *all* may be represented.

6. Spell ten words selected by the superintendent.

PENMANSHIP.—1. Describe the "left" position for writing.

2. Describe the manner of holding the pen.

3. Describe the movements usually employed in writing.

4. Name or write the six principles used in forming the small letters of the alphabet.

5. Analyze A, C.

GEOGRAPHY.—1. Name every State that is bordered for any distance by the Mississippi river. 1% for each

2. Name the five agricultural products that are more largely exported than are any others from the States south of the Ohio river. 2% for each

3. Name five important articles which the United States import from Brazil. Name five countries of South America, each of which touches the Atlantic Ocean. 1% for each

4. What are zones? Name each and give its width. 5 pts, 2% ea.

5. Locate San Francisco, Honolulu, Quito, Moscow, and Vienna. 5 pts, 2% ea.

6. Describe the Rhine river, the Ganges, the Volga, the Nile, and the Amazon. 5 pts, 2% for each

7. Name the four most important exports of the State of Michigan, excluding agricultural products. Where are the richest lead mines of the Northern States? 2% for each

8. Name four important influences that may give to any place a temperature different from that which belongs to its latitude. Give the one chief reason why equatorial regions are warmer than polar regions. 2% for each

9. Name the five greatest mountain systems in the world, and tell where each is 1% for each of 10 pts

10. Where are Birmingham, Rome, Lyons, Constantinople, and Calcutta? and tell for what each is noted. 2% for each

GRAMMAR.—1. Analyze the following sentence: "'Twas in Autumn, and stormy and dark was the night and fast were the windows and doors."

2. What mark of punctuation should be used after the interjection in an exclamatory sentence?

3. In what do personal pronouns and relative pronouns differ?

4. What is the office of each of the italicized words in the following:
    a. He works *well.*
    b. He is *well.*
    c. He looks *well.*
    d. Well is a noun.

5. What is it that distinguishes the subjunctive mode from the other modes? Use correctly in sentences the following clauses:
    a. If he writes well.
    b. If he write well.

6. Correct the errors in the following, giving reasons:
    a. He flew from justice.
    b. We hoped to have seen you before.
    c. I never appreciated before how short life was.
    d. One of you are mistaken.
    e. Why are dust and ashes proud?

7. Define comparison as applied to adjectives. What degree of comparison is expressed by the following: supreme, perfect, bluish, last.

8. State the case of each italicized word in the following, giving reason: *a.* He was appointed *speaker.*
    b. I know *him* to be an honest *man.*
    c. The *speaker* being an able *man*, we had confidence in him.

9. What modifiers may the participle have that the infinitive can not have? Give examples.

10. What classes of words may join adjective clauses to the words they modify?

ARITHMETIC.— 1. Define diameter, circumference, surface, a solid and a triangle. Illustrate each by figure.

2. Reduce ⅔ of an hour and ⅓ of a minute to the decimal of a day.

3. A man owned a farm containg 40 A. 3 R. and 22 sq. rd., and sold it at $40,757 per acre; how much did he receive for it?

4. Reduce ⅞, ¼¼ and ⅘ to a common denominator, by analysis.

5. If a staff 9 feet high casts a shadow 6 feet 9 inches in length, what is the height of a tower whose shadow is 75 feet 6 inches in length? By proportion.

6. What is the interest on $750 for 16 months and 13 days at 8¼ per cent per annum? (Solve by "Six Per Cent. Method.")

7. When it is noon at San Francisco, which is 127 degrees west longitude, what is the time at the 180th degree west longitude?

8. A man bought a house for $8,500. He sold it, losing 18 per cent. on the cost price. For what should he have sold it to gain 24 per cent. on the cost price?

9. The base of a cone is 10 feet in diameter, its height is 30 feet; what are its solid contents?

10. Extract the cube root of 2,299,968.

ANSWERS TO STATE BOARD QUESTIONS PRINTED IN MAY.

HISTORY.— 1. Certain maps and charts which Columbus saw when a student, stories of drift wood and bodies said to have drifted over the ocean to the Madeira Islands, and the ideas of certain learned men, led him to believe that by sailing westward he could reach the eastern shores of China and Japan, attempting which he discovered San Salvador.

2. The Norsemen, inhabitants of Norway and Sweeden and Denmark, who discovered Iceland and Greenland, and claim to have sailed south and discovered the north part of this country, and even as far south as Rhode Island.

3. The West India Company in order to promote the settlement of what is now New York, gave purchasers very absolute power over all the land purchased and over the occupants of it. An attempt, persistently made to exercise these arbitrary powers, by the patroon Van Rensselaer, led to resistance by ths tenants, and resulted in very serious modifications of these rights.

4. The indirect causes—the Navigation Acts, Writs of Assistance, the Stamp Act, and the Mutiny Act. The direct cause was the claim to tax the colonies as and for what Parliment saw fit without any voice of the colonies, which was resisted by the colonies, who declared that taxation without representation was tyranny.

5. Franklin was Agent of Pennsylvania in England, when he assured the Commons that the colonies would never submit to the Stamp Act; he suggested the calling of a general Congress of the colonies; was a member of the II Congress, and a member of the Committee to draft the Declaration, when he remarked that if they did not all hang together, they would all hang separately. He was sent to France, where he served the colonies to great advantage.

6. Wars with the Indians, especially those under the control of Little Turtle, who advised peace, but being forced to battle was defeated by General Wayne. Before this the United States forces suffered severe defeats in Indiana under St. Clair and Harmer.

7. General Winfield Scott, and General Zachary Taylor.

8. The Mexican War was caused by the annexation of Texas to the Union; the annexation was largely promoted by the South, that slavery might have a broader and more general field for extension, and slavery brought about the Civil War.

9. Sherman's March to the Sea. It fatally severed the Confederate forces in the South from those in Virginia and the States bordering on Mason and Dixon's Line.

10. A vast benefit. By relieving the South of the incubus of slavery and slave labor, it has opened up one of the most fertile portions of the country to more general cultivation, and induced in the people of the South those habits of industry and principles of self-dependence which has characterized the North.

READING.—1. Under a careful teacher, pupils of the Third Reader class may be safely allowed to use the small school dictionaries; under the direction of the teacher, the pronunciation of words, as indicated in the dictionary, may be learned gradually; the meanings of words selected by the teacher may be ascertained; and written exercises with words from the reading-lesson in the same and in different senses, may be prepared.

2. The aspirated tone is the whispered tone, which may be more or less vocalized. For an example, see the ghost's address to Hamlet.

3. Punctuation marks are for the purpose of showing the grammatical construction of sentences. Examples: (1) John, Jones the lawyer said he would go. (2) John Jones, the lawyer said he would go. (3) John Jones, the lawyer, said he would go. (4) "John Jones, the lawyer," said he, "would go."

4. The sing-song tone in reading poetry may be avoided by having pupils thoroughly understand the thought or sentiment of the selection before reading it. To aid in this, they may paraphrase the stanzas in oral or written prose.

5. The inflections used in reading are the rising, or upward, the

falling, or downward, and the circumflex, or upward and downward combined. The first is used in questions and in expressions of surprise, amazement, etc.; the second, in assertions, in expression of strong emotions (not interrogative), in announcements, in antithesis, etc ; the third, in irony, mockery, wit, humor, etc.

PHYSIOLOGY.—1. Nerves will heal when cut if placed together again. A severe cut upon the arm does not, when healed, prevent feeling and action in the parts below the cut.

2. The internal or mucous layer of the small intestines, on and between its folds, is covered with a large number of small, hair-like processes. These are covered with an epithelial layer, are composed chiefly of connective tissue, contain lacteals and blood-vessels, and act as absorbents of the digested and nutritive portions of the food.

3. In warm-blooded animals, the constancy of animal heat is necessary to the perpetuation of life. At 120° F the body dies. The skin is the chief organ for preserving an average temperature.

4. The crystalline lens is double convex, the posterior side having the greater curvature. The rays of light are slightly converged on entering the lens, largely converged on leaving it.

5. Because we don't.

6. The epiglottis is a spoon-shaped plate of cartilage at the root of the tongue and the top of the larynx. When swallowing, this covering closes the glottis and prevents the passage of food and drink into the trachea.

7. The heart has two movements—systole and diastole, or contraction and dilation. These alternate in the same chamber and in the upper and lower divisions of the heart.

8. The liver serves three purposes: that of purifying the blood, that of secreting bile for use in digestion, and that of secreting glycogen for nutrition.

9. Other than at the heart, the arteries have no valves. Here the valves are semi lunar. Numerous veins have valves formed by folds of their inner coat. These valves open towards the heart.

GRAMMAR.—1. The principal elements of a sentence are the subject and predicate. Each may be modified by words, phrases, or clauses.

2. *Probably* is a modal adverb, modifying the thought in the clause. *Exceedingly* is an adverb of degree, modifying *honest*.

3. The object of the verb in the active voice becomes the subject in the passive. The subject of the active becomes the agent in the passive. Active—The *boy* struck the *dog*. Passive—The dog was struck by the boy.

4. *a*. I feel bad. The condition of the subject is described, and requires an adjective. *b*. The child behaves badly. *How* he be-

haves is answered by the adverb *badly*. *c*. I had rather go than stay; or, I *would* rather go than stay. The comparative conjunction *than* is required after *rather*.

5. Pianos, valleys, dwarfs, mousetraps, Generals Smith.

6. Writing, written; laying, laid; setting, set; receiving, received.

7. The infinitive expresses the act or state without predicating anything of the subject, and has not person or number. The subject of the infinitive, when it has one, is in the objective case. The subject of the finite verb is always in the nominative case.

8. Complex declarative sentence, "that the moon is not inhabited," is the subordinate clause and also the subject of the sentence; "is believed" is the predicate, unmodified. Of the subordinate clause "moon" is the subject, *is* the copula, and *inhabited* the predicate. "Is inhabited" is modified by the negative adverb *not*. *That* is the subordinate connective, and "it" is the anticipative subject of the sentence.

9. A sentence with a compound subject or predicate is an abridged form of compound sentence. "The boy studies hard and learns fast" is a compound sentence, called by some grammarians a simple sentence with a compound predicate. "Boys and girls like to play," may be stated thus: Boys like to play and girls like to play, the first being the abridged form.

10. Will not the Judge of all the earth do right?

GEOGRAPHY.—1. *a*. Greenland, British America, United States, Mexico, Central America. That portion of the United States called Alaska lies to the northwest of British America. *b*. United States including Alaska, British America, Mexico, Greenland, and Central America.

2. Capital of Great Britain, is London; of Russia, St. Petersburg; of Germany, Berlin; of France, Paris; of Austro Hungary, Vienna; of Italy, Rome; of Spain, Madrid; of Turkey, Constantinople; of Sweden and Norway, Stockholm; of Denmark, Copenhagen.

3. *a*. United States, India, Russia. *b*. Charleston. *c*. China.

4. Brazil is bounded on the north by Venezuela, Guiana, and the Atlantic Ocean; on the east by the Atlantic; on the south by the Atlantic and Uruguay; on the west by Argentine Republic, Paraguay, Bolivia, Peru, Ecuador, and United States of Columbia. Brazil is larger than the United States, exclusive of Alaska; about the size of Australia. Chief exports are coffee, sugar, indigo, timber, india-rubber.

5. Rome is situated on the Tiber, in the central part of the peninsula of Italy: Canton, on the Si-Kiang in the southeastern part of China: Quebec is on the St. Lawrence, in the province of Quebec,

Canada: St. Petersburg, at the mouth of the Neva, in Russia: New Orleans, on the Mississippi, in southern Louisiana.

6. In the Northern States the principal products are corn, wheat, rye, oats, potatoes, and other products belonging to a temperate climate; while in the South the tropical sun and air produce such crops as cotton, sugar, rice, etc.

7. *a*. Russia, Austro-Hungary, German Empire, France, England. *b*. Austro-Hungary, German Empire, Spain, England, Wales, and France.

8. Mississippi River, Gulf of Mexico, Atlantic Ocean, St. George's Channel, Irish Sea. Its cargo would probably be sugar, cotton, or cattle.

9. New York City, Philadelphia, Brooklyn, Chicago.

10. San Francisco is situated in western California, on the Pacific coast; Quito, among the Andes in Ecuador; Tokio, on the island of Niphon, in Japan Empire; Paris, in France, on the Seine; New York, in the southeastern part of New York State, at the mouth of Hudson River.

ARITHMETIC.—1. $\sqrt{(500)^2 + (360)^2} = 616 +$ ft. Because, in the geometrical explanation, we find that after subtracting the square denoted by the square of the first figure of the root, the remainder is almost wholly made up of two equal rectangles, whose length is denoted by the root already found.

2. $1800 + 6 = 300 \times 7 = 2100$
       $2250 + 9 = 250 \times 7 = 1750$
       $3200 + 14 = 228\frac{4}{7} = 1600$
       $2100 + 1750 + 1600 = 5450$

A's cap. $\frac{2100}{5450}$ of \$27450 = \$10577.064+

B's cap. $\frac{1750}{5450}$ of \$27450 = \$8814.22+

C's cap. $\frac{1600}{5450}$ of \$27450 = \$8058.715+

3. $\$1 - (\$1 \times \frac{7}{10} \times \frac{1}{100}) = \$\frac{993}{1000}$, proceeds on \$1.
   $\$1235.40 + \$\frac{993}{1000} = \$1258.13 +$, Ans.

4. $\$1 + (\$1 \times \frac{1}{100} \times \frac{1}{100}) = \$\frac{10001}{10000}$
   $\$6344.25 + \$\frac{10001}{10000} = \$6324.048$, P. W.
   $\$6344.25 - \$6324.048 = \$20.20 +$, Ans.

A debt not due is the amount of its present worth on interest for the time the debt has to run, at legal rate: therefore the difference is the same that exists between the principal and amount.

5. $\$1883 \times \frac{1}{100} \times \frac{1}{1} = \$235.84 +$ int.
   $\$1883 + \$235.84 + = \$2118.84$, Ans.

Simple interest is interest on principal only, while compound interest is interest on principal and interest.

6. 1 lb. 2 oz. $= 18$ oz. 18 oz. a day for 9 mo. $= 162$ oz. a day for 1 mo. 1 yr. 8 mo. $= 20$ mo. $162 + 20 = 8\frac{1}{10}$, Ans.

7. Ans. 73.088. Point off as many in the quotient as those of the dividend exceed those of the divisor.

8. Thousandths. No effect on value; changes form.

9. $4\frac{1}{17} \times 2\frac{1}{4} = \frac{11}{4} \times \frac{41}{17}$; $5\frac{1}{8} - 4\frac{1}{2} = \frac{5}{16}$; $\frac{11}{4} \times \frac{41}{17} \times \frac{19}{10} = 16$, 1st part.
2d part: $\frac{19}{16} = \frac{19}{16}$; $\frac{12}{16} + \frac{11}{16} = 1\frac{11}{16}$. $100 - \frac{111}{16} = \frac{41}{17}$; $\frac{41}{17} \times \frac{1}{2}$
$= 21\frac{11}{16}$, Ans.

10. $\frac{3}{4}$ of $\frac{5}{8} = \frac{5}{16}$; $\frac{5}{16}$ of $219\frac{1}{4}$ A $= 29\frac{1}{4}$ A.

MISCELLANY.

PROCEEDINGS OF THE SOUTHERN INDIANA TEACHERS' ASSOCIATION.

The eighth annual meeting of this Association met in Mitchell, April 2d and 3d, 1885.

April 2d—The Association met in College Hall, and was called to order by the retiring president, A. M. Sweeney. Devotional exercises were conducted by Prof. E. E. Smith, of Purdue University.

The address of welcome was by Hon —— Edwards, of Mitchell; response by the retiring president. President D. S. Kelley, Supt. of Jeffersonville, gave his inaugural, which was very instructive. J. A. Wood was elected recording secretary, and S. B. Boyd and D. H. Ellison enrolling secretaries. Adjourned.

2 P. M.—Paper by John M. Bloss: subject, "Antietam and the Lost Dispatch." This paper was not prepared for the the occasion, but was none the less enjoyed. He stated that the climax of the campaign of 1862 was at Antietam. He then presented the plan of the campaign on the part of the North, beginning February 22d, and its results; also the offensive campaigns of the South, resulting on the eastern end of the great line of battle in the bloody contest at Antietam. The relative positions and strength of the armies of Lee and McClellan were then fully set forth. He then spoke of a very important dispatch which had been lost and which he found, and seeing that it was Lee's Order 191, he immediately sent it to Gen. McClellan. The dispatch disclosed Lee's *whole plan* for the capture of Harper's Ferry. This was found early on September 13th, and Harper's Ferry with its twelve thousand men did not surrender until September 15th, 8 A. M. Prof. Bloss then showed how easy it would have been to save Harper's Ferry, and how possible it was for McClellan with his 110,000 men to have utterly annihilated Lee's army, which the *lost dispatch* showed was divided into five separate armies, and many miles apart.

The paper was a philosophic history of the campaign, and contained much that might be made valuable to the live teacher.

Charles F. Coffin, Supt. New Albany, read a paper on "The Limit of the Practical in Teaching." Mr. Coffin thought that too many mistook what the practical is. Some rejected the difficult subjects on the grounds that they were too abstract and unpractical. They were mistaken in this, as the most abstract subjects were often the most practical. The paper showed much thought and careful preparation.

S. B. Boyd, Supt. Daviess county, then read a very interesting paper on "Our Country Schools." Mr. Boyd showed evidently that he had been among the country schools and saw their needs and capabilities, and gave some good thoughts concerning them.

Mrs. Alice Bridgman, of the Salem High School, read an interesting paper on "Æsthetics in Common School Education." [Printed in full on another page.]

O. T. Dunnagan, Prin. Shoals, opened the discussion of the paper. He fully indorsed the points made, and considered it the duty of all who had the education of children at home to try to instil into their minds the love of the beautiful early in life, as this would be a great barrier against evil influences.

J. A. Wood, Supt. Salem, was appointed to purchase a book for records and write up the history of the Association from its first organization, and leave the book in the hands of the secretary-elect, in which to record the minutes of future meetings.

Committee on Resolutions—A. J. Snoke, Miss Frank C. Simpson, and A. M. Sweeney

Committee on Nomination of Officers—John Cooper, S. B. Boyd, I. M. Bridgman, O. E. Arbuckle, J. K. Beck, John M. Bloss, W. H. Elson, E. E. Smith, W. A. Bell, chairman.

7:30 P. M.—John Cooper, Supt. of Evansville, read a paper on "Primary Instruction." After a few introductory remarks, the speaker described the early methods of teaching the alphabet. He then spoke of the great importance of proper *early* training. If the primary work be properly done the future advancement will be more rapid and thorough. He also gave some good thoughts relative to the preparation for primary teaching. Said the teacher is not valued by the amount of knowledge she has, but by the ability exhibited in mental training; not by the amount *she* can *do*, but by the amount she can lead her *pupils to do*.

Dr. H. Stillson, Prof. Science Southern Indiana Normal College, gave one of his characteristic addresses on "Common School-Room Diseases." He said time would compel him to limit his discussion to the subject of the eye. He suggested several important precautions. The lecture was very interesting and instructive throughout.

NATURAL SCIENCE IN THE ELEMENTARY SCHOOLS,

by O. P. Jenkins, Prof. Natural Science, State Normal, Terre Haute. Mr. Jenkins said: The value of natural science as a means of education is often underrated because of a misconception of what it really is. For example, it is thought sometimes that natural science consists simply in a knowledge of the names of things. A clear conception of the essence of natural science is absolutely necessary to a correct use of it as a means of intellectual development. Our Standard Definer says of science that it embraces those branches of which the subject-matter is either ultimate principles or laws thus arranged in natural order. We might say of natural science that its object is to explain the facts or phenomena that we find in nature.

To explain a fact is to determine its relations, the principles which it involves, the laws that govern its existence. To accomplish this requires the exercise, in turn, of the faculties of *perception, memory,* and *thought,* which include all the recognized classes of mental activity Of these the last is the most important, for in constructing a science we observe, and remember only that we may submit the products of these processes to the reasoning faculty, in order that we may arrive at the law or underlying principle. The ideas and problems expressed in natural objects are the natural food for the growth of mind. The organs of the senses are adapted only to matter and forces of nature. That the mind is also adapted to the solution of these problems, and that they in turn have a peculiar power in expanding the mind is abundantly proven.

There exist reasons for the superiority of natural objects as an educational means in the nature of the objects themselves. One such reason is that they carry in themselves constantly the means for testing independently by observation and experiment every conclusion formed. This necessitates the formation of conclusions only on evidence and correct methods of thinking. Another reason lies in the fact that every natural object exists only by the mutual adaptation of it and all the rest of the matter and forces of nature, each of which has a definite value and an unchangeable method of acting. This is more readily seen in the case of living things, animals and plants. Hence their adaptations, seen in all their organs, form a highly valuable series of problems for the exercise of mental activity. To discover these adaptations and to assign to each element its own proper value forms an exercise unsurpassed for the formation of correct methods of thinking. A third reason for the high value of the study of natural objects is that it drills the mind in the method of nature, that is the method of immutable law. The sooner the mind recognizes this method of law the more intelligent existence becomes. Of the different methods of studying nature only one should be found in any scheme of education, that is the modern scientific method. This has been well defined as the "method of common sense." Refined, developed, drilled common sense applied to the study of nature has in two hundred years brought the race from a a state of ignorance which had hardly varied in historic times to a knowledge before not even conceived. This method is revolutionizing the methods of thinking in many other departments of knowledge, and must in time permeate all.

Beside the world of nature's being managed by natural laws, our whole social and civilized fabric is woven through and through by natural science. One expresses it, "Modern civilization rests on physical science." Need it be insisted further that the method which is becoming the habit of thought of the masters of thinking and the knowledge which has been the means of so great development of the human race, and which now constitutes in so large a measure the very fiber of our civilized life should be found prominent in a list of means for the education of the individual. What dare we offer him in preference to this?

The very limited extent to which natural objects are made use of in the elementary schools in general is well known. Where they are used, often they are very improperly used, and the work is not systematic and earnest. The following would seem to be the main points to be insisted upon in the use of natural objects as a means of education:

1. To give power to observe carefully and accurately.
2. To give ability to discover true relations.
3. To give power to discover adaptations.
4. To form correct methods of thinking.
5. To beget an interest in natural objects.
6. To obtain a knowledge of the forms of matter and the forces among which man dwells of which he makes use.

These ends have not always been secured, but the fault was not with the natural objects but with the use of them. The most common errors in science teaching, each of which is fully able to defeat the very end in view in the use of natural science, are the following:

1. Studying things solely for their names.
2. Studying only books on the objects, and not the objects themselves. Observations and conclusions ready-made *prevent* the intellectual activity of making them.
3. Similar to this last is the giving by the teacher the descriptions and explanations which the pupil should make independently.
4. The sensational and sentimental methods of appealing to the child's emotions of wonder, or of sugar-coating good wholesome facts by disguising them in silly stories.
5. Selection of foreign objects instead of those within reach.
6. The most comprehensive and insidious error is that of making information about the subject the end, instead of that of intellectual development.

The method to be pursued in general outline is determined, it would seem, by the objects which have just been insisted upon. The method should consist:

1. In setting the pupil to observe most carefully the natural objects for himself.

2. For the most part the real object must be used.

3. The pupil should discover as far as possible the explanation of each fact for himself.

4. To accomplish this the pupils must be set to work in a definite way.

5. The instruction should almost wholly be limited to how to go to work.

6. The work should proceed slowly.

7. The work given out should be within the capacity of the pupil, the relative amount of seeing and explaining depending on the age of the pupil.

Where shall we obtain suitable objects? They abound. Every yard contains enough for a long course.

A list was given suggesting a large number completely within the reach of all. As an illustration of a method of treating one of these objects the cat was taken. A printed slip containing an outline suggesting questions in regard to the cat, which might be used according to the principles announced in the paper. It was insisted that the slip should be used only as a suggestion as to the manner by which the teacher was to get the pupil to study, and that in this it was not the cat that was of importance, but the development and training of the mind of the pupil. Adjourned.

April 3d—Devotional exercises were conducted by J. A. Wood, Supt. Salem. E. A. Bryan, Pres. Vincennes University, read a paper on "The Progress of Educational Thought." [This paper will be printed in the Journal.]

D. E. Hunter, Supt. Washington, discussed the subject treated in the paper. He gave an account of the first educational convention he ever attended. Said there were only three teachers present, and the only question discussed was concerning how much they would agree to teach a three months school for.

J. K. Beck, Prin. Preparatory Department State University, read a paper—subject, "Will-Power." Mr. Beck discussed the various powers of the mind, their relations to each other, and the importance of their proper cultivation. He gave some good thoughts concerning the office of the will, and how to develop a strong will-power.

Prof. R. H. Holbrook, Vice-Pres. National Normal University, Lebanon, Ohio, gave a lecture on "Independent Normalism as a Phase of the New Education." He said, and went on to prove, that there *is* something new in education. He said the whole philosophy of education may be illustrated by the familiar example, the *corn stalk.* There are three things in growth, viz., reception, assimila-

3

tion, and reproduction. The lecture was very earnest, and was listened to with marked attention.

By a vote of 37 to 32 (Vincennes and Madison) it was decided to hold the next meeting of the Association at Vincennes. It was left to the executive committee to set the *time* for the next meeting.

2 P. M.—In the absence of the president, the Association was called to order by vice-president J. A. Wood J M. Olcott, of Greencastle, presented the following memorial on the death of President Thompson:

When God speaks it is for man to be silent. In his still voice He has called to himself one of our number. Prof. Chas. O. Thompson, of the Rose Polytechnic Institute at Terre Haute, is dead. While we bow in humble submission to the will of Providence in this as to us in other mysterious manifestations, we would not forget to record our appreciation of the character of Prof. Thompson, in the which we have recognized the true *man*, the scholar, the teacher, and the christian. Therefore,

Resolved, That as an Association we deeply deplore the loss to our State by his death; that we sympathize with the family of the deceased in their bereavement; that a copy of this sentiment be spread upon our records, and a copy sent to the family of the deceased.

Miss Ellen J. Strader, of Bloomington, gave a talk on "Primary Teaching." Miss Strader insisted on constant use of the blackboard in all primary work. She said: Be accurate. Do not try to teach what you do not well understand. Have neatness and insist on system in all work. Promptness is a great essential in primary work. Teach proper handling of chalk and brush.

Miss Alice Whitaker, of Spencer, gave a talk on the same subject. She gave an outline of the plan of primary work in the Spencer schools, and described the methods followed in carrying out the plan.

A. H Kennedy, Supt. Rockport, read a paper on "Education and the Spirit of the Age." He spoke, (1) As to how the spirit of early ages had changed; (2) The present age ideal and practical. (3) Needs of having things handy and practical; (4) What does the practical man admire? (5) Origin of the high school and its progress; (6) Result of the present system of high schools; (7) Demands of of the age not in harmony with the spirit of the age; (8) How the *spirit* of the age may be made to meet the *demands* of the age.

A. J. Snoke, Supt. Princeton, read a paper on "Negative Factors in the Educational Problems." Mr. Snoke said that the frequent changes of teachers and supervision has a tendency to cripple the schools, because it gives rise to change in course of study and change in text-books. A lack of scholarship is a serious clog in our schools.

Teaching must be looked to as a permanent profession by those who engage therein.

Miscellaneous.—The report of the committee on resolutions was read by A. J. Snoke. Treasurer J. P. Funk read his report, showing a balance of ten or twelve dollars in his hands.

The following officers were elected for the ensuing year:

President—R. A. Ogg, New Albany.

Vice-Presidents—1. W. E. Lugenbeel, Mitchell; 2. W. F. Hoffman, Washington; 3. Lydia Middleton, Madison.

Executive Committee—E. A. Bryan; chairman, Vincennes; J. A. Woodburn, Bloomington; S. E. Harwood, Spencer; Mrs. R. A. Moffitt, Rushville; Laura Overbay, Franklin.

Recording Secretary—Mrs. Alice Bridgman, Salem.

Treasurer—J. P. Funk, Corydon.

The number who enrolled and paid their annual fee was 83.

The Association, which was one of the most interesting ever held in Southern Indiana, then adjourned.

J. A. WOOD, *Secretary.*

INDIANA TEACHERS' READING CIRCLE.

OUTLINE OF

Work in Brooks' Mental Science, for June, 1885—Subject: Culture of the Understanding. Pages 274-318.

I. TERMS TO BE STUDIED.

1. Progress of Truth.	6. Proximate genera.
2. Thought Studies.	7. " Par excellence."
3. Notions.	8. Recondite.
4. Notative.	9. Illegitimate inferences.
5. Marks.	

II. ITEMS—PROFESSIONAL.

1. Pages 274-7.	6. Relation of Judgment to Memory.
2. Distinct Conceptions, p. 279	7. Value of Comparison.
3. Logical Definition.	8. The Study of Mental Arithmetic.
4. Value of Classification.	9. Reading, p. 305.
5. The Use of Outlines.	10. Culture of Inductive Reasoning.

III. SUMMARIES.

1. Summarize Rules of Logical Division.
2. Summarize Rules of Logical Definition.
3. Summarize Methods of Culture in Generalization.
4. Summarize the means of culture of Deductive Reasoning.
5. Summarize the studies involving Inductive Reasoning.

IV. QUOTATIONS TO BE REMEMBERED.

1. By the power of thought man becomes master of the world.
2. Man should be a truth-lover, a truth-seeker, and a truth-finder;

and the object of education should be to develop this taste and ability, and make him both a lover of thought and a thinker.

3. Other things being equal, the man of best thought-power will be the most successful in the business of life.

4. A large experience deepens and broadens the significance of of general terms.

5. In order to become a naturalist, one must have the power of classification well developed.

6. Judgment lies at the basis of all the sciences.

7. Every truth is bound to some other truth by the thread of related thought.

8. Euclid has done more to develop the logical faculty of the world than any (other) book ever written.

9. The Philosophic Essayist has a wonderful power to stimulate to thinking.

METHODS OF INSTRUCTION.

Geography.—What is Structural Geography? What relation does it bear to political geography? What relation to vegetation and climate? What relation has the structure of the earth's surface to the other physical sciences? To history?

Method of Study.—What mental faculty is most employed in geographical study? How must the child be prepared to imagine correctly what he can not see,—such as mountain ranges, lakes, etc.? What are the three methods of expressing geographical ideas that should be employed by the pupil? After the child has mastered the geographical elements, how should he proceed in the study of the surface of the earth? What is the place of mathematical geography? What use can be made of moulding in teaching geography? What would be an abuse of it? How would you teach the location of the different plants, animals, minerals, etc., on the earth? What relation has this knowledge to the knowledge of races of men, degree of civilization, location of cities, etc., etc.? What countries should be studied thoroughly? Why? By what method?

OUTLINES OF GENERAL HISTORY FOR JUNE.
Barnes' General History—Pages 203-270.

The tales which make up most of the early history of Rome have been differently viewed by three successive classes of critics. At first and for many centuries these narrations were accepted and gravely taught as reliable history. An examination into their incongruities and absurdities led later reviewers to discard them *in toto* with disgust, as being the veriest trash and containing no truth whatever. Then it was that Niebuhr arose. Admitting the claims that the early legends are not statements of fact, he yet held that they are of very great value to the world, as illustrating the spirit, the manners and customs, the religious belief and other characteristics of the race with whom they originated. And his view is the view of the world to-day.

There is an additional reason for the study of these narrations by the teacher and the student. They are told over and over in admired poems. They are portrayed in painting and sculpture. They are common material for illustration in oratory. They are subjects of exercises in translation in school text-books. Though subordinated to the facts of history, they will be of greater value to the reader than the history itself.

First Week.—1. Greece and Italy, earliest settlement (page 13); Æneas. 2. Romulus and Remus; Tarpeia; The Temple of Janus, when closed; The Horatii and Curatii; Tullia; Lucretia; Horatius; Mucius; The Seven Kings. 3. Patrician and plebeian; Agrippa's fable, and its results; Tribunes, Decemvirs and Censors; Agrarian laws, and the Twelve Tables. 4. Coriolanus; Cincinnatus; Quintus Curtius; Pyrrhus.

Second Week.—1. The First Punic War, its cause and its results; Regulus. 2. The Second Punic War; The Career of Hannibal; Favian policy. 3. The Third Punic War, and the fall of Carthage; Cato. 4. Growth of the Empire.

Third Week.—1. Cornelia and the Gracchi; Jugurtha, the Cimbri and the Teutones. (The Opera of Norma will be of interest to readers at this point.) 2. The Civil Wars of Marius and Sulla; The Gladiators; Pompey and the Pirates; Mithridates again; Cataline. 3. The First Triumvirate. 4. Cæsar in the East: his government; his assassination. 5. The Second Triumvirate; Antony and Cleopatra; Actium and the Suicides (Shakespeare's Antony and Cleopatra, and Addison's All for Love may be read with profit.)

Fourth Week.—1. Imperial Rome; The Twelve Cæsars. 2. The Five Good Emperors. 3. The decline of the Empire. 4. The spread of Christianity. 5. The Great Migrations; The Barbarian Scourge; The Fall of Rome.

The year 476 is the date usually taken to mark the commencement of the Dark Ages—the 1000 years of night bridging between the old civilization and the new; between the Cæsars and Columbus.

NEWTON COUNTY.—A county normal will be held at Kentland, beginning July 6th. The principal instructors are G. H. Walker and Emma Cox, in connection with Co. Supt. Will H. Hershman. The principal instructor for the 2-week institute that will follow the normal is Howard Sandison, of the State Normal.

THE De PAUW NORMAL SCHOOL.

The trustees of De Pauw University have decided to open a normal department at the beginning of next school year.

S. S. Parr, as heretofore announced in the Journal, will be at the head of the department, and will be Professor of Educational Psychology.

Arnold Tompkins, a graduate of the State Normal School, and for several years past Supt. of the Franklin schools, has also been elected a member of the faculty, and will have charge of Grammar and Arithmetic. Mr. Tompkins is a clear headed, incisive thinker, and will do good work.

W. H. Mace, a graduate of the State Normal, and later a graduate of Michigan University, is the third man of the faculty, and will have special charge of History and Geography. Mr. Mace has had successful experience and will do good work.

Joseph Carhart, for many years in the State Normal School, but already a member of the De Pauw faculty, will teach Reading and Orthography.

Other branches will be taught in connection with the regular college classes.

This makes provision for first-class work all along the line, and gives assurance of thoroughness on a sound basis.

HUNTINGTON.—Supt. J. W. Caldwell is closing up his first year as superintendent in a very satisfactory manner. He and his entire corps of teachers have been re-elected. The high school will send out this year 16 graduates, 11 of whom are boys. Did it ever before happen that a majority of a graduating class from a high school was boys?

D. E. Hunter, after superintending the schools of Washington for eight years, has tendered his resignation. He leaves the schools in good condition, and is highly appreciated by the best citizens of the place. A local paper in its comments upon his services says, "Prof. Hunter has done a noble work, and for his untiring labor in our behalf we are profoundly thankful."

MISHAWAKA.—One of the neatest programs for commencement exercises that we have ever seen, is issued this year by the Mishawaka high school. The graduating exercises of eight young ladies took place in Burt's Opera Hall on Friday evening, May 22d. Everything passed off in the happiest manner. The people are well pleased with the good work of Supt. Elias Boltz.

THE Delphi public schools closed on May 28th, after a very successful year's work. There are eight graduates from the high school.

CHAUNCEY.—The public school of Chauncey, near La Fayette, closed a very prosperous year under the management of Mr. E. R. Smith, on May 8th. Nine young ladies completed the grammar school course and held very creditable commencement exercises. The diplomas were presented in a very happy speech by Prof. E. E. Smith, of Purdue University. Attendance over 200.

ST. JOSEPH COUNTY.—The teachers of this county have an excel-lent library, which is kept at the county superintendent's office. By contributing a small annual fee a teacher can thus have access to all the good books he can find time to read. This is one of the best or-ganized counties in the state.

President Jordan, of the State University, writes that he can recom-mend heartily several well educated young men and women as teach-ers—most of them graduates of the university, and several of them having had experience. Those wishing to secure such persons would do well to write to President Jordan.

THE NORTHERN INDIANA NORMAL at Valparaiso is still "unusually prosperous." It seems that the time is never coming when it can not be said of this school, "larger this term than any previous correspond-ing term." The numerous friends of the principal, H. B. Brown, will be glad to learn that his health was "never better."

MITCHELL.—C. W. McClure has closed his first year as superin-tendent with entire satisfaction to his patrons. He is an earnest worker. He was one of the happy applicants who secured a state license.

THE NORMAL SCHOOL, under the principalship of W. E. Lugen-bed, is well attended, and is doing earnest, efficient work. An ex-cellent spirit prevails and energy characterizes every exercise.

PURDUE UNIVERSITY has advertised for bids for the erection of a new shop for the mechanical department, to cost $15,000. The graduating class at Purdue numbers eleven this year, three ladies and eight gentlemen.

HENDRICKS COUNTY has graduated from the county schools this year *one hundred twelve* students. The programs received indicate a lively interest on the part of all parties concerned. Supt. A. E. Rogers is doing a good work.

ADAMS COUNTY has 20 teachers holding 36-month certificates. About 40 teachers have taken the reading circle course. G. W. A. Luckey will continue in charge of the Decatur schools. Co. Supt. Snow has been hard at work.

The Greencastle high school will graduate 35 students. This is an unusual class for a place of the size, and a college town at that.

PAY UP!—*If you are still on the delinquent list, please settle at once, that last year's books may be closed. Money sent directly to the editor will be credited to the proper agent.*

Educators will be glad to learn that Macmillan & Co. purpose issuing immediately an American Edition of Fitch's admirable Lectures on Teaching, with an Introductory Preface by Pres. Hunter, of the Normal College, New York.

LOGANSPORT.—A good judge of schools who recently visited the Logansport schools said: "They are capital. I visited fifteen or sixteen rooms, and they were *all* good. Walts is a quiet sort of fellow, but I tell you he knows how to make good schools."

MADISON COUNTY turned out 40 graduates this year. Supt. Crittenberger is marking close and making a high standard. The educational work in this county is in good condition.

The *Normal Teacher*, published at Indianapolis, is to be enlarged to 16 pages. W. F. H. Henry is editor and proprietor.

PERSONAL.

W. A. Fisk has closed a successful year's work at Liberty Mills.

W. T. Gooden, a former teacher, is now editor of the Ripley Co. Journal.

Albert H. Worrell, of the State Normal, will have charge at Cartersburg next year.

C. L. Hottel has closed a successful year's work as principal of the Brownstown schools.

B. M. C. Hobbs, of Ridgeville, has been round visiting the various educational institutions.

W. T. Field, formerly a teacher in this state, is now editing a paper in Williamsburg, Kansas.

Samuel Lilly has successfully closed his ninth year at G'port as superintendent. He deserves promotion.

I. B. Mount recently read a very carefully prepared and well considered paper on "Indiana in the War," before the Salud teachers' institute.

John G. Newkirk, Professor of History, International and Constitutional Law in the State University, will do institute work the coming season.

Joseph Carhart, Professor of Reading and Orato· in De Pauw University, formerly of the State Normal School, will engage to do work in institutes and normals this summer.

Arnold Tompkins, Supt. of the Franklin schools, and his wife, teacher in the high school, have resigned their places to accept positions in connection with De Pauw University. They are both first class teachers.

Mrs. L. M. Wilson has been elected Supt. of the West DesMoines schools. Mrs. Wilson will have the management of eight different school buildings and a large corps of teachers. Why not give women a better show for the higher places in this state?

Wm. Irelan, who has been for many years located at Burnett's Creek and is well known as a leading teacher in Northern Indiana, has taken charge of a church at Lawrence, Kan. In Mr. Irelan Indiana loses an efficient educator and a valuable citizen.

George P. Brown has tendered his resignation as president of the State Normal School, which has been accepted, to take place at the close of the present school year.

Some trouble has recently arisen between Mr. Brown and his faculty as to the exercise of authority on the part of the president in cases of discipline, the faculty contending that they should be allowed to share in deciding important cases. Mr. Brown takes the ground that in case of difference of opinion between the president and the faculty, the president's view should prevail, as he is held chiefly responsible for the conduct of the school. Some members of the faculty have felt that Mr. Brown's discipline was not sufficiently rigid, and that on some occasions when there was trouble between a student and his teacher Mr. Brown would take sides with the student. Mr. Brown claims on the other hand, that while his ideas of discipline are somewhat liberal, and that while endeavoring to reconcile differences (sometimes when the teacher seemed too exacting,) he has always endeavored to support the authority of the teacher. He says that he has frequently supported the teacher's view for the sake of the general effect upon the discipline of the school, when he felt that the teacher's view was wrong.

The board of trustees held a meeting in April, and after hearing both sides re-elected Mr. Brown and all the faculty, with the hope that time would heal all troubles, and that no resignations would become necessary.

Mr. Brown, however, has tendered his resignation, with the statement that he had expected to take this step at no distant day for the purpose of engaging in other work, and that this little trouble had simply hastened it.

At the meeting of the trustees in June, when the resignation was accepted, they passed resolutions expressing regret at "the seeming necessity which leads to the retirement of President Brown from the charge of the school," and stating that "the board recognizes the fact that during the six years' term of his presidency the efficiency of the school has been greatly increased, its enrollment enlarged and its influence and usefulness extended; that the board entertains a high respect for his ability as a teacher and an administrator, and a profound appreciation of his life-long devotion to the cause of education; and that in accepting his resignation the members of the board would unanimously assure him and the public of their thorough confidence in his ability as an educator, and in his character as a man and gentleman, of their personal regard, and their earnest wish for his future welfare."

The Journal has given the above as fairly as it is able to state the case, and does not care to comment. Mr. Brown doubtless has some faults, but no one ever accused him of being a fool, or of inefficiency. He has filled several responsible educational positions in this state, and has filled them all with marked ability. He has done a memorable work for the Normal School that he may well be proud of, and his retirement is a loss not only to the school but to the state.

The board has placed Vice-President W. W. Parsons in charge of the school, and will not elect a president for some time yet, perhaps for a year. Prof. Parsons is a growing man and an able man, and without much question will ultimately be made president.

GEMS OF THOUGHT.

Mind is from God.—*Zoroaster.*

The mind is the man.—*Tyrtæus.*

We live not in body, but in mind.—*Spinsippus.*

A great mind becomes a great fortune.—*Seneca.*

The mind only is true wealth.—*Adolph of Nassau.*

A good mind is a kingdom in itself.—*R. Leighton.*

It is the mind that ennobles, not the blood.—*Vega.*

A vacant mind is an invitation to vice.—*B. Gilpin.*

The best empire is the empire of the mind.—*Julian.*

It is through the mind the man knoweth God.—*Theurgus.*

As sight is in the eye, so is the mind in the soul.—*Sophicles.*

The mind grows narrower as the soul grows corrupt.—*Rousseau.*

He that doubts the existence of mind, by doubting proves it.—*Colton.*

A man may know his own mind and still not know a great deal.—*C. P. Day.*

The sufferings of the mind are more severe than the pains of the body.—*Cicero.*

Old minds are like old horses; you must exercise them if you wish to keep them in working order.—*John Adams.*

As the mind must govern the hands, so in every society the man of intelligence must direct the man of labor.—*Dr. Johnson.*

BOOK TABLE.

Hutchinson's Physiology and Hygiene, by Joseph C. Hutchinson, M. D., LL. D. New York: Clark & Maynard. J. D. Williams, of Chicago, Western Agent.

Text-books on this branch of study are generally written by a Doctor who knows the subject thoroughly, but who does not know how to teach or write for boys and girls; or by a Pedogogue who knows how to teach but has only a superficial knowledge of the subject. Dr. Hutchinson combines a thorough professional knowledge with arare ability to put his thoughts in clear, concise, simple language, avoiding just as far as possible the use of technical terms. His book is one of the very best extant.

The Laws of Health, by the same House, is a smaller book by the same author, and is especially adapted to use in the common schools. Its treatment of stimulants and narcotics is full, clear, and satisfactory. The mechanical part of these books is all that can be desired.

BUSINESS NOTICES.

THE I. B. & W. RAILWAY will sell round trip tickets to members of the G. A. R. and families, and the "Woman's Relief Corps," to attend a grand meeting at Portland, Me., good going from June 15-22, for one fare and $3. For all information address H. M. Bronson, Gen'l Ticket Ag't, Indianapolis.

THE MONON ROUTE do not propose to be left in the lurch on tourist travel the coming summer, and will, at an early day, change the train now known as the Frankfort Accommodation and make it a through train to Grand Rapids. There are good reasons for saying that it can be made a paying arrangement for both roads.

TEACHING HISTORY.—Topical study and topical recitation has now almost entirely supplanted all other methods, and is attended with most satisfactory results. As an auxiliary to this plan of instruction, THE NORMAL BOOK CONCERN, of Ladoga, Ind., announces the issue of a book, known as UNITED STATES HISTORY OUTLINED. By C. M. Lemon. The work promises to be a complete, systematic topic list of U. S. History. Such a book will relieve the over-tasked teacher of much arduous work, and greatly aid the pupil. Orders will be filled by mail at 25 cents for cloth bound, and 15 cents for paper.

PENNSYLVANIA EDUCATIONAL BUREAU. — *Business transacted in every State and Territory—Old and Reliable.*—PROF. L. B. LANDIS—*Dear Sir :* By becoming a member of the Pa. Ed. Bureau, I secured in a short time a very pleasant position in this institution. Promptness and business-like management characterize the Bureau, and I am prepared to give it my hearty and conscientious recommendation.

Yours most respectfully, JOHN LEAR,
Prof. of Natural Sciences, Central University, Pella, Iowa.
Address L. B. LANDIS, Manager, 631 Hamilton St., Allentown, Pa. 3-4t

The shortest and best route to Fort Wayne from Indianapolis is *via* Muncie.

TEACHERS desiring to attend a *Normal School*, or those wishing a situation or an increase of salary, should send for a sample copy of "*The Educational World.*" Address, W. SAYLER, *Editor, Logansport, Ind.* 1-12t.

INSTITUTE WORK.—Prof. W. H. Venable may be engaged to teach and lecture at Institutes in June, July or August. His favorite subjects are History, Literature, Rhetoric, and Pedagogics. Address him at Station C, Cincinnati. 3-4t

THE INDIANAPOLIS, DECATUR & SPRINGFIELD RAILROAD, which for several years past has been under the management of the I. B. & W. Road, has recently resumed an independent existence. Three trains are now run each way, close connections are made for St. Louis, and the road and equipments are in first-class order. John S. Lazarus, Indianapolis, Gen'l Passenger and Freight Agent.

DUNLAP'S "CHAMPION" STYLOGRAPHIC PEN.—A person who has never used a Stylographic Pen, can not possibly know its value or convenience, or he would certainly procure one at any price. We have used a Pen, presented to us by Mr. L. E. Dunlap, of Boston, Mass., for over two years, and we now intend to send for one of the new "Champion" Pens, recently patented by Mr. Dunlap, as we are advised that it contains valuable improvements; one of the improvements being a compound spiral spring, formed from a tube of hard rubber, while other Stylographic Pens have fine gold wire or metallic springs, which soon rot and corrode.

This newly invented Pen is unanimously endorsed by the trade as giving perfect satisfaction to their customers, and many say, it is the only Stylographic Pen worth having at any price.

In order to successfully introduce to the public this new and valuable Pen, the manufacturers (Dunlap Stylograph Co.,) 296 Washington Street, Boston, Mass., offer (for a short time only) to send by return mail, to any address in the United States, a Champion Pen, 6 months supply of ink, and a beautiful gold-mounted pencil, on receipt of the price of the Pen, which is $2.00 each for plain, and $2.50 each for gold-mounted.

The Champion Pen is the same in style and finish as Pens sold everywhere at $3.50 and $4.00.

INDIANA
SCHOOL JOURNAL.

| Vol. XXX. | JULY, 1885. | No. 7. |

THE VALUE OF CYCLOPÆDIAS IN THE SCHOOL-ROOM—THE BEST MANNER OF USING THEM.

PRIZE ESSAY.

[The readers of the Journal will remember that last January Hiram Hadley, of Indianapolis, agent for Johnson's Encyclopædia, offered as a premium a set of Johnson's Encyclopædia, worth $42, to the person who would write the best essay on "The value of Cyclopædias in the School-room and the best manner of using them."

Fourteen persons entered the list, among them some of the best educational men of the state. A committee, consisting of Geo. P. Brown, Lewis H. Jones, and James Baldwin, carefully examined and graded these essays according to a plan agreed upon, and were unanimous in awarding the premium to W. W. Parsons, of the State Normal School.

The essays were signed with fictitious names so that the committee did not know the real author until after the award was made.

The following is the *prize essay.*—ED.]

THE value of any instrument of education, and also the best method of employing it, are to be determined in part by the nature of the instrument itself. Therefore, it will assist in the discussion of each branch of this subject, if the essentials of a cyclopædia be set forth.

The subject-matter of a cyclopædia designed for general use, should be an abstract of the permanently valuable knowledge accumulated by the race. Whatever is of transient or local interest only has no legitimate place in the work. Nor is it designed to be a source of exhaustive information upon the entire circle of human knowledge. The true cyclopædia is a compendium, embracing in the most compact form the essential phases will greatly contribute to this form of intellectual discipline. The ability to investigate subjects in all their departments and connections must be given by the school. The disposition to remain satisfied with a partial knowledge of a subject must be displaced by the spirit of investigation; and the habit of patient, persistent, thorough study must be established. Systematic use of the cyclopædia in the school-room, it is held, will promote these ends.

It remains to state some of the principles to be observed and the methods to be followed in the use of cyclopædias in the school-room.

The course of study in the common public schools extends through a period of twelve years. With vanishing distinctions, the three equal divisions of this period correspond to the three comprehensive phases of mind unfolding. While the cyclopædia may occasionally be used to advantage in the highest of the primary grades, it can render little important service in primary instruction. The child of from six to ten years is mastering the individual—the particular in the narrowest sense. He is acquiring the use of the simplest instruments of learning. Use of the cyclopædia in connection with the subjects of study in the school, involves the comprehension of what is abstract and general, or the comparison and organization of particulars. For neither of these processes, beyond their most elementary phases, is the primary pupil prepared.

In the four intermediate grades, the cyclopædia may be made very important means of instruction. This is the period for cultivating all the powers of acquisition and retention. The pupil has begun to acquire under the connections of thought. The fact phase, and to considerable extent the logical side, of geography, reading, history, physiology, and other studies are receiving attention. Most of the subjects studied during these four years furnish excellent means for teaching the use of cyclopædias and other references. The manner and the habit of using these may be established during this period of the pupil's school life, by the following steps:—

1. The teacher may read to the pupils from the cyclopædia upon the subject under consideration. The special matters of

information to be learned may be enforced by repeated statement in the teacher's language. This practice will excite the interest of the pupils in the new source of knowledge, and furnish the outlines of a method for rendering it available in the future.

2. A simple explanation of the arrangement of the topics, accompanied by exercises in finding these as occasions arise, will prepare the pupils to begin the use of the cyclopædia under the direct guidance of the teacher.

3. Articles to be consulted may be referred to by the teacher, the heading and page being given. Pupils may be required to present in recitation a summary of the information thus acquired. In this way opportunity will be given the teacher to judge how far the pupil has been able to use the reference intelligently.

4. At a later stage only the topic for investigation need be assigned, the teacher holding the pupil responsible for the important matter found under it.

In these ways, it is believed, the pupil will not only form the habit of consulting the cyclopædia, but by degrees will acquire the power to use it independently.

In the high school, general history, literature, and every branch of science will require the use of the cyclopædia. It should become a habit with the advanced student to use it as systematically as he consults the dictionary. This should be required. A reliable cyclopædia is a part of the necessary furniture of every school room in which instruction is given above the primary grades. The school must not fail to encourage a spirit of investigation that will lead to the habitual and systematic use of standard reference books.

PERSONALITY IN TEACHING VS. INDIVIDUALITY.

JOSEPH CARHART, OF DE PAUW UNIVERSITY.

As a starting point permit me to distinguish between the two words, individuality and personality. That we may start from the same point, and keep together on this short journey, I take the liberty of calling to mind, what you already know, the derivation of the words.

The ending, *ity*, common to both, means the *condition* or *quality of*. *In*, occurring in the word individuality, means *not*. *Dividual*, from *dividuus*, means *divisible*. Add together the three meanings and we have, for the meaning of individuality, the state or quality of being indivisible,—not separable into parts. The individuality of any one then is that quality which is not divided between him and others,—that characteristic which he does not share in common with his fellows,—that peculiar somewhat which makes him a *distinctive, isolated* being.

The word `person is derived from *per, through*, and *sonare, to sound*. Add to these the meaning expressed by the common ending of the two words, personality and individuality, and we have, for the meaning of personality, the state or condition of being *sounded through*.

The word person was originally applied to the actor, whose voice, while performing in a species of drama, sounded through the mask which concealed his countenance. The drama itself, usually called a *mask*, was sometimes designated by the term *persona*, thus hinting that it was not an end in itself, but a means of indicating some state or condition of society of which it was the image.

I am aware that this derived meaning is not the one in which the word personality is usually employed, at the present time, to express, but there is a relation which the individual sustains to the All which the word personality, as above explained, expresses, and, for the want of a better, you will permit the use of that term in the way indicated, provided an important meaning is thereby expressed.

Indeed, some authoritative writers, Mr. Emerson and Mr. Wm. T. Harris among them, use the word individual to express that which makes one a particular, distinctive, isolated something, and the word person to express the ethical character of the individual,—that condition whereby he ceases to be a mere individual, an isolated, distinctive fact, and becomes a part of the All,—whereby he becomes a being who represents not only his particular but his universal self, an instrument through which the rationality of his race expresses itself.

Individuality and personality, with this distinction, like the comprehension and extension of a general notion, are in inverse ratio to each other,—the greater the personality the less the individuality, and *vice versa.*

Let us make an application of these thoughts, first, to the subject of education, the child; and second, to the agent of his education, the teacher.

Let us for a moment consider the child before he reaches the educative age,—while as a babe he lies upon his mother's bosom. At this period, subjectively considered he is neither an individual nor a person,—he is an embryo. He knows not the difference between that little hand and the breast which thrills responsive to its baby touch. He does not distinguish himself from the objects by which he is surrounded. His little body is not distinct from the cradle in which it lies. Father, mother, lamp, ceiling, self constitute an indivisible, undistinguishable, conglomerate, chaotic mass. The world is without form and void. But shortly his attention is arrested by that little hand which passes before his face,—he becomes conscious that he moves that hand, and that it is something other than the toy it grasps. The embryo is becoming an individual.

A few short years pass and, starting out of a deep revery, he makes the astounding statement: "Papa, I know how it is. There is something in me that thinks. And that's me. Aint it?"

Ah, my little "trailing cloud of glory," that's a tremendous announcement! You are conscious of the difference between the *ego* and the *non-ego.* You will lose that consciousness. What you now see intuitively you will lose, to find again among the fogs and mists of speculation when you have become a groping philosopher. But you have made a great stride upon your onward way, the goal of which is education. You have made yourself an individual. But an individual is "cabined, cribbed, confined,—shut in" by many limitations. You have reduced yourself to a point; we will make you "free and broad as the encasing air." There is something in you that thinks and that's you; but there is something outside of you that thinks and that is you also. That within you which thinks is a part of that without you which thinks. We will unite that within you which thinks to that without you which thinks, and thus make you a freeman of the whole estate of reason. That within you which thinks has no vitality as yet; that without you which thinks has made itself valid by posting itself in the institutions of society: the family, the school, the church, the state and business society. You have made yourself an individual by separating yourself from the universe; we will make you a person by connecting you with the universe. The family and the school are intended to make you an intelligent member of the other institutions.

And so we send you to school, to the end that that within, may be united to that without, which thinks,—to the end that your individuality may be swallowed up in that higher, deeper, broader condition of personality. By learning to obey the laws of the family and the school you will learn to subordinate your individual whims and caprices to the reason of the All, expressed in the other institutions.

The "system" you will find in the school you will not understand at first,—some of your teachers don't understand it. To you it will seem arbitrary that you are required to sit, stand, move, and perform other acts, in unison with your fellows. But be not deceived, my boy. All of this, to you, and to some of your teachers, "meaningless machinery," has the deepest meaning. It means that you are to become an ethical being,—that there is to be produced in you that condition whereby you may unite with your fellow-men in all the relations of life, and thus become a person,—a sharer in the life of the All. The condition which this "meaningless machinery" is calculated to produce in you is not less valuable than the power you are to acquire by mastering "the technicalities of learning,"—reading, writing and arithmetic. "The technicalities of learning" will enable you, through books, to master the thoughts of your race. But this is of no value until you have mastered yourself. The "meaningless machinery" is intended to give you that self-mastery.

So much for the individuality and personality of the child. What of the individuality and personality of the teacher? Manifestly this: He must be that which he would have his pupil become. "Like teacher, like school." The teacher must be one who has buried the idiosyncracies of the individual under the rationality of the person. The teacher must have a broad general culture. Undoubtedly. The teacher must have a deep insight into the ethical order of the world, which he is preparing his pupil to enter, and the broad culture mentioned will give him that insight. But why stop with this general culture? If it is necessary to know something of the institutions for which the child is preparing, if it is right to teach him that in these relations the caprice of the one must be subordinated to the reason of the many, does it not follow that the teacher should have a thorough understanding of the school, the institution which he employs as a means of preparing the child to become an intelligent member of those which lie beyond.

The pupil will imitate his teacher, not only in small matters but in great. The teacher may be to his pupil an example in acquiring personality. He may take up into himself the educational thought of his fellow-teachers, and thus enlarge his teaching personality. He may learn from the lawyer, the physician, and the minister that he who would be a professional man must, in addition to a broad general culture, be master of the system which embodies the accumulated wisdom of his brethren in that particular calling. The minister who substitutes his individual notions for the system of theology promulgated by his church often finds himself, "under the "system," deprived of his charge, by those who administer the "system." The lawyer who ignores even the technicalities of the legal "system," is in danger, not only of losing his case but of being ruled out of court. The physician who substitutes individuality for the medical system, prescribed by the schools, is accused of homicide, and if he goes unhung it is not the fault of the regular practitioners who testify against him. The teacher, whose individuality is so great that he can not subordinate himself to a system, sometimes commits menticide, but he goes unhung, probably because a jury of twelve men can not be found who believe that his fellow-teachers have sufficient knowledge of the system of school teaching to give competent testimony concerning the crime committed.

Instead of the facts warranting the conclusion that the profession of teaching does not rank with the so-called "learned professions" because they ignore "system," while the teacher is made subservient to a system, they appear to me to point decidedly in the opposite direction.

The lawyer, the minister and the doctor introduce some innovations, make some new discoveries, which they add to the common stock of knowledge, vary to some extent the "system" which, at the outset, was their capital,—but these modifications are not what make them professional men. These discoveries and modifications are, to each of them, a mere drop in the bucket. They are professional men because they have mastered the common thought of their professi n. The more thoroughly they have mastered that common thought, the better qualified they are to make useful discoveries; the more implicitly they have followed the "system," the more value attaches to their innovations when introduced.

The reason of the race has, for many generations, busied itself with the school problem. It has embodied the results of its thinking in the noble "system" which we of to-day inherit. It has posited its deepest convictions, on this subject, in such institutions as the State Normal School at Terre Haute, and its legitimate and vigorous daughter, the Normal School at Richmond.

It is true that such institutions, to the extent that they realize their purpose reduce the individuality,—the caprice, the whim, the idiosyncracy—of the teacher to a minimum; but they enlarge his personality. The student who enters them loses himself, but if he r main long enough, he also finds himself. He is astonished at the proportions of the person he finds when compared with the diminutive stature of the individual he lost.

There is something within him that thinks the school, something without him has thought the school; he sees a correspondence between the subjective and the objective. The "system" is not imposed upon the school but is the necessary form in which the laws that inhere in the very nature of the school express themselves. He does not comply with the laws of the school from necessity. They are the laws which the reason of the All has discovered in the school. But the reason of the All has become his reason. In obeying these laws he experiences the fullest freedom, for he is thereby obeying his highest self. This highest self is his *personality*, in distinction from his lowest self, which is his *individuality*.

"EXPERIMENTS OF LIGHT."

W. H. VENABLE.

"GOD, on the first day of creation, created light only, giving to that work an entire day, in which no material substance was created. So must we likewise from experience of every kind, first endeavor to discover true causes and axioms; and seek for experiments of Light, not for experiments of Fruit. For axioms rightly discovered and established supply practice with its instruments, not one by one, but in clusters, and draw after them trains and troops of works."

This text, from that inspired philosophical bible, Bacon's *Novum Organum*, suggests a sermon not more important to the scientific explorer than to the practical educator. That ignorant men should fail to see the worth of "Experiments of Light" is to be expected, for they do not reason far enough to comprehend general principles. But that educated men—men educated to educate others—should hold a prejudice against such "experiments" is almost incredible. Yet we know that many teachers *do* mistrust and disparage speculative discussions on pedagogics, and emphatically call for "experiments of fruit" *before* "experiments of light."

It is noticeable that the majority of those who attend teachers' institutes and normal schools, seek methods rather than systems, and are impatient with even the most fruitful axioms, though grateful for even the barrenest rule or regulation to imitate. Young teachers are apt to regard the very terms "Theory and Practice" as antithetical. What is theoretical they assume is impractical. To such an opinion a wise rebuke is to be found in a very ancient Hindoo poem, in which the Deity himself is made to say, "Children only, and not the learned, speak of the speculative and the practical doctrines as two."

All intelligent practice must grow out of theory; that is to say, thought must precede correct action. The workman most bungles who does what he is told without knowing why he does it. The teacher who follows his master's advice, not comprehending the motive, aim and end of that advice, can never succeed. Such a teacher is an automaton—a mechanism of springs and wheels that must soon run down and can not wind itself up again.

Imitating what another does is not *doing*, but only pretending to do. The teacher's art like all arts depends on its science. How profoundly true and how encouraging is Bacon's assertion that "theories supply practice with its instruments, *not one by one, but in clusters, and draw after them trains and troops of works.*"

No sadder delusion can becloud the brain than that broad, philosophical thinking unfits the thinker for practical details of work. Experience proves that the men who comprehend subjects in their general relations are the men who set a true value on particulars. The anatomist does not fully appreciate the structure and office of any bodily organ until he knows the plan of the whole body.

How may a teacher train a mind if he doesn't know what mind is? How can he educate without conceiving an idea of education in the abstract? In a word, what is it to acquire the teacher's profession if it be not to master a special science, namely, the science of teaching?

To possess a good education is not to be a good educator. The teacher, of course, should possess knowledge—the more the better—for, as Goethe says, "There is nothing more frightful than a teacher who knows only what his scholars are intended to know." But no amount of learning minus the science of education can make a person master of the teacher's *profession*. The distinctive possession that distinguishes the educator from other educated men is the possession of the principles of pedagogics, theoretic and applied.

The physician who thoroughly understands anatomy, physiology, chemistry, medicine, surgery, who has studied the body in health and disease, is prepared to practice his art.

The lawyer who comprehends the fundamental principles of law and justice, who realizes the full meaning of his text-books, is ready to undertake a suit in court.

The teacher who has patiently examined the history, philosophy and literature of education, who has formed some definite conception of the human faculties, and of why and how they may be developed best, may begin to teach school.

The objection that the region of speculative pedagogics is a land of fogs, should incite explorers to clearer discoveries. If we must walk in the fog, it is better to light a lantern. Better, it would seem, to pursue the divine way recommended by Bacon, and illuminate our way. And if the teacher must choose between even the visionary and the empirical, is it not barely possible that the visionary may sometimes prove the more hopeful of the two? Happier he who sees visions and dreams dreams of professional progress, than he who is content to plod on, not knowing or caring whither his steps tend, not sure that they tend any way except around a tread-mill.

CINCINNATI, OHIO.

SCIENCE IN OUR PUBLIC SCHOOLS.

FOR twenty-five cents, a person can be provided with a horse-shoe magnet. Magnetize two darning-needles by drawing them from end to end along one of the ends of the magnet. Then suspend one of the needles with a silk thread; take the other in your hand and bring the eye-end of it near the eye-end of the suspended needle, and it retreats. Bring the points near each other, and the one suspended retreats also. Now bring the dissimilar ends near each other, and they attract each other. In the first instance we have repulsion; and in the second attraction. The experiment can be varied by balancing one of the needles on your thumb-nail, then proceeding as before. Much can be said by the teacher or pupil with the magnet and this impressive experiment, concerning magnetic poles, magnetic attraction and repulsion, magnetization, induction, kinds of magnets, etc., etc.

You can illustrate statical or frictional electricity with a great variety of experiments. A glass tube rubbed with a silk handkerchief, or a stick or rod of sealing wax rubbed with flannel, or a gutta-percha comb passed through the hair briskly,—each of these when rubbed or excited as stated will attract bits of paper, a suspended pith ball, or a yardstick suspended by a silk thread. The suspended pith ball will be immediately repelled after it is attracted, showing the attractive and repellant nature of frictional electricity. A multitude of interesting facts and beautiful ideas can be shown by these experiments. A notion seems to prevail that in order to perform experiments in electricity very expensive apparatus is needed, but the ingenious teacher or the pupils under his guidance can construct almost all of the necessary apparatus. A teacher who is a success in the school-room certainly has enough contrivance to make some apparatus to illustrate a few common-sense principles of every-day life.

By referring to some work upon natural philosophy any teacher can make, with a few cents, a simple galvanic battery illustrating dynamical or chemical electricity. With this single cell battery a spark can be obtained, a magnetized needle deflected, induction shown, etc.

It appears that there can be no question as to the utility of the study of the natural sciences, at least elementary philosophy and chemistry. The objections in a great measure are from those ignorant of the sciences; especially their practical application. It is certainly patent to every mind upon the slightest reflection that a practical knowledge of the common phenomena that stare us in the face every day are just as necessary to make useful and practical business men as to know the dry technicalities of grammar as usually taught. Which is the most important to have, a practical knowledge of the common pump, or to know why we use 300 in extracting the cube root? Which is explained the most frequently? Is there no advantage in knowing something about latent heat, the steam engine, lightning-rods, and the telegraph? The gas of coal mines, and the gas forming what is termed damps in wells, which is so destructive to human life, can, with a few cents, be made even by pupils, and their properties noted. Don't these facts come under the domain and practical operations of human existence? The study of these subjects afford excellent opportunities for discipline and culture. I don't undervalue the study of mathematics in the least because I have witnessed the beautiful effects of mental discipline from rigid mathematical drill. But I do claim that a knowledge of those practical facts over which we stumble every day are just as necessary to the attainment of business power.

Scientific experiments constitute one of the best means of exciting an interest and arousing a curiosity among the pupils either by a regular class or an occasional experiment. They also afford advantages of securing culture and refinement besides the illustrations of scientific principles. Throw the responsibility of making apparatus and the explanation of experiments upon the pupils and they will be as busy as bees in hunting up materials for apparatus and in investigating the text-books for facts. Their minds will be so wholly taken up, so absorbed with the beautiful and brilliant experiments that they will not have the least possible time to loiter around in idleness and listen to the street-corner vulgarity and profanity. It seems evident beyond all cavil that if the minds of children could be diverted in a pure and healthful channel from the rough and unrefined vagabondism so prevalent everywhere, it ought to be done by all means, and would certainly be a great blessing to rising humanity.—*Ex.*

✝ MUSIC IN THE PUBLIC SCHOOLS.

BY W. T. GIFFE, SUPT. OF MUSIC, LOGANSPORT, IND.

No civilization can prosper without music. We must have it in the churches, and we ought to have it in every home. We request it at our funerals and engage it for our festivities. In fact, the more the public becomes educated, the more it demands the ministry of music. Stop for a moment and think what a set of beggars the public are constantly making of themselves on the hands of persons accomplished in the art of music. They are constantly hunting up the singers and players and calling on them for music at church fairs, church benefits, public and private charities, society schemes, festivals and funerals ad infinitum; and as a remuneration, a few "thank you's," mixed too often with false praise, is generally all that is given. If the public would take as much interest in furthering the means for making singers as they do in using them after they are made, it would not only show a better spirit of reciprocity but it would soon increase the supply of singers and players, and the necessary demands of the public for musical aid, as a charity, would not be as it now is, a burden put upon a few, but rather it might be shared by many.

To enumerate the reasons for making vocal music a branch of study and practice in the public schools, would be an endless task; but here are a few that should be of interest to all educators and patrons of the public schools:

1. The training of the voice and the study of elementary principles should be commenced in early youth. After a child has reached his maturity his inclinations lead only to that which directly contributes to his business or his pet inclinations. He soon tires of the essentials in learning to sing. He has no time to wait for cumulative processes; and if nature has not endowed him with a voice fully equipped and ready to meet practical demands on short notice, he is quite apt to yield the undertaking before it is fairly begun.

2. The public school can be made to furnish an elementary musical and singing practice to the rich and poor alike, and with very little expense in money or time. What a grand thing it would be for us all, as a people, if the children could grow up in the atmosphere of song in the school-room! It would enable many a heart to tune itself to sweet melody and many a tongue to chant the songs of love, duty, hope and benevolence, that would otherwise be listless and dumb.

3. The wonderful utility and influence for good that well regulated music has in the school-room is not usually understood by school boards and the public. Its sanitary effects, its soften-

ing influence, its recreative tendencies, its power to quicken the inertia of the school, are things only understood by the teachers and others whose privilege it is to observe all the bearings of school work.

But the time is coming, and I think it will soon be here, when the sentiment in favor of music, or that branch of the art that embraces singing, will overcome every objection, and we shall have music in the school-room the same as any other branch of study that we now find in the curriculum. Objectors may say it is useless and foolish to spend in singing, time that is needed in getting a knowledge of the "three R's;" but such objections can not long avail against the fact that, as a rule, our best schools —and by this I mean the public schools that send out the most thorough scholars—are schools that have music in their curriculum. Another fact, or rather observation made by myself and the teachers under my charge, is worthy of mention in this connection, viz: the pupils who make the heartiest efforts in music almost invariably stand highest in every other study—the "three R's" included. Notice I use the word "effort." I do not say that those who do the best singing stand highest, for this is not always true. Nature has given a large amount of musical talent to some very lazy people, and these people usually excel in that part of music that requires no special effort or labor at their hands, and in schools they usually find their names near the bottom of the record.

It is the pupil that applies himself in the music lesson that gets from it power and purpose to do his other work well. In some future article I may follow out this theme and show more specifically the great help the well regulated teaching of music is to the public school, and how every teacher, without being a singer or musician, can efficiently conduct the study and practice of singing in the public schools.

In the face of all the sentimentalism and gush over the poor saloon keeper who would gladly quit the business if he could, there are ten seeking entrance to every one that quits.

2

DEPARTMENT OF PEDAGOGY.

[This Department is conducted by GEO. P. BROWN, ex-Pres. State Normal School.]

See preceding article †

SCIENCE OF SCHOOL TEACHING—III.

IT has been said that the primary activities of mind are Discrimination, Memory, Identification, and Constructive Imagination. Constructiveness is of two kinds: (1) The imitation of a given model; and, (2) the invention of a new combination. The power of imitation is developed very early. Nearly all of the intentional acts of an infant are imitations of the acts of others. To imitate is to construct after a given model. Much of the work of a primary school involves constructing from a model. All writing and drawing and physical exercise, oral reading, singing, much of the number and language work are of this nature. This might be called mechanical construction.

The higher form of the creative imagination is invention. This power is of later development than imitation. Long continued practice in constructing from a model must precede any intelligent invention. The mind must have a large store of these constructions and must have acquired some power to classify before it can invent. Invention is the making of new combinations without the assistance of a model. In imitation in the higher forms, the model is constructed by the imagination by the aid of verbal descriptions, or something else which is external to the mind. This image thus constructed serves as the model or idea which objective construction is to realize. But when the mind, out of the material it possesses independently constructs its own ideal or image the process is invention. Much that passes for inventive drawing in the schools has little or nothing of invention in it. It is oftentimes the representation of a remembered model. The inventive exercises with colored cards etc. in the primary schools are a tentative, or "cut-and-try" method of procedure; it being a happy accident if anything of merit results. This is the beginning of invention. The perfection of invention is this tentative process regulated by a fixed purpose in the mind and by certain principles and laws of procedure that the mind acknowledges.

The invention of the child and that of a Morse or an Edison are widely separated. Discovery is not the synthesis of elements into a new whole, but it is the revealing of things through analysis. In its higher forms it involves the invention of hypotheses which are tested by experiment. Invention and discovery are terms often intimately associated, but they name very different processes.

These four processes, Discrimination, Retention, Identification and Construction are the intellectual processes employed in learning. Reasoning, judging, generalizing, classifying, inferring are different processes by which things are identified. A large chapter in the Science of Teaching consists of the consideration of the conditions and laws of these processes, as they are performed in the different stages of the mind's development.

SCHOOL DISCIPLINE.

THE popular significance of this phrase makes it name that group of influences that have for their end securing obedience to the rules of the school. There are two kinds of obedience. One is genuine, the other spurious. We will all admit that the aim of school discipline should be to secure genuine obedience. When is obedience genuine?

The primary significance of the word *obey* is *to give ear to.* Obedience is more, however, than mere mechanical hearing. It is hearing in that deeper and fuller meaning of receiving, and of harmonizing one's thoughts and conduct with what is received. Genuine obedience is therefore willing and cheerful obedience. It is always rational obedience; by which is meant that the intelligence justifies and prompts the obedience. It is willing and cheerful because the feelings accord with the judgment. Genuine obedience is free obedience. One does as he pleases. He prefers to obey rather than to disobey. Implicit obedience is in accord with perfect freedom when the reason and the feelings prompt the obedience. The condition of this desire to obey is the judgment that obedience is due. Unless one *thinks* that he he ought to obey he may not *feel* that he ought.

The first movement in the process of securing genuine obedience is to convince the judgment that obedience is due. The next step is to persuade the will to do what the judgment dictates. This is done by stimulating desires in accord with obedience and repressing those in conflict with it.

Spurious obedience is obedience secured by compulsion or affection, and is wanting in either the judgment or the desire to obey, or in both.

· It not unfrequently happens that the judgment element is wanting. Pupils will often obey the requirements of the school because of their affection for the teacher. The desire prompts the will to act without any previous judgment as to the rightness of the act. This desire is prompted by the knowledge that it is the wish of the teacher that the pupil obey.

Obedience thus secured is of but little value as education, but may serve an important office in supplying the needful conditions for training in genuine obedience.

Another sort of spurious obedience is that which is prompted by fear. There are not a few who hold that the first duty of the pupil is obedience, *nolens volens*. First obey, and wait for the reason. I remember that a school-master from a distant city that was thought by some of us to be entitled to proclaim the laws of the school, did, some years ago, give to an assembly of teachers a recipe for breaking in a bad boy. He held that the child's first duty was obedience. He recommended that the bad boy be flogged until he would obey any sort of command however unreasonable. He related his own experience. A boy was not readily obedient to commands. He ordered him to walk around the room for no other purpose than to test his willingness to obey. On his refusal to go, he flogged him until he went. He then ordered him to run around the room. This the boy refused to do, and the same process of breaking in was continued. He then ordered him to hop around the room on one foot, and flogged him until he did it. Finally, he boasted, the spirit of the boy was so subdued that he would go around the room on all fours when ordered to do so. After that he had no trouble with him, for the boy had learned "that his first duty was to obey."

I have heard the same doctrine affirmed for the government of a school of young men and young women, within the last six months, by one high in authority. I do not think that he would advocate the same *process* of breaking in, but the *spirit* of the process would be the same. He would frighten the student with expulsion instead of with the whip.

This is spurious obedience. It is mere "lip service." It is mechanical compliance without the spirit of compliance. Obedience thus secured is but little better in its influence upon the character than persistent disobedience. The latter will bring its own consequences in time, and it is probable that through the more natural discipline of consequences reform may result. But this spurious kind of obedience may possibly serve, sometimes, as a condition for the inculcation of genuine obedience. It is frequently the case that the teacher finds himself obliged to depend upon authority to secure that attention to instruction that is necessary to genuine obedience. The pupil who is the victim of passion and caprice, sometimes needs that his will be re-enforced by punishment. But this should ever be regarded as a temporary means to the end of rational obedience. To obey because one does not dare to do otherwise may be the *first step* toward true obedience, but that is all that it can be.

The ideal which the teacher should ever have in view is that the result of discipline should be a cheerful and willing obedience to law. This requires that the pupil shall form a correct judgment of what the right is, and that the desire shall be awakened to have the right prevail. This condition of mind is the result of growth. The process is a slow one, and every step in it must be so taken that the teacher will have the judgment of the pupil working upon his side. Children are few that will stand out long against their own conviction and the kind and intelligent persuasion of an earnest teacher.

In nine cases out of ten it is the fault of the teacher when obedience can be secured only by the exercise of authority and the infliction of punishment.

COUNTY INSTITUTES.

THE season for the County Teachers' Institute is at hand. It is time for the exhortation which the Journal has annually delivered during the last decade, that these institutes be made as profitable as possible. Nearly five thousand dollars is paid out yearly by the state, and probably five times as much more by the teachers of the state to defray the expenses incident to these institutes. This is not a large sum, but it is too much to squander.

How can the institute be made most profitable with the means at the command of the county superintendent?

Our advice is: (1) that the superintendent employ one good institute worker for the week, and rely upon him for the principal part of the work. He or she should be required to conduct at least two exercises each half-day, which should include all of the most important subjects. The less important exercises should be distributed among the best workers in the county, and they should be notified in time to enable them to make the needful preparation.

(2) The superintendent should use whatever means are necessary to secure a full attendance of his teachers during the entire session. Every teacher in the county should know that he is expected to be in attendance on the morning of the first day and to remain till the close.

(3) Keep those features that are merely entertaining out of the day program. Make provision for them at the evening sessions.

(4) Insist upon punctual and continuous attendance of all the members. A free-and-easy institute is an abomination. Make the institute a model school in all matters of attendance and deportment. This is one of the surest ways of securing interest. Besides, it will set up a standard of school behavior that will be very helpful to young teachers, and not a few old ones.

(5) Do not have many heavy lectures in the evening. Let the evening exercises be light and entertaining.

(6) Pay the principal instructor enough to secure the best talent available. A tax of fifty cents or a dollar will be cheerfully paid by each teacher, provided he can thereby secure full value received

for the time and money and labor expended in attending the institute.

(7) "Make things go." Let there be no lagging anywhere. If the superintendent is fully alive and interested his interest will be contagious.

THE SCHOOL ROOM.

[This Department is conducted by Geo. F. Bass, Supervising Prin. Indianapolis schools.]

————:o:————

EMPHASIS.

"The robins have come. I heard them singing this morning. Do you think they will build a nest in the apple-tree this year?" How would you get a pupil to emphasize the proper word or words in the above sentences?

THE above is a question given in an examination of teachers on "methods." The sentences were taken from a Third Reader, hence they were written for pupils about nine years old. The chances are that an *average* nine year old pupil will put the emphasis where it belongs, without any help from the teacher, because he comprehends the meaning. But the under-average pupil must be considered. Any body can teach a smart pupil; it is the dull one who tests the teacher's skill, and he is the one most in need of skilful teaching. He reads, putting his emphasis just where it happens to fal, because he does not understand what he is trying to read. He *might* put the emphasis on the proper words and yet not understand what he reads. Do not be deceived by reading that *sounds* well.

We have heard some teachers *tell* their pupils to "say the word robins harder," and we have heard the pupils say it *harder*, and then they were asked to say it "smoother," and they read it *smoother*. Then they were asked to read it "nicely," (whatever that may mean), and they tried it, and succeeded, for I heard the teacher say they were "beautiful" readers. They *did* read well while the teacher was present to pull out the proper "stops" and bear down on the "soft pedal" at the proper time. Give them a new piece and a new teacher who would not *tell* what words to emphasize and they would not read so "beautifully." This is one of the ways *not* to do. Proper emphasis comes from a clear understanding of the passage to be read, *not* from practice in emphasizing. The child must properly interpret the passage before he can read it intelligently. When he is unable to do this he should be aided by the teacher.

A WAY TO DO.

Referring to the sentences given at the beginning of this article the teacher says, "*What* came?" Every child will read silently and in a short time every one has decided. "Well, now read so as to tell me what has come." Nine pupils of every ten will read correctly on first trial; but what shall be done with those who fail? One boy reads emphasizing *come*. The teacher very quietly remarks that she did not ask what they did. She asks again, "What have come?" and the pupil says "*robins.*" He is then asked to read again and tell what have come. He will probably succeed this time. If he does not, "try, try again."

Referring to the second sentence the teacher asks, "How do you know they have come?" The pupil understands that he must read in such a way as to answer the question. "In the third, the boy asks whether I think they will build a nest in a certain place, read so as to show *what* place," says the teacher. This idea, carried out in detail, will create a habit in the children, of looking for the *meaning* first, and then reading so as to express it.

COUNTING FINGERS.

WHY not allow a pupil to count his fingers while adding? They are convenient; they are always with him. He wishes to add 9 and 8, and he has forgotten what the result is. What is easier or more natural than to count the fingers? With his left thumb he touches the first finger of his left hand and says "ten," then touches the second finger and says, "eleven;" the third, "twelve;" the fourth, "thirteen." He is now once around, and as he carries his thumb back to his first finger, he thinks "one more round." Perfectly natural, isn't it, and by the "object" method, too! Yet there are some teachers who seem to

think it a sin for a pupil to count his fingers. They say to their
pupils, "You must never count your fingers." I once saw a
pupil trying to avoid this sin by nonding his head for every *one*
he added. Ĥe added very rapidly, so it was very interesting to
see him do it. His adding might have been called head-work.
Who has not made groups of marks in one corner of his slate,
or near the bottom of the black-board, in order to ascertain the
result of six times nine? Why do we fall into these "sinful"
ways so easily? Is it because "man is prone to evil?"

"There is a time for every thing under the sun," and counting the fingers is not an exception. But the time is *not* when
one is adding a column of figures. If a person must stop to spell
words while trying to read, we say he can not read: so when a
pupil stops to count his fingers or any other objects, we say he
has not learned to add. Adding is giving the results of combinations that have previously been learned.

A child gets his first ideas of number by means of objects.
He gets his ideas very early. He probably gets the idea of *one*
first. It is certain that he soon appreciates a difference between
one thing and *two* things. If you doubt it, give little three-year-
old Johnny *one* stick of candy, and at the same time give his six-
year-old sister *two* sticks. He will protest in a way that will leave
no doubts in your mind as to his appreciating that there is a material difference between *one* and *two*.

Since the child gets his idea of number by his experience with
objects, the time to count fingers and other objects is when he is
learning the combinations. When he forgets the combination, 9
and 8, he does a very natural and proper thing by counting his
fingers. But he is not *adding* when he does it. He must learn
to name the result without the use of objects. Ĥhe should first,
in case he has forgotten 9 + 8, be referred to the "law of endings" (explained in last month's issue), and if this fails to call
up the result, there are only three things left to do: teacher tell
him, refer to the table, or count fingers or other objects. If the
teacher tells him or refers him to the table, he must take it on
faith; but if he counts the objects he gets the result by his own
experience, which is, probably, more convincing and impressive

than either of the other ways. A teacher should *never* hesitate in referring to objects when she sees that by so doing the fact will be more clearly understood.

A METHOD IN ADDITION.

IF you have board room, send your intermediate and advanced classes to it, and prepare for some work in addition. (If you do dot have this room, use the slate, or the scratchbooks.) Have the pupils to write the numbers to be added as you pronounce them; they would appear thus:

235	234	234	234	234	234	234
987	987	987	987	987	987	987
Etc.	Ete.	Etc.	Etc.	Etc.	Etc.	Etc.

When the columns are written have the pupils face you and give each one a separate and distinct number, requesting them not to turn until each is supplied with a number different from those of the others; at a given signal have all turn, write the numbers given beneath the column, and add.

The numbers might be thus: 987, 376, 768, 375, 937, 879, 675, all different. Ask the pupils to turn as they get the results and pronounce distinctly the numbers 1, 2, 3, 4, 5, etc., as they finish the additions in order. When all are through call for the results by numbers; as no two pupils can have same result, it follows that there must be a test applied in some manner. The writer has used the following test with good results, and commends it to the careful trial of those in need of a sure and speedy one: Have all turn, strike out two or three numbers that you shall name, then have them to add the remaining numbers, omitting the numbers struck out; when this is done have the pupils to take the last sum from the first one; if the difference equals the sum of the numbers struck out, then the work is correct, otherwise it is wrong. It will be noticed that it will answer every purpose to have but one number struch out; in the case of a ledger column instead of striking out a number it would be well simply to place a strip of paper over a number during the second addition, and on raising the paper, if the difference equals the number beneath it, the additions are correct.

The reason for giving different numbers is to prevent all chances for copying, and to make each pupil independent of his fellow. Try it, and if you do not like it, try something better; only be sure that your pupils are able to add.—*Country and Village School.*

VARYING A READING LESSON.

Cut from some newspaper or magazine a narative story that is interesting and not too difficult for the class to read as easily as they would the regular lesson in the reader. Select all the difficult words in it, and copy them on the blackboard, to be pronounced and defined by the class. If there are names of persons in the story, put those on the hoard also, and everything else which could be made a profitable study.

Divide the story into as many paragraphs or parts as there are pupils in the class, and give each a scrap cut from the paper, and require him to study it carefully. Of course he will have no idea of its connection with the story.

Recitation time comes. Spend the first part in reading what they were to prepare from the board. Then have the class commence reading, requiring them so to arrange the paragraphs given them as to make good sense. The pupil who has the scrap on which the subject of the story is written begins to read. The others read whenever they see their paragraphs are needed to make good sense and so continue until the narrative is completed. Care, however, should be taken at first to cut the story in such a way as to have the connection easily seen; but, after they have had some experience the work should be gradually made more difficult. The teacher should always have a copy of the complete story, so as to be able to prompt the pupils if necessary. After the pupils have put together the whole tale, call upon some one to tell it again in his own words.

For the next reading lesson require them to write the story from memory. The papers should be taken charge of by the teacher, all mistakes underlined, and the same corrected by the pupil. The exercise obliges them not only to understand what they have to read, but it is also a good language lesson. Pupils

.like such a lesson; it requires them to give the closest attention to every paragraph read, also to observe the plot of the story, or they will be unable to read when their "turn" comes, to tell what they have read, or to write it out afterward.— *W. C. Crossley, Texas.*

PRIMARY DEPARTMENT.

[This Department is conducted by HOWARD SANDISON, Professor of Methods, State Normal School.]

——:oc:——

The real subject in education is the individual mind of each child, with its acquired habits and inherited tendencies. An evident proposition, then, is: If real teaching is done, each mind, with its peculiar habits and inherited tendencies, must be understood by the teacher; with its double corollary:—

(1) The number of pupils under the charge of a primary teacher should range between twenty and thirty. (2) The pupils should remain under the charge of a given teacher more than ten months.

The second proposition is: Mind being an organism, the heart (sensibilities) is no less an avenue to the intellect, than is the intellect to the heart and will; with its corollary:—

Suspicion and severity can never enable the teacher to obtain a standing place in the child-mind.

The third proposition is: Two rival powers compose the mind—the *carrying power*—memory (the servant) and the *thinking power* (the master); with its double corollary:—

(1) The aim of education is to make the mind strong and skilled as a thinking power, and not to make it full as a carrying power. (2) The most practical education is that which sends the child into the business world with power to observe closely and to think (reflect) accurately upon what he observes.

——•——

IN entering upon a consideration of the problems of primary work, it is desired to touch briefly upon the relation of the kindergarten to that work. In the primary school the pupil begins to deal with the two main avenues of knowledge—reading and writing.

The main difficulty of the child in learning to read is that he is not skilled in distinguishing various forms, as presented by the words and letters, and has not formed the habit of applying one correct name to any given form, i. e., the eye and the ear are untrained.

In writing the difficulty is also two-fold, first in distinguishing the form, and second in making the form, on account of an unpracticed hand that can not trace the given line, even if its form and direction are clearly seen. In the kindergarten, however, the eye and ear are thoroughly trained, and the hands are regularly exercised not only in drawing and molding, but in a great variety of work, requiring accuracy of eye and hand. By means of this training, the child will, in the primary grade, have the power of distinguishing the forms of words and letters rapidly, and the writing will have become merely the application of an art already acquired. In like manner, that which is done in the kindergarten in color and form, prepares the child to observe and interpret in a degree, all that nature and art present on every hand; while the songs and games lay the foundation for music and language, bring the child into sympathy with birds and animals, and interest him in plants, minerals, and the various occupations of man, thus developing language and providing an interesting basis for all forms of general lessons.

It would thus appear that the true function of the kindergarten is to awaken and sharpen the powers of the mind, and to introduce the child to the attractive in nature, against the time he is required to enter upon the formal work of the primary school.

Subjoined is a stenographic report of an exercise on color, given by Miss Estelle Husted, to a class of thirteen, ages ranging from five to seven, in the kindergarten of the State Normal School.

The lesson given is a review. The comments following it are by the author. The lesson, though peculiar to the kindergarten, will suggest to the thoughtful primary teacher many devices for lessons in form, color, number and language in the primary grades.

LESSON.

(Teacher exhibits a number of different colored balls.)

Teacher. What colored ball have you?
Pupils. Blue.
Teacher. What color is this?
Pupils. Yellow.
T. And this? P. Green.
T. And this? P. Orange.
T. And this? P. Red.
T. And this? P. Purple.
T. And this? P. Yellow.

T.   And this?   P.   Blue.

T.   And this?   P.   Purple.

T.   And this?   P.   Green.

T.   Now you may tell me how many purple balls I have.

P.   You have two purple balls.

T.   How many blue balls?   P.   Two.

T.   How many red balls?   P.   Two.

T.   How many green balls?   P.   Three.

T.   Please count the green balls.   P.   One, two, three.

T.   How many green balls?   P.   Three.

T.   How many yellow balls?   P.   Three.

T.   (Giving the balls to the pupils)—Now I am going to ask you to name something that is blue.   P.   The violet is blue.

T.   We do not call the violet blue, we call it purple.   Name something that is blue.   P.   The plum.

T.   Yes, we have blue plums.   What can you name that is blue, Bertha?   B.   The sky.

T.   What color is the sky?   P.   The sky is blue.

T.   Now you may tell me something that is green.   P.   The grass.

T.   The grass is what?   P.   The grass is green.

T.   Name something else that is green.   P.   The trees.

T.   What about the trees?   P.   The trees are green.

T.   What else is green?   P.   The ball is green.

T.   Now tell me something that is red.   P.   Roses are red.

T.   Tell me something else that is red.   P.   Apples are red.

T.   And something else.   P.   The folding paper is red.

T.   And now you may tell me something that is purple.   P. The violet is purple.

T.   Can you tell me anything else?   P.   The goods on Florence's dress.

T.   How many think Florence's dress is purple?   (Most of the pupils think it is blue.)

T.   Yes, It is dark blue.   We have different shades of blue, and this is dark blue.   (The teacher here exhibits several shades of blue.)

T.   Tell me something that is this color.   (Holding up an orange colored ball.)   P.   The sun is that color.

T.   Now we will sing our little song.

(The children sing.)

SONG.

"My ball is like the heavens blue,
    And mine is like the leaves green hue.
Mine is like the opening rose,
    And mine the violet when it blows.
Mine, the yellow buttercup
    That holds the dew the birds drink up.
And mine is like the sun so bright
    That makes this world so fair and light."

T. When we sing about the violet, what colored ball must come up? P. Purple.

T. When we sing about the leaves, what colored ball comes up? P. Green.

T. Now all put your balls down. When we sing about the heavens, what colored ball must come up? P. Blue.

T. When we sing about the rose? P. The red balls must come up.

(The children sing the same song, each bringing up his ball on the proper word. They sing again, putting the ball down on the proper word.)

T. We have found out that flowers are like our balls, now tell me something else that is like them. P. Fruit is like our balls.

T. Now tell me what fruit is like this ball? (Holding up a red ball.) P. Cherries.

T. What have we like this ball? P. Apples.

T. And like this? P. Oranges.

T. And this? P. Pears.

T. And this? P. The plums.

T. What have we like this? P. Lemons.

T. And this? P. Grapes.

T. And what like this? P. Apples.

T. You may name the balls. P. Cherry, lemon, plum, orange, apple, grape.

T. Bertha, you may sell yours. (The pupil takes the ball, walking slowly around the room, singing.)

"Cherries ripe, cherries ripe,
    Who will buy by cherries ripe?"

(All the pupils sing.)

"Cherries ripe, cherries ripe,
We will buy your cherries ripe."

(The pupil selling the fruit then gives it to one and he places it in his pocket. Each pupil in turn sells his fruit until all are sold.)

T. Now I suppose you all have very good memories and can tell me just where each of the balls is. What was the first fruit sold? P. The cherry.

T. Who sold the cherry? P. Bertha sold the cherry.

T. Where is the cherry? P. Florence has it.

T. Florence, have you the cherry? (Florence has the cherry and places it on the table.)

T. The next fruit sold was what? P. The Lemon.

T. Who sold it? P. Eunice.

T. Who can tell me where that lemon is? P. Ralph has the lemon.

(Each fruit is found in its turn and laid on the table.)

At the time of first giving this lesson on the First Gift the child is supposed to know the form—round—to have found out that the ball is active, and some of its activities. And through several exercises sympathetically given he has learned that "our balls are round just like our heads," "our balls are made of nice soft wool," and has had several lessons on the different directions in which our ball can move—i. e., "from right to left," "from front to back," "up and down," and "round and round."

We are now ready to give him color, which is the salient characterestic of the First Gift. Through similarity in form and contrast in color we abstract the color from the form, and apply it to other objects.

In the first lesson on color, we find that in each object—i. e., the ball and the fruit to which it is compared—we have two qualities common to both—those of form and color.

Cherries are round and red. The balls are round and red.

Apples are round and green. The balls are round and green.

The lessons in the first gift *must* be given sympathetically, as we now reach the child by interesting him, and his interest must be gained through his sympathies. We would start in some such manner as this:

Ah! here comes that nice kind old Market Woman.   Let us see what she has brought to us.

Such delicious fruit—and shall we buy some and then have a party?   (The teacher here takes the six different colored balls.)

Ah! what beautiful red fruit.   I am sure it must be good. What can we call this *red* fruit?   (The child suggests the cherry.) Why yes! it is a cherry.

After selling the fruit the children must remember to whom each kind of fruit was sold, and can be allowed to guess, and if the guess is correct must be cheered.

This lesson trains the memory and offers a very good opportunity for the children to begin to classify—both by color and under the typical form round.

We are now prepared to give another exercise in color.   In the last the child could plainly see the resemblance.   In this exercise the objects are not as much suggestive, having only one common quality—that of color.   In the lesson given the memory of the child is strengthened by remembering the words, and his attention kept by watching for his time for singing to come. In this as in all of our exercises we appeal to his three faculties. His thought by the words—His feelings by the music—His will by the activity.   ESTELLE HUSTED.

DIVISION OF THE STATE TEACHERS' ASSOCIATION.

Editor Indiana School Journal:

The article of Prof. Treudley, in the June number of the School Journal, reviving the plan for a change in the method of conducting the State Teachers' Association, strikes me as being timely.   The matter can now receive careful consideration by the teachers of the state before the next meeting, so that all can act thoughtfully.   Finding considerable opposition to the division at the time it was proposed by me, I yielded temporarily.   But I think now, especially after the advantages indicated by Prof. Treudley, as I thought at the time, that the suggestion is a judicious one and that the change will be productive of much good.   Let us hear from the teachers, so that the matter can be acted upon at the next meeting.   E. E. SMITH.

3

EDITORIAL.

Persons sending money for this Journal can send amounts less than $1 in *two* and *one* cent postage stamps; no others can be used.

In asking to have the address of your Journal changed, please give the *old* address as well as the new, naming the county as well as the state.

An agent is wanted to raise a club for the Journal in every township in the State. Send for terms.

PAY UP!—*If you are still on the delinquent list, please settle at once, that last year's books may be closed. Money sent directly to the editor will be credited to the proper agent.*

Special attention is called to the articles composing the body of this issue of the Journal. Each one will repay a careful reading.

PRESIDENT JORDAN'S IDEAL UNIVERSITY.—Pres. Jordan has published in the *Indiana Student* an address which contains his ideal of a university—the one at which he is aiming. He desires to make the State University "the school of the masters"—that is, he desires to have each branch of study taught by a *master*—one who is eminent in his special department.

THE PAID-UP LIST —Reader, are you on the *paid* list? Nearly all the *5000* readers of the Journal are on this list, and the remainder with few exceptions should be. The school year is now ended, and all old accounts should be settled at once. This is urged for the good of all parties. Teachers *can not afford* to let the subscriptions to their educational papers run after the time agreed upon for payment has passed. We are sure that most of these delinquencies are the result of forgetfulness or carelessness, and not dishonesty, but the pecuniary effect upon us is the same in either case.

THE READING CIRCLE —Some months ago the editor of the Journal sent a circular letter to each county superintenent asking questions concerning the Reading Circle. The answers were submitted to the Reading Circle Board and have had their effect in determining the action of the board for the future. With but one or two exceptions the "Circle" was heartily endorsed and commended in unqualified terms. A few thought the mental science a little difficult—but this is not surprising, as the study of this subject always means *hard work*. The prospects for the coming year are flattering. Let no institute or teacher escape.

HOWARD SANDISON, of the State Normal School, has been engaged to take charge of the Primary Department of this journal instead of Lewis H. Jones, whose duties as Supt. of the Indianapolis schools make it necessary to give up the place he has filled so well.

Mr. Sandison is the Prof. of Methods and the Science of Teaching in the State Normal School, and has no superior in his department of work in this country. Having charge of the Model School and the word done in it he has not only the theory but the practical side. He will be assisted in his work by his associate teachers in his department, and thus will be added variety. The editor confidently believes that this department alone will be worth to teachers more than the price of the Journal.

INDIANA'S EDUCATIONAL EXHIBIT AT NEW ORLEANS received many high compliments. Its work from the country schools was generally conceded to be the best on exhibition. Several of the cities made excellent displays. Supt. Holcombe, who had general charge, deserves much credit for his efficient management; and A. E. Buckley, who had direct supervision, also did excellent service. The following letter from Mr. Buckley is certainly a high compliment to John P. Mather, Supt. of the Warsaw schools :

EDUCATIONAL DEPARTMENT OF INDIANA, }
EXPOSITION, NEW ORLEANS, May 15, 1885. }

To the Superintendent and Board of Education of Warsaw Schools :

GENTLEMEN :—The Commissioner of Education from Japan, Mr. Ichizo Hattori, who is also one of the Committee of Examination and Awards at the World's Exposition, makes a request of the U. S. Bureau of Education, and they to me, for "The Analysis of Plants" and "The Analysis of Birds" from the Warsaw City Schools. This is no mean compliment to you, and to the State of Indiana. If you

will part with this work of your schools, (and I trust you will), please
take action in the matter, and I will deliver this school work to the
Commissioner to take back with him to the Government Educational
Bureau of Japan.

Yours, most truly,   A. E. BUCKLEY.

THE NATIONAL EDUCATIONAL ASSOCIATION.

The National Association will convene in Saratoga, N. Y., July
14-18. The program is full of good things. The leading educational men of the state will be there, and Indiana should be well
represented.

The hotel rates are as low as usually provided on such occasions,
and the railroads give reduced rates. All the leading connecting
lines sell round trip tickets, for one and one-third frre. The round
trip from Indianapolis is $25.

The following from the pen of Dr. Harris we heartily endorse:

I have regarded the meetings of the National Educational Association as precious opportunities for meeting prominent persons engaged in the work of education. Interesting questions have been
discussed at every session; but I have never thought that the specially professional papers and discussions, though most numerous,
were most profitable. Papers stimulating to broader views, or deeper
culture, or greater enthusiasm have seemed to be of greater service.
To me the sight of large numbers of representative teachers and superintendents has proved the attractive feature of the annual meeting—I should say—the sight of the friendly greeting, the opportunity
for comparison of views on matters of practical and speculative interest.

Saratoga is of all places in the country the best equipped for personal accommodation of conventions of any sort; it is moreover
accessible to all parts of the country by the directest lines of railway.
From it as a centre one may visit the famous places of summer resort or the oldest cities of the land by making six-hour trips to the
east or south.

It is hoped that these considerations will move teachers in all parts
of the country to attend this coming meeting.   WM. T. HARRIS.

LOCAL SCHOOL TAX CONSTITUTIONAL.

The Supreme Court has unanimously decided the local tax for
tuition purposes *valid and constitutional.*

The fact that the same law in different words was in 1854 decided
unconstitutional by Judge Perkins, rendered the result in this case

very doubtful. It is a good sign when our courts will look beyond the mere letter and interpret laws according to their intent and spirit. No greater calamity could have befallen this state than to have had this tax pronounced invalid.

The following synopsis of the decision is taken from the *Indianapolis Journal:*

A case of vital importance affecting the common school system was decided yesterday by the Supreme Court. A tax-payer in Vevay resisted the assessment by the Common Council of what is known as the tuition tax, which is levied for the payment of teachers. He claims that the statute authorizing the levy is unconstitutional, and that the tax could only be imposed by the Legislature, which has no authority to delegate the power to local school corporations. The constitutional provision which it is claimed inhibits the statute, reads: "Knowledge and learning generally diffused throughout a community being essential to the preservation of free government, it shall be the duty of the General Assembly to encourage by all suitable means moral, intellectual, scientific and agricultural improvement, and to provide by law for a general and uniform system of common schools, wherein tuition shall be without charge and free and equally open to all." Judge Elliott, in the decision on the case, remarks that it is the great duty of courts, when called upon to interpret the Constitution, to give effect to the intention of the people as expressed in the instrument. The purpose of the people was to build up a great and beneficent system in which tuition shall be "without charge, and equally free to all." "We should wander from our post of duty," Judge Elliott says, "if we should give a meaning to the language of the people that would defeat what we know beyond a doubt was their leading purpose. We know that to hold that there must be for the whole state one law, governing alike populous districts and sparsely inhabited localities, making the same provisions for one as for the other, would defeat the great purpose of the Constitution. It is simply and absolutely impracticable for a general law to justly and adequately provide for the necessities of all the governmental subdivisions of the state. It is possible and only possible to build up an efficient system by leaving local school matters, under proper general laws, to the people of the different localities. The system to be successfully maintained should be so intrusted to the people of the different localities. We know it is part of the history of one of the most important institutions of our state, for we can not be ignorant of the fact that the schools suffer severely from a different system, and have greatly prospered under the present. The provision that the Legislature shall 'provide by law for a general and uniform system of common schools' does not mean that the Legislature must directly and by a statute levy all taxes for each locality, nor that they shall provide rules for every school district in the state. The reasonable interpretation of this language is that the Legislature shall by a general law provide for conducting schools and securing revenues from taxation for their support through the instrumentalities of government. These instrumentalities are such political sub-divisions as townships, towns and cities, and they are instrumentalities to which local governmental powers may be delegated. There is not a word in the entire article of the Constitution that directly or indirectly prohibits the Legislature from making use of these agencies of government in the administration of local school affairs. We have ascertained and decided," Judge Elliott says, "that when the Legislature makes provision for the government and support of the common schools by providing suitable machinery, and committing the details of its operation to local affairs, they do provide for a system of schools. Is the system a general and uniform one? is then the question. A system which grants to all the various sub-divisions of the state equal and uniform rights and privileges, leaving only to local authorities the right to govern local affairs, is a general and uniform system. The fact that there is a difference in the methods of local government does not disprove that the system is a general one. The Legislature could not devise a scheme that would meet the wants and necessities of each district. The people never intended that the Legislature should undertake to do such an impracticable thing."

The constitutionality of the law is completely affirmed, and any doubt about the validity of the tuition tax is set at rest.

QUESTIONS AND ANSWERS.

QUESTIONS PREPARED BY STATE BOARD FOR MAY.

SCIENCE OF TEACHING.—1. What are the three distinct forms of action of which the soul is capable? State their general order of dependence.

2. Into what distinct faculties can the intellectual power be separated?

3. What is the order in which these faculties become active?

4. Which should the child learn first, the thing or the word naming the thing? Why?

5. What evil will result if this law is not observed?

READING.—What is articulation? Why should the teacher pay careful attention to it?

2. Name two things that a child should be able to do before attempting to read a lesson.

3 For what is the circumflex used? Give examples.

4. Ought teachers to pronounce difficult words for pupils in a Fourth Reader class? Why?

5. Name three American poets and three poems written by each.

6. Read a paragraph selected by the superintendent.

PHYSIOLOGY.—1. What is reflex action? Illustrate.

2. What are the functions of the liver?

3. What is the blind spot in the eye?

4. Describe the pulse. How is it produced?

5. Describe the structure of a gland. Name five of the largest.

6. Describe the lymphatic system.

7. Describe white and gray nerve matter.

8. What common actions tend to injure the eyesight?

9. Describe the eustachian tube.

10. Describe the composition of bones.

HISTORY.—1. What four nations made explorations in this country? Which one is the "historic nation?"　　　　　　5 pts

2. From what country did the "Pilgrim Fathers" sail to this? Why did they come?　　　　　　5, 5

3. What effect in bringing on the Revolutionary War had the eloquence of Patrick Henry?　　　　　　10

4. What similarity as to political parties was shown in the electoral votes for Washington and for Monroe at his second election? 10

5. What General did effective service upon both the American and British sides during the Revolution? How did he change from one to the other?　　　　　　5, 5

6. What event in the administration of Pierce had a great influence in causing the Civil War?　　　　　　10

7. Why was McClellan superseded in command of the Army of the Potomac by Burnside? What was the result of the battle of Fredericksburg?　　　　　　7, 3

8. Describe briefly the battle of Gettysburg.　　　　　　10

9. What important purchase was made by the United States after the Civil War? What important commercial treaty was made? 5, 5

10. What important commercial event took place early in Grant's administration? What amendment was made then to the Constitution?　　　　　　5, 5

ORTHOGRAPHY.—1. Define Orthography and Orthoëpy.

2 What is the use of diacritical marks? To what grades of pupils should it be taught?

3. Illustrate the difference between phonic spelling and diacritical marking.

4. Accent the following words: Telegraphy, precedence, recess, European, executor.

5. What principle governs the division of words into syllables?

6. Spell ten words selected by the superintendent.

PENMANSHIP.—1. What space should be allowed between words?

2. Define horizontal, vertical and oblique lines.

3. What is an angle? Define the kinds of angles used in writing.

4. What is the unit of measure for the height of letters?

5. What letters extend two spaces above the line? What three spaces?

NOTE.—Your writing in answering these questions will be taken as a specimen of your penmanship, and will be marked 50 or below, according to merit.

GEOGRAPHY.—1. Name in regular order all waters through which a vessel loaded with wheat at Philadelphia, would pass in reaching Liverpool.   1% each

2. Name five countries of S. A. through which the Andes Mountains extend.   2% each

3. Draw a map of Ohio, locating its three chief rivers and its five largest cities.   2% for form, and 1% each for rivers and cities.

4. In what direction from Chicago is Boston? Ecuador from Iceland? Manchester from London? Isthmus of Suez from Gulf of California? St. Petersburg from Canton?   2% for each

5. Define lake, bay, gulf, strait, isthmus.   2% each

6. In what zone is each of the following: Cuba, Moscow, Paris, Rio Janeiro, Baffin Bay, Melbourne, Cape Verd, Japan Islands, Portland (Oregon), Winnipeg?   1% each

7. What is the greatest cotton market of the United States? The greatest rice market? For what is Minneapolis noted? Where is Mobile? Locate Galveston

8. Name the five largest rivers of the western hemisphere.

9. Explain the annual rise of the Nile. What are the productions of the Nile valley?   6% and 4%

10. Name the most important coal fields of the United States.

ARITHMETIC.—1. What is the difference between a divisor and a multiple of a number?

2. Show why the division or multiplication of both terms of a fraction by the same number does not change its value.

3. Time is 7 hr. 57 min. $26\frac{2}{3}$ sec. later at St. Petersburg than at New Orleans, and the longitude of the former is $30°$, 19 min. 46 sec. E.; what is the longitude of the latter?

4 The Julian calendar assumed the year to be 365 da. 6 hr., instead of 365 da. 5 hr. 48 min. and 48 seconds, its true length; in how many years was a day gained?

5. $5\frac{1}{3}-2\frac{5}{8} \times 1\frac{1}{4}-3\frac{7}{10} \times 3\frac{1}{11} \times 8\frac{1}{2}-16\frac{1}{4}=$what? Define the processes necessary in this example.

6   $9 \div 00075=$? How is the order of any quotient figure determined as soon as it is set down?

7. The duty on 1800 yards of silk was $337.50, at 25 per cent. *ad valorem;* what was the invoice price per yard? And what must I charge per yard to clear 20 per cent?

8. A man sold flour at an advance of 13⅓ per cent.; he invested the proceeds in flour again, and sold this lot at a profit of 24 per cent., realizing $3,952.50. How much did each lot cost him?

9. A tree 51 feet high was broken by the wind; ⅔ of the part that fell was equal to ¾ of the stump; how long was each?

10. What would be the cost of fencing a square field of 8 A, 2 R, 9 P, at 65 cents per rod?

GRAMMAR.—1. Define a phrase. Name and illustrate two differ-ent kinds of phrases.

2. Name and give examples of the different kinds of modifiers which the subject of a sentence may have.

3. What changes are made in the regular verb to indicate person and number? Where are they found?

4. Parse the adverbs in the following:
 a. "Tell how he formed your shining frame."
 b. "This is the spot where brave men fell."
 c. "He lay where he fell."

5. State two ways of forming the possessive case. Write the pos-sessive of Henry, Charles, Moses, boys.

6. What is an abstract noun? Show that a participial noun is abstract.

7. Analyze: "Where is Abel, thy brother?" Parse *where* and *brother*.

8. Punctuate the following sentences, and give reasons:
 a. That the earth is round no one doubts
 b. The truth of the matter it is thought will soon appear
 c. His words were these I can not be false to my country.

9. Use the word *what* as a noun, an interrogative, a relative pronoun, and an adverb.

10. Give the synopsis of the verb lay in all the different forms in which it can be conjugated.

ANSWERS TO STATE BOARD QUESTIONS PRINTED IN JUNE.

HISTORY.—1. Because for many years the Portuguese had been the most active European nation in prosecuting researches in and for new countries, which they did under the sanction and protection cf the Pope.

2. The Connecticut Colony. A Royal Charter.

3. The English government having abolished all taxes on the Colonies except that on tea—which was retained solely to enforce

the principle of the right to tax—had so arranged that the price of tea, tax included, should be less in America than in England, and sent a cargo to Boston to be sold under these conditions. The colonists, indignantly resisting the claim of Great Britain to tax them without representation, would not be cajoled into a tacit acquiescence even by their own pecuniary profit, refused to buy, and a party disguised as Indians emptied the entire cargo into the ocean.

4. They acted rather as suggestions to him to modify his plans, and as incentives to more urgent and patient efforts. Fully impressed with the magnitude of the effort made by the colonies, and with the power with which they had to contend, he was prepared for defeats, which really less than he often anticipated, were against his physical preparations, rather than against his moral force.

5. The real inventor of the steamboat was John Fitch, who tested his boat in the Delaware River some years before Fulton built the Clermont and tested it on the Hudson River.

6. The principal cause was the impressment of persons on American vessels, claimed by Great Britain as subject to service to her as seamen. The subject was wholly ignored by the Treaty, Great Britain tacitly acknowledging that she had no right in the case, to be given up.

7. The annexation of Texas was a pet measure of the South, as the Territory was in every way suitable for slave labor, and offered a flattering means of offsetting the growth of free States in the North. The North largely was opposed to its annexation on this ground, but, being made a party measure, it was carried, adding intensity to the abolition feeling in the North, and exciting that bitter and rancorous feeling which eventually culminated in the Civil War.

8. That their slaves were essentially, and under the Constitution, property. As such it was just and feasible to declare them contraband of war, and, recognizing the fact of their humanity, declare them free.

9. That between the Monitor and Merrimac.

10. England and France, having acknowledged the Confederate States as belligerents, the Southern government sent Messrs. Mason and Slidell as commissioners to these countries seeking aid, moral and material. Avoiding the blockade of the southern coast, they sailed from Havanna on the British steamer Trent. Capt. Wilkes, of the Union Navy, followed the Trent in the San Jacinto, took off Mason and Slidell and brought them to the United States. England demanded their release and a proper apology, which was promptly made, and the gentlemen returned to England. The disavowal was satisfactory to England and the moral effect advantageous to the North.

READING.—1.   Accent is stress of voice placed upon a syllable in a word ; emphasis, stress of voice placed upon a word or expression. The former is designed for pronunciation ; the latter, to develop the thought contained in the sentence or discourse, by rendering some part of it specially significant.

2.   Emphasis is variously classified, according to the purpose of the author.   Thus we have *primary* and *secondary* emphasis; *impassioned* and *unimpassioned* emphasis ; emphasis *proper* and *accentuated* emphasis ; emphasis of *force, quality, stress, pitch, rate*, etc.

3.   *Pitch* relates to *high* and *low* in the voice; *force*, to loudness or to energy—*stress* is but a mode of applying *force; rate* has reference to the rapidity or slowness of utterance.

4.   A monotone is a repetition of the same stress, time and voice in a sentence.   Example: "Bless the Lord, O my soul ! and all that is within me, bless His holy name."

5.   The principal object to be gained in teaching reading is to enable the pupil rapidly to interpret and realize the thought expressed by the words read.

6.   If a child does not call the words of the reading lesson at sight, he does not know those words ; hence, time which should be given to the realization of the thought is taken up in its interpretation.

PHYSIOLOGY.—1.   The difference between distilled and fermented liquors lies chiefly in the strength, the object of distillation being to obtain the liquor in a more condensed form, *i. e.*, with a larger per cent. of alcohol.

2.   The digestive fluids are the *saliva*, an alkaline liquid operative upon starch in the mouth ; the *gastric juice*, an acid chiefly operative upon proteids and caseine in the stomach ; the *pancreatic juice*, an alkali operative on starches, proteids and fats in the intestines ; the *intestinal juice*, supposed to be alkaline, also operative in the intestines ; and the *bile*, also somewhat alkaline, operative in the intestines in emulsifying fats.

4.   The diaphragm is a convex fan-shaped muscle attached to the spinal column and radiating to the front wall of the cavity of the trunk, thus separating the chest from the abdomen.   The æsophagus passes through and is attached to it, thus forming a support for the left side of the stomach.   It is an important organ of respiration.

5.   Paralysis is the loss of power of motion in any part of the body.

8.   In the infant many bones are represented by cartilage ; the muscular and nervous tissue is soft and lacks compactness ; the teeth are in a state of change ; the body increases considerably in size from healthy growth ; the heart beats more rapidly, etc.

9.   Various things produce unwholesome air in the school-room : lack of proper ventilation, uncleanliness of pupils, foul cellars, im-

pure breath due to decaying teeth or to disordered stomachs, damp clothing, etc., etc.

GEOGRAPHY.—1. Wisconsin, Illinois, Kentucky, Tennessee, Mississippi, Louisiana, Arkansas, Missouri, Iowa, Minnesota.

2. Cotton, sugar, rice, tobacco, sweet-potatoes.

3. (*a*) Coffee, sugar, india-rubber, hides, dye-woods. (*b*) Guiana, Brazil, Uruguay, Argentine Republic, Patagonia.

4. Zones are climatic belts on the earth's surface, extending parallel to the equator. Torrid, width, 47 degrees; two temperate, each 43 degrees wide; two frigid, each 23½ degrees wide.

5. San Francisco is situated on the western coast of California, at the entrance of San Francisco Bay; Honolulu, capital of the kingdom of Hawaii, is on the island of Oahu; Quito is in the Andes of Ecuador, near the equator; Moscow is in the central part of Russia; Vienna, the capital of the Austro-Hungarian Monarchy, is on the Danube river, in the western part of Austria.

6. The Rhine river rises in the Swiss Alps, flows north and northwest through Germany and Holland, into the North Sea; the Ganges rises in the Himalaya mountains, flows through the northern part of the peninsula of Hindostan, in a southeasterly direction, into the Bay of Bengal; the Volga rises in the north central part of Russia, flows east and southeast into the Caspian Sea; the Nile is the outlet of Victoria and Albert Lakes in central Africa, flows north into the Mediterranean Sea; the Amazon rises in the Peruvian Andes, flows north and east into the Atlantic Ocean.

7. (*a*) Copper, iron, salt, pine lumber. (*b*) Near the Mississippi river, where Wisconsin, Illinois, and Iowa join.

8. (*a*) Elevation; prevailing winds, ocean currents, general slope of the country. (*b*) Because the equatorial regions lie directly exposed to the sun's rays throughout the entire year.

9. The Andes Mountains traverse the western part of South America from north to south; the Rocky Mountains traverse the western part of North America from northwest to southwest; the Himalayas with their parallel chains traverse the central part of Asia from east to west; the chief mountain system of Europe, including the Alps, Pyrenees and Balkan chains, extends across the center of the continent from east to west; the Atlas mountain system of Africa traverses the northern coast from west to east.

10. Birmingham is situated in the central part of England, and is noted for its manufacture of machinery and hardware; Rome, in the western part of Italy, on the Tiber, is noted for its splendid ruins and as the world's art-center; Lyons, in the eastern part of France, on the Rhone river, noted for its manufacture of silk goods; Constantinople, in the southeastern part of Turkey, on the Bosphorus,

celebrated for its fine harbor; Calcutta, situated on the Hoogly river, the western mouth of the Ganges, greatest center of foreign trade in Asia.

GRAMMAR.—1. This is a compound sentence, consisting of three simple sentences; viz , "It (the time) was in Autumn," "the night was stormy and dark," and "the windows and doors were fast." Of the first member, *It* is the subject, *was*, the copula, and *in autumn* the attributive complement. Of the second member, *night* is the subject, modified by *the*, definite article: *was* is the copula, combined with the compound attributive complement *stormy* and *dark*, etc , etc.

2. An exclamation point is usually placed after an interjection; as. "Hurrah! we have won the game." If the interjection forms a part of the sentence, the exclamation point is placed at the end, and a comma is placed after the interjection.

3. Personal pronouns distinguish grammatical person by their form; as, I, thou, him, etc. Personal pronouns can not be used as connectives. The relative pronoun has one form for all persons and is used as a connective in a subordinate clause.

4. (*a*) An adverb of manner modifying *works*. (*b*) An adjective modifying *he*. (*c*) An adjective, describes his outward appearance, and modifies *he*. (*d*) A *noun* and the subject of the sentence.

5. The subjunctive mode generally expresses what is thought of as doubtful or conditional. (*a*) If he writes well, it is .the result of long practice. (*b*) If he write well, he may succeed.

6. (*a*) He fled from justice. (*b*) We hoped to see you before. The *hoping* was in the past, and the *seeing* was *present* with reference to that time. (*c*) I never appreciated before how short life *is*. "Life is short," expresses a universal truth and requires the *present tense*. (*d*) One of you is mistaken. *One*, not *you*, is the subject. (*e*) Why *is* dust and ashes proud? These two nouns express unity of idea and require a singular verb.

7. *Supreme* and *perfect* are superlative in meaning, *bluish* expresses a degree less than the positive, or "less than blue," and *last* is the superlative of *late*.

8. (*a*) Predicate noun after *was appointed*. (*b*) *Him* is the object of *know* and subject of the infinitive *to be*. *Man* must be in the same case as *him* by predication. (*c*) Speaker is nominative absolute before the participle *being*, and *man* is predicate nominative after *being*.

9. Participles and infinitives may have, in the main, the same modifiers. The participle may have an adjective modifier, the infinitive can not; as, "The reason of *John's* leaving school was not made known." *Leaving* is modified by the possessive *John's*.

10. Relative pronouns, subordinate conjunctions, and sometimes conjunctive adverbs.

SCIENCE OF TEACHING —1. The imagination is that power of the mind by which we form mental images, either by uniting different parts and making a new whole, or by imagining something different from anything we have ever seen or heard, or by forming in the mind a picture of something that we have simply heard described; the memory is that power by which we retain and recall knowledge.

2. Imagination is a power of the mind largely used in the study of geography. By it the child is made to *see* the mountain, the river, the city, the desert, the Indian, when the physical eye has never looked upon them.

3 Proper exercise is an essential element of growth of any faculty.

4. A proper development of the powers of the body and mind is education. All the exercises of a well regulated school have a tendency to fix habits and develop power which we call education.

5. By awakening a lively interest in a subject it is easily fixed in the mind and a habit of mind is thus easily formed—the same end may be reached by frequent repetition.

6. Repetition by itself takes much time when interest is lacking, and should not be relied upon. Interest is the chief element and should be aroused at any cost.

ARITHMETIC.—2. $\frac{2}{3}$ of 60 min. $=$ 40 min. 40 min. $+ \frac{1}{2}$ min. $=$ 40.5 min. 1 day $=$ 1440 min. 40.5 min. $\div$ 1440 min. $=$ .028125 da., Ans.

3. 40 A. 3 R. 22 sq. rd. $=$ 40$\frac{11}{16}$ A. \$40.757 $\times$ 40$\frac{11}{16}$ $=$ \$1666.35 $+$, Ans.

4. $1 = \frac{11}{11}$. $\frac{1}{3} = \frac{1}{6}$ of $\frac{11}{11} = \frac{7}{6}$. $\frac{7}{8} = 7 \times \frac{7}{18} = \frac{11}{11}$. $\frac{1}{18} = \frac{1}{18}$ of $\frac{11}{11} = \frac{1}{18}$. $\frac{11}{11} = 11 \times \frac{7}{18} = \frac{11}{11}$. $\frac{1}{7} = \frac{1}{7}$ of $\frac{11}{11} = \frac{1}{18}$. $\frac{5}{6} = 6 \times \frac{7}{18} = \frac{11}{11}$.

5. 6 ft. 9 in. $=$ 6.75 ft. 75 ft. 6 in. $=$ 75.5 ft.

Shadow Shadow Hight Hight

6.75 ft. : 75.5 ft. : : 9 ft. : ———. $\frac{75.5 \times 9}{6.75} = 100\frac{2}{3}$ ft., Ans.

6. Take $\frac{1}{2}$ the number of months and call it cents; $\frac{1}{6}$ the number of days and call it mills. $16 + 2 = 8 = \$.08 : \frac{1}{6}$ of $13 = 2\frac{1}{6} = \$.002\frac{1}{6}$. \$.08 $+$ \$.002$\frac{1}{6}$ $=$ \$.082$\frac{1}{6}$, int. on \$1 at 6%. \$.082$\frac{1}{6}$ $\times$ 750 $=$ \$61.625, int. on \$750 at 6%. $\frac{7}{5}$ of \$61.625 $=$ \$87.30 $+$, Ans.

7. $180° - 127° = 53°$. $53° \div 15 = 3$ hr. 32 min. 12 hr. $- 3$ hr. 32 min. $= 28$ min. after 8 A. M.

8. 124% of \$8500 $=$ \$10540, Ans.

9. $10 \times 10 \times .7854 \times 30 \times \frac{1}{3} = 785.4$, Ans.

10. $\sqrt{2299968} = 132$.

VINCENNES UNIVERSITY.—The catalogue for 1884-5 shows the school to be in a prosperous condition under the presidency of E. A. Bryan.

MISCELLANY.

LIST OF COUNTY SUPERINTENDENTS OF INDIANA.

Elected June 1, 1885, for a term of Two Years.

COUNTY.	NAME.	POST OFFICE.
Adams	John F. Snow	Decatur.
Allen	*George F. Felts	Ft. Wayne.
Bartholomew	*Amos Burns	Columbus.
Benton	Benjamin F. Johnson	Fowler.
Blackford	Lewis Willman	Hartford City.
Boone	Harvey M. LaFollette	Lebanon.
Brown	Simon P. Neidigh	Nashville.
Carroll	*James L. Johnson	Burlington.
Cass	David D. Fickle	Logansport.
Clark	John P. Carr	Charlestown.
Clay	*Mastin S. Wilkinson	Center Point.
Clinton	*William S. Sims	Mulberry.
Crawford	*James Bobbit	English.
Daviess	Samuel B. Boyd	Washington.
Dearborn	Harvey B. Hill	Aurora.
Decatur	John H. Bobbitt	Greensburg.
De Kalb	C. M. Merica	Auburn.
Delaware	John O. Lewellen	Muncie.
Dubois	Andrew M. Sweeney	Jasper.
Elkhart	*S. F. Spohn	Elkhart.
Fayette	Josiah S. Gamble	Connersville.
Floyd	*Levi H. Scott	New Albany.
Fountain	James Bingham	Covington.
Franklin	Michael A. Mess	Brookville.
Fulton	*Frank D. Haimbaugh	Rochester.
Gibson	*W. D. Robinson	Princeton.
Grant	George A. Osborne	Marion.
Greene	*J. S. Ogg	Bloomfield.
Hamilton	*Ellis A. Hutchens	Noblesville.
Hancock	*William H. Glascock	Greenfield.
Harrison	C. W. Thomas	Corydon.
Hendricks	Addison E. Rogers	Clayton.
Henry	William R. Wilson	New Castle.
Howard	John W. Barnes	Kokomo.
Huntington	*Alonzo D. Mohler	Huntington.
Jackson	James B. Hamilton	Brownstown.
Jasper	David M. Nelson	Rensselaer.
Jay	William J. Houck	Portland.
Jefferson	Orlando E. Arbuckle	Madison.

Jennings	Samuel W. Conbov	Vernon.
Johnson	*H. D. Voris	Trafalgar.
Knox	Wm H. Penningto	Vincennes.
Kosciusk	Samuel D. Angli	Warsaw.
LaGrange	Enoch G. Macha	LaGrange.
Lake	Frank E. Cooper	Crown Point.
LaPorte	Warren A. Hosmer	LaPorte.
Lawrenc	David H. Ellison	Mitchell.
Madisor	Dale J. Crittenberger	Anderson.
Marion	*William B. Flick	Indianapolis.
Marshall	Thomas Shake	Plymouth.
Martin	*W, T. Mitchel	Dover Hill.
Miami	*A. J. Dipboy	Peru.
Monroe	*John B. Hazel	Bloomington.
Montgomery	*William T. Fry	Crawfordsville.
Morgan	*James H. Henry	Martinsville.
Newton	Wm. H. Hershma	Kentland.
Noble	*W. B. Van Gorder	Albion.
Ohio	*F. A. Withers	Rising Sun.
Orange	George W. Faucette	Orangeville.
Owen	*Winfield S. Williams	Spencer.
Parke	William H. Elson	Rockville.
Perry	Israel Whitehead	Rome.
Pike	*James E. Mount	Petersburgh.
Porte	Homer W. Porter	Valparaiso.
Posey	James Kilroy	Mt Vernon.
Pulask	*John H. Reddick	Winamac.
Putnam	Leonidas E. Smedley	Greencastle.
Randolph	Henry V. Bower	Winchester.
Ripley	George W. Young	Napoleon.
Rush	John L. Shauck	Rushville.
Scott	*William M. Whitso	Austin.
Shelby	Douglas Dobbins	Shelbyville.
Spence	John W. Nours	Rockport.
Starke	*W. B. Sinclair	San Pierre.
St. Josep	Calvin Moon	South Bend.
Steuben	Robert V. Carlir	Angola.
Sulliva	James A. Marlow	Sullivan.
Switzerlan	Marion C. Walder	Vevay.
Tippecano	W. H. Caulkins	Lafayette.
Tipton	Frank B. Crocket	Tipton.
Union	Clarence W. Osborn	College Corner, Ohio.
Vanderburgh	Ernst D. McAvoy	Evansville.
Vermillior	A. J. Johnsor	Newport.
Vigo	*Harvey W. Curry	Sandford.

Wabash ....*John N. Myers.........Wabash.
Warren...........*Calvin T. Brown ..... .Williamsport.
Warrick .... William W. Fuller.....Boonville.
Washington....... W. C. Snyder.........Salem.
Wayne........... John C. Macpherson....Richmond.
Wells .... William H. Ernst......Bluffton.
White............*John Rothrock ....Monticello.
Whitley ....*Alexander Knisely......Columbia City.

*Newly Elected.

NORTHERN INDIANA TEACHERS' ASSOCIATION.

The third annual session of the Northern Indiana Teachers' Association will be held on Island Park in Sylvan Lake, Rome City, Ind., July 21st, 22d, 23d and 24th, 1885.

PROGRAM.

Tuesday Evening, July 21.—7:30. Address of retiring President: J. K. Waltz, Supt. of schools, Logansport.

8:00—Inaugural Address: President D. W. Thomas, Superintendent of schools, Wabash. Appointing committees.

Wednesday Forenoon.—8:45. Miscellaneous business.

9:00—A paper: Miss Lizzie Morden, Principal of 10th St. School, Logansport. Subject: The Use and Abuse of the Grube Method of Numbers.

9:30—Discussion: E. B Myers, Prin. 4th Ward School, Elkhart; John P. Mather, Supt. public schools, Warsaw.

9:50—General discussion. Rest.

10:20—A paper: Lewis H. Jones, Supt. of Schools, Indianapolis. Subject: How far can a Knowledge of Mental Science be Utilized by the Common School Teacher?

10:50—Discussion: Geo. P. Brown, ex-Pres. State Normal School, Terre Haute; W. A. Bell, Editor of School Journal, Indianapolis. General discussion.

11:30—(*a*) Report of Committees. (*b*) Miscellaneous business.

Thursday Forenoon —8:30. Miscellaneous business.

8:45—A paper: W. H. Banta, Supt. Schools, Valparaiso. Subject: New Departures in Education.

9:15—Discussion: Hon. John W. Holcombe, State Supt. Public Instruction; E. E. Smith, Purdue University, La Fayette. General discussion. Rest.

9:40—A paper: Miss Adda Baylor, High School, Wabash. Subject: True Knowledge and its Functions.

10:10—Discussion: John M. Bloss, Supt. Schools, Muncie; Mrs. Jennie Goodwin, High School, Kendallville. Rest.

4

10:35—A paper: H. M. Lafollette, Supt. Schools, Boone county. Subject: How to Cultivate a Love for Reading Good Books.

11:05—Discussion: D. M. Nelson, Supt. Schools, Jasper county; T. J. Sanders, Supt. Schools, Butler. General discussion.

Friday Forenoon.—8:45. Miscellaneous business.

9:00– A paper: W. H. Sims, Supt. Schools, Goshen. Subject: The Relation of the First Four to the Remaining Years of the Course of Study.

9:30—Discussion: Sheridan Cox, Supt. Schools, Kokomo; Miss Esse Bissel, Prin. Washington School, South Bend. General discussion. Rest.

10:15—A paper: W. W. Parsons, Pres. State Normal School, Terre Haute. Subject: The Organization of Knowledge.

10:35—Discussion: D. D. Luke, Supt. Schools, Ligonier; R. I. Hamilton, Supt. Schools, Anderson. General discussion. Miscellaneous business.

NOTE.—The papers are limited to 30 minutes, and discussions to 10 minutes.

HOTEL RATES.—Island Park House and Assembly Hotel, $1.50 per day, or when two persons occupy the same room $1.25 per day. Spring Beach Hotel $2.00 for any time less than a week, or $9.00 per week.

RAILWAYS.—The Grand Rapids & Indiana Railway and connecting lines will sell return trip tickets for one fare and a third.

Island Park is the most delightful summer resort in the West, and it is confidently hoped that the attractive influences of this beautiful place, combined with the attractions presented in the program, will serve to bring together a very large and enthusiastic gathering of teachers from the northern part of the state. The Island Park Assembly will also be in session, and will offer to the teachers afternoon and evening lectures by some of the best talent in the field.

T. B. SWARTZ, Ch'n Ex. Com. N. I. T. A.

ELKHART, IND.

PURDUE UNIVERSITY.—The *eleventh* commencement of this institution was held on June *11th*, with *eleven* graduates. After the delivery of the orations—which showed fine thought and good expression, State Supt. Holcombe delivered a brief but unusually appropriate and suggestive address. This was followed by the presentation of the diplomas by President Smart in a neat speech. On Thursday evening Pres. Smart gave his annual reception, which was largely attended by the faculty and students. The faculty numbers seventeen members, with four assistants. Enrollment the past year: College, 127; Preparatory, 132; total, 259.

Fort Wayne graduated twenty from its high school and twelve from its training school.

QUERY.—When did the Civil Year begin in September? When was it changed? Who will answer?

The Terre Haute Literary Club have published a "memorial" to Chas. O. Thompson, in pamphlet form.

STATE NORMAL SCHOOL.—A good judge who attended the commencement exercises of this school says they were the best performances of the kind he ever listened to.

A tri-county normal will be held at Gosport. J. H. Henry, Supt. of Morgan county; W. S. Williams, Supt. of Owen county, and L. B. Griffin of Mooresville are the principal teachers. Six weeks, beginning July 13th.

"The Stenograph" is a machine for writing "short-hand." It easily beats the most rapid short-hand reporter. The machine is simple and can be easily mastered. Its use is taught in the Indianapolis Business University.

TERRE HAUTE.—The high school graduated 21, and the commencement occasion was one long to be remembered. The school is very large and very popular. W. W. Byers is Prin., and W. H. Wiley still holds the reins as Supt.

VALPARAISO NORMAL SCHOOL AND BUSINESS INSTITUTE is averaging over *1200* in attendance. It is always "booming." The phenomenal success of this school can only be explained on the score of merit. H. B. Brown is the power behind the throne.

The convention of county superintendents that met June 29th and 30th was one of the largest ever held in the state. *Sixty-three* responded to the first roll-call. The new superintendents on the whole improved the average of the convention, and the meeting as the Journal goes to press promises to be a most profitable one.

SOUTHERN INDIANA NORMAL COLLEGE.—This institution is located at Mitchell, and is one of the most prosperous schools in the state. The attendance is good, the interest is excellent, the energy of the teachers is unsurpassed, and the harmony complete. W. E. Lugenbeel, the President, is an active, energetic, effective instructor.

RICHMOND NORMAL SCHOOL.—The closing exercises of the Richmond Normal School took place in the First Baptist Church June 11th and 12th. The class numbers sixteen. An unusually fine selection of subjects, which were very creditably discussed. The certificates were presented and an excellent address made by Co. Supt. J. C. Macpherson. A valuable feature of this school is the access of its pupils to a library of over 12,000 volumes.

HUNTINGTON.— A crowd 1200 strong greeted the Huntington high school class of '85, June 18th, the occasion being the commencement exercises of the largest class (11 boys and 5 girls—16 in all) ever graduated. That the audience remained almost unbroken from 8 to 11¼ P. M. is evidence of the interest manifested. Miss Emma Purviance, of the above class, attended school from the primary department through a course of 12 years, and during all that time was never absent or tardy. Is there a case in the state that equals Miss Emma's record? J. W. Caldwell is superintendent.

PERSONAL.

D. W. Thomas still holds the fort at Wabash.

A. Whiteleather has been re-elected at Bourbon.

A. W. Dunkle will continue in charge at Delphi.

G. G. Manning has again been endorsed at Peru.

W. O. Warrick will remain next year at Worthington.

L. A. Canada is teaching in the high school at Winchester.

A. J. Johnson, of Southport, is to take the Milton schools.

G. F. Kenaston has been continued at the head at Attica.

E. H. Butler seems to be a fixture as Supt. at Winchester.

W. H. Sims will enter his second year as Supt. at Goshen.

J. F. Martin will have charge at Greenfield again next year.

K. Vander Maaten will be principal of the Portland high school.

John P. Mather will engineer the schools another year at Warsaw.

J. M. McBroom will remain at the head of the Edinburg high school.

Elias Boltz has been retained as superintendent of the Mishawaka schools.

Dr. J. S. Irwin has been re-elected at Fort Wayne—just as we expected.

R. I. Hamilton will continue to enforce the "Hamiltonian system" at Anderson.

W. P. Shannon will remain in charge of the Greensburg schools another year.

J. C. Eagle has been re-elected Supt. of the Edinburg schools for a seventh year.

J. K. Walts is about 14 years old at Logansport, and has arranged for another year.

Charles Hewett seems to have a life lease on the Knightstown schools, and yet was never known to attend an educational meeting out of his own town.

A. D. Moffitt is principal of the new normal school to be located at Worthington.

A. Jones has been elected principal of the Zionsville schools for the coming year.

W. W. Wirt will serve his second year as superintendent of the Portland schools.

John H. Bobbitt was elected Supt. of the Decatur county schools for the fourth time.

John M. Bloss has been re-elected Supt. of the Muncie schools by unanimous consent.

J. C. Black closed a very successful year as principal of the Logansport high school.

C. W. Harvey has done so well at New Castle that he has been re-elected for another year.

J. C. Gregg, after a second business rest, has again been re-elected to take charge of the Brazil schools.

C. H. Wood, the new Supt. of the New Harmony schools, has just closed a successful normal at Winchester.

R. W. Wood, last year of Milton, Wayne Co., has been elected superintendent of the schools of Jeffersonville.

James Du Shane remains in charge of the South Bend schools— with Charles Bartlett principal of the high school.

F. S. Caldwell, of New Amsterdam, has been elected Supt. of the Winchester high school *vice* C. H. Wood, resigned.

J. D. White, a leading teacher of Decatur county, received a state certificate at the late examination by the State Board.

✓ W. N. Brown, of the Indianapolis high school, has been elected Assistant Professor of Mathematics in De Pauw University.

John Goodison, well known to many teachers in Northern Indiana, has accepted a place in the Michigan State Normal School.

J. B. Starr has been promoted from the principalship of a ward building to the superintendency of the New Albany schools.

P. H. Kirsch, a graduate of the State Normal, late superintendent at Rensselaer, has been elected Supt. of the Franklin schools.

Wallace C. Palmer has been promoted from the principalship of the high school to the superintendency of the Columbia City schools.

J. M. Olcott has completed a successful year's work as Supt. of the schools at Greencastle, and has been re-elected for next year.

W. A. Bowles, formerly Supt. of the Shelbyville schools, is now Supt. of schools at Dallas, Texas. Of course he is doing good work.

T. J. Sanders, Supt. of the Butler schools, who recently received a state license, is hard at work studying for a degree at the Wooster, Ohio, University.

A. C. Goodwin, for many years superintendent of Clark county, has been re-elected superintendent of the Owensboro, Ky., schools.

W. C. Barnhart, well known in Indiana, has been re-elected Supt. of the Mt. Vernon, Ill., schools, and heartily endorsed by the best citizens.

J. T. Merrill has been in the Lafayette schools about twenty years, most of the time as superintendent. He is the oldest superintendent in the State.

Prof. J. C. Ridpath, Vice-President of De Pauw University, has tendered his resignation and will devote himself to writing a "History of the World."

D. M. Nelson has been unanimously re-elected Supt. of Jasper county schools. This is a deserved compliment to an energetic and thorough man.

S. S. Parr, Principal of the De Pauw Normal School, has sold his Minnesota Educational paper, and will devote himself entirely to the school work.

O. C. Charlton, of Lebanon, who received a state certificate at the last examination, has been elected Professor of Natural Science, of Ottowa University, Kansas.

W. B. Powell, for many years Supt. of the Aurora, Ill., schools, and author of "How to Talk" and "How to Write," has recently been elected Supt. of the schools of Washington City.

Supt. B. F. Johnson, of Benton county, has been re-elected by a board of opposite politics and when the struggle was a warm one. This is a deserved compliment to a faithful and competent man.

In Tippecanoe county the trustees seem to believe in civil service reform, *i. e.*, when you have a good man, hold on to him. W. H. Caulkins has been the *fifth* time re-elected county superintendent.

Dr. Lemuel Moss, late President of the State University, is now located in Chicago as secretary of a manufacturing company. He has sold his magnificent library of 2700 volumes to Judge D. P. Baldwin, of Logansport.

Lewis H. Jones, who was in April re-elected superintendent of the Indianapolis schools, has recently had his salary advanced from $2500 to $2750 for the coming year. This is *substantial* proof that Mr. Jones is filling the bill

Charles F. Coffin, for several years past Supt. of the New Albany schools, has tendered his resignation, with a view of entering the legal profession. Mr. Coffin is comparatively a young man, and has rapidly advanced to a high place in the profession. It is to be regretted, from an educational stand-point, that he has decided to change his line of work. He is capable of making a success in any field of work he may choose.

E. C. White, Supt. at Albion, was offered the schools at Carthage, Mo., but the Albion people acted wisely and raised his salary and retained him for home consumption. Good. Mr. White has just issued a little book, a cut from which can be seen on cover page.

W. B. Flick, who has been elected superintendent of Marion county, has not been engaged in active school work for several years, but was formerly one of the best teachers in the county. Having served as trustee in the interregnum he has not lost his interest in the work.

D. E. Hunter, as superintendent, gave an annual address to the Washington high school, May 24th. His subject was, as usual, a unique one—"A lesson from the hymn book." The history of the origin of many of our oldest and best hymns, as well as the lessons derived, are both interesting and profitable study.

J. A. Wood, after eight years' service as superintendent of the schools at Washington, Ind., will locate in Kansas next year. J. M. Bridgman is promoted from the principalship of the high school to fill the vacancy created by Mr. Wood's retirement, and Mrs. Alice Bridgman will have charge of the Washington high school.

Rev. L. G Hay, of Indianapolis, an old-time teacher, for many years a missionary in India, for several years past a business man, and always a christian gentleman, has accepted the principalship of a seminary for young ladies at Terre Haute, to be opened next fall under the auspices of the Presbyterian church. As this is the only school of the class in Indiana it should be well patronized.

H. S. Tarbell, for many years the efficient Superintendent of the Indianapolis schools, at the close of his first year as Superintendent of the Providence, R. I., schools, has been re-elected, and had his salary advanced from $3000 to $4000. One of his daughters, Miss Leria, is a teacher in the State Normal School of Rhode Island, and the other at the Graylock Boys' Institute at South Williamstown, Massachusetts.

Geo. P. Brown, who has just resigned the presidency of the State Normal School, has not yet determined his course for the immediate future. While he has in view some literary work, he may for a time engage in something that will give more activity, and thus recuperate his health. It is pleasant to note the confidence of the trustees as expressed in their resolution when his resignation was accepted. It is also pleasant to note (and it must be a source of pleasure to Mr. Brown,) that the great body of students who have come in contact with him hold in high regard and appreciate the service he has rendered them. Mr. Brown has done a valuable work for the normal and for the state at large which is highly appreciated and will not be forgotten.

W. W. Parsons has been unanimously elected President of the State Normal School *vice* Geo. P. Brown, resigned. It is rather remarkable that the trustees, the faculty, the students, and the alumni of the institution, and the leading teachers of the state were almost a unit in favor of Mr. Parsons for the place. This action insures the continuance of the high standing of the school, which for strictly professional work has no superior and few equals in the United States. Mr. Parsons is a graduate of both the regular and the advance course of the school, and besides a few years of successful experience outside, has been a teacher in the school for the past twelve years. For the last two years he has been vice-president. He, therefore, knows thoroughly the work and the spirit of the school, and is in hearty sympathy with its plan, scope, and aim. His success is insured from the beginning.

BOOK TABLE.

How to Build a House is the the title of a little pamphlet containing a good variety of designs for houses, published by George W. Ogilvie, 230 Lake Street, Chicago.

Biographical and Literary Games with Cards, by Walter Wallace, of Columbus, Ind.

Mr. Wallace has arranged these cards and planned these games in such a manner as to teach about 500 different facts. He desires to secure agents for the sale of the cards.

Writing and Drawing Charts for Schools and Families, published by Fink & Adams, Portland, Ind.

These charts contain the principles and elements of these subjects carefully and systematically arranged, and must be of help to both teacher and student.

The *Blue Book*, giving a list of all the cities and towns of Indiana, with the names of the township trustee, the school board, superintendent and teachers, together with the salaries paid, is a very useful little book. It names "*probable* vacancies." The arrangement of the book is not so good as it might be, but still it gives valuable information pertaining to schools and teachers in good form. T. A. De Weese, of South Bend, Ind., is the author and publisher.

The Power and Authority of School Officers and Teachers in the Management of Public Schools. New York: Harper & Brothers: W. J. Button, Chicago, Western Agent.

The above is a collection of decisions bearing upon the powers and authority of school officers and teachers. The facts of each case are stated, and then the opinion of the court is given. The cases cover the whole field of school work. The book will be of use to any one connected with schools, and it will be of special value to school officers.

Saddler's Hand-Book of Arithmetic, by W. H. Saddler, 6 & 8 N. Charles Street, Baltimore, Md.

This book contains the greatest number of problems of any book we have seen. There are more than 5000 problems in the book. Instead of lengthy rules, solutions and definitions, inductive questions are substituted. It seems to be a step in the right direction to break up the habit of solving problems by *sample*. The book is not a self-instructor: it needs to be accompanied by a live, wide-awake teacher.

Elements of Natural Philosophy, by Elroy M. Avery, Ph. D. New York: Sheldon & Co. Alex. Forbes, Chicago, Western Agent.

This has been regarded as one of the best books on the subject since its publication six years ago; but in order to use every new thought and be up to the times in every particular, the author has carefully revised the entire book. The entire chapter on Electricity and Magnetism has been rewritten, and it is safe to say that no elementary treatise stands ahead of it. The book is fully and aptly illustrated, and with its added chapter on the Relation of Electricity to Heat and Mechanical Work, leaves nothing to be added. It must be seen to be appreciated. Sample copies for examination 75 cts.

Pestalozzi's Leonard and Gertrude is the title of a small volume which has been added by Ginn, Heath & Co. to their series of Educational Classics.

It is a greatly abridged translation of an epoch-making book, the first edition of which was printed in 1781. In the century which has elapsed since its first publication the attention of teachers has been increasingly attracted to its remarkable author and the fundamental principles he enunciated. Those not familiar with the language of the original will rejoice that this well made and inexpensive translation places within their reach the opportunity of studying some of Pestalozzi's ideas in regard to educational questions. The position which he has given Gertrude in the small community of Bonnal (which typifies the world) ought to gratify those who claim the most for women.

BUSINESS NOTICES.

The C. C. & I. ("Bee Line") Railway will sell round trip tickets to the National Teachers' Association at Saratoga at $25, good till August 31st, and allow a stop over at Niagara Falls. This is the shortest, quickest, and best route East.

THE NEW DECATUR ROUTE.—Solid trains between Indianapolis and Peoria, including Pullman Palace Sleeping and Reclining Chair Cars at reduced rates. This is the quickest line and is always on time. The shortest possible route to Kansas City, with only one change of cars. For lowest fares and full information apply to Newby & Jordan, agents, I. D. & S. R'y, 136 South Illinois street, Indianapolis. 7-tf

AMHERST COLLEGE Summer School of Languages.—Begins on Monday, July 6th, and continues five weeks. Superior advantages for the acquisition of Foreign Languages. Twelve Departments—Nineteen Teachers. Religious Service in French on Sunday. Location one of the most beautiful and healthful in New England. Tuition $15.00. For information and program, address Prof. W. L. MONTAGUE, Amherst College, Amherst, Mass.

EXCURSION RATES FOR FOURTH OF JULY, 1885.—The C, St. L. & P., J., M. & I., and I. &. V. Railroads will sell cheap excursion tickets to and from all stations on their respective lines, on July 2d, 3d and 4th, good to return until July 6th, inclusive. This will be an excellent opportunity afforded the people living along the roads named above to visit friends at a distance, or form pic-nic or excursion parties for the purpose of enjoying the Nation's Birthday.

CEDAR LAKE, IND.—For information of those who have never visited this charming resort, will state that it is located on the line of the Monon Route, L., N. A. & C. R'y, 38 miles south of Chicago, and is a beautiful sheet of water—fed by springs and surrounded by a magnificent grove of oak and maple trees—alive with game fish, such as bass and pickerel. There are good hotel accommodations. There are plenty of row-boats and several small steamers on the lake, and the dancing platforms, swings, etc., are in first-class condition. Round trip tickets from Indianapolis, $4.35, good for seven days; at $5 85, tickets good until October 31, 1885.

INDIANA
SCHOOL JOURNAL.

| Vol. XXX. | AUGUST, 1885. | No. 8. |

THE MORAL EDUCATION OF THE YOUNG.

[Address delivered before the last State Teachers' Association.]

REV. O. C. McCULLOCH.

THIS subject which I am to present to you,—the moral education of the young,—is one peculiarly related to educational associations. It is one in which I am interested as a teacher with you, standing upon the same platform, recognizing you, like myself, as one of the graces. You remember there were originally three graces, now there are four. Originally there were medicine, law, and the ministry, to which we now admit, very gladly admit, the teacher. And so I stand upon the same platform with you interested in the young. The moral educa tion of the young certainly belongs to a complete school system. This is true, because you have the children so much of their time, because the common school system is one of the institutions of the land, because it is absolutely impossible to develop the mind without instructing in morals. We may analyze the human mind according to the best received system of psychology; we may map out the mind very much as Spurzheim pictures faculties on the exterior of the head, or as Ferrier localizes the functions of the brain; we may say there is an education of the intellect, an education of the feelings, and an education of the will; but after all nature recognizes no such divisions; these are only conveniences. Human nature acts as a whole. You can not touch one without touching all. "Touch but one," says Whittier, "of the thousand strings of life, and the jarring note will fun through all." It would be impossible, then, for any school system to avoid teaching in some way morals or immorals to the young. The very neglect to teach them would be an immoral teaching. But I am happy in saying that it seems to me that the common school system of this country is one of the most potent forces in the moral education of the young. * * *

I most certainly believe that instruction in promptitude, punctuality, correct thinking and statement, in self-control and in social equality are most valuable in the moral education of the young. But beyond that, I should say that the schools fail to emphasize this as a part of their duty. It is taken up, you may say, indirectly, almost unconsciously, incidentally; not as a direct thing. It will hardly be assumed that the function of the school as commonly understood is to teach right and wrong as to their distinctions, is to make felt the binding obligation of right. Yet I can hardly see how this teaching of morals can be left out, because, if this were not so, we should simply educate a faculty and not the whole man. The intellect has no moral quality in itself. We know this, that it is possible to educate a good burglar, that it is possible to educate one so that he will be able to use the last results of scientific thought, and yet be a bad man, when the emphasis is laid on that. Therefore it would seem to be important that those to whom is committed such great responsibilities and trust on the part of the public should see to it that these years are not spent in such a way that when scholars are turned out upon society they become part of a criminal class, but rather that graduation from a public institution shall inferentially carry with it the thought, Here is a good man; here is a good woman; for, you remember, Matthew Arnold said, "Conduct is three fourths of life." Yes, that is so, and the one thing that we are concerned with as citizens, as members of society is how our men and women act. We will allow the largest divergence, if you please, of religious opinion; we are content that society shall divide itself up into political parties *ad libitum*, but we must have observance of law and a recognition of obligation, speaking truth one with another. We must have personal purity; we must have self-control; we must have a recognition of the rights of others in person and property. Therefore it seems to me if, turning over to you this vast amount of money to educate our children and intrusting these souls to you in their pliable condition, you do not give our boys and girls education in the science of conduct, so that they will as by an instinct do the right thing and hate the wrong thing, we have illy spent the money and have done injustice to ourselves in trusting you with our children.

If I were to criticise the development of this age, I should say that it had cultivated what I call sympathetic emotion, and had neglected the moral education of its young. Let me explain this. Christianity entered the world and its gift to it was sympathetic emotion. Imaginatively it entered into every heart, it took upon itself the sorrow and the suffering of everything. "Do unto others," it says, "as you would that they should do unto you." This peculiarity of sympathetic imagination, reading another person's life as you read your own by the power of sympathy, is the secret,—one of the secrets of Jesus Christ; a delicate consideration for others' feelings, a sense of obligation on the part of the strong to care for the weak. He entered the world with this thought, and now for eighteen hundred years, this thought of sympathetic emotion has been part of our mind and of our heart until every Christmas tide it wells up into a great feeling. We can not bear to think that we sit at any table over-loaded when others are hungry, or that pleasure is in our hearts when others are sad; and to the extent that we know a need, we feel a certain obligation to meet it. Even when we do not know of it, the great undefined mass of sorrow and ill and evil in the world rolls over upon our sensitive souls, and we search out the cause which we know not. Now this emphasis has been laid upon sympathetic emotion, upon peace, good will, love and affection and generous response to appeal uttered or unexpressed. This has been developed and it is peculiarly the Christian idea. It is, as it were, the one element which Jesus Christ added to the old Hebrew religion;—what Prof. Seelye has called "enthusiasm for humanity."

But Christianity was developed out of the old Hebrew idea of righteousness, of doing what was right, and the gift which the

Hebrew nation made to the world *par excellence* was just this: that there is in society a power that makes for righteousness, that hates that which is evil and will not tolerate it. That power that makes for righteousness, that force, you will recognize as being, according to Matthew Arnold, the central thought of the Hebrew religion, and Christ touched this with emotion, and upon the basis of this righteousness, built up also the thought of sympathetic emotion, so that we think that it is not only necessary to to do what is right, but also to see that rightness and justice and truth are done in love and through love to all.

Now I do think, my friends, that there is a neglect of that which underlies this sympathetic emotion, namely, the moral education, the recognition of the moral principle in life, its place and its value. It seems to me that we have cultivated, especially in our homes, our children's natures, until their eyes fill with tears at sight of sorrow and their hearts bound toward that which needs them; but that we have neglected this instruction in the moral principle of things. Now while the home has emphasized this thought of sympathetic emotion, the school system of this land, as I understand it, has emphasized the intellect and has given an immense impetus to intellectual development. I said a moment ago, and it seems to me true, that there is nothing moral in the intellect itself, that there is no connection between honor and the distance from here to the sun. I might be able to answer nine questions in the Peloponnesian war and give the exact diameter of the moon, and have eleven examples correctly done in decimal fractions, and not be any nearer to speaking truth, doing justice and being personally right. There is no connection between the two.

Have we not then to begin a scientific system of instruction in morals and incorporate that in our schools? In our schools, I say, because I consider that the educative influence of the schools is greater far than is the educative influence of the home. The home, as I understand it, has the first and most important years of life. At three months old, we will say, the most important part of life is already past. At three years old, affirms Mr. Spencer and Mr. Darwin, the child is in possession of all the principles of life, and that thereafter it is only a question of their application. But you take them at six or seven years old, and have them for six, eight or ten years, six hours a day. Nay, more than that, for you exercise a control over their going and their coming, and fully one-third of the whole number of hours of the day belong to the school and the school discipline, and the school government. Therefore we charge you to take this up as part of your duty, the instruction of our children in the moral principles of life.

And here I turn to another thought in connection with this subject. The discovery of the law of gravitation was a great epoch; the discovery of the laws of planetary motion also. The Darwinian laws of development through natural selection, let us say, marks an epoch. Is it any less an epoch, the discovery that the moral principles of society are part of the very constitu-tution of nature? That morality, that right and wrong, do not rest upon the distinctions made by a personal will, that they do not rest upon the authoritative statement made by the Bible or other sacred books, but are part of the very constitution of na-ture? This is the second thought which I bring to you. This discovery is due in part to the intuitions, if you please, of Mr. Emerson; it is due to the comparative studies of Mr. Spencer and others, that what may be called the Science of Morality is taking its place now among the recognized studies of the world. There is a scientific basis for morality. If I make a command to a child, and he says "Why?" what am I to say? I may say, first, putting it upon my own personal will, "You must do it because I say it." Suppose the child goes beyond that and says, "Why do you say it?" I may say, "Well, public opinion says it; the law has affirmed it; the Bible has uttered it." That will do for a time. By and by comes a question as to the validity of public opinion and as to the correct interpretation, or, if you please, as to the authority itself, of the Bible. What then? You must be able to go beyond that and say, "In the very nature of things; among the necessary conditions of social life, as neces-sary as are physical laws to physical nature, are these moral principles." We recognize the place and power of the physical forces and of their methods and laws of action. Light, heat, chemical affinity, gravitation, electricity, magnetism, all these are recognized. No one doubts that they are part of the very nature of things. Wherever things are, there these forces are. By their interplay, there has been built up this physical condition, there has . been woven this beautiful fabric—what Goethe calls the "garment of God."

All elements combine in certain relations. Two and two do not more necessarily make four than do certain combinations of oxygen and hydrogen make water. Go back into the ancient periods before brooding time began, and water would have combined in just that way, and when the last drop shall have gone ·from this earth, the mist will be but water in just such exact combination. No one questions that. No one questions that heat is a mode of motion; electricity, magnetism, light, modes of motion. No one questions gravitation. You would not doubt for a second if I should step off this platform I would fall. You know the law which draws me toward the earth's center. But do you know, do you believe that what are called the moral principles are just as much a condition of the nature of things as these physical forces? Do you believe that truth is just as much a force in society as gravitation is in matter? Do you believe that justice is just as much a necessary condition of social combination as is attraction in the planetary system? Do you believe that it is just as impossible to evade or avoid the penalties from the breaking of one as it is from the breaking of the other? Do you believe that if I tell a lie a certain ill will come to me in the way of a penalty that is just as quick in its action, just as unerring as would be the result if I step off a precipice? If you do not believe this, you have not read this late science of morality. Lying at the heart of every crystal is a moral law. The stars move along lines of rectitude. Right and wrong are no less a part of the nature of things to us than are these physical forces. This is the scientific basis of morality. This is the new commandment from Sinai. The ancients felt this. The ancients felt their way out into a recognition of this moral order through pain and penalty. They found out at last that one may not meddle with the great spiritual forces. No public opinion can make right wrong nor wrong right. No vested right, though of a thousand years continuance, can give a thief a right to his property. No mind will recognize it as a property right, though by law upon law and in the very constitution itself it should be embodied as a great truth. Yes, this is the new science of morality; "the data of ethics." Right, justice, truth, personal purity, patriotism, honor and honesty;—these are the spiritual forces of morality which build up society to make it happy and good; which perfect character; which place men and women upon their feet, just as the chemical forces, just as the forces of motion and light make us men and women of perfect physical condition and stature. I can but hint these things. If you care to do so, you can read of this in Emerson's "Sovereignty of Ethics" and in his "Perpetual Forces." These are based, not on painful gropings after these truths, but by direct insight into the fact that the bases of society are moral. Or if you will take it further, you will find in Mr. Spencer's "Sociology" this thing worked out by experiment and the comparative method, to show us that ethics do not rest upon personal will, are not matters of public opinion, do not rest upon the authority of anything, but that they are a part of the very nature of things. Upon this nature of things, out of it, grows custom, grows law, grows governmental recognition, grows religious affirmation of what is right, and denunciation of what is wrong. Our ten commandments are but the welling up out of the heart of nature of these great spiritual forces of morality uttered amid the fire of Sinai. As one says whom I have already quoted,—

> "Out of the heart of nature rolled
> The burdens of the Bible old;
> Like the volcano's tongue of flame
> The litanies of nations came;
> Up from the burning core below,
> The canticles of joy and woe."

Now, I think from this basis may be projected a science of morality which may be incorporated into your schools and school systems. It is very true, that you may not be able to *mark* for this. On such a system as this you may construct a system of teaching, not the dry bones of any formulated system, but something which shall recognize all the while that you are dealing with something which can not be moved; "On the solid ground of nature," says Wordsworth, "rests the mind that builds for aye." When I know that I speak truth, that I am but uttering the veracity of every atom of this great globe; then it seems to me I have a force behind me which will help me to be faithful to my truth. If I simply say what by common consent has been recognized as true, then I may find that the movable elements in us may change that standard and I may have to adjust my conduct to new conditions. But when I have heard what nature has said, the great God speaking through it and affirming it, I ask not your voices as to what I shall say, nor your opinions as to the results of it. I then simply say what is said to me. I lean my ear to catch the whisper of Heavenly Truth, bend my eye to watch its distinctions in rectitude. Then I know that the elements of society combine according to a golden rule, and that truth and the great moral distinctions are not a caprice of the will and not an imaginative utterance of my mind, but the voice of nature and of nature's God.

The method of teaching such a science, or the formation of it into a system, the technicalities of it, I have no time to talk to you about to-day; only this, be sure that it must come. We demand of you, we tax-payers and parents, that you give us a place in your school system for instruction in conduct. I see my boys and girls but a little time in the day. I know very well that you will protect them from outside influences. I have no question but what they will understand fractions and the rule of three and equation of payments. I do not doubt that some of the abstrusities of grammar may ultimately penetrate into their darkened brains; but unless you can make them recognize the distinction in nature between right and wrong; unless you can make them feel the sacred obligation of the right; unless you can teach them that they had better die than lie, or be false to themselves and the highest principles, then I have done wrong in giving so much of their early years to you.

Now I appeal to you who are oldest and wisest here that you

take this up. I would have you study Emerson's works with just this one thought of finding therein the scientific basis of morality. I would have you become familiar with his "Perpetual Forces" and his "Sovereignty of Ethics." I would have you read Spencer's "Data of Ethics" and "Social Statistics."

> "So near is grandeur to our dust, so close is God to man,
> When duty whispers, 'Lo, thou must,' the youth replies, 'I can.'"

You will find everything respond to it. The magnetic needle turns toward the pole, turn it howsoever you will. Present these truths, not as the utterance of parent or teacher, not as the capricious commandment of some stern law giver, but as the very necessary voice of God, and you will find the response then is quick and immediate. A sense of justice and fairness and a certain disposition to say and recognize the truth will be seen, which will make itself felt in the relation between teacher and scholar. Teach it how you will. Teach it by story; give incidents of moral courage; tell of every patriot; tell them of every true man, history is full of examples of such. Pass by the current gossip of the day. Ask them not to pay so much attention to who is president or who has a post office, but to give heed to the great names which come down in history. From Chaucer to Whittier let the greatest thoughts of the greatest minds become familiar to them. And then little by little as by an instinct, in every questionable transaction, the needle of the moral sentiment will point to that which is right; in every question of selfishness, the balance will lean, not to expediency, but to right. Thus you shall find that the truths of nature are the truths of the soul, and that they have become possessed with a moral furnishing which shall pass through mind through memory into the very nature of the soul itself.

CULTIVATING INATTENTION.

S. S. PARR, PRIN. DE PAUW NORMAL SCHOOL.

CARELESSNESS is a personal calamity of great magnitude. As society becomes more complex, the fatality of carelessness increases to such an extent that the thoroughly careless person is as much of a failure as the more pronounced kinds of the weak-minded. Carelessness rests at bottom on inattention as a confirmed mental habit. Whatever cultivates inattention fosters carelessness.

The permanent results of all education are the habits formed by it. School-education is not an exception to this general rule. Whatever the school or teacher, the formation of habit goes on. Thus the results of a poor, bad or indifferent school can never be merely negative. A positive residiuum of habit will always remain. Knowledge, from its very nature, is of no value except it be directed by right habits and right modes of action. A good example of this fact was the "paleontological dead beat" who lately victimized numerous Indiana scientists, by purloining the choicest specimens from their cabinets. He had a comprehensive and exact knowledge of geology, paleontology, botany and literature. And yet he was a common vagabond and thief, because of bad moral habits. The world is full of people who possess plenty of knowledge, but whose mental habits utterly incapacitate them for any efficient use of it. Habit, as Matthew Arnold rightly suggests, is not the last word in culture. He would no doubt have added that it is the last word in school-education.

An important question, then, always is, "What habit does this course of action tend to form?" There are many kinds of teaching and learning that cultivate the habit of inattention and thus of general mental incapacity. There are school-rooms that unwittingly, perhaps, have full-rigged curricula arranged to graduate their pupils into this misfortune. Many apparently harmless practices destroy the power of observation, memory, and thought.

When a boy works at the blackboard with crayon in one hand and eraser in the other; when he takes half a dozen trials at one simple piece of work before he gets it correct, and then had passed the point of certainty before he began, he is receiving an efficient lesson in this bad habit.

Repetitions, stumblings, second trials at what ought to be done with the first effort are matters of the same general class. There are schools where the children can no more read, spell, recite, make statements and the like correctly at first trial than they can fly. They can not trust their eyes, their memories, or any of their faculties. They are certain of nothing—habitual blunderers, incapable of attending to anything, and so incapacitated for the actual affairs of life that they would better never have seen the inside of a school-house.

All kindness is not kind. There is a spurious variety that prefers present ease and comfort to ultimate good, because the latter is troublesome and sometimes unpleasant. Of such kind is that good nature that desires suavity and comity of pleasant feeling at all hazards, and thus allows eleven-twelfths of the class to dawdle while the one-twelfth recites to the teacher. Such class-work is only one-twelfth as good as that of a tutor, since in that case the pupil attends twelve-twelfths of his time. Class-recitation is not merely designed to economize time. The members of the class are to learn to concentrate their minds on the subject of the lesson amid the misunderstandings, the wrong constructions, the one-sidedness of view, and the clash of opinions, as well as the distracting elements of behavior, of the recitation. They also should reap the benefit that comes from the contact of mind with mind. The recitation of individuals, without the attention of their fellows, completely defeats both these purposes and goes to the opposite end of cultivating inattention and diffusiveness of mental energy.

The range of practices that destroy the power of attention is wide. Among them may be named: habitual concert-reading, spelling, and other kinds of concert-recitation; discussions with individuals, that are foreign to the point of the lesson; failure to test individual pupils as to the preparation of each point of the lesson; low-voiced recitation that is not heard by all members of a class; bad distribution of work, by which a few of the class do most or all of the reciting; allowing pupils to come to class unprepared, and thus sit through recitation without understanding the points and being able to participate in the discussion; sending part of the class to the blackboard, while some remain in their seats, and then giving all the attention to those at the board, etc., etc. This list might be extended indefinitely. In general, whatever allows attention in all members of a class to flag or cease is to be avoided as calculated to cultivate the worst of mental habits.

One reason self-made men are such a power is that they have never had their minds crippled by any of this execrable drill. Whatever they have done, they have done with their might, that is, with attentive and vigorously active faculties—a feature well worthy of study and imitation in the school-room.

The recitation by no means covers the worst sins against the habit of energetic attention. The most flagrant abuses arise out of misdirected and undirected study-hours. Our sorry paraphrase of the saying "and teach the young idea how to shoot," into the somewhat vulgar form "and teach the young idea how to shoot—spit-balls," gives a volume of evidence against us in not directing well the hours between recitations. As the scale descends toward the primary school, the failure grows. Poor primary child! It comes to school with senses keen and the power of attention well trained within its limits. Mother nature never allows interest to flag and so never allows attention to lag. But alas! how little have our primary schools yet learned of nature's methods in this regard. A child were better on the river's bank soiling its chubby hands in mud-pies than sitting in a careless school-room. The mud-pies would engross its mind with an energy that would bring culture.

The test of good work is the attention it stirs. The teacher who pronounces a word or sentence, reads a statement, dictates a problem, states a direction five times and then goes around to the individuals of her class and tells it over the sixth time, may be as good as the Savior of men in intention, but she is a very demon in the results she thus invites. Whoever destroys one's power of attention destroys his power of reaching results. Humboldt, Dickens, Agassiz, and scores of others have attested the transcendant power of consecutive attention. The success of men in every walk of life depends on this power more than any other. The ability to think a political, social or business problem through to the end, and trace cause, results, tendencies, and relations can be had only on the prior condition of habitual atten tion. How all important, then, that every kind of action which destroys it should be avoided in the school-room!

THAT LAW AND THAT DECISION.

FRIEND BELL:—I have just been informed by Hon. Granville C. Moore, that the Court has by a full and strong decision sustained the law of '67, which provided for local taxation for school purposes. This being true, it has occurred to me that your younger readers who were not in the struggle of former and darker days might be interested in knowing some of the remarkable things connected with this law, so I send the following:

When the school system was inaugurated in 1852, there was a wise provision in the law, authorizing the several school corporations, namely; township, towns, and cities to levy local taxes, to supplement the general reserve and thus lengthen the school term one, two or four months as circumstances demanded. Immediately the "common school system" was happily put into operation throughout the state. All were pleased, many were enthusiastic and jubilant over the prospect of placing their beloved Indiana along side of the more progressive states: Things went well for a short time;—the State Teachers' Association was organized, the Indiana School Journal was established, institutes were being held, and school houses of tolerable size and convenience were being built in the cities, and all was moving on to higher and better work, when lo! in 1855 (in the case of "Greencastle Township *v.* Black"), the Supreme Court decided the provision of the law authorizing townships to levy taxes, *unconstitutional.* "*Unconstitutional!*"—fatal word! Following up this fatal policy the same court in 1857 decided the provision authorizing cities and towns to levy taxes, "*unconstitutional.*" The system was practically crushed; and the court, in the language of Pope, was "damned to eternal fame." As long as the history of education in Indiana remains, so long will remain the remembrance of these odious decisions and the name of the judge (Perkins) who rendered them.

As above stated the system was practically crushed,—a fine

system, with officers, houses, appliances, etc., but with no money to pay the teachers. Schools in cities that were running nine months in the year dropped down to five, four, or three. Many of the best teachers left the state, others quit the profession, some going to farming, merchandise, others to book agencies, etc., etc. In the words of the late brilliant and scholarly Prof. Hinkle, while they found that "it was unconstitutional to *educate* in Indiana, it was not unconstitutional to *emigrate*," and so they went. This was the condition, and this condition gave Indiana through a decade of years, a reputation that took another decade to wipe out. The teachers (those who staid), and other friends of education, realizing this condition, went to work to secure an amendment to the Constitution guaranteeing the funds declared null. So in 1861, an amendment guaranteeing these funds was introduced into the Legislature, but not being acted on in 1863, it was null; and so another amendment was introduced in 1865, but by some strange oversight or perversity, the word *township* was omitted; so despairing of this slow and botching process, the writer, then State Superintendent, went in 1867 before the Committees on Education in the Legislature and asked them to consider heroic treatment, namely, *the re-enactment of the law decided unconstitutional in* 1855–7. This looked bold, almost rash, but after several meetings, a great deal of argument, and no little planning, the committees agreed to bring in a bill to that effect. The chief points in the argument, which I presented to the committees, were two: 1. That a general tax which would raise revenue sufficient to run the schools six months in the rural districts, would raise an excess of revenue in the cities, and thus work an injustice to them. 2. Public sentiment concerning the common school system had greatly changed from 1857 to 1867, and hence, (1) did not believe any one would have the hardihood to bring suit against the law in the next ten years—and (2) if suit should be brought, the court would in all probability hold the law constitutional.

The law was passed, and the people rejoiced, and the school system revived, and Indiana bounded forward with the strides of a giant, till for years she has been at the front. Eighteen years have elapsed before any "mossy back," any enemy of his race, has had the hardihood to attack this law, and happily when attacked, the court, as predicted, has declared the law CONSTI- TUTIONAL.

Praises to an overruling Providence that has led the court to sustain a law and thereby a system which has blessed millions and is to bless millions more, yet to be.

Yours truly,   GEORGE W. HOSS.

BAKER UNIVERSITY, BALLWIN, KAN., June 24, '85.

SOME AIMS IN SCHOOL MANAGEMENT.

BY E. E. SMITH.

THE school is the bridge over which the child is to pass from inefficiency to efficiency, from ignorance to knowledge, from strength to power, from impulse to reason.   It is, then, only an expedient.   The child enters upon the bridge a possibility; he is expected to leave it an actuality.   The law of school life is therefore the law of change—change in child-nature.

This change is to be a definite one—with distinct aims—under the operation of a clearly-defined purpose.   The first of these aims, it seems to the writer, is to teach it to submit to rightly- constituted authority.   Without this disposition it can not be a good citizen, for its spirit will be in rebellion against the very compact by which society is held together.

"Give me the child," says Edward Everett, "whose heart has embraced without violence the gentle love of obedience, in whom the sprightliness of youth has not encroached on deference for authority, and I would rather have him for my son, though at the age of twelve he should have the alphabet to learn, than be compelled to struggle with the caprice of a self-willed, obsti- nate youth, whose bosom has become a viper's nest of unamiable passions, although in early attainments he may be the wonder of the day."

This first aim looks to submission to a power beyond the child's self.   The second should look to its control by a power within itself—to a properly regulated will.   Without this power no child or man is safe. At one moment, when passion is at the flood, he is a wild beast; at another, when passion is at the ebb, he is a remorseful and despondent human being. In neither case is he in the best condition to do the work expected of him by industry, by society, by the church or by the state.

Habit and sentiment combined pretty much master the world. But they master the world because they master individuals. Hence the importance of fixing right habits and implanting proper sentiments in the young. And the duty of giving attention to this is imperative upon the school because of the purpose for which it was established and maintained—to *prepare* the child for useful citizenship.

The following habits would seem to rise out of the nature of the school as an organism:

Punctuality, that promises may be faithfully kept.

Good Order, that due respect may be paid to the rights of others.

Regularity, that things about the home and in business may be done systematically and economically.

Industry, that each may feel that that only belongs to him which is his by right of faithful effort.

Self-Denial, in order to a spirit willing to bear a part of the burdens of those who are unable to carry all their own burdens.

Self-Direction of Effort, that essential individuality may be developed, and with it a spirit of proper independence and a sense of personal responsibility for the condition of public affairs.

Obedience to the Dictates of Conscience, that each may promptly yield to the higher law of right.

As complementary to this work, there may be sown in the school the seeds of

Love, the master passion of the intelligent universe and the guardian angel of the home.

Truth, the acme of human effort and the defender of right.

Honor, The safe-guard of society.

Patriotism, the respect for and the spirit to defend that by which the individual has become what he is.

Faithful Labor, the measure of self-respect.

By thus combining internal and external motive forces, we may assist the child to such development that the world will meet it with a hearty welcome rather than with a cold shrug or a tantalizing quiz. Why should the world so generally think the graduate of the common school or of the college *needs experience before he can be trusted?*

SURDUE UNIVERSITY.

DEPARTMENT OF PEDAGOGY.

[This Department is conducted by GEO. P. BROWN, ex-Pres. State Normal School.]

THE READING CIRCLE.

THE experience of the past year with the Teachers' Reading Circle in this state is valuable more for the possibilities that have been revealed than for the actual work accomplished. If the Board of Directors shall have the wisdom needful to properly direct the course of study in the future the Reading Circle will become the principal institution in the state for the professional education of teachers. There is no reason why a large class of teachers who have ability and perseverance enough to pursue the work that ought to be laid out for them should not acquire all the knowledge that is essential to success in the teaching art, provided they already know the subjects to be taught. The knowledge that is strictly professional,—that sets off the teaching vocation from others and is peculiar to the teacher, can be acquired by every one who will pursue diligently and persistently a course of study and practice such as the Reading Circle Board should prescribe. The Reading Circle should be to the teachers of the state in the way of technical knowledge and training what the Chatauqua Circle is in the way of general culture to the people of the country. It will not dispense with the need of normal schools for the young and ignorant, but it will give to the experienced and capable teachers in the ranks an opportunity for self-culture and training that may be of infinitely more value to them than any normal school instruction they can receive.

2

It seems to us clear that the work of a teachers' reading circle should be something distinctive in its character. Prominent among the early studies of the course should be the study of the mind.

The great error in the method of study of this important subject at this time, both in the schools and in the Reading Circle, is that students devote their time, not to the study of their own minds, but to the study of what some one else has said about the mind. They study mind as they studied, a few years ago, botany and chemistry,—viz., from books.

The only legitimate use of a book in mental science is to direct the student how to study his own mental processes and how to observe the mental processes of others,—especially of children. When he devotes his time and energy to the learning of a mass of abstract terms, even if he apprehends their meaning, and understands what the author says, he is far from having any power to examine his own mental processes and know for himself the truth. His knowledge is all second-hand. He knows that some one else says this or that about the mind.

The great need of the teachers of this country is a manual of mental science especially adapted to the needs of the teacher of children and youth, that shall make clear to the student of it the method by which he must pursue the study of his own mind, and lead him step by step along the way, and which shall, furthermore, give him full and plain directions how to study the minds of others. We shall never have anything worthy of the name of a science of teaching until we know more facts about the mental processes of children. And we shall not know more about the children until we learn better how to observe them.

What progress could be made in educational science in the next decade if every teacher were an intelligent observer of the mental activities of his pupils, and would keep a careful record of his observations!

The study of mental science is fundamental to all rational procedure in teaching. Knowing the mind, the next subject in this line of study is the science and art of school teaching. Here, again, is great need of a proper manual. The nearest approach to such a manual that has yet been published is Bain's Education as a Science. This is practically beyond the intellectual ken of the mass of teachers. It bristles all over with good things, but does not seem to have been prepared as a manual to instruct the ignorant. It was written rather for schools from the stand-point of a scholar. It is built, too, upon a theory of mind that is unsatisfactory to most teachers. A book containing matter of the nature of Mr. Bain's book,—but simplified and better arranged, and built upon the Platonic theory of mind, would be an invaluable addition to every teacher's professional library. Why does not such a book appear? The *study* of the art of teaching should follow the study of the science. The practice of the art generally precedes the study of both.

Accompanying this line of professional study should be a line of study for general culture. In literature there should be one manual that should be carefully studied and a number of "literary classics" so arranged in the course as to illustrate, amplify and impress the principal literary epochs as treated in the manual. A compendium of history should precede and one of the natural sciences should follow the literary study in the course.

This is substantially the course adopted for Indiana. Our plan of organization has been followed pretty closely by other states, but most of them have varied materially from our course of instruction. The reason for this I have not yet been able to discover.

It is to be hoped that the Board of Directors will devise some plan by which the work of the circles will be better supervised and directed than it has been, and more thorough and systematic study be pursued.

MORAL TRAINING IN THE SCHOOLS.

IT has been said and often repeated in these columns that the teacher should see three leading purposes in the school: (1) To train the will, and especially that element that is called the volition,—the executive function of the soul. Any may choose rightly, but if his choice is never executed there will be little influence upon the character. The great end of the school is to train the child *to do.* To put forth effort,—to make the other faculties obedient to the will, when directed toward the accomplishment of a worthy purpose;—to make it the habit of the mind so to act;—this is the commanding function of the teacher. (2) The purpose of the school second in importance is the formation of right habits of observation and thought. This is intellectual training. It can not be secured without an accompanying discipline of will, but it trains the will only so far as to direct and maintain intellectual effort. This might be called the intellectual will. Right methods and habits of observation and thought are fundamental to the formation of proper motives. We call the result of this intellectual training *intelligence.* Intelligence will direct the soul to the formation of rational motives. We are tempted here to stop long enough to say parenthetically, that much of the confusion that arises in the minds of many in considering the relation of the will to motive, and the dependence of our choice upon the motive that stimulates it, would cease to exist, or at least be greatly lessened, if we would always consider that the motive itself is a thing of our own creation. *What we are* will determine the motives by which we are governed. Am I obedient to the strongest motive? Yes. But who makes one motive stronger than another? I myself. (3) The third purpose of the school is information,—to gain knowledge. But let us be careful how we separate knowledge from power. Knowledge *is* power is the old maxim. And so it is. At least they can not be separated. The man of greatest knowledge is the man of greatest intellectual power. Information existing in the mind as isolated facts is not knowledge until it is organized. This organization is possible only after a generalization so comprehensive as to reduce the multitude of facts to one. It may be possible in thought to separate the *power* of generalizing from the *act,* but there can be no manifestation of the power without the act; and the act is an act of knowledge. So it would seem that any attempt to set off power from knowledge and increase one without adding to the other is futile. He whose generalizations are most far-reaching and truest has greatest intellectual power.

Character is what results from the realization of all of these purposes. He is a man of character whose disciplined will is guided by an intelligence begotten of comprehensive knowledge. The end of the school, as of all education, is character.

But each of these aims of the school admits of subdivisions. One of these is called Moral Training. By moral education is meant that attainment which holds one obedient to the commands of duty. He is morally educated who always does as he ought to do. Moral training is the training of the will to choose the right in the face of temptation to choose the wrong. This might be called the moral will.

The school trains the intellectual will by enforcing attention. Concentration is matured into a habit when voluntary attention, which is attention resulting from a conscious effort of will, is changed to involuntary or spontaneous attention, which is an automatic act of the will.

The moral will is strengthened by enforcing punctuality, regularity, order, industry, and especially by leading the child to choose acts of kindness, benevolence, justice, politeness, etc., towards his fellows.

What are proper methods to employ in the common school to enforce moral conduct? The discussion of this question must be deferred to a future time.

PROBLEM AND SOLUTION.—"Required the size of a square field, the number of rails in the fence, about which is equal to the number of acres in the field, the number of rails to the rod being given?"

Having seen no easier solution, I submit my own for what it is worth: The number of rails to the rod multiplied by two equals the length of one side of the field in miles. Demonstration:—

Let x = the number of acres, also of miles.
" m = the length of one side of field in miles.
" n = the number of rails to the rod.
(1) $x = \text{acres} = 640 \, m^2$.
(2) $x = \text{rails} = 1280 \, m \, n$.
(3) $640 \, m^2 = 1280 \, m \, n$.
$\therefore \quad m = 2 \, n$.   A. J. KINNAMAN.

DANVILLE, IND.

PRIMARY DEPARTMENT.

[This Department is conducted by HOWARD SANDISON, Professor of Methods in the State Normal School.]

——:x:——

The real subject in education is the individual mind of each child, with its acquired habits and inherited tendencies. An evident proposition, then, is: If real teaching is done, each mind, with its peculiar habits and inherited tendencies, must be understood by the teacher; with its double corollary:—

(1) The number of pupils under the charge of a primary teacher should range between twenty and thirty. (2) The pupils should remain under the charge of a given teacher more than ten months.

The second proposition is: Mind being an organism, the heart (sensibilities) is no less an avenue to the intellect, than is the intellect to the heart and will; with its corollary:—

Suspicion and severity can never enable the teacher to obtain a standing place in the child-mind.

The third proposition is: Two rival powers compose the mind—the *carrying power*— memory (the servant) and the *thinking power* (the master); with its double corollary:—

(1) The aim of education is to make the mind strong and skilled as a thinking power, and not to make it full as a carrying power. (2) The most practical education is that which sends the child into the business world with power to observe closely and to think (reflect) accurately upon what he observes.

PRIMARY MISCELLANY.

WOULD the principle that *the best way to obtain a clear conception of an object, is to draw or make it,* justify printing in primary reading work?

——o——

Not enough regard is paid to inherited tendencies and habits in children. The unskillful teacher tries to make a given way a key to every mind.

——o——

If the teacher assists the child to that which the child itself is able to obtain, the tendency is to make the child dependent. If teaching becomes a "pouring-in" process the pupil is likely to have little real knowledge, and less power. The aim in primary teaching is not to fill the mind, but to train it.

——o——

Since the sensibility is the avenue to the intellect, if the pupil is led to put his heart into the work, discipline is reduced to the minimum, and the acquisition of power is raised to the maximum.

THE TEACHING OF "A" AND "THE."

THERE are three methods of presenting these words, which will be stated in the order of their value, beginning with the one of least worth:

1. To teach the sounds of these words as given by the dictionary, and to hold the pupils rigidly to this pronunciation.

2. To teach the words, giving "a" and "the" their name sounds, on the assumption that the pupils will naturally acquire the proper pronunciation.

3. To omit all direct teaching in regard to the pronunciation of these words, as separate words. First, on the ground that the directions given for their pronunciation by the dictionary are based upon the observed habit of both children and adults; and, secondly, on the assumption that the pupils will naturally and readily continue their already acquired habit of pronouncing these words when they are presented as printed forms, in connection with the words that they modify, without any direct instruction.

FOUR EXAMINATION QUESTIONS.

1. What reasons would you give for not teaching figures during the first year of school?

2. Do you believe in teaching whole numbers, fractions, and the units of the measures (tables), along side by side? Why, or why not? (In dealing with numbers from one to one hundred.)

3. What principle might be urged against such work?

4. How would you teach the *notation* of the fraction *one-sixth?* (Second year work. The *idea* and oral term of one-sixth having been taught during the first year, in connection with the number six.)

A STUDENT'S ANSWERS.

1. When the child enters school, he has a very limited knowledge of the ideas and oral expressions of numbers, and these must be made his own before the expressions in written or printed form can be made of any use to him; hence he must obtain the ideas and oral expressions first. We might, however, give the pupil the figure 2, as soon as he has the idea and the oral name for two, but this would make the work too complex for the state of development of the mind, and figures should be avoided until the second year.

2. Yes. Because, with objects, fractions are as easy to learn

as whole numbers; the fraction one-half is easier than the number three, while dealing with the number two, and by using two halves in their relations the idea of two is strengthened, and the way for three and thirds prepared. And so on for higher numbers. By the use of the units of measure in connection with each number as taught, as, two pts. are a qt.; a sheet folded into two leaves is a folio, etc., with the number two, the field of applying the idea of two is extended, thus tending to free the mind in thinking of number. Also, information of measures is gained, incidentally, without taxing the powers of the mind unduly. Thus, the work in whole numbers, fractions, and the units of measure, mutually supplement and strengthen each other.

3. Some might claim that by taking so many things to the child's mind at once, we would confuse him, and injure his memory, taking for their ground the principle that one thing should be taught at a time—the psychological principle that those things are best remembered that are longest and most frequently before the mind. I think, however, that these persons forget that all these things are related ideas, and that, if they are taught together, when one of them is presented it is the tendency of the mind to think of the others; and that it is most natural for the mind, in acquiring knowledge, to go from a known to its nearest related unknown.

4. Notation, of course, implies a knowledge of the idea and of the oral expression. In teaching the notation of *one-sixth*, as given in the second year grade in connection with the *whole number six*, I would present to the sight one-sixth of something, as of an apple. The direct work on the notation or the symbol, would then consist of three kinds of work:

(*a.*) Holding before the class one-sixth, I would say, "I will place on the board something which stands for this," writing as I said it the symbol, ⅙. This, in connection with other sixths, I would repeat until there were a number of such symbols upon the board.

(*b.*) Having various sixths upon the table, desks, etc., I would next have the pupils associate the symbols upon the board with that which they signified, by pointing to the symbols and asking the pupils to show me something that each symbol named.

(*c.*) The third kind of work would be for the teacher to lead the class to associate the various sixths with their symbol, ⅙, by taking in his hand one-sixth, or pointing to it and saying, "Make on the board something that shows how much this is. This would be repeated until the pupils acquired some facility in representing sixths. Of course, all of the three kinds of work need not be taken in one lesson.

ORAL, (*i. e.*) EARLY PRIMARY TEACHING—I.

Aim.—In preparing for a lesson, it is essential to see clearly the end to be attained; to fix the mental eye on a definite object, that the mental steps may be sure and direct. The teacher is therefore to consider first the aim, and secondly the best means of attaining it.

Every lesson should instruct the children, that is, it should carry to their minds and fix, some knowledge that was not there before. A real lesson, however, always trains, educates. It draws forth the powers of the mind to discover the knowledge, to seize it, to hold it, and to assimilate it; while by the exercise, the powers are strengthened and sharpened for future work.

Illustration of the Educative Lesson.—Take, for example, a lesson on the rivers of New England. The teacher throws up roughly with molding sand the surface of the region, calling particular attention to the high land. The children are led to examine very closely, and to look through the molding to the real surface, by reference to their own surroundings, and to note on slates or board, in simple language, what they see. They are then shown by familiar illustration, the character of the surface, that there are many depressions; that it is rocky, with a porous covering; that there is an abrupt break between the high and the coast land;—thus leading them to see for themselves that the rain-fall does not run off quickly, but fills the depressions, and flows out from them in whatever direction the land dips; that it soaks in until it comes to the rock, following the dip of the rock, coming out at the lowest places and uniting there from many directions, and flowing off together in the direction of the slope of the land, thus forming many streams and rivers. These, they will be led to see, will soon wear through their earthy bottoms, and flow off over rocky beds, leaving at the junction of the high and the low lands a break, and that from the break they flow in a comparatively level bed to the sea. They are then led to infer the main uses of the rivers.

The region is then placed upon board or slate, roughly, in both vertical and horizontal outline, and the molding and outlines compared with the map. The children then point out on the molding the probable position and direction of flow of the rivers, and compare with the map. From the map, the names of the rivers are then obtained. These are fixed in memory by repetition, as the teacher or pupils point to the molding and map. The pupils are then required to point out the probable locations of manufactories, and the parts that are fitted for navigation, on both the molding and the map. In conclusion, the class are called upon to describe the position and uses of each, as it is pointed out.

In a lesson of this kind many powers of mind are employed: *imagination*, in picturing; *comparison, association,* and *inference* in reasoning as to the course of the water, location of manufacturing establishments, etc.; *language*, in the oral and written statement of the facts gained; and every power employed is disciplined by the exercise, and rendered more easy of control by the child's will.

Moreover, many new words are added to the child's vocabulary that will be of use in reading and language work, and geographically, a real picture, however imperfect, will be retained by the mind. Such is an example of an *educative* lesson.

ILLUSTRATION OF THE INSTRUCTIVE LESSON.—By the instruction method the same material may be dealt with, without any distinct aim at education, but simply with a view to instruct. The teacher employs mainly the map, and the children are called upon to notice the high and low land (in colors), the location of the high land, lakes, etc. From the map they are to see the direction of the high land, and of the rivers.   The names of the main rivers having been learned from the map, the teacher explains their relative importance, uses, the location of manufac- turing places, etc.   This information is written upon slate and blackboard, and repeated until it is fixed in memory, and then with map, slate, and board work away, the pupils are questioned upon the information until the teacher is satisfied that it is pro- ducible on demand.

Such a lesson is of some advantage, but its main aim is evi- dently to put statements into the mind as if it were a vessel, rather than to lead the mind to seek and grasp knowledge for itself, as if it were a living thing.   There is little exercise of the imagination, the map being studied more as the real thing, than as a means; there is no comparing or associating of unknown things with those already familiar, no inferring; and the language employed is meagre, and almost wholly supplied by the map, not being an outgrowth of their own original thinking.   Such a les- son is instructive, not educative.

It is to be noticed that both lessons give the same information, and require that it shall be impressed by repetition and question- ing.   But the aducative lesson makes the information a means to training, not an end in itself.   The demand of the age, of school systems, and of examinations, is generally the instructive lesson, for it gives facts which are always producible on demand; while the educative lesson tends, in connection with its facts, to give training, which is nly to a degree, producible on demand.

A member of Parliament, who was visiting a training school in England, had the difference between *training* and *instruction* explained thus: "The training teacher said, 'Sir, you perceive that the children are now reading part of the history of the op- pression of the children of Israel in Egypt, and the next part of the chapter they are about to read is regarding their use of straw in making bricks, etc.   Now, Sir, I believe they do not know why straw was used, nor do they know whether the bricks in Egypt were dried in the sun or burned as in this country.'   A few questions were put to the children, which proved that they did not know it, as the master supposed.   The trainer then said to the member of Parliament, 'Were I to tell them, seeing they do not know, that would be *instructing;* but I shall not tell them, and I shall cause them to tell me the nature of the clay in Egypt compared with that in England, and whether the bricks were burned or dried there, and that will be *education.*'

The teacher repeated the fact that straw was used in making bricks in Egypt, as the children read from the Bible, but, of course, they were ignorant of the reason. He then *brought out from them,* by analogy, the difficulty of breaking a bunch of straw, however thin—what the effect would be of layers of straw in parallel lines, being mixed with clay, while yet in a soft state, and afterwards dried—that the straw would render the bricks more tenacious, or at least less liable to break. He then brought out from the children that the bricks were not burned in Egypt, seeing, as they told him, that if so, the straw used would have been of no service, as in the process of burning the bricks, the straw would be reduced to ashes; that straw in this country would be of no use in making bricks, seeing that we burn them, and that we could not get them sufficiently dried in ordinary seasons by the sun, even in summer.

From the nature of the climate of Egypt, with which they were familiar, it having been brought out in their geography lessons, they inferred that the bricks might be dried in the sun— also that the clay could not be so firm, or solid, or tenacious as ours, since they required straw to strengthen it. They therefore thought that the clay in Egyyt must be more sandy than ours, seeing that our bricklayers did not require straw to strengthen the bricks. Thus the mode of drying bricks in Egypt, and the nature of their clay compared with ours, was determined by *analogy* and *familiar illustration* without *telling.*"

No primary teacher (and indeed no teacher) should be satisfied with the power and practice of loading that pack-horse of the mind—the memory—instead of training the mind. Every lesson should be made educative. To be able to do this the primary teacher needs to cultivate herself in several distinct lines:

1. The habit of connecting new teaching with some object or fact familiar to the children.

2. The habit of noticing matters that may be useful in illustrating.

3. The practice of drawing roughly but rapidly on the blackboard.

4. The practice of modeling in sand, clay and putty.

5. The study of the arts of :—

   a. Describing vividly and exactly.

   b. Questioning clearly.

   c. Expressing herself in simple, correct language.

BUSY WORK.

BUSY WORK should be all that its name implies. It should be work done in a business-like way, because of the interest and pleasure in it. It should not be employed simply for the purpose of keeping the children quiet.

During the first six weeks of the school year the ingenuity of the teacher will be taxed in order to keep the little fingers and minds busy when not in recitation. The slate and pencil are a source of pleasure to all children, but their use, *without constant supervision*, should be withheld until correct habits of position both of the hand and the body have been formed.

The busy work of the little folks should have some relation to their class-work. The subjects of Color, Form, and Size will furnish a variety of exercises for desk-work :—

1. Cards of different colors assorted and arranged in pleasing forms.

2. Bundles of worsteds for matching colors.

3. Mrs. Hailman's beads strung on shoe-strings. (These may be arranged according to form or color.)

4. Molding in clay the different solids and objects which resemble these solids.

5. Bundles of colored sticks which can be arranged according to color or can be used to represent plain surfaces or angles, or any common object.

6. Paper folding and cutting. Twice a week the children may bring a pair of small round-pointed scissors and may fold and cut paper, keeping the scraps on the slate to be taken up in the waste-basket.

7. Having learned to use the slate and pencil correctly, pupils may bring to school leaves from trees and plants in their yards; placing these on the slate they may draw the outline and supply the veins from observation.

8. In the same way animals and objects cut from colored card-board may be traced and finished.

9. Having traced and finished a leaf or animal on the slate, it may be erased and drawn'from memory.

The number of exercises which may be written is infinite and varied.

In each kind of work the pupils should receive assistance and direction for a time. Fifteen minutes a day spent by the teacher in this way at the beginning of the year will repay her amply before its close by their ability to work quietly, to work independently of their neighbors. If possible each bit of work should be examined by the teacher and approved if it can be done honestly.

FANNIE S. BURT.

THE SCHOOL ROOM.

[This Department is conducted by GEO. F. BASS, Supervising Prin. Indianapolis schools.]

OPENING EXERCISE.

A PRIMARY TEACHER was asked to write something on the above subject for the Journal. She said she did not have any "regular" opening exercise; said they just sang some nice little songs to put them in a good humor, and then recited some beautiful little poem; and that she frequently read a poem or story that had a point in it which the children could grasp. She stated, further, that if she attempted to moralize on what she read "everything fell flat."

She was asked for a story or poem with a point in it. She gave the following, that had been clipped from the children's column of a newspaper. She says now that if one of her children begins to growl or frown and he is asked *where he lives*, it stops his growling and puts smiles where frowns were.

WHERE DO YOU LIVE?

I knew a man, and his name was Horner,
Who used to live on Grumble Corner,
Grumble Corner in Cross-Patch Town,
And he never was seen without a frown.
He grumbled at this; he grumbled at that;
He grumbled at the dog; he grumbled at the cat;
He grumbled at morning; he grumbled at night;
And to grumble and growl were his chief delight.

He grumbled so much at his wife that she
Began to grumble as well as he;
And all the children, wherever they went,
Reflected their parents' discontent.
If the sky was dark and betokened rain,
Then Mr. Horner was sure to complain;
And if there was never a cloud about,
He'd grumble because of a threatened drought.

His meals were never to suit his taste;
He grumbled at having to eat in haste;
The bread was poor, or the meat was tough,
Or else he hadn't half enough.
No matter how hard his wife might try
To please her husband, with scornful eye
He'd look around, and then, with a scowl
At something or other, begin to growl.

One day, as I loitered along the street,
My old acquaintance I chanced to meet,
Whose face was without the look of care
And the ugly frown that it used to wear.
"I may be mistaken, perhaps," I said,
As, after saluting, I turned my head;
"But it is, and isn't it, the Mr. Horner
Who lived for so long on Grumble Corner?"

I met him next day; and I met him again,
In melting weather, in pouring rain,
When stocks were up, and when stocks were down;
But a smile somehow had replaced the frown.
It puzzled me much; and so, one day,
I seized his hand in a friendly way,
And said, "Mr. Horner, I'd like to know
What can have happened to change you so?"

He laughed a laugh that was good to hear,
For it told of a conscience clean and clear;
And he said, with none of the old-time dread;
"Why, I've changed my residence, that is all!"
"Changed your residence?" "Yes," said Horner,
"It wasn't healthy on Grumble Corner,
And so I moved; 'twas a change complete;
And you'll find me now on Thanksgiving Street!"

Now, every day as I move along
The streets so filled with the busy throng,
I watch each face, and can always tell
Where men and women and children dwell.
And many a discontented mourner
Is spending his days on Grumble Corner,
Sour and sad, whom I long to entreat
To take a house on Thanksgiving Street.

"OH, SIT DOWN."

THEY were analyzing. The sentence under consideration was, "In Africa lives the gorilla." The pupil stood on one foot and held to a desk with one hand and said, "This is a sentence, because it expresses a thought in words. *In* is the subject because it names that of which something is thought. Africa is the pred——" "Oh, sit down," said the teacher. He sat down. It did not trouble him much. All he had to do was to let go of the desk and relax his muscles just a little more, and down he went. The teacher then called on some one who she knew had more "back-bone." He stood up like a gentleman and put out his words with a snap that showed he was wide-awake. He disposed of the sentence satisfactorily and *"beautifully."* But what became of the boy who sat down. He simply *sat.* He sat as far *down* as possible. The back of his head touched the back of the desk behind him and his feet reached so far under the desk in front of him that he amused himself and annoyed a sensitive girl who sat in front of him by kicking her feet.

"Did he discover his mistake in analysis?" No. The teacher did not tell him to. He was told to sit. "They that are sick need a physician." This boy was sick. His case should have been diagnosed. His teacher should have felt his pulse and looked at his tongue any how. The boy who did not need to recite is the one that did the reciting. The teacher did not teach. We often say that a teacher must know the individual peculiarities of the pupils. Why must these peculiarities be known? That the individual may be taught. It is common to say, "Teach the pupils to think." "To think" does not mean to recite. If this boy had been told to "stand up" instead of to "sit down," it would have been better. It would have been still better for the teacher to have taken him in his crooked condition and questioned him in regard to the sentence until his activity of thought would have made him straighten up. It is the business of the teacher to take the pupil where he is and lead him on. When this boy said, "*In* is the subject," etc., the teacher should have asked "What *is* a subject?" If the pupil does not know, tell him. He is then ready for this question; "*What* lives in Africa?" He now has something to think about. If he answers the question he must *think*. He reads the sentence and *judges* what word names the thing that lives in Africa. By this means he might get some good out of analysis. But given as a mere form—as a something to say, it is worse than nothing. Analysis, parsing, etc., are not ends but means to gain an end; viz., the cultivation of the power to think.

CORRECTING MISTAKES.

"A teacher should not allow a word to be mispronounced, or an error in grammar to be made, without correcting it at once."

The author of the above probably meant the right thing. In our judgment he has been misunderstood by many teachers. Suppose a pupil is asked to explain the following problem: A can do a piece of work in 4 days, and B can do it in 3 days. If they both work together, how long will it take them to do the work?

The pupil says, "Sense (since) A can do the work——" Here he is called to a halt by the teacher and fifteen swinging hands. He wonders what has happened. A pupil is given permission to tell him. He is informed that he said *sense* for *since*. He starts out again: "Sĕn—*since*", and he has put so much force on the

3

pronunciation of the word that he has almost forgotten what he intended to say, but presently he rallies, in spite of his teacher's encouraging remarks, such as, "Well, hurry. We can't wait all day." He starts again : "Sĕn—since A does the work in 4 days, ¼ of the work is wat (what) he——" Up go the hands, and the teacher allows some pupil to correct him, after which he is told to try again. He does try again, but he is getting disgusted. He begins to weaken. He begins at the beginning with his mind fixed on *what*. He is hoping to get under such headway by the time he reaches the *what* that his momentum will help to carry him over. He says, "Sence A can do——" He has stranded on since. After correction, he tries again, and just as he got under headway he struck the word *of*, which he called *uv*. This produced more consternation. He still survived and tried again, but his explanation had passed out of his mind and he said some *curious* things and gave the queer answer that they could both do the work in 7 days. *This* did not seem to trouble the pupils any, but they noticed that he crossed his legs and stood on one foot and said *is* for *are*, *wat* for *what*, *uv* for *of*, etc.

These habits of bad pronunciation were acquired before he entered school and are of long standing. They can not be broken up at once. They must be broken up as they were made—little by little. Allow him to explain his problem without interruption. Give him credit for his work. Then criticise the mistakes in pronunciation, grammar, etc. Simply correct him and see whether he *can* pronounce the words correctly, and that he sees why his grammar was wrong. "Learn to labor and to wait." Teachers are often unwilling to *wait*. They usually *labor* enough.

QUESTIONS.

BY WILLIAM M. GIFFIN, N. J.

[Only Geographical answers to be given.]

What has a mouth but can not bite ?
What has an arm but can not write ?
What has a foot but can not walk ?
What has a head but can not talk ?

What has a bank with no money in?
What has a top that can not spin?
What has a neck but has no head?
What never sleeps but has a bed?
What hook will never catch a fish?
What has a basin but not a dish?
Where are the locks keys do not turn?
Where are the capes that are not worn?
. What has a branch but has no leaves?
What has no locks but has some keys?
What always falls but gets no scratches?
What is the ball that no one catches?
What is quite long but is not tall?
What has a base but plays no ball?
What are the poles that nobody climbs?
Where are the boys to answer these rhymes?

—School Journal.

NORMALS.

J. B. Evans has a working normal of about 30 at New Ross.

J. W. Cantley is conducting a normal nearly 100 strong at Dayton.

Thos. Shakes has at Plymouth one of the largest normals in the state.

M. W. Harrison and H. E. Coe have a normal of about 60 at Auburn.

Messrs. Machan and Munson are teaching a good normal at La Grange.

R. G. Boone and A. Rosenberger have a good summer normal at Westfield.

R. I. Hamilton and — ———— are holding an excellent normal at Anderson.

J. O. Lewellen and W. H. H. Shoemaker have a normal of about 75 at Muncie.

J. W. Adair, assisted by J. B. Humphreys and W. C. Palmer, are holding a large normal at Columbia City.

E. C. White and W. P. Denny, assisted by Supt. Van Gorder, are doing good work for nearly 100 teachers at Albion.

Tipton county normal is in session with an enrollment of 30. Teachers are doing excellent work under direction of F. A. Crockett, county superintendent.

W. H. Elson and Lin. N. Hadley have a large normal at Rockville. That the most ground possible may be covered, not only each lesson for the entire term, but the main headings of each lesson are printed in advance.

EDITORIAL.

Persons sending money for this Journal can send amounts less than $1 in *two* and *one* cent postage stamps; no others can be used.

In asking to have the address of your Journal changed, please give the *old* address as well as the new, naming the county as well as the state.

An agent is wanted to raise a club for the Journal in every township in the State. Send for terms.

PAY UP!—*If you are still on the delinquent list, please settle at once, that last year's books may be closed. Money sent directly to the editor will be credited to the proper agent.*

BAD, BAD, BAD.—The salary of the Superintendent has been reduced in New Albany from $1500 to $1000, and in Washington from $1200 to $900

THIS MONTH'S JOURNAL.—The editor calls special attention to every article in this issue of the Journal. Almost every one is worthy of not only a careful reading but of many readings and careful *study*. They are all of a high order and go to the core of the subject treated.

Is the purpose of the public school to teach the "legal" branches, to teach morality, to teach "business," or to teach the child? If the latter, is it the duty of the teacher to do all teaching? If not, is the child to be taught partly by the parent and partly by itself? In short, what are the different factors in the school work and what their relations? Who will give us a brief article answering these questions separately?

NATIONAL ASSOCIATION.—The reports from the National Association are all flattering. While the attendance was not so large as that of last year, it was much larger than usual. The Indiana delegation so far as reported were, State Supt. Holcombe, L. H. Jones, Geo. P. Brown and wife, S. S. Parr, E. E. Smith, Mary E. Nicholson, Nebraska Cropsey, Ada Duzan, Jas. H. Smart and wife. State Supt. Holcombe was elected principal of the Primary Section.

Several of these persons took active part in the work, and did credit to themselves and the state. The address of Mr. Holcombe and the discussion of Dr. Harris's paper by Mr. Jones deserve special mention. Mr. Brown was re-elected Secretary of the Council. Mr. Smith acted as Asst. Secretary of the General Association. Mr. Sheldon, author of "Object Lessons," etc., was chosen President for the next year. It was decided to hold the next meeting at either Topeka or Denver.

———

A CURIOUS NUMBER —Here is something to scratch your head over. A very curious number is 142,857, which, multiplied by 1, 2, 3, 4, 5, and 6, gives the same figures in the same order, beginning at a different point; but, if multiplied by 7, gives all nines:

$$142,857 \times 1 = 142,857$$
$$142,857 \times 2 = 285,714$$
$$142,857 \times 3 = 428,571$$
$$142,857 \times 4 = 571,428$$
$$142,857 \times 5 = 714,285$$
$$142,857 \times 6 = 857,142$$
$$142,857 \times 7 = 999,999$$

Multiply 142,857 by 8 and you have 1,142, 856. Then add the first figure to the last and you have 142,857, the original number, with figures exactly the same as at the start.

———

INSTITUTES.—The season of the institutes is here, and over *seventy* of the ninety-two will be held in August. It is of great importance that the time in these meetings be used to the best advantage. The teachers who are required to attend have a right to expect the most possible in the time. To this end no time should be wasted in "organizing"—ten minutes are all sufficient. The Supt. in many cases can sit at his desk and enroll the names while the work proceeds. Why wait for a motion to appoint a secretary, or a counter, or a critic, or to adjourn? Why read the minutes at all? The institute is a school under the control of the Supt., and not a literary society. The program should be carefully prepared and each person who is expected to give an exercise should be notified in time to make careful preparation, that the teachers may have the best.

QUESTIONS AND ANSWERS.

—————*D*—————.

READING.—1. Name three things essential to the correct reading of a sentence.

2. Give a good method of conducting a reading exercise in the Fifth Grade.

3 What is the distinction between didactic and emotional reading?

4. What are some of the reasons in favor of occasional concert reading?

5. How would you keep children from reading poetry in a sing-song tone?

6. Read a paragraph of prose and a stanza of poetry selected by the superintendent.

GEOGRAPHY.—1. Draw an outline of the State of Kentucky, indicating its chief rivers.

2. In what direction from London are the following cities: Edinburgh, Herat, Milwaukee, Melbourne, and Canton?

3. Indicate three great wheat regions of the earth, and two famous for the production of rice.

4. Contrast the chief products of the Gulf States with those of the Central States, and give your reasons for the difference.

5. Locate ten cities situated on the Great Lakes.

6. Explain the annual rise and fall of the Nile, and explain the relation of this to the fertility of the Nile Valley.

7. Where are the Himalaya Mountains? What is their influence on the climate of Southern and Central Asia?

8. Name five great cities of the world, between 40 and 50 degrees north latitude.

9. Describe the Danube River, and locate the Caucasus Mountains, the Adriatic Sea, and the Cape Verde Islands.

10. What are some of the most important exports of China? Of Brazil? Of British India?

ARITHMETIC.—1. Wheeling, in Virginia, is in longitude $80°\ 42'$ west: the mouth of the Columbia River is in longitude $124°$ west; when it is 1 P. M. local time at Wheeling, what is the time at the mouth of the Columbia River? How find the difference in distance between two places when the difference in time is given?   5, 5

2. Divide the L. C. M. of 9, 10, 24, 25, 32 and 45 by the G. C. D. of 120, 168 and 1,768.   Mul. 4, D. 4, Quo. 2.

3. What is the effect of multiplying the denominator of a fraction without changing the numerator? Illustrate by an example.   5, 5

4. Divide $1\frac{3}{2\frac{1}{2}}$ by $5\frac{7}{84\frac{7}{4}}$ Ans. 10

5. What will 1 A. 3 R. 16 P. 25 sq. yd. of land cost at 25 cents per square foot?   Proc. 5, ans. 5

6. Find the cost of $\frac{3}{4}$ of a ℔. Troy at $1.25 per grain.   Ans. 10

7. Find the interest of $57.85 for 2 yr. 3 mos. 23 days at 5 %.   5
     Define compound interest.   5

8. A merchant imports 75 cases of indigo, gross weight 196 ℔. each; allow 15 % for tare; what was the duty at 5c. per ℔.? What is duty?   5, 6

9. In the reprint of a book consisting of 810 pages, 50 lines are contained in a page instead of 40, and 72 letters in a line instead of 60. Of how many pages will the new edition consist? Solve by proportion.   Statement 5, ans. 5

10. The side of a cubical vessel is 1 foot; find the side of another cubical vessel that shall contain 3 times as much.   Ans. 10

TEACHING.—1. What should be the nature of the instruction in Geography in the first three years?

2. Give reasons for teaching children words before they know the letters of the alphabet.

3. Why should the teacher never scold his pupils?

4. Name three objections to concert recitations.

5. What is a habit? How is a habit formed?

PHYSIOLOGY.—1. Describe the epiglottis.

2. What effect is produced by the loss of sleep?

3. Describe the salivary glands.

4. Describe the structure of the lungs.

5. What is the cause of animal heat? What is the natural temperature of man?

6. Describe the retina.

7. Describe the Eustachian tube.

8. What is the blind spot of the eye?

9. Describe the lymphatic system.

10. Describe the structure of the teeth.

U. S. HISTORY.—1. What discoveries made west and north of the Ohio river show this country to have been early inhabited by a more civilized people than the Indians?   10

2. What river famous in the history of John Smith was also famous in the Civil War?   10

3. What three kinds of government obtained among the English colonies? What was the peculiarity of the Connecticut colony?
                                      2, 2, 2, 4

4. How did Washington become the Commander in Chief of the American army?   10

5. Name five difficulties that Washington's Administration had to contend with. How were they met?   10 pts

6. What bold and successful attack of an important city was made by the British in the war of 1812, which the Confederates attempted to repeat?   10

7. What was the Kansas-Nebraska bill? What connection had it with the Civil War?   5, 5

8. What was the first overt act in the War of the Secession? What effect did it have on the South? What on the North? 2, 4, 4

9. How did Hood's invasion of Tennessee in 1864 aid Sherman in his march through Georgia to the sea? What was Gen. Thomas's mode of procedure at the battle of Nashville?   5, 5

10. What principle as to appointment to, and removal from office entered largely into the last presidential election?   10

PENMANSHIP.—1. Describe the position which you regard best for writing in school.

2. What is meant by form?

3. In what manner does a careful study of form aid in making a good penman?

4. How many kinds of lines are used in writing? Define each.

5. Analyze a, b, g, r, B.

NOTE.—Your writing in answering these questions will be taken as a specimen of your penmanship, and will be marked 90 or below, according to merit.

ORTHOGRAPHY.—1. Into what two general classes are the letters divided?

2   Give a table of the short vowels, illustrating the use of each.

3. Mark diacritically the following words: onward, easily, aisle, leisure and patron.

4. In what ways can the sound of o in not be represented?

5. Spell twenty words selected by the County Superintendent.

GRAMMAR.—1. Define a modifier. Illustrate in sentences the different kinds of modifiers that the subject of a sentence may have.

2. What is the order of elements in the interrogative sentence?

3. State the office of each subordinate clause in the following: (a) We are anxious that you shall be satisfied. (b.) And now, where shade and fountain meet, herds of horses and cattle feed. (c. The play's the thing wherein I'll catch the conscience of the king.

4. Select two irregular verbs and give all the participial forms of each.

5. State the case of the italicized words in the following sentences, giving reasons: (a.) We think *General Grant* a *hero*. (b.) I saw John, the *boy* who rings the bell.

6. Correct errors in the following, giving reasons: (a.) I can do this work easier than that. (b.) I do not like such a warm day. (c.) All persons are not industrious.

7. Analyze "If a man be gracious, it shows that he is a citizen of the world."

8. Use the following conjunctions to connect the members of a compound sentence. State the kind of relation shown by each : *And, but, or.*

9. Class the pronouns and the subordinate clauses in the following: (a.) I know who you are. (b.) I know the man whom you saw.

10. State how the passive voice is made from the active.

ANSWERS TO STATE BOARD QUESTIONS PRINTED IN JULY:

PHYSIOLOGY.—1. There are two classes of fibers connecting the nerve-centers with the surface of the body—the afferent and the efferent, or the sensory and the motor. An impression transmitted along the former to the spinal cord (one of the nerve centers) may, owing to some injury, to some preoccupation of the mind, or to sleep, etc., not be transmitted to the brain but *reflected* along the motor fibre, thus producing action of which the mind is unconscious. These reflex actions sometimes seem to have a definite purpose, at other times they are irregular, spasmodic and indefinite in character. Thus, you may pinch the toe of a sleeping person who will quickly remove the foot and yet be totally unconscious of the act.

2. The chief function of the liver is the formation and storage of *glycogen*, a substance having the same chemical formula as starch, doubtless formed from the grape sugar in the nutritive materials carried to the liver by the portal vein, and serving a valuable purpose in the various tissues of the body, both between meals and in the absence of food. A second purpose of the liver is the secretion of the *bile*, a substance of value in intestinal digestion, and also because of its absence from the blood.

3. Light only arouses the sensation of vision when it falls upon the terminal organs of the optic nerve. There being a point of the retina—just where the optic nerve enters—where there are neither rods nor cones but only nerve fibres, this spot is insensitive to light, and hence called the *blind spot.*

4. The beatings of the pulse are due to the successive waves of blood transmitted through the arteries from the left ventricle.

5. The essential parts of a gland are usually secreting cells with smaller and larger ducts to carry off the secretion. Some of the chief glands of the body are the liver, the pancreas, the spleen, the salivary and peptic glands, etc.

6 The lymphatics are of two kinds—the lacteals and the lymphatics proper. The former absorb nutritive materials from the intestines and pass it through the mesenteric mesh to the thoracic duct. The latter originate partly in mere interstices between the

tissues of certain organs and partly in minute channels within certain organs. These unite to form the lymphatic capillaries, those the lymphatic trunks, the latter emptying their contents, directly or indirectly, into the sub-clavian veins.

8. The following are some of the more common actions tending to injure the sight : Reading by a dim light, holding the book or paper read too near the eye, reading, etc., with the face toward the light so that the rays fall as much upon the eye as upon the object looked at, long-continued use of the eye in gazing at minute objects, straining the eyes by children whose defective vision has been overlooked by the relatives and by the teacher, etc.

READING.—1. Articulation is usually defined as the distinct utterance of the several sounds and the several syllables which form the oral word. The latter is more properly termed enunciation. The teacher should give careful attention to articulation, as thereby only can pure and correct English be perpetuated (for sounds can not be printed) and thought accurately expressed.

2. Two things which a child should be able to do before attempting to read a lesson are : (1) to recognize its words at sight; (2) to know the meaning of its words as used in the lesson.

4. To the question whether the teacher should pronounce difficult words for the pupils of a fourth reader class, only a conditional answer can be given. If the pupils have been instructed properly in the use of the diacritical marks and the word is of such a character that a reasonable effort on their part should enable them to acquire its pronunciation, then they should not have that done for them which they can do for themselves, *provided* a proper reference book has been furnished the school. If, however, the word be unusually difficult, or be not found in the reference book, or there be no reference book for the school, it is usually wise for the teacher to give assistance. Just how much pupils should be assisted, or whether they should be assisted at all, is clearly a question of local conditions.

5. Three American poets are Wm. Cullen Bryant, Alice Cary and Jno. G. Whittier. Three poems of each are: Of Bryant, "Thanatopsis," "The Flood of Years," "The Future Life"; of Alice Cary, "Pictures of Memory," "A Dying Hymn," "Lyra"; of Whittier, "Snow Bound," "The Barefoot Boy," "Maud Muller."

HISTORY —1. (*a*) Spanish, English, French, and Dutch. (*b*) English.

2. They sailed from Holland, where they had been for nearly twelve years. In the petition to the King for a charter, they set forth as the chief causes for their coming to America, the conversion of the Indians, and the promotion of the commercial interests of Great Britain : added to these was, what has become historically the chief

cause, freedom for themselves to worship God according to the dictates of their own consciences.

3. It aroused the sluggish antagonism of the Virginians into a lively and growing opposition to the acts of Parliament and the despotism of the Royal Governor, an influence which he carried from the local field into the general one of the country.

4. Washington was elected unanimously, and Monroe at his second election, from the actual fusion of all parties, received all the electoral votes but one, from New Hampshire.

5. Benedict Arnold. While stationed at Philadelphia, recovering from a wound, his measures were so arbitrary and oppressive that he was threatened by a mob, and eventually convicted by a court martial to be publicly reprimanded by Gen. Washington, who performed the unpleasant duty in a singularly kind manner Arnold, however, was irritated by the fact of the court martial, and the failure to recognize his services especially against Burgoyne, and being approached by the British, who knew of his feelings, he yielded to a strong temptation and became a traitor to a cause which his heart and his judgment both still approved.

6. The passage of the Kansas-Nebraska Bill on the ground of Squatter Sovereignty. This led to the serious Border Warfare, which in time excited an intense feeling in the North antagonistic to the Southern ideas of Slavery.

7. The slowness with which he seemed to move in all his operations, and the deliberate character of his study of all the situations of both armies. The northern people, as well as the government, becoming impatient, he was superseded by Gen. Burnside. The Northern Army in their assaults of the town in the rear were most murderously slaughtered, losing over twelve thousand slain, nearly half of whom fell at the stone wall which protected the town.

8 Lee having in the tide of his successes penetrated into Penn., was returning south and east to threaten Baltimore and distract the attention of Meade, when he was suddenly met by Union cavalry near Gettysburg. Here one of the most bloody and important battles of the Civil War occupied three days, with varying fortune to the two sides until Gen. Meade, after a Federal loss of 23,000, succeeded in driving Lee south of the Pennsylvania lines, with probably a still heavier loss in men and materials, and an irrecoverable one in prestige, for all attempts at a Northern invasion were at once regarded as futile.

9. The purchase of Alaska, at the suggestion of Wm. H. Seward, for $7,200,000 in gold. The Commercial Treaty made by Anson Burlingame with China.

10. The opening of the Pacific Railroad. The 15th amendment, which guarantees to all the right of suffrage, without distinction as to race, color, or previous condition of servitude.

GEOGRAPHY.—1. Delaware River, Delaware Bay, Atlantic Ocean, St. George's Channel, Irish Sea, River Mersey.

2. United States of Colombia, Ecuador, Peru, Bolivia, Chili.

3. (*a*) Great Miami River in the western part of Ohio, Scioto in the central part, and Muskingum in the eastern part, all flow mainly toward the south, into the Ohio River. (*b*) Cincinnati, in the southwestern part of Ohio, on the Ohio River; Cleveland, on Lake Erie; Columbus in the centre, on the Scioto; Toledo in the northwestern part, at the mouth of the Maumee; Dayton, in the western part, on the Great Miami.

4. Boston is east of Chicago; Ecuador southwest from Iceland; Manchester northwest of London; Isthmus of Suez is east from the Gulf of California, in the same latitude; St. Petersburg is northwest from Canton.

5. A lake is a body of water lying in a basin of the land. A bay is an arm of some larger body of water extending into the land. A gulf is an arm of the ocean extending into the land. A strait is a narrow passage of water connecting two larger bodies of water. An isthmus is a narrow neck of land connecting two larger bodies of land, and separating two bodies of water.

6. Cuba, Rio Janeiro, and Cape Verd are in the Torrid Zone; Moscow, Paris, Japan Islands, Portland (Oregon), Winnepeg are in the North Temperate Zone; Baffin Bay is in the North Frigid Zone; Melbourne is in the South Temperate Zone.

7. New Orleans is the greatest cotton market in the United States; Charleston is the first rice market; Minneapolis, situated at the Falls of St. Anthony on the Mississippi, contains the largest flouring mills in the United States, and is the seat of the Minnesota State University; Mobile is in the southern part of Alabama, at the head of Mobile Bay; Galveston, at the entrance of Galveston Bay, in southeastern part of Texas.

8. Amazon, Mississippi, Missouri, La Plata, Mackenzie.

9. (*a*) The Nile is the outlet of large lakes, which, owing to heavy periodical rains, annually discharge so large a body of water as to overflow the valley of the Nile, whose waters rise gradually from June till the middle of September. (*b*) Wheat and other grains, cotton, indigo, and a variety of fruits.

10. In the Alleghany Mountains. In the Ohio basin, chiefly in the States of Indiana and Illinois; in Missouri and adjacent States west of the Mississippi River; in Michigan.

GRAMMAR.—1. (*a*) A combination of words that does not express a complete thought. (*b*) We sat down *on a rock covered with moss*. *On a rock* is a prepositional phrase; *covered with moss*, a participial phrase.

2.   *a.* An adjective; as, *Ripe* fruit is wholesome.

    b. A possessive noun; as, The *boy's* composition was good.

    c. A possessive pronoun; as, *Their* efforts were unsuccessful.

    d. An appositive; as, Victor Hugo, the *novelist*, is dead.

    e. A participle; as, A penny *saved* is a penny earned.

    f. An infinitive; as, A desire *to excel* is commendable.

    g. A phrase; as, One *of my friends* came.

    h. A clause; as, The boy *who is honest* will be trusted.

3.   *Est*, or *st*, is usually added to the verb, or to one of the auxiliaries, when the subject is in the second person singular. *S* is usually added to a verb in the present tense of the indicative mode, when the subject is in the third person singular.

4.   *a. How* is a conjunctive adverb of manner, modifying *formed*. *b.* In this sentence, *where* is equivalent to *in which*, and modifies *fell. c. Where* is a conjunctive adverb of place, and modifies *fell*.

5.   By the apostrophe and s, and by the apostrophe alone; as, Henry's, Charles's, Moses', boys'.

6.   An abstract noun is the name of a quality or an attribute. Some grammarians also call the names of actions abstract nouns, since the idea of predication is not found in participles and infinitives.

7.   Abel, thy brother, is *where?* Simple interrogative sentence; of which the subject nom. is *Abel*, modified by the appositive *brother; brother* is modified by the possessive pronoun *thy; is* is the pred. verb (or copula), modified by the interrogative adverb of place, *where. Abel, thy brother.* is the logical subject, and *is where*, the logical predicate.

8.   *a.* That the earth is round, no one doubts. The clauses are transposed. *b.* The truth if the matter, it is thought, will soon appear. Parenthetical expressions are set off by commas. *c.* His words were these: "I can not be false to my country." A formal quotation is preceded by a colon.

9.   *a. What* (noun) is sometimes an interrogative pronoun.

    b. What (interrogative pronoun) are you doing?

    c. I heard *what* (relative) you said.

    d. What (adverb) by entreaty and *what* by threatening, I
      succeeded.

10.   I lay, I laid, I shall lay, I have laid, I had laid, I shall have laid. If I lay, if I laid, if I had laid. I may lay, I might lay, I may have laid, I might have laid.

SCIENCE OF TEACHING.—1. Thinking, feeling and willing, are the three distinct forms of action of which the soul is capable. They are named in the order of their dependence.

2. The intellectual power may be separated into the perceptives, representatives and reflectisve.

3. These faculties become active in the order named above.

4. The thing should be learned before the word naming it; because the child will learn the word more easily and thoroughly when it means something to him

5. If the word is learned before the thing, the child is apt to get the word, as a word, and not as the sign of something. Every word learned should call up its appropriate idea.

ARITHMETIC.—1. A *divisor* of a number is any factor of that number, while a *multiple* of a number is a product obtained by taking the number as a factor any number of times.

2. In multiplying both terms of a fraction by the number the value remains unchanged, for by multiplying the numerator increases the number of parts in the same ratio as multiplying the denominator decreases the size of the parts.

3. 7 hr. 57 min. 26.4 sec. $\times$ 15 = 119°—21'—36'' dif. in Long.

$$\frac{30° - 19' \, 46''}{89° - 1' - 50''} = \text{the Long. of N. O.}$$

4. 365 d. —6 h. — 365 da. 5 h. 48 min. 48 sec. = 11 min. — 12 sec., or 672 sec gained in 1 yr. 1 da. = 86400 sec. 86400 sec. ÷ 672 = 128$\frac{4}{7}$ yr. or 128 yr. 6 mo. 25 da, 17 h. 8 min. 34$\frac{2}{7}$ sec.

5. Arithmetical method. $\frac{3.4}{5} - \frac{3.7}{8} = \frac{7}{8}$. $\frac{7}{8} \times \frac{3.4}{5} = \frac{3.4}{8}$. $\frac{3.4}{8} - \frac{44}{8} = \frac{7.3.4}{8}$, or $\frac{34.5}{8}$. $\frac{34.5}{8} \times \frac{44}{8} = \frac{5.5.5.5}{8}$. $\frac{5.5.5.5}{8} \times \frac{3.4}{8} = \frac{21.5.5.5.4}{8}$. $\frac{21.5.5.5.4}{8} - 16\frac{1}{2}$, or $\frac{34.5}{8} = \frac{1.7.0.5.4.4}{8}$, or $285\frac{1}{2}\frac{3.4.4}{8}$, Ans. Processes necessary, multiplication and subtraction.

Algebraical method. $\frac{3.4}{5} - \frac{1.7}{4} \times \frac{3.4}{5} - \frac{44}{8} \times \frac{7.7}{8} \times \frac{7.3}{5} - \frac{6.5}{4} = \frac{3.7}{5} - \frac{34.3}{8} - \frac{7.7.7}{8.8.8} 1 - + \frac{1.7}{8} = \frac{1.1.7.3}{7.6.0} - \frac{44.5.0}{7.6.0} - \frac{1.3.7.1.1}{7.6.0} - \frac{44.7.7}{7.6.0} = -111\frac{1}{8}\frac{3.4}{8}$, Ans.

6. .9÷.00075=1200. Order of quo. figure is known by position of partial dividend from caret.

7. 25% or $\frac{1}{4}$=$337.50. $\frac{4}{1}$=4$\times$$337.50=$1350, value of silk.
$1350÷1800=$.75, invoice price per yard.
$1350, value, +$337.50, duty,=$1687.50.
$1687.50+20%, or $\frac{1}{5}$ of itself,=$2025.
$2025÷1800=$1.12$\frac{1}{2}$, selling price.

8. 124%=$395250. 1%=31 875. 100%=$3187.50, cost of second lot.
113$\frac{1}{2}$%=$\frac{1}{11}$. $\frac{1}{11}$=$3187.50. $\frac{1}{15}$=$\frac{1}{17}$ of 3187.50=$187.5.
$\frac{1}{11}$=$\times$$187.5=$2812.50, cost of first lot.

9. $\frac{2}{3}$ of fallen part=$\frac{1}{4}$ of stump. $\frac{1}{3}$ of fallen part=$\frac{1}{6}$ of stump. $\frac{1}{2}$ of fallen part=$\frac{1}{8}$ of stump. $\frac{1}{2}$, or fallen part+$\frac{1}{8}$ or stump=$\frac{1}{5}$, the 51 feet. $\frac{1}{6}$=3 ft. $\frac{1}{8}$=8$\times$3 ft.=24 ft. or stump. $\frac{3}{8}$=9$\times$3 ft.=27 ft., the fallen part.

10. 8 A 2 R 9 P (or sq. rd.)=1369 sq. rd. $\sqrt{1369}$=37 rd., one side of field. 37$\times$4=148 rd., distance around. 148 rd.$\times$65 cts.=$96.20.

Prof. C R Barnes, of the chair of Botany in Purdue University, has obtained a year's leave of absence, which he will spend in advanced study at Harvard University.

MISCELLANY.

LOGANSPORT.—The report of the schools shows them in unusually good condition. Supt. J. K. Walts is still at the head.

Any one wishing to secure the volumes of this Journal for 1880 and 1881, should correspond with D. M. Geeting, Washington, Ind.

WAYNE COUNTY.—The manual of this county is one of the largest, one of the most complete, yet published in this state. It gets out of the usual line and does great credit to the venerable Supt., John C. Macpherson.

The Concord Summer School of Philosophy opened its usual course of lectures on July 16th. Not the least attractive feature are the lectures by Prof. Denton J Snyder upon "Gœthe's *Faust*," and "*Wilhelm Meister* as a Whole."

BROWN COUNTY had an average percent of enrollment of 73 instead of 23, as published some time ago in the Journal. The mistake was in the State Superintendent's report. Thirty counties in the state are lower than Brown in the above regard.

The Richmond Normal School closed its summer term July 19th, enthusiastically. The attendance had been good, the work satisfactory, general good feeling prevailed, and the prospects for the next year were bright. Cyrus W. Hodgin is principal.

THE WESTMINSTER SEMINARY for young ladies, at Fort Wayne, under the principalship of Miss Carrie B Sharp and Mrs. D. B. Wells, will open Sept. 10th, with new facilities and increased prospects and confidence of success. The school deserves the highest success.

LADOGA.—The normal school here is running smoothly and seems to be doing good work. The principal, A. F. Knots, reports an attendance of nearly 200 the present term. The commercial department of this school is very complete, and the *actual business* transactions required make a needful preparation for practical life.

The Parke county normal opened in the public school building at Rockville on July 13th, under the charge of county superintendent Elson and L. N. Hadley. The course is very thorough and was outlined for each day upon a neat program issued beforehand. The teachers of this county have as fine an educational spirit as can be found in this country.

LA FAYETTE.—Several of the teachers in the La Fayette public schools have been in continuous service from twelve to twenty years. Miss A. E. Stratton, principal of the Jencks school, has been in since 1861, and Miss M. Hazelett, principal of the Centennial School since 1866; while Mrs. O. H. Gadscombe, one of the best in the corps to-day, has "fought the good fight" since 1853!

St. Joseph County is, fortunately, still under the supervision of Calvin Moon. The county is thoroughly organized. Every school in city and county will open Sept. 7th. Many of the old teachers when they settled for last year contracted for next year. Two months prior to the opening of the schools not a half-dozen out of the hundred and ten schools were unsupplied with teachers. This is business.

De Pauw University will this fall take the lead among first-class universities in organizing a distinct and complete Normal School, on a par with the schools of Law, Medicine, and Divinity. The corps of instructors are able and will without doubt do thorough work and maintain a high standard. With Parr, Tompkins, Mace, and Carhart as special instructors, and the collateral accessories the school must be a success from the beginning.

Clay County.—The institute in this county was held this year at Clay City, beginning July 20—first of the season. It opened with an unusual attendance the first day. The interest and the temperature of the weather were both at about 98 degrees. S. S. Parr, of De Pauw Normal, was the chief instructor. Evening lectures were by W. A. Bell, J. W. Holcombe, and S. S. Parr. Supt. Wilkinson has good reason to congratulate himself on the auspicious opening of his first institute.

The "Spencer Class," of Frankfort, organized in 1880, has issued an unusually interesting program for the coming year. Among the subjects for discussion are "The Unity of the Human Race," by C. E. Newlin; "The Hebrew Character," by M. E. S. Boone; "Political Influence of Christianity," by S. H. Doyal; "Liberalism as a Social Force," by R. G. Boone; "The Relation of History to Tradition," by E. H. Staley.

The Northern Indiana Association was held at Rome City as per program. The attendance was not large, but about as large as ever before. Several excellent papers were read and the meeting was profitable. With a hope of increasing the attendance the place of meeting will be changed, probably to Maxinkuckee. T. B. Swartz, Supt. of the Elkhart schools, was elected president for next year, and D. D. Luke, Supt. of the schools at Ligonier, was elected chairman of the executive committee.

Shelbyville.—That W. H. Fertich, Supt. of the Shelbyville schools, was sued by a patron for causing a little girl to be locked out of a school-room on a cold morning last winter, has been extensively published, and that at the recent trial he was fined $1, has also been published. The trustees of the schools now publish a full explanation of facts fully relieving themselves and the Supt. from fault in the matter. They claim that the impression that has gone out, that the little girl was locked out in the cold, is absolutely false. While the door was locked during opening exerçises, the hall into which the door opened contained a good stove and was proven to be not less than 65 degrees at that time.

The girl went home not in accordance with the rules, but against them, and she lived only four squares away. The Supt. was a half-mile away in another building at the time, and was in no way responsible for whatever was done.

The jury was out 21½ hours and stood 7 to 5 in favor of acquittal, but finally brought in a compromise verdict making a fine of $1.00. The case has been appealed to the Supreme Court.

COUNTY INSTITUTES TO BE HELD.

August 3—Gibson county, Princeton. W. D. Robinson.
" 10—Clark county, Charlestown. John P. Carr.
" —Boone county, Lebanon. H. M. La Follette.
" —Floyd county, New Albany. L. H. Scott.
" —Jackson county, Brownstown. J. B. Hamilton.
" —Jay county, Portland. W. J. Houck.
" —Madison county, Anderson. D J. Crittenberger.
" —Newton county, Kentland. W. H. Hershman.
" —Ohio county, Rising Sun. F. A. Withers.
" —Parke county, Rockville. W. H. Elson.
" —Putnam county, Greencastle. L. E. Smedley.
" —Tipton county, Tipton. F. B. Crockett.
" —Posey county, Mt. Vernon. James Kilroy.
" 17—Bartholomew county, Columbus. Amos Burns.
" —Cass county, Logansport. D. D. Fickle.
" —Daviess county, Washington. S. B. Boyd.
" —Delaware county, Muncie. John O. Lewellen.
" —Dubois county, Jasper. A. M. Sweeney.
" —Fayette county, Connersville. J. S. Gamble.
" —Grant county, Marion. G. A. Osborne.
" —Hamilton county, Noblesville. E. A. Hutchens.
" —Henry county, New Castle. W. R. Wilson.
" —Jefferson county, Madison. O. E. Arbuckle.
" —Pulaski county, Winamac. J. H. Reddick.
" —Rush county, Rushville. W. L. Shauck.
" —St. Joseph county, Mishawaka. Calvin Moon.
" —Sullivan county, Sullivan. Jas. A. Marlow.
" —Switzerland county, Vevay. M. C. Walden.
" —Wabash county, Wabash. John N. Myers.
" —Warren county, Williamsport. C. T. Brown.
" —Wayne county, Richmond. J. C. Macpherson.
" 24—Blackford county, Hartford City. Lewis Willman.
" —Brown county, Nashville. S. P. Neidigh.
" —Carroll county, Delphi. J. L. Johnson.
" —Crawford county, Marengo. James Bobbitt.
" —Decatur county, Greensburg. John H. Bobbitt.
" —Elkhart county, Goshen. S. F. Spohn.
" —Franklin county, Brookville. M. A. Mess.
" —Fulton county, Rochester. F. D. Haimbaugh.
" —Hancock county, Greenfield. W. H. Glasscock.

August 24—Harrison county, Corydon. C. W. Thomas.
"   —Huntington county, Huntington. A. D. Mohler.
"   —Jasper county, Rensselaer. D. M. Nelson.
"   —Jennings county, North Vernon. S. W. Conboy.
"   —Johnson county, Franklin. H. D. Voris.
"   —Knox county, Vincennes. W. H. Pennington.
"   —La Grange county, La Grange. Enoch G. Machan.
"   —La Porte county, La Porte. W. A. Hosmer.
"   —Lawrence county, Bedford. D. H. Ellison.
"   .   —Marion county, Indianapolis W. B. Flick.
"   —Miami county, Peru. A. J. Dipboye.
"   —Monroe county, Bloomington. J. B. Hazel.
"   —Montgomery county, Crawfordsville. W. T. Fry.
"   —Morgan county, Martinsville. J. H. Henry.
"   —Perry county, Cannelton. Israel Whitehead.
"   —Randolph county, Winchester. H. W. Bowers.
"   —Ripley county, Versailles. Geo. W. Young.
"   —Scott county, Scottsburg W. M. Whitson.
"   —Shelby county, Shelbyville. Douglas Dobbins.
"   —Union county, Liberty. C. W. Osborne.
"   —Warrick county, Boonville. W. W. Fuller.
"   —Washington county, Salem. W. C. Snyder.
"   —White county, Monticello. John Rothrock.
"   31—Adams county, Decatur. J. F. Snow.
"   —Allen county, Ft. Wayne. G. F. Felts.
"   —Benton county, Fowler. B. F. Johnson.
"   —Clinton county, Frankfort. W. S. Sims.
"   —Hendricks county, Danville. A. E. Rogers.
"   —Howard county, Kokomo. J. W. Barnes.
"   —Martin county, ———. W. T. Mitchel.
"   —Marshall county, Plymouth. Thomas Shakes.
"   —Noble county, Albion. W. B. Van Gorder.
"   —Owen county, Spencer. W. S. Williams.
"   —Spencer county, Rockport. J. W. Nourse.
"   —Wells county, Bluffton. W. H. Ernst.
September 7—Dearborn county, Lawrenceburg. H. B. Hill.
"   —Dekalb county, Auburn. C. M. Merica.
"   —Fountain county, Covington. James Bingham.
"   —Green county, Bloomfield. J. S Ogg.
"   —Tippecanoe county, La Fayette. W. H. Caulkins.
"   —Vigo county, Terre Haute. H. W Curry.
"   24—Kosciusko county, Warsaw. S. D. Auglin.
October   —Whitley county, Columbia City. Alex. Knisely.
November 9—Steuben county, Angola. R. V. Carlin.
"   23—Porter county, Valparaiso. H. W. Porter.
December —Lake county, Crown Point. Frank Cooper.

GEMS OF THOUGHT.

Boys flying kites haul in their white-winged birds—
You can't do that way when you're flying words.
"Careful with fire," is good advice, you know,
"Careful with words," is ten times doubly so;
Thoughts unexpressed may sometimes fall back dead,
But God himself can't kill them when they're said.
                                    —*Will Carleton.*

"The heart benevolent and kind the most resembles God."

> Unless we act in the living present,
> There is naught that we can save;
> The future is not ours for labor,
> Though our hearts be ever so brave.　　　*—Anon.*

Whoever looks for a friend without imperfections, will never find what he seeks.—*Franklin.*

Every man is a volume, if you know how to read him.—*Channing.*

> Our life is short, but to expand that span
> To vast eternity, is virtue's work.　　*—Shakspeare.*

> When any great design thou dost intend,
> Think on the means, the manner, and the end.

He grieves more than is necessary, who grieves before it is necessary.—*Seneca.*

They that know no evil will suspect none.—*Ben Johnson.*

> Happy were men, if they but understood
> There is no safety but in doing good.　*— John Fountain.*

An ounce of pluck is worth a pound of luck.—*Garfield.*

Be not simply good, be good for something.—*Thoreau.*

When a man has not a good reason for doing a thing, he has one good reason for letting it alone.—*Sir Walter Scott.*

Keep company with the good, and you will be one of them.—*Cervantes.*

> Absence of occupation is not rest;
> A mind quite vacant is a mind distressed.—*Cowper.*

PERSONAL.

M. T. Moss is in charge at Carbon.

B. J. Bogue is re-elected at La Grange.

R. W. Moss will hold sway at Taunton.

Jas. R. Hart is re-elected at Thorntown.

Henry H. Miller is principal at Bremen.

Alice Wilson is principal at Knightsville.

A. B. Stevens will continue Supt. at Angola.

C. W. Crouse remains in charge at Harmony.

W. H. Chillson will be principal at Clay City.

Geo. E. Long is principal of the Roann schools.

A. Hildebrand will continue at Vevay next year.

T. J. Shea, a Normalite, has charge at Lexington.

Maurice Markle is head director at Bowling Green.

Lum. R. Melcher is principal of the Vevay high school.

W. D. Chambers will teach in Scottsburg the coming year.

L. F. Kenoyer, of Illinois, will have charge at Centre Point.

J. A. Carnagey is re-elected Prin\ of the high school at Madison.

E. R. Smith has been re-elected principal of the Chauncy schools.

E. M. Morrison takes the principalship of the Burlington schools.

A. E. Dawson will continue in charge of the high school at Rochester this year.

Victoria A. Adams, of Vt., has been elected principal of the Warsaw high school.

W. B. Creager has been retained in charge of the Sullivan schools at an increased salary.

B. W. Everman, late Supt. of Carroll county, has been elected curator of the State University.

B. F. Moon will succeed W. M. Sinclair at Monticello. Mr. Sinclair goes to Caldwell, Kansas.

W. P. Denny, late Supt. of Noble county, will go to Ann Arbor in the fall to attend the Law School.

W. E. Netherton, late Supt. of Pulaski county, voluntarily resigned his place to accept a $1500 salary:

M. W. Harrison is to retain the superintendency at Auburn, and H. E. Coe is to have the high school.

J. L. Rippetoe has been elected for his *seventeenth* year as superintendent of the Connersville schools.

S. E. Miller has been chosen for the nineteenth consecutive time as Supt. of the Michigan City schools.

J. B. Evans will continue in charge of the New Ross schools. His summer normal has been very successful.

Jos. W. Anderson, formerly a teacher of this state, is now located at Seattle, Washington Territory, and is doing well.

T. D. Tharp, who was for many years Supt. of Grant county, is now pastor of Simpson M. E. Church at Ft. Wayne.

Mary C. Brown, a State Normal graduate of the class of '84, has found a preqious "Jewell," and has laid aside the "birch."

J. H. Martin has given excellent satisfaction as superintendent of the Madison schools, and is re-elected for the coming year.

S. C. Hanson has resigned the principalship of Green Hill Seminary to accept the superintendency of the Williamsport schools.

C. L. Hottel has been re-elected principal of the Brownstown schools. He recently closed a very successful summer normal.

E. C. Clarke, who has been doing excellent work at Huntingburg has accepted the superintendency at Boonville—increased salary.

Prof. Chas. K. Adams, of Michigan University, has been elected President of Cornell University, in place of A. D. White, resigned.

S. S. Roth, a former superintendent of Wells county, is now principal of one of the district schools in Pittsburgh, Penn., at a salary of $1200.

C. M. Lemon has been continued in charge of the public schools of Ladoga. Mr. Lemon's work for the past year has been highly complimented.

J. Fraise Richard, who was last year principal of the Logansport Normal, is now engaged in institute work in this state and Kentucky. He does good work.

Prof. Geo. W. Hoss, former State Supt. of Indiana, and for many years editor of this Journal, is pleased with his professorship in Baldwin University, Kansas.

Thos. J. Bryant, formerly president of the Indianapolis Business College, is now conducting a Commercial Department connected with Hartsville College.

Aura E. Smith, a State Normal graduate of '84, was married to Howard Walls, June 30th. Mr. Walls has engaged to teach in the Bourbon schools next year.

J. O. Lewellen was re-elected Supt. of Delaware county with emphasis; i. e., they elected him and at the same time made him a present of an elegant office chair.

Lilly Ragan, of Clayton, Hendricks county, was awarded the Levy Baker prize for manuscript showing highest scholarship of graduate from the common schools for 1884–5.

W. F. Hoffman, who for the past three years has been principal of the Washington high school, has been elected superintendent of the schools *vice* D. E. Hunter resigned.

John Hancock, LL. D., for many years the efficient and popular superintendent of the Dayton, O., schools, has accepted the superintendency of the Chillicothe, O., schools.

Hiram Hadley, who is well and favorably known to the teachers of this state, has agreed to take charge of the Bloomingdale Academy. He will be assisted by his wife, who is also an experienced and successful teacher. If the school does not prosper in such hands it would better be permanently closed.

J. P. Wickersham, for eight years State Supt. of Pennsylvania, has been engaged by the executive committee to make the annual address before the next State Teachers' Association..

O. L. Kelso, a graduate of both the State University and the State Normal School, resigns the principalship of the high school at Anderson to accept a corresponding place at Richmond at an increased salary.

Rev. L. N. Albright, of Fostoria, Ohio, has been chosen president of De Pauw Female College at New Albany. He is a graduate of Delaware College, O., and has filled several responsible positions with ability.

Eli F. Brown, who is well and favorably known in this state, has been elected superintendent of the Paducah, Ky., schools. Mr. Brown is an excellent teacher, and Indiana loses a valuable worker from its educational corps.

A. H. Morris, late Supt. of Hamilton county, at the recent State Convention of County Superintendents, read a paper on "The Ex-County Superintendent." The paper came late in the session, after most of the superintendents had gone, which is much to be regretted, as it was the raciest, wittiest paper of the session, and contained some very valuable suggestions. The relation of the old to the new superintendent was most happily discussed.

W. W. May, of Salem, a teacher well and favorably known in Southern Indiana, died very suddenly of heart disease. The deceased, a gray-haired man himself, was a son of Jas. G. May, who is the oldest active teacher in the state, and is still in good health.

Prof. L. S. Thompson, of Purdue University, is teaching the Art Department of the Monteagle summer normal school with marked success. Monteagle is not far from Nashvile, on the top of the Cumberland Mountains, and is represented as being a delightful place.

J. M. Cantley, late Supt. of Montgomery county, (and by the way he was one of the best superintendents in the state), has been appointed principal of the 9th St. School at Evansville, at a salary of $1000. He is now teaching a summer normal numbering nearly 100 at Darlington.

D. E. Hunter, so well known to Indiana teachers, has concluded to emigrate to Texas the coming year. The point selected is Terrell, a thriving place of 5000 inhabitants, 30 miles east of Dallas. He writes that Texas is a big thing—as big as "all out doors." He has been elected Supt. of the Terrell schools.

George Sand, a graduate of the State Normal School, and for the past two years a teacher in Bartholomew county, left home last May, saying he was going into the country for a short time, and has not been heard of since. He took no clothing except what he wore and had but little money. It is feared that he is suffering from temporary insanity. Any word of his whereabouts will be gladly received by his wife, who is now at Plymouth.

BOOK TABLE.

Harpers' Bazar stands at the head of fashion magazines, and is what every lady delights to read and examine.

The Current of Chicago has established itself as a first-class literary weekly. It ranks with the best papers of its class in the entire country.

The Atlantic, published by Houghton, Mifflin & Co., Boston, is a standard monthly magazine of the highest rank. It is not illustrated, but the space is all filled with the best thoughts of the best thinkers and writers of the land. It is an old and tried friend.

Harpers' Weekly, edited by Geo. William Curtiss, is the first illustrated weekly of this country. Its reading matter is of the best quality and its illustrations are unequalled. Thos. Nast illustrates no other paper. His cartoons alone are worth the subscription price.

The Wide-Awake, published by D. Lathrop & Co , of Boston, is without doubt one of the very best magazines for boys and girls published on either side of the Atlantic. It numbers among its contributors many of the best writers in the country. It ought to be in every home in which there are young people.

E. E. White, Supt. of the Albion schools, has just published a "*Hand-Book for Teachers*." It gives outlines, dates, and headings in U. S. History, Literature, Arithmetic, Grammar, and Civil Government. It is a neat pamphlet and will be helpful to teachers, especially in conducting reviews. Price 25c.

The Book Lover, by James Baldwin, Ph. D. Chicago: Jansen, McClurg & Co.

The above is a valuable little book for parents, teachers and scholars. Courses of reading and schemes of practical study are clearly presented. Lists of suitable books for the young and the more mature are given. The author gives some very valuable hints on the formation and use of libraries. The book is a safe guide to the best reading, and is worthy a place in every library.

The author of this book is our esteemed friend Jas. Baldwin, Supt. of the Rushville schools, this state. The readers of the Journla will remember with pleasure his occasional contributions.

New Physical Geography for Grammar and High Schools, by Jas. Monteith. New York and Chicago: A. S. Barnes & Co. Cyrus Smith, Indianapolis.

The following are some of the good features of this little book: It contains only 144 pages. The language is clear and concise; so that a higher grammar grade pupil can understand it. It is full of well executed illustrations. It contains the latest discoveries and statistics made by British and U. S Governments on the subjects of which it treats. While it is not so large and expensive as most books on this subject, it contains all that is necessary for ordinary high and grammar schools.

The Sentence and Word Book, by James Johonnot. New York: D. Appleton & Co.

In teaching reading by the word and sentence method, teachers find it difficult to get a sufficient number of sentences with words expressing ideas with which the child is acquainted. This little book will remove the difficulty. It will be of great service to the teacher in all primary language work. The first twelve pages of the book are in script, which is thought to be enough script for one term. It contains over 400 quotations from good authors. These will have a tendency to cultivate the literary taste of the pupils. The book will save the primary teacher much drudgery and make language work a pleasant exercise for the pupils.

English Literature, by Kellogg. New York: Clark & Maynard. J. D. Williams, Chicago, Western Agent.

The chief points that make this a valuable book to the student are, its grouping of authors so that their relations to one another are easily seen; a description of their surroundings and other influences that made them write what they did; its suggestions as to how to study the subject; its selections being mostly those not found in books of selections.

The author of the book is one of the authors of Reed & Kellogg's grammars, and the kind of work to which the grammars will lead, is presented in this book. The aim of the author seems to have been to make the pupil do his own thinking.

U. S. History, by Horace E. Scudder. Philadelphia: J. H. Butler.

After a careful examination we have no hesitation in saying that this is a very excellent school history. Its type is clear and it is printed on good heavy paper. It is written in a simple style so that a 14 year old pupil may understand it without an interpreter. This is no small matter to the teacher. The arrangement of matter, the good pictures, the topical analyses and excellent maps are also important features of the book. The difficult words to pronounce are analyzed and the unfamiliar are defined. A very complete index at the close of the book is very valuable. School officers and teachers would do well to examine this book.

Modern Electricity and Magnetism, by Elroy M. Avery, Ph. D. New York and Chicago: Sheldon & Co.

In this age of multiplex telegraphy, telephony, electric lights, electric railways, electric motors, etc , etc., a book giving a special treatise on electricity and magnetism seems a necessity. This little book is not made up on "the scrap book plan." The author keeps constantly before the reader the underlying principles.

Elementary Physiology, by Richard J Dunglison, M. D. Boston: Porter & Coates. F. S. Cable, Chicago, Western Agent.

☞ The above is a very neat little book of 200 pages, printed on good paper with clear type. It contains sufficient physiology for elementary classes. There are numerous illustrations in the book and they are very good. The book was written for the purpose of showing the effect of alcohol and tobacco on the human system. At the close of each chapter the effects of alcohol and tobacco are given on the organs considered in the chapter. This is by no means a small point.

BUSINESS NOTICES.

INDIANA
SCHOOL JOURNAL.

Vol. XXX.   SEPTEMBER, 1885.   No. 9.

*"HOW FAR CAN THE KNOWLEDGE OF MENTAL SCIENCE BE UTILIZED BY THE COMMON SCHOOL TEACHER?"

LEWIS H. JONES, SUPT. INDIANAPOLIS SCHOOLS.

THE subject assigned to me must of necessity be limited greatly for treatment in thirty minutes. I shall attempt rather to illustrate the uses, to the common school teacher, of some of the facts and principles of his vocation, which the knowledge of mental science gives him, than to make an exhaustive, analytic treatment of my entire theme.

My first inquiry, then is, What are some of the more useful of the facts and principles of his vocation, that the common school teacher may obtain through the study of mental science?

In the discussion of this phase of my theme it will be necessary to give at first a general treatment, and then a specific one.

First, then, the student of mental science is confronted with the *difference* between the mind as a subject of study, and those other subjects with which he is already more familiar.

What *mind* or *spirit* is in its *essence*, can only be known by the study of its attributes. Its attributes are found by study to be those of *action* or *condition*. These are classified as acts or states of *thinking*, *feeling*, or *choosing*. These acts or states become known to the student of mental science by identification and interpretation through his own consciousness. Thus each stu-

---

* Read before the Northern Indiana Teachers' Association.

dent experiences for himself the states which his text describes, and thus he knows without any doubt the exact spiritual nature of these processes. The spiritual nature of these *processes* establishes the spiritual nature of the *mind,* and raises its character above the material surroundings in which it temporarily exists.

One who has experienced the higher and purer pleasures of thought, or the more refined and elevated forms of the nobler emotions, or has exulted in consciousness at the moment of successful achievement, never again doubts the nobleness of a spiritual nature capable of such chastened and refined delights. Now, mental science, properly studied, shows each pupil to be a spirit, capable of a development which makes these noble mental states possible.

If mental science had no other lesson for the common school teacher, this were enough to secure its place in a course of professional study.

It teaches us to see in each child-pupil the possible man or woman, with all the rights and possibilities of the rich, unfolding life; and who shall dare stand in the presence of these undeveloped spirits without the feeling of reverence for such natures and the responsibility for their right development, which every true teacher feels in his school? "I love God and little children," said the German poet. "Of such is the kingdom of heaven," said the Great Teacher.

The student of mental science sees why each should have said what so naturally fell from his lips in the sweet presence of little children.

Thus far I have tried to show that the study of mental science reveals to the teacher the exact nature of the child-pupil whom he is to educate,—namely, that he is an undeveloped spirit, with all the possibilities of an immortal life before him. This being the teacher is to educate, by leading him into and through the varied phases of high thinking, noble feeling, and heroic acting. Thus far I have been general in my treatment of the theme assigned.

I must at this point become specific. In order to do so successfully, I must make a few general statements and announce a few definitions of terms, without stopping to establish by proofs

·the former or to defend the latter. I shall be brief in these, that I may spend the remainder of the time allotted to me chiefly in exemplification by specific instance.

Theorizers upon education have not yet agreed as to what is the proper function of the common school. Some claim that it is entirely for the purpose of developing the spirit, without much reference to the bread-and-butter side of life; others claim that its function is to make the future man or woman self-sustaining in this life; others, still, claim that it is the function of the common school to make each of its graduates a good citizen,—whatever that may mean; while the most appropriate definition of its function will include something of all these properly combined and appropriately related.

I suggest, therefore, for use during the remainder of this discussion, the following definition of the true purpose of the school: To develop and train; to form an ideal conception of the purpose of living and the worth of the soul, and to teach so much of the arts and sciences as will fit the possessor for the practical duties of life.

It is also necessary to define certain of the terms used in this definition. By *development* of the mind, I mean the bringing of it through a series of definite actions into a state of comparative perfection,—i. e., the realizing of its ideal nature. By *training* I mean the securing, through appropriate practice, facility in doing. These two things—*development* and *training*—constitute *education*—*half* of what the school should give. The *other half* is *instruction*,—"so much knowledge of the arts and sciences systematically known as shall fit the possessor for the practical duties of life." This also divides itself naturally into *its* two parts,—knowing things as facts, and knowing them as related to business pursuits and social usages.

Now our subject is in definite shape for specific treatment. What help does mental science offer to the teacher in learning how to develop and train the mind of his pupils, and in learning how to teach the important facts of the arts and sciences to his pupils in their proper relations to business and social life? Let us see. First, mental science teaches that spirit is perfected by spiritual growth; that spiritual growth is the result of spiritual *food* and spiritual *exercise;* that truth of fact or truth of principle is the food required; that the activity required in mastering truth is the exercise required for healthy growth.

Mental science is even more specific than this: it shows that special forms of truth are fit food for the nourishment of special phases of one's mind power; i. e., facts of the physical world for the sensuous phase of spirit-life; remembered ideas are the food for that phase of the mind called imagination; the inner meaning of things is the proper food for the reason. And mental science teaches that this struggle for the mastery of truth, brings the soul or mind through different degrees of development to perfection; does not change the *nature,* but brings it in fact into that state of perfection which was originally designed for it. So much for development.

What now does mental science have to say concerning training—the other phase of education? Mental science completely answers this question by stating the one law which governs the training of the mind,—namely, that the mind tends to act again more readily in any way in which it has acted with intelligence and intensity; it even goes further, and shows that the degree of training received is in direct ratio to the number of repetitions and the intelligence and intensity of the action.

This law of training is sufficiently explicit for the common school teacher. It is comprehensive enough to cover the whole range of mind activity, whether the matter be that of repetition in physical processes, as of penmanship or drawing: or of processes of mind as pure spirit, as adding or subtracting, multiplying or dividing. The law is the same for all: one intelligent understanding and then *much intelligent repetition.*

Thus mental science answers perfectly all questions as to the development and training which the common school should be expected to give to its pupils.

What does mental science offer in the realm of instruction, that can be utilized by the common school teacher? The answer is that it is quite as explicit and serviceable here as in the matters of development and training. Mental science reveals

the fact or law that truth so mastered as to become proper food
for the mind is also mastered for practical use in business or social life : and that if the amount of intelligent repetition that is
needed for training be given, the truth so learned will be thereby
permanently fixed in memory.   So here again the law for learning is *much* INTELLIGENT *repetition* of the act of learning—this
time with a special emphasis on the *intelligence* of the action.

Mental science is even more explicit than this.   It states precisely what power of the mind is capable of making any particular
acquisition, prescribes the laws which control the action of such
power, the conditions under which it acts and indicates the kind
of stimulus or motive required to excite its appropriate action.
Thus ideas of color are possible only by the use of the eye, form
by the use of the eye or of the sense of touch.   The constructions of the imagination can be made only after the component
ideas have been acquired by the appropriate powers; the resem-
blances and differences can only be determined by the action of
the reason.   Now, since all subject matter to be taught is easily
resolvable into sense-ideas, new mental constructions, or relations of some kind, it is easy to see that the student who has
mastered the facts of mental science as applied to teaching can,
by the necessary preparation, present to each power its own kind
of knowledge, supply the appropriate conditions and stimulus,
and secure the intended result.

It is believed confidently by the writer that every claim thus
far made for the usefulness of a knowledge of mental science to
the teacher is valid: yet it may be said by some that there is implied in it a closer study of it than is usual with the common
school teacher.   This is granted.   It has been intended to state
in how far a knowledge of mental science may be utilized by the
common school teacher who has studied it to some purpose.
But it is also claimed that many teachers who have attempted
the study are not conscious of the vast increase of power that
has come to them through its study.

There remains, therefore, to this discussion one point,—i. e.,
to state the unconscious power which the acquisition of a knowledge of mental science gives to a teacher: and in the discussion

of this phase of the subject it will be seen that the result claimed will be the result from a less close and exhaustive study of the subject than that required for the results claimed in the preceding part of the discussion; and for this reason the advantages will be shared by a much larger number of the common school teachers than will be the case with the others. I refer now to the general culture of the teacher himself, which may be gained through the study of mental science.

I shall refer to but two phases of this culture. First, the close self-examination necessary in the interpretation of his text through his own consciousness, cultivates his power of attention, directs his attention to the true nature and value of *any* object of thought, and has a peculiarly refining and elevating effect on his character. This increased personal worth can not fail to be felt for good in every movement of his in the school room.

Second, the close study of the mind's processes will increase the teachers' power to understand the situation at any moment, whether of instruction or discipline, through his better knowledge of the principles and laws of *inductive reasoning*. Reasoning by induction is the crowning act of an intelligent mind; and its constant instantaneous and intelligent use gives to the teacher that valuable sixth sense—common sense.

A teacher is said to have tact. But tact is either inherited or acquired. If inherited in this generation, it was acquired in some previous one. Whenever acquired it was learned through much practice in inductive reasoning. One may learn to have tact. The chief difference between the inexperienced teacher and the experienced one is that the latter has added largely to his inherited tact, through long practice in inductive reasoning on the facts of the school room.

Inductive reasoning or induction is a process of interpretation of facts through some principle of adaptation,—the new knowledge thus obtained being the product of the reasoning and not wholly the result of the observation.

Its whole basis is the principle of adaptation. Through this principle of adaptation one thing is so related to another that to the mind that is cognizant of this relation each is the natural sign of the other—the suggestion of the other. Thus, a peculiar look on the face indicates the state of the mind; a particular tone of the voice expresses a peculiar emotion.

Following these known relations of facts, we are enabled to know much that the senses can not at the moment obtain. Practice in interpretation of existing facts through these natural relations gives in time a readiness in understanding the situation that might easily be mistaken for inherited tact. The hostess at an evening party passes among the guests saying the graceful and appropriate thing to each only through the power of ready interpretation of the facts presented to her as she passes from one to another.

In no other place is this power to reason inductively of such importance as in the school room. The occasions for its use are legion and the advantage of being an adept in its practice very large. One teacher devoid of tact,—i. e., who does not reason inductively with readiness and accuracy says, "I hear somebody talking," and thus advertises her inability to detect the offender. Another, as soon as she hears the sound, knows it is the voice of a boy, that it comes from the northeast corner of the room, that there are only two boys in that corner, and that one of these never does a disorderly act. She is, therefore, able, by the conscious or unconscious application of the laws of "agreement, difference and concomitant variations," to call John Doe at once to account for his misdeed, without disturbing any other pupil. or accusing the innocent: and the mental comment of every pupil, including the offender, is, that Miss Blank *knows her business.*

I entered a school some days since while an exercise was in progress. A boy in the class at study muttered an expletive more forcible than elegant concerning a difficulty in his lesson. Before the sound died away, I knew, by the signs, which boy it was. The teacher had the same opportunity to know, but was slow at interpreting signs. She was at a loss to know how to proceed; for the disorder was so marked that every pupil had taken notice of it, and she felt that she must do something. She went to the best girl in her room and made her tell who had caused the disorder, thus punishing *her* much more than she afterward punished the *boy*. The pupils all felt that she had to ask for what she should have known for herself.

The exact process referred to here may be outlined precisely as follows: One experiences in his own consciousness certain feelings, certain forms of thought, or certain determinations or choices. He manifests these naturally in some look on his face, some tone in his voice, or some definite change of his bodily conditions. Thus his own mental states and their appropriate outward manifestations are, from long usage, firmly associated. Now, when such a person sees in another the same outward manifestations, he instantly reasons inductively that similarity of manifestation indicates similarity of causes; and thus he has at once the key to the mental states of the other person. This is the method of reasoning by which the teacher is enabled instantly to know through the outward manifestation precisely what is the mental attitude of each pupil, whether with reference to questions of instruction or matters of conduct. Now, even a slight study of mental science deepens one's experiences, and sharpens his observing powers, and thus unconsciously to himself, perhaps, greatly increases his tact in the school room. True, this tact can much of it be gained by experience. But experience in teaching is sometimes gained at a deadly expense, especially when one trifles with immortal souls. Mental science offers the only known means of securing a part at least of the necessary tact for the business of the school room, before beginning its arduous duties; or it is a helpful accompaniment to such experience.

In the Union Depot at Indianapolis, fourteen railways converge and one hundred car-wheel inspectors find employment. The cheerful sound of the inspector's hammer may be heard at all hours of day or night, as he tests the wheels of the coaches that have just arrived. On a certain day, no defects had been found until late in the afternoon, when a small break was noticed in the rim of a wheel. The inspector, whose business is one of constant reasoning by induction, almost instantaneously went through the following train of reasoning: This is caused by some defect in one of the tracks; but which one? He looked up: it was a Pan-Handle train, and he quickly excluded from his calculations the other thirteen tracks. He looked again: it was the right-hand wheel; therefore he would expect the defect in the right-hand rail of the track. There were now three remaining possibilities: a broken rail, a misplaced switch, or a loose frog. How should he know which? He instantly saw that it was the second wheel of the forward truck. But a broken rail, or a misplaced switch would have affected the first. He further saw that the distance between the wheels was about the same as the length of the right arm of one of the frogs on the Pan-Handle road. So, in much less time than it takes to tell it, a man was despatched to *fasten down the right arm of the frog on the Pan-Handle road at the Bee Line Junction;* and further trouble was averted by this prompt action.

Here every principle of inductive reasoning was unconsciously applied by one who had unconsciously learned them from long experience in his business. So the teacher may gain this power by experience; but, as was said before, it is a costly matter for her to experiment on human souls. Mental science offers the opportunity to the teacher of becoming an expert in such reasoning by an explanation of its principles and methods.

In these ways and thus far, is it believed that a "knowledge of Mental Science may be utilized by the Common School Teacher."

PURPOSES IN TEACHING HISTORY.

E. E. SMITH, PURDUE UNIVERSITY.

THE first purpose in the study of history is the acquisition of knowledge. An animal serves its purpose as a living mechanism, and dies. It inherited no learning from its ancestors, it leaves nothing to posterity. But a man is heir to all that his race has learned since it came into existence. Through history he comes into possession of a large portion of his property. Here he learns of the character, the deeds, the experiences, the outcome of men as individuals and men aggregated into the family, society and the state. Through these he learns of the forces operative in intelligent life, of the method of their action, and of their tendencies and results.

But the knowledge thus acquired may be of little practical value. Isolated or unorganized knowledge, that is, knowledge not shown in its relations of cause and effect, of time and space, of coördination and subordination, is largely valueless knowledge. It may be presented with a great show of learning on the part of the teacher, with much quotation from eminent authors, and with much glibness of tongue on the part of both instructor and pupils; but unless the facts be acquired by systematic "digging," by pleasant but earnest research with a definite purpose in view, no amount of glamour thrown over them can make them of value. Anecdote, incident, geographical setting, literary and biographical side-lights,—all are useful in adding interest and vivacity to the work; but they must not take the place of that acquaintance with books, with events as viewed by able critics and as operative upon the associated life of the time, or of that personal investigation and individual formation of opinion, which alone can make history operative through the lives of those studying it. Hence the importance of using such forms or methods as will enable the pupil to obtain and properly associate the largest number of necessary facts in the shortest amount of time.

Just here, by way of parenthesis, it may be remarked that two mistakes are liable to be made. The one is that of ignoring method, order and the economy of time by systematic analysis and by a general direction being given to the pupil's work. This mistake is commonly made by the indolent teacher, by the teacher whose mind has not had logical training, or by the "æsthetic" teacher who thinks it important to convince his pupils that he is the greatest literary and historic critic of the age, and that they are next to him. The other mistake is that of losing sight of the real spirit and genius of the historic page in the mechanical contrivances to acquire its content for mental digestion. Neither pupil nor teacher must ever lose sight of the fact that history *is* history, and not fiction; that it is the presentation of the human life of the age,—of that life's struggles, victories, mistakes, defeats, accomplishments, influence, so that the student of its pages may read the signs of the times and forecast the future by the past.   Such mistake is likely to be made by the teacher who lacks the true spirit of teaching, who is not superior to the means used for accomplishing his ends, or who fails to perceive the real purpose of the work he is doing.

But beside the purposes of acquiring historic facts and of grouping them logically and philosophically, another aim should be had by the teacher of history.   He should keep before the pupil constantly and yet without too perceptible effort, that the great fact in all history is the human spirit; that the soul of man is superior to its physiological and physical environment; that intelligence has conquered nature, has shortened time, has made the laws of the material world subservient to its purpose; and that the progress of man's spirit, when under the influence of the great moral law within, has produced the best things for the individual and the best things for the race.

And, finally, the purpose of history is not fully accomplished until the pupil, after having become posted upon the great events and their relations to those that preceded and those that followed them, after having witnessed the strange drama of human life with its shifting scenes and interesting characters, after having perceived the things that make men and nations great and the things that weaken and degrade both, is eager himself to enter into the making of history of which he feels assured he shall not be ashamed.   Filled with a desire to lead men and to control events, he is yet conscious of the responsibility to his fellows and to God thereby incurred.   Thus he hesitates not to act when and where duty calls; he is prepared to act wisely and virtuously; and he is inspired by the best motives to think, to do, and to trust.

WHAT IS GEOGRAPHY?

J. T. SCOVELL, FORMER PROF. IN STATE NORMAL SCHOOL.

GEOGRAPHY means a description of the earth.   It is such a general description of the earth as may enable the student to see all its parts in their relations, forming one grand organism which serves as the dwelling place for man, and which furnishes him with materials for food, clothing and shelter, and for all the necessaries, comforts and luxuries of life. In chemistry and physics, astronomy and geology, botany, zoology, etc., the earth is studied in detail, but in geography, which includes ideas from every domain of science, it is studied in a general way in its relation to man. From chemistry come ideas of the units of matter, and of the different kinds of matter, which variously combined form the earth, air, and soil, and from which plants and animals are built up. From physics come ideas of the forces, attraction and heat, and that from their joint action on matter arise all the phenomena of the material world. Heat is more variable than attraction and seems more important. It keeps the air a gas, and water a liquid; it aids in breaking down the rocks into soil, it stimulates the growth of plants, and quickens animal life. Such writers as Tyndall and Huxley attribute all material phenomena, all the activities of life, and all the industries of society to energy derived from the sun. Heat and those conditions which modify its intensity and distribution are the most important subjects of geographical study. From astronomy come ideas of the relation of the earth to other bodies, and data for the accurate measurement of time and space and for actual location. To understand the present condition of the earth we must know something of its history. From geology come ideas of the successive changes through which the earth has passed in its development from a fiery mist to a revolving sphere clothed with verdure and teeming with life, and from geology comes some explanation of the formation of oceans and continents, of mountains and plains, of rocks and soils, and of the gradual evolution of the higher forms of plant and animal life. Botany, zoology, and other branches of science each contribute valuable ideas to geography.

The idea to be emphasized is that geography is a physical science, made up of ideas derived from every branch of scientific study.

Geography is the only natural science subject taught in the ungraded schools, or in the lower departments of the graded schools. As the great majority of children never go beyond these lower grades, it is very important that geography should be well taught in such schools, so that the child may gain correct ideas of the world in which he lives. Geography, if well taught, more than any other subject opens the world to the inquiring mind of childhood. It helps the child to understand many of the natural phenomena around him, it encourages a spirit of investigation, it enlarges his ideas of the world, and lessens his estimation of himself, and helps him to adjust himself to nature's laws.

If the foregoing is a correct idea of geography is it wonderful that the noted geographers of the world° are so few in number, or that geography is the most poorly taught subject in the public schools? The teacher who would do good work in geography should know more about geography than is written in any textbook on the subject; he should read and study some good book on each of the sciences mentioned. Dana's Geology—or, Le Cont's Geology and Loomis on Meteorology are especially valuable books for the teacher of geography.

The study of man in a general way, and of his relations to the earth seems a matter of history, but is usually made a part of geography. Under this department are studied the races of mankind, languages, religions, the various industries of society, the grades of culture, forms of government and kindred topics.

NEW TELESCOPES AND THEIR PROSPECTIVE REVELATIONS.

BY DANIEL KIRKWOOD.

THE improvement of the telescope, from the first rude instrument constructed by Galileo to the gigantic reflector of Lord Rosse and the great equatorials of recent manufacture, has been a slow and gradual process. But have we reached, or nearly reached, the limit of our progress? Has the Rosse telescope fully realized the expectations of astronomers? and what may be expected from the magnificent instrument now in process of construction for the Lick observatory in California?

The obstacles to be overcome in the use of high magnifying powers are clouds, fogs, dust, etc., together with the agitations of the atmosphere resulting from currents and other causes. The greater the magnifying power of the telescope, the greater, of course, is the trouble from these various causes. The unfavorable atmospheric conditions at Parsonstown, Ireland, have rendered the greatest reflector ever built almost a total failure. The obvious and only remedy for difficulties of this nature is the location of observatories at great elevations above the level of the sea. Mount Hamilton, California, was selected by Professors Newcomb, Holden and Burnam, after a careful trial of several months. The altitude of the observatory site is 4440 feet, or more than five-sixths of a mile. The distance from the coast is such that fogs from the Pacific rarely if ever reach it; and the dust of the denser strata of the atmosphere is left below. With the great three-foot telescope, therefore, when completed and in position, we may reasonably expect most important and interesting discoveries.

PROBABLE ACHIEVEMENTS OF THE LICK TELESCOPE.

The zone of minor planets between Mars and Jupiter will perhaps be a fruitful field of discovery for many years to come; and members smaller than any yet detected may be found by telescopes of greater magnifying power. For anything we know to the contrary a similar zone may exist between Jupiter and Saturn, the larger members of which may be discovered by improved means of observation.

As yet the Uranian and Neptunian systems are but imperfectly known. Efforts have been made by more than one astronomer to detect spots or at least variations of brightness on the surfaces of those distant planets. Thus far, however, nothing has been found sufficiently definite to fix the periods of rotation. To all observers the disk of Neptune appears perfectly circular; that is, no polar compression has been hitherto noticed. In this regard the measurements of Uranus have been strangely contradictory; some finding the disk without any polar flattening whatever, and others assigning it a high degree of compression. The satellites of these planets are too small and remote to be seen by ordinary telescopes. The discovery of new members by higher magnifying power in the pure atmosphere of Mount Hamilton is by no means improbable.

If a planet exist beyond the orbit of Neptune its brightness is not probably greater than that of a star of the tenth magnitude. Under favorable circumstances, however, a telescope of great power might be expected to give it a measurable disk and thus render its detection comparatively easy.

What the great instrument about to be employed on Mount Hamilton may accomplish in the field of sidereal astronomy can now scarcely be conjectured. The discoveries of the last half century will ever be memorable in the annals of astronomy: those of the next, we may reasonably hope, will be equally brilliant.

PRIMARY DEPARTMENT.

[This Department is conducted by HOWARD SANDISON, Professor of Methods in the State Normal School]

————:o:————

The real subject in education is the individual mind of each child, with its acquired habits and inherited tendencies An evident proposition, then, is: If real teaching is done, each mind, with its peculiar habits and inherited tendencies, must be understood by the teacher; with its double corollary:—

(1) The number of pupils under the charge of a primary teacher should range between twenty and thirty. (2) The pupils should remain under the charge of a given teacher more than ten months.

The second proposition is: Mind being an organism, the heart (sensibilities) is no less an avenue to the intellect than is the intellect to the heart and will; with its corollary:—

Suspicion and severity can never enable the teacher to obtain a standing place in the child-mind.

The third proposition is: Two rival powers compose the mind— the *carrying power*—memory (the servant) and the *thinking power* (the master); with its double corollary:—

(1) The aim of education is to make the mind strong and skilled as a thinking power, and not to make it full as a carrying power. (2) The most practical education is that which sends the child into the business world with power to observe closely and to think (reflect) accurately upon what he observes

————•————

[Below are set forth the reflections of a young teacher on the work of a primary room, after observing the work.]

1 I was particularly impressed with the discipline of the room, the controlling power seeming to be a reverence for the teacher by the pupils and a love and sympathy of each pupil for his schoolmates and for the teacher. The idea of sympathy and tenderness was exhibited many times in the work, especially with the I's.

2. I think the silent signals used by the teacher a valuable aid in securing attention, and I was impressed with the quiet manner of the teacher in all her work. It reminds one of the fact that if the teacher wishes a quiet school, she herself must set

the example; and I think the efficiency of that rule of action is demonstrated in this room.

3. I think the gymnastics practiced in this room, together with the attention given to position while in seat, in class, when standing, and at all times, is not only conducive to health, but affords most excellent discipline for the little ones.

4. I was impressed with the idea that the teacher must direct all the work in the primary school; telling the pupils when to begin and when to stop studying the subjects; and also that the work must be changed frequently, for the child-mind soon wearies of one kind of work. In this way the pupils are kept busy all the time.

5. I see that much care must be given pupils beginning writing. Position in seat and of holding pencil, etc., should have especial care. I see the advantage of having the board ruled as it is in this room, and of tracing the letters in learning to write.

6. I think that neatness is sought after in all the work. It may be seen in the arrangement of apparatus for cleaning slates and boards, as well as that for illustrating work; and in all work by pupils and teacher on board and slates.

7. I see the teacher uses the principle of activity in allowing the pupils to do everything they can do themselves, with only suggestions from the teacher, and that the pupils are sometimes shown, in a measure, the responsibility of the teacher, by being allowed to take her place in an exercise.

8. I have been impressed with the *necessity* of apparatus.

9. I see that design is given the children, or rather, developed in them, by allowing them to make pretty combinations with sticks, blocks, etc.

10. I see that in teaching words to the pupils, as well as in all other subjects, the work is made objective, in so far as it can be.

11. I have been impressed with the thought that the real names of forms—such as, triangle, cone, prism, etc.—can and ought to be given to pupils of this age, when these words can be made objective to them, so that they thoroughly understand the forms which they name.

12. Interest and a friendly rivalry are created by sometimes displaying work of merit by some pupil.

13. The music of the room certainly adds much to its life and pleasure; besides, a certain culture comes from it, not otherwise attainable.

14. The moral element of the school is made prominent in the "morning exercise," and the selections committed not only store the mind with good thoughts, but also afford 'discipline to the memory.

15. I see that the basis for arithmetic is laid in the number work.

ORAL WORK—GENERAL LESSONS—II.

MATERIAL—PLAN.

In the beginning work in general lessons, the subjects selected should be, to some extent, familiar, and, to insure interest, the work should commence with animals, since the study of living things affords most pleasure to young children.

However familiar the object selected may be, the first feeling of the teacher usually is that she knows nothing of it, or at least, nothing that will be of use to the pupils. Experience will show that this feeling is justified only in part—the teacher always knowing, if only because she has lived longer, a great deal more than the pupils upon the given subject; her knowledge of it will, however, be found to be defective in certain respects, when tested.

The first impulse will be to take a cyclopedia, or some special work and "read up" on the subject. To do this in the beginning, however, would be a mistake, for it would lead to the habit of depending upon others, instead of thinking for one's self—a habit fatal to vigor and freshness in teaching, and one that has its reflex influence upon the pupils.

The things for the teacher to do when preparing for an oral lesson are four:

1. To quietly and carefully *search her own mind* so as to obtain all that her previous experience and observation have fur-

2

nished upon the subject. *This should always be the first step.* Whatever is obtained in this way should be carefully written in simple language and arranged in proper form.

By taking this as the first step, the teacher is able to determine exactly where her knowledge is defective, and is thus enabled to examine books with a definite purpose of improving herself upon just those points that are required. The teacher who desires to have the pupils *observe* and *reflect upon what they observe,* must constantly furnish examples by giving them the results of her own observations and reflections.

2. To place in *proper sequence* the material obtained from her own experience and from books.

3. To *prune the material* so arranged until that which remains is an example of "The survival of the fittest."

4. To *organize,* in the form of a *written plan,* the material and method of the lesson.

There are many teachers, who are highly efficient, and who believe in the efficacy of written plans, and yet who do not, as a rule, prepare written plans for their lessons. This is because they have served their apprenticeship in written plans, and by their work with them their minds have acquired the habit of spontaneously organizing the material and method of a lesson into a logical *mental plan.* This is the real aim of written plans. They are not to be thought of as a direct and immediate means of conducting a recitation according to directions set down in them; but as a means of forming the *mental habit* of systematically organizing the matter and method of a lesson. They, therefore, belong to the period of the teacher's preparation. Written plans should be resorted to, however, as often as practicable, in the every-day work, in order to reinforce the mental habit referred to, and not for the purpose of using them as guides in the actual recitation. The class of teachers referred to understand this and employ the written plan in its proper place, and to fulfill its true function.

There are some teachers, however, who dismiss summarily the idea of written plans. These are usually of three classes:

1. Those superintendents who consider that they have nothing additional to learn in education, and who, in practice, hold

that the inspiration and skill of their teachers, are to be derived from the grade work and oral suggestions that they promulgate from month to month.

This assistance from month to month is, of course, good and requisite; but taken alone, without painstaking preparation on the part of each teacher for each lesson, it tends to produce a class of imitators.

2. Those teachers who are too indolent to prepare adequately for their work, considering that their responsibility commences at the moment that school begins in the morning, and ends the moment that school closes in the evening.

3. Those superintendents and teachers who hold that the teacher should inform herself well upon the subject, and without any planning, go before the class, and "Trust to the inspiration of the moment." The claim of these is that to prepare written plans for lessons makes the teaching mechanical. Such a criticism indicates a mistaken view of the *true function* of written plans or "notes on lessons."

A farmer once told his sons, when he was about to pass from the scenes of earth, that, concealed beneath the soil in the farm that he was about to leave them, was a great treasure. After their father had passed away, the sons carefully and patiently spaded up every foot of the ground, but found no treasure. Their next crops, however, were found to be more valuable a hundred fold. The treasure that their father meant *was the effect of their careful, thorough work.*

So it is with the written plan. The value of the plan *is in the planning*. The purpose of the written plan is accomplished *before the recitation begins*. To employ it as a guide, and consult it during the progress of the recitation, would be a violation of the spirit of teaching as a psychological art. The attention of the teacher, during the recitation, must be concentrated upon the minds of the pupils, in order that she may read their true condition at each step, and change and adapt her work *as their difficulties change.* To attempt at the same time to consult at each step the suggestions of a written plan, is to disregard the principle that *the mind has but a given quantum of energy;* and it is also to despise the lesson of spirit and interest by thrusting between the mind addressing and the minds addressed, a barrier, thereby making the communion of their minds even more mediate than it must of necessity be.

The true course for the teacher is not merely to inform herself upon the subject, and then go before the class "Trusting to the inspiration of the moment." There is no inspiration in the moment, under such circumstances. The course for the teacher, as demanded by the interest and the interests of the children, is:

1. To gather carefully the material for the lesson.

2. To reflect carefully upon its arrangement, the order and method of presenting the ideas, and to determine, in the main, the illustrations, etc., thus obtaining a *mental plan*.

3. To reduce this mental plan to a *written plan*, ("Writing makes the exact man") in order to test more carefully the mental plan, and to insure a better organization of the lesson.

4. To go before the class and conduct the recitation without the aid of the written plan, or if using it at all, obtaining only the main headings, thus insuring that true inspiration and confidence, and that thorough organization that come from *careful preparation;* and at the same time allowing that freedom which enables the teacher to adapt the work to the changing needs of the class.

But the reply is that the city teacher with eight or ten daily recitations, and the country teacher with from ten to twenty-five can not take the time for such preparation. Admitting that to be true, it may still be said that such should be the preparation for at least one recitation daily, (the most difficult one) and its beneficial effects will be felt in all recitations.

On the supposition that the horse is the animal selected for the oral lesson, the organization of the lesson could be presented in a written plan somewhat as follows:

PLAN.

I. *Subject.*—The *individual minds* of the pupils.

II. *Design.*—1. To give the mind strength and skill by training it to observe common animals and to reflect upon what it observes. 2. To give (incidentally) certain knowledge of the horse.

III. *Condition of Training.*—*Self-activity* of the pupil.

IV. *Exercise-ground.*—The *idea horse.*

V. *The Basis.*—(The basis consists of the ideas already possessed by the child, that are related to the subject and employed by the teacher.)—Knowledge of various four-footed animals; ability to count to four; experience as to some of the uses, food, and homes of horses; knowledge as to glue and as to a certain kind of furniture.

VI. *Steps.*—(A step is the advance of the mind, from an idea possessed to the one to be gained.)

1.   Advance of the mind to the thought—The horse is a quadruped.

a.   *Method.*—Refer to their experience as to number of feet; present pictures; have the feet counted; have the thought that it is a *four-footed* animal expressed; state that there is another word that may be used instead of "four-footed," writing upon the board the word *quadruped ;* have other quadrupeds named; write the sentence, and have the children repeat it and then write it.

2.   Advance of the mind to correct ideas as to the use, food, and home of the horse.

a.   *Method.*—Refer to the children's experience in regard to these points; obtain from them what it eats, what it does for man, and where it lives in winter and in summer; supplement that which is thus obtained; organize the information as it is received; have the children help form the sentence; write it upon the board; have the children read it and then write it.

3.   Advance of the mind to ideas as to the use of the horse after its death.

a.   *Method.*—Obtain from the children the various materials used in furniture, and in this way indicate the use of horse-hair; lead them to talk of glue and its uses; lead them to see that it may be made from the hoofs and some parts of the flesh; add the word *sinews* to their vocabularies; lead them to point out sinews in their own bodies; organize the information as it is given; with the help of the children form the sentences required, and then write them on the board; have the sentences read and written by the children as before; have all of the sentences of the lesson read; by questioning, lead the pupils to express themselves freely upon all the points, noting carefully their language.

Many other ideas concerning the horse could be presented; the aim has been, however, not to give a full treatment, but merely to suggest the nature of a written plan that the teacher may prepare in giving oral lessons on animals.

PRACTICAL LESSON.

The following is a stenographic report of a lesson in reading in the First Year Grade. The children had been in school about nine months. The lesson, and the statement of the aim, are by Mrs. F. S. Burt.

(The teacher relates the following, placing the words in italics on the board; the children, in concert, spelling each in turn as it is written.)

ONCE there were two little girls. The name of one was *Kate* and the name of the other was *Nell.*

They lived in a very pleasant house which had a very pleasant yard around it. Out in the yard there was a large *tree* and under the tree was a swing. The little girls could go there and swing almost any time in the morning or in the afternoon, because the swing was in the shade.

Sometimes they did not go alone, but took their *dolls* with them. Sometimes they took their little *cat* and she liked to swing too. She had such a funny name and they gave her that funny name because she was so *black*. They called her a name that means black. They called her *Jet.* (This is a new word to you, so you may try and see if you can pronounce it.)

(The children spell the word phonetically, thus obtaining the correct pronunciation.)

Now Jet means black. Generally she was a very *nice* cat and the little girls liked her because she was so nice, but one day she was very hungry. She had had some *milk* but she had not had quite enough, so she went into the house, walked through the dining-room and through the kitchen, into the pantry, and there she saw a *table* and on the table was a *pan.* In the pan she thought she might find some more milk. There really was no milk in the pan. It was something else. It was *cream,* and she liked cream very much. It was not a small pan, it was *large* and it was *full* of cream. She was walking along on the table when she thought she would take a *peep* into the pan, so she put her paws on the edge of the pan and the first she knew she *fell* right into the cream. When she found herself in the cream, she took a *hop* and came right out, but when she came out they could not call her *Jet,* because she was not black any longer. She was very *white.*

(The teacher places the following sentences on the board:)

Was she a good cat? Alice may read the sentences.

(The pupil reads.)

What color was she? There is a new word in that. What is it? You may spell it.

(The pupils spell c-o-l-o-r.)

She was black.

What was her name?

Her name was Jet.

(The pupils read the sentences in concert.)

T.   I wonder if you could draw me a picture of a table and the pan of milk and the cat.   How many could do that ?

(All the pupils think they can do so, and draw the outlines on their slates, after which the teacher examines them.)

The results to be secured by lessons of this kind are :

1.   In ability to recall the forms of words.

2.   The ability to read sentences (in script) readily and intelligently.

3.   The development of the imagination.

4.   Habits of correct language.

5.   Habits of attention.

DEPARTMENT OF PEDAGOGY.

[This Department is conducted by S. S. PARR, Principal De Pauw Normal School.]

——:o:——

WHAT A DEFINITION IS.

THE definition plays a great part in our present school-education.   That it is entitled to so much consideration may seriously be questioned.   An intelligent use of definitions requires an understanding of what they are and how they are made.   Here are some typical definitions as they are used in school and school-books :   "A noun is a word which names an object."   "Multiplication is the process of taking one number as many times as there are units in another."   "The equator is an imaginary line encircling the earth midway between the poles," etc.

A definition embodies three elements :   1. The thing defined.   2. The class to which it belongs.   3. The mark which distinguishes it from the other members of the class.   It involves directly and indirectly exact observation, the selection and use of names, the action of memory and imagination, and of one of the highest forms of the judgment   As an example of the formal definition, nothing is better than the time-worn one, "Man is a rational animal."   The thing defined is the class of objects known as man ; the class to which man is said to belong is the class animal; the distinguishing mark of the class man is the possession of rational intelligence.

Every definition must possess these elements, with one possible exception. They may not always be stated as in the typical illustration we have given. Indeed, except for purposes of rhetorical illustration, the only place where such compact formal definitions are. attempted is in school-books and school-rooms. The science-men depend much on the definition as an instrument, but they avoid merely formal ones like the examples given. Herbert Spencer or Prof. Fiske will take three or more chapters of a large book to define life, force, mind, etc. Darwin wrote a book in two large volumes to define evolution. These scientific definitions are full and complete. They embrace the three elements named in their highest sense.

A great many of our so-called definitions are not such at all. They are mere statements and should be so regarded. A child is incapable of making, understanding or using a scientific definition. The three examples given above are spurious definitions, or mere statements. The first classifies the noun as a kind of word. It utterly fails to give the basis of the classification. To call chairs, tables, sofas, wash-stands, etc., furniture, is a similar act. The second is also a mere statement. Multiplication is much more than taking one number as many times as there are units in another. This statement will not cover algebraic multiplication, nor multiplication of either decimal or common fractions. Besides, this objection to it as a precise statement, it fails to state the process of multiplication in any except the loosest kind of way. The third is open to similar objections. If we are to have definitions at all, they must be more exact and comprehensive. As loose, general statements about the noun, multiplication and the equator, these three are well enough. They, may be, are not the best ones that could be used, but still they are near enough the truth for use with the undeveloped minds of children. The child learns just as much, if he says the noun is a part of speech, or all names are called nouns, or significant designations of objects are called nouns, etc. Such statements are about alike in value. Each expresses some relation of the object, but is not by any means a definition.

When we say chairs, tables, sofas, wash-stands, etc., are furniture, we have made a simple classification of the objects. This
is of value, for, if we understand what we are talking about, to
be able to classify is an important step in one's knowledge. We
have no need of definitions and do not have any such, whatever
we may please ourselves with saying, until we not only make a
classification but also attempt to explain it or show the bases upon
which the division is made. An example of this is found in such
a definition of multiplication as this : Multiplication is a combination of equals, or the increase of the number of equal parts,
by means of remembered results in one act. Here multiplication
is said to be a kind of combination. The basis of this division of
all combinations into multiplication and a something other which
we have agreed to call addition, is the *way* in which the combination is made, viz., by means of remembered results. In the
other kind of combination, we do not employ remembered results
in one act. We believe this definition will stand the fire of criticism, as to correctness. But what child could understand it?
Our readers will doubtless have to consider it carefully to understand fully what is meant.

The point of this article is that we need to call things by their
right names. Thereby we come nearer the truth and save falling into many loose and incorrect ways of thought and expression. Exact speech begets exact ideas. We have nothing to
gain and much to lose by calling a somewhat loose general statement a "definition."

THAT "FIRST DAY."

"WELL begun is half done." "A good beginning makes a
good ending." "To start well is to run well." These are popular sayings that emphasize the importance of starting off on the
right foot in any sort of undertaking. The "first day" in school
will have come to many teachers before the close of the month.
It should be the "good beginning" mentioned in the proverb.
To fail on that eventful day might cause failure of the whole
term's work and produce mischievous results without end.

What then are some of the means that will insure prompt success on that day? Surely any formula that will help success is worthy of attention!

The first day should not in general be different from other days of the term. Pupils and teacher are generally new and strange to one another. The pupils are unacquainted with one another, although they may not have been separated but a few weeks. Lessons, classes, and behavior have not settled down to their wonted grooves. The teacher has yet to make individual acquaintances, settle the program and get the machinery to running smoothly. These features constitute the difference between the "first day" and any other day.

The successful teacher thinks over the first day carefully beforehand and comes to its difficulties with a definite plan. This plan provides a well-considered order of exercises and work—calling the roll, opening exercises, division of pupils into classes, providing lessons, the securing of books by those who need them, busy or study-work for those who are not reciting, etc. Part of this well-considered order of exercises is the program of recitations and study. True it is that the ideal program the teacher takes with her to the school-room may need changes that almost or quite revolutionize it. That is no matter. A program is a necessary part of a thoughtful plan which may itself need change every hour of the day. This, however, does not reduce the value of the plan and program, and of careful thought about the work.

Careful planners in any undertaking are almost always successful. Hap-hazard workers who depend on the spirit and inspiration of the moment are often unsuccessful. Careful planning in the school-room is what good book-keeping is to a business house; what a chart of the ocean is to the captain of a ship; and what a careful plan is to a battle or a compaign.

First, then, think the work through and have a definite, consecutive plan. This needs to be flexible. Many young teachers think that their plans and methods are to follow the type of the hand of steel and be perfectly inflexible. Pupils and school-house, stove, fuel, seats and all must, they think, bend to *their* methods and plans; but there is a total and innate depravity in all these things, and one is always safe in predicting they won't conform.

Second, keep cool and act with as much rapidity as orderly procedure and circumstances will permit. The children can not then say, as the writer has heard, "The teacher was flustrated."

Third, be kind and do not snap anybody up. This is the day of all days for impressions. Good impressions well set to-day will last all term,—so will bad ones. The fact that children are the creatures of their feelings and impressions lends great force to the need of good impressions.

Next, put every mother's child to some kind of work, as per the plan, and keep him there, and the demon of mischief will not get loose. An employed child is an interested child, and an interested child is a well-behaved and easily controlled child.

Lastly, the first day should be just as effective as the tenth or fiftieth day. Frittering away two or three days in "getting started" is not only a waste of time, but also a very bad policy. It is disorganizing and demoralizing. It allows evil tendencies to crop out. "That bad boy" and "that saucy girl" have time and opportunity to let their habits and inclinations loose, to the great detriment of the school and discomfort of the teacher.

HOW MUCH WRITTEN SPELLING, AND WHY?

No GOOD teacher confines spelling to mere technical spelling, i. e., to merely giving the letters of words in their proper order. Several other elements are to be introduced parallel with technical spelling:—pronunciation, accentuation, use of capitals and punctuation marks, division into syllables, the use of diacritical marks, meaning, use in original sentence, and, for the older classes, the derivation of important words. The presence of these parallel elements of instruction has much to do in determining the question of how much written spelling and how much oral. The purpose of instruction in the several elements that have been named is not mere technical spelling, but the broader and more significant end of facility in the use of words. A large share of the pupils' work in school is the endeavor to learn written forms of language corresponding to oral forms already known. This is especially so of spelling. The obvious conclusion from these facts is that most spelling should be written.

Another basis for determining the relative amount of these two kinds of spelling is found in the way the mind acts. We learn to spell for accuracy in writing and not for accuracy in oral spelling. In the actual business of life, the only oral spelling used is in the school room, and in spelling out words through the telephone to make them understood, or in occasionally spelling out a name or other word to identify it or make it plain. In all written spelling we depend more largely on the memory of the eye. That is we recall the word as it presents itself to the eye on the page. For this there are two reasons. First, the images presented by the eye are more definite and distinct than those presented by the ear. Colors and forms are permanent; the eye rests upon them as long as it pleases. But sounds are fleeting and must be repeated every time they are experienced. A second reason is found in the fact that the spoken word gives no key to the written form, in the majority of English words. The presence of many silent letters and the representation of several sounds by the same letter are the cause of this.

A law of mind should be viewed with these facts in reaching a conclusion. The more forms of mind-activity that are brought into action the better the object, whatever it may be, will be learned and the more readily it will be remembered.

Both forms of spelling, then, should be used, since the use of the one will reënforce the value of the other. Oral spelling is not so valuable as written spelling as a means of fastening the forms of words in memory. But taking all the things done—pronunciation, giving meaning, use, etc.—many of the exercises should be oral. Estimating roughly the relative amount of spelling-proper, one is not far wrong if he makes three-fourths of it written and one-fourth oral, including in this one-fourth reviews. However, if we consider all kinds of exercises that come along with the spelling (those named above), no such relative amounts ought to be observed. Fully half of all will be better done orally than in writing. No exact rule can be given, since such matters must be left to circumstances and the judgment of the teacher.

SOME THINGS TO BE ASSUMED.

SITUATIONS arise in which one ought not to assume anything, but this policy is not correct in matters of school-instruction. To assume that the child's mind is a blank when he first comes to school will involve serious error. The fact is that quite a broad foundation has already been laid. The first five years of a child's life yield a larger return of positive knowledge than any other in his history. By the time he enters school, he has laid the foundation for everything he will ever learn thereafter. The elements of language, geography, number, and general knowledge have been laid surely and solidly by nature's method. Observation teaches well what comes within its scope. The school may make the mistake of teaching empty words, but not so the spontaneous teaching the child receives before entering.

One of the chief aims, especially of primary instruction, is to organize, systematize and fill out the spontaneous knowledge brought to school. A pupil of six years of age knows oral language quite well within the field where he has used it. He has a vocabulary of from 200 to 500 words, and can make sentences and other forms to express his thought. If he has always heard correct language, his speech will be correct. But as not more than one child in one thousand does hear correct speech, as a rule, the use of some incorrect forms will have been learned. So in geography, the six-year-old knows many facts. He has observed hill, dale, running stream, pond, the formation of soil by rains, day and night, the change of seasons, etc. All this will probably need filling out and systematizing.

The first duty of the teacher is to find out how much the pupil knows and not attempt to teach ideas that are already well-known. The effect is the same as that which results from forcing food on an already full stomach. Disgust arises instead of interest, and the child is prejudiced against that instruction which is really needed beyond what he already knows. Lessons designed to teach what the horse or any other common object is and is like are of this sort. The usual contemptuous comment from the pupil is, "Oh! I knew [more likely know'd] that long ago." No description of the object, for the purpose of giving an idea of it, is needed. It is already familiar. Imagine the disgust of a popular audience, if a lecturer should regale them with such astounding facts as that water flows down hill; we breathe the air; snow is white; grass grows! The disgust of children at being "hauled and mauled" over such common places must be no less measured.

This large field of knowledge must be assumed, but assumed only when an examination has been made to ascertain how much of it really exists, and where it is strong and where weak. We can never hope to do as well in our schools as nature does in hers, so we gain nothing by attempting to do over what she has already done.

THE SCHOOL ROOM.

[This Department is conducted by Geo. F. Bass, Supervising Prin. Indianapolis schools.]

————:o:————

THE FIRST DAY.

"FIRST impressions are most lasting." The manner of the teacher on the first day—and often during the first hour of the day—usually settles the question whether he is master of the situation.

The teacher, therefore, should make previous careful preparation for this day's work. In making this preparation the following should be consideration:—(1) Condition of school-room, school-yard and out-buildings. (2) Probable number of pupils and their classification. (3) List of books to be used. (4) A map of the school-room. (5) Program for the day's work.

1. The condition of the school-room, school-yard and out-buildings will necessitate a visit to the premises before the day of opening. This visit should be made several days before the opening of school, so that if it is found that repairs are needed

they may be made before the opening of school. The school-room should be clean; the floors may need scrubbing and the windows may need washing; the walls may need whitewashing; the boards may need blackening; the yard may have rank weeds in it. They should be removed. The out-house may need attention. It should be made scrupulously clean and kept so. All marks should be obliterated. Of course these marks never should have been there. Make a resolution that none shall be there at the close of your school.

2. The probable number and classification can generally be obtained from records kept by the preceding teacher. These facts will be of advantage because you will be better enabled to arrange for seating the pupils; also for assigning lessons in the proper place in each subject.

3. The list of books can be had usually from a manual prepared by the superintendent. This manual should be in the hands of every teacher, for from it he can get the course of study, rules and regulations, and often many valuable suggestions.

4. A map of the school-room, showing the location of each seat will be valuable to the teacher on the first day. He may pass slips of paper to each pupil upon which may be written the pupil's name, number of row, and number of seat. By means of this map and papers, he will be enabled to look a pupil in the face and call his name. The teacher may get time at noon to write these names on the map, which will be still better. By the close of the second day the ordinary teacher will be able to call each pupil by name. The map, then, of course, is useless. There is no one thing gives one as much power over his pupils as the ability to early call each by name.

5. Program for the first day's work is very important. The main thing to be kept in mind in preparing it is, get everybody at work as soon as possible.

The teacher should decide upon some *definite* plan of procedure and *follow* it. Do not have the whole school wait while you write the name of each pupil, or while you write a list of books that each needs. Do not ask them to sit quietly for an hour with their hands folded. Give every one something to do.

It is hoped that no teacher will try try to ad*o*pt the above, but that he will try to ad*a*pt it.

A WAY.

ANY child who can read three figures can learn in a very short time to read any number of figures; but it is almo*s*t useless to teach more than three figures.

By using objects and bunches of tens, a pupil may be led to see what he means when he says "One hundred twenty-three." But he may be taught to read the number, 123, without the use of objects or without knowing what it means.   He may be *told* that counting from the right, the third figure is always hundreds; and he remembers it; always calls it so and is always right; but but if he knows what it means, he knows more and is stronger because other powers of the mind have been called into action in getting the meaning.

Now when he can read 123, write in groups something of this sort—123—324—536.   Place the hand over any two of them and ask him to read the other *one*.   This will not trouble him. Do this until he has read each group of these.   Next tell him what to call each group, and write *M* over millions, *T* over thousands, and *U* over units.   Have him read several numbers this way.

Erase all the numbers and dictate some for him to write.   It will be found that the difficulty of reading and writing numbers will disappear under some such plan as the above.

WHERE.

IT is so easy to leave out the *where* in teaching history, that almost every teacher does it to a greater extent than he suspects. There are so many questions given in history beginning, "Give an account of."   To-give-an-account-of in history should include the space relation, but frequently it does not include it.   The teacher should see that it does.   For example, when a pupil gives an account of the battle of Bunker Hill and fails to give the *where*, let the teacher ask questions that will call up the locality. In what State, as now named, was this battle fought? Where is this State?

· Many pupils and teachers do not like history because, so they say, they can not remember the dates. Yet there is probably more time spent on the dates than anything else. It is barely possible that there are more persons who can tell what occurred in 1620 than there are who can tell where it occurred. The same might be said of many other common dates. For example, 1565; 1607; 1608; 1754; 1763; 1775; 1776; 1861.

Try your pupils on this point.

EDITORIAL.

Persons sending money for this Journal can send amounts less than $1 in *two* and *one* cent postage stamps; no others can be used.

In asking to have the address of your Journal changed, please give the *old* address as well as the new, naming the county as well as the state.

An agent is wanted to raise a club for the Journal in every township in the State. Send for terms.

PAY UP!—*If you are still on the delinquent list, please settle at once, that last year's books may be closed. Money sent directly to the editor will be credited to the proper agent.*

INSTITUTES.—It is customary to report every institute "the best ever held." While this statement becomes a little monotonous, especially when it is repeated every year, and may not always be true, in the main it is true.

It is entirely safe to say that never before were the institutes so largely attended, never before was there so much interest on the part of the teachers, never before were there so many capable institute workers in the field, never before was there so much money spent for help in institutes, never before was there so much excellent work done and so little time "fooled away." The world does move and teachers move with it.

All reports of institutes are crowded out of this issue for want of space.

3

THE READING CIRCLE.—The "Outlines" appear in this number of the Journal, though many of the Circles will not begin their work till October. Thousands of teachers are taking the work and the results must be most beneficial.

TEACHING DIACRITICAL MARKS.

That diacritical marks are of great importance no one doubts. That they should be taught to the children in the school no one will doubt. · But that they should be taught as they are and when they are, is certainly questionable. In most schools the teaching of these marks is begun in the lowest primary grade. Primary charts and primers are printed with the sounds of the letters all marked.

The *theory* is that children learn to pronounce words correctly by means of these marks, but the *fact* is that they do no such thing. You tell me that small children *can* be taught to pronounce new words correctly by means of these marks. I admit that it can be done and is *sometimes* done, but it is done at a great sacrifice of time. The fact is that in ninety-nine cases out of a hundred the children learn the correct pronunciation of words, if they do not already know them, from the teacher. It is a part of the teacher's work to teach the new words as they occur as to their form, pronunciation and meaning.

Diacritical marks are not known outside our school-books and the dictionary. If we wish the correct pronunciation of a new word we go to the dictionary, and when we go to the dictionary we need a knowledge of these marks. As they are used only in connection with the dictionary the time to study them is in about the fourth year of school, when the use of the dictionary is taught. A few of the more common ones may be taught earlier, perhaps, but this everlasting drill upon these marks, years before the child can make any practical use of them, is a mistake. The time thus spent is not entirely lost, but it could be spent in ways vastly more profitable to the children. "Think on these things." ·

PROTECT THE HEALTH OF THE CHILDREN.

Within a few weeks thousands of children will be gathered into schools that they may be educated, and it is of great importance that school house and school premises be put in good hygienic condition. Next to moral character the health of the child is of most importance, and the child in getting an education should not be required to sacrifice or impair its health.

It is a fact that through the inattention of teachers and trustees to hygienic laws the seeds of disease are sown and the health of thousands of children is undermined, every school year. Many of our schools, as located and conducted, should be named "institutions for the slaughter of the innocents."

The State Board of Health has wisely taken this matter in hand, and it should be sustained in its endeavor to protect the children.

The following rules have been adopted by the State Board of Health and have been sent to all trustees. Teachers should use their influence in every proper way to have trustees comply with all these suggestions. With such an effort all over the state, the beneficial results can hardly be estimated. These are the Board of Health Rules:

1. To clean out all sources of water supply, and place them in good condition; and where houses have no supply of their own, to at once furnish one.

2. In the absence of a better system, to prepare the windows and transoms so that ventilation can be had without causing draughts of cold air to come in contact with the pupils.

3. To place the buildings in good repair, with tight floors, good roofs and under-pinning.

4. To see that the yard and grounds do not admit of standing water, and to prepare gravel or board walks to keep the children's feet out of the mud.

5. Suitable water closets for each of the sexes should be provided with every school house. They should be situated far enough away from the house to secure privacy, and not be a nuisance. They should be kept in good repair, cleaned and disinfected at least twice a month.

6. The rooms should be so warmed that all may be kept comfortable; stoves and furnaces safe and in good order.

7. The rooms should not be overcrowded. Not less than 14 square feet of floor space and 215 cubic feet for breathing space should be allowed each pupil.

8. Blackboards should never be placed between the windows, and the surface of the boards should be a dead black, not glossy.

9. The light should, if possible, be admitted from the rear of the pupil; never from the front.

10. Desks and seats of different heights should be furnished, to suit the sizes and ages of the pupils.

TREE PLANTING.

The Journal desires to call the attention of the committee on "tree planting," appointed by the State Teachers' Association, to the fact that it is very desirable that a day shall soon be named for the fall planting of trees. The day named in the spring always comes as a matter of necessity, after most of the country schools are closed, and so its general observance has been impossible. Let a day be named late in October, or even in November, and let the same effort be put forth to induce teachers and trustees to engage in the work that has been put forth in the spring, and the results will be four-fold what they have ever been before. The country schools as well as the city schools will be in session, and teachers can with little trouble arouse an interest and secure co-operation. Will the committee look to this matter at once?

QUESTIONS AND ANSWERS.

QUESTIONS PREPARED BY STATE BOARD FOR JULY.

ARITHMETIC.—1. A man bought stock at 25% below par, and sold it at 20% above par; what per cent. did he make?   Proc. 5, ans. 5

2. There is a circular field 40 rods in diameter; what is its circumference? How many acres does it contain?   5, 5

3. How many bushels of wheat will fill a bin 8 feet long, 5 feet wide, and 4 feet deep? How find the area of a circle?   5, 5

4. What is the interest of $75.50 from June 12, 1869, to August 6, 1870, at 7½%? What is the difference between simple and compound interest?   5, 5

5. If 8 men cut 84 cords of wood in 12 days, working 7 hours a day, how many men will cut 150 cords in 10 days, working 5 hours a day? By proportion.   Statement 5, ans. 5

6. A house is 40 feet high from the ground to the eaves, and it is required to find the length of a ladder which will reach the eaves, supposing the foot of the ladder can not be placed nearer the house than 30 feet. In extracting the square root, why double the root already found?   5, 5

7. What is the cube root of .074256? How find the trial divisor in extracting the cube root?   5, 5

8. A and B trading in partnership for two years, make each year a profit of $1,200; A's capital the first year was 2½ times B's, and the second year it was 1¼ times B's; what is each partner's share of the profits?   Analysis 5, ans. 5

9. How many rods of fence will inclose 10 acres in the form of a square?   10

10. How many yards of carpeting ¾ of a yard wide will it take to cover a floor 18½ feet long and 15 feet wide? What will be its cost at $2.75 per yard?   5, 5

GEOGRAPHY.—1 What portion of the earth's surface has no sunlight falling directly upon it at the time of our mid-summer?   10

2. What river forms the larger part of the boundary between Virginia and Maryland? What large river flows through Maryland into Chesapeake Bay? 5, 5

3. Mention a country of South America that is wholly north of the Equator, one wholly south of the Equator, one crossed by the Equator, and the largest country of South America? 2, 2, 2, 2, 2

4. What mountain range between France and Spain? What boundary do the Ural Mountains form? 5, 5

5. Where are the following islands? Newfoundland, Ceylon, Hayti, Candia, Porto Rico. 2, 2, 2, 2, 2

6. Describe briefly the successive changes in the character of vegetation encountered in passing from the base of a high mountain in the torrid zone to its summit. 10

7. Name the zones that touch North America, and specify the portion of the continent in each. 5, 5

8. Name five large rivers of Asia. Five important ranges of mountains in Asia. 5, 5

9. Describe the river Rhine, and name all the countries it borders or crosses. 5, 5

10. Name two cities of Europe noted for the production of silk. Two for the manufacture of cutlery. Where is Herat? 2, 2, 2, 2, 2

U. S. HISTORY.—1. What characteristics distinguish the settlers of New England from those of Virginia? 10

2. What was the form of government prepared for the Carolinas at their settlement? What was its fate? 7, 3

3. How were the *Writs of Assistance* and the *Mutiny Act* received? 10

4. What immediate causes led to the Declaration of Independence? 10

5. What two famous laws, passed in the administration of John Adams, led to the success of the republican (or democratic) party at the next presidential election? 5, 5

6. Describe the two great movements of our armies in the Mexican war. 10

7. What territory was purchased by the United States to correct an error in the boundary of the Mexican cession? 10

8. After what President was a capital in Africa named? 10

9. How did Sherman's march to the sea so materially tend to the closing of the war? 10

10. Name those whom you regard as occupying the following positions in this country, in point of character, not time: First orator, first historian, first poet, first naturalist, first novelist. 5 pts, 2 each

PHYSIOLOGY.—1. Describe the cerebellum.

2 Make a diagram of the bones of the leg, naming each bone.

3. Describe the optic nerve.

4. What is reflex action?

5. Describe the cilia in the air passages.

6. Distinguish between arteries and veins.

7. Make a diagram of the heart, showing the course of the blood through it.

8. How does the composition of bones vary with the age of the person?

9. Describe the gastric juice and its functions.

10. What is fermentation?

SCIENCE OF TEACHING.—1. What is the imagination?

2. What use can be made of the imagination in teaching geography?

3. State the different purposes the teacher should have in conducting a recitation in the Second Reader.

4. Name the characteristics of a good recitation.

5. What are the evil effects of punishment as a motive to study?

PENMANSHIP —1. Name the five elements used in forming the principles in writing.

2. Describe the *hand rest.*

3. Describe the *fore-arm* movement.

4. What is a space in height? What are the short letters?

5. Write the capital letters formed from the seventh principle.

NOTE.—Your writing in answering these questions will be taken as a specimen of your penmanship, and will be marked 50 or below, according to merit.

READING.—1. What preparation should be made by the teacher before attempting to teach a class to read a selection from the Fifth Reader?

2. Mention five uses of the dictionary in the preparation of a a reading lesson.

3. Name five American authors that you would recommend children to read.

4. Of what use are punctuation marks? What incorrect view of this is sometimes taken?

5. What is essential to the correct silent reading of a selection?

6. Read a paragraph of prose and a stanza of poetry selected by the superintendent.

ORTHOGRAPHY.—1. When is *es* added to words ending in *o* to form the plural? Give two examples.

2. What is the rule for separating words into syllables? Apply the rule you have given to the following: *Baker, addition, miner, passable, adherence.*

3. Into what general classes are the letters divided as to sounds? Give examples.

4. Show the meaning of the following words by using them correctly in sentences: Proceed, precede, populace, populous, capitol, capital, virtue, virtu, surplice, surplus.

5. Mark the following words diacritically: Laughing, leisure, seine, aged, patronize.

6. Spell and accent the following words correctly: Legeble, metalic, supercileous, sylable, marener, milinery, traveller, chimneys, transative.

GRAMMAR.—1. Illustrate in sentences the different kinds of modifiers each sentence element may have.

2. Write two sentences interrogative in form and declarative in meaning. What is the purpose of such sentences?

3. What is the leading difference between a compound and complex sentence?

4. Define and illustrate the different kinds of clauses as to their office used in the complex sentence.

5. State the office of each infinitive in the following sentences:

    (*a*) The farm is to be sold.

    (*b*) The jailer is supposed to have set the prisoner free.

    (*c*) And they who came to scoff remained to pray.

6. What is the gender of collective nouns?

7. Name and give examples of all the parts of speech that perform in addition to a conjunctive office some other office in the sentence.

8. Correct, giving reasons:

    (*a*) What do you ask for them apples?

    (*b*) This is the more preferable of the two.

    (*c*) He is the best of the two.

9. Parse the underscored words in the following:

      "It is written on the rose,

      In its glory's full array."

10. What distinction should be made between the present perfect tense and the past tense?

ANSWERS TO BOARD QUESTIONS PRINTED IN AUGUST.

HISTORY.—1. The remains of the remarkable works left by the so-called Mound Builders, to be found especially in Ohio and Indiana. Works of a similar character—largely—discovered of late years in Europe, open up an ethnological question of great value, and of exceeding interest.

2. The Chickahominy.

3. *a.* The Royal, the Proprietary, and the Constitutional. *b.* It

was the first colony known in history, as governed by a constitution framed by the people.

4. By election by the Continental Congress, superceding Gen. Artemus Ward, who held his commission from the Colony of Massachusetts.

5. The treasury was empty and the Union had no credit; the Indians were fiercely hostile; African pirates attacked our shipping and imprisoned our citizens or sold them to slavery; Spain refused us the right of navigating the Mississippi; and England refused to send a minister to represent her or to make commercial treaties with us. The remedies were—Congress agreed to pay all the state and national debt contracted for the war, taxes were levied on imported goods and on the distillation of spirits, and a mint and national bank were established—all which restored credit and enabled Congress to pay the debts. Anthony Wayne eventually defeated the Indians, breaking up their alliance with the British; a treaty was made with Spain giving the United States the free navigation of the Mississippi; John Jay made a treaty with England, unpopular, but effective in many respects; a treaty was made with Algiers releasing our citizens and opening up the commerce of the Mediterranean to our vessels.

6. In the war of 1812, Gen. Rose attacked and captured the City of Washington, burned the Capitol and many public and private buildings, including the congressional library. In the civil war the Southern army under Beauregard attempted to seize upon Washington, trusting to force Congress to recognize the Confederacy.

7. A bill originated by Douglass, organizing the Territories of Kansas and Nebraska, on the principle of squatter sovereignty, which gave to the inhabitants of each territory the right to decide the question of slavery within its own borders, and whether it should be admitted as a free or a slave state. As this principle destroyed the Missouri Compromise it excited violent hostility in a large part of the North, strengthening the parties in opposition to slavery to a resistance to every movement that looked to the extension, or even to the perpetuation of slavery, an opposition that largely incited the South to rebel.

8. The attack upon and capture of Fort Sumter under Beauregard. It compelled the South to feel that they had made a step that admitted no retreat, and compelled even Union men to join in the secession movement; while in the North the mass of the people regarded not only the existence of the Union, but almost their own to be menaced, and united them in a determined effort to break down the rebellion.

9. Hood, by his position and the forces under his control, prevented Sherman from making any move towards the East, lest the Confederate forces should strengthen and harrass him in his rear

and repossess themselves of the territory which they had lost. Gen. Thomas, by his Fabian policy, held Hood in the neighborhood of Nashville until Sherman had so far effected his movement as to make it impossible for Hood to follow him. In the meantime he so strengthened himself and his army that when he attacked Hood it was to annihilate him and his army, leaving nothing in the South to carry on the rebellion. •

10. Civil Service Reform.

READING —1. Three things necessary to the correct oral reading of a sentence are,—recognition of the words at sight, knowledge of the meaning of the words, understanding of the thought and sentiment to be expressed.

2. Pupils of the fifth grade are supposed to be pretty well grounded in pronunciation, enunciation, recognition of words, the knowledge of most simple words, ordinary emphasis, etc., so that attention is now to be given chiefly to acquiring power to interpret quickly, to realize in thought and feeling, and to express in proper manner that which is upon the printed page. It follows that special attention is to be given to the character of the piece to be read, to its surroundings, relations, etc , and to the culture of the voice. Hence, in conducting a reading lesson in the Fourth Reader, teacher and pupils are at liberty to go outside of the reader into geography, history, literature, in preparing for the recitation. In conducting the recitation, the materials they acquired may be used first to give a proper setting to the selection. Then, under the direction of the teacher, the attention of the whole class may be concentrated upon a single verse or stanza, or a single sentence, in silence, each endeavoring to form a correct idea in his mind as to the thought or sentiment to be expressed. One pupil, then, may be called upon to rise and state his understanding of the passage selected. If all agree in the interpretation, the pupil may read the passage so as to express the meaning agreed upon.

3. Didactic reading is concerned chiefly with the thought or meaning of the selection; emotional reading with the sentiment contained in it. •

4. Occasional concert reading may tend to encourage diffident pupils, to correct errors in individual members of the class, and to develop accuracy of expression by repetition.

PHYSIOLOGY.—1. The epiglottis is a spoon-shaped piece of cartilage at the base of the tongue. As its name indicates (*epi*—upon), it rests upon the glottis, or opening to the wind-pipe, when food is passing through the pharynx to the gullet, thus preventing strangulation.

2. Loss of sleep produces drowsiness, stupidity from lack of mental tone, lack of accurate control of the mental powers and, at times, extreme nervousness.

3. The salivary glands are small bodies situated at the upper angle of the jaw, underneath the jaw, and underneath the tongue. These, with certain buccal glands secrete the saliva, designed to moisten the food, to bring out its savors, to change its starch to grape sugar, and to facilitate swallowing.

4 The lungs are bodies situated in the chest, on either side the heart and great blood-vessels. The right has three lobes, the left two,—both lungs being somewhat conical in shape, with apex above and concave bases. They are composed of bronchial tubes, air vesicles and cells, two sets of blood-vessels, and connective tissue.

5. Animal heat is due, in part, to the movements of the body itself, all friction resulting in heat; in part, to chemical changes in the food and in the tissues of the body; and in part to heat carried in by food eaten at a higher temperature than that of the body.

6. The retina is the inner and sensitive coat of the eye, composed essentially of rods, cones, and other nervous tissue. It receives the rays of light reflected from objects and conveys knowledge of the image thus made to the brain through the optic nerve.

7. The Eustachian tube is a canal that opens at one end into the pharynx and at the other into the middle ear. It conveys air (received through the nostrils) into the middle ear, thus aiding in the transmission of sound vibrations from the *membrana tympani* to the fluids of the internal ear.

8. (The answer to this question, as also to the 9th, will be found in last month's Journal)

10. A tooth is composed of bone, dentine and enamel. Its parts are the root, the neck, and the crown. Dentine, the chief substance in the tooth, is softest in the center and hardens toward the surface. The tooth is fed while growing by blood-vessels which, with its nerves, enter the tooth through a small opening at the base of the root. When the tooth is matured, the blood-vessels are absorbed, and hence when a tooth is once decayed, nature does not rebuild it.

GEOGRAPHY.—2. From London, Edinburgh is northwest; Herat, Canton, and Melbourne are southeast; Milwaukee is southwest.

3. Three great wheat regions are the Central United States, Southern Russia, and the plains of India; two famous for the production of rice are China and the South Atlantic United States, especially South Carolina.

4. The chief products of the Gulf States are cotton, sugar-cane, and tropical fruits, while those of the Central States are corn, wheat and other grains. The difference in productions is due to differences in soil, latitude, and other climatic conditions.

5. Milwaukee and Racine, in the eastern part of Wisconsin, on Lake Michigan; Chicago, in northeastern part of Illinois, on Lake Michigan; Toledo and Cleveland, in the northern part of Ohio, on

Lake Erie; Erie, in the northwestern part of Pennsylvania, on Lake Erie; Buffalo, in the western part of New York, on Lake Erie; Oswego, in the northern part of New York, on Lake Ontario; Toronto, in Canada, on the northwestern shore of Lake Ontario; Kingston, in Canada, at the east end of Lake Ontario.

6. The annual rise and fall of the Nile is due to the periodic overflow of the equatorial lakes in the rainy season, the Nile being fed by these lakes. The inundation spreads vast deposits of alluvial soil over the land in the Nile basin; hence its great fertility.

7. The Himalaya Mountains are situated north of India, extending east and west. By intercepting the moist winds from the Indian Ocean, they cause the country south of them to be subject to heavy rainfalls, while that to the north is valueless and cold. Hence the southern plains are extremely fertile, while Central Asia is barren.

8. New York, Paris, Vienna, Constantinople, Chicago.

9. *a.* The Danube River rises in the Black Forest, flows in a general easterly direction, through the Austro-Hungarian Monarchy, into the Black Sea. *b.* The Caucasus Mountains extend east and west from the Black to the Caspian Sea, and form part of the boundary between Europe and Asia. *c.* The Adriatic Sea is an arm of the Mediterranean, east of Italy. *d.* The Cape Verde Islands are in the Atlantic Ocean, due west from Cape Verde, on the coast of Africa.

10. The important exports of China are tea, silk, and manufactures; of Brazil, are coffee, sugar, diamonds, and dye-woods; of British India, are cotton, sugar, opium, indigo, and spices.

GRAMMAR.—1. A modifier is a word, phrase, or clause used to qualify or limit the meaning of some other part of the sentence.

1. An adjective; as, The *green* leaves are fading.
2. A noun in the possessive; as, The *man's* coat fits well.
3. A possessive pronoun; as, *His* courage failed him.
4. An appositive; as, The ruler, *Agamemnon*, was angry.
5. A participle; as, Sampson, *shorn* of his locks, lost his strength.
6. An infinitive; as, A promise *to pay* should be as good as the cash.
7. A phrase; as, Relics *of the Mound-Builders* are eagerly sought.
8. A clause; as, The horse *that carries his head high* makes a good appearance.

2. The simple form of the verb, or the first auxiliary, usually comes before the subject; as, *Is* he well? *Did* John go yesterday? If the subject is an interrogative pronoun, the order of words is not changed; as, Who comes here?

3.   *a.* An adverb, modifying *anxious.*
     b. An adverb, modifying *feed.*
     c. An adjective, modifying *thing.*

5. *a. General Grant* is direct object of *think*; *hero* is also in the objective case, called the attributive or factitive object of *think*. *b.* "I saw John, the *boy* who rings the bell." *Boy* is in the objective case, in apposition with *John*, which is the object of *saw*.

6. *a.* "I can do this work *more easily*." An adverb is required to modify *can do. b.* "I do not like such a warm day," is used by good writers; but many grammarians consider this use of *such* incorrect, and express the degree of warmth by *so;* as, I do not like *so* warm a day. *c. Not* all persons are industrious. The thought is to exclude *some* of a class. "All persons are not industrious," excludes *everybody* from industry.

7. This is a complex declarative sentence, of which the subject is the conditional clause, "If a man is gracious," and the predicate, "shows that he is a citizen of the world." *Shows* is the pred. verb, modified by the objective clause, "that he is a citizen of the world." Of the objective clause, *he* is the sub. nom. and *is* the pred. verb; *is* is combined with the phrase, "a citizen of the world," of which *citizen* is the principal word, modified by the article *a* and prep. phrase "of the world." *That* is the connective of the object clause. *It* is the *anticipative* subject of the sentence, etc.

8. Copulative: The rains descended *and* the floods came.
Adversative: I go, *but* I return again.
Disjunctive: One must study *or* he can not make progress.

9. *a. I* and *you* are personal pronouns. *Who* is an interrogative (or responsive) pronoun, used in indirect question. *Whom* is a relative pronoun. *b.* "Who you are," is a clause of indirect question and the object of *know.* "Whom you saw," is a relative clause, used as an adjective, modifying the noun *man.*

10. The object, in the active voice, becomes the subject in the passive, and the subject in the active voice becomes the agent in the passive. Active: Lightning struck the tree.
Passive: The tree was struck by lightning.

SCIENCE OF TEACHING.—1. The work the first three years in geography should be largely oral and objective. Simple lessons in direction, surface, actual observation and illustration of the natural divisions of land and water, simple map·drawing, actual journeys and ideal journeys greatly extended, should be the chief work. Lead through the imagination from what can be seen to what can not be seen.

2. A word is the *sign* of an idea. The child has ideas and knows the oral sign, and the first work of the primary teacher is to give him the *written* or *printed sign.* Letters and sounds are not signs of these ideas, and if presented with the sign (the word) only tend to confuse. It is a mistake to attempt to teach letters or sounds until many words have been learned and put into sentences.

3. A teacher should never scold because it puts both teacher and pupils in a state of mind that defeats all the great purposes of the school.

4. The objections to concert recitation are: (1) It tends to sing-song tone of voice. (2) It fails to reach the individual pupil and make him feel independent. (3) It encourages shirking.

5. A habit is a *tendency* or a disposition to act or think in a given direction. Repetion makes habit.

ARITHMETIC.—1. $124°$ W.—$(80°\ 42'$ W.$)=33°\ 58'$, difference of longitude. $(33°\ 58')+15=2$ h. 15 min. 52 sec. 1 o'clock$=13$ h. 13 h.—$(2$ h. 15 min. 52 sec.$)=10$ h. 44 min. 8 sec. A. M.

2. Mul 480; Div. 8; Quo. 60.

3. It divides the fraction. $\frac{1}{4\times3}=\frac{1}{3}$. $\frac{1}{4}$ is $\frac{1}{3}$ of $\frac{1}{3}$.

4. $\frac{1\frac{3}{4}}{2\frac{1}{4}}+\frac{5\frac{1}{3}}{84\frac{1}{2}}=\frac{\frac{1}{3}}{\frac{2}{3}}+\frac{\frac{3}{4}}{1\frac{1}{4}\frac{3}{4}}=\frac{1}{3}\times\frac{3}{4}\times\frac{7}{16}\times2\frac{1}{4}\frac{1}{4}=11$, Ans.

5. Reduce given number to sq. yd. Multiply by price per sq. yd. $3719 25, Ans.

6. $\frac{4}{5}$ of $5760\times$1.25$=$5760, Ans.

7. 2 yr. 3 mo. 23 da. $=2\frac{1}{4}\frac{7}{1}\frac{3}{2}$ yr. $57.85\times.05\times2\frac{1}{4}\frac{7}{1}\frac{3}{2}=6.684+ Ans.

8. 85% of 196 lb.$=166.6$ lb. $166.6\times$.05$=$8.33, duty per case. $8.33 $\times75=$624.75, Ans.

9. $\left.\begin{array}{l}50:40\\72:60\end{array}\right\}::810.$ $\frac{12\times40\times810}{50\times72}=540$ pages.

10. $\sqrt[3]{1728\times3}=17+$in.

MISCELLANY.

O. E. Sewell is principal of the Mt. Vernon high school.

A very successful normal has just closed at New Providence, Ind., under the care of J. G. Scott and J. R. Weathers.

P. A. Allen, Supt. of the schools at Bluffton, has issued his annual report, which shows his schools in excellent condition.

Mrs. Eudora Hailman will open a permanent kindergarten for the training of kindergartners at Laporte, Ind., Oct. 5th. See adv.

WABASH will expend $200 for a referenee library. Just as "like as not" Supt. D. W. Thomas has had something to do with this.

HUNTINGTON is refitting its school building and extending its library facilities. J. W. Caldwell is giving good satisfaction as superintendent.

E. E. Stevens, a graduate of Franklin College, and for the past two years principal of the Franklin schools, is the new superintendent at Rising Sun.

The address of W. H. Sims before the graduating class of Goshen high school, as printed in "The Weekly News" of that place, contains many good points.

The normal at Marion, under the principalship of Prof. Joseph Tingley, has been remarkably successful. The Professor is greatly encouraged and is looking forward hopefully.

We have just received from the Dixon Crucible Co , of Jersey City, a cedar box containing specimens of eight varieties of their excellent pencils. The pencils and the box containing them are a work of art.

The Normal School at Portland has closed its most pro year, the enrollment reaching 450, and the prospects for 1885-6 flattering. The principal, Geo. Suman, is a quiet man, but he seems to understand his business and attend to it.

Indiana teachers who have recently gone to Kansas: George P. Brown, O. C. Charlton, Homer Charles, D. S. Kelly, Morgan Caraway, Geo. Caraway, Dora Montgomery, Dora and Fannie Stretch. Kansas is getting rich at Indiana's expense.

RICHMOND NORMAL SCHOOL.—This school has succeeded far beyond the earnest anticipations of its best friends. It has just closed a very successful summer term. It has won for itself by its adherence to scientific and psychological principles in methods and thought a place in front, equal to the best.

MISHAWAKA.—The report that comes from the Mishawaka schools, of which Elias Boltz is the worthy superintendent, is very excellent. 151 volumes, purchased from the proceeds of entertainments given by the pupils, have been added to the high school library. During the year just closed 59 pupils were neither tardy nor absent, while the percent of attendance in all the schools was 95. A record to be framed with red lines.

THE AMERICAN NORMAL SCHOOL, located at Logansport, has had some new blood infused into it and is favored with an increased attendance. The summer term has been well attended and those in charge are much encouraged. The proprietors and associate principals are W. S. Sayler, who has been there some time; C. E Kercher and W. S. Harshman, both of the Angola Normal; and E. M. C. Hobbs, a graduate of the State Normal. These gentlemen are assisted by several efficient teachers.

The former students of the State Normal School will be pleased to learn that Dr. J. T Scovell will revise and republish his *Lessons on Geography.* This is one of the best short expositions of the subject yet published for school use. It gives the main points in the *science* of geography as adapted for the common schools. The view of the subject is that geography is a physical science, and that the consideration of government, people, and civilization, usually made part of geography, properly belong to history. A line should be drawn between the subjects as thus indicated. The new work will be used in De Pauw University Normal School. Those who want copies can get them of Dr. Scovell.

W. A. BELL—*Dear Sir :* I wish to approve the plan for the division of labor in the State Teachers' Association. Mr. Treudley's suggestions, as endorsed by Mr. E. E. Smith, are good ones. I can see no danger in doing section work each forenoon and evening. That better results can be gotten in this way, I am convinced, and it would remove the annoyance of conflict with the general work, such as our high school section caused last year.

May we not have the general topics in the main sessions, and the special topics in the sections?

Very truly   SAMUEL E. HARWOOD.

SPENCER, IND.

THAT CURIOUS NUMBER AGAIN.—You may continue the scratching of your head about the number 142857, mentioned on page 463 of the August number of the School Journal, and you will find that if you subtract 1 (unit) from the product of 1, 2, 3, 4, 5, 6, 7 times 142857 and place this *one* to the left side of the number (prefix) you will have the product of 8, 9, 10, 11, 12, 13, 14 times the number.

Subtract 2 instead of 1, and prefix this same 2 to the number and you have 15, 16, 17, 18, 19, 20, 21 times the number.

Continue in this manner, subtracting 3 and placing in the million's place, and you have 22, 23, 24, 25, 26, 27, 28 times that number.

Subtract 4 and prefix to the number, and you have 29, 30, 31, 32, 33, 34, 35 times that number. Who will explain?

M. MAYERSTEIN, La Fayette, Ind.

NORTHERN INDIANA TEACHERS' ASSOCIATION.

The Northern Association met at Rome City July 21–24, and the program heretofore printed in the Journal was with few exceptions carried out. J. K. Waltz, the retiring president, made an excellent address on "Elementary Instruction." The president-elect, D. W. Thomas, gave an inaugural full of suggestive thought on "How to Develop the Power of Thought." "The Use and Abuse of the Grube Method" was well discussed by Miss Lizzie Morden. She advocated the system when it is well taught.

L. H. Jones's paper speaks for itself, as it appears in full in this issue of the Journal. It will well repay reading and re-reading.

D. D. Luke, in the discussion of this paper, showed that he has made a careful study of mental science.

Miss Ada Baylor, of Wabash, read an interesting paper on "True Knowledge and its Functions."

H. M. La Follette, Supt of Boone county, read a most excellent paper on "How to Cultivate a Love for Reading Good Books." It will be printed in full in the Journal. T. J. Sanders, in the discussion of this paper, added some good thoughts.

W. H. Sims, Supt. of the Goshen schools, read a paper on "The Relation of the First Four to the Remaining Years of the Course of Study." The writer placed great stress on the fact that the great purpose of the schools is to develop character, and insisted that the place to begin this work is in the primary grades. The paper was full of good thought.

The officers for the coming year are: President, T. B. Swartz, Supt. of Elkhart schools; Vice-Presidents, T. J. Sanders and Mrs.

N. G. Dakin; Treasurer, A. B. Stevens; Secretary, Jno. P. Mather; Executive Committee, D. D. Luke, chairman, S. E. Miller, H. M. La Follette, Lizzie Morden, and Ada Baylor.

The attendance was not large, the entire enrollment not exceeding sixty; and yet no fault was found with the Chair'n of the Executive Committee, T. B. Swartz, who made a good program and did all he could to have a successful meeting.

There was a general sentiment in favor of trying some other place of meeting with a view of increasing the attendance. The time and place of holding the next meeting was left with the Executive Committee, with a tacit understanding that it would probably be held at Maxinkuckee, about the first of July.

D. D. Luke did faithful work as Secretary,

INDIANA TEACHERS' READING CIRCLE—OUTLINES.

ENGLISH LITERATURE.
First Month——Smith's, pp. 11–26.

Our English forefathers first settled permanently in America in 1607. Their ancestors first came to England from the German lands in 449. The original stock came from the Aryan plains of Asia at time whose history is unrecorded. The modern student of history is little given to cramming his mind with dates. Yet the years when our race crossed the German Ocean and the Atlantic, and that of the great Norman conquest—1066—nearly midway between, like the date of our immortal Declaration of Independence, will always be learned to be remembered.

When the English first came to live in America they brought many books of great authors. When their race first came over to England they brought none. Have we no composition dating back to the time when our forefathers lived in the old German country? I think we have, though some very rare old English gentlemen will swear by the Queen that Beowulf was composed in Surrey. At all events, the scene of Beowulf is laid in old Germany, and it is the oldest composition in the Old English language; and wherever and whenever it may have taken its present form, the tale was doubtless told by our light-haired, rosy-cheeked, and rather rascally progenitors before they came to England.

And so we are to begin at the beginning, and read something about Grendel and Hrothgar and the great hero. The name of the author of the poem is unknown, which is no great loss. It would probably be hard to pronounce, anyway. Next comes Caedmon; and we can make up our mind to suit ourselves as to whether Milton borrowed from him, when the evidence is all in. Then come Alfred,—the sinless man and monarch, according to Bede's history, and Bede himself; and later on, Geoffrey, with his tales of Sabrina and King Lear. Of the value of their works in old time, it is difficult to form an adequate conception. But they are written in the dead Old English, and have been wholly superseded. Hence they are now of no more practical use than burnt gunpowder, though they are subjects of great interest to lovers of literature.

The Norman conquest caused the union of two languages,—the formation of a double language, whose "heterogeneous materials" were shaped by Chaucer "into a symmetrical structure." We are told of the latter's contemporaries, and of the sources from which he drew some of his materials. Perhaps it would have been just as well if he had *not* "drawn" some of these. However, we are not compelled to read all of the Canterbury Tales, and so great a work must not be condemned on account of a few blemishes characteristic of its time

Mandeville, the somewhat mendacious traveler, and Wiclif, the Morning Star of the Reformation, with his Bible translations, his Eighteen Propositions and his Trialogues, now appear, as the fathers of English prose.

A careful study of the text-book will repay the teacher, as the work is thoroughly condensed. The Introduction to Webster's Unabridged Dictionary will afford valuable and entertaining supplementary reading on the same topics. H. M. SKINNER.

————:o:————

BROOKS' MENTAL SCIENCE.
Subject: Intuition——Pages 319–344.

I. TERMS TO BE STUDIED.—1. Reason and Reasoning, p. 320. 2. Complement, pp. 320, 322. 3. Opposition, pp. 234–5. 4. Contingent and Necessary, p. 329. 5. Logically and Chronologically, pp 332–4. 6. Quantitative, p. 333. 7. Cause and Occasion, p. 340.

II. ITEMS OF PROFESSIONAL IMPORT.—1. Relation of Intuition to Memory, p. 323. 2. Relation of Intuition to Imagination, p. 323. 3. Nature of Identity, pp 336–8. 4. Nature of Cause, p. 344.

III. SUMMARIES —1. The Tests of Primary Truths. 2. The Primary Ideas. 3. The Elements of Space. 4. The Elements of Time. 5. The Classes of Identity.

IV. QUOTATIONS.—1. "There are three sorts of ideas in mind: (*a*) Adventitious ideas—those acquired through the senses; (*b*) Factitious ideas—those constructed from materials furnished by the senses; (*c*) Those which are native-born, original, innate, [intuitive, B.]"—*Descartes.*

2. "No general truth is intuitional."—*Hamilton.*

3. "Reasoning is a development of intuition: a course of reasoning is a succession of intuitions."—*Hamilton.*

4. "No conflict ever occurs between the intuitions of one man and those of another."—*Hamilton.*

5. Axioms are of two kinds: (1) Mathematical; (for examples see common texts); (2) Metaphysical. Ex.—(*a*) Space and time exist; and all other things exist in space and time. (*b*) Every body occupies space. (*c*) No body can be in two places at once. (*d*) Every change corresponds, in nature, to the cause producing it."

6. "Identity is a relation between our cognitions of things, not between things themselves."—*Hamilton.*

7. "Intuition is to the understanding, what perception is to sensation."—*Morell.*

4

8. "Hardly shall you find any one so bad but he desires the credit of being thought good."—*South.*

9 "Causat on is the law of connection between physical facts; spontaniety, the ground of connection between mental facts."—*Bascom.*

10. "What space is to material facts, conscience is to intellectual facts. To occupy space is to have physical existence; to occupy consciousness is to have intellectual existence; to occupy neither is not to exist."—*Bascom.*

11. "The power of cognizing beauty may be cultivated by exercise. The study of beauty has a tendency to refine and ennoble the mind."—*Alden.*

12. "Time is that in which things persist, or succession takes place. Space is that in which bodies are situated and motion takes place."—*Schuyler.* R. G. BOONE.

————:o:————

SCIENCE OF TEACHING.
Hewett's Pedagogy——Pages 9—75.

The work for the first month will be found outlined in the text-book, on pages viii, 14, 38, and 48. Subsequent outlines will be prepared by Prof. Geo. P. Brown.

Members of the Indiana Teachers' Reading Circle who had partially completed the course of reading for last year but were not prepared for examination at the time of the regular annual examination in June, will be given an opportunity to pass examination upon the work of both the first and the second year at the annual examination next summer.

The expense of holding a special examination for the accommodation of such members this year would be greater than the board of Directors feel warranted in making. J. J. MILLS,

August 24, 1885. President Board of Directors.

————————

THE NATIONAL TEACHERS' ASSOCIATION.

OPENING EXERCISES—ATTENDANCE—INDIANA FOLKS—THE COMMON SCHOOL AND MORALITY—OFFICERS—CO-OPERATIVE ASSOCIATIONS.

————

The National Teachers' Association was called to order on the evening of July 14th, at Saratoga, N. Y, by President L. Soldan. Prof. E. E. Smith, of La Fayette, Ind., was elected Asst. Secretary.

Addresses of welcome were made by the Secretary of the Board of Regents of New York, and by the Superintendent of the Saratoga schools,—the former delivering a very fine address, in every way worthy of the occasion. The response for the West was by Supt. B. A. Hinsdale, of Cleveland, O.

The paper for the evening, upon "The Ideal Schoolmaster," was written by Gen. Thos. Morgan, of Providence, R. I. It was very dull and prosy—one of those "always-room-for-one-more" (point) documents that a weary but patient audience is sometimes forced to swallow.

The attendance of Saratoga people was quite large, but of teachers quite small. It is very doubtful if the fees received will pay expenses. Especially was the absence of delegates from the West and South noticeable.

Those present from Indiana were, Hon. John W. Holcombe, Pres. J. H. Smart, Supt. Lewis H. Jones, Prof. E. E. Smith, Prof. W. M. Goss, Miss N. Cropsey, Geo. P. Brown and wife, Ada Duzan, Prof. W. N. Hailman and wife. Mary E. Nicholson, Mrs. E. A. Blaker, May Wright Sewall, Lillie J. Martin, and Prof. S. S. Parr.

While mentioning incidentals we may say that it seemed to be the general opinion that Pres. Soldan made a grave mistake in taking the meeting to Saratoga; that there was apparent to the writer a very strong current of feeling that the National Association is being run for the benefit of certain interests; and that there is more wire-working to the square inch at Saratoga than the most fertile imagination could have conceived.

The Kindergarten Section of the Saratoga Summer Normal School is under the charge of three Indiana people, Prof. and Mrs. W. N. Hailman and Mrs. E. A. Blaker, is doing excellent work, and sustains a reputation that the instructors may well be proud of.

The annual address by the President of the Association, F. Louis Soldan, was a strong presentation of the contrast and the struggle between the fixed and the progressive principles of human life, the development of civilization due to the adjustment between these in different ages, and the fact that the only hope of harmony between the antagonistic interests and designs of humanity lies in the superior education of the masses. Inasmuch as the perpetuity of states and of the nation is brought into question by these antagonisms, education has risen to the importance of a national issue.

J. W. Stearns, LL. D., of Madison, Wis., read a paper on "The Common School and Morality." The paper placed the basis of moral instruction in the school in the mechanical virtues. Dr. G. Stanley Hall, in discussing it, argued for a physiological basis of morality. Dr. E. E. White thought that no very high moral purpose could come from a system not based upon the great truths of the christian religion.

Dr. Wm. T. Harris presented a very fine paper upon "Psychological Inquiry." An abstract of this paper will not satisfy any one. In discussing it, Prof. Lewis H. Jones, of Indianapolis, said, in substance: "The paper we have just listened to seems to be constructed about two leading ideas: (1) the true nature of the mind; (2) the mode of study of the mind necessitated by this nature The first was expressed by the statement that the primary fact of the mind is self-activity. The second, in the statement that the facts of mind can only be known by the study of the states of self through introspection by consciousness; and through this self-study the interpretation of the mental states of others by inferences.

On the first point the speaker thought the paper made too much of self-activity and not enough of the fact that the mind is capable of becoming, through self activity, self-directive, and by this means to obtain rational freedom through education. The second point, Prof. Jones said that he had never heard so clear a statement of what seemed to him the true method of psychological inquiry. Study of this work as manifested by teachers in the school-room showed three kinds of teachers: (1) the unconscious but yet partially successful teacher; (2) the teacher half-conscious of the principles involved in his work, but yet stumbling from lack of clear light; (3) the teacher who has passed through the first two stages into that wherein the end is fully seen from the beginning, and who thus walks in the light of great principles."

Col. F. W. Parker failed to be on hand with his promised old tune set to new music under the head of "The Philosophy of Learning to Do by Doing," and so Dr. A. D. Mayo, of Boston, evidently counting upon the Colonel's absence, was prepared with a very good paper upon "How to Learn." Among the excellent things said by the Doctor are the following: "What we are individually is the least part of us; only that little angle in which we are differentiated from the glorious common human nature whereby we are made in the image of Almighty God. So, while it is necessary that we should hold up in the new schools of our newland the adage of wise old Comenius, we shall make the worst failure of the ages if we shall fall into the conceit that we are set up here on this Western Continent to begin from the beginning and make all things new. * * * Why, in our education, can we not take up one good thing without dropping another? * * There is an absurd provincialism in a new country that does not know there has been any life of the ages before; where man stands up a creature without a past; to whom history is only a last year's almanac; in whose light all the mighty achievements of mankind are matters of stolid indifference."

The paper was discussed by Profs. W. N. Hailman, of La Porte, Ind., Z. Richards, of Washington, D. C., and Edward Brooks, of Pennsylvania.

Excellent papers were read also by Miss Clara Conway, of Memphis, Tenn., and by Prof. C. K. Wead, of Ann Arbor, Mich.,—the former upon "The Child's Environment," the latter upon "The Teaching of Physics in the Common Schools."

OFFICERS FOR NEXT YEAR, ETC.—The Committee on Nominations reported the following officers for next year, whose selection met with pretty general approval: *President*, N. A. Calkins, of New York; *Secretary*, W. E. Sheldon, of Massachusetts; *Treasurer*, E. C. Hewitt, of Illinois; 12 *Vice-Presidents; Counsellors-at-Large*, John Eaton, D. C., and Dr. E. E. White, of Cincinnati, Ohio. In the executive committee for the Department of Higher Instruction, Prof. E. E. Smith, of Indiana, was elected for the three years term. Dr. J. H. Smart, of Indiana, was re-elected a member of the National Council of Education, his time having expired. Hon. John W. Holcombe was elected President of the Department of Elementary Instruction.

The President elect was authorized to appoint a committee of experienced teachers to co-operate with other bodies and endeavor to ascertain how physics-teaching in our schools may be improved and made more uniform throughout the country

CO-OPERATING ASSOCIATIONS.—Prof. E. E. Smith, of La Fayette, Ind., make the following motion, which was read for information and afterwards taken up and referred to the Executive Committee for action as recommended:

WHEREAS, It is evident that the territory of the United States is too large to be embraced in the meetings of one teachers' association; and whereas, the motto of all teachers' gatherings should be "the greatest good to the greatest number," and especially to that large majority of teachers whose pay is limited in amount; therefore,

Resolved, That a committee of five be appointed by the Chair to take into consideration and ascertain, by correspondence or otherwise, the advisability of aiding in the organization of a limited number of co-operating but self-regulating Teachers' Associations in various portions of the United States. This committee to report at the meeting of the National Association one year from this time.

This resolution was discussed among the members with a great deal of interest, meeting with hearty approval in its purpose on the part of some and earnest opposition on the part of others. The step proposed is regarded with serious apprehension by many, but it was generally agreed that an investigation of the matter may be productive of good.

May Wright Sewall, of Indianapolis, made a report of some interest upon the " Higher Education of Women." The report was also signed by Dr. W. T. Harris and by W. E. Sheldon, A. M., of Boston, and was adopted by the association.

Denver, Col., and Topeka, Kan., endeavored to get up a musical soiree by presenting bids for the next place of meeting of the association. Their *billet doux* were referred to the Executive Committee. The general feeling seemed to be in favor of Topeka, though the presentation of the two names resulted in a tie vote.

Dr. Bicknell presented the report of the Committee on Education at the New Orleans Exhibit, which, after some discussion, was referred to the Executive Committee.

The usual vote of thanks for privileges extended was passed, a general jubilee of the elder brethren was indulged in, the retiring President introduced his successor, and the latter, with some timely remarks, closed *sine die* the 25th annual session of the association.

JOHN REX.

PERSONAL.

John Myrick goes to Hazelton.

A.▐J. Snoke remains at Princeton.

E. O. Ellis is principal at Fairmount.

Robert Taylor is principal at Shelburn.

J. W. Runcie takes charge at Ft. Branch.

A. M. Ward is principal of the Merom schools.

Harvey Lucas has been retained at Owensville.

George E. Long will continue in charge at Roann.

W. S. Ellis is principal of the schools at Alexandria.

E. A. Hinshaw will succeed N. W. Bryant at Acton.

V. E. Livengood will remain in charge at Covington.

H. S. McRae remains in charge of the Marion schools.

W. S. Wood remains in charge of the Seymour schools.

Minnie Brunker has charge of the schools at Farmersburg.

J. F. Scull will continue in charge of the Rochester schools.

L. M. Sniff is the new principal of the Angola Normal School.

Lizzie Remster is the new principal of the Veedersburg schools.

A. W. Dunkle has been six years at Delphi. He will continue.

Jesse Lewis has been elected principal of the schools at Sylvania.

W. W. Black will have charge of the schools of Flora next year.

W. F. L. Sanders has a good hold on the schools of Cambridge City.

V. McKnight, of Cortland, is principal of one of the Jeffersonville schools.

D. W. Thomas is entering his *thirteenth* year as superintendent at Wabash.

H. W. Graham will continue as principal of the Camden schools another year.

N. W. Bryant will have charge of the schools of Mapleton the coming year.

W. H. Warbel will be principal of the schools at Liberty Mills the coming year.

R. J. Aley, of Spencer, will enter the State University as a Junior this coming fall.

P. A. Allen has been retained as superintendent at Bluffton, at an increased salary.

Emma Cox, a graduate of the State Normal, is principal of the schools at Morocco.

J. G. Scott will remain as principal of the schools at New Providence, another year.

W. H. Cain will enter upon his eighth year's service as principal of the Carlisle schools.

Geo. W. Dealand has been elected for the fifth time to take charge of the Perrysville schools.

J. E. Mannix, of Vincennes, will remove to Elk Point, Dakota, to take charge of the schools.

A. M. Huyck, a graduate of Michigan University, will remain in charge of the Wabash high school.

A. E. Davisson is the principal of the high school at Rochester, not A. E. Dawson, as printed last month.

Walter S. Smith, formerly so well known in Indiana, still remains principal of the seminary at Owenton, Ky.

Supt. Robinson, of Gibson county, has arranged for an exposition of school work at the next county institute.

Mr. — Shafer, of Springfield, Ind., formerly of Thorntown, has been elected superintendent of the schools at Attica.

H. C. Montgomery, after teaching two years in Kentucky. returns to take the principalship of the Seymour high school.

Wm. M. Craig, for many years superintendent of the Rockville schools, will this year have the schools at Waveland.

B. F. Moore, a recent graduate of the State Normal School, will have charge of the Monticello schools the coming year.

Samuel E. Harwood, at an increased salary, will remain at Spencer another year. Most of his teachers will also remain.

Z. T. Emerson, one of the ablest teachers in Southern Indiana, has resigned his position at Booneville to go into business.

W. S. Almond, superintendent of the Vernon schools, has the sympathy of a large circle of friends in the loss of his wife.

W. H. Mushlitz, late superintendent of Clinton county, has been elected principal of the Fulton Avenue school in Evansville.

Walter Wallace, of Columbus, Ind., has revised his biographical and literary games with cards and has much improved them.

Elmer Henry, of Howard county, and a graduate of the State Normal School, will teach in the Peru high school next year.

J. H. Layne, formerly principal of the Anderson high school, is now the efficient superintendent of the Danville (Ill.) school.

J. I. Hopkins, well known in Indiana, is now teacher of the Classics and Higher Mathematics in Orange College, Starke, Fla.

F. W. Reubelt, for several years past superintendent at Noblesville, has been elected to take charge of the Rensselaer schools

J. B. Roberts has given up the Indianapolis Female Seminary and accepted a position in the faculty of the Indianapolis high school

A. N. Higgins, who has for several years had charge of the Veedersburg schools, has been elected prin. of the Waynetown schools.

Oakland City has a new school-house, seven rooms. N. C. Johnson, who recently received a state certificate, will be retained for the third year.

J. B. Starr, the new superintendent of the New Albany schools, will receive a salary of $1200, instead of $1000, as stated in last month's Journal.

W. C. Washburn, formerly superintendent of the Charlestown schools, has been for three years past principal of the 18th district school, Cincinnati.

Mrs. Emma Mont. McRae remains as principal of the Marion high school, at an increased salary. She has spent a part of the summer at Boston, studying.

J. C. Black was tendered the superintendency of the Attica schools, but the Logansport board increased his salary, and so he will remain as principal of their high school.

J. A. Zeller, for many years principal of the high school at Evansville, and for two years superintendent at Richmond, has accepted the principalship of the La Fayette high school.

P. P. Stults, for eleven years superintendent at Rising Sun, but for the last three years at Mt. Vernon, has been re-elected for *two years* at the latter place, having his salary increased to $1500.

Smith (now *Leigh*) Hunt, formerly one of the leading teachers of Whitley county, is now president of the Iowa Agricultural College. He was recently married to Miss Jessie Noble, of Des Moines.

Homer W. Charles, one of the live teachers of Wabash county, has accepted the superintendency of the schools of Sedgwick, Kan. Indiana loses and Kansas gains a good teacher and a good man.

Geo. H. Caraway, a graduate of the State Normal School, has accepted the superintendency of the schools of Great Bend, Kansas. Alice Hogue, of Howard county, as a "better-half" will assist him.

Chas. Fagan, late principal of the Goodland schools, goes to the Indian Territory in the employ of the government to take charge of a school among the Osage Indians. He will be accompanied by John Roberts, another Newton county teacher.

A. H. Morris, late Supt. of Hamilton county, has been appointed Superintendent of the Soldiers' Orphans' Home, at Knightstown. This is a most fitting appointment—the right man in the right place.

Miss Mary Nicholson, the new principal of the Indianapolis Training School, did her first year's work in such a manner as to secure the hearty commendation of the superintendent and a re-election by the board.

The next President of the National Teachers' Association, to be held probably at Denver, next summer, is N. A. Calkins, Supt. of primary schools, New York City, and not Mr. Sheldon, as stated last month.

W. A. Boles, formerly of Shelbyville, this state, will open a select school for both sexes at Dallas, Texas. The school is intended to be sufficiently comprehensive to admit all grades from primary to the high school.

S. S. Parr, now at the head of the Normal Department of De Pauw University, has sold *School Education,* which he owned and edited for the three years he lived in Minnesota. His successor is Sanford Niles, who, in Prof. Parr's opinion, is an able man.

Geo. C. Hubbard, principal of the lower seminary at Madison, has made a collection of the flora of Jefferson county, which is one of the finest in the state. It excels not only in the extent of the collection, but also in the manner of its arrangement and display.

D. S. Kelley, for several years past Supt. of the Jeffersonville schools, has been elected to the chair of Natural History in the Kansas State Normal School, at Emporia. Mr. Kelley was one of Indiana's live teachers, and is a valuable acquisition to any state.

E. M. Chaplin, for many years the agent in Northern Indiana for Van Antwerp, Bragg & Co., is now doing business on his own account, with headquarters at Warsaw. Any one in need of reading charts, writing charts, or anatomical charts, can be made happy by writing to him.

W. M. Croan, formerly superintendent of Madison county schools, this state, but for two years past superintendent of Western Normal College, situated at Shenandoah, Iowa, has not only sustained the reputation he achieved in Indiana, but has won an enviable success in the management of the Western Normal College.

Prof. Thompson, who occupies the chair of art in Purdue University, has formed a class of young men at Monteagle, Tenn., who study nothing save caricatures. They aim to perform for newspapers the kind of work done by Nast and others who enliven the pictorial press with cartoons. This is the first class of its kind in the country of which we have any knowledge. It is a field, but one in which there are but few aspirants, and it offers substantial and ready employment to men of ability.

D. Eckley Hunter, who leaves Indiana for Texas the next year, is one of the oldest and best known Hoosier teachers. He was a charter member of the State Association and has not missed a single meeting; he has been a contributor and subscriber to THE INDIANA SCHOOL JOURNAL from its earliest infancy—having in his possession a complete file from the first issue. He has always taken an active part in all educational reforms, and the Indiana system of education which is among the best, owes not a little to him. In his departure, the state is a loser. To his new home Mr. Hunter bears with him the best wishes of a host of warm Indiana friends.

Geo. P. Brown, late president of the State Normal School, has accepted an agency for A. S. Barnes & Co., and will make his headquarters at Topeka, Kan. For many years Mr. Brown has been among the leading educational spirits of the state, and his loss will be widely felt. Whether as superintendent of the Richmond schools, as principal of the Indianapolis high school, as superintendent of the Indianapolis schools, as president of the State Normal School, or as a member of the State Board of Education, he has done his work with ability. He has done much for the educational interest of the state, and he leaves behind him a host of friends who regret his removal from the state and wish him eminent success in his new field of labor.

Charles E. Bickmore, formerly a teacher in this state, died near Hamilton, O., July 27th. He fell from an apple tree July 24th and received injuries that resulted in his death. Mr. Bickmore was a native of Maine; but he had spent the greater part of his life teaching in Ohio, Indiana and Kentucky. He was a graduate of the Ind. State Normal. For several years he was connected with the schools of Rising Sun and of Logansport. During the last two years he had been superintendent of the schools at Catlettsburg, Ky. Owing to his reticent manner and modest disposition, he did not attain the positions to which his abilities as an instructor and a disciplinarian entitled him; but his influence for good was, perhaps, none the less potent on that account. He labored for the good of others, not only in the school room, but out of it as well. Those who knew him best most highly appreciated his worth to the world. In his death the cause of education has lost one of its most earnest, unselfish and conscientious workers.

BOOK TABLE.

Walter Wallace's Biographical and Literary Cards have been revised and greatly improved in appearance and in the rules. See advertisement.

The Fountain is a youth's monthly magazine published at York, Penn. Vol. 3, No 1, which has just reached us, is full of interesting matter for boys and girls. We find articles on birds, flowers, and animals. In the history line is a description of Westminster Abbey. It is in every way worthy the boys and girls who may read it. W. H. Shelly, publisher.

Vocal Drill Book for Schools. By W. T. Giffe. Published by the author, at Logansport, Ind.

The author has taught music in the public schools of Logansport for several years past, and h s book has grown out of his experience. The book is filled with music, much of it original, well adapted to the different grades of school. The words also have been selected with care and are well adapted to the music and the grade.

The author claims as a special merit of his book that the exercises are so graded and the explanations and suggestions to teachers are so full that teachers who know little of musical notation can teach this important branch successfully. The author takes a new departure in objecting to beating time with the hand. The book is certainly a good one, and teachers would do well to examine it.

William Cobbett's English Grammar, with notes by Robt. Waters, Principal of the West Hoboken Public School, consists of a series of twenty-one letters, addressed to his son, who had just reached the age of fourteen years. The main facts of Grammar are stated in simple, intelligible language, so that one of mature mind may understand them without the aid of an instructor. Cobbett does not enter into the minute classification, which characterizes the later English Grammars; but the notes of Prof. Waters furnish what is lacking in this particular. One reads the book through with a great deal of interest and is glad to place it among his books of frequent reference. In addition to the twenty-one letters, there are " six lessons, intended to prevent statesmen from using false grammar, and from writing in an awkward manner "—a consummation devoutly to be wished.

A. S. Barnes & Co., publishers: Chicago and New York.

New Elementary Geometry. By Edward Olney. New York and Chicago: Sheldon & Co.

This book is intended to take the place of Olney's Geometry, now in use. The work in the first part of the book has been much simplified, to more readily reach the grasp of the pupil, and gradually lead him to the more difficult reasoning. The demonstrations in the first part of the book have been arranged so that each step occupies a separate paragraph. The subject of Parallels is treated in a somewhat new manner, enabling the author to put some of the longer demonstrations in fewer words. In the early part of the work definite references to former principles are made, by question marks, which will be found a great help in securing individual thought.

In addition, a larger number of problems has been given, also leading the pupil to original investigation—a feature much to be commended. The figures are in white lines on a black ground, which make them stand out clear and well defined.

The mechanical work is equal to the best in every respect, and school men would do well to examine.

BUSINESS NOTICES.

LA PORTE KINDERGARTEN TRAINING SCHOOL.—This school offers superior advantages to ladies desiring to become Kindergartners. Send for circulars, to Mrs. EUDORA HAILMAN, La Porte, Ind.　　　　9-2t

The Grand Rapids & Indiana Railroad leads up into the best fishing section of the country. The road is appropriately named " The Fishing Line." C. L. Lockwood, Grand Rapids, is Gen. Pass. and Ticket Agent.

Do not fail to read the list of excellent books published by Houghton, Mifflin & Co., of Boston, to be found in this number of the Journal. No other house in the country gives the public so many works of a high literary character.

TEACHERS desiring to attend a *Normal School*, or those wishing a situation or an increase of salary, should send for a sample copy of "*The Educational World.*" Address, W. SAYLER, *Editor, Logansport, Ind.*　　　　1-12t.

GRAND EXCURSION TO NIAGARA FALLS VIA "THE BEE LINE ROUTE."— The C. C. C. & I. R'y ("Bee Line") will run their Annual Excursion to Niagara Falls and Return on Tuesday, September 8th, 1885. The entire train, consisting of Coaches and Reclining Chair Cars, will run through to the Falls

without change. Fare for the round trip only $5 00. The "Bee Line" is the
only direct line from Indianapolis to Niagara Falls. For full particulars call on
or address W. J. Nichols, District Passenger Agent, No. 2 Bates House, Indianapolis, Ind.

DAKOTA EXCURSION.—The I. D. & S. R'y announce round trip tickets from
principal points on that road to Dickinson, Devil's Lake, and Grand Forks,
Dakota, at rates ranging from $19.50 to $23.00, good 40 days, with stop-over
at St. Paul and points on the Northern Pacific and Manitoba R. R's. These
tickets will be sold for night train leaving Indianapolis at 10:50 P. M. August
24, and for 8:30 A. M. train from Indianapolis August 25. About 2000 miles
for a little better than $20.00. This will be the only excursion to the North-
west this fall.

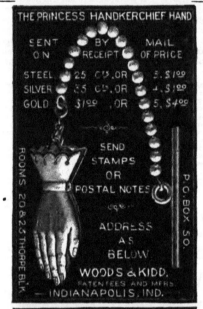

INDIANA
SCHOOL JOURNAL.

| Vol. XXX. | GCTOBER, 1885. | No. 10. |

HORACE MANN.

J. B. WISELY.

[Read before the Owen County Teachers' Instttute.]

FAR away to the eastward, in the good old educational "Bay State," and not a great distance from the City of Boston, lies the little village of Franklin; named after the great father of American Philosophy, who in token of the respect shown his name offered the little town a bell for their church; but afterwards learning, as he said in his quaint way, that they "preferred sense to sound," he gave them a small public library instead. That library was the spiritual father of the son of a poor farmer who lived near by, and gave to him that thirst for knowledge and culture which resulted in giving to the world HORACE MANN. More than three-quarters of a century ago that little library planted the seed, and to-day we are enjoying the ripe fruit.

Up to the age of twenty he was engaged, most of his time, in manual toil, for the support of a widowed mother, spending his leisure moments in gleaning mental strength from the public library and poorly managed public school of Franklin. It was in this pure country atmosphere, while struggling against those difficulties which opposed themselves to his very existence, that he imbibed that spirit of endurance and persistent perseverance which afterwards made his life a success. Here his muscles were strengthened and his sinews hardened for that Herculean task which awaited him.

In 1816 he entered Brown University at Providence, R. I., and after three years of the closest application and most economical living he graduated with credit to his efforts. In his final thesis on "The Progressive Character of the Human Race," he struck the key-note of his life and foreshadowed the fields of his labor. The life energy of Mr. Mann flowed in two main channels: a political and an educational, the current of the latter much stronger than the former. Aalong with these he carried that spirit of philanthropy which should be a characteristic of every life.

He chose for his profession the Law, a profession which his conscience would not allow him to practice, believing, as he did, that no one is justified in advocating a cause, unless he is thoroughly convinced of its truth and justice. And being a public speaker of no mean ability he was naturally prompted to enter the political arena. In this field of labor his actions were characterized as having at their foundation a desire to better the condition of his fellow-citizens. He was a warm supporter of temperance, assisting it with a speech whenever an occasion offered. While in his state legislature, he was a member and part of the time chairman of the committee which revised the state statutes of Massachusetts. In 1848 he filled the vacancy in Congress caused by the death of John Q. Adams. He was a bitter enemy of slavery, in the opposition of which he might be said to be the immediate forerunner of Wendell Phillips. He engaged in a discussion with Daniel Webster relative to this subject in 1850. The friends of Mr. Webster succeeded just at this time in defeating Mr. Mann's renomination to Congress, but he appealed to the people and was re-elected as an Independent Anti-Slavery candidate, a fact which shows his popularity in his own state.

* * * * * * * *

But it is not of his political life that I wish particularly to speak, nor is it the purpose of this paper to perpetuate the memory of his political usefulness, for it is unimportant compared with his great life-work. It is as an *educator* that we wish to remember HORACE MANN.

While in the legislature he was a warm supporter of every movement which looked toward the advancement of educational interests. But when in 1837 he was placed in command of his 80,000 children, as he was pleased to call them, by being chosen Secretary of the State Board of Education, he threw his whole life into its public school system, which succeeded in placing it at the head of educational schemes in the United States. No one ever recognized more fully the responsibility of a position than he, and surely no one ever labored more faithfully and un- selfishly to discharge every duty belonging to his office. He had only one object in the world, and that was to reform and improve the public school system of his native state. And comprehending his purpose clearly, he went to work with that *earn. estness* and *faith* which remove mountains.

Envious ambition mocked his toils and intellectual tricksters laughed at his ideas, but in spite of unrelenting opposition he kept the even tenor of his way, and as Napoleon moulded France, so he shaped the education of his state in accordance with his own model. He did not stand aloof weaving fine-spun theories for others to unravel and apply, but he *worked*, among the common schools and common teachers, making progress by the sweat of his brow. For eleven *long* years he spent all the time he could possibly spare from his other duties, in holding educational conventions and teachers' institutes; teaching all day and lecturing at night. He spared no pains in discovering the weak points in his school system, and he was tireless in his efforts to secure means to strengthen them; even making a six months visit to Europe, at his own expense, in order to glean the products of experience in that country.

His annual reports were complete and valuable educational documents, especially his Seventh Annual Report, which contained his observations on the schools of Europe, and was read by educators the world round. His *Common School Journal*, published for ten years, had almost as wide a circulation. Here also he found opportunity to use his philanthropic spirit, and schools for poor children, asylums and hospitals embodied his thought.

* * * * * * * *

But we who owe something to Normal Schools, may perhaps remember HORACE MANN in a somewhat different and nearer relation. We may, perhaps, have caught some of his inspiration and life without being conscious of it.

He saw that the state had taken it into its power to educate the children, within its own boundaries; that it used as a means to this end the common schools; that in order to have good schools the state *must* have well trained teachers; and he held that as the state had created the school for this noble purpose, it should also supply the means of MAKING THE SCHOOL A SUCCESS. *Schools for training teachers was the thought;* and although Mr. Mann was not the first advocate of Normal Schools in America, he *was* the first who had the *energy* and *courage* to bring about a practical result of this thought.

In 1838 he received from Edward Dwight an offer to appropriate $10,000, for the purpose of establishing a State Normal School, provided that the state would appropriate an equal amount for the same purpose. By dint of great exertion he succeeded in obtaining the co-óperation of the state, and on July 3, 1839, the first Normal School in America opened its doors in Lexington, Massachusetts.

Mr. Mann had succeeded in accomplishing something in America which had never been done, in the doing of which there is some honor. He now had an equally difficult task to perform; viz, to support it. He proved himself equal to the task, however, and succeed in establishing another in his own state, besides planning for hundreds of others outside of it.

Mr. Mann did not live to see the end of his great work, nor indeed has the end of it yet been reached, but we see the effects of it in the hundreds of normal schools which dot our land, and in the army of trained teachers that go out every day to battle with *ignorance* and *vice*.

In 1852 Mr. Mann took charge of Antioch College, Yellow Springs, Ohio, where he spent the remainder of his days in earnest efforts to build up that institution.

* * * * * * * *

In reviewing the life of a great character it is interesting to inquire into his motives, powers, and actions, and see what were the elements of his success, for it is only in so doing that we are benefited.

Mr. Mann's whole life was characterized by an honesty and earnestness which is convincing. He never undertook anything until he was thoroughly convinced that it was the right thing to do, and then he went about it with that whole-soul spirit which convinced every one with whom he met of his sincerity of purpose at least. He was self-sacrificing. Nothing, honorable, was too expensive if it would assist in accomplishing that which he believed to be beneficial and right. It is said that during a great part of the time which he acted as secretary of the board of education, his work averaged *fifteen* hours per day. He very often supplied funds from his own salary or borrowed money on his own credit to carry out his educational schemes. The legislature fixed his salary as secretary at $1500 per year, of which he said: "Well, it will probably leave me about $500 for my *ordinary expenses* and *services* after defraying the *extraordinary* expenses, but I will be revenged on them; I *will do them more than* $1500 *worth of good.*"

He was always a friend of morality, public charities, education, and the welfare of the poor and ignorant, because coming from that class he knew how to sympathize with them, and he also recognized these as the influences which had lifted him to his present condition. It was probably the contemplation of this thought that gave him his humble spirit; for certainly no man ever lived more in accordance with the passage of scripture which says that "One should not think more highly of himself than he ought to think," than did he; for so far from being a bigot, he always rather underestimated his abilities. His prayer was, "Give me good health, a clear head, and a heart overflowing with love for humanity."

It is the contemplation of such virtues, so clearly set forth in such a life, that leads us to respect and reverence "the great teacher" and "father of normal schools."

Begin with what is already well known to the pupil in the lesson or upon the subject, and proceed to the unknown by single, easy, and natural steps, letting the known explain the unknown.

CHAUCER AND HIS TIMES.

MATTIE CURL DENNIS.

THERE were two great passions that inspired the life of the Middle Ages; the one was religious enthusiasm, the other, the enthusiasm of war: the former was the inspiration which caused pilgrimages to the Holy Sepulcher, fought the Crusades, fostered monasteries and built massive cathedrals; the latter perpetuated knighthood, protected feudal castles and furnished them with lordly occupants.

The spirit of the one had, at the time of Chaucer, degenerated into church bigotry and superstitious favoritism; that of the other, into the supreme selfishness and violent extravagancies of fourteenth century chivalry.

The work that gave soul to the middle ages had been completed, and men without a purpose had no alternative but to decay. They strove to prop crumbling institutions with the pageantry of ornament, and so, extravagance in dress, in architecture, in all departments of social, civil and religious life became a passion with them, and only added one more certainty to their downfall. There were still the great universities, filled with students and many learned priests and bishops, but scholarship had become scholasticism and religion fanaticism.

But, a new era, with a new thought in it, that had been hid away amid the rocks and caves of the Waldenses, or, perhaps, sung in the Grecian streets by Homer, was about to break in upon the age; the battle of Crescy and Poitiers had been fought; the truce of Bretigny signed; and Richard the Second had announced to the Parliament of 1389 that he was now old enough to manage his own affairs. In the peace which ensued, the plowman released from his bow had time to reflect; Wat Tyler and the Peasant rebellion had not failed of his purpose. Lollardism was becoming not only deep seated but widespread; the masses were becoming tired of a religion that gave them only stones for bread, and of a government that swallowed up their income with taxation. Wyclif's germ of civil and religious freedom was planted in no uncertain soil; and although it took 140 years for it to take root, it grew nevertheless. It was under these circumstances that Chaucer lived and wrote.

The blood of the intruding Dane, the conquering Norman, and the unconquerable Saxon was rapidly becoming one; there was a general upgrowth in the minds of the masses, in favor of English thought expressed in the English tongue, and by the middle of the 14th century there was a growing disuse of the French language even among the nobler classes; and English soon became the language of courts of law and the grammar schools, and in 1363 it was used by the Chancellor in opening Parliament; bishops now began to preach in English, and the tracts of Wyclif made it once more a literary tongue, which it had ceased to be since the time of the Saxon chroniclers.

Language is always a leveler; common sympathy was fast making a people one who could not help having common interests; camps and courts and priests could not long be sustained, independent of the plowmen, and the plowman in this case was an Englishman who had not forgotten the stern baron who had driven him from his home. But as yet the language was only in a *formative* state; each particular locality and caste having a dialect peculiar to itself. The Vision of Pier's Plowman and Wyclif's Bible and tracts were written in dialects; but thought was awakened; and if a great thought is given to any age or nation, some master mind will grapple with it and finally express it so that all ages will understand. It was preeminently the work of Chaucer to express the idea of freedom in English poetry in a language which he *organized* rather than *invented;* it is thus that he established a recognized English tongue; and, so he has given an impetus to the world's civilization that can be claimed for no other writer of the English language.

At once page to a Maid of Honor, pensioner of the King's bounty, member of Parliament, private messenger for the King, patron of the renowned John of Gaunt, the friend of Lollardy(?) both his social and official position furnished him rare opportunity for observation and information in the different ranks of life. These things combined with his scholarly attainments and fixed habits of industry give us a clue to the products of his pen.

Chaucer was born in London, perhaps, in 1340, and died in 1400, his life reaching from four years after the battle of Crecy, which was fought during the prosperous part of the reign of Edward the Third, to the downfall of Richard the Second, in 1399, and the accession of Henry the Fourth. He filled so many places of public trust and did it through so many years of his life that Taine has well said, "a history of his life is a history of his income." His broad human sympathies, his genial wit, his rare humor, his vein of sarcasm, his seeming integrity, his power to select, to adapt, and to appropriate all available material, his great love of nature, his relish for books, and withal the possession of that divine something that inspires every true poet and makes him one of the world's teachers—all these things add to the charm and temper of his writings and have made him a model for poets from Spencer to Tennyson.

That in the first years of his authorship, he drew largely from others is true; but Matthew Arnold says that "the ground-work of literary genius is a work of synthesis and expression, that the genius lies in dealing divinely with the ideas, and not in the ideas themselves." This is the office of true genius, to make the common-place things of life seem and really be surrounded with a halo of beauty; to arouse us from the *ennui* of routine and so freshen and deepen every-day life; this Chaucer succeeded in doing. Lowell says, "There is a pervading wholesomeness in the writings of Chaucer—a vernal property that soothes and refreshes in a way of which no other man has ever found the secret."

How much of his earlier inspiration he may have drawn from the great French and Italian authors is unknown; on some of his missions to Italy he probably met both Boccacio and Petrarch, and Dante had only been dead a few years. Froissart, Machault, and the author of the Romance of the Rose were among the great French leaders in the literature of the age, and their works were all at his command; at home and contemporary with him was the "Moral Gower," of whom Marsh says, "of original imaginative power his poems possessed not the slightest trace."

Wherever he may have obtained his material, he possessed the rare faculty of making it his own; whether he found it *raw* or in pure lumps of gold, it passed through his own alembic, was touched by the depth and tenderness of his own heart, and made to shine with the beauty of his own poetic taste before he adopted it.

While Chaucer has written for all time, because he has struck the key of the universal heart, yet he is still a poet of the decaying strength of the Middle Ages; poetry in his day was largely made up of the formalities and heartlessness of courts and the crabbedness of clerks: again, he has Mediæval notions in style and expression, he often seems content with triteness both in style and figure, mixes up things, and seems to lack an eye for literary perspective; these and many other defects may be found in the lines of Chaucer. He seems, sometimes, rather an eager listener at the door of opportunity, than master of ceremonies within.

Controversial notions exist as to his social and religious tenets; he was, at least, out of harmony with the prevailing church dogmas, and, although the prowess of chivalry had passed away with the necessity for it, yet, that high religious expression of man's thought for woman's mission had not by any means died out, nor did it ever die on English soil, and whatever may have been Chaucer's private opinion of the women of his circle, his Legend of Fair Women shows that he was still the Christian Knight at heart in his better thoughts, and whatever may have been his success or failure in his struggle toward ideal manhood, still,—

> "He is the poet of the dawn, who wrote
> The Canterbury tales, and his old age
> Made beautiful with song; and as I read
> I hear the crowing cock, I hear the note
> Of lark and linnet, and from every page
> Rise odors of plowed field or flowery mead."

THE MAGNETIC NEEDLE.

THOMAS BAGOT.

WE may assume the earth to be an immense magnet whose force, in the main, is probably due to the circulation around it of currents of electricity produced by the unequal heating of different parts of its surface by the rays of the sun. The poles of this magnet are in the vicinity of the extremities of its axis, but are by no means identical with them, and are called, respectively, the north magnetic pole and the south magnetic pole in order to distinguish them from the geographic poles. At the present time the north magnetic pole is situated, approximately, in lat. 70 degrees north and long. 97 west from Greenwich, and the south magnetic pole when approached by Ross in 1831 was not far from lat. 75 degrees south and long. 154 east from Greenwich. Both of these poles are doubtless slowly revolving around the earth's axis, completing a revolution in perhaps about three centuries, more or less.

If a magnetized steel bar (magnetic needle) be delicately poised on a vertical pin at any point on the surface of the earth, the south pole of the needle will be attracted by the north magnetic pole of the earth, and the north pole of the needle by the south magnetic pole of the earth (the preponderance of attraction being in favor of the nearer magnetic pole), and the direction assumed by the needle will indicate the position of the pole exerting the greater influence upon it. The lines marked by the direction of the needle on different parts of the earth are called magnetic meridians, and these coincide with the true meridians in comparatively few places, since they all converge toward the magnetic poles instead of the geographic poles. Generally speaking, therefore, it is absurd to consider the magnetic needle as pointing due north.

The difference in direction of the magnetic meridian and true meridian at any point is called the declination (variation) of the needle at that point. If the needle point to the east of the true meridian, the declination is said to be *east;* if to the west, the declination is said to be *west.* The size of the angle determines the amount of declination, which varies with the locality from 0 to several degrees, east or west.

Lines passing through places where the magnetic meridian and true meridian correspond in direction, are called agonic lines or agones. There are three of these lines on the earth: (1) The western agone passing through the western part of Hudson's Bay southeast through the eastern part of Lake Superior, eastern Michigan, central Ohio, western West Virginia, Virginia, North Carolina, and eastern South Carolina, into the Atlantic, just east of the West Indies, and through the eastern part of Brazil in South America; (2) the eastern agone extending through eastern Europe, southwestern Asia, the Indian Ocean, and Australia; and (3) the agonic oval, which was formerly a loop of the eastern agone, in the eastern part of Asia, enclosing the Japan Isles and portions of China and Siberia.

' Lines east and west of the agones, running through places having the same declination, are called isogonic lines or isogones. The isogones and agones bear a relation to one another similar to that existing between geographic meridians, but there are frequent exceptions to the general rule of direction. The isogones of 1 degree east and 1 degree west declination lie near the agones, those of 2 degrees east and west are more remote, and so on. In the United States the isogone of 20 degrees west declination passes through the vicinity of the northeast corner of Maine this year, and the isogone of 20 degrees east lies in the northwestern part of Washington Territory.

As we have said, the magnetic poles are probably in constant motion around the axis of the earth, and the direction of revolution seems to be from east to west at the present time (although, judging from the phenomena merely, the contrary is not impossible), and as a consequence the agone and isogones in the United States (except in the extreme west, of late) have been slowly sweeping westward ever since the westward movement of the pole began, which was about the beginning of the present century in the eastern part of the United States, but later further west. In the vicinity of the Rocky Mountains the needle is stationary at the present time, indicating that it has just reached its eastern elongation and will soon begin to move to the west as it is doing further east, while along the Pacific coast east declination is still increasing in some places.

The change of declination caused by the movement of the magnetic pole is called the *secular* change, and the annual amount of it (although not often constant) may be determined for any locality by a succession of observations with sufficiently long intervals between them. Then, having the declination of the needle at the particular place for a given year, the declination for any former or subsequent year (neither to be too remote) may be determined with sufficient accuracy for general purposes by multiplying the annual change by the number of years that have elapsed or will elapse, and adding or subtracting the product as the declination of the place is increasing or decreasing.

The magnetic needle was used on land by the Chinese ten or twelve centuries before Christ and perhaps earlier, but they do not seem to have employed it in navigation to any great extent until the third or fourth century of our era. From China a knowledge of the needle and its uses passed to India, thence probably to Arabia and other countries adjoining, and was later carried westward into Europe some time before the year 1100, A. D.

There is strong probability, too, that the declination was discovered at a very early date, since in many parts of the earth the needle diverged so much from the true meridian that the divergence could not possibly have been overlooked by attentive observers in these parts.

Later, however, and naturally, too, the discovery was made that the declination changes with changes of position in particular directions on the earth's surface. How early this discovery was made is not known, but Columbus gives us the first record from his own observation, having in his voyage of 1492 noticed that he passed from east declination to west declination. The agone at that time probably ran southwest through the eastern Atlantic, passing through the Azores, until it reached about 18 degrees of north latitude and then curved westward toward the West Indies.

Until early in the seventeenth century, however, the declination of the needle was supposed to remain constant at every particular place, and the discovery of secular change is due to Gellibrand, of Gresham College, in England. There are other peculiarities of the needle, the discovery of which is due, in some instances, to modern scientific investigation and research.

One of these is the *diurnal* change of declination. Between 11 and 12 o'clock, P. M., the north end of the needle begins to move from west to east, and continues in this direction until about 8 o'clock in the morning, at which time the movement reverses and the north end moves westward until about 4 o'clock, P. M., when it changes again and the needle retraces its path, arriving at the starting point a short time before midnight on the succeeding night.

This excursion of the needle is about twice as great in summer as in winter, hence an *annual* change of declination may be mentioned. As it seldom exceeds one-sixth of a degree (one-twelfth on each side of the main position of the needle for the day), however, it is discovered in ordinary operations with magnetic instruments.

The needle is also affected by various kinds of magnetic disturbances. During an aurora the needle frequently exhibits great restlessness and sometimes shifts itself several degrees out of its normal direction, and occasionally a thunder storm affects it sensibly.

In addition to all these things, the needle is thrown out of position by the nearness to it of beds of iron ore, by even small masses of steel or iron, or by electricity excited in the glass that usually serves as a cover for it.

So far, we have considered the habits of the magnetic needle in a horizontal plane only, but let us now turn our attention to its action in a vertical plane.

If a small steel bar be suspended by a thread and carefully balanced, it will keep a horizontal position on any part of the earth to which it may be taken, but once it is magnetized one end will rise and the other will fall, except on a line about midway between the magnetic poles of the earth. North of this line (magnetic equator) the north end (south pole) of the bar will sink lower and lower as we go further north until we reach the north magnetic pole, when the needle will be in a vertical position. The reverse is true in the southern magnetic hemisphere. In surveying instruments used in the northern hemisphere a small counterpoise is placed on the south half of the needle to keep it in a horizontal position, but south of the magnetic equator the counterpoise is placed on the north half.

This deviation from a horizontal position is called the *dip* or *inclination* of the needle, and as this increases from the magnetic equator both north and south, we have isoclinic lines or lines of equal inclination cutting, generally at nearly right angles, the isogonic lines or lines of equal declination. The isoclinics are shifting their position, too, like the isogones, but their excursions are generally confined to narrow limits. In the year 1671 the needle at Paris, France, was inclined 75 degrees to the horizontal, but now it is inclined only about 67 degrees. This seems to indicate that the north magnetic pole has been getting further away from Paris while revolving around the axis of the earth.

The magnetic equator crosses the geographic equator at an angle of about twelve degrees, lying generally north of it in the eastern hemisphere and south of it in the western hemisphere. It varies somewhat from a perfect circle. The isoclinics run more or less nearly parallel to it, and all are moving slowly from year to year.

In general, the needle is affected in the vertical plane by the same agencies that influence it in the horizontal plane, and it acts similarly in both cases. It has been observed that during an auroral display the needle points directly to the place where the rays or streamers of the aurora converge. A "magnetic storm" always takes place during an aurora, and the converse, that every magnetic storm indicates an auroral display, is doubtless true, even though the aurora may not be visible at the point where the storm is observed.

The fact has been discovered that the intensity of magnetic action is greatest when the earth is nearest the sun, so it is probable that the sun exercises an important influence over terrestrial magnetism apart from that mentioned at the opening of this article. This influence is further proved by an intimate connection now known to exist between magnetic storms and sun spots, and hence between these spots and auroras.

But let us leave this wonderland in which we find ourselves. The objects around us contain too much mystery to be understood at present. In course of time science will remove the veil and, having determined all about them, will reveal all about them. Let us be patient and wait.

NEW MARION, IND.

DEPARTMENT OF PEDAGOGY.

[This Department is conducted by S. S. PARR, Principal De Pauw Normal School.]

—:o:—'

THE BRACE METHOD OF TEACHING SUBJECTS.

ONE of the prevailing modes of school-work is the brace method. It is a lineal descendent of the sausage-link method of diagraming sentences, of blesssed memory! From sentences the eruption spread until it now covers all subjects. Like most fashions it has a grain of reason at the bottom. But it is a caricature on methods, because it does exactly what caricature does in the field of wit and humor, viz., exaggerate one feature out of all proportion to the others with which it co-exists. Caricature seizes on some feature of its subject and exaggerates it until the absurdity becomes so evident that we involuntarily laugh. The brace-method exaggerates the features of classification and of specializing points to the eye.

A few years ago a bright young man went to Le Mars, Iowa, and created a great sensation for a time by applying the brace-method to partisan journalism. He started the Le Mars *Sentinel*` and berated his political opponents in very common billingsgate, which would never have been heard of beyond his own door-yard, had it not been for the novelty of the way in which he specialized his epithets to the reader's eye. In place of calling them ''poltroons, cowards, thieves, cravens, cringing curs, lick-spittles and hireling dogs,'' writing his words consecutively as in ordinary composition, he specialized each word to the reader's eye. This at first sight rendered ordinary abuse very startling indeed. For a man to be called a poltroon, cur and coward in the ordinary way does not amount to much, but when he becomes a

> ''poltroon,
> coward,
> thief,
> craven,
> cringing cur,
> lick-spittle,
> and hireling dog,''

the matter becomes serious at once. But the vein soon gave out. When the novelty of the display to the eye wore off the happy thought was done and the paper lost its audience.

Take for example this tame statement about the noun: "Nouns are classified as proper and common; normal an abnormal; class, collective and mass-nouns; quality, action, condition and relation-nouns; the noun has the grammatical attributes of person, gender, number and case."

It states a few of the more common classifications of the noun and recites the grammatical attributes that belong to it. Such a statement might be made by any one who had made a sufficient study of the noun. Or it might be committed to memory and recited by a pupil to whom it had been furnished ready-made. In the latter case it would have small value. In the former it would be a suggestion of what ground had been gone over in the study of the noun.

But focus the method of diagraming upon it and it becomes imposing and important. It then meets one's eye as,—

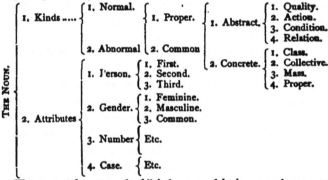

The term "brace-method" is here used in its generic sense to include all such ways of specializing to the eye. There are many of these. But they are all alike whether they employ braces or figures, or figures and letters. The above is not changed by writing it thus:—

THE NOUN.

I. Kinds.
    1. Normal.
    2. Abnormal.
        1^1 Proper.
        2^1 Common.
            1^2 Abstract.
                1^8 Quality.
                2^8 Action.
                3^8 Condition.
                4^8 Relation.

2^2 Concrete.
$\quad$ 1^3 Class.
$\quad$ 2^3 Collective.
$\quad$ 3^3 Mass.
II. Attributes. $\qquad$ 4^3 Proper.
$\quad$ 1. Person.
$\qquad$ 1^1 First.
$\qquad$ 2^1 Second.
$\qquad$ 3^1 Third.
$\quad$ 2. Gender, Etc., Etc.

We do not care to use up further space in illustration. What is given may stand for all that is possible in this line. The farther such work goes the more it multiplies classifications and the less it specializes to the eye. Like too profuse use of italics, it defeats its own purpose. A certain amount of classification is necessary. The example given above is one that is correct and it is good so far as it goes. But classification must not usurp the place that justly belongs to observation, memory, imagination, and judgment. The brace-method exaggerates the value of classification and mistakes the fact that only a limited amount of specializing to the eye can be done. Further, a tame statement is still tame although lionized by white paper, printer's marks and a prominent place. A certain amount of such work is profitable and should find a place in good teaching. To be of most value, diagrams and brace-arrangements should be made by the pupil for himself. Our text-books err in furnishing these parts of the statement of subjects ready-made. To lift one over a stile gives him no strength. He must jump it for himself to get any value out of the exercise.

Not only does the brace-method exaggerate certain features, it is often illogical and confusing. Somebody made a gibe at the Adams family in Massachusetts by classifying the people as "Men, women, children, and the *Adamses.*" Our friends the brace-makers often unconsciously perpetrate such "gags." We have repeatedly seen such classifications (in some kind of brace) as: "Nouns are proper, common and abstract;" "Fractions are common, decimal and compound;" "Springs are constant, periodic and mineral;" etc., etc. These are quite as ridiculous as the "Men, women, children and *Adamses.*"

2

If teachers understood definitely that the value of classification depends on its logical consistency, on the clear perception of the various bases of classification, and on the explanation of the classification after it is made, they would avoid all such "bulls" as those given. They would not then follow the example of the little boy who "counted the black pigs, the white pigs, the spotted pigs, and the one that ran around so fast I could hardly count it."

Another serious charge against the brace-system is that it magnifies mere verbal statement and fosters the habit of memorizing words without ideas. This is probably the most serious damage it does. A diagram or brace arrangement generally represents the husks of intelligence. Those who run to braces and subdivisions as naturally as a pumpkin vine runs through a fence, are generally speaking those who fill themselves on husks and then flatter their feelings by congratulating themselves that they are full.

THE SENTENCE METHOD.

THE educational papers report that the sentence-method is having a redivivus in some quarters. A few institute conductors have taken the sentence-method under their wing and proceeded to demolish the word-method and other methods before their institutes. This demolition is usually very witty and entertaining. Fun is easily made of anything holy or unholy, good or bad. But ridicule is not reason, and we shall do well to examine the relative merits of methods before we pull down and set up in a promiscuous way.

The sentence-method takes the sentence as the unit of teaching. The alleged reason for this is that that which the sentence expresses, i. e., the thought, is the natural unit of the child's mental activity. Because this is so, say its advocates, the child should learn to read sentences and not words. We are told that the child should learn to read sentences at a glance, and hence the sentence should be the unit.

If one shut his eyes to all other considerations, the reasoning of any specializer will seem irrefutable. Values, it must not be lost sight of, are always comparative. This is true of methods.

The sentence-method can be made to succeed. Patience, skill, perseverance, tact, will insure the success of even inferior methods. But that application of method is best which reduces difficulties to the minimum, and provides for the most economic realization of purpose. A gradation of the difficulties of primary reading seems best reached by the word method. Primary reading deals with *written* words. It is concerned very little with the thought, except incidentally. The thought of the two readers that are distinctively primary—the first and second—is supposed to be familiar to the child; so are the oral words. If this is not true, the books are at fault. The problem of teaching, then, for primary reading, is the rapid, interested and sure acquisition of written words. In this particular, primary reading is peculiar. All other primary subjects are used, more than anything else, to organize the knowledge the child already has and develop his mind. Secondly, of course, they give knowledge and give a great deal of it, but that is incidental. The sentence is a unit too large in size, too complicated in structure, and involving too many elements to be taught economically. "One at a time," so far as possible, is a maxim that applies to difficulties in school-work. The word offers many difficulties less than the sentence. To be logical the sentence-method must teach the sentence as a whole and then descend to the words that are its parts. Whatever method be taken there must be numberless repetitions in order to fix forms on memory. Sentences are more difficult to repeat in a variety of ways than words, though, perhaps, the sentence is capable of a greater variety. Variety is a powerful factor in sustaining interest. Greater variety is possible with the word than with the sentence. Owing to its greater size and complexity, the sentence must be dwelt upon longer than the word. Thus reading becomes cause for weariness.

Finally, the pure sentence-method is an absurdity, because an impossibility. It would require the learning of every possible sentence in the English language, as one has to learn every word, separately. As the permutations of one hundred and twenty thousand words are infinite, this would be impossible. The sentence-method is forced to descend to the word at once.

The word-method is now in general use. It is logical and practical. The only thing to be learned, if the first reader is what it ought to be, is the written word. Ways of representing it to the eye are numerous and easily obtainable. Cards containing words to be taught are easily made; many kinds of word-hunting at the board, on slates and in books are possible; the word may be built up in a great variety of ways. The child may read sentences as soon as he has sufficient words to form *one*, and as fast as he learns new words sufficient, he may read other sentences. We thus keep all the benefits of the sentence-method without its disadvantages.

PRIMARY DEPARTMENT.

[This Department is conducted by HOWARD SANDISON, Professor of Methods in the State Normal School.]

———:o:———

r The real subject in education is the individual mind of each child, with its acquired habits and inherited tendencies. An evident proposition, then, is: If real teaching is done, each mind, with its peculiar habits and inherited tendencies, must be understood by the teacher; with its double corollary:—

(1) The number of pupils under the charge of a primary teacher should range between twenty and thirty. (2) The pupils should remain under the charge of a given teacher more than ten months.

The second proposition is: Mind being an organism, the heart (sensibilities) is no less an avenue to the intellect, than is the intellect to the heart and will; with its corollary:—

Suspicion and severity can never enable the teacher to obtain a standing place in the child-mind.

The third proposition is: Two rival powers compose the mind—the *carrying power*—memory (the servant) and the *thinking power* (the master); with its double corollary:—

(1) The aim of education is to make the mind strong and skilled as a thinking power, and not to make it full as a carrying power. (2) The most practical education is that which sends the child into the business world with power to observe closely and to think (reflect) accurately upon what he observes.

———◆———

THE NUMBER OF PUPILS TO A TEACHER.

IF each individual mind is the teacher's subject, the inference is obvious—that the number of pupils under the charge of one teacher should be small enough for the teacher to become thoroughly acquainted with the capacities and defects of each mind, while it should not be so small as to deprive the pupils of the advantage which comes from the contact of mind with various different minds.

It may, perhaps, be safely held that the suitable number of

pupils for a teacher vibrates between twenty and thirty, owing to the teacher's penetration in comprehending character and its needs. It is a serious, not to say irreparable injury to a community, when a school board, under the idea that it is a stroke of economy and a gain to the people, place one hundred children in charge of two teachers at an annual expense to the taxpayers of one thousand dollars, instead of employing *to educate* them, four teachers, with twenty-five to a room, at an annual expense of two thousand dollars.

If it is true, as is held, that numbers higher than about thirty shut off attention to individual minds, then a little reflection makes it obvious that the second procedure would be far more economical to the community.

In the first place, the attempt of the teacher to deal with fifty children makes it impossible to give that attention to the peculiar nature and needs of each child, that the parent has the right to demand when he hands him over to the care of the school, and pays for that care. The problem is to reach and teach the mind of *each* child. Anything other than this would be manifest injustice to some families of those represented by the fifty pupils. With fifty children one teacher can not understand the individual minds and needs well enough to teach to each mind each branch of study well and neglect no one of them; and this is not taking into account the subject of discipline and moral culture, which are very much complicated by numbers. The teacher has neither the knowledge of the minds nor the time to adapt herself and her work to each mind, and she is, therefore, compelled to address the minds as a mass, to pour out knowledge before them and let those who can, adapt themselves to it, and the others remain without even this kind of help. The result is an attempt to inform to a given extent, each month, and not to educate, because *to educate* requires that each mind shall be understood. In this way but little interest is aroused in the pupils; and the process of cramming is received at first with protest, then with indifference, and at last the hundred pupils of the two teachers pass out of school, none of them educated in the sense that education is development; some few—those who needed it least—well instructed perhaps; others but fairly instructed; and still others, perhaps fifty out of the hundred—and they the ones who needed training most—with little or nothing in the way of intellectual or moral power, and worse than this, indifferent to education and its value, the effect of the schools having been to make them contented in their ignorance and lack of power.

The question naturally arises—In which case has the school board done most good to the community? Which course would be true economy? Would the community have been richer in having expended only one thousand dollars, and in having received the children back into the active walks of life as above described, which is no untrue picture, or in having spent two thousand dollars, thus insuring a sufficient number of teachers to give individual attention to the needs of the children, and receiving them at last from the schools with their moral and intellectual powers well trained, with minds active, skillful and capable; with new longings and new capacities for satisfying those longings; with minds as receptive and skilled as each individual case is capable of being made. Which is worth more to a neighborhood, one thousand dollars each year, or one hundred children morally and intellectually strong?

If individual minds are the subject of education, is it not a proper inference that school boards should see to it that the number in charge of each teacher is small enough to enable the teacher to read each mind and then adapt herself and her work to each mind?

WHAT IS NUMBER TO THE CHILD?

CURRIE says in his Infant-Education, that number is a property of things which the child observes very early, so that he may be exercised upon it as soon as he enters the infant school, (kindergarten.) He may be subjected to a mental training of a very considerable extent by basing his early work on the observation of objects.

It has also been said that "Number is the limitation of objects by ones." That is, by the idea *one* (unity), objects, either mental or material, may be limited, just as material objects are limited by the ideas *red, hard, blue, rough,* etc.

Thus,—objects of various colors and qualities may be placed upon the table, and the requests made: Show me the *red* objects; point out the things that are *hard;* bring to the desk all the *blue* things that you see; which of the objects upon the table are *rough?* etc.

In like manner, the objects having been arranged into *ones, twos, threes,* etc., it may be said: Show me the *one* balls, the *one* cubes; point out all the *two* spheres; take in your hand a *three*-prisms, etc.

It is thus evident that objects are as definitely limited by the ideas *one, two,* etc., as by the ideas *red, hard,* etc.

STAGES IN PRESENTING NUMBER AND ARITHMETIC.

NUMBER and ARITHMETIC may be presented in *four* stages, determined by the stages of the pupil's mental growth.

During the first year of school life, the pupil's mind is in that stage in which he is not able to think number except it be presented to his senses in concrete form. This may be called the *Stage of Perception.* As color, form, and all other qualities of objects must be presented to the senses before the mind can get a correct conception of them, so must numbered objects be used to bring the idea of number into the mind. Nature has ordained that numbered objects *must* be used as a means of teaching number, so the teacher is not to choose whether or not she will use them in the work; but to teach number successfully, she must conform to the laws and plans of nature.

Objects are not to be used *to explain figures,* in order that figures may be used in giving knowledge of the different processes. They should be used to give knowledge of number, and the relations existing in number. Thus the pupil will be enabled to deal with the different processes without any knowledge of the symbols of numbers.

Since it is essential that objects be used in teaching number, the kinds of objects that may be used may now be considered.

Objects which are highly novel and interesting should not be selected, for the novelty of them will cause the child to concentrate the greater part of his attention upon the object, rather than upon the idea of number that is to be gained, and thus the mental energy of the child will be divided.

All objects having form as their characteristic attributes, either 'of wood or. paper—including paper-folding, or involving drawing —such as the *square*, *triangle*, etc.; units of measure—as bushel, dollar, yard, etc.; objects in groups—as brace, double, triple, etc.; kinds of minerals; parts of animals and plants; parts of the room — window-panes, doors, etc.; miscellaneous objects; the abacus; and any other objects that can be readily obtained and successfully used.

Some teachers may think it useless to have such variety and numbers of objects, on the ground that they cause the appearance of disorder in the room, and therefore confine their work to the use of the abacus alone. But this is objectionable, as the child, being compelled to apply all number to these objects constantly, will get the idea that number belongs to these objects only.

This stage is not limited necessarily to the first year of school-life, but may be lengthened or shortened in accordance with the child's mental strength.

The second stage is the *Stage of Imagination*, into which the child is led gradually from the first stage. This stage occupies about the second and third years of school. During this time the child is sufficiently strong mentally to think numbered objects with the objects *absent from the senses*. By questions, the teacher may test whether the pupil is able to do this; if not, he must for a longer time, continue in the work of the first stage. In this second stage, the pupil is given power to apply number in its relations, to absent objects and to think number accurately and rapidly. No attention was given to rapidity of thought in the first stage.

Figures are used in the second stage at first by the teacher, then by the pupil to express his ideas.

The third stage is the *Stage of Transition ;* this occupies about the fourth year of school-life. During this time the pupil emerges gradually into the almost uniform use of figures, by means of which he sees the same relations existing in numbers that he found when objects were used. Work similar to that of the preceding stage, is however largely used, the transition being made *gradually* to the application of figures.

The fourth and last stage is the *Stage of Symbols and Rules*, occupying the period of time extending from the fourth year to the close of arithmetic work. The truths which the child has learned previously by means of objects, either present to the senses or absent, are now presented to him by means of symbols and rules. By means of these he is enabled to recall truths which have been presented, and does not need to perceive nor image objects in concrete form. The pupil is now able to solve all problems presented to him by means of reasoning. If he is led skillfully, he may discover for himself every thought in the science of numbers that is appropriate to his stage of mental development. This he should be left to do alone—without undue assistance from the teacher, this being the law of mental growth.

Rensselaer, Ind. LOTTA HESTER.

PRACTICE IN ORAL READING.

PRACTICE in Reading is of two kinds—individual and simultaneous.

Individual practice is what is chiefly and in many cases, exclusively relied on in schools to form the pupil's reading—a fact sufficient in itself to account for the imperfect results so often attained. Where there is no model presented for his imitation, and little or no instruction is given him in reading, practice is as likely to confirm in the pupil a bad style, as to impart to him a good one. This is the first fault then, often observable in reading practice—that it is expected to accomplish what by itself it never can. Another defect common to the practice of reading in our common schools is that it fails to accustom the pupil to continuous reading. He can not feel the same interest in a subject in the description of which he reads only a detached sentence. It is continuous reading that he will have to practice in after-life if he reads at all, either for his own instruction or for that of others; to give him the habit, therefore, of sustaining his attention, and to give him command over his voice, he should be accustomed to the reading of paragraphs.

The principle of simultaneous practice is that the inferior readers of a class are compelled to conform, for the time, to the standard of the better readers. It influences the reading of the class favorably in three ways:—

1. In the point of distinctness; the mere effort required from all to keep together improving their articulation.

2. It improves the rate of reading where it is defective. The quick reader it moderates; the sluggish it stimulates; drawing both by a power of sympathy which they can not resist, to abandon for a time their peculiarities.

3. It tends to remove asperities of tone and modulation.

Simultaneous reading involves little thought work, and is mechanical in its nature and should be used sparingly, and always intelligently—to accomplish one of the three purposes indicated.

—Adapted from Currie.

OPENING EXERCISES—THIRD AND FOURTH GRADES.

THE opening exercises consist of singing devotional songs, repetition of the Lord's Prayer, Bible verses, alphabetically arranged, alternating with the XXIII Psalm or the Ten Commandments, and the morning lesson. The Lord's Prayer and the Psalm may be sung as a chant for variety.

BIBLE VERSES.

These verses are selected by the pupils in the following manner: Each child is prepared on a certain day with a bible verse beginning with "A." The pupils select from these the one which they can most easily understand.

Examples: "A good name is rather to be chosen than great riches and loving favor than silver or gold." "Do unto others as you would have them do unto you." "Even a child is known by his doings whether his works be pure or whether they be right." "Lying lips are an abomination to the Lord, but they that speak truth are his delight."

After the selection has been made, the pupils are allowed to give their own thought of the meaning. The teacher by illustration, makes the meaning more plain.

Illustration: "Go to the ant, thou sluggard, consider her ways and be wise; which, having no guide, overseer or ruler, provideth her meat in the summer and gathereth her food in the harvest."

Lead the pupils to observe the ant-hill, tell them about its wonderful structure, its builders, their queen, workers and warriors. Lead the pupils to apply the meaning to themselves. The work on the ant can be done as rest work on the previous day.

MORNING LESSON.

This lesson consists in a portion of a bible story, read or told by the teacher, in simple and attractive language. Last year the teacher selected one story for each month, occasionally changing the story for a parable or emblem, or had the pupils select and commit verses containing certain thoughts; as, love, truth, obedience, etc. Birthday verses, the longest and shortest verse, also give pleasing variety.

Manner of procedure: 1. Read or narrate a portion of the story. 2. Question the pupils on the leading points. 3. Lead pupils to give their own thought of its meaning and application. 4. Write upon the board the bible precept found in or suggested by the lesson. 5. After the entire story has been given, let the children give or write the story and its lesson to them.

Each day allow one or more of the pupils to give the story of the previous day, in order that they may more plainly see the connection between the old and the new. Show pictures representing the scene when possible. Make all descriptions vivid and real.

The following stories were taken last year in the order given:

1. The Garden and its Inhabitants.
2. Joseph and his Brethren.
3. The Wandering Children of Israel. Balaam's Ass.
4. Gideon.

5. Samson, Samuel and Saul.
6. The Shepherd Boy that became a King.
7. Solomon and the Queen of Sheba.
   Emblem. "Consider the lilies," etc.
8. Queen Esther.
9. Daniel.
10. The Great Teacher. ·

The following gives the divisions of the first story for each day of the month :

The Garden and its Inhabitants.

a. Description as beautifully given by Frothingham in his "Stories of the Patriarchs."
b. Outside the Gates.
c. Quarrel of the First Brothers.
d. Death of Abel. Cain's Flight.
e. The Ark and the Flood.
f. The Tower of Babel.
g. Abraham's Childhood.
h. Abraham's Journey.
i. Visit of the Angels.
j. Destruction of Sodom.
k. Lot's Escape.
l. Sacrifice of Isaac.
m. Isaac's Two Sons.
n. Jacob cheats Esau of his Birthright.
o. Jacob receives his Father's Blessing.
p. Jacob's Flight.
q. His Dream.
r. History of his Twenty Years' Life with his Uncle.
s. His Return.
t. Meeting of the Brothers.
u. Review and Application to Us.

The stories were given in this order, that pupils might study the stories in connection with the country in which they are located. "The Children of Israel" was studied at this time because the Third Grade were studying and molding the peninsula of Arabia. The Fourth Grade were studying and molding Africa. The desert where the Israelites wandered forty years, the place where they were supposed to have crossed the Red Sea, the mount where Moses received the Ten Commandments, and Egypt could be located, thus adding interest to both story and country. In the study of Daniel a description of Babylon, its walls, gates, towers and hanging gardens, make it more real. Representing the positions of the armies in sand, when David killed Goliah, will add interest also.

Some books, valuable for their simple, attractive language and illustrations are: "Stories of the Patriarchs," "Joseph and his Brethren," "Line upon Line, Precept upon Precept," "Stories of David," "Descriptions of Jerusalem," "John the Baptist," "Christ's Teaching and Death," "Ben Hur," "The Bible," Extracts from "Far Off" and "Near at Home," etc.

Cora Hill.

THE SCHOOL ROOM.

[This Department is conducted by Geo. F. Bass, Supervising Prin. Indianapolis schools.]

LITTLE THINGS.

"STRAWS show which way the wind blows." The little things in the school room make or spoil the school. The neatness of the school room has much to do with the school. "A place for every thing and every thing in its place" should be the rule of the school room.

Under the general head of Neatness of Room might be mentioned the following: Order of the desks—teacher's and pupils'; order of floor; curtains; erasers; pointers; black-board work, by teacher and pupils.

Every teacher who expects to teach neatness and order to the pupils "must be what he expects them to become." The teacher's desk should be a model of neatness and order. Each article about the desk should be in its appropriate place when not in use. If books, paper, pens, jack-knives, string, tops, etc., are in the desk as if left by a cyclone, how can the teacher expect the pupils to put their books away carefully? On the other hand, let the teacher have a place for each article and carefully place it there,—the pupils will catch the spirit, and it will be comparatively easy to get them to form the habit of keeping their desks orderly. At the close of each day the teacher should give the pupils time to put their "things" away carefully; at the same time he should arrange his own desk. It is better to say "come boys" than "go boys."

Paper, apple-pealings, nut-shells, etc., should be kept off the floor. The floor should be kept as clean as circumstances will permit. Some mud will, of necessity, be carried in sometimes; but it is never necessary to allow any of the above named things to fall on the floor.

If the teacher is careful about such things the pupils will learn to be so. If, when he sees a piece of paper on the floor, he picks it up, pupils will do so too, and there will soon be a public sentiment in favor of keeping the floor clean. Very little need to be said about it.

Curtains should be about the same height, except when they need to be different to protect the eyes from the direct rays of the sun. Have them hang straight, not "lop-sided." Erasers and pointers should not be left in one corner of the room, so that when a pupil needs to use one he must walk half-way around the room to get it. The teacher should see that they are distributed at the beginning of the day. Much time may be saved in this way. Besides, a habit that will be of great value in the future, is formed.

The black-board work should show care. Avoid "slip-shod" work. Do not allow large, awkward letters and figures put on the board. Have pupils economize space by making figures of a reasonable size. Have a plan of placing examples and other work on the board, and stick to it until it is mastered. Writing need not be Spencerian, but it should be legible and neat.

FRACTIONS.

ANY fifth grade pupil of average ability ought to be able to understand all the necessary and ordinary processes of "common fractions."

If properly presented by objects, he can understand what the numerator and denominator each means. Cut a sheet of paper into four equal pieces, and draw a horizontal line on the board, placing a figure 4 under it, and say, "That shows how many equal parts into which the paper is divided." Have a pupil take three of them and place the figure 3 above the line and say, "That shows the number of parts taken." If the association of these figures with objects be kept up long enough, the *meaning* of numerator and denominator can not be forgotten; but, even after this, if all their force is spent on learning a formal definition of these terms, the meaning may be entirely lost.

Addition of fractions is sometimes troublesome because pupils do not see the "sense in it." Teachers should show the "sense in it." It will take time, but what of it? It takes time to raise a stalk of corn. Growth is slow. We wish to add $\frac{1}{2}$ and $\frac{1}{3}$. Draw a horizontal line on the board and divide it into two equal parts. Draw another of the same length under it and divide it into three equal parts. Now draw a line equal to $\frac{1}{2}$ of the first and another equal to $\frac{1}{3}$ of the second. Place them together end to end and compare with the whole line. "What part of the whole line have we?" A pupil of only a moderate amount of ingenuity will soon be able to see that we have just $\frac{5}{6}$ of the whole line. It is then time for the teacher to ask such questions. as the following: "How many sixths of the line does one-half of it equal?" "How many sixths does one-third equal?" We are now ready to say that $\frac{1}{2} = \frac{3}{6}$ and $\frac{1}{3} = \frac{2}{6}$; and it is easily seen that if we add the numerators and place the result over the like (common) denominators, that we have really added. Pupils now see the "sense in it" and where the rule came from, and they can add. The only thing now left to do is, add, add, add.

READ AS THEY TALK.

"A TEACHER should teach children to read as they talk." This is an old saying and it is as true as it is old, but the saying of it does not help the teacher in teaching reading nor the child in learning to read. It has been said in institutes by the instructors, and the teachers have gone to their schools and said it, and yet there is not one pupil in a thousand nor one teacher in a hundred who reads as he talks. Why? Because he does not think before he reads, as he does before he talks. A little girl was asked why she talked so much, and she answered, "Betause I's dot somefin to say." Let us read because we have something to say, then we will read as we talk. But to get something to say from our reading, will require some study on the part of the pupils and more on the part of the teacher as to how to guide them in their study. It is not enough to *tell* the pupils to study their reading. It is about on a par with telling a six-year-old to study his a–b–c's.

Teachers should furnish their pupils with questions or topics as guides for a general study of the lesson, and during the recitation they should ask questions upon each sentence that would compel the pupil to get the thought of each sentence. The pupil should then express his thought by reading orally the sentence under consideration. Use oral reading as a *means* not as an *end.*

BRIEF NOTES.

WHO?—Who should do the thinking, the teacher or the pupil? Leave the exercise to the pupil. The teacher should guide, not tell. He should think for himself, but not for the pupil. Question in such a way as to make the pupil do the thinking. It does not help a pupil any in thinking, for a teacher to tell him what he (the teacher) thinks. Stop it.

PRONUNCIATION.—Look in Webster's Dictionary for the pronunciation of the following: Bombast, vagary, bellows, carbine, exhaust, abstract, concrete, bestial, almond, concave, accoustics, persist. You may be surprised before you have finished the list. Teachers should study Webster more than they do, especially the "front part."

TEN LARGEST CITIES.—Teach the children the ten largest cities in the U. S. By the last census they are: (1) New York, (2) Philadelphia, (3) Brooklyn, (4) Chicago, (5) Boston, (6) St. Louis, (7) Baltimore, (8) Cincinnati, (9) San Francisco, (10) New Orleans. These are named in the order of their size.

OFFICIAL DEPARTMENT.

State Supt. Holcombe, recently submitted to the Attorney General the following question :

"The term of A, a county superintendent, expired June 2, and B, his successor, was elected and qualified on the same day. On May 29 A had held teachers' examinations, and after the expiration of his term of office he granted licenses and issued certificates to several teachers. B demanded the manuscripts of said candidates, that he might examine them, which A refused to give up, saying that he had destroyed them. Is this granting of licenses and issuing of certificates legal ?

Answer: The power and authority of an outgoing superintendent ends when his successor is elected and qualified. When a new superintendent is elected and qualified his predecessor is no longer an officer either *de facto* or *de jure*, and all acts performed by him as such superintendent after the termination of his office are illegal and void." Numerous authorities are cited.

This ruling will affect many counties and make much trouble. In some counties, the outgoing superintendent issued the licenses by mutual agreement with the new superintendent. It is clear from the above that licenses issued by the old superintendent *after the new superintendent had qualified*, are illegal.

TEACHERS' READING CIRCLE—ANSWERS TO CORRESPONDENTS.

1. You ask to whom you, as county manager, are to send the fees collected from the members of the Reading Circle. You should retain the fees in your possession until Nov. 30, 1885, at which time you will be required to make full report of names enrolled and moneys collected. A blank will be furnished you for the report.

2. You inform me that you pursued the advanced course, last year, and desire to know what work you will be expected to do this year. I think that Seelye's Hickock was intended to be a full equivalent for Brooks's Mental Science. Hence I would suggest a further study or review of Seelye, together with all the work assigned to the present year except the work in Brooks.

3. You ask if a circle may pursue the work of last year instead of the present year's work. I answer, yes—though I should not like to encourage such a plan. An examination on last year's work will be held in June, 1886, in connection with the regular examination, and certificates will be issued on satisfactory examinations. Since any four years will constitute a course, I can not see why you should not make the work of 1884-5 count for one of the years. However, if you pursue that work, you will deprive yourself of the advantages of

3

the township institute reviews, unless you pursue the work of both years together; and that will be a greater undertaking than I should advise teachers to enter upon, unless a large portion of the work of 1884-5 be review work. In the latter case it might be advisable to prepare for both examinations in 1886.

4. You inquire when the results of the Reading Circle examination will be announced. I am unable to give you this information, at present. The MSS are in the hands of the committee.

5. To your inquiry as to published outlines of work, I would reply that the work for each month of the year has been *assigned*, and the apportionment is published in the Outline of Township Institute Work just issued by the Department. We will endeavor to have all the monthly outlines prepared and published promptly; but should any teacher fail to receive the publications containing these, he need not be in doubt as to the lesson assigned.

6. You inquire if members who prefer to review last year's work during the coming year will be required to pay the yearly dues—25 cents—this year. Certainly they will, if they desire to be considered members of the organization. The annual dues are necessary to membership, and are assessed without reference to the nature of the work pursued.

The above are from my recent replies to inquiries.

HUBERT M. SKINNER,
Sec. and Treas. T. R. C.

ANSWER TO QUERIES.—*Ed. School Journal:* Mr. M. Mayerstein, of Lafayette, Ind., mentions certain curi us roperties of the number 142857, and asks, "Who can explain?" The explanation is simple enough. To subtract one and prefix one to a number consisting of six figures, adds 999,999 to it. But 999 999 is exactly seven times the given number. To add seven times a number to once the number, of course gives eight times the number; to twice the number gives nine times the number, and so on. To subtract two and prefix two, adds twice as much as in the first case, and hence produces respectively, 15, 16, 17 times the number, etc.

Yellow Springs, Ohio. C. B. PALMER.

A CURIOSITY—IS ONE EQUAL TO TWO?

$$\text{Let } x = y \qquad \text{Let } x = 5 \qquad \text{Then } y = 5$$
$$x^2 = x y \qquad \text{Then } 5 = 5$$
$$x^2 - y^2 = x y - y^2 \qquad 5^2 = 5 \times 5$$
$$(x + y)(x - y) = y(x - y) \quad 5^2 - 5^2 = 5 \times 5 - 5$$
$$x + y = y \quad (5+5)(5-5) = 5(5-5)$$
$$2y = y \qquad 5 + 5 = 5$$
$$2 = 1 \qquad 10 = 5$$
$$\text{or } 2 = 1$$

L. E. D. (?)

EDITORIAL.

THE OUTLINES to the Reading Circle printed last month, are reprinted this month, to accommodate several hundred subscribers whom we could not supply with the September Journal.

ATTENTION is called to the article on Chaucer, by Mrs. Dennis. She will furnish a series of articles to accompany the work of the Reading Circle in Literature. Mrs. Dennis is a member of the Reading Circle Board, and is abundantly able to render valuable aid in this direction.

LITERARY SOCIETIES in connection with district schools can be made the means of much good. A wise teacher can so direct them as to secure much reading and general culture on the part of the older pupils and interested citizens. Every teacher should feel bound to do something, *outside of school*, to benefit the community in which he lives.

THE JOURNAL'S PROSPERITY.—The friends of the Journal (and they were never before so numerous or so ardent) will be glad to know that notwithstanding the unprecedented competition its circulation has steadily increased. During the past three months the *bona fide* subscription list has been increased about *one thousand*, notwithstanding the fact that all names are dropped at the termination of the term of subscription. This is the best possible indication that the Journal contains what teachers want. This substantial endorsement is highly appreciated.

"STOP MY JOURNAL."— Teachers need not be at the trouble of asking to have the Journal stopped at the end of the time subscribed for, as it stops then by our rule of business. The Journal is able to live without forcing itself upon its subscribers beyond the time named in the terms of subscription. The law that gives an editor the power to collect for a paper sent beyond the time contracted and paid for is unjust and should be repealed.

The Journal will be continued gladly, if the request is made, even when it is not convenient to make advance payment. The Journal's course is good sense, good business, and simple justice.

TOWNSHIP TRUSTEES GONE WRONG.

Every reader of the Journal has learned, ere this, through his county paper, that a few trustees have issued warrants on their townships for large sums of money, and have shared the proceeds of these warrants with the rascally agents who concocted the scheme. How many trustees may have been led astray can not now be stated, but certainly not nearly as many as would be inferred by the amount of criticism the disclosures have caused. Up to date only *ten* have been detected, and as the whole number is about one thousand, not counting the trustees of cities, the percent is very small.

Some of these trustees (now in Canada) have issued warrants to the amount of $30,000 and $40 000, but it is very doubtful whether the townships will be bound to pay anything beyond the value of goods actually received, which will be a comparatively small amount. Of course the feeling against these trustees is very intense. The almost universal opinion is that the present law gives the trustee too much absolute power and should be changed. Here lies the danger. Because a few men have abused the confidence reposed in them the many must suffer. To limit the power of the few the fear is that so many restrictions will be placed upon trustees that they will not be able to furnish to the schools much that they really need.

While there is a great deal of excellent "school supplies" there is a great deal offered to trustees that is practically worthless for public school use, and the prices are ofte extortionate. Trustees should first be sure that an article is *needed*, and then take time to learn that the price is *reasonable*. The amount that these few absconding trustees have stolen is nothing comp'red with what trustees through ignorance and hasty action have *wasted*.

CONCERNING INSTITUTES.

The reports of institutes have been cut down to the minimum. Lack of space makes this necessary. As stated in last month's issue the institutes this year have been much better than ever before. There can be no doubt as to this, and yet all institutes have not been equally good. A great deal of time is yet wasted in "organizing," in waiting for motions, in enrolling, in reading minutes, in waiting for order, etc. The institute is not a literary society, but a *school*, of which the county superintendent is principal. If the superintendent will simply select a secretary, a person to preside in his absence, the necessary committees, etc., he will save time and give just as good satisfaction. By passing slips of paper the enrollment can be made in five minutes. As a rule the reading of minutes is a waste of time. Teachers must take their own notes if they are to be benefited by them. Except in a few instances where the minutes are printed no *use* is made of them. If the minutes are to be printed, let a committee correct them, and thus save time.

The instruction has been *good*—much better than ever before. As a rule one or more persons from abroad have been employed, and the work done by resident teachers has been generally carefully prepared and well received. In a few counties may still be found a "committee on program," whose duty it is to arrange and assign the work from day to day. It is not fair for either instructors or institute, to ask persons to give lessons which have not been carefully prepared. Instructors should be notified weeks in advance, so that they may be able to make the best possible preparation. Teachers who spend time and money to attend these institutes ought not to be asked to waste their time in listening to *impromptu* exercises. "The best is none too good."

The general testimony of superintendents is that it is best to have at least one good worker, for the entire week, from abroad. Even if the stranger is no better than the home talent, he presents his lessons in new form and adds the zest of novelty. We have heard some excellent lessons from resident instructors, that were not appreciated, simply because the teachers for years, in institutes, associations, and township meetings, had grown accustomed to their manners and general thought.

While the average attendance has been better than in former years, some counties are still subject to criticism. It is a bad indication when not more than 50 per cent. of the teachers make their appearance on the first day, and when the irregularity is such that not more than 75 per cent. are present at any one time. It is also a bad indication for both teachers and superintendent when the exercises are frequently disturbed by persons passing in and out—and still worse when at the close of a recess the next exercise must begin with one-third of the seats vacant.

There certainly is no reason why all the rules of a well organized school should not be observed in an institute.

A MODEL COUNTY.—Supt. D. M. Nelson, of Jasper county, announced that his institute would open on Monday morning at 9 o'clock. When the hands of the clock indicated nine he rang his bell, conducted his opening exercises, made his *little* speech, and at exactly ten minutes past nine Howard Sandison, of the State Normal School, was on the floor giving the first lesson, with *ninety five* teachers in their seats, (one hundred and five is the whole number of teachers employed in this county), and at noon 111 teachers had enrolled their names. The work of Monday forenoon was as full and complete as that of any other half day session of the week. In no other county have we seen teachers actually *run* for fear of being tardy. Other counties may have done as well, but they have not come under our observation. Many others have done nearly as well—excellently well. Jasper county is singled out in this way not for the purpose of giving it special praise, however deserving it may may be, but to show what is attainable in this regard.

TIME TO HOLD INSTITUTES.—There seems to be a tendency toward holding county institutes in the month of August. Whether this is wise or otherwise is not quite clear. In those counties in which the great bulk of the schools begin in October or November, a later date for the institute would be better. The State of Pennsylvania contains only 67 counties, and 31 of these hold their annual county institute in December, and only *two* in August. Indiana contains 92 counties, and over 75 of these hold their institutes in August.

The subject will admit of careful thought and consideration.

QUESTIONS AND ANSWERS.

QUESTIONS PREPARED BY STATE BOARD FOR AUGUST.

READING.—1. Why should pupils be required to make a thought analysis of a lesson before reading it orally?

2. Describe the alphabet method of teaching reading, and state in what respects inferior to either the phonetic or word method.

3. What is a good method of conducting the recitation of a Fourth Reader class?

4. How can a knowledge of American literature be obtained by the reading classes of our public schools?

5. Name five American poets and mention at least one selection from the works of those named.

6. Read a paragraph of prose and a stanza of poetry selected by the superintendent.

PENMANSHIP.—1. What letters are but one space in height?

2. What is the height of r and s? Of t and d?

3. What is meant by principles in penmanship?

4. Where should we begin in forming the small letters? Where end?

5. Analyze u, v, c, p, W.

NOTE.—Your writing in answering these questions will be taken as a specimen of your penmanship, and will be marked 50 or below, according to merit.

ARITHMETIC.—1. What is arithmetic? Notation? Numeration? The Arabic Notation? The Roman Notation?   5 pts, 2 each.

2. What is the interest of $41,361.18 at 6χ for 5 years, 7 months, 3 days?   Ans. 10

3. A note of $345.60, dated Feb. 5, 1863, was paid Aug. 20, 1865, and the amount was $407,088.; what was the rate per cent.? Give the rule.   Rule 5, ans. 5

4. What is the face of a note dated July 5, 1871, and payable in 4 months, to produce $811, when discounted at 9%? Define bank discount.   Ans. 5, def. 5

5. How large a draft, payable in 60 days after sight, can be bought for $798.80, exchange being 1¼% premium, and interest 8%? Process 5, ans. 5

6. From the sum of 64.5 and 0.5 take their product. 5, 5

7. What will 2 pk., 7 qt. of chestnuts cost at $3.12½ a bushel? Solve by aliquots. Proc. 5, ans. 5

8. If 32 men can dig a ditch 40 r.l. long, 6 ft. wide and 3 ft. deep in 9 days, working 8 hours a day, how many men can dig a ditch 15 rd. long, 4½ feet wide and 2 feet deep in 12 days, working 6 hours a day? Ans. 10

9. A, B, and C are partners in business. A's capital is twice B's and three times C's, and their profits in business are $4,675. What is the share of each? Analysis 5, ans. 5

10. Two boys start from the same point, and one walks 96 rods due north, and the other 72 rods due east. How far are they apart? Ans. 10

GEOGRAPHY.—1. Name three races of people found in Asia, and name all the oceans that border that continent.

2. Name four of the chief productions of the East India Islands, and locate their largest city.

3. Name five important islands in the Mediterranean Sea; five important seaports in the same.

4. Where are the following: English Channel, Baltic Sea, Amsterdam, Port Natal, and British Guiana?

5. Name the form of government in each of the following countries: China, Brazil, France, Russia, and Mexico.

6. Describe the influence of the Andes mountains on the climate and vegetation of S. A., in not more than ten lines.

7. Sketch the outline of Illinois, showing the Illinois River, the location of Chicago, Bloomington, Springfield, and Peoria.

8. Name five rivers of the U. S. that are of great value on account of their navigability. Five of them that are valuable chiefly for water-power.

9. Suppose a vessel at Pittsburg: What could be obtained there which it would be profitable to ship to New Orleans? What could you profitably take on as a completion of the load at Cincinnati?

10. What relation do the winds sustain to the distribution of moisture over the earth?

GRAMMAR.—1. Illustrate in sentences five uses of the pronoun. Designate.

2. Punctuate the following, giving reasons:
    a. There is a fierce conflict between good and evil but good is in the ascendant and must triumph.
    b. Avoid affectation it is a contemptible weakness.

3. What relative words join adjective clauses to the words they modify? Give examples.

4. In what respects are the participle and infin:tive alike? How are they different, and how do they both differ from the verb?

5. Write sentences illustrating the singular and plural uses of the collective noun. State what determines the number of such nouns.

6. Correct the errors in the following, giving reasons:
   a. Give it to whomever comes.
   b. Whom did you suppose it was?
   c Whoever I send will go.

7. How does the subjunctive differ from the other modes?

8. Analyze—"Full many a gem of purest ray serene
            The dark unfathomed caves of ocean bear."

9. State the office of the underscored words in the follow:ng: "For it is wrong to steal"

10. How does a *clause* differ from a sentence?

ORTHOGRAPHY.—1. Name the mutes. Why are they so called?

2. Give a table of the long vowels, illustrating the use of each by naming a word in which it is found.

3. What is a primitive word? Give five.

4 Show the meaning of the following words by using them correctly in sentences: Principal, principle; vein, vain, sailo:, sailer, canon, cannon, elicit, illicit.

5 Give the proper diacritical marking of the following words: Kerosene, gouge, forehead, victuals, Indiana.

6. Give the correct spelling of the following words, and mark the accent: Sator, dominear, grammar, gutteral, coersion, cinamon, chimnies, potatos, substract.on, Teusday.

PHYSIOLOGY.—1. How is alcohol produced in fermented liquors?
2. Describe the structure of a gland. Name five of the largest.
3. Describe the structure and growth of the hair.
4 Make a diagram of the cavities of the heart.
5. Describe a vertebra.
6. Describe the structure of the nose.
7. How is nearsightedness produced?
8. Describe the bones of the ear.
9. Describe the crystalline lens.
10. What is the pulse? How often does the pulse beat?

SCIENCE OF TEACHING.—1. Define curiosity. Discriminate between curiosity that is genuine and that which is spurious.

2. How would you proceed to fix an idea in the mind of the pupil so that it will be remembered?

3. Why can not a pupil study or recite effectively when there is intense activity of the emotions?

4. Why is it not well to engage in severe study immediately after a full meal?

5. Why should not prizes be offered to pupils as a motive to study?

U. S. HISTORY.—1. When and where did the first legislative body assemble in America? 5, 5

2. Tell briefly the story of the Charter Oak. 10

3. As tea with the tax added was cheaper in America than in England, why d d the Americans destroy it in Boston harbor?   10

4. Name one Pole, two Frenchmen and two Germans who gave effectual aid to the Americans in the Revolutionary war.   5 pts.

4. What State was not represented in the Constitutional Convention?   10

6. What c lebrated national song was compos d in the midst of a battle of the war of 1812? What of its author?   5, 2, 3

7. What event occurred in 1848 that led to the rapid settlement of an important part of the territory gained from Mexico?   10

8. What State was permanently divided in the time of the civil war? By whom was it divided? Under what name was the new State admitted?   3, 4, 3

9. What important political event occurred in 1876 which seemed to make an amendment to the Constitution desirable? How was it settled?   5, 5

10. What connection had the expulsion of the Moors from Spain with the discovery of America by Columbus?   10

ANSWERS TO BOARD QUESTIONS PRINTED IN SEPTEMBER.

PHYSIOLOGY.—1. The cerebellum is one of the three chief divisions of the lower or smaller brain, and is situated in the posterior and lower part of the skull. It is composed of gray and white nervous matter, the white being internal. Its chief function is to regulate the muscular movements of the body,—it being the source of the acquired automatic motions of the body, such as standing and walking.

2. Bones of the Lower Limb.
- Upper. — *Femur.*
- Middle. — *Patella. Tibia. Fibula. 7 Tarsals.*
- Lower. — *5 Metatarsals. 14 Phalanges.*

3. The optic is the second pair of cranial nerves. They spring from the optic thalami and the corpora quadrigemina, unite and in part exchange fibres in the optic commissure underneath the front of the cerebrum, and thence pass as separate trunks to the eye-balls. The retina is the expansion of an optic nerve, in part.

4. Reflex action is action stimulated by a nerve center without the direct or conscious intervention of the brain.

5. The cilia of the air passages are motor tissues, essentially composed of cells, upon the surface of which are fine threads having a constant outward motion. They are of special value in that they bring up from the deeper portions of the lungs such fluids, etc., as are likely to prove noxious.

6. Arteries carry blood away from the heart; veins toward the heart.

8. The skeleton of the body is at first larg:ly cartilaginous, with calcified nuclei here and there. It is thus quite tough, has a larger proportion of animal matter, and is rather more solid in structure. As the person reaches and passes middle life, however, the proportion of lime is larger and the skeleton more brittle.

9. The gastric juice is secreted by the peptic glands in the walls of the stomach toward the pyloric end. It is acid and slightly bitter in taste. Its precise composition can not be given, because it can not be obtained free from admixture with mucous and saliva. Its special function is to act upon albuminoids—proteids and casein—and prepare them by chemical change for digestion.

10. Fermentation is a chemical change produced in certain organic bodies by means of substances known as ferments. By some, these changes are attributed to the development of living organisms in the bodies through the action of the ferments; by others they are attributed to certain conditions in the fermenting substances themselves. The various kinds of fermentation commonly spoken of are the alcoholic, lactic, saccharine, mucous, butyric, putrefactive and acetic. Alcohol arrests fermentation.

READING.—1. The preparation to be made by the teacher before attempting to teach a class to read a selection from the Fifth Reader, depends very much upon the selection. Some selections require the knowledge of physical surroundings; others, of subjective purposes, thought or sentiment; others, especially of voice culture, etc. (See suggestions in last month's Journal.)

2. Five uses of the dictionary in the preparation of a reading lesson may be: to get a knowledge of the meaning, pronunciation and synonyms of words, to learn something of mythology, biography, etc.

3. Five American authors whose works children may safely read are Louise M. Olcott, "Grace Greenwood," Hawthorne, "Oliver Optic," Abbott, Trowbridge, etc.

4. Punctuation marks are to indicate the grammatical relations of the parts of a sentence. Their bearing upon the expression of the sentence is small. The length of pause can not be regulated by them.

5. For the correct silent reading of a sentence there is necessary (1) the interpretation of the thought, (2) the realization of the thought and sentiment, (3) a strong predisposition of sympathy or antagonism.

HISTORY.—1. Hardy, stern in character, unflinching in their devotion to duty and to their convictions, religious and political, the New Englanders came to a barren and sterile country to enjoy civi and religious liberty, and educate their children; in all this they differed from the settlers of Virginia, who were gentlemen by birth, unused to labor, and idle, poor, and emigrating in hopes of making large fortunes with which to return home to live in luxury.

2. It was a scheme originated by Lord Shaftesbury and John Locke, based upon the Aristocratic idea; the country was divided into large estates to which were attached hereditary titles carrying with them great privileges and immunities. No provision in this scheme being made for the benefit of the common people who had come to a wilderness to improve their condition and promote their political rights, and the entire condition of the country and its surroundings being utterly opposed to the success of such a scheme, it failed.

3. The *Writs of Assistance*, authorizing any custom's officer to enter any man's house in search of smuggled goods, were resisted as violating the right of each man to hold his house sacred against the entrance of even the King. The *Mutiny Act*, which compelled the colonists to supply all provisions and quarters for the soldiers sent to enforce the laws of Parliament, and which they regarded as intended to enslave them, they resisted with the utmost indignation.

4. After the destruction of the tea in Boston Harbor, the British government retaliated by appointing Gen. Gage as Governor of Massachusetts, which could not fail to arouse the utmost opposition and excitement. The port of Boston was closed by act of Parliament, destroying all business and causing great distress. The Governor of Virginia dissolved the Assembly which had protested against these measures. Rebellion against these tyrannous acts led to such active warfare on the part of the colonists as compelled the Second Continental Congress to issue the Declaration of Independence as setting forth the action by which they had been driven and the course of Great Britain which had compelled them to it.

5. The Alien and Sedition Laws.

6. Gen. Taylor was sent to hold the territory between the Rio Grande and the Neuces, in dispute between Mexico and Texas. In obeying orders he won the battles of Palo Alto and Resaca de la Palma, captured Monterey, and fought the battle of Buena Vista with a few thousand soldiers, overcoming Santa Anna with 20,000. Gen. Scott, ordered to take chief command in Mexico, bombarded and took San Juan de Ulloa, fought the battle of Cerro Gordo, driving off Santa Anna hastily, took Puebla without resistance, and storming the heights before the City of Mexico, Contreras, Cherubusco, and Chapultepec, eventually captured the City, which virtually closed the war.

7. That lying south of the Gila River, now known as the Gadsden Purchase.

8. President Monroe; the Capital being Monrovia.

9. By separating the forces in the Gulf States from those in the north part of the Confederacy; by leaving Hood to be literally destroyed with his army by Thomas; and by the moral effect of showing the South how utterly unable they were to hold their own territory.

10. This must be answered according to the judgment of each candidate, who should, however, be required to give sound reasons for his opinion.

GEOGRAPHY.—1. The South Frigid Zone.

2. (*a*) The Potomac. (*b*) The Susquehanna.

3. (*a*) Venezuela. (*b*) Peru. (*c*) Ecuador. (*d*) Brazil.

4. (*a*) Pyrenees. (*b*) The Ural Mountains form a portion of the boundary between Europe and Asia.

5. Newfoundland is situated east of the Gulf of St. Lawrence, on the east coast of British America; Ceylon is southeast of India, in the Indian Ocean; Hayti is east of Cuba; Candia is southeast of Greece, in the Mediterranean Sea; Porto Rico is one of the Greater Antilles, situated east of Hayti.

6. On the lower slopes of a mountain in the Torrid Zone the vegetation is tropical like that in the surrounding country; between 4000 and 8000 feet grow the plants of the warm temperate zone, the trees being a lustrous, evergreen foliage; from 8,000 to 10,000 feet the deciduous forests of the temperate zone appear; above this altitude is found only such vegetation as belongs to the cold-temperate and polar zones, the summits are rock covered by perpetual snow.

7. The North Frigid Zone, in which are islands and a portion of Alaska, British America and Greenland; the North Temperate Zone, including the remaining part of British America, all of the United States, and a portion of Mexico; the Torrid Zone, embracing the southern half of Mexico and Central America, together with the islands of the West Indies.

8. (*a*) Yang tse Kiang, Yenisei, Hoang-Ho, Lena, Indus. (*b*) Himalayyas, Kuen-lun, Thian-Shan, Khin-gan, Altai.

9. The river Rhine takes its rise in the Swiss Alps, flows in a northerly direction across Germany and Holland, into the North Sea.

10. (*a*) Lyons, Milan. (*b*) Sheffield, Birmingham. (*c*) Herat is situated in the northwestern part of Afghanistan.

GRAMMAR.—1. The subject and predicate each may be modified by a word, a phrase, or a clause. Subject modifiers: 1. *Large* trees are in the forest; 2. The flowers *on the prairies* look beautiful; 3. The letter *which he sent* was lost. Predicates modified: 1. Industry produces *wealth;* 2. The children are playing *in the water;* 3. I think *he has not come.*

2. 1. Shall we gather strength by irresolution and inaction? 2. Who can count the number of the stars? 3. Variety of expression and emphasis.

3. The propositions of a compound sentence are of *equal rank.* The complex sentence consists of *one principal* proposition and one or more subordinate clauses.

4. The different kinds of clauses in a complex sentence are:
    1. Adjective; as, *He whom thou lovest is sick.*
    2. Adverbial; as, He died *that we might live.*
    3. Substantive; as, He convinced me that I was wrong.

5. *a.* An adjective modifying *form.*
    b. An adverb modifying *is supposed.*
    c. An adverb denoting purpose.

6. A collective noun, when used in the plural form, or when it represents the collection as a unit, is of the neuter gender; otherwise the gender corresponds to the sex of the individuals composing the collection.

7. *a.* Relative pronoun; as, Uneasy lies the head *that* wears a crown. *b.* Conjunctive adverb; as, Make hay *while* the sun shines.

8. *a.* What do you ask for *these* apples? The pronoun *them* should not be used for the adjectives *these* and *those.* *b.* This is the *preferable* of the two. Preferable implies choice and can not be compared. *c.* He is the *better* of the two. The *comparative* degree is ordinarily used when two objects are considered.

9. *a.* *It* is a pronoun, third, singular, nominative, subject of the verb *is written.* The antecedent of *it* is indefinite. *b.* *Is written* is a verb, irregular, transitive, passive voice, indicative, present, third, singular, to agree with its object *it.* *Array* is a noun, common, neuter, third, singular, and object of the preposition *in.*

10. The *present tense* represents what is taking place at the present time, or it is used to express a universal truth. The *present perfect tense* relates to an action *completed* in the present time, or to a condition of affairs that has continued up to the present.

SCIENCE OF TEACHING.—1. Imagination is that power of the mind by which we make new creations out of materials already in the mind, and *picture* to ourselves places and things which we have not seen.

2. In teaching geography the imagination enables the pupil to *see* with the mind the mountain, the river, the city, the people, etc., which he has read of or heard described, but which he has not seen.

3. The *chief* purpose in hearing a recitation in the Second Reader, is to secure facility in recognizing words and their relations to one another in the sentence given, and to give proper expression to the thought thus represented. Other purposes are spelling, pronunciation, and the learning of new words.

4. The characteristics of a good recitation are : (1) a clear statement of what the text gives; (2) in a good tone of voice; (3) with some collateral facts not found in the text. Children should be encouraged to get something outside.

5. ' Punishment as a motive to study is a failure. It puts the mind in a condition farthest removed from that required for the best study. Punishment distracts the mind and irritates the feelings; study requires concentration of mind and composure.

ARITHMETIC.—1. $75\% = $ cost; $120\% = $ selling price.

$$120\% - 75\% = 45\%, \text{ gain.}$$
$$45\% \text{ is what } \% \text{ of } 75\%.$$
$$45\% = 60\% \text{ of } 75\%. \quad \text{Ans. } 60\%.$$

2. 3.1416×40 rd. $= 125.664$ rd., circumference.
(40 rd., or diameter,)$^2 \times .7854 = 1256.64$ sq. rd.
1256.64 sq. rd. $\div 160$ sq. rd. $= 7.854$ A. Ans.

3. $\frac{1 \times \frac{5}{8} \times \frac{7}{1} \cdot \frac{1}{0} \cdot \frac{7}{4} \frac{1}{4}}{}= 128.57 +$ bu. Sq. of diameter $\times .7854$.

4. 1 yr. 1 mo. 24 da. $= \frac{6 8}{6 0}$ yr.
$\$75.50 \times .075 \times \frac{6 8}{6 0} = \$6.51 +$ int.

5. 84 cd. : 150 cd.
10 da. : 12 da. : : 8 men :
5 hr. : 7 hr. Ans., 24 men.

6. $\sqrt{(40 \text{ ft.})^2 + (30 \text{ ft.})^2} = 50$ ft., Ans.

7. $\sqrt[3]{.074256} = .4203 +$, Ans.

8. Since A's capital is $2\frac{1}{2} \times$ B's, then their gain must be in the ratio of 2 to 5.
B gets $\frac{2}{7}$ of gain, or ($\$1200,) = \$342\frac{6}{7}$, first year.
A " $\frac{5}{7}$ " " " $= 857\frac{1}{7}$, "
B " $\frac{2}{7}$ " " " $= 480$, second year.
A " $\frac{5}{7}$ " " " $= 720$, " "
$\$342\frac{6}{7} + \$480 = \$822\frac{6}{7}$, B's gain.
$\$857\frac{1}{7}$ $|$ $\$720 = \$1577\frac{1}{7}$, A's gain.

9. $\sqrt{10 \text{ A} \times 160}$ sq rd. $= 40$ length of one side.
4×40 rd. $= 160$ rd., Ans.

10. $\frac{11 \frac{9}{10} \times 11}{3} = 41\frac{1}{3}$ yd. $\$2.75 \times 41\frac{1}{3}$ (yd.) $= \$113\frac{2}{3} \frac{1}{3}$.

MISCELLANY.

√ The new Mechanics' Shop at Purdue University is completed and occupied.

WABASH COLLEGE has opened in good trim and will continue to do the high order of work for which it is noted. Dr. Tuttle seems to retain his original vigor and energy.

THE HOME AND SCHOOL VISITOR, a youth's paper published by D. H. Goble, of Greensburg, Ind., is a great success, and its success is merited. The issue for October is 26,000.

Purdue University opened on the 10th of September, with a fine attendance. The Faculty is enlarged this year by the addition of Miss Nellie Jones, instructor in French and German.

The *Parke County Teacher* is an 8-page 4 column monthly, edited by County Supt. Elson and Lin. H. Hadley, Supt of the Rockville schools. It looks well and reads well, and should be in the hands of every Parke county teacher.

THE BATTLE OF SEDAN, at Cincinnati, Ohio, is a great work of art. It is a grand painting, so true to life that it is impossible to tell where nature stops and art begins Having witnessed this "pictured battle" we freely say that a visit to it will richly repay.

THE RICHMOND NORMAL SCHOOL has opened its third year with an attendance above the expectations of its friends. There are now thoroughly organized, classes in each of the three years' courses. The principal, C. W. Hodgin, is confident and happy.

NORTHERN INDIANA NORMAL SCHOOL, at Valparaiso, was never before in a more flourishing condtion. Everything is booming. Co lege Hill is literally *alive* The popular principa , H. B. Brown, is "hale and hearty" notwithstandi g his continuous labors. He has promised to get married after the close of this school year. The Journal has been advising this move for lo ! these many years.

NORMAL DEPARTMENT OF DE PAUW UNIVERSITY.—This school opened with 26 students, besides a class of 8 in didactics, made up of Seniors, Juniors, and irregulars. This is not a *boom*, but the number is by no means discouraging. The State Normal opened with 14; and had but 37 the second term ; and the now mammoth Valparaiso Normal opened with only 35 The number is as large as the Principal, S. S. Parr, expected. May it *grow*.

EARLHAM COLLEGE has opened with 177 students—91 of them in the college departmen:. This is the largest number ever in the college classes at one time. The faculty has b en increased this ye r by the election of Geo. T. Cox, A B., ch. of History, and Mary Binford Bruner, A. B., M. D., an Earlham graduate, lecturer on Hygiene Mary E. Harris, educated at Vassar, has been elected Lady Principal. Pres J. J. Mil s seems to be the man for the place.

WARSAW.—The school buildings here are in excellent condition and are kept so. The teachers' platforms are neatly carpeted and the aisles are covered with matting. An excellent reference library has been provided, chiefly by means of concerts, festivals, etc. Every room is furnished with magazines suited to the grade. These are paid for by teachers and pupils. In no other schools in the state, so far as known, is so much done in the direction of encouraging children to read. Supt. Mather is doing a good work.

THE STATE NORMAL SCHOOL opened the new year Tuesday, Sept. 1st, with the largest Fall attendance it has ever had. The enrollment for the Fall term of 1884 was 301 ; for the present term it will exceed 350. The entering class numbers 140, among whom are fifteen graduates of commissioned high schools, four college or university graduates, and a large number of experienced teachers holding twenty four and thirty-six months license. The large attendance during this the smallest term of the year, the harmony and united action of the faculty, and the spirit that prevails among the students assure the most prosperous year in the history of the institution.

[Republished from September Journal.]

INDIANA TEACHERS' READING CIRCLE—OUTLINES.

ENGLISH LITERATURE.

First Month——Smith's, pp. 11–28.

Our English forefathers first settled permanently in America in 1607. Their ancestors first came to England from the German lands in 449. The original stock came from the Aryan plains of Asia at a time whose history is unrecorded. The modern student of history is little given to cramming his mind with dates. Yet the year when our race crossed the German Ocean and the Atlantic, and that of the great Norman conquest—1066—nearly midway between, like the date of our immortal Declaration of Independence, will always be learned to be remembered.

When the English first came to live in America they brought many books of great authors. When their race first came over to England they brought none. Have we no composition dating back to the time when our forefathers lived in the old German country? I think we have, though some very rare old English gentlemen will swear by the Queen that Beowulf was composed in Surrey. At all events, the scene of Beowulf is laid in old Germany, and it is the oldest composition in the Old English language; and wherever and whenever it may have taken its present form, the tale was doubtless told by our light-haired, rosy-cheeked, and rather rascally progenitors before they came to England.

And so we are to begin at the beginning, and read something about Grendel and Hrothgar and the great hero. The name of the author of the poem is unknown, which is no great loss. It would probably be hard to pronouce, anyway. Next comes Caedmon; and we can make up our mind to suit ourselves as to whether Milton borrowed from him, when the evidence is all in. Then come Alfred,—the sinless man and monarch, according to Bede's history, and Bede himself; and later on, Geoffrey, with his tales of Sabrina and King Lear. Of the value of their works in old time, it is difficult to form an adequate conception. But they are written in the dead Old English, and have been wholly superseded. Hence they are now of no more practical use than burnt gunpowder, though they are subjects of great interest to lovers of literature.

The Norman conquest caused the union of two languages,—the formation of a double language, whose "heterogeneous materials" were shaped by Chaucer "into a symmetrical structure." We are told of the latter's contemporaries, and of the sources from which he drew some of his materials. Perhaps it would have been just as well if he had *not* "drawn" some of these. However, we are not compelled to read all of the Canterbury Tales, and so great a work must not be condemned on account of a few blemishes characteristic of its time.

Mandeville, the somewhat mendacious traveler, and Wiclif, the Morning Star of the Reformation, with his Bible translations, his Eighteen Propositions and his Trialogues, now appear, as the fathers of English prose.

A careful study of the text-book will repay the teacher, as the work is thoroughly condensed. The Introduction to Webster's Unabridged Dictionary will afford valuable and entertaining supplementary reading on the same topics.　　　　　　　　H. M. SKINNER.

———:o:———

BROOKS' MENTAL SCIENCE.

Subject: Intuition———Pages 319—344.

I. TERMS TO BE STUDIED.—1. Reason and Reasoning, page 320. 2. Complement, pp. 320, 322. 3. Opposition, pp. 234–5. 4 Contingent and Necessary, p. 329. 5. Logically and Chronologicall, pp. 332–4. 6. Quantitative, p. 333; 7. Cause and Occasion, p. 340.

II. ITEMS OF PROFESSIONAL IMPORT.—1. Relation of Intuition to Memory, p. 323. 2. Relation of Intuition to Imagination, p. 323. 3. Nature of Identity, pp. 336–8. 4. Nature of Cause, p 344.

III. SUMMARIES.—1. The Tests of Primary Truths. 2. The Primary Ideas. 3. The Elements of Space. 4. The Elements of Time. 5. The Classes of Identity.

IV. QUOTATIONS —1. "There are three sorts of ideas in mind : (*a*) Adventitious ideas—those acquired through the senses ; (*b*) Factitious ideas—those constructed from materials furnished by the senses ; (*c*) Those which are native-born, original, innate, [intuitive, B.] —*Descartes.*

2. "No general truth is intuitional."—*Hamilton.*

3. "Reasoning is a development of intuition ; a course of reasoning is a succession of intuitions."—*Hamilton.*

4. "No conflict ever occurs between the intuitions of one man and those of another."—*Hamilton.*

5. Axioms are of two kinds : (1) Mathematical ; (for examples see common texts); (2) Metaphysical. Ex.—(*a*) Space and time exist; and all other things exist in space and time. (*b*) Every body occupies space. (*c*) No body can be in two places at once. (*d*) Every change corresponds, in nature, to the cause producing it."

6 "Identity is a relation between our cognitions of things, not between things themselves."—*Hamilton.*

7. "Intuition is to the understanding, what perception is to sensation."—*Morell.*

8. "Hardly shall you find any one so bad but he desires the credit of being thought good."—*South.*

9. "Causation is the law of connection between physical facts; spontaniety, the ground of connection between mental facts."— *Bascom.*

10. "What space is to material facts, conscience is to intellectual facts. To occupy space is to have physical existence; to occupy

4

consciousness is to have intellectual existence; to occupy neither is not to exist."—*Bascom.*

11. "The power of cognizing beauty may be cultivated by exercise. The study of beauty has a tendency to refine and ennoble the mind."—*Alden.*

12. "Time is that in which things persist, or succession takes place. Space is that in which bodies are situated and motion takes place."—*Schuyler.*   R. G. BOONE.

——:o:——

SCIENCE OF TEACHING.
Hewett's Pedagogy——Pages 9–75.

The work for the first month will be found outlined in the text-book, on pages viii, 14, 38, and 48. Subsequent outlines will be prepared by Prof. Geo. P. Brown.

Members of the Indiana Teachers' Reading Circle who had partially completed the course of reading for last year but were not prepared for examination at the time of the regular annual examination in June, will be given an opportunity to pass examination upon the work of both the first and the second year at the annual examination next summer.

The expense of holding a special examination for the accommodation of such members this year would be greater than the Board of Directors feel warranted in making.   J. I. MILLS,
August 24, 1885.   Pres. Board of Directors.

TO MEMBERS OF INDIANA TEACHERS' READING CIRCLE.—No outlines of work will be published for October. Owing to the fact that a number of county institutes have not yet been held, the organization of the Circle throughout the state is not yet completed. Many members who have recently joined, or who will join hereafter, will not be able to finish the reading assigned in the September outlines before the end of October. By withholding the outlines this month, it is thought that all members may be ready to begin the reading for November together. Outlines will be published in the November educational journals and thereafter regularly.

As the outlines of the first year's work (pp. 13–318) in Brooks' Mental Science, were published last year in the educational periodicals and in the report of the State Superintendent, it is not deemed necessary to republish them this year. New members will therefore refer to the School Journal for October, 1884, or to the Educational Weekly for October, 1884, or to State Supt. Holcombe's Report for 1884 (Part I, p. 151), for the first months's work in Mental Science. The pages of the text-book assigned for the first month are 13–40.

J. J. MILLS, Pres. Bd. Directors.

————

THE STATE TEACHERS' ASSOCIATION will open December 29 and close Dec. 31st. The program is nearly complete and is excellent. Let everybody get ready to come.

EDINBURG.—The schools employ ten teachers besides the Supt. The high school numbers about one hundred—perhaps the largest in the state in proportion to the size of the place. No pupil is allowed to graduate from this high school till he shows a license to teach at least one year, from the county superintendent. J. C. Eagle still continues as superintendent.

ED. JOURNAL: One of my attorney friends in Indiana informs me that Judge Perkins did not render both the odious decisions referred to in my article in August number. He states that Perkins rendered the decision in the case of *Lafayette* vs. *Jennee*, and Judge Hovey, the decision in case of *Greencastle Township* vs. *Black*. This correction I deem due the truth of history. Please, therefore, insert, and oblige   Yours,   GEORGE W. HOSS.

PERSONAL.

C. E. Sutton is the new superintendent at Tipton.

G. W. Musser will preside at Linn Grove next year.

F. P. Smith is still in charge of the Bedford schools.

J. T. Graves is principal of the Monticello high school.

J. H. Groves continues as Supt. of the Tell City schools.

Geo. L. Harding, of Leesburg, is now Supt. at Middlebury.

J. P. Dolan is serving his tenth year as principal at Syracuse.

F. P. Hocker will have charge at Monmouth the coming year.

Thos. McCarthy, of Battle Ground, takes the Goodland schools.

A. O. Reubelt has entered upon another year as Supt. at Winamac.

E. J. McAlpine has been four years a. Pierce on, and still stands well.

Alpheus Reynolds will have charge of the Pendleton schools next year.

W. T. Lopp will have charge of the schools at Valley City next year.

O. T. Dunagan will remain as principal of schools at Shoals another year.

O. L. Kelso is making a good start as principal of the Richmond high school.

Horace J. Ridge, of Connersville, is in charge of the Everton schools this year.

F. M. Fuller, of Montgomery county, is now principal of schools at Wellsville, Kan.

W. W. Byers is the efficient, continuous principal of the Terre Haute high school.

L. C. Frame, a graduate of the State University, has charge of the Bloomfield schools.

P. D. Creager, a State Normal graduate, is Supt. at Albion, *vice* C. E. White, resigned.

John P. Mather continues in charge at Warsaw. His schools are in excellent condition.

A. D. Moffet, last year of Tipton, has been elected principal of the Bowling Green schools.

O. P. McAuley, late Supt. of Owen county, is attending school this year at Valparaiso.

C. W. Egner, of Warsaw, is principal of the Spencer high school.

Miss Mary Anderson is making a success in teaching grammar in the Richmond Normal School.

J. B. Wisely, a graduate of the State Normal, has charge of the 7th ward school, Terre Haute.

J. C. Keenan, of l ountain county, is now Supt. of schools of the Kaw Agency, Indian Territory.

S. B. McCracken, a graduate of the State Normal School, is principal of the Delphi high school.

W. F. Axtell, ex-superintendent of Monroe county, is principal of the high school at Washington.

G. A. Hawkins, a graduate of the Valparaiso Normal, is principal of the White River graded school.

Geo. Isham, last year principal of the high school at Monticello, now has the schools at Brookston.

A. H. Votaw, formerly of this state, has for the last eight years been teaching at Westtown, Penn.

Miss Victoria A. Adams is the new Yankee high school principal at Warsaw. She has made a good s art.

Theo. Dingeldey, formerly teacher of German in the Indianapolis high school, is now a teacher in Tell City.

J. Fraise Richard, the well known institute worker and educational writer, still retains his residence at Logansport.

Prof. J. M. Coulter, of Wabash College, is chairman of the Botanical club of the National Scientific Association.

W. T. Gooden, of Osgood, has given up journalism and returned to te ching, and has removed to Tecumseh, Kan.

L. C. Frame and J. W. Walker were joint principals of the Bloomfield normal school, which has been very prosperous.

A. E. Buckley, who had charge of Indiana's educational exhibit at New Orleans, is superintendent of the Butler schools.

Jonathan Rigdon, a graduate of the Danville normal school, has been elected a member of the faculty of his *alma mater*.

Robert Spear, after several years of faithful service, has been promoted to the principalship of the Evansville high school.

James B. Angell, Pres. of Michigan University, has been engaged to make an evening address at the State Teachers' Association.

A. E. Mezzeek, of Terre Haute, makes a plea through the *Indianapolis World* for a state teachers' association for colored teachers.

C. T. Lane is serving his seventh year as principal of the Fort Wayne high school, and the school is in a very prosperous condition.

F. S. Caldwell, a graduate of the Lebanon (O.) Normal, is principal of the high school at Winchester. He will be assisted by L. A. Canada.

C. O. Du Bois, a graduate of the State University, and also a graduate of the State Normal School, is principal of the Crothersville schools.

J. A. Collins, formerly a teacher in our own state, will have charge of the schools of Florence, Kansas, next year. He wishes to be remembered to old friends.

Chas. Fagan, mentioned in last month's Journal, has the superintendency of the schools of the Indian Agency at Pawhuska, Osage Agency, Indian Territory.

Chas. E. Hodgin and wife were, at last accounts, at Colorado City, Texas, on their way to Albuquerque, New Mexico, where they will spend the coming winter.

B A. Ogden, Pres. of the Parke County Teachers' Association, reports progress in the arrangement of the program for the annual meeting November 27th and 28th.

C. M Merica, upt of De Kalb Co., has planned a country school house that is a little ahead of anything yet suggested. "Merica's Model School-House" is certainly a success.

Prof. E. E. Smith, of Purdue University, has been doing some good work among the institutes of the state during the past summer. He does good work and honors Purdue.

R. A. Ogg has entered upon his sixth year as principal of the New Albany high school, at a salary of $1200. He is a good man in a good place. He spent his summer vacation farming.

Prof. D. W. Dennis, of Earlham College, has just published "Notes and Tables for Twenty Weeks in Experimental Chemistry and Imitative Analysis." It is certainly a step in the right direction.

Prof. J. B. Demotte, of De Pauw University, has been doing some very acceptable work in teachers' institutes. It is a pity that his valuable lectures on Hygiene can not be given in every county in the state.

W. H. Wiley went to Terre Haute twenty years ago as principal of one of the ward schools; he was soon made principal of the high school; and for the last sixteen years has been superintendent of the schools. Out of his 101 teachers 99 were present at the county institute the first day.

COUNTY INSTITUTES.

TIPPECANOE CO.—R. G. Boone and Emma Mont. McRae did the work. Nothing more need be said.

CLARKE COUNTY.—This was an excellent institute. With such instructors as C. W. Hodgin, Michael Seiler, W. H. Mace, and others, it could be nothing less.

LA GRANGE CO.—This county has been for several years past, doing an advanced grade work. It did not fall below this year. The chief instructors were Alfred Kirk and Homer Bevans, of Chicago, and D. W. Thomas of Wabash. Supt. Machan keeps step with the times.

NEWTON COUNTY held a two weeks session of institute (annual) at Kentland, commencing August 10, '85. It was conducted by Prof. Howard Sandison, assisted by Miss Emma Cox and Annette Ferris. The work was done entirely after the plan of the State Normal, and the institute was a grand success.

PULASKI COUNTY.—Enrollment 137. Work done principally by Messrs. Beals, Knotts, Reddick, and Reubelt. General satisfaction was given and all went home wiser and happier. The new Supt., J. H. Reddick, is taking hold with intelligence and firmness, and bids fair to make an excellent officer.

GREEN Co —The institute was large and interested. Charles F. Coffin was the principal instructor from abroad. L. C. Frame and J. W. Walker rendered efficient service. Evening lectures were given by Dr. D. S. Jordan, W. A. Bell, C. F. Coffin, and State Supt. Holcombe. Co. Supt. Ogg is taking hold with vigor.

FULTON COUNTY.—Enrollment 170. The institutes in this county are generally good, but this was the best. From Monday morning till Friday evening perfect system marked the order of business. The principal instructors were S. C. Wilson of Ill., W. J. Williams, A. E. Davisson, and Supt. F. A. Haimbaugh. Supt. Haimbaugh is making an excellent record so far.

ORANGE COUNTY.—We have just closed one of the most successful institutes ever held in Orange county. We have 101 schools and enrolled 111 Orange county teachers, beside a number from other counties. Profs. Bloss of Muncie, and Beck of Bloomington were the instructors. Forty-eight subscriptions were taken for the School Journal. Miss Jennie Throop was secretary. ● ● ●

WARRICK COUNTY.—Enrollment 119 the first morning, and 174 for the week—the largest ever made in the county. The principal instructor was W. F. L. Sanders, of Cambridge City, and he gave unqualified satisfaction. Other instructors were Messrs. Clark and Groves. At the close of the institute the retiring Supt., W. W. Fuller, was the recipient from the teachers of a fine gold-headed cane. The new Supt. is starting well.

HENDRICKS COUNTY.—Institute at Danville, August 31st to Sept. 4th, inclusive. Attendance over 200. Instructors: Chas. F. Coffin, New Albany; M. J. Mallery, Danville; Dr. G. Dallis Lind and Miss A. Kate Huron, of Central Normal; other work was given by local talent. Only two teachers are reported as having passed the bounds of this life. The institute unanimously requested Supt. Rogers to secure Chas. F. Coffin's services for next year. This is a new move for Hendricks county, and shows that Mr. Coffin's labors are appreciated. SEC.

BROWN COUNTY.—The Institute convened August 24th. Enrollment 101; average attendance, 85; and yet the county has but 73 schools. A. H. Graham, of Columbus, and J. A. Mitchell, a student of Ann Arbor, gave very satisfactory instruction. Mr. Mitchell closed an interesting and satisfactory five-week normal just before the institute. Supt. Neidigh is giving good satisfaction, as may be. seen from the fact that 30 counties in the state have a lower average enrollment of pupils in school.

CARROLL COUNTY.—The Carroll county institute convened in Delphi August 24th. One hundred fifty-one teachers were enrolled, with an average daily attendance of one hundred thirty-five. A large number of citizens were in constant attendance; the interest throughout the entire session was unusually good. D. E. Hunter, W. W. Black, and Geo. Lacea were the chief instructors. During the week State Supt. Holcómbe, D. S. Jordan, W. A. Bell, Cyrus Smith, J. M. Olcott, E. M. C. Hobbs, and others favored us with their presence and rendered efficient aid. J. L. Johnson is the Co. Supt.

SULLIVAN CO.—"And though its beaming sun has set,
Its light shall linger round us yet."
The institute convened August 17th and continued in session *two weeks*. The first week was conducted on the county normal plan, with mostly home instructors. The second week was institute proper, the leading instructors being O. J. Craig and Miss A. Kate Huron of the Danville (Ind) Normal. The enrollment for the entire session was 160, and of this number 140 belong to the Teacher's Reading Circle. The interest manifested was unusually good, and Superintendent Marlow can congratulate himself on having conducted another *very* successful institute.   SIGEL E. RAINES, Cor. Sec'y.

DELAWARE COUNTY.—The Delaware county institute closed a five weeks' work at Muncie on August 21st. Over 150 teachers were in *regular* attendance, or a considerable number more than the schools of the county employ. This county is one of the best organized in the state the result of energetic, hearty and systematic work on the part of Supt. Lewellen. The instructors for the week were E. E. Smith of Purdue University, Jesse H. Brown of Indianapolis, W. H. H. Shewmaker of Muncie, and H. B. Brown of Valparaiso. Lectures by W. H. Bryan of the State University, and E. E. Smith of Purdue. Fine essays were read by E. K. Hoober, W. E. Driscoll, L. G. Lafter, L. L. Horton, and Miss Kate Garst.

DAVIESS COUNTY.—The meeting this year was unusually large and very successful. Outside of Washington, Daviess county employs about 110 teachers, and the roll-call Monday evening showed 126 present. The intense interest manifested by the teachers in attendance was a fair result of the work done by the different instructors. The workers from Daviess county did good service. Besides instruction in the common school branches, mental science and the principles of teaching received a fair share of the time, thus proving that why we teach is as important as how we teach. The Reading Circle also received an impetus that will carry it along successfully through the entire school year. There will not be less than 100 members in Daviess county.

RIPLEY COUNTY.—The most largely attended and interesting institute ever held in Ripley county closed on August 28th. There was an enrollment of 78 names on Monday before the institute was organized, and 100 names during the day. Total enrollment 206, with an average daily attendance of 150.

The high standing of our schools and institutes can be credited to the executive ability of our worthy Supt., G. W. Young, and to show their appreciation of his efficiency the teachers presented Mr. Young, on Friday of the session, with a gold watch and chain. All who attended the institute went away feeling "that it was good to be there." R. L.

LA PORTE COUNTY.—Institute convened August 24th, with Supt. Hosmer chairman. Instructors: Profs. Sims of Goshen, Giffe of Logansport, Forbes of Chicago, Miller and Hunziker of Michigan City. The home workers were Misses Brown, Smith, Caldwell, Knight, Lingenfelder, and Galbreth. The interest of the session is evinced by the unusually large membership—232.

Among the resolutions two were of special importance: the first, providing for the payment annually, by each teacher, of a specified sum, the amount to be applied to the county institute fund; the second, looking to the formation of a reading circle, to be composed of the teachers of the county. O. S. GALBRETH, Sec'y.

HOWARD COUNTY —The institute began its annual session August 31st and continued to Sept. 4th, inclusive. . It was characterized by the great amount of good work done and the number enrolled, which was 127 the first day and increased to 167 during the week. The instructors during the week were O. J. Craig of Purdue, J. E Locke of Kokomo, and Elmer Henry of the Peru high school. The persons who came in and did incidental work were Supt. Holcombe, Prof. S. S. Parr, C. S. Olcott, E. M. C. · obbs, C. S Ginn, and Cyrus Smith. Mr. Craig spoke to a large number at the Christian Church Thursday evening on the subject of "Christian Science." The lecture was followed by songs and declamations, and a general "good time" was had. The institute was favored throughout with music by the institute chorus class. It was noted as an "era of good feeling."

ELMER BRYAN, } *Secretaries.*
BELLE McFANN, }

MADISON COUNTY.—The Madison county institute this year was one of the most pleasant and most profitable ever held. Supt. Dale J. Crittenberger is thoroughly in earnest in his work, as shown by the excellent spirit of the teachers during the sessions of the institute. He believes in good work and they believe in him. The instructors for the week were Profs. W. W. Parsons, of Terre Haute, and E. E. Smith, of La Fayette; R. I. Hamilton, of Anderson, W. S. Ellis, of Alexandria, with incidental lessons from W. A. Bell, editor School Journal, State Supt. Holcombe, Pres. D. S. Jordan, and Co. Supt. Wilson, of Henry county. Lectures by Profs. Smith, Parsons and Jordan, and also by Hon. W R. Myers, Secretary of State.

Average attendance from 150 to 175.

ADAMS COUNTY —The county institute which was held here last week was largely attended and was a success in every way. The teachers expressed their satisfaction with the institute and with Supt. Snow's work, by presenting him a $15 00 chair at the close of the session.

The Decatur schools began Sept. 7th, with a large attendance. The new $15,000 school house will not be completed in time for any of this year's schools. The district schools will begin near the first of October. The trustees have placed three books, "Pedagogy," "Management," and "Methods" in the district schools, at the township's expense. They are determined to educate the teacher, that better results may be produced and a professional education may be gotten in other ways than by experience.

FLOYD COUNTY —The twenty-first annual session of the Floyd county institute convened in New Albany, August 10th, and continued in session five days. The only regular foreign instructor was W. F. L. Sanders, of Cambridge City. Messrs. Warfel, Olcott, Bell, Bloss, Lugenbeel, and State Supt. Holcombe were present a part of the week and did efficient work. The interest manifested by the teachers was such that the enrollment and attendance constantly increased until the close.

Our punctual and worthy superintendent, L. H. Scott, expressed himself specially pleased with the character of the work done, and the interest manifested; and he well merits the praise of the Floyd county teachers for procuring the services of such an able instructor as W. F. L. Sanders. The teachers of Floyd county mean to hold their own with any in the state. SUBSCRIBER.

SCOTT COUNTY.—The Scott County Teachers' Institute met at the Court House in Scottsburg, August 31, 1885, Will M. Whitson, Co. Supt., presiding. W. H. Mace, of De Pauw University, gave exercises on History, Geography, and the Science of Teaching. E. M.

Teeple, of Charlestown, conducted the exercises in Physiology, Constitution, and American Literature. State Supt. Holcombe addressed the institute, urging the teachers and trustees to use some means to lengthen the school term. Thursday evening he gave an interesting address upon the subject of " Early American Literature." W. D. Chambers gave exercises in Arithmetic, T. J. Shea in Grammar, and S. E. Thomas in Reading.

This was not "the largest institute ever held," but the attendance was fair, the interest good, and the work thorough.

BUSINESS NOTICES.

NEW BOOKS—JUST PUBLISHED. — Barnes' Brief History U. S., revised; Page's Theory and Practice, revised by W. H. Payne, Michigan University; "Watts on the Mind," revised by Prof. Fellows, Iowa University; Barnes' Elementary Geography; Barnes' Complete Geography, *two-book series;* Bardeen's Shorter Course in Rhetoric. Cyrus Smith, Ag't, Indianapolis, Ind.

LA PORTE KINDERGARTEN TRAINING SCHOOL.—This school offers superior advantages to ladies desiring to become Kindergartners. Send for circulars, to Mrs. EUDORA HAILMAN, La Porte, Ind.   9-2t

TEACHERS desiring to attend a *Normal School,* or those wishing a situation or an increase of salary, should send for a sample copy of "*The Educational World.*" Address, W. SAYLER, *Editor, Logansport, Ind.*   1-12t.

AFTER an experience of some years without a Spelling Book, the Public Schools of Cincinnati have re-introduced McGuffey's Speller, placing the Revised edition in five grades of the District Schools. The action of the City Board of Education in adopting McGuffey's Revised Speller was unanimous.

INDIANA

SCHOOL JOURNAL.

Vol. XXX.　　　　NOVEMBER, 1885.　　　　No. 11.

*ESSENTIALS OF THE NEW EDUCATION.

BY W. N. HAILMAN, SUPT. LA PORTE SCHOOLS.

THE confusion concerning this much-used and much-abused term renders desirable an attempt to approach its definition. The undertaking is not without its difficulties, lying in the subject itself, in the deficiencies of educational science, and in the inadequacies of the circumstances surrounding educational practice. The well-known difficulties opposing the definition of *education* oppose us here undiminished, for the scope of the *new* education is the same. To these are added the difficulties brought in by the term *new*. Education, inasmuch as it pertains to the origin and destiny of man, pertains to the Infinite, and in many of its phases, old and new, refuses to be defined. Indeed, the New Education, divested of all transient phases, is simply a new view, a wider and deeper view, of the nature and dignity of man ; a fresh and brighter gleam of light that reveals to us the insufficiency of previous opinions and principles of action, and a surer and nearer road toward our ideals.

From this it appears that the New Education can not be confined to a limited portion of the work. It is not the Kindergarten, nor the "Quincy schools," nor the industrial department of some college, nor the new curriculum of a university. It is a new, more nearly complete statement of principles to be followed in these and all other features of educational work. If such a statement modifies or revolutionizes previous methods of work,

---

*Read before the Frœbel Institute of North America, at Madison, Wis., July, 1884.

this does not alter the matter. The New Education lies in the statement of principles, not in its transient or particular methods, which may be, and probably are as yet, quite imperfect, and much vitiated by influences of "old educations."

It is evident, too, that such a statement must contain much of previous statements, much of "old educations"; for these, however one-sided they may be, were formulated concerning the same infinity, by an equally intense love of the true, the good, and the beautiful. Nay, it is impossible to collate a new, many-sided, quite comprehensive education from the material found in various one-sided views of the subject, without the addition of a single new principle—the newness lying in the greater completeness, in the many sidedness, in the superior comprehensiveness of the new statement; and such a statement would deserve the name *New Education,* though all the disciples of the old formulas that have furnished it material should clamor, "We had this long ago."

Such a statement, even if it should contain a number of phases not previously recognized, yet inasmuch as it does contain the truth of previous one-sided statements, would, under certain circumstances, call forth great confusion of ideas concerning itself. Earnest one-sided persons, blind to all but the phase that rivets their attention, if they are one-sided in the cause of some idea struggling for recognition, and recognized in the new statement, will greet this New Education as their own particular gospel, and will attempt to monopolize it. Others, equally one-sided, but in the service of a phase of truth well established in general recognition, will treat the new statement with contempt and ridicule; for, inasmuch as it contains their truth, they—blind to all else—will accuse it of false pretensions and reprehensible insolence in claiming as its own what has belonged to humanity "from time immemorial."

The circumstances for such a condition of things could scarcely be more favorable than they are now in our own land. In the midst of a great educational revival many are eager to behold the truth, and their very eagerness inclines them to exclaim wild *Eurekas* over every gleam of light. Others, of calmer mood, failing to see adequate cause for this wild joy, do not grant it even the deserved credit of sincerity. This condition of things is aided by the fact that educational circles, as a whole, are just emerging from a period of empiricism into the recognition of a science of education. Hence vast numbers — as unknowing children are apt to laugh over every new thing as something funny — are in a state of perpetual, more or less puerile mirth concerning the new and *quasi*-new things that greet their dazzled view.

On the one hand we find the Kindergarten, the "Quincy Method," Industrial Training, the "Grube Method," — nay, even the kitchen-garden and calisthenics, — claiming that theirs is the New Education. Now the fact is that most of these — some more and some less—represent limited phases of the New Education, *in so far as they do their work in accordance with its principles*. The Kindergarten represents, perhaps, the latest complete statement of the New Education, as applied to the training of children between the ages of three and seven. The "Quincy Method" represents an earlier and less comprehensive statement in its application to school-work. The "Grube Method" is a fragment of an earlier phase in its application to rudimentary arithmetic. The claims of the kitchen-garden and of calisthenics are too flimsy to deserve notice. Industrial training, as such, is an outcome of temporary industrial needs, and has no intrinsic connection with the New Education. The apparent relationship is due mainly to the fact that the New Education finds in manual training an indispensable factor of harmonious development; but in aim and method it differs widely from the industrial training.

On the other hand, we read in journals and hear at teachers' gatherings more or less sweeping denunciations of the very term "New Education." One proves that a certain fundamental principle which enters into the make-up of the New Education, and which he ignorantly believes is claimed as new, is as old as Socrates. Another shows that a certain particular method of doing a limited portion of the work has been practiced in his section for many years. A third condemns the New Education on the basis of its supposed abandonment of books in teaching, its supposed "utter disregard of discipline," and other similar equally groundless imputations, made honestly, but under the influence of constitutional one-sidedness.

Necessarily the character and value of an educational system will depend ultimately on its innermost essence, on its basis, which is its view of the nature and destiny of man. Now, since our views of man and his destiny depend largely on the experience and observation, on the growing knowledge and insight of the race, it is evident that, however far advanced such views may be, they will have their beginnings in the beginnings of human self-consciousness, and that their roots will reach back through all intervening ages to earliest stages of civilization. Hence all, no matter how far they may be behind the new statement in their own practice, will recognize in it much, perhaps all, of what they hold true in theory and upon which their work is based; but many fail to see more. As of yore, the new view, which is in fact merely a fresher, clearer view, comes "not to destroy, but to fulfill," and still "the Pharisees go out and consult together how they might destroy him."

For the New Education of our day, Frœbel is still the foremost exponent. He sees in mankind a growing revelation of God, destined in individual man consciously to approach His perfection. He sees in each individual man a self-conscious, progressive revelation of God, a name around which, to Frœbel and his New Education, there cluster all the brightest ideals of beauty, wisdom, and virtue in ever-approaching, yet ever-receding, perfection. The name of God, however, on account of its infinite subjectivity, gives rise to numberless misconceptions. It will, therefore, be better to translate Frœbel's thought into purely objective terms, declaring *mankind — and respectively man — to be a growing unit, and its destiny conscious progress, conscious expansion into ever higher perfection.*

Stated separately, the salient points of this formula are the following : —

1. Mankind is a unit, having a growing life of its own.

2. Man is a growing unit in whose life the life of mankind finds conscious expression.

3. The life of man is, therefore, subservient to the life of mankind and included in it.

4. The destiny of mankind and, therefore, of man is conscious progress which implies ever fuller conscious adaptation to the laws of being. This again implies a growing insight into the nature of these laws and spontaneous obedience to their requirements, which leads to their control, and hence to the freedom of man.

The first of these propositions, declaring mankind to be a unit with a growing life of its own, places the present upon the shoulders of the past and puts upon it the responsibility of the future. It represents each generation as a pulse in the life of the whole. Its achievements rest upon those of past generations. For the elevation of this basis it has no responsibility, but it alone is responsible for the elevation upon which it places succeeding generations. Its duty is to lose no vantage ground gained by the past, and to gain more; to take not a step backward, but many steps forward. Its progress is the progress of mankind; its sleep, the sleep of mankind; its backsliding, the loss of all who are to come after. However rich the legacy it receives, it should leave a richer. It may enjoy, but it may not waste, and should increase the store. Thus this proposition affirms the law of heredity, but it also affirms the law of evolution, hence the law of progress, in its application to the life of mankind.

The second proposition, declaring each individual man to be a growing unit in whose life the life of mankind finds conscious expression, subjects education to the laws of growth and development. These laws, which in their essence are reducible to the law of attraction of similars, will lead the intellect to the recognition of truth, the spirit to an apprehension of the Infinite, the will and conduct to goodness, to conscious obedience to law. For education there is no escape from this. Whenever, in slavish adherence to custom and cant, it hinders the recognition of truth and perpetuates error; whenever, in cowardly submission to prejudice and dogmatism, it keeps the spirit from a nearer approach to the Infinite; whenever, by interposing the insolent behests of a despotic authority, it clogs the evolution of conscious obedience to law,—it falls short of its ideals or becomes pseudo-education.

Again, the proposition involves the all-sided harmonious culture of man as a unit. Action, in language, play, and work, should keep pace with intellectual and emotional development. Insight and feeling should keep fully abreast in their upward growth into an emancipated will, free obedience to law, which is to show its supremacy in spontaneously good conduct. This last is at all times the highest criterion of harmonious culture. However full the memory, however fertile the imagination, however keen the insight, however tender the feelings, they accuse culture of one-sidedness, and are of little value, unless they enrich, enlighten, and strengthen truly spontaneous good conduct.

The education of our time is still very far from this. The family, the school, the church still vie with each other in efforts at a one-sided hot-house culture in a variety of directions; one belabors certain phases of the will, the other tugs at the intellect, the third strains the feelings. Not one of them reaches the spirit. Thus they produce angular monstrosities, natures at war with themselves, instead of beautifully rounded wholes that shed peace upon their worlds. The problem of the New Education is to find means and adjust circumstances for the all-sided harmonious culture of man as a unit, to establish educational practices that will strengthen him at all times and simultaneously in all the phases of his being. It is to be feared that this problem will remain new for many generations to come.

The third proposition, declaring the life of man to be subservient to the life of mankind, or, at least, included in it, calls for deliberate systematic training into social efficiency. It condemns as inadequate all merely egotistic, all merely centripetal forms of education. There should, indeed, be as much or more *in-coming*, as there is in the most egotistic forms of education; but the current should not stop there. Gathering new vigor, new warmth and intensity in the mighty gulf of self, it should pour out into a broad Atlantic of universal good-will a genial, expansive stream freighted with life for a world. This proposition would seek, as the highest outcome of educational effort, a lofty altruism which finds the interest of self in the interest of all; it would expand narrow individual egotism into a broad race-egotism; it would teach the individual to seek an attainable practical immortality in the life of the race.

From earliest beginnings it would make the social nature of man an object of educational care and activity. It would have him grow surely and steadily into an appreciation of the value of social effort to himself and of his own value to society. In an atmosphere of universal good will, it would bring him up into habits of sympathy, gratitude, and helpfulness, into a condition of rational self-sacrifice and benevolent self-assertion.

There can be little question that the average school of our day does not afford suitable adjustments for such work. It collects individuals in masses, it is true; but it expends a larger part of its energy in effort to secure isolation in the work of the individuals composing the masses. This is the chief object of its seatings, its rules and regulations, the insolent prominence of its masters, and all the numberless expedients to render the pupil blind to his fellows.

Unquestionably, too, the isolation of the pupil in a greater or less degree is frequently desirable in efforts to concentrate his mind upon the solution of problems affecting his individual growth. Yet this isolation should not become paramount. As the individual growth should be subservient to its social value, the isolation should alternate with opportunities for testing and applying the gain of individual power in social efforts in the organized subordination and co-ordination of common endeavor. This will give worthy purposes to isolation—purposes that lie in good-will and that lead away from the shoals of egotism. This problem, too, must remain new for many generations to come.

The last proposition finds in conscious progress the destiny of mankind, and, therefore, of man, in whom mankind lives. Inasmuch as this implies ever fuller conscious adaptation to the laws of being, it calls for ever-growing insight into these laws. Hence the study of these laws in their manifestations in nature and life is one of the chief concerns of an education that would foster that conscious progress. It is easy to see that this gives to the nature-studies, such as the various departments of exact and empirical science, as well as to the life-studies, such as history, language, and literature, a significance and fascination which must remain ever new.

Again, this adaptation is to be not merely verbal, but must become real. ' The power of insight is to be exercised in life, must become conscious obedience to the laws discovered, full mastership of their inner and outer manifestations, of self and world. This reality of adaptation, this continuous, progressive translation of insight into will and conduct, can be attained only in action, in practice for which the education we seek must afford constant opportunities. These opportunities should be adapted as nearly as possible to the learner's power, in order that they may aid the evolution of faith—faith in self, in his surroundings, in nature, in God. They should, too, be free from temptation to evil, leading outward and upward, strengthening the good. All else is hindrance. The supplying of these opportunities constitutes the adjustment of surroundings, which is the main business of education. The difficulties of this adjustment, in view of the ever-shifting status of our own and the learner's insight and power, will surely keep this phase of education, too, forever fresh and new.

In the limits of this essay I can only indicate some of the proximate requirements of a school education based upon these principles. In the first place, courses of study must have for their center the child, and *not* the subjects of instruction. All that is done at any time must be done for the child's sake. The subjects of study must always adapt themselves to the child's wants and needs. This calls for a concentric, spherical arrangement of the materials of instruction and practice, in which a free outlook in all directions is secured at all times for the child, who is at the centre. Wherever we take hold of the course it should be a well-rounded whole, never an angular fragment. In this, classification must be made on the basis of power, and *not* of technical advancement. The latter is easy to get when the former has been secured, but not *vice versa.* In no case should power be sacrificed to technical advancement.

The practice of cutting up subjects, and parceling them out with reference to the various subdivisions of arbitrarily fixed periods of school-life, is pernicious. It compels the child to pass through the entire curriculum, if it is in search of a rounded, harmonious education. Yet very few children can afford to do this. The curriculum should be rounded, harmonious at all stages. It should open to the child always the whole subject and all subjects within the limits of the child's scope and power. Every new circle should not so much complete the knowledge previously gained; but, starting again from the same centre, the child, it should extend this knowledge to wider fields and greater depths; and at all times the development of tact and skill, of taste and foresight, in the applications, should keep pace with the new acquisitions. Thus in due time science will be reached on the side of knowledge, and art on the side of skill.

Again, the practice of leading all streams toward the college or university is pernicious. In one sense the school, at each and every stage, should be a university. It should open for the child the avenues to all categories of knowledge and mastership. Whatever it can grasp and handle of the relationships of form and color, number and size, natural history and geography, social and historical data, language and music, should enrich and strengthen its life at school from the day of its entrance to the day of its leaving. Thus, alone, will every day and every hour spent in school become in the child's life a precious seed, which, at successive stages of growth and development, will yield bounteous harvests of all that makes life worth living.

The methods of teaching should at all times furnish opportunities and incentives for discovery and application, for finding and doing. Whatever the pupil may have found, he should have the opportunity to use it at once in accomplishing some spontaneous purpose of pleasure and profit. Upon the very heels of every discovery there should come the activities of using and inventing, creating a thirst for new discovery, for other steps onward.

Thus the child should not be compelled to the doleful and profitless task of learning to read solely for the sake of acquiring this art. From the very beginning the legitimate purpose of reading—the gaining of information and enjoyment—should be uppermost in the child's mind. The child must want to learn the art for the sake of the good it gains in it from its own immediate life. The child must have an object whose attainment renders necessary the acquisition of this art. The same is true of all other studies. Not the teacher's purpose, but the child's, must lead. His ingenuity will find ample play in the judicious adjustment of surroundings, keeping opportunities and incentives in the direction of right development, and supplying with the least possible delay and friction the growing needs and wants of the pupil.

Similarly, I might point out in fuller detail the demands of the New Education, here set forth, with reference to the æsthetic, ethical, and social training of the child; but I reserve this for some future occasion, believing that I have sufficiently indicated the far-reaching changes in ordinary school life that must follow in the train of a full and nnreserved acceptance of the principles of the New Education.

CAN YOUR PUPILS ADD?

ESSE B. DAKIN.

Not long since at a teachers' meeting the question was asked, "What is the greatest defect in our mathematics as taught?" Various answers were given. One teacher said, "We don't have time enough to solve all the examples; there are so many given in the text books that we have no time left to dwell upon the principle involved in their solution." Another said, "The pupils promoted from lower grades have not given any time to the analysis of problems, and in the higher grades are unable to give a logical analysis of any problem." A third answers that there were too many "methods" taught. For example, one method of computing interest, thoroughly understood and firmly fixed in the mind by a great number of examples is much better than a partial understanding and imperfect drill in several methods. Other teachers answered the question in much the same view as quoted above, all agreeing that the *time* was lacking to do the amonnt of work laid down in the catalogue.

Do any of these answers reach the difficulty? We think not. Surely the first is not correct, for, if properly taught, each example is an elucidation of a principle, and the more examples given the pupil, the more familiar the principle becomes. Indeed, since we learn by doing, the example, the application of the principle, are the essential part of the text-book.

· Neither can the second answer be wholly correct, for, since analysis is simply giving the steps of a solution with the reasons therefor, if a pupil can solve a problem, without aid, he can give the analysis.

The third answer is good, but does not reach the root of the difficulty. The teacher who thought "pupils will have time for all the examples in the text-book and for all the "methods" given, if they are well drilled in the foundation of arithmetic, *addition*," pointed out the true defect. Here we have the weak point. If your pupils "haven't time" to solve all the problems in percentage, interest, or insurance, find out if they can *add*. Send the class to the board with an example in multiplication and watch closely. How many will you see counting their fin⁻ gers to add the number they are "carrying"? Or, ask a pupil to add two numbers and observe his fingers.

The test was made recently with a pupil of moderate ability. The teacher asked, "How much is 9 and 5?" The child's hands flew behind her back, the fingers and thumb of one hand counted and the answer "14" was given with a triumphant air. "Very good. How much is 5 and 9?" continues the teacher. Again all the fingers and one thumb were counted and the result, 14. The child had no idea of *adding* the numbers; neither did she recognize the number, 9 and 5, when given in the reverse order, 5 and 9. Yet this pupil could "do examples in fractions."

These tests are simple, but reliant. Try them in your schools.

The results may be disheartening, but should be welcome if they open our eyes to the importance of *addition.* It is the basis of all rapid, accurate, mathematical work. The so-called *four* fundamental operations of arithmetic are but forms of *one* operation, addition. What is subtraction but finding what number added to another will produce a given sum? If we subtract 5 from 9 wh it do we do but/ascertain what number added to 5 will produce 9?

Multiplication is but "a short method of finding the sum of several numbers," while division is finding how many times we add equal numbers to produce a given number, the dividend.

No wonder pupils "haven't time" to solve many problems, when the simplest operation consumes much time and mental strength; the principle involved in the example is lost sight of in the laborious work of adding, subtracting, or dividing.

Drills in addition should be given daily in *all* grades. If asked what we consider the most important part of arithmetic, imitating the famous orator who thought action the beginning and end of true elocution, we answer, addition, *addition*, ADDI-TION.

TEACHERS' WAGES WHEN SCHOOLS ARE CLOSED ON ACCOUNT OF DANGEROUS DISEASES.

A DECISION by our Superintendent of Public Instruction was published last spring, to the effect that, if any school should be closed by order of the Board of Health or the School Board, by reason of some dangerous disease, the teachers would not be entitled to pay for the time thus lost.

I was surprised at the decision, not merely because I thought it to be unjust and contrary to the general law of contracts, but more especially because it is the reverse of a decision given by the Supreme Court of Michigan in a case exactly parallel. The case is reported in 43 Mich. p. 480.

Franklin S. Dewey vs. *Union School District of the City of Alpena.* The plaintiff was regularly hired to serve as teacher for ten months. He entered upon his duties Sept. 2d, and continued up to Dec. 10th, at which time the officers closed the schools, on account of the prevalence of small-pox in the city, and kept them closed for the same reason until March 17th. They were then reopened and the plaintiff renewed his duties. The district refused to pay him for the period of suspension and he brought this action to recover it.

The decision of the Circuit Court was against him, but he appealed to the Supreme Court and the verdict of the lower court was reversed.

The *decisive* point of the decision is as follows: "Beyond controversy the closing of the schools was a wise and timely expedient. But the defense interposed could not rest on that. It must appear that observance of the contract by the district was caused to be impossible by the act of God. It is not enough that great difficulties were encountered, or that there existed urgent and satisfactory reasons for stopping the schools. This is all the evidence tended to show. The contract between the parties was for positive and for lawful objects. On one side school buildings and pupils were to be provided, and on the other, personal service as teacher. The plaintiff continued ready to perform, but the district refused to open its school-houses and allow the attendance of pupils, and it thereby prevented performance by the plaintiff.

Admitting that the circumstances justified the officers, there is yet no rule of justice which will entitle the district to visit its own misfortunes upon the plaintiff. He was not at fault. He had no agency in bringing about the state of things which rendered it eminently prudent to dismiss the schools. It was the misfortune of the district, and the district and not the plaintiff ought to bear it. The occasion which was presented to the district was not within the principle contended for. It was not one of absolute necessity, but of strong expedience.

To let in the defense that the suspension precluded recovery, the agreement must have provided for it. But the district did not stipulate for the right to discontinue the plaintiff's pay upon the judgment of the officers, however discreet and fair, that a stoppage of the schools is found a needful measure to prevent their invasion by disease, or to stay or oppose its spread or progress in the community; and the contract can not be regarded as tacitly subject to such a condition.

The judgment is reversed with costs and a new trial granted."

But a new trial was not asked for by the school board. They paid the teacher his full claim with interest.

The Supreme Court was unanimous in its decision and so satisfied of its justice that when the school board's attorneys stated, "That is our case," Chief Justice Cooley replied at once, "Then we don't care to hear the other side," and they did not hear it.

The decision of our State Superintendent of which we complain is unjust to the teachers of the state, and its author will, we hope, pardon a humble member of the profession for raising his feeble voice in self-defense.

Teachers should bear in mind that the decisions of our State Superintendent, given under the advice of the Attorney General and published in our educational journals, carry with them no judicial authority whatever. But school boards are frequently guided by them in their dealings with teachers, and for this reason we have spoken.

We close this discussion by asking for one more decision. If the small-pox should break out in the neighborhood of the offices of the Supt. of Public Instruction and the Attorney General, and prevail so extensively that those offices should be closed temporarily by the Board of Health, would the salaries of those officers cease? The teachers will wait anxiously for this decision.

Elkhart, Ind. E. B. Myers.

Fear is born of evil. In a perfect state there is no fear. When children obey because they are afraid to do wrong they obey from a spirit of evil. *You can not make a child good by making him afraid to be bad.* Fear stands in the same relation to its possessor that chains do to a crimal. The clanking of iron never converted a sinner. The hard threats of fear never made a child good. Laws are for the unruly. Making a child afraid to do wrong may keep him from doing wrong for a time, but unless *better* motives come in, he will not be made better. "Let not fear create the God of childhood."—*Ex.*

THE SCHOOL ROOM.

[This Department is conducted by GEO. F. BASS, Supervising Prin. Indianapolis schools.]

——:o:——

WHY WRONG?

THERE is as much value in knowing *why* we are wrong as in knowing what is right. A pupil should be be convinced of the "error of his ways."

"An agent received $315 to invest in goods after deducting his commission at 5 per cent. What did he invest in goods?"

A pupil solved the above as follows: 5 per cent. of $315=$15.75; $315—$15.75=$299.25, Ans.

When he had finished explaining it, hands were flying in the air, and the teacher called on some other member of the class. He explained as follows: "$315 includes the amount expended and his commission; then, it is $105 per cent. of the amount expended. One per cent. is $\frac{1}{105}$th of $315, and 100 per cent. is 100 times that, which is $300."

This explanation may have some "lame places" in it, but in the main it is right and the majority of the class agree that it is right. The teacher now asks the first pupil if he sees. He says he does and he probably does see something, but it may be a very different thing from what the teacher thinks he sees. I once heard a teacher say, "Well, what do you see?" "I see that I am wrong," said the pupil. This seems acknowledgment enough to satisfy the most fastideous; but it did not satisfy *this* teacher. He said, "Why are you wrong?"

The pupil laughed a laugh that showed bashfulness coupled with weakness and said, "Because." He thought he ought to know and supposed he did know, but "could not tell."

The teacher, very patiently, led the pupil by skillful questions to see his mistake. The questions were similar to the following: "Question—Upon what is commission computed? Ans.—Upon amount of money collected or expended. Ques.—If commission is computed upon anything else will the work be wrong? Ans.— Yes. Ques.—Upon what did you compute commission? Ans. —Upon the $315. Ques.—What is the $315? Ans.—It is the sum of the amount expended and the commission. Ques.—Why is your work wrong? Ans.—Because I computed commission upon the wrong sum.

Now the pupil has been led through all the mental processes he must make to intelligently solve the given problem. He now knows he is wrong because he has violated a principle of commission. This is all that is wrong with his work. A teacher who thus works with the individual will make thinkers of his pupils. There is morality in this kind of teaching. A pupil thus taught will form the habit of acting right for right's sake—not as a matter of expediency.

THE TEN GREAT NOVELS.

Ivanhoe, Jane Eyre, Pickwick, Vanity Fair, Les Miserables, Don Quixote, Last Days of Pompeii, Egyptian Princess, Consuelo, Adam Bede.

How many school teachers have read them? This question was asked in an institute held in one of the most progressive counties in this state. There were about 150 teachers in attendance. Of this number, 35 percent had read Jane Eyre. This was the largest per percent on any one book. The lowest percent was on Egyptian Princess, 1.4 percent. The average on all was 19.3 percent.

What does this mean? Is it an argument for the introduction of literary studies into the school course of study?

Jugs hold only a certain quantity. If more is pressed in an equal amount runs away. Jugs have different capacities; some are quite large and others very small. If a precious liquid is to be put into a hundred jugs, of different sizes, the pourer would be careful to stop pouring when the jug was full. Teachers, do you see the application? No two of your pupils have equal powers of *holding*. If you attempt to make them all learn the same amount, some will not be full enough, and others will be too full for utterance.. You can't cram either jugs or children. Grade your lessons according to the child's capacities.

REPEATERS.

TEACHERS have frequently been criticised for repeating the answers of their pupils. As, for example, Who discovered America? Answer by pupil, "Columbus." Teacher, "Columbus." In what year? Pu., "In 1492." T., "In 1492," and so on. Why do they persist in doing this? Echo answers why? The only excuse I could ever find for myself is, the pupil spoke so low or indistinctly that I feared the class did not hear. This is a poor excuse. It would be better to have the pupil say it again for the purpose of saying it so that the entire class might hear. The pupil should be made to feel that he must speak loud enough and distinctly enough the *first* time for the entire class to hear. The repeating of the answer each time by the teacher will not make him feel so.

But pupils have a habit of repeating a part of almost every answer they give,—e. g. Name the products of India. Ans., "Cotton, tea—cotton, tea, coffee—cotton, tea, coffee, sugar-cane, pepper—cotton, tea, etc." Why do they do this? It may be the force of habit, but this habit has been formed by trying to recite a poorly prepared lesson. Let us have the pupils adopt the rule they adopt in playing marble—"No-tryances-over." Let them feel that they must say the right thing at first trial and that they are to say it once only. When they have said *cotton*, if they can not instantly think what to say next, take time to think of it, but not repeat what has been said.

There is another senseless repetition made by pupils. If one pupil were to name the products of a country and there were five to name and he should happen to omit one, the hands will come up. When a pupil is called upon he names the whole list instead of saying, "he omitted *tea*."

Repetition is too valuable to be wasted in this way.

EXPLOSIVENESS.

SOMETIMES teachers put their questions out with so much explosiveness, that when the name of a pupil is called he feels as if he had been shot at and not missed either. Not long ago we

2

witnessed a performance of this sort. The teacher said, "*Mary,*
how do you reduce a common fraction to a decimal?" Mary
bounced out of her seat, caught her breath, looked at the ceiling,
at the teacher, down her nose and at the floor, gasped, and was
about to say "I don't know," when the teacher said in a very
pleasant and quieting tone, "All think how to reduce a common fraction to a decimal." This gave Mary a chance to think
too, and in a moment her countenance brightened and her answer was ready.

The teacher gave her an oportunity to answer, which she
seemed to do with great satisfaction. The teacher's second request should have come first. Give the pupils a chance to think.
Do not force them into the habit of bouncing up and beginning
to talk before they have something to say. Do not startle children with a question, unless there is a special reason for doing
so.

MATHEMATICAL LANGUAGE.

PUPILS do not seem to understand that $2+4=6$ is a sentence
and should express a truth. Such expressions as the following
are frequently seen and often accepted by very good teachers:
$2\frac{2}{3}=\frac{8}{3}\div8=\frac{1}{3}$. If this were written in words it would make a
peculiarly constructed sentence. "Two and two-thirds are equal
to eight-thirds divided by eight are equal to one-third." What is
the subject of the second *are?*

Such expressions as the above should not be accepted. Take
this one as it stands and it means nothing. The example of
which it is supposed to be the solution is, "$\frac{8}{3}\div8=$what?" The
following is better: $2\frac{2}{3}=\frac{8}{3}$: $\frac{8}{3}\div8=\frac{1}{3}$.

SENSIBLE.—"How does it happen that there are so many old
maids among the school teachers," asked a reporter of a school
teacher the other day. "Because school teachers are, as a rule, women of sense, and no woman will give up a $60 position for a $10
man," was the reply.—*Michigan City Dispatch.*

PRIMARY DEPARTMENT.

[This Department is conducted by HOWARD SAXDISON, Professor of Methods in the State Normal School.]

———:o:———

The real subject in education is the individual mind of each child, with its acquired habits and inherited tendencies. An evident proposition, then, is: If real teaching is done, each mind, with its peculiar habits and inherited tendencies, must be understood by the teacher; with its double corollary:—

(1) The number of pupils under the charge of a primary teacher should range between twenty and thirty. (2) The pupils should remain under the charge of a given teacher more than ten months.

The second proposition is: Mind being an organism, the heart (sensibilities) is no less an avenue to the intellect, than is the intellect to the heart and will; with its corollary:—

Suspicion and severity can never enable the teacher to obtain a standing place in the child-mind.

The third proposition is: Two rival powers compose the mind—the *carrying power*—memory (the servant) and the *thinking power* (the master); with its double corollary:—

(1) The aim of education is to make the mind strong and skilled as a thinking power, and not to make it full as a carrying power. (2) The most practical education is that which sends the child into the business world with power to observe closely and to think (reflect) accurately upon what he observes.

———•◆•———

READING.

WEBSTER defines reading in two ways:

1. To go over, as characters or words, and utter aloud, or recite to one's self inaudibly.

2. To take in the sense of. Hence to know fully; to comprehend.

Who is't can *read* a woman.—*Shakespeare.*

The first definition attracts the attention first, and in accordance with the usual habit of teachers of accepting without question that which is given upon authority, we have adopted the first definition as an expression of what is meant by reading in the schools. The significant part of the definition—*to go over*—seems to have escaped us. The learned lexicographer has unwittingly given the two characteristics of reading as generally taught in our schools:

1. *To go over;* i. e., to miss, to neglect the *thought*—the *essence.*

2. *To utter aloud;* i. e., to pronounce, to call words.

Years of work of this kind finally made the results so manifest that teachers could no longer ignore them. When it was seen that the majority of those who had taken the work in the public schools could not read, in the home circle, selections from the newspapers in an intelligent manner; and when it was observed that the attempt to read a passage of Scripture in the Sabbath-school, or a set of resolutions at a public meeting, was equally a failure, the cause began to be sought for. Why is it, it began to be asked, that the modulation, emphasis and inflection of our pupils are so good in their conversation and so mechanical in their reading? The answer that was finally evolved was that in conversation the pupil is complete master of the thought and feeling that he is expressing, and that the expression itself is in the back-ground, the mind giving very slight consideration to it. This fundamental thought of reading then came into view — *Thought governs expression;* if the thought is thoroughly mastered, and the attention is concentrated upon the thought, the oral expression will be natural and will take care of itself. (Except in the case of pronunciation, enunciation, articulation; and faults in these respects should be corrected in conversational exercises, not in reading.)

If the attention is turned upon the expression the inevitable result is a mechanical expression. However graceful one's movements may be, if his attention is called to them, and he is conscious that others are observing them, they at once become some-what mechanical. So it is with oral expression. If the pressure is constantly in the direction of oral reading and attention is, to a large degree, called to its excellencies and its defects, the oral reading will, by force of the mind's nature, become mechanical.

If, however, the stress is placed upon the thought—that which determines the oral expression—the tendency is for it to become free and natural. Reading should be taught in such a way that the thought is made prominent while the printed expression is in the back-ground, as are the oral words in conversation. Oral reading is to be, largely, a *means* by which the teacher peers down into the thinking of the pupil.

Real reading, then, is that indicated by Webster's second definition— *Taking in the sense of.* If a child comprehends the thought of a paragraph, he has *read* it, in the most important sense, even if he has not attempted the oral expression.

PROMOTION OF TEACHERS WITH THEIR CLASSES.

If it be admitted that the individual mind is the subject of the teacher's work, then a proper inference is that the teacher should remain long enough with the pupils to be able to see into their peculiarities of disposition and environment. This can not be well accomplished in six months, nor in one year, and the thought that arises is that the teachers of the country schools should not be changed so often, and that the teachers in the city schools should be promoted with their classes. Viewing this principle alone—that time gives the teacher the opportunity to know the minds of the pupils—the thought would be that the pupil should have but one teacher during school-life. But another principle—that the pupil's mind gains greater breadth and power by coming into contact with different minds—seems to require variety in teachers. With the two principles in consideration it may be held that there should be two or three changes of teachers during the school course.

It is obvious, of course, that if the teacher is inefficient, the sooner the change is made the better; on the supposition, however, that the school boards and superintendents do not complicate the selection of teachers by geographical, family, and other arbitrary considerations, but make moral and intellectual fitness the sole test—a supposition which in theory may be permitted—a greater length of time with a given class than is now allowed would be a gain, inasmuch as it would necessarily result in the teacher's gaining a more intimate acquaintance with the individual minds of the pupils.

ORAL LESSONS.

1. *Variety.* The tendency to organize all lessons of the same kind on one order of topics, is one that the teacher, especially a beginner, is likely to acquire. Those on animals, for example, will be arranged under:

    a. Place.
    b. Description.
    c. Habits.
    d. Uses.

Those on common subjects, as the chair, poker, etc., under:

    a. Material.

    b. Parts.

    c. Uses.

While such an order may be the very best, it should not be rigidly adhered to, because, the children having become familiar with the order, anticipate the next point, which to a degree deprives the lesson of interest. The teacher having gathered the materials for the lesson, should consider carefully, how the method may be varied without a loss of discipline or clearness. One who is to lead the minds of little children should not rest content until she can organize the materials on any kind of a subject, in several different ways. This is required for two reasons—freedom on the part of the teacher, in adapting the material to the needs of the children, and variety, as a source of interest to the children.

2. *Reflection on one's own work.* Having given a lesson, the teacher on inspecting it will recall that at one point the children seemed interested and attentive, while at another stage of the lesson they were quite the reverse; she will not fail to observe that some points were eagerly considered, and that others made but a slight impression. The teacher should thus reflect upon a number of lessons, jotting down the points obtained for future guidance.

Such a study of her work will suggest some such conclusions as the following:

a. The children are always greatly interested in their own experiences and those of the other pupils and of the teacher.

b. They watch with great interest the progress of any experiment.

c. The actual *growth* of a sketch or of a map enchains their attention much more than those presented in a completed state.

Thus would the teacher gain confidence in her own resources and an incentive to prepare herself *to draw at the blackboard in the presence of the class.*

PRACTICAL LESSON.

(Stenographic Report.)

SPELLING—SECOND YEAR GRADE.

Teacher places on the black-board the following words:

Ship, sails, steam, masts, cells.

T.   (Pointing to first word.)   Pronounce this word.   Pupils pronounce.   Ship.

T.   Who is ready with a story?   Jane may tell us one.

J.   The ship sails on the ocean.

Teacher places sentence on the board.

T.   You may read this sentence.

P.   "The ship sails on the ocean."

T.   I think Jane has used two of our words; what ones are they?

P.   She has used the words, "ship" and "sails."

T.   Pronounce the next word.

Pupils pronounce.   Steam.

T.   Who has a sentence ready?

P.   "Steam is strong."

T.   How do you know it is strong?

P.   Because it makes the engines and boats go.

T.   What does steam do for us?

P.   It makes us warm in winter.

Teacher places the sentence, "Steam is strong," on the board.

T.   Read the sentence.

Pupils read.   "Steam is strong."

T.   Pronounce the next word.

P.   Masts.

Who can give a sentence?

P.   The sails are put on the masts.

Teacher places sentence on the board and has the pupils read as before.

T.   Pronounce this word.

Pupils pronounce.   "Cells."

T.   Can some one ask me a question about this word?

P.   Are the cells made of wax?

T.   I like that question.   Has any one another?

T. Who has anything to do with those cells?

P. The bees.

T. Now I would like to have you put the word "bees" into the sentence, so that I will know what kind of cells you mean.

P. Does the bee make the cells?

Teacher places sentence on the board.

T. What do I need at the end of this sentence?

P. A question mark.

T. Now read all the sentences carefully.

Pupils read.

> "The ship sails on the ocean."
> "Steam is strong."
> "The sails are put on the masts."
> "Does the bee make the cells?"

T. I wish you to copy these sentences just as carefully and as nicely as you can.

The pupils copy the sentences on their slates and the teacher examines the work. They then erase their work and the teacher dictates the same sentences to them, after having erased them from the board.

The pupils also write their names and the date.

The teacher then examines the work and the pupils make the proper corrections, giving the corrections orally.

EXPLANATORY.—Spelling, in the second grade, deals with sentences rather than with words. An eminent educator says: "Sentences are the written forms of thought expression, and the stimulus of the thought enables the child to recall the word-forms in writing just as it does in reading."

In the preparation of the lesson, the sentences are written a number of times on the slates. While this is being done the teacher passes from one desk to another in order to see that no mistakes are repeated. Incorrect or careless work is erased at once by the teacher. The first work done in preparing the les. son was the discussion of a picture on the wall which had excited the interest of the pupils.

The results to be secured by a series of lessons of this character are:

1.   Habits of thought and attention.
2.   Correct habits of language both spoken and written.
3.   The proper use of capitals and punctuation marks.

MRS. FANNIE BURT.

FIRST THREE MONTHS IN NUMBER WORK.

THE number work in the first three months may be made incidental in connection with form.   The main purpose during this period may be to teach form, (elementary geometry.)

The sphere, cube, cylinder, prism, square, triangle, etc., are presented at different times, and the pupil is given a clear idea of them as wholes, also a clear idea of surfaces, lines, angles, corners, etc.

In doing this, number must of necessity be incidentally brought in.   Yet the number work must be subordinate: the principal aim of the work being to make the ideas of form more clear to the mind.   The nature of this work may be shown in taking the triangular prism, as an example: This prism is shown to the child, he observes it carefully, and by skillful questioning on the part of the teacher, the child is led to describe it, which description consists in giving its lines, faces, angles, corners, etc.   The teacher, of course, gives the child the correct name of each when the child has a clear idea of it.

In this work the child is using his perceptive faculties, and strengthening his powers of observation.

The child is then ready to make a similar prism of moulding clay.   In this part of the work he is taught carefulness and accuracy, using his fingers to shape and smooth the form with which he is working.   So far the child has been gaining the idea of form.

Next he is required to point out or name objects in the room that are similar to the triangular prism.   Also, to name objects at home, on the streets, or elsewhere of similar shape, perhaps describing something about some of them.

Then he is required to draw objects that are similar to the prism described.   In this work he is applying his knowledge of triangular prisms, and training his eye and hand, as well as gaining language. The child is now ready to begin number work with this object.

The, prism may be placed before him, and such questions as the following may be asked;—(each teacher must be judge of the kind and number of questions, and be governed by the development of the child's mind, and the circumstances under which he is working.)

How many prisms do you see? (Taking it away.) Now how many? One prism less one prism is how many prisms?

How many faces do you see? (Changing.) How many now? How many faces on the sides of the prism? How many on the ends? How many in all? (Using numbers as wholes, not counting.)

How many corners do you see? Now how many?

Point out two corners.

Point out the two upper corners.

Point out the two lower corners.

How many corners in all?

The questioning can be continued as long as the teacher thinks best.

Upper, lower, front, back, right, left, etc., are taught with form rather than with number.

In the child's answers his language must be guarded, and every answer must be a full, clear, complete sentence.

Richmond.   PENINA HILL.

DEPARTMENT OF PEDAGOGY.

[This Department is conducted by S. S. PARR, Principal De Pauw Normal School.]

——:o:——

THE MODIFIED GRUBE METHOD.

TO TEACH THE NUMBERS FROM ONE TO ONE HUNDRED.

THE pure Grube method in primary number is an instrument of too keen edge and too complicated make-up for any teacher but an expert. It is very likely, in the hands of an ordinary teacher, to become a dead formula. A modified form of this method is less liable to become machine-like. There are many variations of it possible. One of the most efficient is this:—

1.   Teach the numbers from 1 to 100.

2.   The addition of all combinations of the digits into groups of two figures each.

3.   Subtraction of these groups.

4.   All the constant additions involved in multiplication by the nine digits.

5.   Multiplication involving the nine digits by means of re-membered results from constant addition.

6.   Division as the converse of multiplication.

This plan makes the work cumulative and continuous.   Each step is based on those that precede and prepare the way for it.

This series of exercises may be extended, with some change to suit the conditions, through numbers of two figures each.

In teaching primary number, three stages naturally arise :—

1.   Sight-numbers or numbered objects.   These are to be continued until each number is thoroughly learned by sight.

2.   Concrete numbers or number applied to particular objects which are not present to the sight.

3.   Abstract number, that is, number thought apart from any particular object.

Nothing has been said about the oral and written words that express number, nor about the figures by means of which the pro-cesses of number are represented.   One direction with reference to these will suffice.   Figures should not be introduced before the number itself is learned, as the introduction of a new element distracts the mind by dividing the attention.   Of course, we are assuming that no one will fall into the gross error of failure to distinguish between numbers, which are ideas in the mind and figures which are marks—material objects—outside of it.

One of the best devices yet invented for teaching number is the Decimal Board.   This is a board eighteen inches or two feet long and a foot wide, as per the accompanying cut.

The first set of holes are just large enough to receive a single tooth-pick or small match ; in the second set the holes are of a size to receive a single bundle of ten tooth-picks or ten matches; in the third line, the holes are cut sufficiently large to take in a bundle made up of ten of the smaller bundles. Such an arrangement provides for building up to thousands. This is as far as numbered objects need to be used.

The numbers from one to nine are to be taught as sight-groups by means of the holes and tooth-picks. These groups are formed by the addition of one to each preceding group, the method by which the mind is forced to learn the contents of groups. The most economical way of teaching these groups seems to be as follows:

1. Attentive observation of the group.

2. Put the group into the child's hand and let him match it. This involves discrimination.

3. Number-hunting, that is, picking the number from among others. This involves discrimination and memory.

4. Reproduction from memory. This adds to discrimination and memory, the element of conception or generalized idea.

Each of these is capable of many drill-devices. The number of such devices necessary will depend on the amount of drill and on the variety that will be required. The law of repetition requires that the idea shall be before the attention often enough to make its impress on the power of retention. The number of repetitions required for this depends on the intensity of attention, which in its turn depends on the principle of interest. In repetition, that element which is the principal condition of interest is variety of form.

When the number and its word-expressions are learned, the same process which taught the number may, in a general way be applied to learning the use of the figure to express it.

The "decimal-board" bridges over a troublesome difficulty. When the number nine is learned, the child readily sees that, if one more is added, he must bunch the ten ones into one ten in order to find a place for it. The formation of the tens from one to nine and the grouping into the second set of holes is easy and has no new elements except that each *one* is now made up of ten parts which are themselves *ones*. The representation of tens by figures involves the new idea of more than one value for each digit and of the necessity for some way of showing this. The child would better discover these ideas for himself, under the teacher's guidance. He will not perhaps discover that we show the *tens-value* of the several digits by placing them in the second place on the left, but he will discover the necessity for some means of designating the *tens value.* The third set of holes are used for teaching huñdreds. A hundred is a one made up of ten tens—bundles, etc. No new principle enters into the teaching of hundreds or their representation.

One of the most necessary elements is the tests to be employed by the teacher to see when work is done. A sight-group of numbered objects is not known sufficiently well until the child can recognize it as quick as flash and that without any conscious counting. He must not only recognize 3, 5, 7, 9, etc., marks or objects, 3, 5, 7, 9, etc., sounds, touches, or motions, but conversely. The moment any figure is seen, the child should be able to form its corresponding number. When these results are reached, the next step, addition of the numbers expressed by the digits, is due and not before in the present plan.

CONCERNING INDIVIDUALITY.

WE hear a great deal said about the pupil's individuality. Much of it is cant. Not one person in a hundred can tell what he means by the pupil's individuality. The schools are terrorized with the charge that they repress individuality. This is the more demoralizing because it relates to a vague undefined something that can not be confronted and refuted. What is this individuality that the schools are said to repress? We are not helped by being told that we "stretch everything on the same bed," nor by the statement that we "put round pegs in square holes and square pegs in round holes," nor even by that lucidly clinching diagnosis that we "grind everything through the same mill."

A close scrutiny of these criticisms shows that they all relate to the child's idiosyncrasies. Lop-sidedness of mind is individuality; so are inherited weaknesses of this or that faculty, and acquired habits of body and mind. Mental squinting and other obliquity of vision, club-foot of the moral nature, and hobbling on all sorts of crutches are dignified with the praise of a term that depends for its value on its vagueness and, perhaps, on a real emptiness of meaning.

We submit whether or not one of the chief values of education is that it lops off such "individuality." Certainly, the more such peculiarities are lopped off the better. Any system of education that would increase them is deserving a place in the vagaries of a madman. If these things are individuality, then the typical individual is the imbecile or the savage. All culture has for its purpose the repression of this kind of individualism.

The purpose of school-education, as of other kinds, is to realize in the individual the type of his species. This is the very reverse of the individualism we have cited. It is the individual minus his idiosyncrasies but fully developed on the side of those faculties and elements that are common to all men. These constitute his *true* individuality. They constitute him a person, as the others constitute him a thing. The highest type of difference arises from the cultivation of the common faculties; the lowest possible type from the cultivation of idiosyncrasies. Cultured men of a high type differ more widely than savages. The differences of savages are mainly physical, and even there they are greatly surpassed by their civilized brethren.

A current misconception exists as to what constitutes originality. Odd and fantastic modes of action, thought and speech are called original. People who resurrect worn out ideas and forms of expression are said to be possessed of originality. Crudities and whims are elevated to the same level. A sophomoric disregard for fact and a corresponding exuberance of loud-colored fancy are charged to a bump of originality. Indeed, we have known cases of downright literary and linguistic stealing palmed off on good-natured and somewhat obtuse people, charged to the same account.

The fact behind these sayings and criticisms on the school seems to be that the fault lies in the teaching skill. The differentiation needs to take place in it, so as to accommodate it to the individual. The same mode of procedure is too often applied to the hale and hearty mind that is applied to the one that is crippled. The end sought, the means employed and the results to be reached are the same in both, but there the sameness ceases. The common element is to be developed; the other is to be repressed.

A special form of the general criticism is found in the fact that all pupils are made to study the same lesson. Two things may be true: either the teaching may be at fault or the subject is not well differentiated and variety is thus lacking in the matter. Sometimes pupils have, as they think, incapacities for subjects. In ninety-nine cases out of a hundred, these are prejudices. If they really existed, that would be reason, if no other, for giving training in the subjects which are their ground. What would be thought of the trainer who would carry the young athlete over all the stiles because his legs were weak!

The teacher needs to grip firmly the principle that the true individuality of the pupil is found in the common element in his mind with others, and that this is the true subject to be developed, while all idiosyncracies should be subjected to the pruning knife.

THREE THINGS THE TEACHER MUST KNOW.

KNOWING precedes doing. The latter is, however, a corrective of the former; that is, our theoretical knowledge is always under process of readjustment by our experience. What is here called theoretical knowledge includes those facts and principles that have been discovered little by little by the race. To disregard these would be to set out blindly and make the same trials and the same mistakes that the generations before us made in bringing knowledge to its present condition. Experience shows three kinds of knowledge of the individual pupil to be absolutely necessary to his teaching:—

First, a knowledge of his "pre existent state of mind." This means two things. The ideas that are in the mind at any given time must be understood before the teacher can proceed intelligently to form a new idea. That is, if one desires to teach the ascending zones of vegetation on the Andes or the Alps, the prior knowledge to be obtained is that of the ideas already in the pupil's mind, which bear directly on the topic to be taught. Like the merchant who lays in a stock of new goods, the teacher must take an inventory of what is already on hand. A failure to do this involves duplication, confusion and, at last, failure. This inventory is on the side of the intellect. The emotions and will are likewise to be scheduled. As no two minds present the same furnishing of ideas, so no two are alike in the way they regard a given topic. What excites lively interest in one is received with indifference by another. One pupil believes it is of value; another thinks his time lost in mastering it. Parents, by unguarded and ignorant remarks often prejudice the minds of their children about topics or subjects. The will presents as great differences. Some minds, by ill-training or no training are as scraggled as the vine that runs wild in a shut-in corner which renders it lop-sided and half-paralyzed. All these come under the head of "pre-existent states of mind."

Second, the teacher must know with what rapidity the individual mind acts. The difference between the dull boy and the bright boy is at first mainly one of rapidity of mental action. This difference becomes cause for other differences of even more serious nature. After a time the dull boy becomes a confirmed mental coward by being always outstripped in the race. Slowness is not weakness until it produces this cowardice. How often do we hear the dull pupil paralyzed by "Hurry! hurry! You are *so* slow!"

Dullness arises from other causes than slowness, but this, we think, is the chief one.

Third, the teacher must study the individual mind to know what stimuli to apply to bring it into prompt and efficient action. The knowledge in any two given minds may be the same, their processes *must* be the same and, with the same material, they will reach results that differ only in unimportant details; but the stimuli will vary with each. The motives to be appealed to depend on idiosyncrasies of the individual, on the immediate circumstances of the school and recitation and on the personality of the teacher. Among what we term stimuli is the mode of presenting the subject—the method. This is all important and must be varied somewhat with each pupil.

An understanding of these three elements of successful teaching will be a source of great power and satisfaction to the teacher. They render pointed and effective the injunction—so often laid upon the teacher—to "study the individual pupil."

OFFICIAL DEPARTMENT.

SALARIES OF TEACHERS.

JUDGE HORD HOLDS THAT THEY CAN NOT BE ATTACHED OR GARNISHEED.

State Superintendent Holcombe has addressed certain inquiries to the Attorney-General regarding the right of creditors to attach or garnishee the salaries of school teachers, and Judge Hord has given a legal opinion on that matter, which, together with the question, are as follows:

"Can the salary of a teacher in the common schools of the state be attached or garnisheed in the hands of a school trustee?"

Answer—Municipal corporations deriving their authority from the law for receiving and disbursing public funds, are not chargeable as garnishees in the absence of an express statute authorizing such proceeding. A school township is a municipal corporation, and such township and its officers in control of the common school fund are not suject to garnishment. So long as the school fund for the payment of teachers remains in the hands of a disbursing officer, it is as much the money of the state as if it had not been drawn from the state treasury until paid over by the officer to the persons entitled to it. The fund can not in any legal sense be considered a part of his effects.

2. Does the statute abrogate the statutory rule and permit the salaries of teachers to be garnisheed in the hands of officers with whom the school fund is intrusted for educational purposes?

Answer—It is my opinion that the salary of a teacher in the common schools of the state can not be garnisheed in the hands of a school trustee by a creditor of such teacher.

A WORD ON "SCHOOL FIGHTS."

No one can commit a meaner offense than to try to break up a school because he does not like the teacher. The school is a public

3

institution established for the benefit of the people; and any one who does anything to impair its efficiency, on account of a private grudge, violates the first duties of good citizenship. He might as well advise people not to pay their taxes because he dislikes the county treasurer, as try to hinder his tenants or friends from sending their children to the public school because he dislikes the teacher or school authorities. Such conduct is beyond the reach of the law, but should bring upon the person guilty of it the contempt of all good men. The Secessionists left the Union because their candidates were not elected. This is the same spirit manifested in small matters.

J. W. HOLCOMBE.

EDITORIAL.

SENDING MONEY.—Send by express, money order, postal note, or registered letter at our risk Do not send 5-ct. or 10-ct. stamps. Do not send *checks* except on large cities, as it costs from 10 to 25 cts. to collect.

W. F. L. Sanders, Supt. of the Cambridge City schools, has agreed to w ite a series of practical articles for the Journal on Arithmetic, beginning next month. Mr. Sanders has but few equals in the state in this special line of work. Those who have had the pleasure of hearing him treat this subject in institutes will hail with gladness this announ-ement.

THE JOURNAL is glad to be able to announce another addition to its corps of *regular* contributors. Cyrus W. Hodgin, principal of the Richmond Normal School, has been engaged to write regularly. Mr. Hodgin is recognized as one of the ablest instructors of the state, and will add strength to the Journal's corps of able contributors.

No other educational paper in the United States employs so large a number of regular contributors; and it will be noticed that each of these is eminent in his special department.

This insures a good variety of the freshest and best matter for each issue.

WANTED—*June* and *September* Journals for 1885. Any one having one or both these numbers in good condition will confer a great favor upon persons who desire to complete their files by sending them to this office. Doubtless many of the Journal readers have one or both these copies *extra* which they receive 1 as sample copies at institutes; others having read them do not care to preserve their files complete and would be willing to part with them.

We will be glad to extend the time of subscription *one month*, of any one, for each of the above named Journals returned. Please send name and address, that due credit may be given.

Please send at once, and confer a special favor

INDIANA READING CIRCLE EXHIBIT AT ST. LOUIS —Hubert M. Skinner, the efficient secretary of the Reading Circle Board, has been at no little trouble to make an exhibit of the Indiana Reading Circle at the St. Louis Exposition. He visited St Louis in person, and secured an appropriate alcove and displayed in an attractive way the "Indiana Plan," the text-books used, together with all blanks, explanations and suggestions, necessary to a complete understanding of the system.

This will add to Indiana's already respectable educational standing, and Mr. Skinner deserves the thanks of Indiana teachers.

WHAT WORDS TO SPELL —The Journal wishes to again enter its protest against the custom that requires children to spell *all* the words found in their daily lessons. The spelling of proper names, whether of persons, places, or things, as well as technical and scientific words, excepting only those of unusual note and frequent use, should not be required. A vast deal of time is "fooled away" in learning to spell words, the spelling of which will never be required in after life, simply because they may come up in *examination*. In practical life we only spell the words that we have to *write*, and the class of words referred to above almost never occur in written composition.

How much wiser it would be to occupy the time of the children in drills upon the words that enter into every-day life. The words that are always used and generally misspelled are such words as: happy, copy, too, sure, balance, there, till, separate, precede, exceed, supersede, allege, salable, judgment, etc , etc

Words like these are the words to spell and drill upon, and when they are learned there will be little time left to devote to those words which seldom or never enter written composition, though some of them may occasionally be employed in oral speech.

GEMS OF THOUGHT.

To err is human ; to forgive, divine.—*Pope.*

" I wasted Time, and now Time doth waste me."

They that will not be counselled can not be helped.

The eyes of other people are the eyes that ruin us.—*Franklin.*

That man lives twice, who lives the first life well.—*Rob't Herrick.*

I'd rather be right than be President of the United States.—*Henry Clay.*

'If you do what you should not, you must bear what you would not.—*Franklin.*

> He prayeth well who loveth well,
>   Both man and bird and beast;
> He prayeth best who loveth best,
>   All things both great and small;
> For the dear God who loveth us,
>   He made and loveth all.　　　　*—Coleridge.*

The talent of success is nothing more than doing what you can do *well*, and doing *well* whatever you do, without a thought of fame.—*Longfellow.*

> Truth crushed to earth, will rise again;
> The eternal years of God are hers:
> But error, wounded, writhes in pain,
> And dies amid his worshipers.　　　*—Bryant.*

"Seek the right though the wrong be tempting,
  Speak the truth at any cost."

There's room enough on every hand
For men of muscle, brain, and nerve.—*Wallace Bruce.*

> Do not look for wrong and evil,
>   You will find them if you do;
> As you measure for your neighbor,
>   He will measure back to you.　　　*—Alice Cary.*

There is no substitute for thorough-going, ardent, sincere earnestness.—*Dickens.*

> —Know whate'er
> Beyond its natural power hurries on
> The sanguine tide; whether the frequent bowl,
> High seasoned fare, or exercise to toil
> Protracted, spurs to its last stage tired life,
> And sows the temples with untimely snow.
> 　　　　　　　　*—Dr. John Armstrong.*

Ignorance breeds monsters to fill up all the vacancies of the soul that are unoccupied by the virtues of knowledge. He who dethrones the idea of law bids chaos welcome in its stead.—*Horace Mann.*

QUESTIONS AND ANSWERS.

QUESTIONS PREPARED BY STATE BOARD FOR SEPTEMBER.

SCIENCE OF TEACHING.—1. What is attention?

2. What is spelling? Its first stage?

3. Which should be taught first, elementary drawing or writing? Why?

4. Why is the word-method in reading preferable to the phonic?

5. What reason would you give for teaching the figures during the first year in number work?

These questions are based on the Reading Circle work of last season.

PHYSIOLOGY.—Describe in detail the alimentary canal and the structure of its different parts. Describe the digestive fluids, their functions and the glands which secrete them. Trace a piece of bread and butter from the mouth till its nutritive part enters the circulation.

- Answer must not exceed three pages.

HISTORY.—Give an account of the causes that led to the Civil War; the circumstances connected with its opening; the changes of policy on the part of the North during its prosecution; the events that marked its close, and the eonstruction policies adopted for the restoration of the Union as a whole.

Answer not to exceed three pages. To be marked on character of work rather than on sphcific points.

PENMANSHIP.— I. Write the stem (or semi extended) letters. What instruction would you give to a class before writing the letter "*h*"? 2 pts, 5 each.

2. State, in order, the steps you would take in giving a lesson to a class in penmanship.

3. Write the capital letters which may be formed from the seventh principle.

4. Name and make the principles used in forming the small letters.

5. In what order should the letters be presented to a class of beginners? What should determine the order? 2 pts, 5 each.

The answers to these questions should be wrtten with ink, as a specimen of penmanship, and marked 50 or below, according to merit.

ORTHOGRAPHY.—I. Define the terms penult, antepenult, and ultimatl.

2. Spell the plurals of the following words: Folio, negro, money, wife, atlas.

3. Of what value is the spelling-book as a text-book in school?

4. When do the letters *c* and *g* have the hard sound?

5. What is a syllable? Write a word in which a single letter forms a syllable.

6. Spell, accent, and mark diacritically ten words dictated by the superintendent. 50

GEOGRAPHY.—I. Define equator, latitude, longitude. What is the largest number of degrees of latitude that any place can have? Of longitude? 5 pts, 2 each.

2. Select two South American seaports and name the most important articles that each would contribute to a cargo intended for the U. S. markets.

. Sketch an outline map of France, showing the position of countries that touch it.

. Where is Trieste? Tokio? Bogota? Galveston? Newport?

5. Describe the climate of Italy. Locate three of the chief cities.

6. Compare and contrast Siberia and Hindostan with respect to climate, productions, and civilization.

7. Name all the large bodies of water that touch Europe.

8. Sketch the Mississippi river, with its five most important tributaries.

9. Explain the great prosperity of New York City.

10. Locate the most important copper mines in the United States.

GRAMMAR.—1. What are the principal parts of the verb? Why so called?

2. Give the principal parts of *go, do, see, rise, lie* (recline).

3. When is a noun in the nominative case?

4. Give the general rules for the formation of possessives, singular and plural.

5. What is meant by "comparison of adjectives?"

6. Give reasons for the number of verbs in the following sentences:
    a. The general and the statesman *is* dead.
    b. The jury *was* dismissed.
    c. The class *is* large.

7. Correct, if necessary:
    a. He don't hear you.
    b. Everybody should think twice before they speak.
    c. America was discovered during Ferdinand's and Isabella's reign.
    d. We were comparing Cæsar and Napoleon's victories.
    e. I can not think but what God is good.

8. Analyze: "When letters were first used is not certainly known."

9. Use "that" as a pronoun; as a conjunction, and as an adjective.

10. What does the moode of verbes denote? The voice? The tense?

READING.—1. Give a good method for testing the ability of pupils to call words at sight.

2. What is a good plan to pursue when teaching children the meaning of words?

3 What are the advantages and disadvantages of concert reading?

4. Which method do you prefer, the word, phonic, or alphabetic? Why?

5. Name three living American poets, and name one poem written by each.

6. Read a stanza of poetry and a paragraph of prose selected by the superintendent.

ARITHMETIC.—1. What is the cube root of 912673? Of what orders is the square of a number composed of tens and units? 5, 5.

2. A stock buyer wishes to invest the same amount of money in sheep at $3 each, hogs at $14 each, and cows at $21 each, as he does in beef cattle at $48 each. What is the smallest possible amount which he can invest in each? What is the difference between a divisor and a multiple of a number? 5, 5.

3. Multiply 15 thousandths by 15 hundredths, and from the product take 15 millionths. 5, 5.

4. A man sold a piece of cloth for $24, and thereby lost 25 per cent.; if he had sold it for $34 would he have gained or lost, and what per cent.? 5, 5.

5. If 40 yards of carpeting, ¾ of a yard wide will cover a floor, how many yards of matting, 1½ yards wide will cover a floor of equal size? 5, 5.

6. When it is 9:30 P. M. at New York (74° W.), in what longitude is it 11:45 P. M.? proc. 5, ans. 5.

7. A note of $1,250, dated July 5, 1868, was paid June 1, 1870, with interest at 8 per cent.; what was the amount paid? ans. 10.

8. At $7.62½ a cord, what will be the cost of a pile of wood 85 ft. 6 in. long, 8 ft. 4 in. high, and 5 ft. wide? 10

9. Divide 88 ℔. 16 pwt. 17 gr. by 54. ans. 10.

10. What is $\frac{1}{3} \times \frac{1-\frac{1}{3}}{2} \times \frac{2-\frac{1}{3}}{3} \times \frac{3-\frac{1}{3}}{5} \times \frac{4-\frac{1}{3}}{4}$ equal to? Ans. 10.

ANSWERS TO BOARD QUESTIONS PRINTED IN OCTOBER.

HISTORY.—1. In June, 1619, Gov. Yeardley, of Virginia, believing that the colonists should assist in their own government, called, at Jamestown, the first legislative body that ever met in America, consisting of the Governor, Council, and burgesses chosen from the various plantations. Its laws were valid only when ratified by the London Company, while on the other hand orders from the Company were without force until ratified by this Assembly.

2. The Royal Charter which united the Connecticut colonists, giving them rights beyond those given to any other colony, was demanded by Gov. Andrus after having been in force some twenty-four years. While an animated debate was taking place, in the presence of a large crowd who had gathered to take a last look at the Charter, the lights were suddenly put out, and when relit, the Charter was gone, Wm. Wadsworth having seized and hid it in the hollow of a tree, afterwards known as the "Charter Oak." Andrus declared the government at an end, and wrote *Finis* at the end of the minutes.

3. Had the Americans been willing to buy the tea under these circumstances it would have shown to the world that their refusal to pay taxes without representation was not based upon principle; whereas a determination to resist until the principle was recognized lay at the very foundation of the matter, and the tea was destroyed to show this feeling.

4. Kosciusko, La Fayette, Count Rochambeau, De Kalb, and Steuben.

5. Rhode Island.

6. The Star Spangled Banner, Francis S. Key.

7. The discovery of gold in California

8. Virginia. The people of the western part of the state, in two conventions, one held before, and one after the secession of Virginia, declared West Virginia independent of Virginia, and it was admitted into the Union under this title in 1863.

9. The trouble involved in the Presidential election, the result depending upon the legality of the votes in certain states. By a Joint Electoral Commission, composed of five Senators, five Representatives, and five Judges of the Supreme Court, who by a vote of 8 to 7 declared Hays and Wheeler elected by one majority in the Electoral College.

10. When Columbus first applied to the Spanish Monarchs for aid to prosecute his discovery of a west passage to the Indies, those monarchs were engaged in warfare with the Moors, who held Granada and other parts of Spain, the warfare being carried on largely from a religious motive to rid the country of the heretics and unbelievers, who were regarded as even worse than heathen. When the Moors were expelled the monarchs, especially Isabella, listened to the petitions of Columbus, whose discoveries if successful promised to add largely to the domain of the Church, and especially to that and the coffers of Spain, now thoroughly empty. Selling her personal jewels, Isabella enabled Columbus to prosecute his voyages with success.

SCIENCE OF TEACHING.—1. Curiosity is the feeling which arises from knowing part of a fact, coupled with the desire to know more or all of it. Curiosity results in that attent condition of the intellect we call interest, and when carried into a habit takes expression in that form of asking questions designated inquistiveness. Genuine curiosity is that which arises from intelligent judgment and good motives; spurious, that which is either assumed, or which depends on unintelligent judgment or bad motives.

2. An idea is fixed in memory by clear and decided perception, the condition of which is attention, definite classification or conception, pointed statement or definition, and lucid explanation. These

processes of acquisition are greatly re-enforced by applying and illustrating the idea, putting it into various forms of statement and by repetition in the way of drill. The value of each of these depends on the amount of attention with which it is done.

3. A pupil can not study or recite effectively when "laboring under strong emotions," because the attention is absorbed by it. Attention is incapable of division under such condition. Strong emotion absorbs, likewise, the mind's energy.

4. A person has a limited amount of nervous energy at any given time. This is not sufficient to habitually carry on at once active thinking and digestion. If this energy is expended on thinking, immediately after a meal, digestion will be retarded. Such action impairs the digestive organs by too long continued distention, arrest of the secretions, etc. Hence study should be omitted for a time after a full meal.

5. Prize-giving cultivates wrong motives. Study and other school-work should be done because of interest in it, and because it is the thing to be done, i. e., a duty. Prizes cultivate wrong habits. The school prepares for the world, and there no formal prizes incite to work. Prize-competition generally reduces itself to a very few members of a class and has very little effect on the rest. As a mode of control, prize-giving is fictitious and does not comport with even moderately high aims in education. It is a confession of weakness— the teacher buys what should be obtained otherwise. Finally, it is a premium put on lying and deceit.

READING.—1. The emphasis, inflection, tone of voice, kind of voice, etc., all depend upon the thought or the sentiment to be expressed. A careful analysis of a selection to be read fixes in the mind the thought and the feeling to be expressed, thus tending to arouse similar emotions in the reader and so make his oral reading more natural and more correct. In connection with such aid as the pupil obtains from such analysis, he should also have the help of training in voice-culture and in position.

2. The alphabet method of teaching reading has, as its first object, the form, name and order of the letters of the alphabet; as its second object, the sounds of these letters alone and in combination; and as its third object, the association of these letters and sounds as combined into words with the ideas which those words are designed to symbolize. It thus proceeds arbitrarily from the unknown and meaningless to the known; from the parts to the whole, as form and as symbol, the value of neither of which is as yet perceived by the child; and goes upon the assumption that the word is a synthesis of its letters. It also makes the word itself more prominent than the idea represented, when the latter is all that gives the former any

value. If anything, it is less arbitrary than the phonic method, though both are at variance with the natural method of growth of the child-mind.

3. (For answer to this question, see Sept. School Journal)

4. The reading classes in our public schools can acquire a knowledge of American literature in various ways:

(*a*) For the higher classes, one day in each week may be given to the study of authors and their works. [A method of doing this was indicated in the School Journal for January, 1880; also for February, April, and June, 1881.]

(*b*) For the lower classes, the committing of appropriate selections; the relating of incidents which they persuaded older members of the family to select and read to them ; the relating to them of other incidents, in connection with pieces assigned them, by the teacher; the recitation in concert each morning of memory gems written upon the black-board by the teacher, etc.

(*c*) In addition to this, in connection with the regular recitations in reading, a brief biography or some interesting facts of an author may be given, suggestions may be made by the teacher of an instructive work which it would pay the pupils to read, etc , etc. In short, there are numberless ways in which the appetites of the pupils might be whetted by the shrewd teacher. Thus tell them the old German legend of Peter Klaus, and then suggest Washington Irving's "Rip Van Winkle."

5. Five American poets and one selection from each : Longfellow, "Evangeline"; Bryant, "The Flood of Years"; Poe, "The Bells"; John G. Holland, "Kathrina"; Alice Cary, "Pictures of Memory."

PHYSIOLOGY.—1. Alcohol in fermented liquors is produced by the decomposition of grape sugar, or glucose.

2. Glands are composed of cells of various shapes, into which bloodvessels pass and out of which ducts carry its secretions, and veins or lymphatics its worn out or unused material. Among the glands of the body may be named the liver, the pancreas, the spleen, the salivary glands, the thyroid gland, etc.

3 A hair consists of a root and stem. The root is fixed in a fold or depression of the cuticle and receives its nourishment from the true skin. The stem grows upward from the root by the formation of new cells beneath. From without inward the stem is composed of (*a*) the hair cuticle, (*b*) the cortex, (*c*) usually, the medulla.

5. A vertebra is one of the bones which, united, form the backbone, or spinal column. It is made up, anteriorily, cf a body, solid and somewhat cylindrical in form ; posteriorly, of an arch, called the neural arch, and various processes, seven in number. To the twelve dorsal vertebræ the ribs are attached.

The nose is composed partly of bones, partly of cartilage, and partly of muscles, skin, etc. It has two cavities or nostrils, opening anteriorily into the atmosphere and posteriorly into the pharynx. Ducts from the lakes of the eyes empty surplus tears into its upper part.

7. With some persons, near-sightedness is a natural defect; with others, it is the result of the habit of holding the book too near the face, of stooping over too much in reading or writing at the desk, etc., etc.

8. There are, in early life, four bones in each ear. In later life, one of these, the orbicular, unites with the stapes, and is then no longer styled a separate bone. They are stretched across the middle chamber of the ear and convey sounds made upon the *membrana tympani* to the inner ear

9. The crystalline lens is a small, double-convex, transparent and colorless lens, situated in the eye just back of the circular opening in the iris. Its posterior surface is more curved than its anterior surface, it is contained within a capsula, and its shape is constantly varying with the distance from us of the object examined, so as always to bring the rays of light to a focus upon the retina.

10. The pulse is the waves of blood sent along the arteries by the contraction of the left ventricle of the heart. The rapidity or the slowness with which these waves succeed each other, together with their volume, is a very good criterion by which to test the condition of the health of an individual.

GEOGRAPHY.—1. (*a*) Malyas, Mongolians, Caucassians. (*b*) Arctic, Pacific, Indian.

2. (*a*) Coffee, sugar, spices, rare woods. (*b*) Manila, on the western coast of the island of Luzon, (one of the Philippines) is the largest city.

3. (*a*) Corsica, Sardinia, Sicily, Candia and Cyprus. (*b*) Naples, Valencia; Marseilles, Genoa, Palermo.

4. The English Channel separates England from France. The Baltic Sea separates Sweden from Russia and Prussia. Amsterdam is situated on an arm of the Zuyder Zee in Holland. Port Natal is on the southeast coast of Africa, in the colony of Natal. British Guiana is the western division of the country of Guiana, in the northern part of South America.

5. The government in China and Russia is an absolute monarchy; in Brazil, a limited monarchy; in France and Mexico, republican.

6. The Andes mountains in the central part arrest the moisture of the warm winds and cause rainfall on the eastern slopes. In the south, westerly winds prevail, and there is a heavy rainfall on the western slopes, while on the eastern side, desert regions occur. On

the eastern slope of the tropical Andes occurs at different elevations the vegetation peculiar to every zone.

8. (*a*) Mississippi, Missouri, Ohio, Hudson, Arkansas. (*b*) Merrimac, Kennebec, Saco, Androscoggin, Genesee.

9. Coal, iron and petroleum could be profitably taken from Pittsburgh, while wheat and dressed meats would be found in Cincinnati.

10. The moisture of the ocean when evaporated, is circulated by the impulsive force of the winds, and falling upon the lands is distributed over the continents.

GRAMMAR.—1. (1) Subject; as, *You* are mistaken.

(2) Object; as, The ball struck *him*.

(3) Possessive; as, *Her* dress is becoming.

(4) Predicate; as, It is *I*.

(5) Indirect object; as, Give *me* liberty, or give *me* death.

2. (1) There is a fierce conflict between good and evil; but good is in the ascendant, and must triumph.

(2) Avoid affectation: it is a contemptible weakness.

3. (1) Relative pronoun; as, The tree *which* I planted is growing.

(2) Relative adverb; as, He visited the place *where* the battle was fought.

4. Both may be used as nouns, adjectives, or adverbs. They may have the same modifiers. They differ from each other chiefly in form, and are unlike the finite verb in that they do not predicate anything.

5. (1) The *army* (singular) is on the march.

(2) The *audience* (plural) were well pleased.

(3) Several committees (plural form) were appointed.

6. (1) Give it to *whoever comes*. The object of *to* is the clause that follows.

(2) Who do you suppose it was. *Who* is nom. by predication after *was*.

(3) *Whomsoever* I send will go. *Whomsoever* is the object of *send*.

7. The subjunctive states not what is real, but what is doubtful; or a mere supposition or conception of the mind.

8. This is a simple declarative sentence, of which 'The dark unfathomed caves of ocean" is the logical subject; "bear full many a gem of purest ray serene" is the logical predicate; "Caves" is the subject nominative, modified by the adjectives "dark" and "unfathomed," and also by the prep. phrase "of ocean"; the predicate verb is "bear," modified by the object "gem"; "gem' 's modified by the complex adjective "many a," and by the prep. phrase "of purest ray serene," of which "ray" is the principal word, modified by the

adjectives "purest" and "serene"; "full" is an adverb, and modifies the compl x adjective "many a."

9. (1) *For* is a conjunction, introducing the sentence. (2) *To steal* is used as a noun and the subject of *is*.

10. A clause is a dependent proposition and does not express a complete thought.

ARITHMETIC.—2. 5 yr. 7 mo. 5 da. = $\frac{671}{120}$ yr. $41,361.18×.06×$\frac{671}{120}$ yr. =$13876.675 int., Ans.

3. 2 yr. 6 mo. 15 da.=$\frac{51}{24}$ yr. $407.088, am't.—$345.60, prin.,=$61.488, int. $61.488÷($345.60×.01×$\frac{51}{24}$ yr.)=7%, Ans.

4. 4 mo.+3 da. = $\frac{43}{120}$ yr.; $1×.09×$\frac{43}{120}$=$\frac{43}{120}$. $1—$\frac{43}{120}$=$.96925. $811+$96825=$836.728, face of note.

5. $1 — $.014 = $.986, proceeds of $1. discounted for 63 days. $.986+ $.0125=$.9985, cost of $1. $798.80+$.9980=$800, face.

6. (64.5+.5)—(64.5×.5)=32.75, Ans. (If decimal point be wrong, it should be, (64.5+.05)—(64.5×.05)=61.325, Ans.)

7.

	$3.125 = cost per bu.
2 pk. = $\frac{1}{2}$ bu.	$1.5625
4 qt. = $\frac{1}{2}$ of 2 pk.	.390625
2 qt. = $\frac{1}{2}$ of 4 qt.	.1953125
I qt. = $\frac{1}{2}$ of 2 qt.	.09765625
	$2.246+, Ans.

8. 40 rd. : 15 rd.
   6 ft. : 4.5 ft.
   3 ft. : 2 ft. : 32 min. : : (?).
   12 da. : 9 da.
   6 hr. : 8 hr. Ans., 6 men.

9. Their property bears the same relation as 6, 3, 2.
   $\frac{6}{11}$ A's; $\frac{3}{11}$ B's; $\frac{2}{11}$ C's.
   $\frac{6}{11}$ of $4675 = $2550, A's.
   $\frac{3}{11}$ "   "   = $1275, B's.
   $\frac{2}{11}$ "   "   = $850, C's.

10. $\sqrt{96^2 \mid 72^2}$ = 120 rd., Ans.

MISCELLANY.

INDIANA TEACHERS' READING CIRCLE—OUTLINES.

BROOKS' MENTAL SCIENCE FOR NOV., 1885.

Subject: Intuitions of the Beautiful, pp. 345-370.

I. TERMS TO BE UNDERSTOOD.—1. "Hogarth's Line of Beauty," p. 351. 2. Ruskin's Idea of Beauty, p. 352. 3. Character as defined, p. 353. 4. Moral Sublimity, p 358. 5. Incongruous, p. 361.

II. SUMMARIES.—1. Subjective Theories of the Beautiful. 2. Objective Theories of the Beautiful. 3. Elements of Sublimity.

4. Elements of the Ludicrous. 5. Forms of the Ludicrous. 6. Elements of Taste.

III. CLASSIFICATION OF WRITERS AS TO THE "IDEA OF BEAUTY." 1. Holding the Subjective Theory: Sir G. Mackenzie, Sir Thomas Brown, Upham, Lord Jeffrey, Sir Archibald Alison, Thomas Reid, Victor Cousin, Kant, Schiller, Fichte, Alexander Bain. 2. Holding the Objective Theory: Galen, Marmontel, Earl Shaftesbury, Hutcheson, Hogarth, Aristotle, Augustine, Crousez, Andre, Hume (?) Kames. 3. Holding the Spiritual Theory: Schelling, Hegel, Jouffroy, Dr. Ruhlert, Plato, Dr. Hickock, Ruskin.

IV. CONCERNING "TASTE."—1. "Taste is the power of discerning and relishing the beautiful."—*Reid.*

2. "Judgment in respect to the beautiful we call *taste*, in respect to the right, conscience."—*Haven.*

3. "Taste is that faculty or those faculties of the mind, which are affected with, or form a judgment of the works of imagination and the elegant arts "—*Burke.*

4. "Taste consists in the improvement of the internal senses, viz., sense of novelty, sublimity, beauty, imitation, harmony, etc."—*Gerard.*

5. By taste is meant—

> " * * * * * those internal powers,
> Active and strong and feelingly alive
> To each fine impression." —*Akenside.*

6. "A lively sensibility is the basis of a correct taste; but persons of the liveliest sensibility are not always, perhaps not generally, persons of the nicest taste. Like every other faculty of the mind, taste requires cultivation."—*Haven.*

7. "Varieties of taste depend far more upon differences of culture and the influence of fashion, than upon differences of mental nature."—*Munsell.*

8. "In uncultured minds the emotional element of taste predominates; in cultivated, the intellectual element."—*Munsell.*

9. "Imagination and taste are sometimes confounded. Imagination creates; taste judges of the creation. A fertile imagination may be combined with a very imperfect taste; a correct taste with weak imagination."—*Wayland.*

10 "The books, statues, pictures and edifices which have received the approbation and admiration of all cultivated minds, form a practical standard of taste."—*Alden.*

V. CONCERNING ÆSTHETICS IN GENERAL —1. "The study of beauty has a tendency to refine and ennoble the mind."—*Alden.*

2. For acquaintance with the beautiful, read Milton's "Comus" and the "Fourth Book of Paradise Lost."

3. "The æsthetic activities in general may be expected to play an increasing part in human life as evolution advances."—*Herbert Spencer.*

SCIENCE OF TEACHING.
Hewett's Pedagogy——Pages 75 to 116.

WORK FOR SEPTEMBER AND OCTOBER.—The work for the first month included Hewett's Pedagogy, pp. 9–75. It comprised a brief review of the psychology of education and a consideration of what education is. The mental-science course of last year furnishes all the facts necessary for the review. The work done included, we believe, Brooks' Mental Science, pp. 13–318. The consideration of what education is on its practical side was met, at least in part by the study of Parker's Talks on Teaching.

WORK FOR NOVEMBER —The work for this month comprises two general topics: the Kinds of Education and the Teacher. Each of these ideas is to be logically unfolded, its limitations fixed, both as a whole and as made of parts, its place in each student's system of knowledge fixed, and its practical application made, so far as possible, to the real problems of the school-room

TERMS AND IDEAS IN THE FIRST.—Each of the following sets of terms needs careful discrimination: Development Education, breaking (as of animals), training (as of mere drill); culture, "physical," "intellectual," "moral" and "spiritual," as applied to education; "spontaneous" and "formal," as applied to education; the education of the family, of the church, of polite society, of the business world, of politics, and of the school; as a science and as an art.

TERMS AND IDEAS IN THE SECOND.—Teacher and learner; desire to do good, love for the work, "enthusiasm for humanity," desire for a career; and personal adaptation, as applied to the teacher.

Those who care to study deeper than an examination of terms and a mastery of the text bearing on the kinds of education, will find the best treatise in Rosenkranz' "Pedagogics as a System," pp. 98 to 148, taken in connection with Mr. Harris' Notes. Address Jones & Co., publishers, St. Louis. Price $1.50.

A study of the typical teacher will be best accomplished in one volume in Quick's "Educational Reformers." It furnishes sketches of Locke, Montaigne, Ratisch, Basedow, Rousseau, Pestalozzi, and of their ideals of what the teacher should be and become. Robert Clarke & Co., Cincinnati, publish a Reading Circle Edition at $1 00.

OUTLINE OF THE CONCEPTION OF THE TEACHER.—I. As a person: Good health; perfect body; good character; mental ability. II. As a professional person: Adaptation to pursuit; knowledge of material on which education is wrought; knowledge of ideas (in the form of "subjects") as the means by which the pupil's minds are to be developed; correct ideals of the results to be wrought. III. As a citizen: A person of influence in his or her locality; properly paid; not a recluse, but a "citizen of the world"; a forceful personality in the family, church, society and the state.

QUOTATIONS BEARING ON THE TEACHER.—"The governor [teacher], then, must be able to sympathize with his pupil, and, on his account should be young. * ' * * as young as possible consistent with his having attained necessary discretion and sagacity. * * * There are not things enough in common between childhood and manhood to form a solid attachment at so great a distance."—*Quick's Paraphrase of Rousseau.*

"The present race of school-masters sacrifice the essence of true teaching to separate and disconnected teaching in a complete jumble of subjects. By dishing up fragments of all kinds of truths, they destroy the spirit of truth itself, and extinguish the power of self-dependence which, without that spiri , can not exist."—*Pestalozzi.*

"Every one can teach; and, moreover, can teach that what he does not know himself."—*Jacotot's Paradox.*

"It is not boards, nor superintendents, nor committees that decide the character of S.: it is the teacher; and the teacher should be the center of dignity and the depository of power."—*Gail Hamilton.*

"To refine manners, develop thought, and fill young souls with noble aspirations is the every-day duty of his [the teacher's] high calling. He is intrusted by the state with one of its most tender cares, and it looks to him almost wholly for the accomplishment of what is really its highest and noblest ambition—the formation of minds such as will enhance its society, perfect its laws, and adorn its history."—*Walsh, Lawyer in the School-Room.*

————:o:————

ENGLISH LITERATURE.
Smith's Outlines ———— Pages 29–69.

1. GOWER.—Story-telling first represented in our literature by him. He belongs to an older school than does Chaucer. He is touched by the French influence, not by Italian. His tales are told with a special moral. His three great works were written in three different languages, French, Latin, and English. This shows the unsettled state of our literary language. Gower was a careful writer of English, but he mingles allegory, morality, the sciences, the philosophy of Aristotle, all the studies of the day with comic or tragic tales as illustrations. Hence the tales are less attractive and even become wearisome, not only from their length but the smoothness of the verse.

2. CHAUCER.—His Times. (*a*) The physical and social condition of the people. (*b*) The religious and political agitation.

The causes of the development of religious poetry before the story-telling poetry which culminated in Chaucer, were the pretensions of the Friars and cries for truth and purity in life and in the church, and a movement for the equal rights of man against the class system of the middle ages. In addition to these there were causes growing out of the misery of the English people on account of the French wars, and also the ravages of the great pl gue. In their misery and terror they fled to religion. The "Vision of Piers the Plowman," being essentially religious, reflects the conditions of the English people.

The Normans brought a historical taste with them to England. Out of the historical literature created by them grew story-telling.

Characteristics of Chaucer as a writer: 1. Variety and power of diction. 2. Invention. 3. A borrower, but like Shakespe re lending to all that he borrows the wonderful influence of his own fancy. 4. A painter of nature. The grass, the birds, the flowers—all natui e revealed its lf to his penetrating eye. 5. Character painter. His "pilgrims" seem each a separate portrait as to costume, disposition, habits, antecedents. Each character is typical. 6. He is an artist. He is full of emotion and joy in his own thoughts. He writes for the pleasure of writing. 7. He made English a means of poetry. I e welded the various elements in the language into one tool for the use of literature.   EMMA MONT. McRAE.

COMMISSIONED HIGH SCHOOLS.—The State Board at a recent meeting commissioned the high schools of the following places to send graduates to the State University without examination, viz:

Auburn, Aurora, Anderson, Amboy, Bedford, Bloomington, Bloomfield, Bluffton, Brookville, Brownstown, Butler, Brazil, Cambridge C ty, Connersville, Covington, Columbus, Columbia City, Crown Point, Crawfordsville, Decatur, Dublin, Delphi, Edinburg, Elkhart, Evansville, Franklin, Frankfort, Fort Wayne, Goshen, Greensburg, Greencastle, Huntington, Indianapolis, Jeffersonville, Kokomo, Kendallvill , Lawrenceburg, Logansport, Lafayette, La Porte, Lagrange, Madison, Marion, Martinsville, Muncie, Mishawaka, Monticello, New Castle, N w Albany, Noblesville, Peru, Peters urg, Portland, Princeton, Rensselaer, Richmond, Rockport, Rochester, Rushville, Salem, Seymour, Spencer, Shannon, South Bend, Sullivan, Shelbyville, Tipton, Terre Haute, Union City, Valparaiso, Vevay, Vincennes, Wabash, Washington, Winchester.

AMERICAN NORMAL COLLEGE.—This school, located at Logansport, seems to be getting a firm footing. It has recently again been reorganized. The principal, Walter Sayler, retires, B. B Bigler having purchased his interest in the school. The present proprietors are Charles E. Kircher, principal; W. S. Harshman, secretary; E. M. C. Hobbs, treasurer; B. B. Bigler, librarian. The present management starts out with a determination to do work that will merit success.

4

QUERY.—What letters are never doubled?

A joint township institute will be held at Fortville, Nov. 21st.

The Whitley county institute has been postponed till the holidays.

Supt. W. S. Sims has issued a very complete manual of the Clinton county schools.

The Steuben county institute will open at Angola November 9th—R. N. Carlin, Supt.

The Normal Department of De Pauw, under the direction of S. S. Parr, is moving on satisfactorily.

Houghton, Mifflin & Co., of Boston, publish a large list of the best literary works. Send for catalogue.

The City Superintendents of Indiana and Ohio will hold a meeting at Richmond November 5th, 6th, and 7th.

The State Normal School continues to run smoothly under the direction of its new principal, W. W. Parsons.

The Department of English and History in Purdue University, is remarkably popular under the direction of E. E. Smith.

"The Purdue" is the name of the college paper at Purdue University. The first number for this academic year looks well and reads well.

SPENCER.—The reports show that the schools have started well. The local papers are freely used, which is a good step. Supt. Harwood is a worker.

"The Public School" is the name of the paper published for the teachers of Tippecanoe county by Supt. W. H. Caulkins. It is filled with good things.

MONTGOMERY COUNTY.—The teachers will hold a two days' association November 27-8. A good program has been provided and a large attendance is expected.

Mrs. Eudora Hailman opened a training school for kindergartners at La Porte October 5th. Mrs. Hailman has earned a high standing among kindergarten teachers.

The Calendar of the La Porte schools for 1884-5 is at hand. It is characteristic of the able Supt., W. N. Hailman, and contains much that is instructive and suggestive.

NOBLESVILLE.—The schools are full to overflowing, and the work is being pushed with vigor. The high school has enrolled 82. Supt. G. F. Kenaston is making a good start.

VALPARAISO.—The schools here are prosperous. They have been under the supervision of W. H. Banta for twelve or fifteen years. He is assisted by a good corps of teachers.

The teachers of Parke county will hold their regular annual association the Friday and Saturday following Thanksgiving. This date belongs to Parke county for such meetings by right of discovery and occupation.

The Kosciusko county institute was ably taught by J. Fraise Richard, of Logansport; Prof J. B. Demott, of Depauw; H. B. Brown, and others. The attendance was not large but the interest was good. Supt. Anglin is a hard worker.

The *Practical Teacher*, of Chicago, Col. F. W. Parker, editor, has been sold to E. L. Kellogg & Co., of New York, and will be combined with "The Teachers' Institute." Chicago seems to be a bad climate for educational papers.

BLOOMINGDALE ACADEMY is reported as starting out with a good attendance and excellent prospects. With Hiram Hadiey and his wife, both superior teachers, in charge, the school deserves success, and certainly must win its way.

BOURBON.—The annual report for 1884-5 shows the schools of this enterprising little town to be in good condition. A new school building adds very much to the facilities for making a good school. Supt. A. Whiteleather seems to be doing a good work.

The North Central and South American Exposition will open at New Orleans November 10th and continue till March 31st. This will afford another opportunity to visit, at low rates, the "Sunny South," and see one of the most interesting cities in America.

SHELBYVILLE.—The report from the schools for October indicates an increased attendance over any previous year, and a healthy condition of the schools. The trustees, the great bulk of the people, and the superintendent, W. H. Fertich, are working in perfect harmony.

The *Journal of Education*, which has for nearly eleven years past been published at 16 Hawley street, Boston, has outgrown its old quarters and removed to No. 3 Somerset street. This is good news and the proprietor and editor-in-chief, Thomas W. Bicknell, is to be congratulated.

The State Teachers' Association will meet Tuesday, December 29th. The program is about complete and is excellent. In addition to good home talent, Jas. B. Angell, Pres. Michigan University, and J. P. Wickersham, for 18 years State Supt. of Pennsylvania, will be present and lecture. Let ev ry teacher plan to attend.

OWEN COUNTY.—The Board of Education at its Sept. meeting unanimously passed the following resolution:

"We, the trustees of Owen county, do favor and adopt the following resolution: 'That we will use our influence among our teachers for the suppression of dram-drinking, card-playing, dancing, and the use of profane language by them.'"

ALLEN COUNTY.—The institute which closed October 30th was one of the best ever held. The chief workers were W. W. Parsons and Chas. F. Coffin. The attendance was large and interest excellent. Over 150 teachers, outside of Ft. Wayne, joined the Reading Circle. This is splendid. The teachers voted to tax themselves $2.00 each to pay able instructors to conduct a 4-week normal next summer. The. Supt. subscribed $25 to this purpose. The new Supt., Geo. F. Felts, is making an excellent start.

The Fo t Wayne College opened its fall term Sept. 14th. The class of students in attendance is unusually good. Tne course of study has been revised and extended, and few institutions of similar grade are better prepared for good thorough work. A fine new building was erected last summer and is now fully occupied. Teachers desiring to qualify themselves for higher positions will find the Normal course exceedingly thorough and practical. A teachers' reading circle will be organized Nov 23d, and evening sessions will be held to discuss the topics prescribed in this course.

HONOR SCHOLARSHIPS.—Hereafter the trustees of the State University will award, each year, t) the best tudent in the Senior Class of each of the commissioned high schools of the state, an "Honor Scholarship," which shall entitle the holder to the benefits of the University, free of all fees except the library fee, the laboratory fee, and the fee for graduation. This exemption amounts to $15.00 per year, or $60 00 for the entire course. Similar scholarships will also be given to the best three students in the Senior Year of the Pr :paratory School. Further details will be given to those specially interested in this matter.

TIPPECANOE COUNTY.—Purdue University has a Freshman class which numbers 75 students; a Sophomore class numbering 28; a Junior class numbering 9, and a Senior class numbering 16. The Freshman class last year numbered 67.

The La Fayette high school numbers nearly 100 members, a very decided increase over the attendance last year. J. A. Zeller is doing very efficient and very satisfactory work as Principal.

The Chauncey public school, near La Fayette, numbers this year 224 pupils, the largest enrollment it has ever had. E. R. Smith continues as principal, assisted by Worth Reed, Ava Cory, Josie Warnack, and J. Doty.

Prof. E. E. Smith, of Purdue University, lectured to the teachers' association of White county, at Brookston, on October 17th.

The superintendent of Tippecanoe county travels over more than five hundred square miles of territory in visiting the different schools of that county.

The Faculty of Purdue University, by majority vote, have at last decided to permit the students of that institution to join and attend the meetings of College Secret Fraternies. Pres. Smart announced the fact to the students in chapel on Sept. 30th, but stated that the permission granted was limited to students of the Junior and Senior classes.

STATE UNIVERSITY.—The trustees hereafter will award, each year, an "honor scholarship" to the best student in the Senior class of each commissioned high school. The University classes are as follows: Seniors, 20; Juniors, 25; Sophomores, 46; Freshman, 84. President Jordan is complimented on every hand, and is rapidly popularizing the University.

XENIA —J. Goodykoontz, who has charge of these schools, makes one of his characteristic reports, giving information to parents and teachers, in a neat 3 column, 4·page sheet, entitled " The· Public School."

The Proceedings, with all the addresses of the second meeting of the Frœbel Institute, held at Madison, Wis., July 1884, in neat pamphlet form, can be had of Supt. W. N Hailman, of La Porte.

Dr. W. T. Harris, of Concord, Mass.; L. H. Jones, Supt. of the Indianapolis schools, and W. H. Ernst, Supt. of Well; county, have been appointed visitors to the State Normal School.

SPENCER.—This township reading circle enrolls 21 members, and includes all the Spencer teachers. Samuel E. Harwood, Supt. of the Spencer schools, is an active and efficient worker.

PERSONAL.

A. T. Reid has charge at Oxford.

M. S. Smith is principal of the Kewanna schools,

J. C. Comstock has control at Michigantown this year.

J. S. White is principal of the Noblesville high school.

F. S. Mulkey is in charge of the schools at Leavenworth.

R. H. Harney continues in charge of the Lebanon schools.

Bailey Martin, of the State Normal, is principal of the Franklin high school.

R. D. Mellen is the name of the new Supt. of Warrick county. His address is Boonville.

S. S. Hamill, the elocutionist, has recently fallen heir to a neat little fortune, amounting to about $166,000.

Geo. W. Weimer is principal of the Cochran schools. The published report shows the schools in good condition.

W. D. Howells, the novelist, has accepted an offer of $10,000 a year to write exclusively for the Harper publicat ons.

D. S. Kelley, late superintendent of the Jeffersonville schools, is now at work as Prof of Natural History in the State Normal School at Emporia, Kansas.

E. C. White, late principal of the Albion schools, has gone to Callao, South Amer ca, to take charge of the schools at a salary of $1500 and traveling expenses.

M. F. Cowdery, formerly Supt. of the Sandusky, O., schools. and one of Ohio's ablest educators, died recently at his home in Sandusky. His book on Morals was one of the first and is still one of the best for school use.

A E. Mourer, a teacher of high character and much respected, in Wabash county, recently departed this life. The teachers of Chester township at their October meeting passed a series of highly complimentary resolutions with reference to their late co-laborer.

BOOK TABLE.

The Earlhamite has donned a new coat and improved its looks

Mind in Natnre, is the name of a new magazine of a high literary character.

The Hillsdale Advance, edited by Prof. Fisk, of Hillsdale College, Mich., should be in the hands of every friend of this excellent institution.

The School-Music Journal, published by F. H. Gilson, Boston, is a monthly devoted to music in schools and methods of teaching. The first number looks well.

Lessons in Geography, by J. T. Scovell, of Terre Haute, has been revised, enlarged to 80 pages and reissued. It is very suggestive. Used in connection with an ordinary geography it will give a student a good idea of physical geography.

The Popular Science Monthly is what its name indicates It treat; a great variety of topics in a style free from technic lities, within the comprehension of all. It discusses subjects that pertain t> every-day life and is valuable to any intelligent reader. Published by D. Appleton & Co. Price $5.

Grammar and Analysis Made Easy and Attractive by Diagrams. By F. V. Irish. Published by the author, at Lima, Ohio.

This little book of 118 pages contains about 600 different sentences, diagrammed by Prof. Irish's "Improved Straight-line System."

These include all the difficult sentences in Harvey's Grammar, with numerous sentences from other grammars.

The Century Magazine, published by the Century Company, New York City, continues to rank with the best monthlies of the world. The best writers contribute to it and it is richly and profusely illustrated. Its circulation is much above *one hundred thousand*, and extends to both continents. Its articles on the late war, by active participants on both sides, has added much to its popularity and circulation.

The Wide-Awake, published by D. Lothrop & Co., of Boston, with its years loses none of its attractions. Entering upon its 22d volume it offers to its readers six illustrated serials by as many well-known writers, among whom we find Harriet Prescott Spofford and Charles Egbert Craddock. In its C. Y. F. R. U. department a series of articles on American authors makes it valuable as well as entertaining. A year's subscription to this magazine makes a valuable Christmas gift.

Barnes's Elementary Geography. By James Monteith. New York and Chicago: A. S. Barnes & Co. Cyrus Smith, Indianapolis, Ag't for Indiana and Michigan.

This is a marked improvement on the old book by the same author. It is primary not only in name and size, but in matter and method, which is a good deal to say for a "primary geography." The book contains excellent maps and is beautifully illustrated. It is a very attractive little book.

Cæsar's Gallic War. Seven Books. Edited by J. H. and W. F. Allen and J. B. Greenough. Revised; with notes and dissertations, fully illustrated, on Cæsar's Gallic Campaigns and the Roman milita y art, by H. P. Judson, principal high school, Troy, N. Y. Boston: Ginn & Company.

Among the features that contribute to the interest and excellence of this new book are, the picture of the Roman Legionary in full armor, the diagrams illustrating the movements of the armies in celebrated battles, the large amount of information on the military affairs of the Romans, judicious notes with reference to Harkness's and Gildersleeve's Grammars, as well as to Allen and Greenough's, and a superior vocabulary by J. B Greenough.

How we Live: or The Human Body, and How to Take Care of It. By James Johonnot and Eugene Bouton. New York: D. Appleton & Co. C. E. Lane, Chicago, Western Agent.

This is a small book on Physiology, intended for use in the common schools. It aims to present the laws of life in such a simple and interesting way that they will become the guide to living. The effects of alcohol and narcotics on the system receive careful and full consideration. The book is well illustrated and is very attractive in its general appearance.

Tennyson's Poems. Published by T. Y. Crowel , New York.

The announcement of a complete edition of Tennyson's Poems in a single volume is good news to every admirer of the poet-laureate. Such a beautiful book, too—exquisite binding—full gilt, smooth paper, easy print, bordered pages, fine and frequent illustrations, added to the poems of the greatest living poet, and who will not say that $5 00 is a small eq iivalent for so much. Of the contents of the book, nothing need be said ; only its style and general make-up this notice desires to make public. For a holiday gift, nothing could be more desirable.

Howard's Elementary Arithmetic. By Chas. L. Howard. New York : Potter, Ainsworth & Co.

This little book proceeds in a logical way from the concrete to the abstract—embodying the best ideas in the presentation of matter. Formal rules are not given, the author taking the ground that "if principles are understood rules are useless."

The higher book follows the logical methods employed here. The series is certainly an excellent one.

The same house furnishes at low rates number tablets for supplem :ntary work, and standard composition books.

Exercise Manual in Geometry. By Wentworth & Hill. Boston : Ginn, Heath & Co.

This book is aimed to furnish, in convenient form, a large number of exercises for original investigation. A brief and logically arranged syllabus is given, for quick and easy reference, and may be used by either t acher or pupil. The exercises are divided into chapters, and graded,—including a great number of easy problems for beginners and enough harder ones for more advanced pupils. The harder sections may be omitted without destroying the work as a whole. Both plane and solid geometry are included within the scope of the book, and it may be used in connection with any text-book.

8vo. cloth, 250 pp.

Little Arthur's History of France. Published by T. Y. Crowell, New York.

The object of this book is to give to the young reader the more interesting facts in French history in simple language, without wearying him with unnecessary detail. It is uniform in size with Little Arthur's History of England, which has been a very popular child's book for some time. While the name of the author is not given, the date attached to the preface informs us that it is an English book. It is, however, exceedingly fair and honest in its statements. It covers, in time, the history of France from the earliest time that anything is known o' the country, down to the close of the Franco-Prussian war and the formation of the third republic in 1873.

Its style is exceedingly simple, adapting it to the use and pleasure of quite young readers, and the many illustrations present additional charms. Where supplemental reading forms a feature in school work, it would become a very valuable help to the pupil

Barnes's Brief History of the United States   Published by A. S. Barnes & Co., New York and Chicago.

This is not a new book, but only a new edition of a book which has long held a high rank in the educational library. In its mechanical execution, it is hard to conceive that any improvement could be made. Its illustrations are most artistic, bearing so close a resemblance to fine steel engravings that one is only forced from the belief that they are such by the consciousness that it would be pecuniarily impracticable. One of the engravings, oppoeite page 54, representing a puritan couple wending their way to church through the snow and on the constant lookout for their enemies the Indians, is a perfect gem. There are 14 two-page maps, bound in such a manner as to open out whole as a single page. The ground covered is from the earliest time that anything is known of the country or its inhabitants to the funeral of General Grant, which took place August 8th, 1885. The events are narrated in a concise, yet entertaining manner, entering within the grasp of children in the grades for which it is intended.

As a hand-book for teachers using any other history it must be very valuable. An item of importance is that the pages are numbered to correspond with the pages in the old edition, so that a teacher can use both books in the same class at the same time.

Cyrus Smith, Indianapolis, is agent for Indiana.

BUSINESS NOTICES.

Go to Fort Wayne *via* Muncie, and save time.

Don't go to School—until you have seen the special rates to county graduates, young teachers and others preparing to teach, made by the Fort Wayne (Normal Classical and Business) College.   W. F. YOCUM,
     11-3t   Fort Wayne, Ind.

New Books—Just Published. — Barnes' Brief History U. S., revised; Page's Theory and Practice, revised by W. H. Payne, Michigan University; "Watts on the Mind," revised by Prof. Fellows, Iowa University; Barnes' Elementary Geography; Barnes' Complete Geography, *two-book series;* Bardeen's Shorter Course in Rhetoric; Barnes' Popular Reading Charts. A. S. Barnes & Co. Cyrus Smith, Ag't, Indianapolis, Ind.

INDIANA
SCHOOL JOURNAL.

Vol. XXX.   DECEMBER, 1885.   No. 12.

*THE COUNTY SUPERINTENDENT IN THE SCHOOL ROOM.

M. A. MESS, SUPT. FRANKLIN COUNTY.

IN Germany they call him school-inspector, and he is a man of much weight in their school system. When he enters the school, pupils all rise, and when boys meet him on the street they respectfully remove their hats. The very name shows that his work is important. He does not merely visit the schools, he inspects them. The term "visiting schools," with the idea of official inspection, is new to our people, and their notion, that a visit means a fashionable call, has given rise to the opinion that the county superintendent is a superfluous piece of apparatus in our school economy; and, I do not doubt that many acts of ourselves and our predecessors have given proof that their opinion is well founded. If the stories told of our predecessors deserve any credence: That they would seat themselves comfortably in the teacher's chair with their feet on the table or stove, and, taking their paper from their pocket, would fall asleep over it; or, that they would ask some puzzling questions and laugh at the chagrin of pupils and teachers in failing to answer them, the office surely did not gain strength thereby with the people, and the efforts of the Legislatures to abolish it need not surprise us.

How we have been trying for the last four years to show by our work in the school-room, that we are needed, and that our

---

*Read in the Superintendents' State Convention last June.

office, with its incumbent, is not only a necessary piece of furniture, but one of the very pillars of our educational structure, is the theme of this paper. How well we have succeeded in these efforts, is shown by the fact that the people feel the need of us, and the last Legislature, after a single effort to change the mode of election, has, at least, let us severely alone.

I will give the actual practice of one of my experienced fellow-workers in a neighboring county, (to give my own might seem pedantic), with whom I frequently exchange opinions and with whose practice I am in accord. If this work has been wrong I trust it will be corrected here, and our new brethren will at least have learned how not to do.

I will here re-affirm a few principles upon which my neighbor and I base much of our action in the school-room.

1. The county superintendent is, *ex-officio*, a member of every school in the county. His teachers are made acquainted with this, and they understand that his appearance in the school-room must be considered as nothing extraordinary, and it should be attended with the least possible formality; hence he generally enters the school without knocking as do the other members of the school.

2. The teacher is the proper head of the school, and he has no right to surrender his position to any one. The pupils should recognize no one as superior to the teacher in the school-room; hence, whatever suggestions, questions, and other work the superintendent brings before the school, he does by the permission and consent of the teacher. His obtaining that consent in the presence of the school, establishes confidence in him by teacher and pupils, and leaves the impression that he comes there as their friend and fellow-worker, not as puzzler and tyrant. The teacher hereby retains his sense of authority and carries on his work with the confidence of one who is responsible for its management.

3. The county superintendent should correct evident faults of the teacher in the presence of the school. By making the correction he has an opportunity of applying the remedy for the error at once, and of proving to the teacher that the correction

is right and proper, not only in theory but in principle and practice. The school thereby, unconsciously perhaps, becomes the tribunal before which the teacher is put upon his honor to make the correction. My neighbor's plan of work in visiting schools is substantially as follows: When he enters the school, the teacher generally continues his recitation, and they exchange greetings with a nod or a word. After the recitation, they shake hands, exchange a few pleasant words, the teacher hands him the register, which should always be in the school-room when school is in session, and then goes on with his work. After noticing the wants of the school in regard to apparatus and supplies, and inspecting the register, taking from it the statistical items, the superintendent, taking a position, not too prominent, observes the teacher and his work as to *manner*, *means* and *method*.

1. Does the *manner* of conducting classes, the form of questions, the answers of pupils, the position of teacher and pupils at seats, recitations and boards, the form and general appearance of written work, the wording of solutions and other statements, the manner of passing to and from recitation, of dismissing and convening the school, exhibit an air of business, and prove the teacher master of the situation?

2. Does he employ such *means* as tend to establish correct habits of living and thinking in his pupils; such as bring about a normal development of all the faculties of the child's three-fold nature, moral, mental and physical; so that it will grow up not only well-informed in matters that it will use in life, but well-trained in all powers which it must exercise to make it a good, intelligent, worthy member of society?

3. Do his *methods* work out these means? Are they in harmony with correct principles of educational growth? Do they show that he has made a special study of the *child* not as material upon which to work, but as an organism composed of soul and body, whose growth he has to direct?

To illustrate as to manner: The class moves noisily and carelessly to the recitation. The superintendent asks permission to offer a suggestion. The class returns to seats. At the signal, 'one" they rise, at "two" pass, at "three" sit. The class is pleased with something systematic in school tactics; the teacher sees that the suggestion is practicable and productive of discipline; all are instructed; the fault is corrected; yet nobody's pride is wounded.

Again: The teacher permits the violation of principles in arithmetic; by permission the superintendent states the principle or writes it on the board; the pupil who made the mistake repeats the principle and applies it to his case; the class sees his mistake and the teacher, if he be wise, will correct the deficiency and profit by the correction.

Again: The teacher asks leading questions or he reads them *verbatim* from the book. By permission the superintendent asks the same questions in a different form, which requires the pupil to frame his own answer; the same ground of the text-book is covered, yet the pupil is thereby obliged to do his own thinking; new ideas are developed in his mind; his mind grows. The teacher sees that his method has been defective; both he and his pupils have learned a useful lesson without any display of authority on the part of the superintendent.

Again: The teacher makes all of his questions general; the answers are given promiscuously and "in broken doses"; the pupils do not rise to recite. The superintendent asks that John please rise and answer the question; he asks that all who agree with him raise hands; after excusing John he calls upon some one who did not raise the hand, to rise and repeat John's answer. He asks William, who perhaps has not paid strict attention, if he sees the point. William, thinking that he is let off easily, nods his head, when he is asked to rise and state what he sees. By this time the state of mind of the class has been changed from the mere advertence to the subject to *intense concentrated* attention to the particular point under consideration. The eyes of every member sparkle with enthusiasm; the teacher sees that the superintendent's shafts have been leveled at him; and, he seizes the first opportunity of admitting his deficiency in the plan of hearing classes and, unsolicited, promises that a change will be made.

Once more: The teacher is very busy with a class; a pupil

in another portion of the room is out of order. The teacher is asked to please stop a moment. Has the boy in the corner any work to do? He is in the fourth grade and has a geography lesson to prepare; the boy sees that he was caught in his mischief, which under ordinary circumstances is punishment enough; he resumes his work; the teacher has learned that he must assign sufficient definite work to each pupil to occupy his time fully, so that he will have no cause to be idle. The teacher must see what is going on in the room, no matter how intensely interested he may be in his recitation, and must correct misconduct as soon as he discovers it.

Many faults in manner are easily corrected in the written suggestions to be left with the teacher, and in private consultation; such as mispronounced words, ungrammatical expressions, careless commands, defective questions, and doing work for pupils which they can, by fair effort, do themselves.

In regard to the means employed it may be a painful task for the superintendent to suggest, and extremely humiliating for the teacher to receive, that there is much teaching power in a clean shirt-collar and a neck-tie. I had one of the choicest collections of anathemas that could be scraped up in the regions of Pluto, tossed at me by an irate farmer for suggesting that the boys could study with greater ease if their hands were cleaner. Yet it remains true that soap and shoe-blacking are educational forces.

The condition of the out-houses, the floor, the arrangement of books and materials at desks, the care of wraps, the neatness in dress and person of pupils, *all mirror* the teacher as a moulder of habits. A teacher who has not the manhood or womanhood to wage a relentless warfare against the lewdness and vandalism which is carved and scribbled in lamentable profusion about our school premises should resign his position and make room for a person of more grit.

The untiring correction of errors in speech, wherever and under whatever circumstances detected, show that the teacher is determined to lead his pupils to correct habits of thinking and expressing thought. The arrangement of the program, so that each grade shall have its proper portion of the teacher's time and

attention, and the strict adherence to its division in both recitation and study, establishes habits of regularity and punctuality,
and shows that the teacher is a person that knows his business.
Under means may be classed the teacher's preparation. Whether
or not he has made himself worthy of his high office by reaching
a high degree of scholarship does not here enter into consideration; this is tested in the examination. Does he show by
his management that he has made every class, no matter how
familiar the subject, a part of his daily preparation, so that he
can carry on the work freely and intelligently without constant
reference to his text-book to prop up his weakness and carelessness? To show the teacher that it is unnecessary to have a
book in hand, the superintendent rarely takes a book. If he is
unable to gather the thought of a paragraph read by a pupil,
without having a book in hand, something is wrong. The pupil
has been advanced beyond his capacity, or the means of study
have not been provided by the teacher. The superintendent, by
permission, asks for the definition of a few ordinary words, either
by use in a sentence or by synonym; he then has the pupil re-
read the paragraph, substituting synonym, and afterward repeating the sense in his own words. The pupil now discovers the
thought beyond the symbol; his mind is invigorated; the teacher
sees that he has made reading a meaningless task of calling words,
instead of a stimulating exercise in seeking out thought. He has
not wisely led them into habits of close and careful observation,
and thus he has failed to lay the foundation for healthy mental
discipline and symmetrical growth in knowledge.

Lastly: Do his methods of instruction show that he not only
knows the branches which he is to teach, but also the laws of
mind, both in its action and its growth? Does he follow the
right order to stimulate this growth? Does he teach his different grades work which develops the faculties most active at the
time? If his third grade is required to give the analysis of problems in mental arithmetic, which require the reasoning of a
Euclid, he must change his plan. If his instruction in history
is by isolated topics, that convey no related thoughts, the superintendent suggests a plan then and there, by which the pupils

may associate events with places, topics with subjects, and these with epochs and periods, so as to form in their minds a methodical scheme of the subject in hand. They see thus that there is a science of history. If the teacher's methods are not in accordance with correct principles of educational growth; if they do not lead the pupils into channels of self-improvement; if they do not widen their views and increase their power of grasping thought, it is the superintendent's duty, by judicious hints and questions, to put the teacher on the right track.

The foregoing is only indicative of the line of work pursued. The work of the first visit can by judicious economy of time be crowded into a half-day, but it can not fulfill its mission in less time. It furnishes a *basis* for estimating the teacher's worth in the school-room, but it can not be relied upon in drawing conclusions. Without a second visit the work is incomplete and much of the good set on foot in the first visit is lost. The second visit may be shorter, but it is by all means necessary. It shows whether or not the hints of the superintendent have been heeded. The very expectation of it stimulates teacher and pupils to do their best. From his observations on the second visit the superintendent can deduce conclusions upon which the teacher's work in the school-room may be made a potent factor in grading license. The grade in success, with *manner, means,* and *method* as a basis of its computation, is worth fully one-fourth of the entire grade in measuring teaching power.

In conclusion let me say that the superintendent must show by his work in the school-room, that he knows what the school needs to fill its sphere completely as a training place for intelligent citizenship, and that *he* is the prime mover in the work of effectually supplying these needs.

He must show the teacher that his visit means more than a fashionable call; that he will correct faults without reserve; that he will expose all shams and soft formalities; that he will not tolerate fraud in any form.

The teacher must learn that the superintendent is a man who has the courage of his convictions; who has no friends to reward nor enemies to punish; who is under no obligation to any political ring or religious clique; who *tells the truth* for the truth's sake; who has the highest good of the schools at heart, and upon whom the faithful teacher may depend as a firm friend and a wise counselor.

FORMS AND METHODS IN ARITHMETIC.

W. F. L. SANDERS, SUPT. CAMBRIDGE CITY SCHOOLS.

1. A more frequent use and investigation of the general formula—

$$\text{MULTIPLICAND} \times \text{MULTIPLIER} = \text{PRODUCT},$$

would enable teachers to attain great success in teaching several subjects in Arithmetic. Let them introduce the formula by a question like this (written on the black-board)—

$$4 \times 7 = \text{WHAT?},$$

and when the answer (28) is given, let the teacher ask what fundamental process (multiplication) is performed to obtain the result, 28.

2. Next, put the question in this way—

$$4 \times \text{WHAT} = 28?,$$

and when the answer (7) is given, let the teacher ask what fundamental process (division) is performed to obtain the result, 7.

3. Again, put the question in this way—

$$\text{WHAT} \times 7 = 28?,$$

and when the answer (4) is given, let the teacher ask what fundamental process (division) is performed to obtain the result, 4.

4. Now, let the teacher impress upon the minds of the pupils, that when the right-hand side, (the product), of the expression is required, *multiplication* is the process; and when any part (one of the factors) of the left hand side of the expression is required, *division* is the process.

5. To apply the preceding to practical examples, take the following example (or a similar one) :—

Ex. *If a bushel of potatoes cost* 62½ *cents, what will* 18¾ *bu. cost?*

The general principle (or formula) which must now be written on the black-board is—

PRICE PER BUSHEL $\times$ NUMBER OF BUSHELS $=$ COST.

Then, the teacher, referring the class to the example, and asking the two questions—

     (*a*)   What is the price per bushel?

     (*b*)   What is the number of bushels?

may write just beneath the general principle—

$$\$.62\tfrac{1}{2} \times 18\tfrac{3}{4} = \text{WHAT?}$$

Now, let the teacher ask what fundamental process will be used in obtaining the result, and the answer (multiplication) being given, let the process be performed, and beneath the others, there may be written the third expression—

$$\$.62\tfrac{1}{2} \times 18\tfrac{3}{4} = \$11.71\tfrac{7}{8}.$$

6.   Next, take the following example (or a similar one):—

Ex. *If a bushel of potatoes cost 62½ cents, how many bushels may be bought for* $11.71⅞?

Write the general principle on the black-board, thus:—

PRICE PER BUSHEL $\times$ NUMBER OF BUSHELS $=$ COST.

Then let the teacher ask the class which two of these *three parts* in this statement are to be found in the example; the answer, the price per bushel and the sum to be expended (or the cost), being given, let there be written beneath the general principle the following:—

$$\$.62\tfrac{1}{2} \times \text{WHAT} = \$11.71\tfrac{7}{8}?$$

With this, let the teacher compare the question (see Art. 2)—

$$4 \times \text{WHAT} = 28?,$$

and ask what fundamental process is used in obtaining the result; answer (division) being given, let him immediately ask what fundamental process must be used to obtain the result in—

$$\$.62\tfrac{1}{2} \times \text{WHAT} = \$11.71\tfrac{7}{8}?,$$

and the pupils, perceiving the similarity of the two questions, will answer promptly and correctly. At the same time, for fear the pupils will not recognize the fact, the teacher must bring to their minds the idea that in this question a factor is required; and that the process used to obtain it is, of course, *division.* Also, there may be given the usual explanation—that as many bushels may be bought as the number of times $.62\frac{1}{2}$ is contained in $11.71\frac{7}{8}$, which is $18\frac{3}{4}$ times; hence, $18\frac{3}{4}$ bu.

The division necessary to obtain the $18\frac{3}{4}$ is performed, and then there is written on the board the final expression—

$$\$.62\frac{1}{2} \times 18\frac{3}{4} = \$11.71\frac{7}{8}.$$

7. Next, take the example (or a similar one)—

Ex. *If $18\frac{3}{4}$ bushels of potatoes cost $11.71\frac{7}{8}$, what is the price per bushel?*

Again, write the general principle on the board, thus:—

PRICE PER BUSHEL $\times$ NUMBER OF BUSHELS $=$ COST.

Then, let the teacher ask the class which two of the *three parts* are to be found in the example; the answer, the number of bushels and the cost of all, being given, let there be written beneath the general principle the following:—

$$\text{WHAT} \times 18\frac{3}{4} = \$11.71\frac{7}{8}?$$

With this, let the teacher compare the question (see Art. 3)—

$$\text{WHAT} \times 7 = 28?,$$

and ask what fundamental process is used in obtaining the result; the answer (division) being given, let him immediately ask what fundamental process must be used to obtain the result in—

$$\text{WHAT} \times 18\frac{3}{4} = \$11.71\frac{7}{8}?,$$

and the pupils, perceiving the similarity of the two questions, will answer promptly and correctly. At the same time, for fear the class will not recognize the fact, the teacher must bring to their minds the idea that in this question, also, a factor is required; and that the process used to obtain it is, of course, *division*. (See Art. 4). Also, there may be given the usual explanation—that the cost per bushel is found by dividing the amount to be expended by the number of bushels.

HISTORY OF THE ORDINANCE OF 1787.

CYRUS W. HODGIN.

NEARLY one century ago, on the 13th day of July, 1787, the Congress of the United States, in session at New York, among its last acts under the Articles of Confederation, enacted an

Ordinance for the Government of the Territory of the United States north-west of the Ohio River. We know of no legislative enactment, proposed and accomplished in any country, in any age, by monarch, by representatives, or by the people themselves, that has received encomiums so exalted, and at the same time so richly deserved, as this same Ordinance of 1787.

It has been lauded by our great statesmen, great jurists, great orators, and great educators.

In his great speech in reply to Hayne, delivered in the United States Senate in January, 1830, Daniel Webster said of it, "We are accustomed to praise the law-givers of antiquity; we help to perpetuate the fame of Solon and Lycurgus; but I doubt whether one single law of any law-giver, ancient or modern, has produced effects of more distinct, marked, and lasting character than the Ordinance of 1787. We see its consequences at this moment, and we shall never cease to see them, perhaps, while the Ohio shall flow."

Judge Walker, in an address delivered in 1837 at Cincinnati, spoke upon this subject in the following words: "Upon the surpassing excellence of this Ordinance no language of panegyric would be extravagant. It approaches as nearly to absolute perfection as anything to be found in the legislation of mankind; for after the experience of fifty years, it would perhaps be impossible to alter without marring it. In short, it is one of those matchless specimens of sagacious forecast which even the reckless spirit of innovation would not venture to assail. The emigrant knew beforehand that this was a land of the highest political as well as national promise, and under the auspices of another Moses, he journeyed with confidence to his new Canaan."

Chief Justice Chase said of it: "Never, probably, in the history of the world, did a measure of legislation so accurately fulfill, and yet so mightily exceed, the anticipations of the legislators. The Ordinance has well been described as having been a pillar of cloud by day and of fire by night in the settlement and government of the Northwestern States."

Mr. Peter Force, in 1847, in tracing its history, declared: "It has been distinguished as one of the greatest monuments of civil jurisprudence."

About ten years ago, the writer of this article had the great pleasure of hearing a most eloquent address delivered at the Normal School in Terre Haute, by the "silver-tongued orator of the Wabash," Hon. R. W. Thompson. His subject was Education. He quoted the sentence of the Ordinance reading thus: "Religion, morality, and knowledge, being essential to good government and the happiness of mankind, schools and the means of education shall always be encouraged," and then he praised the Ordinance and its supposed author in strains of eloquence difficult to equal, much less to surpass.

George V. N. Lothrop, LL. D., in an address delivered at the annual commencement of the University of Michigan, June 27, 1878, said, substantially: "In advance of the coming millions, it had, as it were, shaped the earth and the heavens of the sleeping empire. The Great Charter of the Northwest had consecrated it irrevocably to human freedom, to religion, learning, and free thought. This one act is the most dominant one in our whole history, since the landing of the Pilgrims. It is the act that became decisive in the Great Rebellion. Without it, so far as human judgment can discover, the victory of free labor would have become impossible."

Notwithstanding all this profusion of praise, the authorship of the Ordinance has been a matter of controversy; and a cloud of mystery has hung over it that has not been cleared away until recently. The explanation has been published, but not in such a way as to reach a large number of readers. It will be our purpose in a future article to present to the readers of the Journal a pretty full account of the exceedingly interesting origin of the Ordinance.

NORMAL SCHOOL, RICHMOND, IND., Oct. 16, '85.

SIR THOMAS MORE.

MATTIE CURL DENNIS.

The force of his own mind makes his way,
A gift that heaven gives him, and which buys
A place next to the King.   [*Henry VIII, Act I, Scene 1.*

God has not often combined charity with enthusiasm; when he has done
e hvs produced his noblest work."

ALEXANDER said, "There are two Alexanders; one, the un-conquered son of Philip; the other, the unrivaled work of Apel-les"; so, it may be said there are two Sir Thomas More—the one, that which church bigotry and cynical criticism has made; the other, the product of impartial history and Holbien's canvas. Emerson says that, "The true hero will always find crises to try his edge." The inimitable life and tragic death of Sir Thomas More emphasizes this proposition. He was born into the temper and times of the Pagan renaissence, at the period when the intel-ligence and spiritual energy that had given soul to the Middle Ages was exhausted. Constantinople had been ravaged and overthrown by the Turks, and the Byzantine commonwealth thus bereft of its glory was deserted by the great scholars who had there found that protection and opportunity which had been denied them in the blood-stained, fluctuating empires of the West. The exiled Greek scholars now found homes in Italy, and Flor-ence, which had once been the seat of freedom and of art, now became the center of the great intellectual revival which was to give a new bent to politics and religion. Philosophy, poetry, and the drama awoke to life on the banks of the Arno, and the energy of Florence—that had been so long and so hopelessly used in the struggle for freedom—took a new impetus in the ambitions of intellect; every vessel which touched the shores of Italy came freighted with manuscripts from the East, which fur-nished intellectual manna for minds that had been dwarfed for centuries; students from all parts of the civilized world crowded the streets of Florence, eager to partake of the New Learning, or, rather, to study the old learning and cause it to take on new form and meaning adapted to the great upheavals in the thought and action which were to be a part of the evolution of the ages, a step in the growth of man.

It was said that "Greece had crossed the Alps," but Greece on this side the Alps was no longer Greece, but Germany, Spain, France, and one day became England, and after that America! England, from her insulated position was slow to become awak-ened to the upgrowth in thought that was soon to startle both church and state; but, finally, the effect of all the great discoveries and inventions that characterized and immortalized the fifteenth century broke in upon her at once; the Crusades and the Wars of the Roses were ended, paper and printing invented, gunpowder and America discovered. England now had abundant opportunity to develop her intellect, spiritual and financial energy: Grocyn of New College, who was pupil to the renowned Greek scholar Chancondylas, returned to England in 1491, after completing his studies in Italy, and began to deliver lectures in Oxford; and with these lectures began a new era in English history. In a short time a cluster of Greek-English students gathered around the English universities; these scholars were encouraged by such men as bishops Langton, Warham, Fisher, and cardinal Morton; among these scholars and leaders in the new thought were Grocyn, Colet, Linacre, Erasmus, and his life-long friend, "the gentle Sir Thomas More."

From the first the revival of letters took a less literary and a more religious turn in England than it had done in Italy, and the awakening of a rational christianity began with the lectures of Colet after his return from his Greek studies in Italy. He had no sympathy with the Platonic mysticism of the learning of the times, and with him began the practical ideas of the gospels that gave the peculiar bent to the theology of the renaissence. Erasmus and More were sharers in these views with Colet; and amid all the vicissitudes of More's eventful life he clung to his religious convictions. At one time his strong religious enthusiasm inclined him to become a Carthusian monk, and he even went so far in physical religion as to wear a hair shirt next his body all his life; but his prevailing good sense and broad humanity saved him even in this age of benefices from the thralldom of church fanaticism.

More was born 1480 (?), and died 1535. He saw three different Kings upon the throne of England, Edward IV, Henry VII, and Henry VIII. He was the son of Sir John More, and his reverence for his father may be learned from the little incident, in which it is said that even when he became the first lawyer and even chancelor of England, that he never failed each morning to kneel for his father's blessing before he began the duties of the day. More lived in that age that "exhibited man's ferocity in civilized life without his simplicity, and the degeneracy of modern manners without their refinements"; he was one of the chief actors in the reign of a King whose character may be summed up in the words of More to Roper : "If my head would win him a castle in France, it would not fail to go"; born in the metropolis, surrounded by the polite circle of that polite age, "the greatest wit in England," a master of the learning of his times, the intimate friend of almost all the learned men of Europe, and one of the greatest diplomatists of his age, admired at foreign courts, loyal to his country and his religion, modest, truthful, and jealous of nothing but the right, seemingly without political ambition, he was the fittest man in Europe to control the destinies of men.

But it is More in his literary character that most concerns us. His reputation as a public lecturer was established when he pronounced his famous speech on St. Augustine, "De Civitate," in the Church of St. Lawrence Jewry; again we meet him in 1504 in the Parliament of Henry VII, in his daring speech in opposition to the granting of a subsidy to King Henry VII, on the marriage of his daughter; again, in the memorable case of the Pope *vs.* Henry VIII, in which More's argument was so convincing that although he won the case for the Pope, yet it gained him the royal favor. Mackintosh says of More that he was the first public speaker worthy of English history. His fragmental history of Edward V and Richard III are really the first worthy English history; it is remarkable for simplicity of style and purity of language, and of its truthfulness Hume says, "No historian of ancient or modern times can possibly have more weight." Hallam says, "It is the first example of good English language, pure and perspicuous, well chosen, without vulgarism or pedantry."

But it is needless to dwell longer on his less important works; he, in common with other authors of even later date, wrote much and perhaps too much. It is well known that his literary fame must rest upon his Utopia; even to-day we can but admire the diamonds shining among the rubbish in this remarkable work, and when we remember that after three hundred years of legislation and enlightenment political economy has failed to find anything better on many points suggested here than the remedies given, we wonder at the sagacity and divination of the author; the questions of crime and its proper punishment, of labor, farming, politics, population, government, are often argued from the standpoint of the wisest nineteenth century legislators, and religion is given as broad bases as though dictated by a Penn or a Williams, and here the immortal Horace Mann may have received some of that divine inspiration that made him one of the broadest humanitarians and noblest teachers of his age.

If any one feels that he has an over-busy life, and that the pressure of daily routine is so great that he must give up intellectual progress, let him remember that the author of the Utopia wrote Erasmus that the time which he gave to writing was taken from that which others allowed for eating and sleeping. It is almost invariably the *busy* man who reads.

Too Much Drill.—Nothing tends to discourage pupils more than constant drill upon the same lesson. Give pupils a variety. Rather let them read a lesson but moderately well, and give them some supplementary reading, than keep them drilling on a lesson until they are tired of it. Many teachers in their anxiety to secure thoroughness fall into this error, and nauseate their pupils with constant and senseless repetition. The child, like the man, delights in acquiring new ideas, in fighting new battles, and in testing its strength in overcoming new difficulties.—*Raub.*

According to the higher interpretation of its function, the teacher finds the recitation a place for probing the mind of the pupil, and ascertaining his power of comprehension of the lesson; correcting his distorted views, developing his expression of thought in his own language, enlarging his vocabulary of words by teaching him how to use the technical terms which human thought has set apart for the expression of accurate ideas.—*W. T. Harris.*

PRIMARY DEPARTMENT.

[This Department is conducted by HOWARD SANDISON, Professor of Methods in the
State Normal School.]

———:o:———

The real subject in education is the individual mind of each child, with its acquired
habits and inherited tendencies. An evident proposition, then, is: If real teaching is
done, each mind, with its peculiar habits and inherited tendencies, must be understood
by the teacher; with its double corollary:—
(1) The number of pupils under the charge of a primary teacher should range between twenty and thirty. (2) The pupils should remain under the charge of a given
teacher more than ten months.
The second proposition is: Mind being an organism, the heart (sensibilities) is no less
an avenue to the intellect, than is the intellect to the heart and will; with its corollary:—
Suspicion and severity can never enable the teacher to obtain a standing place in the
child-mind.
The third proposition is: Two rival powers compose the mind—the *carrying power*—
memory (the servant) and the *thinking power* (the master); with its double corollary:—
(1) The aim of education is to make the mind strong and skilled as a thinking power,
and not to make it full as a carrying power. (2) The most practical education is that
which sends the child into the business world with power to observe closely and to
think (reflect) accurately upon what he observes.

———•———

READING.

WHEN, IN PRIMARY READING, HAS A WORD BEEN LEARNED?

THE true answer to this question is involved in the answers
to two other questions—What is a word? and, What is the
use of a word? A word is an arbitrary sign of an idea;
that is, it is only by arbitrary agreement that a certain familiar
object is called *table;* it might with as good reason have been
called *door.* The only valuable use of a word is to suggest to
the mind an idea. If a word is an arbitrary sign of an idea, it
can be made to suggest its idea only by acts of association. If
the acts of association are weak, the word will suggest its idea
vaguely, if they are strong, the idea will be recalled vividly.

*The root idea in primary reading, then, is strong association of idea
and word.* It is held by some that the main thought of primary
reading is the mastery of the written or printed word. It is said,
the child is familiar with the idea, and with the oral word, and
the thing remaining to be done is to teach him the printed word.
This thought is at the basis of the formal and mechanical reading
work of the schools. It inevitably tends to concentrate the attention of both teacher and child upon words to the comparative
exclusion of ideas. If those holding to the thought that the
mastery of the printed word is the design, employ ideas or objects, it is simply to make vivid the picture of the word. It is

2

true that the printed word must be taught, but as a *means* not as an *end*. It is to be taught only that it may be associated with its idea, and not for itself.

The child in the beginning does, as is said, know two things—the *idea* and the *oral word;* but it is hardly correct that there remains but one thing to do—the mastery of the printed word. There are *two* things to be done:

1. The mastery of the printed word.
2. *The strong association of the idea with the printed word.*

The last is the central idea of primary reading—the one that determines method, means, etc. If it is said that those who say that the mastery of the printed word is the work of a primary school mean to include the second point, the answer is that the results show a very *weak association,* but considerable power to *call words at sight*—thus indicating that the stress of the work has been upon *expression* and not upon the *association of thought with expression.*

There are, however, two ways of associating the printed word with the idea—one indirect, the other direct. In the first, the thought is—the child already knows the idea and the oral word and has associated them; he is now to be led to associate the printed word with the idea *through* the oral word. This assumes that the thing that above all others the child neeeds is the *oral word;* that he is already able by means of association with the idea to call it up, and that his power to call it up must be increased by associating it with the printed word. It is thus seen that the termination is again, power to *to call words at sight,* instead of power to instantly drink in the meaning of words *at sight of them.*

In "The True Order of Studies," the statement is made that "the children must early be taught that the printed word is the sign or picture of the oral word." This idea has been the blight to thought work in primary reading.

In the second way of associating the printed word with the idea, the thought is that nature has already provided the child with one means of suggesting the idea, viz., the oral word, by associating the two directly and frequently, and that the aim of primary reading work is to furnish another means, by the same method—the printed word. This consideration makes the *direct association* of printed word and idea the ruling thought. It furnishes the true ground for deciding as to the means and devices that are to be employed—if they strengthen the direct acts of association they are legitimate; if not, they hinder in the process of reading, which consists essentially in bringing about acts of association between printed words and ideas.

A printed word has been learned, when the association between it and its idea is so strong that the idea (not the sound—the oral word) is instantly suggested at sight of it.

ORAL LESSONS.

It is said by Porter that "the mind has but a given amount of energy." As soon as the teacher approaches the horizon of her knowledge and skill she begins to falter and grow confused. That is, the mental energies are divided—a part going to a consideration of her own limitations, and a part to the real work of the lesson. The problem is to determine how all the mental energies of the teacher may be concentrated upon the minds of the children and their needs. This is especially the question in oral work, for there the teacher may not, to so great an extent as in other work rest upon the knowledge and authority of the book. The three main aids to a well grounded confidence are:

1. A full employment of the teacher's own resources, and a close observation of the effect.

2. A full use of the pupil's knowledge.

3. A definite purpose for each lesson, and a searching inquiry at the close of each lesson as to whether the purpose has been gained.

If the teacher freely draws upon her own resources in her work, i. e., constructs her own illustrations, employs original drawings and interweaves her own experiences that bear upon the lesson, much closer attention will be given by the children than if ready made illustrations are used. Observation and reflection upon the attitude of the children's minds toward that kind of work in which the teacher's experience is involved will tend, on account of the manifest interest and attention of the pupils, to increase the teacher's confidence in herself. There are two kinds of confidence—the confidence of ignorance and the confidence of knowledge and skill. Every teacher should have the second kind, and a study of her own resources and the use of them will do very much toward securing the confidence required for good work. The law of the mind that bears upon this point is, as indicated above—the mind has but a given amount of energy.

If the teacher lacks confidence in herself, she can not concentrate all her energies upon the mental attitude and requirements of the pupils. The question being discussed is—How can the teacher gain a well grounded confidence in herself, so that all the powers of her mind may be turned from her own mental condition to the workings of the children's minds? One answer is— by utilizing her own knowledge to its full extent before employing that from books; by involving personal experiences that are apt; by devising apparatus needed; by performing the experiments required and by drawing the illustrations needed. In this way she more largely puts herself,—her life, into the work, and the advantageous results upon the class will at once inspire her with the proper self-confidence—the confidence of knowledge and skill. Another answer to the question is—by employing to the fullest extent the knowledge that the pupils possess. It has been said that the children learn more during the first six years than they ever can during any other period of corresponding length. Their knowledge extends, also, into every field. The perception of the extent and value of their knowledge, and the reflection that, merely on account of time, hers is of more value, will tend to bring that freedom that oral work requires. The habit that oral teaching demands is that of studying carefully the resources of the pupils and of self.

To this must be added the habit of thoroughly mastering and assimilating the information gained from books, so that it shall become a part of the teacher's own life—and hence of her resources. The confidence arising from knowledge and skill will be increased if the teacher always sets before herself a definite aim, and acquires the habit of asking and answering at the close of each oral lesson—What capacities of mind were strengthened by this lesson? What knowledge was deepened? What knowledge was gained?

LANGUAGE.

I. GENERAL AIM.—The aim or purpose of language work is, in general terms, to train the mind. Specifically it is to give the pupil the power of thinking clearly upon any subject, and of expressing his thoughts in good English *as he thinks them*. It is also the aim to gain the power of interpreting the written page as easily as the spoken language is interpreted.

II. WORK OF FIRST YEAR.—The work of the first year is to be done incidentally in connection with every lesson given. In the first place all errors in oral language should be corrected at the *instant they are made* if the aim of language work is to be realized. The corrections should be made at first by the teacher; because the pupils at this stage have not sufficient knowledge of language to enable them to know what expressions are erroneous and what correct. But the teacher should, during this year, lead them to form the habit of criticising errors, and should require that all criticisms should be made by them to the extent that they are able, in accordance with the principles that the mind grows by self-exercise. The regular and general lessons may be made an exercise-ground in language.

The pupil should be led to tell in good English what he knows about a subject, and then by judicious questioning be led to see more. The first aim in this kind of work, should be power to think and knowledge of the object; second, power in the use of language.

Constructive work in language should also be begun in the first year. It should, however, be very simple. The following is the order in which language studies come in the scale of difficulty: (considering language work as a whole, not merely the first year's work,) oral expression, copy-work, dictation, putting the thought of another in the pupil's own language, original composition.

It will be seen from the above that copy-work is the simplest form of written language work. This should be done in the first year, first from black-board, because it is easier to take it from the board free from all distracting associations than from the book. The work should be increased in difficulty by taking it finally from the book.

In the entire work of the first year the teacher should be content with a single expression for a single idea or thought, e. g., "The earth is round like a ball," is sufficient, although they might be taught it is spherical, globular, or an oblate spheroid. This is in accordance with the thought that it is the nature of mind in acquiring knowledge (1) observe a particular, (2) many particulars, (3) compare, (4) generalize, (5) classify, (6) name and define.　　　　　　　　　　　　　　　STUDENT.

DAILY PREPARATION.

(In relation to government; fret and worry; health, etc., as suggested in the State Board Outline for Township Institute work.)

FEW persons are naturally possessed of a great amount of governing power, but most persons of fair ability, can, by proper training, secure for themselves this necessary qualification of the teacher. Some, it is true, have a nameless something about them that naturally governs or controls the child with seemingly little or no effort on the part of the person. But most teachers are not possessed of this much desired qualification and must do all possible to gain it. This ability must be acquired either by special training or by experience. If by experience it must be either at the expense of the teacher, or at that of his pupils and patrons, and most likely at the expense of both.

The special training that one can get upon the general work of school management is better than any amount of experience without reflection, for it puts him in the right track at once and enables him to build upon the right kind of a foundation, whereas his experience may after all prove to be "a house built upon the sand."

· There are many little things the teacher can do that will help him in governing. To prevent disorder, the teacher should be firm and dignified, should prepare his lessons, should see that his pupils are comfortable and have plenty of work to do; he should thoroughly inspect all work.

There are in almost every school boys who will do little mean things to aggravate and annoy the teacher. The first trial is to find out the possibility of an aggravation, and in case the pupil succeeds in making his teacher evince anger, he has glory enough in having accomplished his object. Now he resolves to repeat the experiment time and again. This, of course, causes more annoyance, and if allowed to go on will make those pupils who, under other circumstances would behave well, try to help overthrow the order of the school. The teacher should manifest no anger or impatience, but should be firm and decided in suppressing such disorder.

A faithful preparation of his lesson will be a great aid to him in this; it will make the government of the school much easier, for if he can lay aside his book and conduct the recitation without it, he will be the better able to keep the remainder of the school in mind, to observe carefully all that is going on, and let them know that he has them in mind and that any disorder whatever will not pass unnoticed. If the teacher is able to do this the pupils would not have so many opportunities to get into mischief. Of course, if the child knows he is not observed and it will not be seen, he will do many a little disorderly thing that he would not be likely to do otherwise.

If the teacher is so busy with her class that she allows the remainder of the school to be disorderly and not check it, she can expect naught but disorder.

The effort has been thus far to show how a preparation of lessons will lessen the burden of government. And just in the degree that it does this, it reduces the fret and worry of teaching. If the government is easy, if we have control over the school, there need be no fret and worry, or very little, if any.

It has often and truly been said that one can not teach what he does not know, and that one can not teach better than he knows. No matter how often we have gone over the work, it is highly possible we have forgotten part of it, perhaps some important points that ought to be brought out, and we need to review it. In order to teach a lesson well we should make a thorough preparation for it. We should know every important point that ought to be brought out, and should be familiar with all our author's thoughts. But this alone is not sufficient; we should study and gain the thoughts of others, for by holding converse with the different authors, we may see their variety of thoughts and expressions.

Different writers present the same subject in different ways, and a form which is comprehensible to one is not to all Different explanations are required to reach the comprehension of all. But it is not enough that the teacher and pupils be possessed of a mass of facts, simply, but to be of benefit to them these facts must be organized and arranged so that they can be used. The teacher should have the points arranged in logical order and have them brought out thus. It is organized knowledge that is power.

The teacher above all others should have a broad, comprehensive knowledge of the branches taught. He is expected not only to assist the pupil to understand the truths in the text-book, but also to select channels of his thinking in respect to a great many other things as well. The teacher having a superficial knowledge is most unfit to do this.

The manner of presenting a subject has much to do with the reception of it. If the teacher has made no preparation for her lesson and must keep her book before her, merely asking questions from it and having them answered in the words of the book, I do not see how she could arouse the least interest or enthusiasm in her work. Her pupils would soon see that she did not know even what she expected them to know, and would soon become careless and neglect their work.

But if she has prepared her lesson, she can discard the text-book altogether and be a living, active power in the school, and not a mere questioner. She can present her lesson in a much more interesting manner. A teacher with no spirit or energy is no teacher at all

The teacher should have something new to present to her pupils—something not found in their books. They seldom fail to remember anything thus presented in connection with their lesson, even if the rest becomes a blank. Zeal is indispensable in teaching.

The health is promoted in so far as the fret and worry of teaching is reduced.

Terre Haute.   FRANCES BALCH.

THE SCHOOL ROOM.

[This Department is conducted by GEO. F. BASS, Supervising Prin. Indianapolis schools.]

COULDN'T READ IT ANY OTHER WAY.

"WHEN I hear people boasting of a work yet undone, and trying to anticipate the credit which belongs only to actual achievement, I call to mind that scene by the brookside; and the wise caution of my uncle in that particular instance takes the form of a proverb of universal application."

The above is taken from Monroe's Fifth Reader. A seventh year pupil read it orally as if he thought *scene* and *caution* the objects of the verb *call*. The teacher, who was using oral reading as a means to ascertain whether the pupil had the thought, asked the following questions, which were answered as follows:

T.   What is the object of the verb *call?*

P.   *Scene* and *caution.*

T.   What is the subject of the verb takes?

P.   After studying a moment, *caution.*

T.   Can it be both object of *call* and subject of *takes?*

P.   It can not. It is *not* the object of *call;* it is the subject of *takes.*

T.   Read it again.

P.   I can not read it any other way.

T.   You can not read it as you did before. Try it.

The pupil did try, but he read it just right, because the thought was so clearly in his mind that he could not help it. It is quite difficult to read a sentence to mean what one thinks it does not mean. If a reader knows and feels what is to be expressed, the expression, so far as meaning is concerned, will take care of itself nine times out of ten.

ENCOURAGE PUPILS.

IT is often stated that an object of the recitation should be to test the pupil's knowledge of the subject. This object seems to have taken hold of the majority of teachers. They are constantly testing. They are not satisfied with a fair question, for they say, "Any one can answer that." They must have a question that no one can answer. I've seen some teachers look disappointed when a "poser" was readily answered. Examiners *seem* to make an effort to think of questions that the pupils will fail on. They often succeed in turning out a whole set of that kind. Why not make the majority of the questions of such a character that the average pupil will do well? Nothing encourages one so much as success. Let the pupils feel that they can do something and they will take hold of a difficult question with double the energy.

DEFINITIONS.

SOME years ago nearly every reader contained lists of definitions at the beginning of each piece. The teachers insisted that these "definitions" must be learned before any attempt at reading was made. Quite frequently the "definition" was more difficult to understand than the word itself. No matter, they must be learned and recited to the teacher. The word had to be spelled too. The boys used to judge of a teacher by what he did on definitions. If he had us learn them as above, we did not like him. But if he had us read, and when we came to the word in the text and could not get the idea, he referred us to the definition and explained it, we liked him and thought him a good teacher. This may have been a narrow basis upon which to judge a teacher, but it was broad enough for us boys. We did despise "to get the definitions." Why? Because they did not mean anything to us. We got only words—empty words. They were hard to get, hard to remember, and of no account when they were remembered.

Book-makers have quit putting those definitions into their books now, and teachers have quit asking for them. But books on other subjects continue *definitions*, and some teachers are yet requiring children to learn them so they can *say* them. Take almost any text-book on grammar and we shall find definitions. Grammar is with us, the "New Education" to the contrary notwithstanding—and it is our duty to teach it in the way to produce the most good.

Within the last year, I have heard pupils *say* that "an adverb is a word used to modify a verb, an adjective, or an adverb," and then say that the word *the* is an adverb modifying the noun lesson. Ask those pupils what a word must do to make it an adverb and they can not tell, yet they can *say* the definition.

Instead of having children learn the definition *verbatim*, have them learn what it means. Is an adverb a principal word or a modifying word? What may it modify? How does it modify? What does a relative pronoun do that a personal does not? How does an adjective differ from an adverb? What is the chief use of the verb? etc.

MEMORANDUM FOR EXERCISE IN CORRECT PRONUNCIATION.— The root of the difficulty was a pile of soot allowed to accumulate on the roof.

The rise of the waters has injured the rice crop, and it may be expected the price will rise.

He had moved his goods to the depot, but his friends bade him not be discouraged, as he would soon be acclimated if he would only stay.

He is an aspirant for Asiatic honors.

The disputants seemed to be conversant with the question, and, if not good financiers, they are, at least, familiar with the problem of finance.

The irrefragible evidence that he was the sole cause of the altercation, indisputably fastened on him the responsibility for the irreparable damage.

His conduct was indicatory of the blatant blackguard, but his complaisant coadjutor, with his incomparable complacency, was even more dangerous.

The physician, after a careful diagnosis, pronounces the patient to be suffering from bronchitis, gastritis, periostitis, and meningitis, caused by the prevalence of mephitis, and has prescribed morphine.

THE HIGHEST LAKE.—The lake that has the highest elevation of any in the world is Green Lake, in Colorado. Its surface is 10,252 feet above the level of the sea. Pine forests surround it, and eternal snows deck the neighboring mountain tops. One of these, Gray's Peak, has an altitude of 14,341 feet. The water of Green Lake is as clear as crystal, and large rock masses and a petrified forest are distinctly visible at the bottom. The branches of the trees are of dazzling whiteness, as though cut in marble. Salmon and trout swim among them. In places the lake is 200 feet deep.

TEACH the pupil to think for himself. Avoid routine. Do not be more anxious to display your own knowledge of the subject under discussion than you are to draw out that of the pupil. Make haste slowly. Be sure of each step before you attempt the next. Be thorough. Do not permit the brightest and most forward in the class to do all the answering. Devote the greater portion of your attention to the dull and backward ones. The smart ones will get along well enough. "They that are whole need not a physician."—*The School Master.*

DEPARTMENT OF PEDAGOGY.

[This Department is conducted by S. S. PARR, Principal De Pauw Normal School.]

—:o:—

RAISING HANDS.

ONE of the badly abused devices of the recitation is the raising of pupils' hands, as a sign of readiness to recite, to criticise a recitation already made, or to assent to some statement given by teacher or pupil. The grosser forms of misuse consist in snapping the fingers (never to be tolerated) and in punching the air with the fist or sawing wildly and aimlessly with the entire arm. It may be questioned seriously whether the whole practice of raising the hands is not detrimental to the true purpose of the recitation. The recitation is a systematic procedure, according to a plan fixed in a general way beforehand, toward a specific point of thought, that is, the point of the lesson. The attention is to be directed without flagging toward this point, and its successful direction is the true criterion of success. Incidental to the main point are a number of processes, among which may be named: Incitation to thought, testing of preparation previously made, supplementing what is deficient, organizing information and thought, and securing full statement of what has been worked out. Whatever in any way distracts the attention of pupils and teacher from the main point, or interferes with these processes, is to be avoided. It is foreign to the purpose and success of the recitation.

Pupils can no more profitably rush at these processes pell-mell than the teacher can profitably aim his efforts at the mass regardless of the individuals who compose it. Raising the hands fosters irrational rushing *en masse* at the subject. Pupils are led by their feelings rather than by what they actually see of the thought. The timid ones are bullied. The energy of attention is transferred from the subject to the bodily motions of teacher and pupil. Besides, practices of the kind named foster habits of unconscious (and conscious) egotism and lying. Those who are not prepared and who really know nothing of the lesson or the particular point raise their hands to save themselves, since they have observed that those who do not do so are often called upon. The competition which results is of the unhealthy sort. Those who need stimulation most are stimulated least, and *vice versa.* The skillful teacher does not need a showing of hands to ascertain who is ready to recite. He knows it from the expression of the countenance.

Dr. Bitmann says: "When the teacher addresses a question to the entire class, there is no need of raising hands. * * * His question may be addressed to any scholar; no one knows but the question may be addressed to him; all can think and pay attention without the interference and dissipation of attention of any kind."

So much on the side of the pupil; in many cases, the teacher relaxes his grasp on the subject, by the practice, and loses his point among the pupils who proceed to wrangle over it like so many dogs over a bone that has been tossed among them.

If it is not best to abandon the habit entirely, the better way, at least, is to use it sparingly, taking care that the raising of the hand shall mean something to the individual pupil.   s. s. p.

OFFICIAL DEPARTMENT.

ABSENCE FROM INSTITUTES—PENALTY.

In : nswer to the question whether a trustee has the right to deduct a day's wages for each day's absence from the township institute, of a teacher who regards Saturday, the day on which the institute is held, as the Sabbath, I will say that I think you should make the deduction, as in the case of other teachers. That is the penalty fixed by the laws of the State. Individuals have a right to their own belief in matters of conscience and religion, but where their private belief conflicts with the public law, they must be willing to suffer the penalty of the law.

THE BIBLE IN THE SCHOOLS.

In answer to your question I refer you to the statute and the opinions of former State Superintendents on the use of the Bible in the schools. Notes 1 and 2 to Sec 4493, page 75, School Law. Under this statute and these opinions I hold that a trustee or school board can not forbid the teacher's reading a chapter of the Bible at the opening of school, but may forbid all comments and other devotional exercises. An assistant teacher could not, probably, be required to be present at such Bible reading, conducted by the principal, but must give the principal all necessary help in moving pupils from room to room, as may be required by such exercise.

HOLIDAYS—TEACHERS' WAGES.

The dismissal of schools for Thanksgiving day and other holidays is not regulated by law or by any authoritative rule. State Supt. Hopkins expressed the opinion that school teachers, if exempted from labor on such days, should be allowed their wages, as is the case with employees in most lines of business. (Note 7 to Sec. 4501, School Law). It may be claimed that where teachers are employed at so much a day, they can not demand pay for days that they do not teach; but I hold that teachers are not employed by the day, and paid their wages day by day; but are employed for the term and are, or ought to be, paid monthly, the specification of so much per day being merely a measure of the amount they are to receive. I think therefore that they are emp'oyed by the month, and that if the trustees order or permit the schools to be dismissed for a holiday, the teachers should not suffer thereby a diminution of their wages. If teachers, without authority from the trustees, dismiss their schools, they may be required to make up the time or submit to a reduction of wages.

ENFORCEMENT OF COURSE OF STUDY.

A course of study have been prescribed by the school authorities for the schools of the township, town, or city, and it is the duty of the teachers of such schools to require all pupils to study the subjects appropriate to their advancement or grade, as d termined by the course of study. And no pupil should be exempted from studying any subject required by the course of study; except on account of sickness or other reason th it may seem sufficient to the trustees, and upon request of parents or guardians.

[The above are selected from my recent decisions]

J. W. HOLCOMBE, *Supt. of Public Instruction.*

GEMS OF THOUGHT.

"We live in deeds not years, in thoughts not breaths;
In feelings, not in figures on a dial.
We should count time by heart-throbs. He most lives
Who thinks most, feels the noblest, acts the best"

I would risk my life, though not my reputation, to exalt my station. I mean to prepare fo futurity —*Alexander Hamilton.*

A man who had reached nearly his four-score years in age was asked how he had succeeded in preserving his youthful vigor to such a remarkable degree. His answer was: "By not allowing myself to look at things through old eyes—I have endeavored to retain the enthusiasm of younger days i everything I have undertaken, and have retained my youth simply because I have never permitted myself to consider myself old."

The tissue of the life to be—
We weave with colors all our own;
And in the field of destiny
We reap as we have sown.   —*Whittier.*

Our true knowledge is to know our own ignorance.—*Charles Kingsley.*

The burden comes light which is cheerfully borne.—*Ovid.*

The small courtesies sweeten life; the greater ennoble it.—*Bovee.*

So live thou here, that when thy life has fled, no one may say of thee, "this man is dead "—*Bicknell.*

Nature and wisdom always say the same.— *Juvenal.*

O, that men should put an enemy in their mouths to steal away their brains.—*Shakespeare.*

EDITORIAL.

THE ELECTRIC STREET RAILWAY.—South Bend now operates its street cars by means of electricity. While this is not the first instance of the kind on record, this is the first city in the United States that has tried the experiment.

DOES THIS MEAN YOU ?—This paragraph is inserted to remind those of our readers who are on the *unpaid* list that their subscription will be due before Jan. 1st. This is not a *dun*, only a *reminder*. Teachers are generally honest but sometimes forget—and sometimes are negligent. Let each one make it a principle to return all borrow:d books, pay all little debts, and if possible begin the new year with a clean record and a clean sheet.

Do not fail to read the program of the State Teachers' Association. It is an excellent one. *One thousand* Hoosier teachers should attend this annual meeting. It will pay in many ways. The chairman of the executive committee, W. H. Elson, has done a good work and deserves much praise. *Do not fail to note that every one, to get reduced rates, must have a certificate from the Railroad Secretary, C. S. Olcott, Chicago,* BEFORE LEAVING HOME.

THE EDUCATIONAL WEEKLY has been sold to The New England Publishing Co., of Boston, and its readers will hereafter be served with the *New England Journal of Education,* with "New England" left off and "Western Edition" substituted. This western edition will devote one page largely to Indiana interests. A western branch office has been established in Chicago, with Mr. Chas. S. Olcott in charge. The movement indicates prosperity and enterprise on the part of the New England Publishing Co., and will doubtless extend the circulation of its excellent publications.

The *Weekly* has made a brave and persistent struggle, but never succeeded in reaching a paying basis. It died as it lived, claiming a circulation and boasting a prosperity which it never enjoyed.

To misrepresent the circulation of their papers seems to be a failing of some editors. When the *Practical Teacher* of Chicago was *"combined"* with the *New York Institute,* a month or two ago, its editor *claimed* a circulation of 6,000, and when *The Institute* had swallowed it Bro. Kellogg went Col. Parker 4,000 better and claimed an additional circulation of a cool 10,000. Some people call this "advertising," but the Journal calls it *lying.*

QUESTIONS AND ANSWERS.

QUESTIONS PREPARED BY STATE BOARD FOR OCTOBER.

[These questions are based on the Reading Circle work of last season.]

SCIENCE OF TEACHING.—1. How does it aid the teacher to comprehend that the imagination creates no new material?

2. How should the child be taught to correct his pronunciation? His articulation?

3. Show how a knowledge of 'the earth's structure is the foundation for other work in geography.

4. What, in the order of simplicity, is the second stage of spelling?

5. In writing should the element or the letter be taken first? Why?

PHYSIOLOGY.—Describe in detail the structure and function of the muscles, and give some account of the hygiene of the muscles. Explain voluntary and involuntary muscular action.

Answer must not exceed three pages.

HISTORY.—Give an account of the formation of the Constitution of the United States, keeping in view the failure of the Articles of Confederation; the conflicting opinions of the two great parties then existing; the means adopted to recommend it to the people, and its adoption.

Answer not to exceed three pages. To be marked on character of work rather than on specific points.

PENMANSHIP.—1. For what purpose would you use the blackboard in teaching penmanship?

2. At what point should the final stroke in all words terminate?

3. What slant should all straight lines make with the base line?

4. Give the length of the following letters above and below the base line: *g, y, q, f, p.*   5 pts, 2 each.

5. Analyze the letters in the word "light."   5 pts, 2 each.

The answers to these questions should be written with ink, as a specimen of penmanship, and marked 50 or below, according to merit.

ORTHOGRAPHY.—1. What principle is employed in the division of words into syllables? Illustrate.

2. What is the use of teaching the sounds of the letters?

3. Ought pupils to be taught to spell words of which they do not know the meaning? Give reasons for your answer.

4. Classify the consonant sound. Is there any other basis of classification besides the one you have taken? If so, what is it?

5. Spell the plurals of the following words: Radius, axis, index, stratum chimney, woman, child, duke, king, deer.

6. Spell, accent, and mark diacritically ten words dictated by the superintendent.   50

GEOGRAPHY.—1. Explain the rapid growth and the continued prosperity of Minneapolis.

2. Write the names of all the States of the United States west of the Mississippi River.

3

3. Write from six to ten lines, describing the physical structure and the climate of South America.

4. Name every country of Europe that is bordered by navigable water (rivers excepted), indicating what body of water in each case.

5. State what conditions of soil and climate are necessary to the successful culture of rice.

6   Draw a map of Indiana, showing its important rivers and its five largest cities.

7. Name two important cities and three chief productions of Brazil.

8. Bound Switzerland and describe the form of government.

9. Name five large rivers of Asia and five of the largest cities.

10. Name four large islands of the West Indies and tell to what government each belongs.

GRAMMAR.—1. About what time in the common school course should a child begin the study of *technical* grammar? Why?

2. What are the differences between the simple and the compound relative pronoun?

3. Make each of the following words or group of words express possession: James, enemy, father-in-law, queen of England, somebody else.

4   I shall receive *who ever* comes. I shall receive *whom ever* comes. Which sentence is correct? Why?

5. Conjugate the verb "be" through the subjunctive and potential moods.

6. Correct, if necessary, and give reasons:
  a. This result, of all others, is most to be dreaded.
  b. This is the more preferable expression.

7. Analyze: Language was given us that we might say pleasant things to one another.

8. What does the italicised word in each of the following modify:
  a. He writes *plainly.*
  b. *Assuredly* he is here.

9. Correct the following sentence, assigning reason: "Whom say ye that I am?"

10. Parse *why* in the sentence: The reason why he came is evident.

READING.—1. What is meant by monotone? When should it be used?

2. What is cadence, and in what respect is it unlike the falling inflection?

3. What is expression? How would you teach it?

4. Write a sentence which asks a question and requires the falling inflection

5. What is emphasis? In what ways may a word or sentence be emphasized?

6. Read a stanza of poetry and a paragraph of prose selected by the superintendent.

ARITHMETIC.—1. The distance from the base of a building to a pole is 145 feet, and a string 225 feet long attached to the top of the pole just reaches the base of the building. What is the height of the pole?   Process 4, ans. 6.

2. If 52 men can dig a trench 355 feet long, 60 feet wide and 8 feet deep in 15 days, how long will a trench be that is 45 feet wide

and 10 feet deep, which 45 men can dig in 25 days? Proc. 5, ans. 5.

3. What are the antecedents of a proportion? Name the consequents n the problem above. 5, 5.

4. D. and G. furnish capital to engage in business, and L. does the work for $\frac{1}{4}$ of the profits; D. contributes \$8,000 and G. \$10,000 of the capital. They gain \$5,400; what is each one's share of the gain? Analysis 4, ans. 6.

5. What is the cubic root of 48,228,544? Proc. 5, ans. 5.

6 What will be the cost in New Orleans of a draft on New York, payable 60 days after sight, for \$5,000, exchange being at $1\frac{1}{4}$ per cent. premium? Analysis 5, ans. 5.

7. What are the present worth and discount of \$3,457.84 payable in 7 mo. 10 da., when money is worth $7\frac{1}{2}$ per cent? 5, 5.

8. What is the interest of \$30.24 for 2 yrs. 8 mo. 15 da., at 8 per cent? (Solve by Aliquot parts) Proc. 5, ans. 5.

9. What number increased by $33\frac{1}{3}$ per cent. itself equals 1200? Analysis 5, ans. 5.

10. Two men dig a ditch for \$53; one man worked $3\frac{1}{2}$ days and dug $14\frac{1}{2}$ rods per day; the other worked as many days as the first dug rods per day. How much did each receive, if they shared in proportion to the time they worked? Ans. 5, 5.

ANSWERS TO BOARD QUESTIONS PRINTED IN NOVEMBER.

ARITHMETIC.—1. $\sqrt[3]{912,673} = 97$, Ans.

2. The L. C. M. of \$3, \$14, \$21, and \$48 = \$336, Ans.

3. $(.015 \times .15) - .000015 = .002235$, Ans.

4. $\$24 = \frac{3}{4}$ of cost.
$\frac{1}{4}$ of cost $= \frac{1}{3}$ of $\$24 = \$8$.
$\frac{4}{4}$. or cost, $= 4 \times \$8 = \$32$.
\$34, selling price, — \$32, cost, = \$2, gain.
\$2 is $6\frac{1}{4}$ % of \$32. Ans., $6\frac{1}{4}$ %.

5. $1\frac{1}{2}$ yd. : $\frac{3}{4}$ yd. : : 40 yd. : (?). 20 yd. Ans.

6. 11 hr. 45 min. — 9 hr. 30 min. = 2 hr. 15 min., difference in time.
2 hr. 15 min. $\times$ 15 = 33°— 45′, difference in longitude.
74° W. — (33°— 45′) = 40°— 15′ W. Long., Ans.

7. 1 yr. 10 mo. 26 da. = $\frac{343}{180}$, time.
\$1250, prin., $\times \frac{8}{100}$. rate, $\times \frac{343}{180}$, time, = $\$190\frac{5}{9}$, interest.
\$1250, prin., + \$190.555, int., = \$1440.555, amount. Ans.

8. [illegible] $\times \$7.62\frac{1}{2} = \$212.219 +$, Ans.

9. 88 lb. 16 pwt. 17 gr. $\div$ 54 = 1 lb. 7 oz. 11 pwt. $10\frac{5}{54}$ gr., Ans.

10. $\frac{1}{3} \times \frac{1-\frac{1}{3}}{2} \times \frac{2-\frac{1}{3}}{3} \times \frac{3-\frac{1}{3}}{5} \times \frac{4-\frac{1}{3}}{4} = \frac{1}{3} \times \frac{1}{3} \times \frac{5}{9} \times \frac{8}{15} \times \frac{11}{12} = \frac{22}{729}$, Ans

HISTORY.—The answer to this question requires an account of the introduction of slavery into Virginia by the Dutch in the year 1619, and its extension into all the colonies north and south. Then follows a statement concerning the growth of the slave trade especially in the northern colonies, Massachusetts being more particularly interested. The difficulties in settling the questions of slavery and the slave trade in the Constitution, and the rapid transfer of all slave interests to the South, and the profit there of slave labor should be mentioned.

The rise of the Abolition party, the passage of the various compromise measures, the annexation of Texas, the Missouri Compromise and its repeal in the Kansas-Nebraska Act, the Fugitive Slave Law, the Dred Scott Decision—should be given as causes leading to the outbreak; the determination of the South to extend the slave territory at all hazards, and its resistance to the election of Mr. Lincoln being the chief immediate causes.

Secondly, sketch the attack upon Fort Sumter; the massacre of the 'Massachusetts troops in Baltimore; the rapid raising of armies in the North and South even while the North had no real sense of the magnitude of the Rebellion; the battle of Bull Run, and those near the Capital of the country.

Thirdly, sketch the changes made in the Northern policy whereby the North assumed the aggressive and offensive line of action, the division of the northern army into corps occupying different sections of the country, and lastly the march of Sherman to the sea, cutting the Confederacy in two, and the surrender of Lee.

Fourthly, then should follow a description of the terms on which final surrenders were made by the South; the assassination of President Lincoln, the disagreement between Johnston and Congress as to the reconstruction policies by which the Southern States were to be restored to their place in the Union, and the principles upon which they were severally based.

Science of Teaching.—1. Attention, in its highest phase, is an act, is the direction of the mind toward an idea or object by means of the will. Attention, as a condition, is that state in which the mind is when it is energetically exercised on an object of thought. Attention, as a condition, and as an act, is capable of several varieties: *a*. Animal attention, like that with which the cat watches a hole, for a mouse; *b*. attention roused by curiosity; *c*. that directed by the will in accordance with a pre-arranged purpose.

2. Spelling is giving the characters of the written word or the names of the letters or sounds of the spoken word in their order, and in their correct form, as they occur in sentences and other parts of discourse, which involves capitalization, punctuation, syllabification, meaning, and pronunciation (involving accent). This is the full meaning of the term, as applied to school-work. Various other meanings are possible. The first stage of school-spelling is the learning of the spoken word as a representative of an idea. The first stage of spelling in practical, every-day reading, in new words, is to learn the form of the written word by the eye, with something of its meaning, and then by means of the dictionary, other books of reference and thought to fill out the points mentioned above

3. Elementary drawing is easier than elementary writing (script), provided the child does not *draw* the letters, because drawing is done with a rigid wrist and writing with a flexible wrist. The latter is more difficult for the pupil to attain than the former. Primary drawing and primary writing usually begin simultaneously and go along together. If possible, the child should learn the flexible wrist and arm first. Acquiring the flexible wrist and arm, after the rigid has become habitual, is exceedingly difficult for most children.

4. The word method in primary reading is preferable to the phonic because the former is the way the child naturally learns words. The word-method teaches words, as wholes and then teaches the parts of the written word, viz the letters which compose it. However, the teaching of letters is deferred by many teachers until a little vocabulary of written words learned as wholes is accumulated. The principle governing this is that of simplicity, or, "One thing at a time." The phonic-method, like the word-method, begins with the spoken word, but unlike the latter, proceeds to analyze it, find the sounds of which it is composed, and then teaches the representation of each sound in the written word as a whole. The method is, in the main, the reverse of that in the word-method. The latter proceeds from the whole spoken word to the whole written word, and then to the parts of each. The former proceeds from the parts of the spoken to the parts of the written word, and then to the written word as a whole.

5. The teaching of figures as representatives of the primary numbers learned the first year might be deferred to the second year, but this is not the most economical procedure. The reasons why this is so are two : ' By teaching the figures with the numbers the work is done little by little ; whereas, if deferred, it accumulates and becomes troublesome from the amount necessary to be done the second year. Less variety is possible if this pla is pursued. Teaching figures with their numbers enables a greater variety of busy-work. The pupils are restricted to work on numbered objects, if they are not taught the figures.

PHYSIOLOGY.—1 The alimentary canal is an extended tube, of one to one and one-half inches in diameter, beginning with the mouth and nostrils and terminating with the anus. It has three enlarged portions,—the mouth and pharynx cavity, the stomach, and the large intestine. It is lined throughout with a mucous membrane, which is a continuation of the external skin. Its parts, in their order from above downward, are the mouth and the nostrils, the pharynx, the æsophagus, the stomach, the small intestine, the large intestine (caecum, ascending, transverse and descending colon, sigmoid flexure, rectum), and the anus.

The digestive apparatus, direct and accessory, in addition to the portions of the alimentary canal named above; consists of the tongue, teeth, salivary glands, located in the mouth; the mucous glands, in the mucous membrane; the peptic glands, in the walls of the stomach; the liver and pancreas, in the abdominal cavity; and the small glands in the walls of the intestines. From the various glands five juices, useful in digestion, are emptied upon the food at various points,—saliva, gastric juice, bile, pancreatic juice, intestinal juice.

A portion of the food, taken into the mouth and chewed with the teeth, is moistened with saliva, whose active ingredient, *ptyalin*, has the power to change 2000 times its own volume of starch into grape sugar. Absorption of the food thus changed begins in the throat and is finished in the stomach. The action of this alkaline juice is stopped by the acidity of the gastric juice of the stomach, when the food reaches the cavity.

The stomach, a conical bag lying transversely in the upper and left portion of the abdominal cavity, receives the food through the gullet and at once begins to churn it and to mingle with it the gastric juice, an acid (hydrochloric), whose associate ingredient, *pepsin*, acts chiefly upon albuminoids (lean meat, cheese, white of egg, gluten of grains, etc.). From the stomach, absorption takes place mainly through the veins into the liver.

From the stomach the undigested and the unabsorbed portions of the food pass, by degrees, through the pyloric orifice into the small intestine. Here change takes place through the operation of three juices,—the bile, the pancreatic juice, and the intestinal juice. The precise function of each of these juices is not known with certainty. The pancreatic juice is supposed to act upon starch undigested by the saliva and upon fats and oils. In this latter work it is doubtless assisted by the bile, whose other function is thought to be a stimulation of the muscular coat of the small intestine. Absorption from the small intestine is by the veins into the liver and by the lacteals into the *receptaculum chyli.*

Digestion is largely finished in the small intestine.

READING.—There are several methods of testing the ability of pupils to call words at sight: (1) The words may be called in the reverse order from that in which they are read; (2) they may be arranged in columns upon the black-board, or at least the more difficult ones, and the pupils may call them as written or as promiscuously selected by the teacher; or, (3) those most commonly mispronounced may be written in short sentences upon the board and the pupils, in turn, required to read these.

2. Plans for teaching children the meaning of words: (*a*) Don't convey the impression, in beginning reading, that the word is the great thing to obtain, and its content the less important thing; (*b*)

require the words to be used in original sentences in the same sense as used in the lesson; (*c*) require them to be used in a different sense— the pupils to state the distinction, if they can; (*d*) put synonyms in the place of the words as used by them, and get the pupils to show why the synonym is not as good a word, etc.

3. In concert reading the teacher is unable to say who is reading to detect who is making the chief mistakes; or to detect the individual deficiencies. Besides, this process is mechanical and does not rest, in principle, upon the true basis for correct reading. Concert reading is not wholly evil, however.

4. Neither the word, the phonic, nor the alphabet method of teaching reading is best, by itself. Each has defects which may be remedied by supplementing it with certain features of the others. A judicious combination is thought to be the best method.

5. Whittier, "Snow Bound"; Holland, "Kathrina", "Bitter Sweet"; Holmes, "Bill and Joe."

GEOGRAPHY.—1. The equator is a great circle equally distant from the poles. Distance north and south from the equator, measured in degrees, is called latitude. Distance east and west from a given meridian, measured in degrees, is called longitude. The greatest number of degrees of latitude that a place can have is ninety. Of longitude, one hundred and eighty.

2. (*a*) Buenos Ayres, exports wool, hides, tallow, live cattle. (*b*) Bahia, coffee, sugar, fruits.

4. Trieste is on the northeast coast of the Adriatic Sea, in the Austro-Hungarian monarchy. Tokio, the capital of Japan, is situated on the island of Hondo. Bogota is situated in the central part of the United States of Columbia, of which state it is the capital. Galveston is situated on an island at the entrance of the Bay of Galveston, on the southern coast of Texas. Newport is on the Island of Rhode Island, at the entrance of Narragansett Bay

5. The climate of Italy is generally considered genial and healthful, but the mortality is large. In some portions the extreme heat of summer parches vegetation, and the marshes exhale pestilential vapors. Yet some districts are delightfully salubrious. Rome is situated near the central part, on the Tiber; Naples, on the Bay of Naples; Genoa, in the northwestern part, on the Gulf of Genoa.

6. Siberia being situated in the northern half of Asia and exposed to the icy winds of the Northern Ocean has a bleak, extremely cold climate. Hindostan, on the southern slopes of the Himalays, in the tropical zone, is very warm, while the moist winds from the Indian Ocean bring copious rains. The only valuable productions of Siberia are minerals and furs; those of Hindostan are numerous, including rice, cotton, flax, indigo and tea. The inhabitants of the former

are half-civilized nomadic tribes; those of the latter have an old civilization, rich in intellectual lore, and now combined with that of England, which is transplanted to this soil.

7. Atlantic and Arctic Oceans, Mediterranean, Black, Caspian, North, Baltic, and White Seas.

9. New York City is advantageously located in a temperate climate, at the entrance of a large navigable river, with an excellent harbor. The surrounding country is rich in agricultural and mineral resources for the needs of a large city. With unsurpassed agricultural, manufacturing, and commercial facilities its prosperity is assured.

10. The richest copper mines in the United States are near Lake Superior and in the northern peninsula of Michigan.

ENGLISH GRAMMAR. — 1. Present Indicative, Past Indicative; Present Participle, Past Participle. These are called principal parts because all forms of the verb may be made from them.

2. Go, went, going, gone.
Do, did, doing, done.
See, saw, seeing, seen.
Rise, rose, rising, risen.
Lie, lay, lying, lain.

3. A noun is in the nominative when it is the subject of a sentence, when it completes the predicate after intransitive or passive verbs, when it represents the person or thing addressed, and when used absolutely before a participle or after an intransitive infinitive.

4. The possessive singular of most nouns is formed by adding the apostrophe and the letter *s*. Nouns that form their plural by adding *s* or *es*, take the apostrophe only, to form the possessive; otherwise they take the apostrophe and the letter *s*.

5. Comparison is a modification of adjectives to express a quality in different degrees.

6. (*a*) General and statesman refer to the same person and require a singular verb. (*b*) A collective noun expresses the idea of unity and requires a singular verb.

7. (*a*) He does not hear you.
(*b*) Everybody should think twice before *he speaks*.
(*c*) America was discovered during Ferdinand and Isabella's reign.
(*d*) We were comparing Cæsar's and Napoleon's victories.
(*e*) I can but think that God is good.

8. This is a complex declarative sentence, of which "When letters were first used" is the subject, "is not certainly known" is the predicate. Of the subordinate clause, "letters" is the subject nom. unmodified; "were used" is the predicate verb, modified by the adverb "first;" "is known," the predicate of the first prin. proposition,

is modified by the adverbs *certainly* and *not*. The subordinate clause is introduced by the conjunctive adverb ''when.''

9. I hear that (conjunction) that (adjective) friend that (pronoun) you mentioned has been sick.

10 Mode represents the *manner* of the action. Tense represents the *time* of the action. Voice shows whether the subject acts or is the receiver of the action.

MISCELLANY.

The winter term of the Richmond Normal has opened "fuller than ever."

The Montgomery county teachers organized a county association November 27–8.

The Boone county teachers held a very profitable association at Thorntown, October 23–4.

‘The Illinois State Teachers' Association will meet at Springfield, December 28th.

The City Supts of Northern Indiana and Southern Michigan will hold a meeting at Elkhart, Dec. 5th.

The National Educational Association will meet next year the second week in July, in Topeka, Kan.

WABASH COUNTY.—The schools are full and running smoothly. Supt. Jno. N. Myers seems to be taking hold well.

The Ripley county teachers held their fourth annual association November 27–8. Supt. Holcombe made the annual addresss.

INTELLIGENCE, edited by E. O. Vaile, of Chicago, is one of the very best educational papers that come to our table. Bro. Vaile wields a trenchant pen, has clear notions of his own, and does not hesitate to express them.

HOUGHTON, MIFFLIN & Co., of Boston, who in past years have issued such beautiful Holmes, Emerson, Longfellow and Whittier Calendars, have added to the list this year calendars for Mrs. Whitney and Mr. Lowell. They are all works of art.

The Parke Co. Teachers' Association held its fifth annual session Nov. 27, 28. It was as usual large and well conducted S S. Parr delivered the annual address. In the oratorical contest Maggie Newton took the first prize and Fora Pickett the second.

FRANKLIN COLLEGE has arranged for a Normal Department, to be opened January 7th, with W. J. Williams in charge. Mr. Williams is well and favorably known. He was in turn principal of the high school, then superintendent of Rochester, and later was county superintendent.

THE VALPARAISO NORMAL in its third week of the present term reached an enrollment exceeding 1500—and still they come. The writer recently had the privilege of looking into the faces of as many of these students as could crowd into a large chapel. It was an inspiring sight. H. B. Brown is still at the head.

THE PORTER CO. INSTITUTE was held Nov. 25-27. It was fairly attended and those present exhibited good interest. Mr. and Mrs. H. A. Ford were the principal instructors. H. B. Brown gave a daily lesson which was highly appreciated. W. A. Bell and State Supt. Holcombe were present two days, each. The list of home workers is large and efficient.

THE STEUBEN CO. INSTITUTE, held Nov. 9-13, was as usual a success. The instructors from abroad and the home workers alike did good work. Mr. and Mrs. H. A. Ford of Detroit, Mich., were the principal instructors. Capt. Ford gave two evening entertainments. Supt. G. J. Luckey, of Pittsburg, Penn., was present one day, and will be long remembered. Supt. R. V. Carlin has a strong hold on the affections of his teachers.

Mrs. Susan B. Jordan, wife of David S. Jordan, President of the State University, died recently at her home in Bloomington, leaving two little children, her husband, and a large circle of loving friends to mourn her loss. Mrs Jordan was a lady of generous culture and a real companion of her husband. Pres. Jordan has the sympathy of friends throughout the state in this saddest of afflictions.

THE NORMAL TEACHER, W. H. F. Henry, editor and proprietor, failed to make its appearance in October. The November issue has printed on it "October and November," but the size is not increased. Out of 16 3-column pages, aside from advertisements and "questions and answers," this issue contains but little more than *two pages* of reading matter for teachers. These are evidently signs of distress, and the friends of the *Teacher* should rally to its assistance.

THE SUPERINTENDENTS of town and city schools of Southwestern Indiana met at Princeton Nov. 14. The following subjects were considered: 1. The Relation of the Superintendent to the Teacher. 2. Examinations—their frequency, kinds, and relation to promotions. Those who participated in the discussion were Supts. Snoke, of Princeton, Stultz of Mt. Vernon, Wood of New Harmony, Johnson of Oakland City, Clark of Henderson, Ky., Lucas of Owensville, Taylor of Vincennes, and Principal McCrea of Princeton. Next meeting will be held at Evansville, Jan. 22-3. All school superintendents are invited to attend.

PURDUE UNIVERSITY.—The new Mechanics Shops at Purdue University, built the past summer at a cost of $9,000 or $10,000, and handsomely supplied with the finest machinery that could be secured for the purpose, were formally dedicated on November 11th. In answer to a large number of printed invitations issued by President Smart, the people of La Fayette and vicinity visited the shops in the afternoon of the day mentioned above, and saw some eighty or ninety students engaged in various lines of handicraft. This Department of the University has been very rapidly developed under President Smart's administration, and it bids fair to become the chief feature of the work at Purdue: Over half the Freshman class is taking this course.

The La Fayette public schools are in a very prosperous condition this year, the number in attendance being considerably increased, notwithstanding the increasing drain by Purdue University, The high school also has a much larger attendance than for years, due in part to confidence in the new principal, and in part to the more convenient location in the centre of the city.

INDIANA TEACHERS' READING CIRCLE—OUTLINES.

SCIENCE OF TEACHING.

Hewett's Pedagogy——Pages 117 to 139.

GENERAL OUTLINE OF PEDAGOGY.—By means of the following diagram, we shall be able to locate ourselves in the subject:

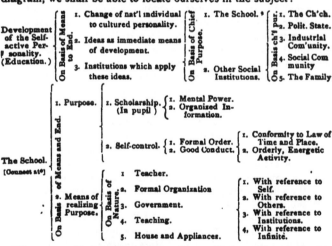

WORK FOR DECEMBER.—The student will do well to make his own the practical directions, pp. 117 to 122, relating to the house, grounds, and mechanical appliances. The teacher should do his duty fully in educating and directing public sentiment aright on these matters.

FORMS AND IDEAS TO BE STUDIED.—Organization, its etymology and meaning. The etymology of the book is faulty. The word *organ-iz at-ion* is derived from *organ*, which is derived from Latin, *organon;* derived from Greek, *organon*, which latter is allied to Greek *ergon*, though not derived from it. *Organon* means "instrument." [See Skeat's Etymological Dictionary, word *organ*.] Idea of an organism.

In what sense is the school an organism? Parts organized— course of study, schools, classes, program, records, instruction, government, and appliances. The agent or doer of the organizing—the law, the school-board, and the teacher. See diagram, for the purpose of this organization, viz., the purpose of the school. On what principles in the pupils are they divided into schools? On what principles on the part of the teachers are the pupils divided into schools? Why not put all the pupils of a graded-school into an assembly-room and send them out to teachers in class-rooms? On what principles in pupils and teacher are pupils divided into classes? In other words, why not have a class of 40 pupils 60 minutes, rather than two classes of 20 pupils each 30 minutes? Define a course of study, tell what elements enter into it and on what basis its subjects are divided into parts, and on what basis arranged in the order of time. Since the whole of any subject can not be taken, what shall determine what parts shall be taken for course of study and what shall be left? [In answering, look at the purpose or the school.] Fix meaning of the logical arrangement of a subject. [See Hill's Rhetoric, on Logical Division.] Also, for meaning of the mind-development, arrangement of a subject. [This means the arrangement of the subject as it is to be taught to the developing mind of the child.] Reasons for the unequal division of time on the program.   S. S. P.

——:o:——

ENGLISH LITERATURE.
Smith's Outlines —— Pages 85—126.

"An astonishing irruption of facts—the discovery of America, the revival of antiquity, the restoration of philosophy, the invention of arts; the development of industries, the march of human curiosity over the whole of the past and the whole of the globe—came to furnish subject-matter, and prose began its reign."—*Taine.*

Sir Thomas More, in his "History of Edward V and Richard III," produced the earliest English history, written in the best English prose of the period. In "Utopia," More presents some impracticable dreams of government, but on the other hand he anticipates many things that have already come to be a part of our civilization, and still others that may in the future, under improved conditions, cease to be sneeringly called "Utopian" ideas and become the realizations of be+ter days.

EDMUND SPENSER.—(*a*) His contemporaries, Sidney and Raleigh, two most accomplished knights of the age, were his friends. Sidney combining as he did the elements of a scholar, a poet and a 'most perfect gentle knight,' exerted a powerfol influence.

"A work so extensively perused as was the Arcadia must have contributed not a little to liberalize and dignify English speech, and to create, among writers, a bold and imaginative use of words. From him, as from a fountain, the most vigorous shoots of the period drew something of their verdure and their strength. Shakespeare was his attentive reader, copied his diction, transferred his ideas—above all, his fine conceptions of female character."—*Welsh.*

Raleigh contributed to the historical and poetical literature of his age. His diversity of tastes hindered excellence in any one direction.

(*b*) Spenser's subject-matter—Chivalry.

"The delicate fancies of old Welsh poetry, the grand ruins of the German epics, the marvelous splendors of the conquered East, all the relics which form centuries of adventure had dispersed among the minds of men, had become gathered into one great dream; and giants, dwarfs, monsters, the whole medley of imaginary creatures, of super-human exploits and splendid follies, were grouped about a unique conception, exalted and sublime lore, like courtiers prostrated at the feet of their king."—*Taine.*

(*c*) Characteristics.— 1. Sincerity. 2. Imagination. 3. Artistic finish. His verse is uniformly and exquisitely musical. 4. Rich description. He presents pictures drawn with the utmost skill.

He stands alone between Chaucer and Shakespeare. His "Fairy Queen" expresses the harmonious beauty of the poet's own heart.

EMMA MONT. McRAE.

——:o:——

BROOKS' MENTAL SCIENCE.

Subject: Intuitions of the Right—pp. 371-389.

I. TERMS TO BE DISTINGUISHED.

1. Rational Idea, page 371.   6. Sophists, page 375.
2. Ethical Element,   "   7. Tautology, page 377.
3. Obligation—Right, p. 373,   8. Logically (distinct), page 378.
4. Triune Conception,   "   9. Sensational School, page 380.
5. Verities—Truths,   "   10. Complacency—Remorse, p. 384.
            11. Absolute—Relation, p. 388.

II SUMMARIES.
1. Theories of the Right.
1. Elements of Conscience.
3. Classification of Authors of Ethical Theories.

III. CONCERNING RIGHT.

1. "Education and fashion are powerful instruments in the culture of the mind; but they do not account for the origin of the idea of Right."—*Haven.*

2. "The idea of Right is not strictly *innate*, but *connate;* the foundation for it being laid in our nature and constitution."—*Haven.*

IV. CONCERNING CONSCIENCE.—1. Definitions: (*a*) "C. is the power of cognizing the moral qualities of actions."—*Wayland, Alden, Haven.* (*b*) "C. is the sense of Right."—*Watson.*

2. Synonyms: "moral faculty," "moral judgment," "faculty of moral perception," "moral sense," susceptibility to moral sense.—*Tenneman.*

3. Illustrations: (*a*) "Reason is the eye of conscience."—*Winslow.* (*b*) 'A good conscience is to the soul what health is to the body."—*Addison.* (*c*) "A good conscience is the only object of universal desire."—*Haven.*

V. CONCERNING MERIT.

1. "Moral law is inconceivable without the ideas of merit and demerit."—*Hopkins.*

2. "One of the keenest griefs a man can have is the consciousness of his own moral unworthiness."—*Wheaton.*

VI GENERAL.

1. "Obligation is to the moral being what instinct is to the animal."—*Hopkins.*

2. "The specific truths of moral science are to be learned by a species of education as really, as are all the specific truths of natural science."—*Winslow.*

3. "One marked peculiarity of the moral emotions, in their relation to the law of habit should be noted: their freshness, vividness, and intensity are not like the other emotions, blunted by frequency of repetition. But, on the contrary, every fresh exercise seems but to heighten their susceptibility, and prepare them to respond to more and still more delicate impressions and distinctions."—*Munsell.*

INDIANA STATE TEACHERS' ASSOCIATION.

XXXII Annual Session—To be held at Plymouth Church, Indianapolis, December 29, 30, and 31, 1885.

GENERAL PROGRAM.

TUESDAY, DEC. 29, 7:30 P. M. 1. Opening Exercises. 2. Address of retiring President, H. B. Hill, Supt. Dearborn county. 3. Inaugural Address, "The Philosophy of Life," E. E. Smith, Chair of English and History, Purdue University. 4. Miscellaneous Business—Appointment of Committees.

WEDNESDAY, 9 A. M.—I. Opening Exercises. 2. Paper—"The Social Influence of the Teacher," John W. Holcombe, Supt. Public Instruction. Discussion opened by Wm. J. Bryan, Prof. of English, University of Indiana. 3. Paper—"The Truancy Problem," Mrs. Mattie Curl Dennis, Richmond. Discussion opened by E. H. Butler, Supt. Winchester schools. 4. Brief Addresses—*a.* "Is it the Aim of the School to Train the Body?" Mrs. Emma Mont. McRae, Prin. Marion high school; John P. Mather, Supt. of Warsaw schools. *b.* "Tenure of Office of the Teacher," Lin H. Hadley, Supt. Rockville schools; B. F. Johnson, Supt. Benton county.

Afternoon, 2:00.—1 Paper—"The Æsthetic Element in Child-Culture," Mrs. S. E. Barnes, La Fayette. Discussion opened by W. N. Hailman, Supt. La Porte schools. 2. Paper—"The Discipline of the Will," S. S. Parr, Prin. De Pauw Normal School. Discussion opened by R. G. Boone, Supt. Frankfort schools. 3. Miscellaneous Business—Appointment of Committee on Officers.

Evening, 7:30.—Popular Address—"The Thinker and the Doer," James B. Angell, Pres. Michigan University.

THURSDAY, 9 A. M.—I. Opening Exercises. 2. Paper—"Organic Relation of the Common School Studies," Howard Sandison, Dept. of Methods, State Normal School. General Discussion. 3. Brief Addresses—*a.* "How Best to Develop Thought Power in Pupils," J. H. Martin, Supt. Madison schools; S. E. Harwood, Supt. Spencer schools. *b.* "Should the State furnish Text-Books for the Pupils?" C. F. Coffin, New Albany. *c.* "Is Instruction Best when Pleasantest?" J B. Ragan, Associate Prin. Richmond Normal School; Elias Boltz, Supt. Mishawaka schools.

Afternoon, 2:00.—1. Annual Address—Hon. Jno. P. Wickersham, ex-Supt. of Public Instruction, Penn. 2. Reports of Committees. 3. Miscellaneous Business.

HOTELS.—Headquarters at the Grand Hotel—Rate $2.00 per day. Tne other Hotels will doubtless give reduced rates also. *Positive arrangements ensure these reduced rates only to those having certificates showing payment of annual dues.*

RAILROADS.—Better railroad facilities than ever before are offered. Reduced rates on nearly all roads in Indiana have been obtained, so that all may secure the reduction in fare for the whole distance. The plan is unlike any heretofore pursued, but if instructions are closely followed no mistakes need occur.

Write at once to the Railroad Secretary for full information and certificates. POSITIVELY NO REDUCED RATES GIVEN TO ANY ONE WHO DOES NOT SECURE A CERTIFICATE BEFORE STARTING. The uniform rate will be one and one-third fares for the round trip. Address at once *with stamp*, C. S. Olcott, R. R. Sec'y, Chicago, Ill.

SPECIAL ATTENTION is called to the following changes since last year: 1. No person can secure reduced rates over any road without first securing a certificate. 2. Applications must reach the secretary not later than Dec. 24. Otherwise they will not be noticed.

PROGRAMS are ready for distribution. For these or other information, address   W. H. ELSON, *Ch'n Ex. Com., Rockville, Ind.*

HIGH SCHOOL SECTION.

TUESDAY, DEC. 29, 9 A. M.—1. "Biology Work in High Schools," Prof. John M. Coulter, Wabash College. 2. "The Value of the Student Spirit to the Profession of Teaching," Prin. Chester E. Lane, Ft. Wayne high school. Discussion led by Supt. E. D. Bosworth, Farmer City, Ill. 3. "Discipline from the Study of Physics," Prin. Robert Spear, Evansville high school. Discussion led by Prin. J. A. Zeller, La Fayette high school.

Afternoon, 2:00.—1. "Chemistry in the High School," Miss Lillie J. Martin, Indianapolis high school. (Illustrated with class in the laboratory.) Discussion led by Supt. F. Treudley, of Union City. 2. "Report of Committee on Course of Study for High Schools," Supt. R. G. Boone, Frankfort, Ch'n. 3. Miscellaneous Business.

NOTE.—Ample time will be given for the discussion of this proposed course of study, and the high school people are expected to talk. It is made to meet the needs of cities having a population not greater than ten thousand.

T. H. DUNN, Crawfordsville, Ch'n Ex. Com.

INDIANA COLLEGE ASSOCIATION.

The following is a partial program of the eighth annual meeting, to be held at the Dennison House, Indianapolis, Dec. 28–29, 1885. Papers are limited to 25 minutes each, to allow time for general discussion.

MONDAY, DEC. 28, 2 P M.—Reports and Routine Business. "The Practical Value of College Degrees," Prof. Alpheus McTaggart, State Normal School. "Methods of Teaching Chemistry to Beginners in a College Course." Several contributors of papers, limited to five minutes each. Irregular Business.

Evening Session, 7:30.—Inaugural Address, Prof. John L. Campbell, Wabash College.

TUESDAY, 9 A. M.—"Medicine and Agriculture as Learned Professions," Dr. Chas. R. Dryer, Ft. Wayne College of Medicine. "The Tendencies of Scientific Investigation," Prof. D. A. Owen, Franklin College

Afternoon Session, 1:30.—"The Use of English in Teaching Foreign Languages," Prof. Allen B. Philpott, State University; Prof. Hans. C. G. Jagemann, Earlham College. Election of Officers and adjournment.   ROBT. B. WARDER, *Sec'y,* Lafayette, Ind.

SUPERINTENDENTS' CONVENTION.

The third meeting of the superintendents of city and town schools of Indiana and Ohio was held at Richmond, November 5, 6, and 7, 1885. The following superintendents and othnr educators were present from Indiana: Dr. John S. Irwin, Fort Wayne; Dr. W. N. Hailman, La Porte; John M. Bloss, Muncie; J. N. Study, Richmond; S. S. Parr, De Pauw University; Sheridan Cox, Kokomo; J. L. Rippetoe, Connersville; F. Treudley, Union City; J. W. Caldwell, Huntington; Miss M. H. McCalla, Bloomington; J. J. Mills and Allen Jay, Earlham College; J. C. Macpherson, Supt. Wayne county; J V. Martin, Greenfield; Eli Jay, T. A. Mott and L C. Harriscn, Richmond; Victor C. Alderson, Dublin; Cyrus W. Hodgin and J. B. Ragan, Richmond Normal School; W. W. Wirt, Portland; N. D. Wolfard, Fountain City; E. H. Butler, Winchester; W. T. Fry and Cyrus Smith, of the State at large. From Ohio: L. R. Klemm, Hamilton; C. L Vancleve, Troy; P. W. Search, Sidney; C. C. Miller, Eaton; P. E. Cromer, Arcanum; H. L. Frank, West Liberty; and P. C. Zemer, Ansonia.

The following subjects were informally discussed: 1, Methods of Promotion ; 2, How to Promote Culture among Teachers; 3, Teachers' Meetings; 4, Examinations; 5, Gradation of Schools: 6, Duties of Janitors

"Methods of Promotion" was given an entire evening. Mr. Caldwell said that in the Huntington schools promotions were made once a year, based upon five written examinations, modified by the pupils' daily recitations and judgment of the teacher and superintendent. Standard for promotion fiom 75 to 85 percent. Superintendent prepares all of the questions.

Supt. Hailman said at La Porte pupils were promoted once a year, but not upon written examinations or recitations, but wholly upon the judgment of the teacher and superintendent. This judgment was based upon the mental power of the pupil. They hold monthly examinations or reviews for the benefit of the pupil and teacher. Have no percent standard for promotion. Teachers prepare the questions for reviews, subject to the superintendent's approval. He has a supernumerary teacher whose business it is to assist in the office work and give extra attention to pupils who are deficient in their work.

Mr. Wirt said that his method of promotion was similar to that of Mr. Caldwell's. Bi-monthly examinations are held in all of the grades except the high school, where they are held at the close of the term. Promotions are made at the close of the year, upon examinations and recitations, each counting one-half. The percent for promotion is 80.

4

J. C. Macpherson said the question of promotion of pupils in the country schools was an unsolved problem, but was demanding attention The question of grading the country schools had been partially solved, but the next important one was to establish a basis for promotions. "Why are pupils nearly always placed in a lower grade when they move from one school to another?" He also stated that he thought the same text-books should be used in the graded schools that are used in the country schools of the same county.

Supt. Bloss said that he made promotions at the end of the year, based upon examinations, modified by the teachers and superintendent's judgment. The basis upon which pupils are promoted is fixed at the close of the year. Examinations are held at irregular intervals, the Supt. making out the questions,—teachers not allowed to grade the papers of their own pupils.

E. W. Search said at Sidney much dependence is placed upon the pupil's daily work. Examinations are reduced to the minimum and are used as the superintendent's "check." Promotions are made once a year, based upon examinations and recitations. All questions are prepared by the superintendent. Have no fixed basis for promotion. Percents are not made the entire test for promotion.

The program for Friday was to visit the public schools of Richmond, the Normal School, and Earlham College. This part of the program was carried out, and gave much pleasure and profit. The public schools are in excellent condition. The Richmond Normal is a demonstration of success. Earlham College was never before so prosperous.

"Culture of Teachers" was exhaustively discussed. The following points were made: Teachers should mingle with people of other professions and business. Teachers should read general literature. The State Teachers' Reading Circle was highly commended. Teachers should study with a view of obtaining broad culture. Personal habits and dress are elements of culture. Cultivate a pleasant countenance. Teachers' associations are means of culture.

On the subject of "Teachers' Meetings," all agreed that the business part should occupy but little time. Many of the superintendents held grade meetings for the purpose of laying out the work of teachers and giving methods of instruction.

The subject of "Examinations" was discussed by nearly all of the superintendents.

On the subject of "Gradation" Supt. Hailman remarked that the discussion should take the line of principles. He has found the question in his experience to be, how to *ungrade* graded schools, so as to adapt them to the wants of the individual pupil, and the stage of his development. Instead of grading on the amount of arithmetic, geography, etc., better grade on the amount of power pupils have over their work, thus making their mental growth the basis of gradation. He would designate what is usually called the Primary Grade as "The Perceptional Stage," in which all knowledge is obtained by contact with *things*. He would call the Grammar "The Conceptional Grade," in which the language expression of thought is the leading idea. The High School, "The Stage of Research—seeking truth." For convenience he preserves the three grades, Primary, Grammar, and High School.

The discussion of this subject took a somewhat philosophical turn, and was further participated in by Parr, Hodgin, Mills, Cromer, and Vancleve.   J. S. Irwin, *Pres.*
E. H. Butler, *Sec'y.*

PERSONAL.

J. W. Love holds the reins at Montezuma.

E. W. Wright is Supt. of the Kendallville schools.

Geo. W. Deland continues in charge at Perrysville.

F. S. Morgenthaler is principal of the schools at Jasper.

C. M. Carpenter, a graduate of the State Normal, is serving his second year as principal of the Bruceville schools.

Mrs. E. D. Kellogg, formerly an Indianapolis teacher, but for twelve or more years past a teacher in Boston, is now teacher of a model department in Charlotte, N. C.

E. E. Smith, of Purdue University, will read a paper on Horticulture and Sanitation at the meeting of the Indiana Horticultural Society, to be held at La Fayette December 1, 2, and 3.

Chas. S. Olcott, late publisher of the *Educational Weekly*, has taken charge of the Western Office of the New England Publishing Co., and will make his headquarters at Chicago.

John G. Overton, who served as Supt. of Montgomery county from the enacting of the superintendency law until June '73, has just been elected to his old position *vice* W. T. Fry, resigned.

John Eaton, U. S. Commissioner of Education, has resigned his office to accept the presidency of Marietta College, Ohio. The best man to fill his place, is James H. Smart, of Indiana.

C. M. Merica, Supt. of DeKalb county, is in the field first. He has already fixed the date of his institute for 1886. It will open Aug. 30th. There is room left for about 40 others that week.

Hon. J. L. M. Curry, who has for years served as commissioner of the Peabody Fund, has vacated the place to accept the appointment of Minister to Spain. The best man in the United States to fill that vacancy is the Hon. E. E. White, of Ohio.

---

written about forty years ago. But notwithstanding this lapse of time and the improvement in "school-keeping," so thoroughly did the author understand the underlying principles and the aims of the work that even to-day it is one of the best books a young teacher can read.

Prof. W. H. Payne, of Michigan University, has recently prepared a new edition in which appears a biographical sketch of the author, and many notes and additions to the original text.

Cyrus Smith, Indianapolis, agent for Indiana and Michigan.

The St. Nicholas has no superior as a youth's magazine. The ablest writers contribute to its pages; it gives a great variety, so as to both instruct and entertain; and it is richly illustrated. What better Christmas present for a boy or girl than a year's subscription to St. Nicholas could possibly be suggested. Published by the Century Co., New York City.

Harpers' Young People is a weekly paper filled with all kinds of good things for boys and girls. Like all of Harpers' periodicals it is first-class of its kind. If allowed to do so it will bring to any family a stream of light and joy fifty-two times a year.

A Primary History of the United States. New York and Chicago: A. S. Barnes & Co. Cyrus Smith, Indianapolis, agent for Indiana and Michigan.

This book, comprised in 225 pages, is what its title indicates. It is primary in matter and manner of treatment, and not simply an abbreviation of a large book. By not attempting everything there is space for a fuller discussion of the more important points. The author has clearly discriminated between simplicity of style and simple thought. The mechanical execution of the book is all that could be desired.

Harpers' Copy-Books embrace some characteristic points worthy of consideration. They are well graded, simple, beautiful, and deserve large patronage. For full porticulars address W. J. Button, Chicago.

Harpers' Basar is the leading fashion paper for ladies in the United States. It not only gives in each issue large numbers of fashion plates of many styles, for both women and children, and a large sheet of patterns, but it gives a good variety of reading matter. No paper pleases ladies better. Address Harper & Bros., New York City.

The Eclectic Manual of Methods for the Assistance of Teachers Cincinnati: Van Antwerp, Bragg & Co.

This s a new book, and embodies the best thought on the subject.

treated. It is the result of the combined labors of several practical teachers and prominent educators. All the common school branches are included. The book is intended for teachers, not pupils. The suggestions and instructions are clear and comprehensive. The different grades are carefully recognized and each step logically taken. Ample illustrations are furnished. While the book will be helpful to all, it will be of special service to the young teacher.

It is written with special reference to the Eclectic Series of Textbooks, but will go almost equally well with any others.

BUSINESS NOTICES.

See the advertisement giving list of books for Young People.

What better Christmas present could be suggested than Webster's Unabridged Dictionary?

It will pay any reader to carefully examine the new advertisements this month. There are several, and no two alike.

An Opportunity.—Teachers can learn short-hand evenings. Thoroughly taught by *mail*. Address A. D. Reser, La Fayette, Ind.

The C. H. & I. is the best route frim Indianapolis to Cincinnati. The track is in good order, the cars are first-class, and the country passed through the "finest out doors."

Readers of the Journal in noticing the advertisement of DePauw University Normal School will please add the fact that students may enter at the beginning of *each* term. The next term begins Jan. 6, 1886. A beginning class will be formed at that time. 12-6t

Don't go to School—until you have seen the special rates to county graduates, young teachers and others preparing to teach, made by the Fort Wayne (Normal Classical and Business) College. W. F. Yocum,
11-3t Fort Wayne, Ind.

The New Decatur Route.—Solid trains between Indianapolis and Peoria, including Pullman Palace Sleeping and Reclining Chair Cars at reduced rates. This is the quickest line and is always on time. The shortest possible route to Kansas City, with only one change of cars. For lowest fares and full information apply to Newby & Jordan, agents, I. D. & S. R'y, 136 South Illinois street, Indianapolis. 7-tf

DE PAUW UNIVERSITY
NORMAL SCHOOL.

A School for the Professional Training of Teachers.

TUITION FREE.

All the advantages of a good Normal School, with the added benefits of the University Libraries, Laboratories, Lectures, Department Work, and Social Culture and Life.

LOCATION. Greencastle is one of the best school-towns in the West. It is located forty miles west of Indianapolis.

PLAN OF ORGANIZATION. The Normal School is an integral part of the University, but is distinct from all other schools. It has its own course of study, instructors, instruction, assembly-room and class-rooms, and provides superior facilities for training in the science and art of school-teaching and government, in connection with the **Advantages** of Instruction in the Collegiate, Special and Professional Schools of a great University. The school is organized to secure the highest type of professional training and to qualify its students to serve as superintendents and principals and to fill other important positions in the public-school service. Ample assembly and recitation-room facilities are provided in the West Building, adjoining the University Library and the well furnished rooms of the Department of Physics.

INSTRUCTORS. (ALEXANDER MARTIN, LL D., President;) S. S. PARR, Principal; Didactics; ARNOLD TOMPKINS, Arithmetic and Grammar; W. H. MACE, Geography and History; JOSEPH CARHART, Orthoepy and Reading. Other subjects are done in the Regular Departments of the University, by Specialists who are at the head of their respective lines of work.

COURSE OF STUDY. Three Courses: the English, the Latin, and the Select or Review Course. The English and the Latin courses extend over three years, and are intended to fit teachers for work in the best high-schools and in all schools below them. The Select or Review course, as its name indicates, is a course of one, two, three or more terms made up of selections from the English and the Latin courses. The student, if reasonably proficient in the common-school essentials, will be allowed to select a course for himself. If a number present themselves at once, asking a certain kind of work not in progress, a class or classes will be formed at any time. This arrangement affords excellent opportunity for review by such teachers as do not have time to take a regular course. High-School and College Graduates will find De Pauw University Normal School especially adapted to their wants.

SPECIAL ADVANTAGES.

1. INSTRUCTION. The Faculty have had special training for their work. The student is part of an organization that has nearly half a hundred competent and experienced instructors.

2. GREAT SOCIAL ADVANTAGES.

3. USE OF A MAGNIFICENT LIBRARY OF SEVERAL THOUSAND VOLUMES. No other Normal School in the West enjoys such advantage

4. LECTURES AND ENTERTAINMENTS.

5. CABINETS. Anatomical and Lithological Cabinets costing several thousand dollars.

6. REDUCED-RAILROAD RATES.

7. AID IN SECURING PLACES.

8. CHEAPNESS OF LIVING. Cheap rates of room-rent and board are offered. The University has erected new and commodious halls for boarding and lodging. These halls furnish rooms that are carpeted, well furnished and provided with all needed comforts, including bath-rooms, steam-heat and gas. These rooms rent at from forty to sixty cents per week. Heat and light are furnished at cost. Table-board will be furnished at the University boarding-halls at $2 00 to $2 75 per week. Improved facilities and purchase of material at wholesale rates render it possible to furnish the most for the money; self boarding at $1 25 and $1 50 per week. Board in private families at corresponding rates. These rates are not surpassed by any school that furnishes good accommodations.

9. BOOKS RENTED. Students who wish to rent books will be accommodated at a low rate. Those who desire to buy their books will receive them at introductory rates, thus insuring a considerable saving in expenses.

10. TUITION FREE. The only charges are an incidental fee of $5 00 per term to cover miscellaneous expenses connected with the school, and one of 25 cents per term for use of the library.

THE SCHOOL YEAR.

Three terms per year. The second term begins January 6, 1886, and ends March 24; the third begins March 31 and ends June 10. Students taking select courses may enter at any time not unreasonably late; but as the aim of the work is organic unity of subjects and lessons, lessons can not well be made up. Hence there is desirability of prompt attendance at the first of any term.

☞ For further information address the Principal,

11-tf

S. S. PARR, Greencastle, Ind.

Announcements:

	Sample Copy and Introduction Price.
Murdoch's Analytic Elocution, (1) - - - -	$1 00
Eclectic Complete Book-keeping, (2) - - -	50
Norton's Chemistry—Complete, (3) - - - -	1 10
White's Oral Lessons in Number, (4) - - -	60
Eclectic School Geometry, (5) - - - - -	60
Ray's New Astronomy, (6) - · - - -	1 20

(1) *Now Ready.* ANALYTIC ELOCUTION, by the well-known veteran Actor, Reader, and Instructor in Elocution, JAMES E. MURDOCH, author of A PLEA FOR SPOKEN LANGUAGE. A complete and practical exposition of the only true and scientific method of developing the speaking voice. Fully illustrated by numerous extracts from the best sources, to which are added seventy pages of selected Readings. 12mo., cloth, half roan, 504 pages.

(2) *Now Ready.* ECLECTIC COMPLETE BOOK-KEEPING. By IRA MAYHEW. e cheapest and most practical work yet offered on this subject. Its methods have been tested by 25 years experience. Double Entry is clearly elucidated. Many new and valuable special forms suggested. 156 pages, half roan. *Key and Blanks also nearly ready.*

(3) *Now Ready.* New edition of Norton's Elements of Chemistry, *completed* by the addition of chapters on *Organic Chemistry.* Half roan, 504 pages, 12mo.

(4) *Ready December* 15. ORAL LESSONS IN NUMBER. For Teachers. By E. E. WHITE, A. M. This work is not simply a Manual for Teachers, but an exhaustive treatise *containing the Exercises to be used* by the Teacher in the instruction of primary classes in Number. It is a Complete and practical Guide, indispensable to every teacher of Arithmetic.

(5) ECLECTIC SCHOOL GEOMETRY. A revision of *Evans's School Geometry,* by J. J. BURNS, A. M., Superintendent of Schools, Dayton, O., formerly Ohio State School Commissioner. In this revision the work is made to conform to the "New Geometry," and is especially adapted to High Schools by the addition of numerous exercises and original demonstrations. 12mo., half roan, 155 pages.

(6) *Ready Jan.* 1, 1885. RAY'S ASTRONOMY, revised by the author, S. H. PEABODY, *Regent of University of Illinois,* and adapted to the progress of astronomical science. All recent established discoveries are included, especially those relating to solar and planetary physics. 12mo., half roan, about 350 pages.

VAN ANTWERP, BRAGG & CO., Publishers, Cin. & New York.
[s-tf]

THE INDIANA UNIVERSITY.

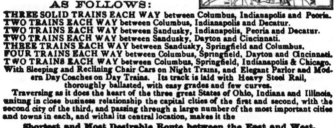

The Northern Indiana Normal School

AND BUSINESS INSTITUTE.
VALPARAISO, INDIANA,

Wishes its patrons and all interested in the Cause of Education,

A Happy New Year.

To the School the past year has been one of unusual prosperity, and the prospects for the future were never more flattering.

The institution has enjoyed a growth and prosperity unparalleled in the history of schools. It was organized September 16th, 1873, with 35 students in attendance. The number has grown until now this is the

LARGEST NORMAL SCHOOL IN THE UNITED STATES.

For this remarkable growth there are many reasons. The principal one, however, is that

The School Accommodates Itself to the Wants of the People,

Instead of compelling them to accommodate themselves to it. To establish such an institution **Three Things Were Necessary :**

1st. That the School possess the same advantages, and that the work be as thorough as at the older and endowed institutions. 2d. That the work be properly arranged. 3d. That the expenses be made less than at any other place. That we have accomplished these three points is acknowledged by all.

THE FOLLOWING COURSES OF STUDY HAVE BEEN ARRANGED: Preparatory, Teachers', Collegiate, Special Science, Engineering, Penmanship, Elocution, Fine Art, Music, Law, Literature, Telegraphic, Phonographic and Review. Each Department is independent within itself, and the fact that there are other departments than the Teachers', makes this none the less a **Special School for Teachers.**

The same is true of each department. While each is independent of the others, yet the student may select a part of his studies from one department, and a part from another, without extra charge. This is a feature that is especially commendable. From the beginning of the school none but experienced teachers have been employed. **New Specialists are Provided for each Department.**

We do not call attention to this boastingly, but because it is supposed that specialists are employed in endowed institutions only. A more complete Library than is found in any other Normal School has been furnished, and an abundance of apparatus for the elucidation of every subject has been supplied. In short, no expense has been spared in providing everything that would, in any way, advance the interest of students.

THE ARRANGEMENT OF THE WORK IS SATISFACTORY. While we have regular courses of study, and where it is at all possible, the student will do well to pursue some one of them, yet the school realizes that there are THOUSANDS OF YOUNG PEOPLE WHO HAVE NOT THE MONEY NOR THE TIME to take a regular course, but wish to pursue special subjects, and must attend school at such times as are convenient for them. THE LARGE MAJORITY OF TEACHERS are engaged in their profession, the greater portion of the year, but desire to improve their vacations, by continuing a course of study, or in reviewing; again, the school meets the wants of a large class of People who have not had the Opportunity of Attending School while young. These realizing the need of some education, and knowing that they must COMMENCE AT THE VERY BEGINNING OF ARITHMETIC, GRAMMAR, etc., yet having an aversion to entering the primary classes in the public schools, can come here and enter classes composed of students of their own age, and stage of advancement. To accommodate all of these different grades, we organize at the beginning of every term, and not at the beginning only, but at different periods during the term, Beginning, Advanced, Regular, Special, and Review Classes

STUDENTS CAN ENTER AT ANY TIME, SELECT THEIR OWN STUDIES, BEGIN WHERE THEY WISH AND ADVANCE AS RAPIDLY AS THEY MAY DESIRE. These are advantages which can not be offered IN SCHOOLS THAT HAVE A SMALL ATTENDANCE.

The Expenses are Much Less Than at Any Other Place!

In order to accomplish this we have erected numerous boarding houses and have arranged and furnished the rooms such as no uninterested parties would do. Good board and well-furnished rooms, $1.70 to $1.90 per week—never exceeding the latter. Tuition, $6 per term. No other institution in the land furnishes equal accommodations at anything like as low rates. We invite the most thorough investigation. In addition to the above, the student has the advantage of one of the **Most Complete Business Colleges in the Land, Without Extra Charge.**

While many schools advertise a business course in connection with their work, yet none of them have ever attempted anything like as extensive a course as is found here.

The result of all these advantages is that no other school of equal age that has one-third as many students FILLING RESPONSIBLE POSITIONS, and that the demand for teachers, and business men trained here is always far greater than we can supply.

CALENDAR.

Second Winter term will open January 15; Spring term, March 25; Summer term, June 3; Fall term, August 26.

For further information send for Catalogue, which will be mailed free.

9-tf   Address,   H. B. BROWN, Principal, or O. P. KINSEY, Associate Prin.

THE INDIANA UNIVERSITY.

BLOOMINGTON, MONROE COUNTY, IND.

Spring Term begins March 30, 1885.

Fall Term begins Sept. 3, 1884. **Winter Term Jan. 5, 1885.**

THREE COLLEGIATE COURSES.

1. The Course in Ancient Classics; 2. The Course in Modern Classics; 3. The Course in General Science.

Also, a Preparatory Course.

The Fall Term begins with the opening of the College Year, Thursday Morning, September 3, 1884. Students to be examined should present themselves two days earlier.

Tuition Free. Contingent Fee, $5 per term. Library Fee required of all, $1.00. Fees must be paid strictly in advance.

Women Admitted to all Courses on same conditions as Men. For Catalogue, and other information, address

A. R. HOWE, *Treasurer.* DAVID S. JORDAN, *President.*

WM. W. SPANGLER, *Secretary.* 9-1y

DO YOU WANT TO TEACH

In the Indiana Public Schools? If you do, now is the time to apply for a position. According to the reports sent in by the school officers and superintendents of the state there will be at least 3,000 vacancies in the state to be filled before September 1, 1885. The "TEACHER'S BLUE BOOK," (just issued), is the only published key to these vacancies. It also gives the name of every school officer in the state, every teacher and salary, and other valuable information. If you want a position in a state which has a reserve school fund of *ten million dollars*, the largest of any state in the Union, send one dollar for the "BLUE BOOK," or a one-cent stamp for descriptive circular. It is endorsed by the State Superintendent of Instruction and every prominent educator who has examined it.

4-2t   Address,   T. A. DE WEESE, PUBLISHER, South Bend, Ind.

UNION CHRISTIAN COLLEGE,

MEROM, SULLIVAN COUNTY, IND.

DEPARTMENTS: CLASSICAL—6 years. SCIENTIFIC—4 years. BIBLICAL—3 years. ACADEMIC—2 years. NORMAL CLASS—Each Spring Term MUSICAL—Instrumental and Vocal. DRAWING and PAINTING. Equal Advantages to both Sexes.

EXPENSES: Tuition $2 per Term—payable in College Script or Cash. Incidental fee $5 per Term, payable in advance. Instrumental Music, Drawing and Painting extra.

Fall Term—10 weeks—begins September 5, 1883.
Winter Term—13 weeks—begins December 5, 1883.
Spring and Normal Term—12 weeks—begins March 12, 1884.

For further particulars, address   REV. E. MUDGE, President, or
10-tf   PROF. B. F. McHENRY, Secretary.

CENTRAL NORMAL COLLEGE,

DANVILLE, INDIANA.

Fall Session begins Tuesday, September 2, 1884.
Tuition $8.00.   Room-rent 50 cents.   Board $1.50.
Board, room-rent and tuition, one term of ten weeks, $27.00.

A healthy, accessible, intelligent community.   NO SALOONS.   A popular, progressive, independent, successful school.   An annual enrollment of over ONE THOUSAND earnest, enthusiastic, moral young people.   All grades of classes.   No examinations.   Students may select their studies, entering at any time.   ROOMS IN PRIVATE FAMILIES.

MRS. F P. ADAMS, Prin.   [8-tf]   J. A. STEELE, Vice-Pres.

SOUTH!

J. M. & I. RAILROAD.

Shortest, Best, and Most Popular Line to

Louisville, Nashville, Memphis, Chattanooga, Atlanta, Mobile & New Orleans.

It is obviously to the advantage of passengers going South to purchase tickets by the direct route. The facilities offered are unequalled.

Palace Sleeping Cars and elegant Parlor Cars run between Chicago and Louisville daily without change.

Through Coaches and Pullman Sleeping Cars between St. Louis and Louisville daily. These are rare advantages. Speed and safety.

Ask your friends if they have ever ridden over the "Jeff" and they will answer, "yes, always take the old reliable"

J. M. & I. R. R.

For information as to rates, route, and time of leaving of trains, please apply to   H. R. DERING, Ass't Pass. Agt., Indianapolis, Ind.

Office northeast corner Washington and Illinois Sts., opposite Bates House.

JAS. McCREA, Manager, Columbus, O.

6-7t   E. A. FORD, Gen'l Pass. Agt., Pittsburgh, Pa.

THE GREAT
PAN-HANDLE ROUTE.

Chicago, St. Louis and Pittsburgh Railway.

Pittsburgh, Cincinnati & St. Louis Railway.

—IS THE—

SHORTEST, QUICKEST AND BEST

—LINE GOING—

EAST, WEST, NORTHWEST & SOUTH.

Unexcelled Through Car Service. Superior Equipment Prompt Connections in Union Depot.

NO TRANSFERS.

PULLMAN CARS THROUGH BETWEEN ALL THE GREAT COMMERCIAL CENTERS.

Pittsburgh, Harrisburg, Baltimore, Washington, Philadelphia, New York, Columbus, Cincinnati, Indianapolis, St. Louis, Chicago, Louisville.

The advantages offered to Passengers via Pan-Handle Route are unequalled. The rates are always as low as by any other line. All modern improvements conduce to speed, comfort and safety. Baggage checked through to destination. Superior service in every respect. Agent of the company will cheerfully furnish information in regard to trains, connections, and rates of fare.   H. R. DEERING,

Ass't Gen'l Pass. Agent, Indianapolis, Ind.

JAMES McREA, Manager, Columbus, Ohio.

6-7t   E. A. FORD, Gen. Pass. Agent, Pittsburgh, Pa.

5

PURDUE UNIVERSITY,

LAFAYETTE, IND.

Fall Term begins Thursday, September 10th, 1885.

FIVE COURSES OF STUDY.

1. A Course in Agriculture and Horticulture. II. A Course in Practical Mechanics and Mechanical Engineering. III. A Course in Industrial Arts. IV. A Course in General Science. V. A Course in Pharmacy.

EXAMINATIONS for Admission will be held in each County, by the County Superintendent, on the last Saturday in August, and at the University September 8th, 1885.

TUITION FREE. Expense for Board, Room, Light, Fuel and Washing, about $50.00 per term. *One Hundred and Fifty Dollars* will pay all necessary expenses for one year at the University. Women are admitted to all departments. The Preparatory class will receive students and thoroughly fit them for entrance to the University classes.

Send for a Catalogue to Registrar Purdue University, or to

JAMES H. SMART, President,

7-3t
LAFAYETTE, IND.

MESERVEY'S
BOOK-KEEPING

Single and Double Entry.   For High Schools and Academies.

MESERVEY'S BOOK-KEEPING,
Single Entry—For Grammar Schools.

Meservey's Text-Books in Book-keeping have been adopted for use in the public schools of more than five hundred and fifty cities and towns and over seventy academies in New England alone. It is also used very extensively in the West. Copies sent for examination on receipt of—for Single Entry, 30 cents. Single and Double Entry, 50 cents.

—o—

STONE'S
HISTORY OF ENGLAND
By A. P. STONE, LL. D.
Superintendent of Schools, City of Springfield, Massachusetts.

The author of this work is widely known as one of the most successful of New England educators. His text book will be found a well-prepared and impartial history of the country, written in a style to interest the pupil in the main historical events without wearying him with a mass of unimportant facts and figures.

A special feature of the book is the prominence given to matters concerning social life and progress, giving the pupils an idea of the manners and habits of the people, and of the state of society at different periods.

It has recently been adopted in the public schools of Boston and Springfield, Mass.; Minneapolis, Min.; Indianapolis, Ind.; Grand Rapids, Mich, etc., etc. Copy sent for examination on receipt of 50 cents

Attention is also invited to Bradbury's Eaton's Series of Arithmetics and Higher Mathematics.

Descriptive Circular of all of above books, with terms for introduction, will be sent on application.

7-3t   Address,   THOMPSON, BROWN & CO., 23 Hawley St., Boston.

THE INDIANA UNIVERSITY.

BLOOMINGTON, MONROE COUNTY, IND.

**Fall Term begins Sept. 3, 1885.   Winter Term, Jan. 5, 1886.
Spring Term begins March 30, 1886.**

THREE COLLEGIATE COURSES.

1. The Course in Ancient Classics; 2. The Course in Modern Classics;
3. The Course in General Science.

Also, a Preparatory Course.

The Fall Term begins with the opening of the College Year, Thursday
Morning, September 3, 1885.   Students to be examined should present
themselves two days earlier.

Tuition Free.   Contingent Fee, $5 per term.   Library Fee required of all,
$1.00.   Fees must be paid strictly in advance.

Women Admitted to all Courses on same conditions as Men.
For Catalogue, and other information, address

A. R. HOWE, *Treasurer.*   DAVID S. JORDAN, *President.*

WM. W. SPANGLER, *Secretary.*   9-1y

SOUTH!

J. M. & I. RAILROAD.

Shortest, Best, and Most Popular Line to

Louisville, Nashville, Memphis, Chattanooga, Atlanta, Mobile & New Orleans.

It is obviously to the advantage of passengers going South to purchase tickets by the direct route. The facilities offered are unequalled.

Palace Sleeping Cars and elegant Parlor Cars run between Chicago and Louisville daily without change.

Through Coaches and Pullman Sleeping Cars between St. Louis and Louisville daily. These are rare advantages. Speed and safety.

Ask your friends if they have ever ridden over the "Jeff" and they will answer, "yes, always take the old reliable"

J. M. & I. R. R.

For information as to rates, route, and time of leaving of trains, please apply to · H. R. DERING, Ass't Pass. Agt., Indianapolis, Ind.

Office northeast corner Washington and Illinois Sts., opposite Bates House.

JAS. McCREA, Manager, Columbus, O.

6-7t   E. A. FORD, Gen'l Pass. Agt., Pittsburgh, Pa.

THE GREAT
PAN-HANDLE ROUTE.

Chicago, St. Louis and Pittsburgh Railway.

Pittsburgh, Cincinnati & St. Louis Railway.

—IS THE—

SHORTEST, QUICKEST AND BEST

—LINE GOING—

EAST, WEST, NORTHWEST & SOUTH.

Unexcelled Through Car Service. Superior Equipment   Prompt Connections in Union Depot.

NO TRANSFERS.

PULLMAN CARS THROUGH BETWEEN ALL THE GREAT COMMERCIAL CENTERS.

Pittsburgh, Harrisburg, Baltimore, Washington, Philadelphia, New York, Columbus, Cincinnati, Indianapolis, St. Louis, Chicago, Louisville.

The advantages offered to Passengers via Pan-Handle Route are unequalled. The rates are always as low as by any other line. All modern improvements conduce to speed, comfort and safety. Baggage checked through to destination. Superior service in every respect. Agent of the company will cheerfully furnish information in regard to trains, connections, and rates of fare.

H. R. DERING,
Ass't Gen'l Pass. Agent, Indianapolis, Ind.

JAMES McREA, Manager, Columbus, Ohio.

6-yt   E. A. FORD, Gen. Pass. Agent, Pittsburgh, Pa.

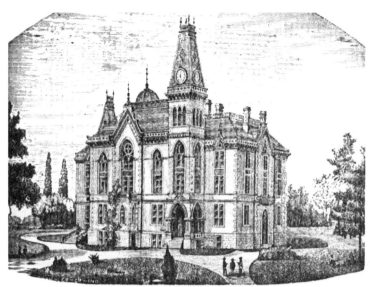

(East Building.)

De Pauw University
Normal School,

GREENCASTLE, IND.

School for the Professional Training of Teachers.

the advantages of a good Normal School, with the added benefits of the University Libraries, Laboratories, Lectures, Department Work, and Social Culture and Life.

FACULTY.

ALEXANDER MARTIN, D. D., LL. D.
PRESIDENT.

S. S. PARR,
(Formerly of the State Normal School Faculty, late State Institute Conductor for Minnesota.)
Principal and Professor of Didactics.

ARNOLD TOMPKINS,
(Graduate of State Normal School and student at State University, late Superintendent of the Franklin School.)
English Grammar and Arithmetic.

W. H. MACE,
(Graduate of State Normal School and Michigan University, late Superintendent of McGregor (Iowa) Schools.)
History and Geography.

JOSEPH CARHART,
(Until recently, for several years, of the faculty of the State Normal School.)
Orthoepy and Reading.

TUITION FREE.

The only charge is an incidental one of $5.00 per term for miscellaneous expenses incurred in conducting the School, and 25 cents Library Fee.

There are no other charges.

GENERAL STATEMENT.

Location. Greencastle is a beautiful little city of five thousand inhabitants, situated forty miles West of Indianapolis and thirty eight miles East of Terre Haute, on the Vandalia and the Indianapolis and St. Louis Railroads, at their intersection by the Louisville and Chicago Road. These ample railroad facilities make ingress and egress rapid, easy and cheap. The town is one of the most beautiful and orderly in the State, and is noted for its good society and pleasant associations. Its location is not surpassed by any school-town in the State.

Plan of Organization. The Normal School is an integral part of the University, established in order to provide superior facilities for training in the science and art of school teaching and goverment, in connection with the advantages of instruction in the collegiate, special and professional schools of a great University. The school is organized to secure the highest type of professional training and to qualify its students to serve as superintendents and principals and to fill other important positions in the public-school service. Ample assembly and recitation room facilities are provided in the West Building, adjoining the University Library and the well-furnished rooms of the department of physics. Its pupils will have the seating, organisation and dicipline, so far as practicable, of the schools in which its members are expected to teach.

Instructors. The Principal and teachers were trained for Normal School work, besides having availed themselves of the higher training of the College and the University. They are fresh from the field of Common School work, and thus familiar with the environment which surrounds the common-schools and the problems which perplex the Common School teacher. Three members have been in the practical work of organizing and superintending schools. The Principal has had a lengthy experience as teacher of didactics and as State Institute conductor, and has thus had good opportunity to study the wants and needs of all classes of teachers. The work in Phyics, Chemistry, Latin and other academic subjects is done in their respective departments.

Courses of Study. Three courses: the English, the Latin and the Select or Review Course. The English and the Latin courses extend over three years, and are intended to fit teachers for work in the best high-schools and in all schools below them. The Select or Review Course, as its name indicates, is a course of one, two, three or more terms made up of selections from the English and the Latin courses. The student, if reasonably proficient in the common-school essentials, will be allowed to select a course for himself. If a number present themselves at once, asking a certain kind of work not in progress, a class or classes will be formed at any time. This arrangement affords excellent opportunity for review by such teachers as do not have time to take a regular course

High-School and College Graduates will find the courses of study in DePauw Normal School especially adapted to their wants. The course in Didactics supplies them with the needed professional work The privilege of selecting studies in the University courses supplies such additional work as they need. The presence of the University proper offers many advantages to those of both classes who are preparing to teach. Diplomas will be conferred on those who complete either of the prescribed courses, and certificates issued to those who take select courses, if they complete any part of the work, for such part or parts as are completed.

SPECIAL ADVANTAGES.

1. **Instruction.** The Faculty have received the best Collegiate and Normal School training, have had extended and successful experience in various grades of public school work, have been selected because of special fitness for the particular departments they have assumed and the Normal School is part of a University which has nearly fifty thoroughly competent and experienced instructors.

2. **Social Advantages.** Students have the advantages of association with from six to eight hundred young men and women from the best families of Indiana and adjoining states; and they may become permanently identified with an institution having a thousand graduates occupying positions of honor and trust in all parts of the world.

3. **Use of Libraries.** Students of the Normal School enjoy the advantages of the nificent University libraries, consisting of several thousand volumes. The general l rooms are located only a few feet from the Normal School assembly-room. The library arranged and catalogued so as to be of easy use for students of all grades of advanceme is open for reference and reading, morning and afternoon, six days in the week.

4. **Laboratories.** Normal students have the advantages of a chemical laborato supplied with facilities for all kinds of qualitative and quantitative analysis: and ca accomodating one hundred students; a large and well equipped laboratory recently fi at an expense of $3,000 furnishes the best facilities for study of physics.

5. **Cabinets.** A complete lithological cabinet consisting of specimens historicall stratigraphically arranged, recently purchased of Prof. Henry A. Ward, of Rochester. York, at an expense of $3,000, furnishes opportunity for practical illustration in physical raphy; an anatomical cabinet, consisting of a manikin of the best French make and an enlarged scale, of such organs of the human body as require illustration, supplies the improved facilities for the study of physiology.

6. **Lectures and Entertainments.** During the year the student has opportunity to to distinguished lecturers and eminent artists who are invited to the University. These tainments are an important aid to social and literary culture.

7. **Cheapness of Living.** Cheap rates of room-rent and board are offered. The U sity has erected new and commodious halls for boarding and lodging. These halls fu rooms that are carpeted, well furnished and provided with all needed comforts including rooms, steam-heat and gas. These rooms rent from forty to sixty cents per week. Hea light are furnished at cost. Table-board will be furnished at the University boarding- $2.00 to 2.75 per week. Improved facilities and purchase of material at wholesale rates re possible to furnish the most for the money; self-boarding at $1.25 and $1.50 per week. private families at corresponding rates. These rates are not surpassed by any schoo furnishes good accomodations.

☞The number of rooms in the Gentlemen's Hall is limited, students should the apply as early as possible. Address the Principal.

8. **Reduced Railroad Rates.** East and West railroad lines carry students the round for one and one fifth fares.

9. **Books Rented.** Students who wish to rent books will be acomodated at a low Those who deire to buy their books will receive them at introductory rates, thus insu considerable saving in expenses.

10. **Aid in Securing Places.** The Normal School through the influence of the number of graduates, patrons and friends residing in all parts of the country, is able to r important aid to worthy students in securing positions.

11. **Tuition Free.** The only charges are an incidental fee of $5.00 per term to cover cellaneous expenses connected with the school, and one of 25 cents per term for use library.

THE SCHOOL YEAR.

Three terms per year. The first begins September 14 and ends December 23; the begins January 6 and ends March 24; the third begins March 31 and ends June 19. taking select courses may enter at any time not unreasonably late; but as the aim of th is organic unity of subjects and lessons, lessons can not well be made up, hence the desi of prompt attendance at the first of any term.

☞For further information see DePauw University Year Book pages 88-91 or add Principal.

S. S. PARR, Greencastle, Ind.

BARNES' NEW READERS,

"THE EDUCATIONAL GEMS OF THE AGE."

The most beautiful and practical set of School Readers ever issued. In point of subject-matter, gradation, type, illustrations, paper, binding, and in every other essential feature which goes to make up the very best, these books represent emphatically the perfection in school book literature.

The prices quoted below are those at which we can supply these Readers to schools, both for first introduction and subsequent use. The figures in the first column represent the exchange prices, where old Readers in use are taken as part pay. The second column gives the rates for introduction, where no old book is taken in exchange.

	Exchange.	Introduction.
BARNES' NEW NATIONAL FIRST READER, - - -	.12	.20
BARNES' NEW NATIONAL SECOND READER, - - -	.21	.35
BARNES' NEW NATIONAL THIRD READER, - - -	.30	.50
BARNES' NEW NATIONAL FOURTH READER, - - -	.42	.70
BARNES' NEW NATIONAL FIFTH READER, - - -	.54	.90

It is difficult to speak in moderate terms of these beautiful books, even if one were so inclined.—*Illinois School Journal.*

The books are gems, in every sense, and the only problem in doubt is, how they can be furnished at the price.— *National Journal of Education.*

HYGIENIC PHYSIOLOGIES,

With Special Reference to Alcoholic Drinks and Narcotics:

	Exchange	Introduction.
STEELE'S HYGIENIC PHYSIOLOGY COMPLETE, - - -	.67	$1.00
HUNT'S HYGIENE FOR YOUNG PEOPLE, - - -	.36	.50
THE CHILD'S HEALTH PRIMER, - - - - -	.18	.30

OTHER LATE AND LEADING BOOKS OF THE NATIONAL SERIES.

BARNES' NEW ARITHMETICS.

This series presents a minimum of theory with a maximum of practice. It adopts the shortest and best methods, and the language is clear and exact.

BARNES' NEW GEOGRAPHIES.

Complete TWO-BOOK series, with latest data, beautiful maps, new standard time, and all other "modern improvements." The plan of TEACHING BY COMPARISON or association of ideas, in this series, is worthy of special attention.

SILL'S LESSONS IN ENGLISH.

Practical, systematic, and complete. Useless verbiage eliminated, and English Grammar treated comprehensively in one convenient sized volume at small cost.

BARNES' BRIEF U. S. HISTORY.

One of the most remarkable text-books ever issued. In many parts of the country it is now more largely used *than all competing Histories combined.*

STEELE'S 14 WEEKS IN EACH SCIENCE.

Embracing Philosophy, Physiology, Chemistry, Zoology, Geology, Astronomy, and Botany.

These books have attained a phenomenal success, and the demand is constantly increasing. They present the cream of the respective studies, and the treatment of the subjects is not only exceedingly practical, but always remarkably interesting to the pupils.

Correspondence cordially invited. Address,

A. S. BARNES & CO.,

34 & 36 Madison St., CHICAGO, ILL.

THE AMERICAN EDUCATIONAL SERIES OF
SCHOOL $\frac{2}{4}$ COLLEGE TEXT-BOOKS.

IVISON, BLAKEMAN, TAYLOR & CO, Publishers,

Invite the attention of Teachers and School Officers to their large
and popular list, embracing many new and carefully
prepared text-books:

Swinton's Spellers.
Swinton's Readers
American Educational Readers
Swinton's Geographies.
Robinson's Arithmetics,
Fish's Arithmetics,
Swinton's Histories.
Spencerian Copy Books.
Kerl's Grammars.
Wells's Shorter Course Gram'r.

Bryant & Stratton's Book-keeping.
Townsend's Civil Government.
Gray's Botanies.
Dana s Geologies.
Eliot & Storer's Chemistry.
Cooley's Chemistry.
Wells's New Natural Philosophy.
Smith's Physiology.
Loomis's Music.
White's Industrial Drawing, etc.
Webster's Dictionaries.

Catalogues and Descriptive Circulars on application.

IVISON, BLAKEMAN, TAYLOR & CO.

753 ana 755 Broadway, New York.　149 Wabash Avenue, Chicago.

[7-3t]

5

MONON ROUTE

LOUISVILLE, NEW ALBANY & CHICAGO RY.

THE SHORTEST AND MOST DIRECT ROUTE FROM

INDIANAPOLIS

To Frankfort, Delphi, Monticello, Michigan City,

CHICAGO,

And all points in Northern Indiana, Michigan, Northern Illinois, Wisconsin, Iowa, Minnesota, Nebraska, Kansas, New Mexico, Dakota, Nevada, Colorado, California and Oregon.

2 THROUGH SOLID TRAINS DAILY 2

From Indianapolis to Chicago; also, to Michigan City. Elegant Pullman Sleeping Cars on Night Trains. BAGGAGE CHECKED TO DESTINATION.

No route can offer you any better accommodations or lower rates than we can. Road and Equipments first-class. Steel Rails, Miller Platforms and Buffers, Air Brakes, and all modern improvements. Superior advantages to Western Emigrants. Land and Tourists' Tickets to all points reached by other lines. If you are going West, Northwest, or North, do not purchase your tickets until you have seen our time-folders or called upon us.

For full and reliable information, Tickets, or Sleeping Car Berths, please call on or write to   .   ROBERT EMMETT,

District Passenger Agent,

Office, 26 South Illinois Street, INDIANAPOLIS, IND.

WM. S. BALDWIN, Gen. Pass. Agt., CHICAGO, ILL.   3-9t

Fort Wayne, Cincinnati and Louisville

RAILROAD.

THE POPULAR ROUTE

NORTH AND SOUTH.

Ft. WAYNE, INDIANAPOLIS, TERRE HAUTE, EVANSVILEE, St. LOUIS.

---

13 MILES SHORTER 13
—BETWEEN—

FORT WAYNE AND INDIANAPOLIS
Than any other Route.

22 MILES SHORTER 22
And quicker by THREE HOURS, between

LOUISVILLE AND FORT WAYNE.

NO CHANGE OF CARS between CINCINNATI AND FORT WAYNE
Via White Water Railroad.

All Trains arrive and depart from Central Union Passenger Station, Cincinnati, corner Third Street and Central Avenue.

DIRECT CONNECTION at Fort Wayne with L. S. & M. S. Trains, for all Points North and East.

ASK FOR TICKETS via *Fort Wayne, Cincinnati & Louisville Railroad.* For sale by all Agents of Connecting Lines, EAST, WEST, NORTH and SOUTH.

W. W. WORTHINGTON,   ROBT. T. KINNAIRD,
General Superintendent.   Gen'l Ticket Agent,
3-tf   FORT WAYNE, IND.

BARNES' NEW READERS,

"THE EDUCATIONAL GEMS OF THE AGE."

The most beautiful and practical set of School Readers ever issued. In point of subject-matter, gradation, type, illustrations, paper, binding, and in every other essential feature which goes to make up the very best, these books represent emphatically the perfection in school book literature.

The prices quoted below are those at which we can supply these Readers to schools, both for first introduction and subsequent use. The figures in the first column represent the exchange prices, where old Readers in use are taken as part pay. The second column gives the rates for introduction, where no old book is taken in exchange.

	Exchange.	Introduction.
BARNES' NEW NATIONAL FIRST READER,	.12	.20
BARNES' NEW NATIONAL SECOND READER,	.21	.35
BARNES' NEW NATIONAL THIRD READER,	.30	.50
BARNES' NEW NATIONAL FOURTH READER,	.42	.70
BARNES' NEW NATIONAL FIFTH READER,	.54	.90

It is difficult to speak in moderate terms of these beautiful books, even if one were so inclined.—*Illinois School Journal.*

The books are gems, in every sense, and the only problem in doubt is, how they can be furnished at the price.— *National Journal of Education.*

HYGIENIC PHYSIOLOGIES,

With Special Reference to Alcoholic Drinks and Narcotics:

	Exchange	Introduction.
STEELE'S HYGIENIC PHYSIOLOGY COMPLETE,	.67	$1.00
HUNT'S HYGIENE FOR YOUNG PEOPLE,	.36	.50
THE CHILD'S HEALTH PRIMER,	.18	.30

OTHER LATE AND LEADING BOOKS OF THE NATIONAL SERIES.

BARNES' NEW ARITHMETICS.

This series presents a minimum of theory with a maximum of practice. It adopts the shortest and best methods, and the language is clear and exact.

BARNES' NEW GEOGRAPHIES.

Complete TWO-BOOK series, with latest data, beautiful maps, new standard time, and all other "modern improvements." The plan of TEACHING BY COMPARISON or association of ideas, in this series, is worthy of special attention.

SILL'S LESSONS IN ENGLISH.

Practical, systematic, and complete. Useless verbiage eliminated, and English Grammar treated comprehensively in one convenient sized volume at small cost.

BARNES' BRIEF U. S. HISTORY.

One of the most remarkable text-books ever issued. In many parts of the country it is now more largely used *than all competing Histories combined.*

STEELE'S 14 WEEKS IN EACH SCIENCE.

Embracing Philosophy, Physiology, Chemistry, Zoology, Geology, Astronomy, and Botany.

These books have attained a phenomenal success, and the demand is constantly increasing. They present the cream of the respective studies, and the treatment of the subjects is not only exceedingly practical, but always remarkably interesting to the pupils.

Correspondence cordially invited. Address,

A. S. BARNES & CO.,

8-   **34 & 36 Madison St., CHICAGO, ILL.**

THE NORMAL SCHOOL.

"Work makes Worth."

After ten terms of successful work, with the same popular faculty but many improvements in the way of a new Commercial Hall, that has not an equal in the state, new apparatus and new reference books, we now feel safe in making the following offer, viz:

To furnish as good instruction, better accommodations, and for less money than any school in this or any other state.

We do not claim to have everything nor to teach everything, *but we do claim* to be able to give perfect satisfaction in the following Departments or refund all money, viz:

CLASSIC, SCIENTIFIC, PREPARATORY, TEACHERS, COMMERCIAL, PLAIN AND ORNAMENTAL PENMANSHIP, CIVIL ENGINEERING, GERMAN, MUSIC, FINE ART, PHONOGRAPHY, TYPEWRITING and TELEGRAPHY.

Our school year opens September 1st and continues the entire year. We shall be pleased to have all who wish to do good honest work with us. Students can enter at any time and find classes to suit.

"THE NORMAL SCHOOL,"

A small paper published by the Normal Publishing Co. and devoted exclusively to the *practical* work of the public school teachers, should be examined by every teacher. Please send for sample copy.

A. F. KNOTTS, Principal,

8-
                                   C. I. N. S., LADOGA, IND.

THE CENTRAL NORMAL COLLEGE

DANVILLE INDIANA.

WILL BEGIN ITS TENTH YEAR SEPTEMBER 1st, 1885.

EXPENSES ARE AT A MINIMUM. Tuition $8.00 for ten weeks; table board $1.50 per week; furnished and carpeted room 50 cents per week.

$27 00, if paid in advance, will secure tuition, board and room-rent for one term of ten weeks.

The advantages offered are unexcelled: No saloons or other contaminating influences; Free Reading Room and Library; all students room in good private houses; an experienced and successful Faculty; the most complete and cheapest BUSINESS COURSE in the country; particular attention is given to backward pupils; *You can enter at any time, have perfect liberty in selecting studies, and advance as rapidly as you are able.*

☞ NEARLY 1,100 DIFFERENT STUDENTS WERE ENROLLED DURING THE PAST YEAR.

Catalogues and full particulars sent free. Address,

Mrs. F. P. ADAMS, President,

8-
                                   DANVILLE, IND.

McGuffey's Revised Readers and Speller.

"Many series of Readers have appeared since the first publication of Mc-Guffey's's, but McGuffey's still more than hold their own in the affection and patronage of the public. The grading of McGuffey's Readers has never been surpassed, nor has the interesting character of the matter. In singleness of purpose, in the adaptation of means to ends, in catching and holding the attention of children, in filling the bill of 'reading made easy,' McGuffey's Readers stand unrivaled and alone."

Superior Features of McGuffey's Revised Readers.

1. Adaptation to the modern methods of teaching.
2. Consistent use of the most familiar system of Diacritical Marks.
3. Introduction of carefully engraved Script Lessons.
4. Unequalled gradation of the Series and of each book of the Series.
5. Greater variety of the best Reading Matter than is found in any other Series. More than two hundred of the best writers represented.
6. Nearly three hundred Illustrations by the best artists.
7. Typography, Printing, and Binding of unrivalled excellence.

EXTENSIVE USE.

McGuffey's Readers have at various times been officially adopted or recommended for use by State Superintendents and Boards of Education in nearly one-half the States in the Union, and are now in general use; in several States they are practically in exclusive use in all the schools.

McGuffey's Revised Readers are now officially adopted or authorized for use in the public schools of

VIRGINIA, WEST VIRGINIA, KENTUCKY, ARKANSAS, SOUTH CAROLINA, LOUISIANA.

Also Adopted, and now used in the Public Schools of

City of New York,	City of Cincinnati,	City of San Francisco,
City of Brooklyn,	City of Saint Louis,	Saint Paul and Minneapolis.
Hoboken, N. J.	Portland, Me.	Chattanooga, Tenn.	Columbus, Ohio.
Paterson, N. J.	Topeka, Kan	Atlanta, Ga.	Sandusky, Ohio.
Calais, Me.	Hyde Park, Mass.	Dallas, Texas.	Dayton, Ohio.
Lewiston, Me.	Joliet, Ill.	Gainesville, Texas.	Toledo, Ohio.
Dubuque, Iowa.	Springfield, Ill.	Murfreesboro, Tenn.	Terre Haute, Ind.
Burlington, Iowa.	Charleston, Ill.	Meridian, Miss.	Evansville, Ind.
Iowa City.	Leavenworth, Ks.	Covington, Ky.	Fort Wayne, Ind.
Sedalia, Mo.	Hutchison, Kan.	Lexington, Ky.	Charlotte, Mich.
St. Joseph, Mo.	Los Angelos, Cal.	Maysville, Ky.	Sturgis, Mich.
Silver City, N. M.	Duluth, Minn	Charlotte, N. C.	Beaver Dam, Wis.

AND THREE THOUSAND OTHER CITIES AND TOWNS.

Adopted for more than One Thousand Counties and Ten Thousand Townships and Special Districts.

Ray's New Arithmetics and Algebras,
Eclectic School Geometry,
White's New Arithmetics,
Schuyler's Complete Algebra,
Milne's Inductive Arithmetics,
Milne's Inductive Algebra,
Harvey's Revised Grammars,
Holbrook's Normal Grammars,
Kidd's New Elocution,
Murdoch's Analytic Elocution,

New Eclectic Geographies.
New Eclectic Penmanship,
Eclectic United States History,
Eclectic Primary History,
Thalheimer's Historical Series,
Ridpath's United States Histories,
Eclectic System of Drawing,
Forbriger's Drawing Tablets,
Eclectic Complete Book-keeping,
Eclectic Physiology and Hygiene.

Complete Descriptive Catalogue and Price List of Eclectic Educational Series sent on application.

VAN ANTWERP, BRAGG & CO., Publishers, Cin. & New York.

[4-tf]

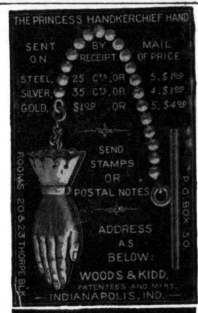

Vol. XXX. 1856-1885 Number 1.

INDIANA

SCHOOL JOURNAL

DEVOTED TO LIBERAL

EDUCATION.

PUBLISHES THE OFFICIAL DECISIONS OF THE

SUPERINTENDENT OF PUBLIC INSTRUCTION.

TABLE OF CONTENTS

Subscription Price, $1.50 Per Annum. Five or more Copies, $1.25 each

INDIANAPOLIS, IND.:

W. A. BELL, Editor & Publisher,

GEO. P. BROWN, Associate Editor.

[Entered as "Second-Class Matter," at the Post-Office, Indianapolis, Ind.]

An Interesting Conversation.

Smith. Good evening, Brown.

Brown. Good evening, Mr. Smith.

Smith. I've been thinking some about going to school somewhere this winter, and have come to talk with you about it.

Brown. Well, I think your resolution a good one. A young man who neglects education in these times will miss it.

Smith. I have saved up a little money, and my father says he can help me if necessary, and I have concluded to invest something in education. But where shall I go, is the question. So many schools are advertised, all claiming to be the best, that I am puzzled to decide.

Brown. I recommend the Fort Wayne College. I have been there myself, and if I had the means would go again.

Smith. Oh, I don't think I would like to go there.

Brown. Why not? It is certainly a good school.

Smith. Well, in the first place the course of study in a college is too antiquated. I can't afford to spend four or five years in turning over the rubbish of a college course.

Brown. Now, my friend, you are quite mistaken. The course of study at the Fort Wayne College is eminently practical and modern. By rubbish I suppose you mean Latin and Greek and Hebrew and Metaphysics and Mythology and such. Well, now in the "*College Preparatory Course*," as they call it, they *do* drill them in Latin and Greek and the other studies of a classical college, and they drill them thoroughly, so that if a student wants to enter DePauw or Bloomington or Ann Arbor or Yale or any of those old colleges he finds himself well prepared for entrance. But if you want only a good, solid business education, you will enter the "*Academic Course*." Here you will find all the modern studies taught by the best modern methods.

Smith. Yes, but how long will it take me to graduate? I understand that in these colleges the way to teach is so poorly understood that the student crawls along at a snail's pace, and, by the time he gets to the end of a study, he has forgotten the beginning of it. How is it that some schools carry the scholar over a whole college course of seven years in the space of three years? Time is money, and I can't afford to spend six or seven years in college when I can get a better education in three years at some other kind of a school.

Brown. Now, Smith, you are a school teacher yourself and a man of sense. You have sometimes, I presume, rushed your scholars over a subject so fast that they failed to comprehend it, and your term's work went for nothing; then you swung to the other extreme, and detained your class so long that they became disgusted with the subject; there is a *golden mean between too fast and too slow*, and I believe they travel in the golden mean at Fort Wayne. The Academic course of study would perhaps occupy you four years, but if you can go faster you will not be kept back by a cast-iron class system.

Smith. Can I take as many studies as I chose?

Brown. Yes.

Smith. Can I enter at any time?

Brown. Yes, though of course the beginning of the term is best.

Smith. If I have to stay out and teach a term or two can I make up the studies in class?

Brown. You can; classes in the same subject begin several times each year.

Smith. Are they very strict in government?

Brown. Moderately so. Students are required to attend classes and chapel and to be fully occupied in school and study hours with school work. Notoriously idle or vicious students, after expostulation fails, are quietly dismissed. All rules are made for the good of the student, and not for the convenience of the teacher.

Smith. Probably the expenses are great.

Brown. Not at all. $2.75 to $3.50 per week will pay all expenses of Board, Room, and Tuition.

Smith. The buildings are old, I hear.

Brown. They *were* old, but now a magnificent brick and stone building is going up, which will afford large, well-ventilated recitation rooms, chapel, library, laboratory, offices, and dining room. The rooms for students are all newly furnished with everything needful.

Smith. Can I study music?

Brown. The music department is unexcelled. Prof. Otto Schmidt is in charge. New music rooms entirely free from interruption and neatly furnished have been provided.

Smith. How about the Teachers' course of study?

Brown. It is one of the best; send for a catalogue and read for yourself.

Smith. How many teachers do they have?

Brown. About ten or twelve.

Smith. And how many students.

Brown. About two hundred.

Smith. Pretty well. At that rate a school of 2000 pupils would require 120 teachers.

Brown. Yes, or else the classes must be very large.

Smith. Is Fort Wayne a desirable place for a school?

Brown. I think so. It is a city of about 30,000 inhabitants; all the first-class lecturers and concert companies visit it, and a student can hear in a single winter several of the celebrities of the world. The citizens take interest in the school. The literary societies of the college are favored with fine audiences, and the most eloquent speakers and accomplished musicians of the city often speak and sing before the students. A year or two in the city is worth a great deal to a young man.

Smith. How about the morals? There are probably a great many saloons and variety theaters and other bad places.

Brown. Yes, there are. But a young man must encounter such places everywhere. I don't know where he can more safely form his character than under the moral and religious influence of such a school. Each teacher seems to have a special regard for the moral growth of the students. A Y. M. C. A. is sustained by the pupils and the associations are of the very best kind.

Smith. When do the terms commence?

Brown. October 6th the fall term begins. Later than usual this year because the new building and the repairs on the old one can not be completed before September 20th, and the Trustees want everything in first-rate order before beginning. Send for a catalogue.

Smith. To what address?

Brown. Send for catalogue to

W. F. YOCUM, Fort Wayne, Ind.

[9-1t]

Vol. XXX. 1856-1885 Number 2.

INDIANA

SCHOOL JOURNAL

DEVOTED TO LIBERAL

EDUCATION.

PUBLISHES THE OFFICIAL DECISIONS OF THE

SUPERINTENDENT OF PUBLIC INSTRUCTION.

TABLE OF CONTENTS

Subscription Price, $1.50 Per Annum.   Five or more Copies, $1.25 each

INDIANAPOLIS, IND.:

W. A. BELL, Editor & Publisher,

GEO. P. BROWN, Associate Editor.

(Entered as "Second-Class Matter," at the Post-Office, Indianapolis, Ind.)

BETWEEN THE

M. BRONSON,
General Ticket Agt.

first-class

higher branches—the Business Depart-
Collegiate Department, and th
pparatus, etc , offered all.
W. E. LUGENBEEL,

Ask your friends if they have ever ridden over the "Jet answer, "yes, always take the old reliable"

Place for Teachers and others to secure a day keeping by Felton's Short Method, and Pen the Spencerian authors.

THE CROWNING

Interesting Conversation.

...evening, Brown.

...nd evening, Mr. Smith.

...been thinking was about going
where this winter, and have done
...th you about it.

...ll, I think your resolution a good
...en who neglects education in
...must it.

...ve saved up a little money, and
...an help me if necessary, and I
...t to invest something in education.
...hi I go, is the question. So many
...ertised, all claiming to be the best,
...rd to decide.

...commend the Fort Wayne College.
...ere myself, and if I had the means
...in.

...don't think I would like to go

...ment? It is certainly a good

...the course of
...I can't af-
...years in turning over
...College course.

...Smith, you are quite mis-
...the Fort Wayne
...and modern. By
...Latin and Greek
...and Mythology and
...College Preparatory
...them in
...the other studies of a clas-
...them thoroughly, so
...DePauw or Bloom-
...any of these old
...well prepared for an-
...only a good, solid busi-
...enter the "Academic
...find all the modern
...modern methods.

...how long will it take me to
...that in these colleges
...understood that the
...pace, and, by the
...study, he has forgot-
...How is it that some
...over a whole college
...in the space of three years?
...I can't afford to spend six or
...when I can get a better ed-
...years at some other kind of a

...Smith, you are a school teacher
...You have some-
...your scholars over a
...failed to comprehend it,
...went for nothing; then you
...became disgusted with the
...between too fast
...believe they travel in the
...Fort Wayne. The Academic
...perhaps occupy you four
...you will not be kept

...take as many studies as I chose?

...time?

...of course the beginning

Smith. If I have to stay out and teach a term
or two can I make up the studies in class?

Brown. You can; classes in the same subject
begin several times each year.

Smith. Are they very strict in government?

Brown. Moderately so. Students are required
to attend classes and chapel and to be fully occupied in school and study hours with school work.
Notoriously idle or vicious students, after expostulation fails, are quietly dismissed. All rules are
made for the good of the student, and not for the
convenience of the teacher.

Smith. Probably the expenses are great.

Brown. Not at all. $2.75 to $3 per week
will pay all expenses of Board, Room, and Tuition.

Smith. The buildings are old, I hear.

Brown. They were old, but now a magnificent
brick and stone building is going up, which will
afford large, well-ventilated recitation rooms,
chapel, library, laboratory, offices, and dining
room. The rooms for students are all newly furnished with everything needful.

Smith. Can I study music?

Brown. The music department is unexcelled.
Prof. Otto Schmidt is in charge. New music
rooms entirely free from interruption and neatly
furnished have been provided.

Smith. How about the Teachers' course of
study?

Brown. It is one of the best; send for a catalogue and read for yourself.

Smith. How many teachers do they have?

Brown. About ten or twelve.

Smith. And how many students.

Brown. About two hundred.

Smith. Pretty well. At that rate a school of
4000 pupils would require 120 teachers.

Brown. Yes, or else the classes must be very
large.

Smith. Is Fort Wayne a desirable place for a
school?

Brown. I think so. It is a city of about 30,000
inhabitants; all the first-class lecturers and concert companies visit it, and a student can hear in
a single winter several of the celebrities of the
world. The citizens take interest in the school.
The literary societies of the college are favored
with fine audiences, and the most eloquent speakers and accomplished musicians of the city often
speak and sing before the students. A year or
two in the city is worth a great deal to a young
man.

Smith. How about the morals? There are
probably a great many saloons and variety theaters and other bad places.

Brown. Yes, there are. But a young man
must encounter such places everywhere. I don't
know where he can more safely form his character than under the moral and religious influence
of such a school. Each teacher seems to have a
special regard for the moral growth of the students. A Y. M. C. A. is sustained by the pupils
and the associations are of the very best kind.

Smith. When do the terms commence?

Brown. October 6th the fall term begins.
Later than usual this year because the new building and the repairs on the old one can not be
completed before September 20th, and the Trustees want everything in first-rate order before
beginning. Send for a catalogue.

Smith. To what address?

Brown. Send for catalogue to

W. F. YOCUM, Fort Wayne, Ind.

[oct]

Vol. XXX. 1856–1885 Number 6.

INDIANA

SCHOOLJOURN

DEVOTED TO LIBERAL

EDUCATION.

PUBLISHES THE OFFICIAL DECISIONS OF THE

SUPERINTENDENT OF PUBLIC INSTRUCTION.

➤ TABLE OF CONTENTS ➤

Subscription Price, $1.50 Per Annum.   Five or more Copies, $1.25 eac

INDIANAPOLIS, IND.:

 W. A. BELL, Editor & Publisher,

GEO. P. BROWN, Associate Editor.

[Entered as "Second-Class Matter," at the Post-Office, Indianapolis, Ind.]

Vol. XXX.   1856-1885   Number 7.

INDIANA

SCHOOL JOURNAL

DEVOTED TO LIBERAL

EDUCATION.

PUBLISHES THE OFFICIAL DECISIONS OF THE

SUPERINTENDENT OF PUBLIC INSTRUCTION,

—TABLE OF CONTENTS—

Subscription Price, $ .50 Per Annum.   Five or more Copies, $1.25 each

INDIANAPOLIS, IND.:

W. A. BELL, Editor and Publisher,

GEO. P. BROWN, Associate Editor.

[Entered as "Second-Class Matter," at the Post-Office, Indianapolis, Ind]

WHITE'S MONTHLY REPORT CARD.

)ort of ....for the

.r ending ....188.......

?s Initials......									
STUDIES.	1st Mo.	2d Mo.	3d Mo.	4th Mo.	5th Mo.	6th Mo.	7th Mo.	8th Mo.	9th Mo.
	Cl. | Ex	Cl. | Ex	Cl. | Ex	Cl. | Ex	Cl. | Ex	Cl. | Ex	Cl. | Ex	Cl. | Ex	Cl. | Ex
aetic									
age									
#									
sphy									
rraphy									
inship.............									
ilogy.............									
ng									
isition.............									
tment									
Absent									
rits for Absence									
Tardy.............									
rits for Tardiness									

nrks:

N. B —Below 70 is poor from 70 to 85 is fair from 85 to 100 is good
Parents, please sign this report, and return the same to the teacher.
Patrons are cordially invited to visit the school

....Teacher.

-Vol. XXX.   1856-1885   Number 8.

INDIANA

SCHOOL JOURNAL

DEVOTED TO LIBERAL

EDUCATION.

PUBLISHES THE OFFICIAL DECISIONS OF THE

SUPERINTENDENT OF PUBLIC INSTRUCTION.

→TABLE OF CONTENTS←

eription Price, $1.50 Per Annum.   *Five or more Copies, $1.25 each*

INDIANAPOLIS, IND.:

W. A. BELL, Editor & Publisher,

GEO. P. BROWN, Associate Editor.

[Entered as " Second-Class Matter," at the Post-Office, Indianapolis, Ind.]

WHITE'S MONTHLY REPORT CARD.

eport of .... for the

ear ending .... 188......

ent's Initials																		
STUDIES.	1st Mo.		2d Mo.		3d Mo.		4th Mo.		5th Mo.		6th Mo.		7th Mo.		8th Mo.		9th Mo.	
	Cl.	Ex	Cl.	Ex	Cl.	Ex	Cl.	Ex	Cl.	Ex	Cl.	Ex	Cl.	Ex	Cl.	Ex	Cl.	Ex
thmetic																		
nguage																		
tory																		
graphy																		
iography																		
manship																		
siology																		
ding																		
rposition																		
ortment																		
ys Absent																		
merits for Absence																		
es Tardy																		
merits for Tardiness																		

marks:

N. B.—Below 70 is poor; from 70 to 85 is fair; from 85 to 100 is good.
Parents, please sign this report, and return the same to the teacher.
Patrons are cordially invited to visit the school.

.... Teacher.

DEVOTED TO LOCAL

EDUCATION.

CONTAINS THE OFFICIAL DECISIONS OF THE

...ERINTENDENT OF PUBLIC INSTRUCTION.

—TABLE OF CONTENTS—

Price, $1.50 Per Annum.   Five or more Copies, $1.25 each.

INDIANAPOLIS, IND.:

DEVOTED TO HIGHER

EDUCATION.

PUBLISHED THE OFFICIAL MEDIUM OF THE

SUPERINTENDENT OF PUBLIC INSTRUCTION.

—TABLE OF CONTENTS—

Subscription Price, $1.50 for Annum.   Five or More Copies, $1.25 each.

INDIANAPOLIS, IND.:

EDUCATION.

PUBLISHED THE OFFICIAL ORGANS OF THE

SUPERINTENDENT OF PUBLIC INSTRUCTION.

—TABLE OF CONTENTS—

Subscription Price, $1.50 Per Annum.   Five or more Copies, $1.25 each.

INDIANAPOLIS, IND.:

1886-1885

IX. Number 1.

INDIANA

SCHOOL JOURNAL

DEVOTED TO LIBERAL

EDUCATION.

CONTAINING THE OFFICIAL BUSINESS OF THE

SUPERINTENDENT OF PUBLIC INSTRUCTION.

TABLE OF CONTENTS.

INDIANAPOLIS, IND.:

W. A. BELL, Editor Publisher,

GEO. P. BROWN, Associate Editor.

(Entered as "Second-Class Matter," at the Post-Office, Indianapolis, Ind.)